THE HERITAGE OF VIRGINIA

THE HERITAGE OF VIRGINIA

THE STORY OF PLACE NAMES
IN THE OLD DOMINION

By James Hagemann

THE
DONNING COMPANY
PUBLISHERS
NORFOLK/VIRGINIA BEACH

Library of Congress Cataloging-in-Publication Data

Hagemann, James A.
    The heritage of Virginia.
    Includes index.
    1. Names, Geographical—Virginia. 2. Virginia—
History, Local. I. Title.
F224.H28   1986   917.55'00142   86-29079
ISBN 0-89865-255-3 (pbk.)

Printed in the United States of America

FOREWORD

For the past fourteen years, I have been accumulating the 1,400 bits and pieces for this collection out of a love for Virginia's history and a curiosity about the origin of the names used for homes and geographical features. Once I got deeply involved, I realized that some terms had to be more closely defined. At the same time, when writing about the people and events, I had to dig into both English and American history. It has been a most fascinating hobby that, at times, bordered on being nosey in order to be as thorough as possible.

The information was gleaned from a multitude of sources, most of them written, some of them unpublished, and occasionally I sought names and dates from badly worn tombstones. Of course, I had plenty of help from personal encounters with those who remembered stories told to them by aging relatives. Help was found everywhere I made my interest known. Total strangers became research assistants to aid me in locating some hidden site while chattering on about a bit of family history or an amusing local anecdote which they "knew for a fact," or "had read somewhere." Close friends, many of my wife's Virginia relations, and helpful librarians volunteered data, much of which was of some value.

Old-timers were the most garrulous about the past, often speaking of things that had happened two or three hundred years ago as if they had lived in those times. Of the old-timers I rather quickly became wary. Local legends may make for fine conversation over a cup of tea in the late afternoon, but as authentic history many of the tales were inaccurate or misleading.

During my collection times, I have visited numerous, venerable sites to see what was left of grand manor houses, humble abodes, abandoned estates, crumbling fortifications, and unused roads. However, my major source was books, especially the published histories of cities, counties, and regions. In every instance, the research librarians were tremendously helpful. It was good to discover that every library, no matter how large or small, has one section set aside for Virginia lore which, I must admit, was designed for geneological research more than the origin of place names. All too often I found a place name without being able to find out why it was selected. That, perhaps, was the most frustrating aspect of the entire search.

Although Virginians tend to have a rather sparce personal fund of accurate knowledge of history, I was pleased to find that so many old homes and buildings have been restored, more or less accurately, to preserve them for the coming generations. Some have been drastically altered to meet modern living requirements and that, in a way, is good because it keeps alive a continuity of habitation and veneration. Many places are gone, of course, victim of the ancient foe, fire. Some have been allowed to rot away, while a few have been picked up and moved to new and "better" locations. Some, being private dwellings, quite naturally, are not open either to the public or to a curious seeker of Virginia lore. All too often, though, original sites have been cleared or mutilated or obliterated for modern buildings or roads. The march of progress, the erosion of time, the ravages of nature, and the total indifference of some people have all conspired to erase many colorful and interesting places. Out of sight is so often out of mind that even the memory of some places has faded away. Fortunately, they have been written about in books, diaries, and manuscripts.

Places in Virginia were named by people from many different countries during nearly four centuries. From the very beginning of the colony, the early settlers came from different countries of the British Isles and from the Continent. During the first decades of the Jamestown settlement, Dutchmen and Poles worked as carpenters and glassmakers, potters and soldiers. Frenchmen were brought over to grow grapes in early wine-making experiments. Settlers came from Germany, Bohemia, Russia, Switzerland, Italy, and Scandinavia. Many were brought involuntarily from Africa and the West Indies. The Old Dominion was the first melting pot of the New World, and the names these people attached to their homes, farms, taverns, rivers, and streams echo the various colors of their imaginations, their whimsies, their loyalties, and their almost universal longing for home.

Many, many names are of Indian origin. As there were at least fifty tribes, there were dozens of dialects of Algonquin, Sioux and Iroquois. No one can be positive about the languages today, and those who dare to give an exact translation are only guessing. Those who tried to explain some words in the seventeenth century usually made matters worse with their phonetic spellings since today we are not certain how Englishmen of that century spoke the King's

English. What matters most, however, is that the Indian heritage has been retained in so many names despite the colonists' attempts in the mid-seventeenth century to remove all "heathen" names. Virginia once belonged to the Indians, and we must never forget that most of us are descendants of immigrants.

This work is not finished, nor can it ever be. There are countless names that have been lost, or, rather, that I have not yet found. I make no claim that this is a complete listing for I have several hundred place names in my card file for which I have been unable to discover any information. As long as the people of Virginia continue to build new homes, new towns and cities, there will be new names to explain and more history to divulge. My collection, then, is only a beginning.

Except where noted, all illustrations came from the extensive collection of the Virginia State Library in Richmond.

James Andrew Hagemann

Hampton, Virginia, 1986

ABINGDON
Arlington County   **Site**

John Alexander came from Scotland in 1659. Within years he owned 7,450 acres of land with two miles of shoreline on the west bank of the Potomac River. It was not until 1741 that a house was erected on the property by John's great-grandson who named his home Abingdon for the English city in Berkshire, near Oxford. He sold 1,000 acres in 1778 to Martha Washington's son, John Parke Custis, which later became the famed Arlington estate of that family. The balance of the tract was purchased in 1837 by Alexander Hunter, then the Marshall of the District of Columbia. When his son, Bushrod W. Hunter, who had inherited the estate, joined the Confederate Army, Abingdon was confiscated by the Federal government. The old house burned in 1930. Ten years later the land was cleared to become Washington's National Airport. *See: Alexandria; Arlington; Summer Hill*

ABINGDON
Washington County   **Town**

First known as Wolf Hills, the land here was patented in 1750 by Dr. Thomas Walker of Castle Hill during his explorations of southwestern Virginia. Black's Fort was erected in 1776, two years before the town of Abingdon was established as the seat of Washington County. It claims to be the oldest incorporated town located on a stream that drains into the Mississippi River. Of more significance, perhaps, is the Barter Theater that was organized here in 1932 by Robert Porterfield as a means to provide theatrical work for performers stranded by the Great Depression. Tickets were exchanged for food or other useable items in a unique bartering system which gave the actors work and provided entertainment for the people of the area. *See: Castle Hill; Washington County*

ABINGDON CHURCH
Gloucester County

Six miles south of Gloucester Court House, the mother church of Abingdon Parish was erected about 1651 on land donated by Augustine Warner of Warner Hall. Some remains of the foundation of this early building can be found, but there is no record of its description. This first church remained in use for about a hundred years. It was replaced by the present building at a new site in 1750. A handsome communion service, still in use, was presented by Maj. Lewis Burwell. *See: Fairfield of Gloucester; Ware Church*

ABRAM'S DELIGHT
Winchester

Abraham Hollingsworth built a frontier cabin in 1729 beside a bountiful spring that was "a delight to behold"—the spring, not the cabin. His family prospered in the area for over 200 years. In 1754 the original log home was replaced by a house of stone that had walls two feet thick, which, at that time, were unusually thick. Many notables, including Lord Fairfax, George Washington, and the Marquis de Lafayette were entertained here by the Hollingsworth family.

ACCOMAC
Accomack County   **Town**

Now the thriving seat of Accomack County, this town began when the courthouse was sited here in 1708. The site was then known as Metomkin, for a local Indian tribe. So many members of the Drummond family lived here or owned property in the region, that the new town was known for many years as Drummondtown. Since the original spelling of the county did not have the final "k", the residents here insist upon spelling the town's name Accomac. *See: Metomkin*

ACCOMACK COUNTY

The entire region of the Eastern Shore was known as "Ye Plantacione at Accawmacke" by the early settlers, using the Indian word meaning "across the water." In 1634 the entire peninsula was formed into a shire and the name was spelled Accomac. When the purists of the House of Burgesses decided to eliminate all "heathen" names, the county was named Northampton. As the territory became more densely settled and complaints arose about the distance to be traveled to the courthouse, the county was divided in half. The lower portion retained the name Northampton and the northern area was called Accomack, a spelling closer to the original Indian word.

For many years court sessions were held in a tavern in a private home at the head of Pungoteague Creek. When this inconvenienced the owner, the court convened in a nearby tavern. Eventually the court records were kept in the village of Onancock, the first official county seat. One of the first county commissioners was Colonel Edmund Scarburgh who was ordered arrested in 1670 for his murder of the Indian chiefs, his way to insure peace with the tribes he had needlessly inflamed. Claiming he was the newly elected Burgess for Accomack County, and was therefore immune from arrest, Governor William Berkeley revoked the county's charter and declared Scarburgh an ordinary citizen. When Scarburgh died in shame the next year, the county was re-established.

Those citizens who lived on the ocean side objected to having the county seat on the bay side. In 1708 a courthouse was erected midway between the two coasts at Drummondtown. Eventually this tiny settlement became a village that took the name Accomac. The present courthouse dates from 1899. *See: Metomkin; Pungoteague; Occohannock; Onancock; Savage Neck*

ACHILLES
Gloucester County

A number of years ago, Achilles' Store was located here, named for the proprietor. When a tiny hamlet developed near the store, the present name was adopted.

AIRVILLE
Gloucester County

Richard Kemp patented 3,500 acres here in 1659, but there is no evidence that he ever used any of it. The Dutch-colonial house of 1756, still standing high above the Ware River, was built by John Dixon of Mount Pleasant. A larger and more imposing Federal wing was added to it in 1840. *See: Church Hill; Isleham; Kempsville; Mount Pleasant; Richneck*

ALBEMARLE COUNTY

One hundred and twenty years after the founding of Jamestown, the Tidewater settlers began to apply for lands in the Piedmont region just east of the Blue Ridge Mountains. According to Thomas Jefferson, his father was "the third or fourth settler about the year 1737, of the part of the country in which I live." At that time, this territory was in Goochland County. A new county, formed in 1744, was named for the second Earl of Albemarle, the titular governor of Virginia at that time. Over the years the county has changed in size and shape. Buckingham and Amherst were carved from it, and later a part of Louisa was added to straighten out the boundary line. Then, in

1777, a slice of Albemarle was contributed to form Fluvanna. The county seat was first at Scottsville on the James River, but, at the time of the last re-alignment of the county lines, the courthouse was erected in Charlottesville. *See: Monticello; Scottsville*

ALBERTA
Brunswick County   **Town**

First known as Walthall's Store, the residents of this town decided that they wanted a name that would not be confused with any other in the state. They assumed that the Canadian province of Alberta was far enough away and so they selected that name for the post office. The Canadian province was named for Prince Albert, the consort of Queen Victoria, who died in 1861, a date that, perhaps by coincidence, marked the selection of the name. *See: Naxera, Victoria*

ALDIE
Loudoun County

Charles F. Mercer laid out this hamlet in 1810. He claimed to be a descendant of the Mercer clan of Scotland whose seat was Aldie Castle.

ALEXANDRIA
Arlington County   **City**

The land upon which this town was laid out was first owned by Robert Howsing in 1657. John Alexander, who surveyed the grant twelve years later, helped erect a fort here in 1675 in defense against the Seneca Indians whose raids helped spark Bacon's Rebellion nineteen years later. A warehouse was built at the head of Hunting Creek in 1731 around which grew the first hamlet which was called Belle Haven (good, safe place). When the settlement was recognized by the House of Burgesses in 1749, it was formally named for John Alexander, the surveyor. Alexandria prospered from trade carried up the Potomac River to the Hunting Creek Warehouse. It became one of the major commercial shipping centers of late colonial times. *See: Abingdon of Arlington; Curles; Little Hunting Creek; Northern Neck*

ALLEGHANY COUNTY

Formed in 1822 from parts of Bath, Botetourt, and Monroe, this county was named for the Allegheny Mountains that rise to the west. For some reason, the mountains are spelled with an "e" and the county with an "a." The name is an Indian word meaning

ALEXANDRIA 1863

"endless," and so they must have seemed to the early pioneers. The county seat is Covington.

ALLEGHENY SPRING
Montgomery County

The water from a spring here contains about thirty different minerals. In the years following the Civil War, it became stylish to drink mineral water as a cure for dyspepsia. It was bottled and sold from about 1870 until 1920. A resort was built to care for 1,000 guests who "took the waters" under the supervision of the resident physician, Dr. Isaac White. Those who stayed also enjoyed a variety of indoor and outdoor activities. Fire and neglect have claimed all of the resort's buildings. The land was subdivided into lots upon which homes were built to create the town of Allegheny Spring.

ALLISONIA
Pulaski County

Charles Allison was an early settler here. Others came to join him and the cluster of homes near his farm developed into a hamlet named Allisonia.

ALTAVISTA
Campbell County

Alta Vista, meaning "high view" in Spanish, was the name of a farm owned by Henry Lane who established a small factory that specialized in cedar chests. Cedar trees grew in wild abundance; the Staunton River

provided power for the machinery. By the turn of the century (1900) it was a mark of affluence to own a genuine Lane cedar chest to store linens since cedar is thought to discourage moths. The factory now makes other furniture but continues its famous item.

In the days before Campbell County was organized, Colonel Charles Lynch, William Preston, Robert Adams, and James Callaway took turns holding court at Alta Vista under a huge walnut tree. They had no legal training and no law books, and they judged local offenders according to what they thought was justice based on common sense. Punishment varied according to the crime. Frequently it was "39 lashes well laid on the bare back," although they were not squeamish about pronouncing the death sentence by hanging if the crime was particularly heinous. When challenged by a prisoner at one session, Colonel Lynch uttered his famous statement, "I am the Law!" This system of quick trials without the benefit of the niceties of properly trained prosecutor and defense attorney became known as the "Lynch Law" since Colonel Lynch was by far the most highly quoted of the four self-appointed magistrates. After the Civil War, when midnight hangings were common in the Southern states, they were called "lynchings," an unfortunate and inaccurate reference to the system of justice employed here prior to the Revolution. Colonel Lynch was a vociferous advocate of fair trials and would not tolerate

3

extra-legal execution by a mob. *See: Chestnut Hill; Lynchburg*

AMELIA COUNTY

This county was organized in 1734 when it was formed from parts of Prince George and Brunswick counties. It was named for Princess Amelia Sophia, the youngest daughter of King George II. The courthouse was erected soon after the organization and the village of Amelia Court House grew around it.

AMHERST COUNTY

Formed in 1761 from Albemarle, this county was named for Jeffery, Lord Amherst, the British commander in the French and Indian War who was acclaimed throughout England as the "Conqueror of Canada." Although he was appointed Governor of Virginia, he never came to the colony but sent deputies who bore the title Lieutenant Governor. The first courthouse was built in a tiny hamlet known as The Oaks which is now the town of Amherst.

AMISSVILLE
Rappahannock County

Joseph Amiss made his home here after he received a grant of land in 1763. The growth of the present village is a more recent happening.

AMPTHILL
Chesterfield County

The land of this estate was sold to Henry Cary, the builder of the Capitol building in Williamsburg, by William Byrd II of Westover. Located on the south bank of the James River, the house was built by Henry Cary II in 1730 who named it for Ampthill Park, a section of Cambridgeshire, England. The estate was inherited by Colonel Archibald Cary in 1749 who was a colorful, forceful man. Those who worked for him in his iron foundry, flourmill, and rope walk called him, secretly, "Old Bruiser" or "Old Irons." In 1929, a collateral descendant, Hundson Cary, acquired the property, dismantled the house, and had it re-erected at its present location at Cary Street and Ampthill Road in Richmond.

ANDERSON'S TAVERN
Prince Edward County   **Site**

Charlie Anderson established a tavern here in 1749 just as the new county jail was built. The tavern became the first courthouse and continued to operate on the old stage road after the county seat was moved a few miles north to Rutledge's Ford. Anderson's Tavern became King's Tavern late in colonial times. *See: King's Tavern*

ANDERSONVILLE
Buckingham County

When the post office was established in Mr. Gary's store, Mr. R. M. Anderson was appointed the first postmaster. This was about 1902.

ANNANDALE
Fairfax County

The Earl of Annandale was a twelfth century knight of Scotland. This possibly might be the source of the name of this populated section of Fairfax County, but more likely it was a coined named selected by a developer.

ANNA RIVER
Orange County

This minor stream begins as a tiny brook near Gordonsville and flows into the Pamunkey River. Most likely it was named for Queen Anne, as were so many other streams in Virginia. However, it could have been named for Lady Anne, the wife of Governor Alexander Spotswood whose home was nearby. *See: Fluvanna River; Rapidan River River*

APPALACHIA
Wise County   **Town**

The Appalachian Mountain range runs more or less parallel to the eastern seaboard from New York to Georgia. Early Spanish explorers are given credit for naming this long string of moderately high mountains; some say the name is of an Indian tribe called Apalchen. These Indians did not live in Wise County, nor anywhere in Virginia, but the mountains are very evident. It is not known who named this town Appalachia, but obviously it refers to the shadowing hills.

APPOMATTOX COUNTY

The county gets its name from the Appomattox River. In 1845 parts of Buckingham, Campbell, Charlotte and Prince Edward counties were put together to form Appomattox. The county seat was sited at the headwaters of the river far inland from the James.

APPOMATTOX COURT HOUSE
Appomattox County **Park**

Here on April 9, 1865 Confederate General Robert E. Lee surrendered to Union General Ulysses S. Grant which ended the Southern states' attempt to create a separate nation.

The surrender took place in the home of Wilmer McLean and memorialized the county seat into a national landmark which is operated today by the National Park Service.

In 1892 the court house burned and the county seat was moved to present-day Appomattox.

APPOMATTOX MANOR
Prince George County

About a decade after the founding of Jamestown, Francis Eppes came to Virginia. A Burgess in the first Assembly of 1619, he was appointed to the Council in 1635. In that year he received a grant of 1,700 acres on the south bank of the James at the mouth of the Appomattox River. Shortly thereafter, he qualified for 650 more acres for transporting his three sons and thirty servants to the colony. The house he built, named Eppington, was pulled down by his grandson in 1751 and replaced by another, finer building which was named Appomattox Manor. Now owned by the National Park Service, the house and grounds are open to the public. *See: City Point; Eppington; Hopewell, Weston*

APPOMATTOX RIVER

In early May 1607, the original Jamestown settlers sailed up this river to the falls, which are rather close to the mouth, and considered planting their settlement there "in the country of Apamatic," as they called the area. They landed a few miles upstream, remained for a few days, and then, deciding that the local geography did not match the requirement written in their instructions from the London Company, sailed back to the main river and settled in an unsatisfactory place that we know today as Jamestown. Although this river is navigable only for a few miles to the falls, it winds westerly into the heart of present-day Virginia.

AQUIA CREEK
Stafford County

Giles Brent was the first settler here. He came from Maryland after being expelled by Lord Baltimore for his political meddling and for marrying the princess of the Piscataway tribe. These Indians lived on both sides of the Potomac River and called this creek *Aquia* which means either "muddy" or "bush nut," depending upon which interpretation one cares to accept at this late date. Brent built his first house at the mouth of the creek in 1647, invited others to join him from Maryland, and, three years later, helped to organize the first Roman Catholic church in Virginia. This was during the days of the English Commonwealth of Oliver Cromwell when the affairs of Virginia were given slight attention by Parliament.

Sandstone, called "free-stone," cut from a quarry near the creek, was used for many public and private buildings. It was used to build the first lighthouse at Cape Henry in 1791 and, found satisfactory and easy to work, was the primary stone of the new Capitol building in the District of Columbia. It has not weathered well and is slowly being replaced. *See: Brentsville; Bristow; Richlands*

ARGALL'S GIFT
Charles City County **Site**

This early settlement, now vanished, was created by Gov. Samuel Argall to commemorate his "gift" of Pocahontas to the colony. In 1613, while still just the captain of a ship named *Treasurer*, he kidnapped the daughter of Powhatan at a village on the upper Potomac by bribing the greedy local chief with a copper kettle. Argall brought Pocahontas to Jamestown as a peace hostage. Many colonists were aghast at his rash action and predicted a bloody war when the Indians sought to rescue her. No war resulted. Powhatan even refused to negotiate a ransom. The Indian maid, no stranger to the English of the earlier days, was quite happy with her captors and, when her father was obviously not interested in making a peace treaty in exchange for her freedom, began to learn English and allowed herself to be instructed in Christianity. In 1614 she was baptised, given the name Rebecca, and married John Rolfe who had assisted the Reverend Alexander Wittaker in her religious instruction. The union brought about eight years of peace between the whites and the natives.

Shortly after Argall became Governor in 1616, he took possession of an abandoned Paspehegh village near Jamestown and shifted people from Martin's Hundred to live in the houses he had paid someone to build. In the Massacre of 1622, directed by Powhatan's successor Opechancanough, Argall's Gift was wiped out, never again to be inhabited by colonists. Two men from Argall's Guift, as it was spelled in the records, were members of the First Assembly of 1619. By then Samuel Argall, having been discovered in many unlawful financial arrangements by which he lined his own pocket, had secretly left Virginia to avoid arrest by the new Governor, Sir George Yeardley. Argall escaped prosecution when he arrived in England but, like his personal town, he faded from the scene and today is little remembered. *See: Littletown; Paspehegh Indians*

ARGYLE
Albemarle County

The lands of this tract were patented in 1741 by John Lewis. The first house was built about 1765 by Colonel Joseph Joplin, an officer in Washington's army who named the place for Argyl, Scotland. Later it was owned by the Bunker family who, it is said, are responsible for a ghost that appears on any wild night in March. The apparition is that of a man who swims his black stallion across the James River, dashes at full gallop to the house, rides through the front door and ties his steed to the newel post of the stairway. His brother, the former master of Argyl, joins him and the two men spend the night in drunken revelry as they did when alive. Today the farm goes by the quiet name River Lawn.

ARK
Gloucester County

This tiny community took its name from the Old Ark Farm that was the major establishment in this region for many years.

ARLINGTON
Arlington County

This familiar estate once belonged to the Custis family who first settled on the Eastern shore in Northampton County on a large tract they called Arlington. The mansion here was built by George Washington Parke Custis who died in 1857. At the outbreak of the Civil War, Arlington was owned by the builder's grandson, G. W. Custis Lee, the eldest son of Mary Custis Lee. It was here that her famous husband, Robert E. Lee, the future Confederate general, decided to resign his commission as a colonel in the U.S. Army and offer his services to Virginia. As a result, the estate was confiscated by the Federal government and was occupied by Northern troops all through the War Between the States.

In June of 1864, Secretary of War Edward Stanton signed a document that stated, "The bodies of all soldiers dying in the Hospitals in the vicinity of Washington and Alexandria will be interred in this cemetery." Veterans of all wars since then have been buried with high honor in Arlington Cemetery. Most famous are the Tombs of the Unknown Soldiers and the grave of President John F. Kennedy. *See: Fort Myer*

ARLINGTON
Northampton County   **Site**

No longer standing and only faintly remembered, this first Arlington was located on Old Plantation Creek on the Eastern shore, a few miles south of the present town of Cape Charles. John Custis II, the son of the immigrant, named the plantation for Lord Arlington who had been of great help in getting John, Sr., and his son "naturalized" after they both had spent many years in Holland. By this action, they regained their rights as Englishmen. John II was just completing his manor house when Governor William Berkeley took refuge with him in 1676 during the height of Bacon's Rebellion. The only remaining trace of this once prosperous farm are the tombs of John Custis II and his grandson, John IV. The stone marking the elder man's resting place says he was "...one of the Council and Major General of Virginia who departed this life ye 29th of January 1696, aged 66 years."

Next to his grave is a stone marking the eternal resting place of a man whose married life was a trial. His wife was the stubborn and headstrong Frances Parke, daughter of Colonel Francis Parke, Esq., whose own life was full of conflict and debts which his son-in-law inherited. The epitaph, written by John IV just before he died, reads, "Under this Marble Tombe lies ye body of the Honorable John Custis, Esqr, of the City of Williamsburg and the Eastern Shore, the place of his nativity. Aged 71 years and yet lived but Seven Years which was the space of time he kept a Batchelor's house at Arlington on the Eastern Shore of Virginia."

The son of John IV was Daniel Parke Custis who, at the age of thirty-seven, married Martha Dandrige (she was eighteen), sired two children and died when the boy and girl were still quite young. The widow, Martha Dandridge Custis, married George Washington who reared the two stepchildren with love and affection. George Washington Park

Custis, Martha's grandson, built the mansion near Washington, D. C., which he named for the Arlington of his ancestors early in the nineteenth century. *See: Arlington of Arlington; Audley; Council; Eltham; Queen's Creek Plantation; White House; Wilsonia*

ARLINGTON COUNTY

This county was that portion of the District of Columbia which was returned to Virginia ("retroceded") in 1847 since it was not needed by the new Federal City. Then called Alexandria County for the largest city in it, the name was changed in 1920 to avoid confusion. It was named for the Custis-Lee estate, Arlington.

ARRINGTON

Nelson County

The major industry here is a soapstone quarry. The first company, organized in 1921, was named the Phoenix Soapstone Company. It was later brought out by other business interests. Nothing has been recorded on why this hamlet is called Arrington. None of the company officers had that name.

ARVONIA

Buckingham County

Obviously a coined name, Arvonia was developed by Evan R. and John R. Williams who began a boom here in 1871, the last the hamlet was to see. The closest settlement to a slate quarry that had been in operation since 1787, Arvonia first came alive when Edward Sims landed a nice contract to supply slate for the roofs of a number of new dormitories at the University of Virginia in 1833. Later, when coal furnaces heated most homes and slate was the best roof to ward off falling sparks, the hamlet prospered. Slate is heavy, however, and the extra bracing required to support the mass added to the cost of building. With the invention of composition shingles, the slate industry fell upon hard times.

ASHBY GAP

Frederick County

Thomas Ashby settled here about 1710 on the road to Winchester. His son, John Ashby, kept a tavern from which he was sent as a messenger to Governor Robert Dinwiddie in 1755 with the sad news of General Braddock's defeat and death. The nearby gap in the mountains, at 1,150 feet above sea level, soon was named for Ashby's Tavern.

ASHLAND

Hanover County   Town

For many years, Ashland was merely a fueling stop on the R. F. & P. Railroad. In 1848 Edwin Robinson, the president of the line, bought 155 acres of wilderness on which was located a mineral spring. Here he built a health spa, complete with a grand ballroom. Richmonders came to dance; others stayed to "take the waters." All were transported on Mr. Robinson's railroad in a packaged deal. His hotel was named Slash Cottage for the local pine trees that were slashed in the wilderness for their sap to make turpentine. A few permanent homes were built, and then a church.

When the spa closed, the villagers discarded the former name Slashes and, in 1855, adopted Ashland, the name of Henry Clay's Kentucky estate. Clay was born in Hanover County near Slash Church. Although he achieved fame elsewhere, the residents of Ashland were proud of the association. The unsold and unused land next to the town was given by the railroad to the Methodist church

HENRY CLAY
ASHLAND, HANOVER COUNTY

as an inducement to move Randolph Macon College here. Today Ashland's major industry is catering to the tourist trade, those who come to visit the nearby theme park, King's Dominion. *See: Slash Church*

ASHLAWN
Albemarle County

This was the home of James Monroe from 1799 until 1825, when he moved to his new estate, Oak Hill. Located not far from Monticello, his friend and neighbor, Thomas Jefferson, had a hand in the purchase of the land. He and Monroe had served together in the Federal government. It is said that the two men communicated with each other by means of a visual signal system since the trees between them were not as thick and tall as they are today. Monroe assisted Jefferson in the founding of the University of Virginia and for a while was a professor who lived on the grounds. He was forced to sell Ash Lawn in 1826 to help pay for Oak Hill. It is now owned by the College of William and Mary and is a mecca for tourists. *See: Oak Hill of Loudoun*

ASSAMOOSICK SWAMP
Sussex County

The southern edge of this swamp, in the eastern third of Sussex County, in the Littleton area, was the early home of the Nottoway Indians. They were present until about 1698. The name Assamoosick appears on very early maps, yet its name is of obscure origin, most probably Indian.

ASSATEAGUE ISLAND
Accomack County

One of the barrier islands off the Eastern Shore, this one was named for the Indians who lived here centuries ago. The word means "stony river," so it is said, although in this tideland region the waterways are anything but stony, tending, rather, to be filled with sand. Now a wild life refuge, the island teems with ducks, geese, swans, and other migrating waterfowl. Bird-watchers come here in droves to see the huge flocks. Assateague is equally famous for its wild ponies whose origin is a mystery. The lighthouse, erected in 1833, is still in service. *See: Occohannock*

ASSAWOMAN
Accomack County

A small tribe of Indians lived on the upper end of Virginia's Eastern Shore on a creek that bears their name today. Many miles north of their village, at what is now called Jenkins Bridge, a church was built in 1687 through the efforts of the Reverend Francis Makemie. It was named Assawoman Church, a name that was dropped in the early eighteenth century and replaced by Emmanuel which was considered to be more appropriate. The suffix *woman* in the Algonquin language appears to have meant a "road" or a "trail." On the lower portion of the Eastern Shore lived the Mattawoman tribe, and across the bay lived the Cuttawomans. *See: Oak Grove; Onancock; Mattawoman; Mount Wharton; New Church*

ATLANTIC
Accomack County

This village on U.S. Highway 13 is named for the nearby ocean. *Atlantic* is thought to be of Greek origin meaning, more or less, the "sea beyond the Atlas Mountains of northwest Africa."

AUDLEY
Clarke County

Warner Washington, a cousin of George, purchased a large tract of land at the northern end of the Shenandoah Valley from Colonel William Fairfax in 1749. He built a house shortly thereafter but replaced it with a larger one in 1774. The choice of the name has two possibilities. Audley End was the home of the Earl of Suffolk, near the English racecourse at Newmarket in East Anglia, which was a favorite royal retreat of King Charles II (who died in 1685). The home of the Earl of Bute, a close advisor to King George III and possibly the king's mother's lover, had a home in London on Audley Street. Lord Bute was England's prime minister for six months in 1762. It is not known if either of these suggestions were the inspiration for Warner Washington to name his Virginia estate Audley, but the name was not changed during the Revolution.

Audley was purchased by George Washington's nephew, Lawrence Lewis, just before he married Nellie Custis, Martha Washington's granddaughter. The wedding was a great social event at Mount Vernon just a short time before the first President died. Both Lawrence and Nellie lived out their happy lives on this Clarke County estate. *See: Eltham; Kenmore; Mount Vernon; White House*

AUGUSTA COUNTY

This county was formed in 1738 from Orange. The territory at its forming extended all the way to the Mississippi River and northward to the Great Lakes. It was named for Princess Augusta, wife of Frederick, Prince of Wales, who was the mother of George III. At the time the county was formed, William Beverley donated twenty-five acres at his mill for the erection of the courthouse and jail in what became the city of Staunton, the present county seat. *See: Manor Mansion*

AUGUSTA MEETING HOUSE
Augusta County

Built of gray field stone in 1749, this church housed a congregation of Presbyterians who had been brought together nine years before by the Reverend John Craig. This rather small body of members owns the largest set of matched communion silver of any church in Virginia. Made in London by Anthony Calame in 1764, the service has three flagons, two patens, and six chalices. *See: Craig's Mill*

AUSTINVILLE
Wythe County

This village was named for Stephen F. Austin, a Yankee, who came here in 1784 and purchased the local lead mine. He remained for thirteen years, leaving to join his father in another mining venture in Missouri. Later he moved to Texas where he planted the first all-American settlement which became the city of Austin, the capital of the Republic of Texas and later of the state.

Near Austinville is an old shot tower built by Thomas Jackson in 1820 to produce balls for ammunition from the local lead supply. When the vein of lead was exhausted, they found zinc, which was mined until 1981. *See: Fort Chiswell; Shot Tower*

AVERETT COLLEGE
Danville

Organized in 1859 as Union Female College, this institution was renamed Roanoke College during the last year of the Civil War when the word "union" was unpleasant to Virginians. Operated under the sponsorship of the Baptist Association of Virginia, the college was again renamed in 1917 to honor two benefactors from the Averett family.

AXTON
Henry County

The early name for this hamlet was Old Center. When the post office was established, it was named for Congressman Axton whose home, Axton Lodge, was nearby.

AYLETTE
King William County

This village near the Mattaponi River originally was part of the land holdings of the Aylett family. The settlement came to life on Tuesdays and Fridays when the people of the region came to meet the stagecoach that ran between Tappahannock and Richmond. Although once in a while the coach delivered or picked up a passenger here, its more important duty was to bring in the mail and newspapers.

This was a family town. The Aylett family owned the tailoring and millinery shops, the tavern, general store, carriage factory, iron foundry, harness, saddler and blacksmith shop, and the ferry that crossed the river. *See: Fairfield of King William*

B

BACK BAY
Virginia Beach

A narrow body of water lies protected behind the dunes that separate it from the Atlantic. It was named, with typical colonial clarity, Back Bay because it was back of the dunes.

BACON'S CASTLE
Surry County

Arthur Allen was a mysterious fellow who came to Virginia in the early 1640s. Some say he was a runaway son of the House of Hanover who adopted the new name to cover the fact that he was Allen Guelph. When he first came to the colony he lived in a modest frame home at Smith's Fort Plantation, then owned by Thomas Warren. During this time he patented the lands of this farm and land at Claremont, married the daughter of Lawrence Baker, and began to plan his manor house which was erected about 1665. Built in the shape of a Greek Cross of typical seventeenth century design, its most impressive features are the two clustered Jacobean chimneys at either end.

The first Arthur Allen died in 1670. The estate was inherited by his son, Maj. Arthur Allen II, who was the Surveyor of Lands of the Colony and was a strong supporter of Governor William Berkeley. He was with the governor on the Eastern Shore in 1676 when the rebel, Nathaniel Bacon, burned Jamestown. The day before this event about seventy followers of Bacon, led by William Rookings, occupied Allen's empty brick house and converted it into a stronghold. They remained there for about three months "Ransacking & making what havoc they pleased both within Dore and without."

Although Bacon died in Gloucester County that October, these rebels held Major Allen's "castle" until the day after Christmas. When the captain of the armed merchantman *Young Prince* dropped anchor offshore and sent an ultimatum to surrender or face an attack by marines at dawn, the renegades slipped off during the night carrying away as much plunder as they could stuff into their pockets or into pillowcases. Rookings was captured and died in jail while waiting to be hanged. Major Allen returned to his despoiled home which, from then on, was called Bacon's Castle. *See: Claremont; Smith's Fort Plantation*

BACON'S QUARTER
Richmond

When the rebel Nathaniel Bacon and his wife came to Virginia in 1674, he bought a working plantation at Curles. Thomas Ballard, who sold the property, also threw in as a bonus a smaller, more distant tract which was then being worked by a sharecropper. Located today within the city of Richmond, this tract was called Bacon's Quarter. This and the plantation at Curles were confiscated by Governor Berkeley after the rebellion had been quelled. The only trace these days is a small steam that runs across the former rebel's bonus which is now called Bacon's Quarter Branch. *See: Curles; Green Spring; Quarter*

BACOVA
Bath County

This is one of several names coined by real estate developers. "Ba" is for Bath, "co" is for County, and "va" is for Virginia.

BANISTER RIVER

This tributary of the Dan was named for Richard Banister, a noted student of Virginia's natural history during the last quarter of the seventeenth century. Born in Twigworth, Gloucestershire, England, in 1650, Banister studied botany and theology at Magdalen College of Oxford University where he earned a master's degree. After ordination in the Anglican church, he was sent to Virginia in 1678 by the Bishop of London. While an under-utilized curate of Bristol Parish, he soon found his way to William Byrd's trading post at the falls of the James River and, with much time on his hands, began his observations of plants and insects. He made many accurate drawings and filled several notebooks with comments which were published years after his death. The books he brought with him formed the basis of the Byrd library at Westover. John Banister was accidentally shot to death by a member of the expedition while he was studying plants along the Roanoke River. His death in May 1692 was mourned on both sides of the Atlantic as a great loss to the world. *See: Bristol Parish; Halifax County; Stone House; Westover*

BARBOURSVILLE
Orange County

This community retains the name of the

once magnificent home of James Barbour, Governor of the Commonwealth during the War of 1812. All that remains of his mansion, designed by Thomas Jefferson about 1817, are the Roman columns that once stood before the main entrance since fire destroyed Barboursville in 1884. James Barbour was a strict conservative who often clashed with his brother, a Jacksonian liberal. Philip Barbour, a Congressman who rose to be the Speaker of the House, was appointed to the U.S. Supreme Court by President Jackson. He, too, lived in a house designed by Jefferson. Located some miles away, it was called Frascati. *See: Catalpa*

BARHAMSVILLE
New Kent County

Bennett Barham built his home here in 1823 at the junction of the stage road to Richmond and the road to Brickhouse on the Pamunkey. The hamlet of Barhamsville developed slowly around Barham's house. About a mile-and-a-half to the east was the site of Doncastle's Ordinary which by this late date had ceased to operate. *See: Brickhouse of New Kent*

BARN ELMS
Middlesex County   Site

Major Robert Beverley came to Virginia about 1663 from Yorkshire, England. He eventually settled in what is now Middlesex County, near the Piankatank River, where he accumulated over 50,000 acres by his death in 1687. In twenty-four years, he became one of the wealthiest planters, owning much personal property which included forty-two slaves. Married twice, he had nine children of whom the most noted were his sons, Peter, the eldest who lived in Gloucester, Harry of Middlesex, and Robert II of King and Queen. The Major was a leader of the Whigs who were known as the "people's party" as opposed to those who stuck closely with the king. In 1677, when Governor Herbert Jeffreys and the Royal Commissioners sent over to investigate Governor Berkeley's handling of Bacon's Rebellion demanded the journal of the House of Burgesses, Major Beverley refused to give it to them. As the Clerk of the House, he said he would not give up the journal without the consent of the members. Jeffreys complained to London of this insubordination and had the clerk removed from office. The storm passed, and the Major was re-elected to the post in 1680. He continued his leadership against the clique

that was blindly loyal to the governors.

However, when tobacco prices fell because of overplanting, Beverley and a number of farmers wanted to outlaw the planting of tobacco for one year. When the House of Burgesses failed to pass the necessary law, Major Robert led a small band of planters into their neighbor's fields and began to cut down the young plants. For this Governor Henry Chicheley had him arrested and placed on a prison ship in the York River under the loose custody of a friendly sheriff. Beverley escaped twice and both times was recaptured. Finally, on bended knee, he begged forgiveness of the Council on May 3, 1684 and went home to Barn Elms to live out his days with a full pardon. His second wife, Mary, by whom he had Robert Beverley II, outlived him for many years. *See: Beverley Park; York Hall*

BARNES JUNCTION
Charlotte County

R. P. Barnes built a store at a crossroads in 1920 in which a post office was established. He succeeded in getting the Greyhound Bus Company to make a stop here and the company named the depot Barnesville. However, the Commonwealth of Virginia recognizes the crossroads hamlet as Barnes Junction on its official road map.

BARRACKS
Albemarle County

Northwest of Charlottesville, a prisoner of war camp was hastily thrown together in 1774 to contain about 4,000 British and Hessian soldiers who were captured after the Battle of Saratoga on October 17th of that year. John Harvie, Jr., of Belmont (now a part of Charlottesville) secured a contract from the Continental Congress to provide the required support for these men. The camp was not ready when the captives arrived in January 1778. The weather was biting cold, the roofless huts were half-filled with snow, and food rations were scant and of poor quality. The prisoners dug the snow from their rude quarters, completed the barracks with materials hewn from the nearby woods, hunted for extra meat, and made the best of a bad situation. Many prisoners escaped but their departures were not reported by Harvie, the supervisor, since he received a stipend of so much per head and, with cheap rations, he made money. A young British captain put the blame where it belonged when he wrote that the American Congress was "misguided and duped by one

11

of their own members, a Colonel Harvie, who is a delegate from this Province."

Many of those who escaped fled to the mountains, later married Virginia women, and became an integral part of the Commonwealth's population. Today many Hessian names are common in Albemarle and Nelson Counties. Thomas Jefferson fraternized with some of the higher ranking officers who, billetted near Monticello, lived rather comfortably. In the spring of 1778 Jefferson suggested that the men quartered at the Barracks plant gardens. He helped procure seeds and tools, but that summer the prisoners were transferred to a new camp in New Jersey without explanation, although the complaints about John Harvie might have had some effect.

The generals at Saratoga were "Gentleman" Johnny Burgoyne and William Phillips. Both of them were exchanged and paroled; they both broke their oaths and fought again. During World War II, another prisoner of war camp was established here for Germans captured in North Africa. *See: Belmont; Blandford Church; Blenheim; Colle; Eniscorthy; Saratoga*

BASIC CITY
Waynesboro   **Obsolete**

Early in the 1900s, a boom town sprang up across the South River from Waynesboro around the Penn Foundry and Car Works that supplied steel wheels and other castings to railroads. A machinist of the works organized the Dawson Manufacturing Company to make steam-powered automobiles. Only one car was ever built and sold. It was designed to carry three people at a claimed twenty-five to thirty miles per hour. The brass steam engine was supplied by an eight-gallon fuel tank and a water tank holding twenty-five gallons. Its performance has not been documented nor has its final resting place. Basic City died completely during the Depression and eventually was annexed by the city of Waynesboro.

BASSETT
Henry County

This is a company village that grew up around the Bassett family's chair factory on the Smith River. Today the factory produces fine quality furniture that is known throughout the county for its excellence of design and workmanship.

BASSETAIRE
King William County   **Obsolete**

Here stood the early home of the Bassett family. It was abandoned in 1730 when Colonel William Bassett moved his family to a new house in New Kent County which he named Eltham. Today this tract is known as Holly Hill. *See: Eltham*

BASTIAN
Bland County

Originally called Parkersburg for an early settler, Parker Hornbarger, the name of this hamlet was changed to Bastian to avoid conflict with the larger city of West Virginia, also a railroad town. E. F. Bastian was an executive of the N & W Railroad who had a home here. The rail line did not pass through Bastian but had its track farther west between Bluefield and Tazewell.

BATH COUNTY

Formed from parts of Augusta, Greenbrier (now in West Virginia), and Botetourt in 1790, this county was named for the famed English city of Bath where hot springs were developed by the Romans in the sixth century. Within Bath County are many warm and hot springs that attract visitors to the famous resorts. The county seat is located at Warm Springs. *See: Hot Springs*

BATTERSEA
Prince George County

This old estate is located within the city of Petersburg. The first house was built by a grandson of the naturalist, John Banister, who bore the same name. This latter-day John Banister was born in Virginia and was sent to England to study law. While at the Inns of Court in London, the house in which he was born was destroyed by fire. The present structure, which he built in 1765 after he had established himself as a successful lawyer, shows some evidence that Thomas Jefferson might have had a hand in its design. But, if that is so as claimed, Jefferson would have been but twenty-one and would not have travelled in France and Italy, the countries which had a great influence on his architectural designs. It is possible that he might have offered advice on post-construction modifications. According to the French Marquis de Chastellux, who wrote of his travels in America during the early Federal period, Battersea "... was decorated in the Italian rather than British or American styles, having three porticoes at three principal entrances, each of them supported by Four Columns."

John Banister was an early supporter of the independence movement as a member of the House of Burgesses. During the Revolution, he rose to the rank of colonel and served with distinction. When General Benedict Arnold came through the area in the summer of 1781, he authorized the vandalization of Battersea. The interior furnishings were destroyed and the house was badly damaged but not burned. After the war Banister served in the Continental Congress and was one of the framers of the Articles of Confederation that bound the newly independent thirteen colonies together prior to the formation of the republic. He signed the Articles for Virginia.

Before Petersburg was incorporated as a town in 1784, Banister's flour mill was an important facility for the people of this part of the Appomattox River valley. The land leading to Battersea was one of the landmarks mentioned in the description of Petersburg's town limits. Colonel John Banister was the first mayor. See: Banister River; Bollingbrook.

BATTERY
Isle of Wight County
Gun emplacements were constructed all over Virginia from 1607 to World War II. The Confederates built many along the James to harass the Union fleet. This one, on the lower south bank of the river, never saw action and was bypassed as ineffective. However, this is the only Virginia community that bears the name Battery, probably because the earthworks for the guns were visible for so many years after the conflict ended. Virginians have difficulty forgetting important things.

BATTLE KNOB
Wythe County
On a rounded top of the local mountains, warriors of the Shawnee and Cherokee nations fought a long, bloody battle in the late eighteenth century with both sides using guns. The Cherokees fortified a spot and held off many attacks but were faced with sure annihilation by a large force when their ammunition ran low. A runner slipped out of the defenses and obtained powder and ball from friendly settlers at Fort Witten down below. Resupplied, the Cherokees won the battle. See: Fort Witten

BATTLETOWN
Clarke County   Site
Major Charles Smith, a wounded veteran of the French and Indian War, came here from Prince William County and built a log cabin with the corners perfectly aligned with the four points of the compass. He built a tavern close by on the post road from Alexandria to the Shenandoah River. Here it became the custom for local youths to engage in boxing and wrestling matches on Saturday afternoons, followed by drinking, gambling, and boasting in the evening. Since this evening activity led to frequent brawls in which everyone took part, the name Battletown was a natural consequence. See: Berryville

BEALTON
Fairfax County
At one time this village was known as Germantown. The Beale family owned a good chunk of land on the outskirts of the settlement which was purchased by the Orange and Alexandria Railroad in 1850. When a depot was decided upon, the railroad surveyor marked his map Beale for the previous owners. The name stuck. John Marshall was born nearby. See: Oak Hill of Loudoun

BEAR CASTLE
Louisa County   Site
Dabney Carr was born at his father's home, Bear Castle, on October 26, 1743. His father, Thomas Carr, was a close associate of Peter Jefferson, both men having been early settlers in this frontier region. Carr and Thomas Jefferson grew up together and were classmates in the Reverend James Maury's school which was equidistant from Shadwell and Bear Castle. Dabney Carr married Jefferson's sister, Martha, and they lived simply and quite happily for eight years during which they had six children. In May 1773, after a brief illness diagnosed as "bilious fever," he died in Charlottesville just as his life was reaching its peak of happiness and his profession as a lawyer was reaping rewards of income and political prominence.

A better speaker than Jefferson, and probably a better lawyer, Carr was pushed to the force by his brother-in-law when they served together in the House of Burgesses. He introduced the resolution that formed the Virginia Committee of Safety, taking an idea proposed by Richard Henry Lee that probably had been written by Jefferson. Still, Carr's forceful presentation and enlightened arguments had much to do with the enthusiastic reception the resolution received during its adoption. Fourteen months after this event, the young Dabney Carr was dead, a great loss

13

to Virginia. He was buried on the grounds of Monticello, the first to lie in the new Jefferson family plot. His body lies near his friend and brother-in-law who lived on for another fifty-three years.

Soon after becoming a widow, Martha Jefferson Carr ran into financial difficulties. Her brother brought her to Monticello and helped raise her children with his own. *See: Carrsbrook; Keswick; Snowden*

BEAVER DAM
Hanover County

Beavers were plentiful throughout Virginia in colonial times, and they still dam streams in isolated woodland areas. It was common for settlers to build their homes beside beaver ponds where fish were plentiful and easy to catch in nets. A few beaver pelts provided income, too. The name Beaver Dam appears in every state that has the proper environment for these busy creatures. When post offices were opened in the early decades of the Federal period, this village, on the main road between northern Virginia and Richmond, was the first to lay claim to the name. *See: New Post*

BEDFORD
King George County

William Fitzhugh came to Virginia in 1670 with John Newton. They shared accommodations for awhile and then both patented large tracts of land in the upper section of Northern Neck. In 1676 William Fitzhugh married Newton's stepdaughter, Sarah Tucker, who was then only eleven years old. The bridegroom promptly packed her off to England for proper schooling. The estate Bedford was established this same year, the house was constructed, and the land was developed into a successful working plantation while the young bride was away. When she returned to Virginia she settled into a happy life and bore her husband five stalwart sons and one daughter (the last child was the girl), almost as if William Fitzhugh had planned all this, too. It was he who, in 1681, began the custom of enclosing his orchard with fences of locust wood which he said was "as desirable as most brick walls and more lasting than any of our bricks." *See: Bedford County; Boscobel; Marmion; Ravensworth*

BEDFORD COUNTY

Formed in 1753 from parts of Lunenburg and Albemarle, this county was named for the fourth Duke of Bedford who was a leading figure in the Privy Council of King George II. When this king made his periodic visits to his ancestral home in Hanover, Germany, the Duke of Bedford advised the Queen Regent, giving him more power and influence in British affairs than the Prime Minister. During the early days of the reign of George III, this Duke of Bedford became the President of the King's Council (in 1763) and was, for all practical purposes, the head of the government since George III did not have much confidence in his other ministers except, perhaps, the Earl of Bute. Lord Bedford supported his king's ending of the subsidy to Frederick, King of Prussia and was opposed to levying additional taxes upon the American colonies to pay for Frederick's wars with Austria. This stand put him on a collision course with the Prime Minister, George Grenville, who fathered the hated Stamp Act of 1765.

The first courthouse of Bedford County was built at New London which, because it had a naturally warm spring, became a social center of note for wealthy Virginians for many years. However, just prior to the Revolution, the county seat was moved to its present location. After the Yorktown surrender, the site of the courthouse was named Liberty. The name lasted one year and then reverted to Bedford Court House. Today it is officially Bedford City to avoid confusion with the Bedford of King George County. *See: Greensville County*

BEL AIR
Prince William County

Major Charles Ewell built a small house on a low hill here in 1740. The view is exceptional. Major Ewell's daughter, Marianne, married Dr. James Craik who became the Surgeon-General of the Continental Army. A granddaughter of the Major married Parson Mason Locke Weems, the man who wrote that epic mixture of fact and fiction entitled *A History of the Life and Death, Virtues and Exploits of General George Washington Equally Honorable to Himself and Exemplary to His Young Countrymen.* Parson Weems authored the fables of the cherry tree and the tossing of the Spanish dollar across the Rappahannock River, neither of which seem to have any basis in truth. *See: Ferry Farm*

BELLE AIR
Charles City County

Built about 1670 not far from the Charles

BEL AIR, PRINCE WILLIAM COUNTY

City County courthouse, this is one of the oldest frame houses still standing in America. In a region where the more common building material was native brick, this house is unique in Tidewater, Virginia for the time. The original heart-pine timbers serve as both a sturdy frame and a quaint interior trim. The land upon which this house was raised is part of the 1,700 acres owned in the middle of the seventeenth century by Thomas Stegge II. *See: Thoroughgood House; Stone House*

BELLE GROVE
Frederick County

This early Federal home, built of native limestone about 1794, saw the Civil War battle of Cedar Creek claim 6,000 lives in October 1864. Union General Phillip Sheridan used the house as his temporary headquarters and wounded were brought here for treatment. The names of soldiers can be seen today where they were scratched into the plaster of the walls. *See: Middletown*

BELLE HAVEN
Accomack County   **Town**

Mr. Bell, an early settler on the Eastern Shore, had a huge outdoor oven on his farm. Known as Bell's Oven, his friends and neighbors applied it to Bell's home. In 1762 the estate was sold and the new owner modified Bell's Oven to Belle Haven, a name that sounded enough like the original to satisfy the neighbors. When a small town grew up on the primary highway, it adopted

the name in 1898 when it applied for incorporation.

BELLEVILLE
Gloucester County

John Booth, a tobacco exporter who shipped his cargoes to London from his own wharf here, built his house on the south side of Mobjack Bay's North River in 1658. He and his partner, John Boswell, had their office in a separate building adjacent to the house. John Booth's grandson, Thomas Booth, built the present house in 1705. It was inherited by his daughter, Frances, who married Warner Throckmorton Taliaferro. During her years at Belleville, this plantation reached its zenith of production and development. Everything used on the place was made here, items ranging from leather to cloth to boats to wrought iron. *See: Church Hill; Mobjack Bay; Toddsbury; Warner Hall*

BELLE VUE
Northampton County

This old house dates back to about 1665. It was erected on the "Secretary's Land," a farm set aside for the personal gain of the Secretary of the colony. Upon this land, on the bay side of the Eastern Shore, a town was to be established as a port for the area. The town did not develop and the port was underutilized. The house remains, however, as evidence that at one time this was the seat of government for the Plantation of Accawmacke. The name Bellevue is prominent in French history as the palace built by Louis XV for his mistress, Madame de Pompadour. *See: Townfields; Tuleries*

BELLFIELD
York County   **Site**

Captain John West received a grant of land, about 2,000 acres, on the York River in 1632 "in right of his son being the first born Christian at Chischiak." When West moved up the river in 1650, he sold this land to Edward Digges, an aggressive planter who first experimented with silk worms before turning to a more reliable cash crop, tobacco. The silk industry never amounted to much in Virginia since the imported silk worms did not thrive on American mulberry leaves. However, part of King Charles II's coronation costume was made of Virginia silk, but that appears to have been the end of production.

Digges made his fortune in tobacco when he developed a mild leaf that sold well in England and Holland. His hogsheads bore the

15

BELLFIELD, YORK COUNTY

brand "E. D. Plantation," a trademark that was continued long after Edward Digges died. His brick manor house, of pretentious size, was a landmark for ships sailing up the York River to Pamunkey Neck and West's plantation. According to an inventory dated August 1682, the house was elaborately furnished. The farm employed 108 slaves of all occupations from house servants to artisans to field hands.

After the Revolution, the Digges family's fortune declined and the estate was sold. In the deed of sale, the name Bellfield appears for the first time so that prior to 1787, the actual name of the plantation is unknown. Most likely it was called the Digges Place or E. D. Plantation. Only the ruins of the manor house exist today, and those are but the foundations. They can be found tucked away in a clearing of the woods beside the Colonial Parkway near Yorktown. *See: Chischiak; West Point*

BELLONA ARSENAL
Chesterfield County   Site

A major arsenal was established by the U.S. Government in 1815 not far from the Midlothian Coal Mines. It was named Bellona for the Roman goddess of war who either was the wife or sister of Mars. The first building of the plant was the powder magazine which had walls five feet thick and was surrounded by a stone wall as high as the magazine's roof. Next came storage facilities for small weapons and the iron cannons that were cast at a foundry adjacent to the arsenal. After barracks for the workers and guards, officers' quarters, workshops, and more storage facilities were constructed, all buildings were connected by a seventeen-foot brick wall that was pierced at intervals for riflemen and had gunports for cannons.

In 1856 Jefferson Davis, then the U.S. Secretary of War, decided to dispose of the entire installation. The selling price was $2,650 for a plant that had cost the taxpayers $200,000 to erect. Moses McArthur, who had served at Bellona for twenty-three years as a sergeant of the guard, bought the arsenal and used the shops to make rifles for the Virginia militia, a move that proved to be most advantageous when the Civil War broke out five years later. Strapped for operating capital, McArthur leased the works to the Confederate Government in 1863 with the proviso that he would be retained as the superintendent.

At the war's end, with no mass market for

new guns and plenty of used ones around, the sergeant sold Bellona to a group of business-men who tore down four of the seven buildings for the bricks which they sold in Richmond for the replacement of those structures burned in the evacuation fire of 1865. Slowly, the remains of the arsenal fell to near ruin. What was left was purchased in 1942 by a private citizen who converted the main building into a private dwelling. *See: Midlothian*

BELLWOOD
Chesterfield County **Obsolete**

Many old-timers remember when the U.S. Army had a supply depot just below Rich-mond during World War II. It was called Bellwood Arsenal since it occupied land formerly owned by James Bellwood, a successful farmer. *See: Defense General Supply Center*

BELMONT
Charlottesville

The southeastern section of Charlottes-ville, nearest to Monticello, was originally owned by John Harvie, a native of Scotland, who settled here about 1740. When Peter Jefferson died in 1757, he named Harvie the guardian of his six minor children, the eldest of whom was Thomas. John Harvie, Sr., one of the first lawyers to practice before the Albemarle County bar, had a hand in the formation of the new county. He died at Belvedere, the Richmond retreat that he had bought from the Byrd family. A portion of the Belmont tract was later purchased by the Gilmer family, who are still active in Charlottesville affairs. At present the entire old farm and house plot is thoroughly covered with modern homes. The site of the old home of Belmont was on the top of the highest knoll

and could be seen from Monticello. *See: Barracks; Belvedere; Pen Park*

BELMONT
Loudoun County

This Belmont was patented in the early eighteenth century by Thomas Lee, the builder of Stratford. About 1800 Ludwell Lee, a former officer of Washington's army, built the present house and lived here until his death in 1836. The name means beautiful hill. *See: Berry Hill; Frying Pan Run; Shuter's Hill*

BELMONT
Stafford County

Thomas Vickers was granted 1,260 acres of land in April 1679 on the north side of the Rappahannock River in return for having transported twenty-six persons to the colony. The grant was not much of a bargain at the time since it was in the part of Virginia that was still inhabited by very unfriendly Indians who were smarting from their defeat in 1676 by Nathaniel Bacon, Jr. The reputa-tion of the Dogues, who lived nearby, was enough to delay any settlement until about 1700 by which time the Indian population had been reduced to a controllable few. Fifty acres of land were given by the Vickers family in 1724 to lay out a town near the courthouse. The manor house of Belmont was built just outside the town in 1761 by John Dixon of Williamsburg who had bought the property of the old farm from Martha Vickers Todd, a descendant of the original patentee. *See: Dogue Indians; Falmouth; Fredericksburg*

BELSPRING
Pulaski County

A large spring in the vicinity was named Bell Spring, probably for its owner. The hamlet that grew near it took the name

Courtesy Defense General Supply Center
BELLWOOD, CHESTERFIELD COUNTY

which, for some unknown reason, is spelled as one word with a letter dropped.

BELVEDERE
Richmond Site

William Byrd built a house on Shoccoe Hill after losing most of his possessions when the James River flooded in April 1685. He was then living in what he called Stone House on the river's edge (its site has never been documented) where he carried on a thriving trade with the settlers of the region and with the Indians, obtaining furs in exchange for tools and cloth. When his son, William II, returned from his schooling in England and his business training in Holland, the young man and his mother chafed at the isolation of Belvedere that was so far up the river from the other James River plantations. The elder Byrd purchased the lands of Westover from Theoderic Bland to which William II (the Black Swan, as he was called) and his mother moved. William Byrd I remained at the Falls to attend to business, living at this home until his death. When the Black Swan inherited Belvedere, he promptly sold it to John Harvie, Sr. of Albemarle County who probably gave it its name. In Italian, *belvedere* means a summer house on a high place. Harvie always referred to this home as his summer place. *See: Belmont of Albemarle; Richmond; Stone House; Westover*

BELVIDERA
Spotsylvania County

The name of this place is of Latin origin, a combination of *bel* meaning "good" and *videre* "to see." Colonel William Daingerfield built his mansion in 1770 on a bluff overlooking the Rappahannock River. The 1,300 acres, on Snow Creek, had been inherited by his wife Sarah from her father, Lawrence Taliaferro. The colonel tried to raise tobacco but gave it up when wheat and corn brought much better prices. He was not a successful manager despite the demand for the grains after the Revolution. Despondent over mounting debts, he killed himself by slitting his throat. Perhaps Colonel Daingerfield could see the future all too well.

BELVOIR
Albemarle County Site

About three miles southwest of Charlottesville lies the site of Belvoir, once the home of John Walker, the eldest son of Dr. Thomas Walker of Castle Hill. Walker was a member of Washington's staff during the Revolution. The first house here, constructed in 1760, was dismantled and moved to another site, known as Maxwell. Colonel Walker then built a much larger home here in 1790 which retained the name. *Belvoir* is French for "beautiful truth." *See: Castle Hill; Locust Hill*

BELVOIR
Fairfax County Site

Colonel William Fairfax came to Virginia in 1734 to act as an agent for his cousin, Thomas, Sixth Lord of Fairfax, the proprietor of Northern Neck. The manor house, originating about 1741, was modernized by the colonel's eldest son, George William Fairfax, sixteen years later. Lawrence Washington, George Washington's elder half brother, married Anne Fairfax, the eldest daughter of Colonel Fairfax and because of this kinship, the general was a frequent visitor to Belvoir in his early teens. It was here that he began his training as a surveyor, taught to him by George William Fairfax who had some engineering background. The future first president always managed to pay a visit to this home when Mary Cary was here. She was the younger sister of his instructor's wife and George Washington was extremely fond of both ladies.

The house and plantation were abandoned in 1774 when the entire Fairfax family returned to England because their ties with royalty would not permit them to be a party to the growing resistance to the king and Parliament. They settled in the English city of Bath where Fairfax then found that he was sympathetic to the Americans after all. He and his wife, Sally, exchanged letters with General Washington all through the Revolutionary War. Washington bought many items from Belvoir when the manor was emptied and its contents were sold after the departure of the Fairfax family, but he could not afford to save everything he wanted. During the next nine years the large house was occupied by squatters who carelessly allowed it to be consumed by fire. When George William Fairfax died in Bath in 1787, his wife lived on for another twenty-five years. She never returned to Virginia. In colonial times, Belvoir was pronounced "BEEV-er." Today the estate is occupied by Fort Belvoir. *See: Carter's Grove; Mount Vernon; Northern Neck*

BENHAMS
Washington County

An early settler, whose last name was Benhams, was a local hero in 1790 during the period of the last Indian uprisings in the east. By quickly racing alone through the forest, he managed to warn others of impending attack. This hamlet honors his memory.

BEN HUR
Lee County
One of the two small producing oil fields in Virginia, this name comes from Lew Wallace's novel of Roman times, *Ben Hur*, which was made into a movie spectacular in the 1960s. Together with the Rose Hill oilfield, nearby in this southwestern county, the combined production is about 3,000 barrels per year. *See: Oilville*

BENNETT'S CHOICE
Nansemond County   Site
After Bennett's Welcome proved to be a success, Edward Bennett, a London merchant, secured another huge tract of land, this time on the east bank of the Nansemond River. His nephew, Richard Bennett, moved down from Bennett's Welcome to become the manager of this plantation when 100 new settlers arrived in Virginia, all of whom had been "transported" at his uncle's expense. Richard was named one of the commissioners to meet with the Maryland delegation to settle the dispute about the boundary between the two colonies. A Puritan, he lead the movement to invite ministers from Boston to help relieve the shortage of clergymen in Tidewater, Virginia. This made him highly popular with the Puritan faction of England who, under Oliver Cromwell, had executed King Charles I at the end of the mother country's civil war.

Richard Bennett, Thomas Stegge, William Claiborne, and Captain Edmund Curtis were appointed commissioners by Cromwell to "reduce Virginia" to a more subservient attitude toward the will of Parliament. The former royal Governor of the colony, William Berkeley, resisted the commissioners but was soon forced to give up his powers and retire to his estate, Green Spring, as a private citizen. The House of Burgesses, careful not to offend Cromwell (who was so busy at home and in Ireland that he ignored Virginia) elected Richard Bennett one of the three men who were Governor during the days of England's Commonwealth. He served for three years beginning in 1652. In the beginning this plantation was called Bennett's Hundred. When the term "hundred" fell out of fashion, it was called Bennett's Choice. Later it was simply Bennett. *See: Belle Air of*

Charles City; Benn's Church; Bennett's Welcome; Denbigh; Green Spring; Occahannock; Swann's Point; Utimara

BENNETT'S WELCOME
Isle of Wight County   Site
Edward Bennett, a prominent London merchant and a member of the Virginia Company, secured a grant for a Particular Plantation in 1621. His two nephews, Richard and Robert, came over to help "plant" the people and to manage the settlement. They established a successful farm on the south bank of the James River along what was then called Shoal Bay (now Burwell's Bay), a wide but rather shallow indentation where the river makes a wide curve. It is across from Mulberry Island and is below Hog Island. The Massacre of 1622 inflicted very heavy casualties here forcing the temporary abandonment of the plantation. In the spring of the next year, a few brave survivors went back and took part in the vigorous military campaign against the local tribes which eliminated the hostile threat. At Bennett's Welcome they put in crops of tobacco and corn and built a system of defenses against possible future attack.

With the success of this settlement, Edward Bennett secured a second grant on the Nansemond River and "transported" 100 more people to "prove out" that grant. Richard moved to the new location while his brother remained in charge of Bennett's Welcome. Robert lived in relative obscurity as a gentleman farmer and left the political activities to his brother.

In 1634 this territory was formed into Warrasqueoc Shire, named for the major tribe that lived on this land before they were eliminated. In 1637 the Indian name was dropped in favor of Isle of Wight County. The present hamlet of Rushmere occupies a part of what once was the thriving settlement and producing farm. *See: Bennett's Choice; Mulberry Island; Nansemond; Shoal Bay; Southside Virginia*

BENN'S CHURCH
Isle of Wight County
When Methodist Bishop Ashbury preached here in 1804, this church was referred to in the records as Benn's Chapel. A distinction was made between Methodists and Anglicans by saying you "went to chapel" if you were a Methodist and "went to church" if you were of the Church of England. This distinction became more common during the days of Queen Victoria. Possibly the name Benn's

Church is a shortened version of Bennett since it was located near Bennett's Welcome. Methodists seldom name their churches for saints, as do Anglicans, Roman Catholics, and Lutherans, although the trend is slowly changing.

BENTONVILLE
Rappahannock County

Benton Roy was the chief of staff of Gen. Hardie's Corps during the Civil War. When the war was over, the local residents decided to honor him. However, they felt Royville did not have the proper ring so they selected the former soldier's first name. *See: Port Royal*

BEN VENUE
Rappahannock County

In the mid-nineteenth century, this was a 5,000 acre farm with a large brick manor house, an overseer's home, and many slave quarters. Twenty miles of stone fences divided the property into special fields. The Civil War ruined the plantation's organization when field hands were hard to find and, when they would work, had to be paid. Ben Venue could not adjust to the postwar economics and declined into bankruptcy. In the new century it was abandoned and finally cut into smaller parcels which were sold for taxes. Ben Venue is Latin for *bene venue*— literally "good coming," but more often translated into "welcome."

BERGTON
Rockingham County

An early name here was West Gap, but the residents objected to a name that honored one person or could be construed as a gap to the west. They selected Dovesville for some obscure reason. That name did not sit too well with the post office since it was too easily confused with Covesville. Therefore, as many of the residents were of German extraction, they combined *berg* the German word for mountain, with *ton* the English short form of town.

BERKELEY
Charles City County

This perfectly situated riverfront estate was first occupied by a group of thirty-nine men under the leadership of Captain John Woodlief. They were sponsored by the Berkeley Company which took its name from Berkeley Castle, England. On the day of their arrival, and following their written instructions, they celebrated a service of thanksgiving on December 4, 1619, a custom that they followed annually. This, then, was the first Thanksgiving in America. Their chaplain, the Reverend George Thorpe, is credited with distilling the first bourbon whiskey from corn that was grown on the place. The men and the Indians who sampled it said it was much better than English ale. In the Massacre of 1622, forty-eight people were killed at Berkeley, many of the victims recent arrivals. As at most exposed farms, it took about a year before resettlement was attempted.

Giles Bland bought the tract from the defunct company in 1637, but he and his heirs lost title to it forever when Bland was hanged as a traitor for his part in Bacon's Rebellion. Benjamin Harrison III of Jordan's Point, while the Attorney-General and Treasurer of the colony, acquired Bland's estate and imme-

Courtesy Malcolm Jamieson

BERKELEY

diately moved into the old house where his son and heir was born.

When Benjamin IV married Anne Carter of Corotoman, he built the present structure. The letters B & A 1726 are still inscribed in a stone of the outer wall. His son, Benjamin V was born in the present manor house in 1730. A signer of the Declaration of Independence, he had quite a fortune to pledge when he affixed his name. After the Revolution, he served as governor of the Commonwealth of Virginia for three terms.

His son, William Henry Harrison, also born at Berkeley, chose a military career, became the governor of the Northwest Territory during Andrew Jackson's presidency, and was elected President (the ninth) with his neighbor, who was born as few miles from here, as his running mate. Their campaign slogan, "Tippicanoe and Tyler too," capitalized on General Harrison's victory over the Shawnees in modern Indiana. President William Harrison wrote his inaugural address at the home of his birth. When he died in office soon after his inauguration, he was succeeded by his Vice President, John Tyler.

Although the twenty-third President, Benjamin Harrison VI was not born here, he was a direct descendant of this James River family.

During the Civil War, the grounds of this estate were occupied by Union troops under General McClellan in the retreat from the disaster of the Peninsula campaign to take Richmond in 1862. An officer, General Daniel Butterfield, in the encampment composed the famous bugle call "Taps," which is widely known. While the army rested at Berkeley, President Lincoln made a field visit to personally confer with General McClellan. (The general ran against Lincoln in 1864 as a Democrat.) During Reconstruction this estate fell into disrepair, and both the house and the farmlands suffered from neglect. They were rescued by a former Union drummer boy who had been with McClellan's army at Berkeley.

In 1907 a Scot, John Jamieson, purchased the place and began to restore the house and grounds. His son, Malcolm Jamieson, continued the careful restoration and brought this historic estate back to life as a working farm of more than 1,000 acres that produces small grains, hay, and sheep. Berkeley is open to the public, but only the first floor of the manor house can be viewed since the Jamieson family makes it their home. *See: Brandon; Corotoman; Eastover; Greenway; Harrison's Landing; Jordan's Point; Sherwood Forest*

BERMUDA HUNDRED
Chesterfield County   Site

Between 1613 and 1619, during the "Peace of Pocahontas," the early settlers fenced in a huge tract of land from the city of Henricus south to the mouth of the Appamattox River. This tract was named Bermuda Hundred by Governor, Sir Thomas Gates, to commemorate the time he had spent shipwrecked in Bermuda while enroute to Virginia. Captain George Yeardley, the commander of militia for Gates and later Governor, settled at the southern end of this enclosed land at the mouth of the Appomattox where it enters the James. When others made their homes on the opposite bank, this portion was called Upper Bermuda Hundred and the other portion (now City Point) was Nether Bermuda Hundred.

When the colony of Virginia was divided into four corporations, Upper and Nether were dropped and it was all Charles City. However, when representatives were selected for the First Assembly in the summer of 1619, Bermuda Hundred as a borough was entitled to send two men who took part in the momentous assembly, the first in America. Bermuda Hundred was badly mauled in the Massacre in 1622 and few people returned. The low land, vulnerable to periodic flooding by the James River, was unattractive even though it was extremely fertile. No traces of the early habitations at Bermuda Hundred can be found today. It is occupied by a modern synthetic fabric plant and one charming farm house of rather recent vintage. A stone marker that one has to search to find honors Sir George Yeardley and his fellow colonists who lived here 360 years ago. *See: City Point; Hopewell*

BERRY HILL
Stafford County   Site

On the north lip of Potomac Creek was Berry Hill, the home of Thomas Ludlow Lee, son of the builder of Stratford. Prior to his arrival, a village of the Petomek Indians was located here. *See: Belmont of Loudoun; Potomac Creek*

BERRYVILLE
Clarke County   Town

Known for many years as Battletown, for the many brawls that took place at a local tavern, this town adopted the name Berryville when it was laid out in 1798 on land owned by Benjamin Berry; *See: Battletown*

21

BEVERLEY PARK
King and Queen County   **Site**

Robert Beverley II was born in his father's home, Barn Elms, in Middlesex County about 1673. He was educated in England, as was the custom in most of the wealthy Virginia families, and then returned to make his mark upon the social and political structure of the colony. Settling in Jamestown where he built a house, he married the sixteen-year-old daughter of William Byrd II. The following year Ursula died while giving birth to their only child. The bereaved Robert never remarried. Inheriting a large piece of land in King and Queen County, he became the clerk of the county court while maintaining his home in Jamestown.

In 1702 he went to London to defend his ownership of land and houses at Point Comfort which the colony of Virginia had decided to condemn for an expansion of Fort George. During his eighteen months in England, he wrote open letters that were critical of the Governor, the Council, and the House of Burgesses which, when published, ruined him politically. Upon his return to the land of his birth, Beverley built a home in King and Queen County and established his estate, Beverley Park. Settling into a spartan life, he wrote his famous *The History and Present State of Virginia* which was printed in England in 1705. His son, William, built Blandfield in Essex County. *See: Blandfield; Sabine Hall*

BEWDLEY
King and Queen County

An imposing brick house of Georgian style was begun in the third quarter of the eighteenth century for Obadiah Marriott. Located on the bank of the Mattaponi River, it was not finished until a half century later. Marriott's fortunes fell in the 1766 exposure of Speaker John Robinson's mishandling of the colony funds, a scandal that hurt many honest gentlemen who had accepted loans from Robinson. Bewdley was completed in the early part of this century and is occupied today. *See: Piscataway*

BEWDLEY
Lancaster County   **Site**

On the north bank of the Rappahannock River once stood Bewdley. It was constructed about 1750 by Major James Ball, a first cousin of Washington's mother. The house was unusual for colonial times since it had two rows of dormer windows, three for the second floor and three for the third, all set into a high, steeply-pitched shingled roof. This house remained in the Ball family until it was destroyed by fire in 1917. *See: Epping Forest; Saint Mary's White Chapel*

BIG LICK
Roanoke County   **Obsolete**

Although this name is no longer used, it was the official name of the city of Roanoke for many years. A marsh here attracted wildlife from all over the region for the natural salt deposits which all animals love to lick. It was an excellent place for hunters to make an easy kill. *See: Roanoke*

BIG STONE GAP
Wise County   **Town**

A gap through Stone Mountain was cut eons ago by the Powell River. The town was sited at the junction of three forks of the river, at a natural route for the rail line for trains to pick up coal from the nearby mines. At first the settlement was called Three Forks. Next it was Imboden. It was chartered in 1882 as Mineral City but, to avoid confusion with Mineral of Louisa County, the present name was adopted in 1888.

BIZARRE
Cumberland County

This minor estate, near Farmville on the Appomattox River, was settled in 1742 by Richard Randolph of Curles. John Randolph of Roanoke Plantation, a grandson of the original owner, took refuge here with his mother when Benedict Arnold's British forces invaded the James River area in the summer of 1781. The long journey from Curles to Bizarre was made almost entirely by small boat.

Bizarre came into the news as the locale of the only major scandal in the Randolph family's closet. It involved Richard (another grandson), Richard's young and rather plain wife, and the wife's attractive and rather active sister, Nancy Mann Randolph of Tuckahoe (keeping it all within the family). Patrick Henry successfully defended Richard and Nancy against a charge of murdering Nancy's child on the night it was born. The case was a series of suppositions since it was never proven that Nancy actually was pregnant or that a child ever had been born to her, but circumstantial evidence was strong in support of these charges. While maternity was not actually established, and the acquittal was based on this point, scandalmongers were certain that Richard was the father and that the bloodstains on a shingle in the woodpile came from the newborn child which Richard supposedly buried in the dark of early morning. Nancy denied all.

Nicely recovered from her "strange sickness" by the time of the trial, she later married the aging Gouverneur Morris of New York, and became the belle of Northern society. Richard never fully recovered from the trial and the scandal that accompanied it. He died within four years, as much from shame, it was supposed, as from any disease. Strangely, the name Bizarre had been given to this farm long before the bizarre events took place. Perhaps the elder Richard Randolph thought that living this far out in the wilderness was reason enough to warrant the unusual name. See: Curles; Rosewell; Tuckahoe

BLACKSBURG
Montgomery County   **Town**

Named for William Black who divided the land into lots to form a town in 1798, this settlement was previously called Draper's Meadows for the home of the leading citizen, Colonel James Patton. When the colonel moved away, Black began his efforts to create the town. Here is located Virginia Polytechnical Institute and State University, better known as V.P.I. See: Draper's Meadow

BLACKSTONE
Nottoway County   **Town**

Many years ago, the settlement here was called Blacks and Whites for two taverns along the road. One was operated by a Mr. Schwartz (which is German for black), the other by a Mr. White. Some say the town was named for Schwartz. Others say it was named in honor of Sir William Blackstone, the English jurist. Possibly both suggestions are true. Near Blackstone is the U.S. Army's huge reservation, Fort Pickett.

BLACK'S TAVERN
Albemarle County   **Site**

About two miles west of Yancey's Mill, on the old Three Chopt Road to Waynesboro, is the site of Black's Tavern, once operated by James Black. He was the son of the Reverend Samuel Black, the pastor of Rockfish Church, and the first Presbyterian minister to settle in Albemarle County. When George Rogers Clark visited his native county in 1777, he passed the first night at Black's Tavern and from there went to the Keswick section of Albemarle to see the cabin in which he was born. When Dr. John Bolling Garrett built his

home here 100 years later, he moved the old tavern behind his large house which he named Seven Oaks. See: White Hall of Albemarle

BLACKWATER RIVER

This river, along with the Nottoway and the Meherrin, form the Chowan River of North Carolina. Although the Blackwater is relatively shallow, it is free of rapids and was a natural waterway to the southeast for barges and rafts. A great many settlers from Edenton moved up this river; later, they sent their produce down it to be sold to the residents of North Carolina's early capital. The name of this river comes from the dark color of the water that is stained by the oaks and cypress trees of the numerous swamps that it drains.

BLADENSFIELD
Westmoreland County

The original estate was patented in May 1653 by John Jenkins who built his house about 1690. When Jenkins died about twenty years later, Bladensfield became a part of Robert "King" Carter's estate, Nomini Hall, which it adjoined. John Peck, who followed the more famous Phillip Fithian as tutor to the Carter children, eloped with one of the girls that he was teaching. This was in 1775. Her father, "Councillor" Carter, was irate at first but he soon relented and gave the couple Bladensfield as a wedding gift. Ann Carter and John Peck lived happily in their two-story house and enjoyed the profits of the 1,000 acres. See: Nomini Hall

BLAIRS
Pittsylvania County

The leading citizen of this settlement was John Blair, the local delegate to the Virginia Assembly. When the Southern Railway decided to add a station and depot to serve the people here, Blair contributed the land. Since there already was a town of Blair in West Virginia, the new station was named Blair's. The minor spelling alteration apparently prevented confusion.

BLAND COUNTY

Formed from parts of Wythe, Tazewell and Giles counties in 1861, this coal-rich region was named for Richard Bland, a Revolutionary leader. The courthouse was built at the little village of Seddon which changed its name to Bland when it was incorporated as a town in 1872. See: Jordan's Point

BLANDFIELD
Essex County

This land was patented in 1688 by Robert Beverley I, but the house was not built until three generations later. William Beverley, the only son of Robert II and his child bride, Ursula Byrd, inherited this property in 1730 but did not get around to having a house built for another forty years. The mansion and numerous connected dependencies had a total of twenty-four rooms. Possibly designed by the noted architect John Ariss, the main brick dwelling is surrounded by a "ha-ha," a ditch that keeps the livestock at a distance without the bother of a fence or wall.

William Beverley named his estate Blandfield in honor of his wife whose maiden name was Bland. It was inherited by their son, Robert III, who was educated in England at Trinity College and remained steadfastly loyal to the Crown. Stubbornly, he remained in Virginia all through the Revolution and kept out of county and state affairs. Although he was a county magistrate in 1775, he declined to serve on the Essex County Committee of Safety and resigned his office, declaring that he would not participate in any public business while a Revolution was raging. After the war he was elected to the General Assembly by his fellow Tories of Essex but, as a matter of principle he declined to take his seat. *See: Barn Elms; Essex County; Manor Mansion*

BLANDFORD CHURCH
Petersburg

This brick church on Well's Hill, now known as Old Blandfield Church, was built between 1734 and 1737. It was named for the town of Blandford which disappeared as a political entity after being annexed by the present city of Petersburg. At the time of its erection, the church was a part of Bristol Parish. British General William Phillips lies buried in the churchyard along with American soldiers of six wars. Phillips was in command of troops sent out by Lord Cornwallis in the summer of 1781 under the control of General Benedict Arnold. The mission was to raid various towns in central Virginia to convince the populace that resistance to the king's forces was not only futile but expensive. In Petersburg, Phillips seized the tobacco and burned it. In a skirmish the general was wounded. Already ill from some unspecified sickness, his wound proved too much for his enfeebled body and he died a few days later. American forces, under Lafayette, continued to clash with his troops all the while he lay dying. His last words were, "Those damned colonials won't even let a gentleman die in peace." He gave no care about the men his troops had killed nor of the suffering the raids had caused to noncombatants and women and children.

Blandford Church was the center of a storm during the seige of Petersburg by General Grant in the winter of 1864-65. Confederates defending the hill used the gravestones as cover from small arms fire but were forced to give up this important high ground when Union shells began to fall. The bombardment badly damaged the old church and set a fire that burned out its interior. Many years after the end of the Civil War, Blandford Church was repaired and turned into a shrine for the fallen men of the Confederacy. The beautiful Tiffany windows were given by each former Confederate state as a memorial to its brave warriors who fought honorably for states rights. *See: Battersea; Blenheim; Bollingbrook; Bristol Parish; Colonial Heights; Petersburg*

BLENHEIM
Albemarle County

This land was part of the original grant of 1730 which John Carter, then the Secretary of the colony, obtained from the Crown. Edward Carter, the Secretary's son, settled on 9,500 acres and named his home for the great manor house in England that was given to Sir John Churchill by Queen Anne for his victory at Blenheim on the Continent. Edward Carter represented this county in the House of Burgesses with Dr. Thomas Walker of Castle Hill from 1767 to 1769, and with George Nicholas in the General Assembly after independence. British General William Phillips, after his capture at Saratoga, lived quite comfortably here with his mistress while his less fortunate troops were confined in the barracks at White Hall.

Described in 1779 by Thomas Anbury, Blenheim "stands on a lofty eminence, commanding a very extensive prospect. The present proprietor, Colonel Carter, possesses a most affluent fortune, and has a variety of seats in situations far surpassing this of Blenheim, which he suffers to go to ruin." General Phillips was paroled later in the Revolution but broke his word "as a Gentleman" and led troops for Lord Cornwallis with the traitor Benedict Arnold. This estate was inherited by Edward Lee, the youngest son of Anne Hill Carter and Harry

Lee. *See: Barracks; Blandford Church; Colle; Corotoman; Saratoga*

BLOOMSBURY
Orange County

Bloomsbury was the estate of the pioneer James Taylor, ancestor of two Presidents, James Madison and Zachary Taylor. A member of Governor Spotswood's expedition west of the Blue Ridge Mountains in 1716, he was one of the Knights of the Golden Horseshoe. *See: Montebello; Swift Run Gap*

BLOXOM
Accomack County   **Town**

William E. Bloxom was an early postmaster here. The town of Bloxom was incorporated in 1953.

BLUEFIELD
Tazewell County   **Town**

First known as Pin Hook, this town grew in 1883 when the Norfolk and Western Railway completed a line to the Pocahontas Coal Mine. When first incorporated a year later, it was named Graham for Thomas Graham, an officer of the railroad. In 1924 it was re-incorporated as Bluefield to match its sister city in West Virginia which it adjoins. The "blue" comes from the abundance of blue stone in this region. Unlike Bristol, which also adjoins another community in the neighboring state, the state boundary does not run down the middle of Main Street.

BLUEMONT
Loudoun County

This hamlet was called Snickersville for a long time. About 1900 the name was changed to Bluemont for the Blue Ridge Mountains that rise west of it. This is the only community in Virginia that is named for the mountains and, in this case, it is a shortened form. *See: Mount; Snicker's Gap*

BLUE RIDGE MOUNTAINS

A very early name for these beautiful, relatively low hills was Blue Ledge Mountains. The old word *ledge* meant *ridge*. The soft blue haze that clings to these famous mountains suggests the descriptive name. These are the second mountains encountered when traveling westward from the Chesapeake Bay. First are the Southwest Mountains. Between them and the Blue Ridge is the Piedmont section of Virginia. West of the Blue Ridge is the Shenandoah Valley which is bounded by the more formidable Alleghanies.

All of these hills and mountains are a part of the Appalachian Range that stretches from New York to Georgia. *See: Southwest Mountains*

BLUE RIDGE PARKWAY

Beginning at Rockfish Gap, the southern terminus of the Skyline Drive, this roadway follows the crests of the Blue Ridge Mountains and the Great Smokey Mountains of Tennessee for a distance of 469 miles, half of which are in Virginia. From Waynesboro to Buena Vista, the parkway is in the George Washington National Forest. From Buena Vista to just east of Roanoke, it is in the Jefferson National Forest. This scenic roadway, begun in 1936, is administered by the National Park Service.

BLUE STONE CASTLE
Mecklenburg County   **Site**

William Byrd II patented land here in 1730 and named the tract for the color of the native rock. The land grant extended for miles along the Roanoke River. Byrd did not build a castle here, nor any other significant dwelling, but liked the sound of the name he gave it. Shortly before the Revolution, William Byrd III played a game of chance with Sir Peyton Skipwith, putting up this land as his gambling stake. Byrd lost. Skipwith added to it many years later and created Prestwould Plantation.

BOLLINGBROOK
Petersburg

When this house was built, about 1725, there was no town of Petersburg. At first there were two separate buildings which were combined into one house by Major Robert Bolling. Twice it was used as temporary headquarters by General William Phillips and General Benedict Arnold, two British officers who headed a large raiding party in 1781. While they occupied Bollingbrook, it was bombarded by Lafayette from his battery on Colonial Heights. The young Frenchman did not know that General Phillips was then dying from a disease complicated by a recent wound. *See: Blandford Church; Blenheim; Cedar Level*

BOLTHROPE
Newport News   **Site**

Five-hundred acres were patented in 1626 by Richard Stevens on the Warwick River just above Denbigh Plantation. Stevens had married the daughter of the Cape Merchant, Abraham Piersey, and when his wife came

25

into her inheritance, Stevens was then the owner of a huge estate in the heart of the populated part of the Peninsula. His son, Captain Samuel Stevens, married the sister of Lord Culpeper shortly after inheriting this large estate. When he died after only a few years of married life with Frances Culpeper, she married Sir William Berkeley, the royal Governor, who then sold off his wife's land to William Cole, a member of the Council.

In 1685, Cole gained title to an adjoining tract held by the Gookin family then known as the Newport's News Plantation. Both parcels of land, when combined, were known as Bolthrope by which it was known until 1766. At about the time of the Declaration of Independence, Cole Digges, through inheritance from both of his grandfathers (William Cole and Edward Digges) combined the lands of Bolthrope, Denbigh, and Newport's News into one huge unit known collectively as Nutmeg Quarter. *See Bellfield; Chippokes; Denbigh; Green Spring; Pear Tree Hall; Newport News*

BON AIR
Chesterfield County   **Site**

In the 1880s a popular resort was established just outside of Richmond. The French name means *good air*. It is now a suburb of the city of Richmond.

BONAPART

See: Galax

BOONE'S MILL
Franklin County   **Town**

Jacob Boone came here in 1782 and built a grist mill on Maggodee Creek. Since it was on the Carolina Road, many people brought their grain to him to be made into flour. Jacob was Daniel Boone's cousin. *See: Mill*

BOROUGH

Once the Virginia Company's charter was changed to permit the granting of land for private ownership (for a modest quit rent paid to the Governor), numerous settlements were established on both sides of the James River. In 1614 the colony was divided into Four Ancient Boroughs—James City, Kecoughtan, Charles City, and the City of Henricus. When plans were revealed for a General Assembly in 1619, the four Boroughs became Four Incorporations within which were eleven boroughs, each named for the major town or plantation within the boun-

daries. Each borough was authorized to send two representatives to Jamestown to formulate new laws that touched on matters peculiar to the colony which had been placed under English Common Law, replacing the harsh martial law of Lord Delaware. Whatever laws the representatives wrote would not take effect until approved by the king's Privy Council.

Full of hope, the twenty-two men met in the Jamestown Church, with the Governor and his Council, on July 30, 1619. The two men from Martin's Brandon were expelled since they had been instructed by John Martin that they could not bind his Particular Plantation to any new laws created in this General Assembly. The remaining twenty men, under the leadership of John Pory, the Secretary of the colony who acted as Speaker of the house, worked for four days. One man died, either from the intense heat or from some disease he had before he arrived in the capital. Many of the laws were approved after a delay of over a year. This gathering was the first attempt to have representative government in America. It convened eighteen months before the Pilgrims landed at Cape Cod. *See: City; Corporations; Martin's Brandon; Shires*

BOSCOBEL
Fairfax County

This was the home of Thomas Fitzhugh, a grandson of William Fitzhugh of Bedford, King George County. The entire family, of Scottish descent, was very loyal to the memory of the Stuart kings of England, particularly Charles II. However, during the Revolution, the Fitzhughs were strongly in favor of independence. Boscobel was a home in Scotland near which, in September 1651, young King Charles II took refuge in an oak tree after his army was defeated at Worcester. The "Boscobel Oak" was often celebrated by the restored King during his reign of twenty-five years. It often appeared on royal medallions. *See: Bedford of King George; Chatham; Kinsale*

BOSTON
Culpeper County

When the residents of this tiny hamlet reached for a name, they chose to honor Boston, Mass. That historic city was named for a major seaport in Lincolnshire, England, from which the Pilgrims tried to sail to Holland. *See: South Boston*

BOSWELL'S TAVERN
Louisa County **Site**
A tavern was built on the main stage road, about 1735, where River Road meets the Three Chopt Road. The Marquis de Chastellux, who travelled in Virginia after the Revolution, described Colonel Boswell, the innkeeper, as a "tall, stout Scotsman . . . who appeared but little prepared to received strangers." Boswell's tavern was renamed The Lafayette Tavern in 1824 when the famous Frenchman stopped here long enough to have the horses of his coach changed. The new name was soon forgotten. The colonial structure has been so often modified over the past 250 years that it bears little resemblance to the original. *See: River Road; Three Chopt Road; Zion Crossroads*

BOTETOURT COUNTY
Norborne Berkeley, Baron de Botetourt, a popular Governor of Virginia for two years, was the next to the last Englishman to hold the job. Succeeded by John Murray, who was Lord Dunmore, Lord Botetourt is the only colonial Governor that Virginians honored by erecting a statue of him in Williamsburg. During his first year in office, 1769, a new county was formed from a part of Augusta and was named for him. While Dunmore was the Governor, Botetourt County was reduced in size to form Fincastle. After the surrender at Yorktown, Fincastle County was eliminated and Botetourt County's lines were re-arranged. However, since a new courthouse had been erected in the town of Fincastle, which was situated in the center of the re-aligned Botetourt County, that town continued to be the county seat. *See: Fincastle; Gloucester County*

BOTTOM'S BRIDGE
New Kent County
The first bridge built here to span the upper reaches of the Chickahominy River was put up shortly after 1700. John Bottom owned the land on both sides of the stream and, since the colonial road that required the bridge went through his land, it was named Bottom's Bridge. Bottom did not own it nor did he bother to keep it in repair. In 1743 the court of Henrico County authorized a new bridge if New Kent County would share the expenses. An agreement was worked out and the new span was built which retained its former name as have many other replacements over the past two centuries.

BOURBON
Fort Eustis
The only existing colonial house still standing on Mulberry Island has an unclear history. The original frame house, brick foundations, and chimneys date to about 1660, according to local historians' guesses. The structure was bricked over some time between 1700 and 1730. Later, the Reverend Robert Webb took bricks from an unused separate kitchen dependency and built a second story on this old dwelling. A keystone brick, possibly a copy of one from the kitchen, is inscribed "Mathew Jones 1727," but when it was actually fired is uncertain and it could be a copy. No court records mention a Mathew Jones House, but several men of that name have lived in the vicinity. One Mathew Jones, who died in Isle of Wight County (just across the James River), mentioned his "new" plantation on Mulberry Island in his will of 1727 but that is all that one can go on. Some call this house "Bourbon," without explanation. It probably is a family name; several men of the Jones family had Bourbon as part of their names. Bourbon whiskey was first made from corn at Berkeley Plantation about 1621. *See: Berkeley; Mulberry Island; Varina*

BOWLERS
Essex County
This area was settled in 1663 by Thomas Bowler. The original house of the mid-seventeenth century still stands. In 1730 a descendant of Bowler was authorized to run a ferry from Bowler's Wharf.

BOWLING GREEN
Caroline County **Town**
The first settler to build a fine home near here was Major John Hoomes who came to this frontier region in 1670. The magnificent oaks still standing at his old home are said to have come from acorns which he brought with him from England because he feared he would not see his favorite trees in Virginia. Bowling on a level patch of finely trimmed grass was a polite pastime, and the Major named his place Bowling Green although it is not known if he actually had such a green at his home. When Caroline County was formed in 1727, Hoomes donated the land for the courthouse, and the county seat adopted the name of the benefactor's establishment. The kind Major did not object and from then on he called his manor Old Mansion. *See: Caroline County; King's Highway; Milford*

BOWMAN'S FOLLY
Accomack County

East of Accomack Court House, on Folly Creek, the first home of Edward Bowman stood in lonely isolation. It was built about 1653 by the man who became the sheriff, a Burgess, and the Major of Militia for the district. He applied the unusual name shortly after his only son died of "slow fever" in 1660. This personal loss made him extremely depressed and from then on he considered his coming to Virginia to have been a terrible folly. The present house was built about Revolutionary times by John Cropper who married Bowman's daughter, Gertrude. The earlier house was torn down for the new home. Cropper acquired his rank as the head of the Eastern Shore militia during peacetime.

BOYCE
Clarke County   **Town**

This town is sited at the intersection of the N & W Railroad line and the Winchester Turnpike. There is no published record about the origin of the name. The town was incorporated in 1910 and possibly owes its name to some railroad official since the N & W named many hamlets during its expansion in the late nineteenth century. This town taps water from a well that provides liquid so cold that no ice is needed with it. Of course, this is also a disadvantage when making hot water. The town's standpipe uses solar energy to take off the chill before it is distributed to the homes, an application of modern technology that was purely accidental.

BOYD'S TAVERN
Albemarle County   **Site**

When known as Shepherd's Ordinary, this was little more than a place to water a horse and buy a drink or a poor meal. The ordinary was sited on the Three Chopt Road at its intersection with the River Road. During the Revolution, it gained a measure of competence by expanding into an inn where food and lodging could be obtained. At that time it was called Boyd's Tavern for the owner, a Mr. Boyd. The original structure burned in 1780 and was quickly replaced by another which also was destroyed by fire in 1868. The present frame building, although probably close to one hundred years old by now, quite possibly was never used as a tavern. *See: Zion Crossroads*

BOYDTON
Mecklenburg County   **Town**

This town, the county seat, was named for Alexander Boyd, a Scot who settled here in 1765. A respected county judge, he died while holding court in 1801. Here was the first location of Randolph Macon College, chartered in 1830 by the Methodist Church of Virginia. When the college was moved to Ashland three years after the end of the Civil War, Boydton lost its major industry and had to be content being the county seat with its erratic flow of visitors who came during court days. In the late 1800s, Boyd Tavern was built which, by the turn of the century, had been expanded into a thirty room lodging house known as the Finch Hotel. It was once one of the state's top attractions for vacationers from the Commonwealth and North Carolina. When America took to the road in automobiles after World War I, and people did not have to select vacation spots that were convenient to the railroads, Finch Hotel went into a serious decline. The building was converted into apartments. By 1970 it was such a serious firetrap that it was condemned and was scheduled for demolition. However, ancestors of Judge Alexander Boyd formed the Boyd Family Memorial Foundation, bought the old hotel, and have converted it into a community center and local museum.

BRANCH

The upper portions of a river are called the *forks* which, in turn, are fed by small streams known as *branches* so that the whole plan can be compared to a tree. In those sections of America which were settled late in the colonial period or during the nineteenth century, a branch is often incorrectly called a creek. A popular drink in Virginia, since 1620, is "bourbon and branch"—that is, bourbon whiskey and plain water. Scotch drinkers, of course, never use this common shorthand term but always order scotch and water in a more civilized manner. *See: Creek; Run*

BRANDON
Prince George County

John Martin came to Virginia in 1607 with the first colonists. In the spring of 1610, he was banished from Jamestown for repeatedly disagreeing with Lord Delaware's policies. He and a few of his supporters moved to the opposite bank of the James River and created his own Particular Plantation a few miles upstream. Investing his own money, Martin built houses and transported new people from home. A severe fire wiped out his buildings, forcing him into bankruptcy. Unsuccessful in collecting debts owed to him, he died, nearly a pauper, in 1632 and was buried at Brandon. His grave remains to be found. After his death, a group of men formed a corporation named Merchant's Hope and bought Martin's plantation.

In 1720 the land was purchased by Nathaniel Harrison who did not live here but remained in his several homes in Warwick and Stafford counties. His son, Nathaniel II, inherited Brandon and elected to live here shortly after marrying the daughter of Colonel Cole Digges. The present house is thought to be designed by Thomas Jefferson, a groomsman at Harrison's wedding, who suggested constructing a main building to connect two older houses that were perfectly aligned. From this resulting manor house one can see the James River at the end of a long, sweeping lawn.

During the Civil War, Union gunboats occasionally fired blasts at the house since it was such an easy, tempting target. Brandon was of no military significance, but was damaged as were many other historic homes in Virginia. Some minor scars of this shelling can be seen today as evidence of Brandon's heritage that spans more years than any estate in any Northern state. *See: Curles; Martin's Brandon; Martin's Hundred; Prince George County; White House*

BRANDY STATION
Culpeper County

Early in the ninetenth century, a tavern here had the word *Brandy* painted in large letters on an outer wall. During the War of 1812, soldiers passing by purchased all the spirits they could afford and named the watering place Brandy House. When the railroad built a local station in 1854, it called it Brandy Station. Here, on June 9, 1863, Jeb Stuart's cavalry was massed for a ceremonial review by the general staff. It was suddenly attacked by Union cavalry under the command of General Alfred Pleasanton. Altogether, about 10,000 mounted troops were engaged, the first real cavalry battle of the Civil War. Prior to this time, cavalry had been used effectively for reconnaissance and minor raids by the well-horsed Southerners who looked upon the Federal cavalry with contempt as a timid group of noncombatants. General Stuart rallied his surprised troopers who fought well but were soon required to break off the action since they had no support. The Northerners lost 936 men, the Confederates 523 in the brief clash. From

then on, the Union cavalry, made bold by the relative success of their attack, became an active, constant threat. It played a vital part in the eventual surrender of General Lee less than two years later. *See: Five Forks*

BREAKS
Buchanan County

The local people here called the deep ravines of the nearby Cumberland Mountains "breaks." A small community was founded here during the nineteenth century which the people decided to call Breaks. Near here is Russel Fork Canyon which is five miles long. Breaks Interstate Park, spread over parts of Virginia and Kentucky, was dedicated for public use in 1955.

BREMO
Henrico County   **Site**

Richard Cocke patented the acreage in 1639 on the north bank of the James River just above the great bends that surround Curles Plantation. This early Bremo was abandoned about fifty years later when the Cocke family decided to get away from the periodic flooding of the James and the malarial marshes that bred swarms of biting insects. They moved farther inland to establish a new family estate which they named Malvern Hills. The abandoned remains of Lower Bremo, as it was later called, were washed away in the great flood of 1771. The name bremo comes from the Cocke family's home village of Braemore in County Wilts, England, not far from the ancient city of Bath. *See: Bremo Recess; Malvern Hills; Mount Pleasant*

BREMO RECESS
Albemarle County

A member of the Cocke family of Malvern Hills received a 1,500-acre grant in Albemarle County on the north bank of the James. Richard H. Cocke built a simple dwelling that he used as a hunting lodge and masculine retreat. He was fussy about marking the corners of his property and at one corner he placed a stone monument into which were carved his initials, RHC, and the inscription from the Bible, "Remove not the landmarks thy forefathers have set thee." Richard Cocke's son, Colonel John Hartwell Cocke, lived in the hunting lodge while his larger, permanent home was being constructed according to a design by his friend, Thomas Jefferson. Situated on a high bank of the river, the formal name of this dwelling is Bremo Bluff, although many times it was referred to by members of the Cocke family as Upper Bremo. *See: Malvern Hills*

BRENTSVILLE
Prince William County

A "Sanctuary for peoples of all religions" was established along the Potomac by King James II as a New World refuge for his fellow Catholics who preferred to live in Virginia rather than in strictly governed Maryland. Those who came here lived close together in a small community. They named their village Brentsville for Giles Brent, the first settler in this region. He helped them form the first Roman Catholic congregation in the Old Dominion.

Beginning in 1822, Brentsville was the seat of Prince William County. Since it was on the extreme eastern edge of the county and was very inconvenient for most people, the courthouse and corresponding public buildings were rebuilt in Manassas in 1892 after a long interval of argument. With the loss of the courthouse, Brentsville went into a severe decline from which it never recovered. Adding to insult, it does not even appear on the Commonwealth's official highway map these days. *See: Dumfries; Marlborough; Prince William County*

BRICK HOUSE
Chesterfield County

The oldest house in this county was built in 1685 by Richard Kennon who came to Virginia prior to 1670. His home was made of brick, suitable to his wealth, while his neighbors had to be content with frame dwellings. He was a merchant at Bermuda Hundred before he received his grant of land between Swift Creek and the Appomattox River, a tract that sometimes is called Conjuror's Neck after an old Indian medicine man who once lived there. Richard Kennon married the daughter of Robert Bolling; his sister married John Bolling, his wife's half brother. They all lived at Cobbs although the plantation house always was known as Brick House. The Kennon children married into other old-line families of the James River society. *See: Bermuda Hundred; Bollingbrook; Cedar Level; Chatsworth; Cobbs Hall; Kippax*

BRICKHOUSE
New Kent County   **Site**

For many years a lonely brick structure stood on the bank of the Pamunkey River. Erected prior to 1650, it was used as the courthouse of New Kent County from 1654 to 1691. When the General Assembly passed an act for the establishment of towns in 1680, a port was to have been created here which was to be named Brickhouse. The port was not successful; no town grew around it. The county seat was moved elsewhere and the brick building stood alone and unused. During Bacon's Rebellion of 1676, William Drummond and William Lawrence, two leaders of the rebel faction, hid in the former courthouse. Alerted at the last possible moment that the Governor's troops were near, they fled. Drummond was captured, taken to Governor Berkeley at Green Spring, and hanged the same day. Lawrence escaped and was never heard from again. *See: Green Spring; Doncastle's Ordinary*

BRIDGEWATER
Rockingham County   **Town**

A covered bridge crossed the North River to serve this community. When the residents decided to get rid of the former name, Dinkletown, they turned to the bridge for inspiration. It has been Bridgewater since 1835. The name is not unique, however. There is a city of that name in Somerset, England, and there are cities and towns of that name in many other states.

BRIDGEWATER COLLEGE
Bridgewater

The oldest coeducational college in the Commonwealth, this school was founded in 1880 with the unwieldy name Spring Creek Normal and Collegiate Institute. Seven years later it was moved to Bridgewater where it was renamed. This is the first college of the Church of the Brethren to grant degrees to its graduates. *See: Nokesville*

BRISTOL
Washington County   **City**

On land owned by Isaac Baker and Evan Shelby, a farm known as Sapling Grove, a town grew around these two pioneer's trading post. It was the only store for miles around. By 1765, Sapling Grove had sufficient population to become a town. During the early Federal period, John Goodson purchased the Sapling Grove farm, the store, much of the land in the town, and put his mark on the community. In 1856, the town's name was changed to Goodson. However, about thirty-five years later, the name was changed to Bristol, either for the city in

England from which port many immigrants sailed to Virginia during colonial days, or for Bristol Parish which extended this far west. As another possibility, John Tayloe, of Hazelwood in Caroline County, was one of the early investors of this frontier property. Since he was the major stockholder in the Bristol Iron Works, he might have planted the idea for the future use of the current name.

The modern city lies so close to the Tennessee border that it has spread into the neighboring state. The Virginia-Tennessee line runs down the middle of the main street to split the city into two separate political entities. However, the community spirit does not worry about the state line. In fact, it makes a great publicity display about it. *See: Bristol Parish*

BRISTOL IRON WORKS
Westmoreland County   Site

On the Rappahannock River, about twenty miles south of the hamlet of Oak Grove, the Bristol Iron Works was erected in 1724. Locally, the project was sponsored by John Tayloe of Caroline County, and John Lomax, a neighbor. They were agents for the John King Company of Bristol, England, which put up much of the front money. The iron works was moderately successful in smelting the low-grade Virginia ore into cast iron pigs which were shipped to England where they were converted into durable goods, many of which were sent back to the colony for sale. The Bristol Iron Works was abandoned after less than five years of operation because of the unexpectedly high cost of the enterprise.

Iron works of major importance, such as the Tredegar mill in Richmond, did not become economically feasible until after the Revolution when better ore was shipped in from the interior of Virginia and a greater market for ironware, steam engines, and rails for the railroads created an expanding market during the nineteenth century. *See: Dumfries; Falling Creek; Falmouth; Foxhall's Mill; Tubal Furnace*

BRISTOL PARISH
Obsolete

In December 1656 the House of Burgesses created an expanded Bristol Parish and gave the vestry the authority to hold court to try all cases that normally would be heard in county courts. Bristol Parish was a special case for the benefit of the people of the interior regions where it was not practical to organize counties because the population was

too thin. Special provision was made to enable either a plaintiff or a defendant to appeal any parish court decision to any established county court. Bristol Parish had been organized in Henrico and Charles City counties since 1643, and this expansion of civil authority was, admittedly, an experiment. There is no written commentary on how the parish court was actually run, how successful it was, or when and why its authority was cancelled. The unique system must not have worked too well since it was not tried again in other remote western areas of the colony. *See: Banister River; Blandford Church*

BRISTOW
Prince William County

The present hamlet of Bristow, near Manassas, many miles from the site of Old Bristow, merely keeps the name alive. When King James II, the last Catholic king of England, created his "sanctuary" on the Potomac River, one of the trustees of the 30,000 acre tract was Robert Bristow of London. He never came to Virginia but attempted to supervise his section from afar, a place known as Bristow Quarter. *See: Brentsville; Marlborough*

BROADWAY
Rockingham County   Town

Those objecting to the revelry of the young people who gathered at this place said they were on "The Broadway to Destruction." Rather disrespectfully, the youngsters liked the idea and called their favorite rendezvous Broadway. In time, a settlement grew here at the best place for a railroad station. The stop was called Broadway Depot. In 1854 the post office dropped "depot," since that was railroad lingo, and officially sanctioned Broadway. The young people, all grown by then, had the last laugh.

BRODNAX
Brunswick County   Town

The Brodnax family owned a large tract of land near the present Mecklenburg-Brunswick county line. Their estate was named Woodlands. When cotton was still king, the Brodnax family owned the state's largest cotton market which was known, far and near, as Brodnax. A village grew near the great warehouses and brokerage office. It was incorporated as a town in 1915. Cotton is no longer grown in commercial quantities in Virginia, having been replaced by edible crops

31

and tobacco which is still an important cash crop in the Commonwealth's economy.

BROMPTON
Fredericksburg

The original section of this house was built about 1730 by Colonel Henry Willis. Thirty years later, the estate, high on a hill overlooking Fredericksburg, was purchased by Colonel Fielding Lewis. His wife, Betty Washington Lewis, was forced to sell it when her husband died while deeply in debt. It was purchased in 1821 by Colonel Lawrence Marye. General Robert E. Lee wisely chose to occupy Marye's Heights during both Civil War battles for the village, placing his artillery on the grounds of Brompton for easy shots that swept the battlefield below. In 1947 this house became the residence of the president of Mary Washington College. *See: Kenmore; Luray*

BROOKNEAL
Campbell County   Town

The Brooks and Neal families settled in this area in the very early years of the eighteenth century. By 1736 they had intermarried and had produced enough descendants to create a small community. When the post office was established to serve them, the name selected was Brookneal. There were some who wanted to call it Nealbrook. *See: Kenbridge*

BROWNSBURG
Rockbridge County

The Reverend Samuel Brown came to this part of Virginia with his own large family. He organized a congregation and supervised the erection of a New Providence Church in 1796. Two years later there were enough people living near the church to form a village which was called Brownsburg for the minister. Of course, many of his children lived here who bore the name Brown.

BROWNSVILLE
Northampton County

Overlooking the broad waters of the Machipongo, with the Atlantic Ocean not too far away, Brownsville was the residence of the Brown family who settled on the Eastern Shore in the late seventeenth century. In the next century, Arthur Upsur Jr. from Essex plantation, just across Machipongo Creek, married Sarah Brown. The Upshur family has been living here ever since. The house is a classic example of the design known as an "Eastern Shore House." *See: Essex; Neville's Neck*

BRUNSWICK COUNTY

Formed in 1720 from parts of Prince George, Surry, and Isle of Wight, this county was named for the Royal House of Brunswick which came into English and Virginia history when George I ascended the throne in 1714. The region had been explored as early as 1650 and was fought over in 1676 when Nathaniel Bacon, the rebel, clashed with the Indians along the Roanoke River. The first courthouse was built in the hamlet of Cochran twelve years after the county was organized, but the county seat was moved eastward to Thomasburg in 1746 when the county was reduced in size to create Lunenburg. Thomasburg lost its prominence when the courthouse was rebuilt in Lawrenceville in 1783 when Greensville County took another slice of Brunswick.

Perhaps the most well known product of this county is a recipe for Brunswick Stew that was first standardized in the late nineteenth century although the dish had been made by country people in all parts of rural Virginia for hundreds of years. One source claims that Queen Victoria named it for her royal ancestors of Brunswick, Germany, since she had a liking for it. Local residents insist that the true inventor of the established formula was a slave, known to everyone as Uncle Jimmy, who belonged to Dr. Creed Haskins whose home was on the Nottoway River. Authentic Brunswick Stew requires squirrel meat as its base to which are added onions, bacon, potatoes, tomatoes, butterbeans, and corn. Some Virginians like to add a dash of sherry. Brunswick Stew is as important to true Virginians as planked shad. *See: Fort Christanna; Lunenburg County; Occaneechee*

BUCHANAN
Botetourt County   Town

Colonel John Buchanan had a large tract of land surveyed here in 1748 and was granted ownership five years later. He established a prosperous farm which he named the Anchor and Hope Plantation, possibly in reference to the hymn that declares Christ to be the anchor on which Christians base their hope. This town, of course, was named for Colonel Buchanan. *See: Kanawha Canal*

BUCHANAN COUNTY

Formed from parts of Tazewell and Russell in 1858, this county was named for James Buchanan who then was President of the United States. A Democrat, he was unable to prevent the Civil War because he could not reconcile the differences between the States Rights and Abolitionist factions in the country. Although he was blamed for his inaction, he was caught in a struggle that made him powerless to avoid the inevitable War Between the States. The courthouse of Buchanan County is at Grundy.

BUCKINGHAM COUNTY

Formed in 1761 from Albemarle, on the south side of the James, the records do not show why the name was chosen. The most probable link is with Buckinghamshire of central England, northwest of London. A number of Virginia counties bear the names of the old shires of the Mother Country.

One also can speculate that Buckingham was named for Buckingham House which the young King George III purchased for his queen, Charlotte. The date of the purchase and the founding of this county coincide. Today the huge structure, the official residence of the kings and queens of England, is known throughout the world as Buckingham Palace.

The territory of Buckingham County was slowly settled. Lying between the James and Appomattox rivers, most of the farms and estates were concentrated on the two waterways. It was not until the twentieth century that an all-weather road system was constructed to permit the farmers of the interior to get their products to the markets in the major population centers of the Commonwealth. The first courthouse was erected, shortly after the county's organization, in the tiny hamlet of Mayville, a name that was replaced by the more cumbersome, but more descriptive, Buckingham Court House.

A minor flurry of excitement put the county in the news in 1830 when gold was discovered near Dillwyn. A gold rush began, but it soon ended when the thin vein played out. Several mines were opened which, even at today's gold prices, have not been reworked. See: Charlottesville; Gold Mines

BUCKLAND
James City County   **Site**

When George Menefie returned from England, cleared of treason charges for his part in the ousting of Governor John Harvey, he acquired 8,000 acres of land on the north bank of the James River near Westover. He called his new home Buckland for Buckland Abbey, a thirteenth century Cistercian

monastery in Devonshire that was modernized in 1581 by Sir Richard Grenville who then sold it to Sir Francis Drake for his permanent home. Menefie's Buckland was a very successful endeavor. See: Harrop; Littletown

BUCKROE
Hampton

Some years prior to 1620, several Frenchmen were brought over to Virginia to establish a vineyard because it would be much cheaper to make wine in the colony than to ship it across the wild Atlantic. Since the entrance to Chesapeake Bay is at the same latitude as central Italy, the London Company assumed that the land near Point Comfort would be a fine place to grow grapes where they would be bathed in the bracing sea air. Although some wine was produced, the experiment was a failure. The vines did not do well and the Frenchmen did not care to live in the exposed location about a mile north of Fort Algernourne. They gave up the project and scattered to other settlements. Following the failed winery, the company "planted" other servants on this beach who were ordered to grow mulberry trees for silkworms. This, too, was a failure when the silkworms did not thrive. The mulberry trees took joyous root, however, and descendants of these shrubs can still be found all over this section of the city of Hampton, growing voluntarily and competing for space and nourishment behind the low dunes.

Records dating before 1617 call this thin stretch of beach, directly opposite the mouth of the bay, Buck Rose or Buck Row. The name possibly comes from a hamlet of Yorkshire, England, a region of the mother country from which many early settlers came. During the 1700s, the land of this former vineyard was owned by the Selden family who created a successful farm. See: Colle; Exeter

BUENA VISTA
Rockbridge County   **City**

During the war with Mexico (1846-48), two battles were fought near the Mexican town of Buena Vista. In the first engagement, Zachary Taylor (later President) was defeated by General Santa Anna. The second battle, about a year later, was a victory for General Winfield Scott over the same opponent. General Scott also had designs on the presidency, but was a poor candidate. Although this Virginia community was not developed until the late 1880s, the name was selected in memory of the two battles. It is Spanish for "beautiful view." Locally, it is pronounced "Bew-na vista."

A group of speculators, certain that Rockbridge County was a source of mineral wealth, planned a grand commercial center here. They built a magnificent hotel, an opera house, fancy homes, and expensive shops. The minerals were not found in commercial quantities, the financial structure of the venture foundered in the Panic of 1893, and the great plans fell apart. The embryonic town remained and slowly grew around the huge, frame hotel that continued to attract vacationers. This hotel still stands and today is the main building of Southern Seminary Junior College. Also still evident is the Victorian structure that served as the land office for the company. For many years it was the town's courthouse; now it is used for the public library.

BUFFALO GAP
Augusta County

American bison roamed as far east as the Piedmont section during the primitive times in Virginia. The coastal Indians often traded shell beads for these fine skins that were used as a part of the outer wall of their lodges or as robes on which to sit or sleep. As the Commonwealth became settled in the early days of the Republic, the huge beasts migrated westward for survival and are more associated with the western plains than the eastern seaboard. They are native to North America. Because they resemble the water buffalo of Asia, which had been seen by world travellers before the New World was colonized, the bison were mistakenly called buffalo, an error that has never been overthrown in the minds of the general public.

A few cattlemen in modern Virginia are breeding bisons for their meat, not so much for the novelty but because bisons produce more meat than other cattle for the same amount of food. They are also quite hardy and can stand bitter winter weather. There also has been successful cross-breeding with cows to create a new animal called a beefalo.

BUFFALO SPRINGS
Mecklenburg County

Colonel William Byrd discovered a group of mineral springs in 1728 during his survey of the Virginia-North Carolina border. He spoke so glowingly about the excellent effect of the water upon the human body that the area attracted settlers. It was not until 1811, however, that John Speed capitalized on the four springs. He built a tavern, several cabins and a large dining room to cater to guests who travelled the eight miles from Clarksville by stagecoach. Business was so good that the property was incorporated as a resort in 1852.

Thomas F. Goode gained control in 1874. To augment the income, he began to bottle the water in a plant that he built near Spring No. 2. Through advertising, Buffalo Mineral Water was shipped all over the world, making the resort famous and Goode wealthy. Because of the high content of lithium, the resort was named Buffalo Lithia Springs. It boasted about its golf course, baseball field, and miles of bridle paths. In the late 1880s, the resort was nearly self-sufficient from the food grown on an adjoining farm.

The resort faded during the Depression. The demand for bottle mineral water dropped off, and the entire enterprise closed in the 1930s. In 1947 the old hotel was moved to the side of U.S. 58 where it was used as a restaurant and night club. Part of the resort property disappeared under the waters of Bugg's Island Lake. Spring No. 2 is maintained by the Corps of Engineers in a small park. *See: Occaneechee; Rich Creek*

BUGG'S ISLAND LAKE
Mecklenburg County

This huge lake was formed in 1953 with the completion of the John H. Kerr Dam. Fed by the Staunton River and Kerr Reservoir, Bugg's Island Lake's thousands of acres of fresh water are a favorite spot for fishermen and boaters. *See: Kerr Reservoir*

BULL ISLAND
York County

There are two islands by this name in Virginia, one on the ocean side of the Eastern Shore and this one, better recorded in history, located in the Poquoson River, an inlet of the York. Early settlers used islands to contain their livestock without having to bother with fences, the first recorded instance being Hog Island in the James River where the Jamestowners put their swine. The York County Bull Island was named for a similar reason. Benjamin Symns and Thomas Eaton, two seventeenth century residents of Elizabeth City (now Hampton) placed a few bulls and cows on the island and let them breed unmolested. Now and then they took an animal for their own use. Both men are remembered for their generosity to the community when, through a legal arrangement, they gave the herd to the town fathers to support the first free school in the colony. Both Syms and Eaton have had schools named for them in Hampton. *See: Hog Island; Poquoson*

BULLPASTURE RIVER
Bath County

The area of Highland and Bath counties, near several excellent rivers that run through lush pasture lands, is a good region for raising stock. The Bullpasture River connects with the Cowpasture River. Nearby, at a lower elevation, is Calfpasture River. *See: Cowpasture River*

BULL RUN
Prince William County

This relatively minor stream, properly called a run, empties into Occoquan Creek. It is primarily known for two Civil War battles fought along its bank. Both times the Union forces were striking to control two important rail lines that came together at Manassas Junction. The first battle was an embarrassing disaster for the Federals who retreated in wild disorder all the way to Washington, D.C. The second fight was better fought, but again it was a Confederate victory. In after-action battle reports, Union generals named the engagements for the objectives; hence, the Yankees called the two clashes the Battles of Manassas Junction. The Southerners were more specific and cited the locale, calling the victories the Battles of Bull Run. *See: Manassas; Run*

BURG

Burg is an ancient term for a fortified place or a walled town. It is German in origin. Commonly it is attached as a suffix to a person's name to identify a locality, such as Lynchburg. *See: Bury; Ville*

BURGESS
Northumberland County

Alfred the Great, the 10th century king of England, organized his regions into *burhs* which roughly correspond to the modern world *borough*. The man who represented the burh was called by the Normans a *burgess*.

The first postmaster for this settlement was a Mr. Burgess who also ran the local store. For many years, until as late as 1950, this hamlet was known as Burgess' Store.

BURKES GARDEN
Tazewell County

At one time this was the site of a minor Revolutionary fort. While in charge of an exploration party in 1748, a Captain Burke buried his breakfast potato peelings near his campfire before leaving for the day's trek. Several years later he came back to find the old campsite covered with vines that had produced many edible potatoes. When a fort was built here, it was called Burke's Garden. During the very late eighteenth century, a number of Germans made their homes in the bowl-shaped valley on the top of Garden Mountain. In the cemetery of Burke's Garden Central Church can be found a number of interestingly carved gravestones of typically German design. Some date to the 1820s.

BURKEVILLE
Nottoway County   **Town**

A tavern was first opened here in 1800 by Anderson Miller who gave up his establishment and sold his license to Samuel Burke after twenty-two years as a tavern keeper. The establishment stood at the intersection of the road to Prince Edward Court House and the road to Moore's Ordinary (now the town of Meherrin). Burke's hostelry sat right on the county line and historic writings often refer to it as Burke's Tavern of Prince Edward County. A small village developed at the intersection of the two roads which was given its name when the Richmond and Danville Railroad crossed the Southside Railroad near the site of the old tavern. Burkeville was sometimes called Burke's Crossing.

BURLINGTON
King William County

This 5,000-acre tract was patented in 1699 by Nathaniel Burwell. When the land and the house upon it were purchased in 1752 by Owne Gwathmey, the name was recorded for the first time in the county records. There is no hint why the name Burlington had been chosen. *See: Carter's Grove; Cownes; Fairfield of Gloucester*

BURNT HOUSE FIELD
Westmoreland County   **Site**

The family burial plot of the Lee family of Westmoreland County is located at Machodoc, a home owned by Richard Lee III which he leased to his brother, Thomas, the builder of Stratford. Thomas Lee was a local justice of the peace who judged several felons for serious crimes. They escaped and set fire to his residence in revenge. Although the house was later replaced by a descendant of Richard Lee on a different site, the burial plot was always identified by the family as being in Burnt House Field. George Lee, who built the new house, called it Mount Pleasant. *See: Chantilly; Machodoc; Mount Pleasant; Stratford*

BURWELL'S LANDING

See: Harrison's Landing

BURY

In England in the sixteenth century, the meeting place of a neighborhood was called the Bury. At this common ground the ranking personage of the area heard complaints from members of the working class and settled disputes. Men and women also were tried for minor offenses such as drunkenness or failure to attend church. Quite often the bury was in a common hall, usually in the manor house of the local squire; sometimes it was a separate building much like our town halls which contain, among other things, a courtroom. The English bury was always identified either with the name of the major estate on which the people worked as vassals or with the name of the landholder. In colonial Virginia, the suffix "bury" did not refer to a common hall or courtroom or a large home but was simply used to give an estate a fancy name that had a good English sound to it, such as Toddsbury or Edmundsbury. *See: Burg; Hundred; Ville*

BUSHFIELD
Westmoreland County

Richard Bushrod acquired this land in 1659 and built his home here. It was all acquired by his son, John, who had married Hannah Keene. She not only outlived her husband but married twice again and saw these two men to their graves. At her request, she was buried between number one and number three. Her eldest son, John Bushrod II, had a daughter who married John Augustine Washington, the future president's younger brother, and they set up housekeeping in a modest house on the land that was later to be known as Mount Vernon.

When George Washington married Martha Custis, and Martha wanted to live in a house on the Potomac River, Bushrod and his wife returned to Bushfield. It was here that their illustrious son, Bushrod Washington, was born in 1762. He was a successful lawyer who, at the age of thirty-six, was appointed to the U.S. Supreme Court by President John Adams. Bushfield was described by Philip Fithian, the tutor of the Carter children at nearby Nomini Hall, as having "the most agreeable situation of any I have seen in Maryland or Virginia; the broad Potowmack, which they account between 7 and 8 miles over, washes its gardens on the North, the River Nomini is within a stone's throw to the west, a level open country on the East . . . There is no marsh near which altogether makes the place exceeding description." The original house in which Justice Washington was born was burned by the British in 1814 on their way to the District of Columbia *See: Mount Vernon; Pecatone*

CALFPASTURE RIVER
Augusta County

A tributary of the Maury River, this stream provides excellent water for cattle who thrive on the abundant pasture lands. Old-timers say that the calves were kept in this lower region until they were strong enough to be moved to higher elevations with the mature herds. *See: Bullpasture River*

CALLAGHAN
Alleghany County

Dennis Callaghan was famous as the landlord of Callaghan's Tavern on stage road and turnpike. A native of County Cork, Ireland, he lived here in the years between the beginning of the republic and the war with Mexico. His son, Oliver, was the first clerk of Alleghany County.

CALLANDS
Pittsylvania County

About 1771 Samuel Callands opened a store here in what was then Chatham, the county seat. When Henry County was cut off from Pittsylvania in 1777, and the county seat was moved to a tiny town called Competition, which was more centrally located, a switch of names took place. Since it was important to keep the name Chatham as the seat of Pittsylvania County government, Competition became Chatham and what had been Chatham was named Callands. The name Competition has disappeared.

CALLAO
Northumberland County

Jacob H. Callaway established a post office in his store and sent in his name for approval. Callaway had already been used in Franklin County so the would-be postmaster offered Callao as a compromise.

CALLAWAY
Franklin County

An iron works was operated here between 1774 and 1779 by Colonel John Donelson, father of Rachel who later became the wife of Andrew Jackson. When Donelson left Virginia to settle in Tennessee, he sold the works to James Callaway who named it the Washington Iron Works. It specialized in farm implements, pots, kettles, and pans. All that is left of the works are crumbled stone walls overgrown with vines. Callaway's name lives on. *See: Evington*

CALVERT
Faquier County

Members of the Calvert family, who came from Calvert County, Maryland, settled here. Once this was Warrenton Junction on Owl Run.

CAMDEN
Caroline County

The present home here was erected in 1859 by William C. Pratt, a descendant of Charles Pratt, the First Earl of Camden, who so strongly supported the idea of American independence that he came to Virginia. The Earl first settled in King George County but his son, John, moved to Caroline in 1790 and built a Georgian frame house. John's son wanted better things. William razed his father's home and built a mansion of Tuscan style, quite unlike other homes of eastern Virginia. A tower, part of the fancy structure, was shot away during the Civil War by Union gunboats working far up the Rappahannock. It was never replaced.

CAMPBELL COUNTY

Formed from a huge chunk of Bedford County in 1781, this county was named for General William Campbell, the hero of the Battle of King's Mountain fought the year before. The courthouse is at Rustburg.

CAMP PEARY
York County

Camp Peary was established in 1942 and was named for Rear Admiral Robert E. Peary, an arctic explorer. The base was opened to train sailors for the Navy's Construction batallions (the famed SeaBees). Over 100,000 people were trained here during World War II. From 1945 until 1947, Camp Peary was used as a supply depot and then was deactivated. The land reverted to the control of the Commonwealth of Virginia. The Federal government resumed occupancy when the Armed Forces Experimental Training Activity (AFETA) was established on the reservation in 1951 which has continued its activities since that year.

During the early eighteenth century, Ripon Hall was built on Poplar Neck, on the shore of the York River, by Edmund Jenings.

Also located here, in later years, was Vaux Hall, of which little is known, and Porto Bello, the farm of Lord Dunmore. None of these dwellings are still standing. Ripon Hall was torn down in 1961. *See: Porto Bello; Ripon Hall*

CAPE

This is an old English word that comes from the Latin *caput*, meaning "head." Gradually it evolved into the word "cape" for an article of clothing worn over the shoulders with a hood to cover the wearer's head. It also evolved as a geographic term for a "headland," a prominent piece of land that extends into a body of navigable water. A cape is always larger than a point which is the tip of a peninsula or some sort of land that protrudes into an ocean, a bay, or a river. The renowned Capes of Virginia are Cape Charles, at the tip of the Eastern Shore, and Cape Henry, the hump of land directly south of it. They form the mouth of the Chesapeake Bay. *See: Peninsula; Spit*

CAPE CHARLES
Northampton County

The southern tip of the Eastern Shore forms the northern edge of the mouth of the Chesapeake Bay. Around this cape are the Smith Isles, named for Captain John Smith who mapped them but did not discover them (they were known to both Italian and Spanish explorers of the 15th century). The Charles for which this cape was named was the Duke of York, second son of King James I.

The famed Cape Charles lighthouse is actually on Smith Island. The town of Cape Charles, about fifteen miles up the peninsula on the bay side, came into being as the eastern terminus of the Willoughby Spit-Cape Charles ferry late in the nineteenth century. Therefore, when the colonials referred to Cape Charles, they always meant the tip of the Eastern Shore. The Duke of York, who gave his name to this cape, later became King Charles I who was executed by Cromwell in 1649.

CAPE HENRY
Fort Story

On the rounded hump of land that forms the southern edge of the mouth of the Chesapeake Bay, the newly arrived Jamestown settlers first set foot on Virginia soil on April 29, 1607, after five weary months at sea. As thirty of them enjoyed the feel of solid land again, they were suddenly attacked by local natives (probably the Chesapeakes who

lived nearby). The Indians were quite alarmed to see white men again. Years before, Spanish adventurers had been in the lower bay. They treated the Indians with cruelty in the name of their religion, giving rise to the prophecy that some day another tribe from across the great water would return and destroy all of the native inhabitants. In the brief attack, two of the Englishmen were wounded by arrows and, given the lack of knowledge about infection in those days, probably died later. The politically-minded newcomers named the place for Henry, Prince of Wales, the eldest son of the reigning monarch, James I. Prince Henry did not live long enough to wear the English crown. Instead, it was inherited by his younger brother, Charles, Duke of York.

CAPITOL LANDING
York County   Site

Near the head of Queen's Creek, about a mile-and-a-half from the capitol building in Williamsburg, a landing was established to handle the freight and passengers that were lightered up from the vessels anchored in the York River. For the convenience of important travellers, a royal cottage stood near the landing where ladies and gentlemen could refresh themselves before continuing their journey by land to Williamsburg. A number of royal Governors made their initial step onto Virginia soil at Capitol Landing amid much pomp and ceremony. *See: Porto Bello; Trebell's Landing*

CAPPAHOSIC
Gloucester County   Site

The name comes from the Cappahosic Indian village that was located here. In 1608 Powhatan offered to make Captain John Smith the "King of the Cappahosic Tribe" in exchange for "two great guns and a grindstone," as Smith wrote in his book four years later. A house and wharf were built here in 1712 by Captain John Stubbs who also was licensed to operate a ferry across the York River. After his death, William Thornton continued to operate Stubb's Ferry. This is a convenient place to cross between the great estates along the north bank of the York and the road from Chiskiak to Williamsburg. The toll allowed under the law of 1748 was one shilling, three pence for a horse and rider, about the price of a very good meal in those days. *See: Purton*

CAROLINA

The northern 170 miles of North Carolina were a part of the Virginia colony under the terms of the first charter which established the colony's jurisdiction 200 miles north and south of Point Comfort. This extended seaward to include, and later exclude, Bermuda. The first English settlers who came to Virginia in 1581 stayed for a year on Roanoke Island of the Outer Banks but gave up under Indian pressure and went home. The next settlers to come to this same place in 1585 included a number of women, one of whom gave birth to Virginia Dare, the first English girl born in America. This colony disappeared completely, leaving behind only the criptic message "Croatan" carved into a tree. Since both the islands of the Outer Banks and the neighboring Indians were hostile to settlement, the next attempt was ordered to avoid this area and try elsewhere (Jamestown in 1607).

The lands around Albemarle Sound remained unsettled until 1653 when the Virginia House of Burgesses offered 100 acres of land to anyone who would settle permanently on the Chowan River. Although colonists were wary, gradually enough moved to require some sort of government by 1664. This was only a year before Charles II rewarded eight of his favorite courtiers, who had helped him regain his throne, with a tremendous land grant. In gratitude, they called it Carolina, a Latinized version of the name Charles.

This enormous grant extended from the present borders of Virginia to the top of Florida, then owned by the Spanish, and stretched from the Atlantic west to the "South Sea." In response to a request by the proprietors, Governor William Berkeley of Virginia sent his good friend William Drummond down to be the first governor of Carolina, giving him the title of Lieutenant Governor of Virginia since Berkeley was responsible for this territory, too, as the only resident agent of the king. In 1691, fifteen years after Berkeley hanged Drummond for his part in Bacon's Rebellion, the Albemarle Colony was assigned to the Carolina Province which had been established in Charleston. This was a highly unpopular change since the people of that area all had migrated from Virginia and had nothing in common with the plantation aristocrats of southern Carolina who had established themselves into a local nobility of landed barons.

The great resentment against the Charles-ton governors led to a split between northern and southern Carolina in 1712 and a new governor for the northern section lived in New Bern on the Chowan River. The boundary line between these two parts of Carolina was first surveyed in 1730, but the agreed line was not firmly established until 1815. *See: Governor's Land; Green Spring; Maryland; West Virginia; Virginia*

CAROLINE COUNTY

Formed in 1727 from parts of Essex, King and Queen, and King William, this county was named for Queen Caroline, the wife of George II. The county seat is at Bowling Green. George Rogers Clark, the Conqueror of the Northwest Territory spent his youth in this county. *See: Bowling Green*

CARROLL COUNTY

Formed in 1842 from Grayson, this county was named for Charles Carroll, one of the signers of the Declaration of Independence. He was not a member of the Virginia delegation but represented North Carolina. The courthouse is at Hillsville.

CARRSBROOK
Albemarle County

This land was part of the estate of Dabney Carr, a close friend of Thomas Jefferson. The house was built in 1794 by Peter Carr, Dabney's son who became Jefferson's ward, later served as his private secretary, and was a help to the retired President during the founding of the University of Virginia. The name Carrsbrook is reminiscent of Caris-brooke Castle, once the prison of King Charles I on the Isle of Wight during the English civil war. *See: Bear Castle*

CARRSVILLE
Isle of Wight County

Jonas Johnston Carr lived here prior to the Revolution. His descendants have remained in the vicinity ever since. A son of Jonas, Elias Carr, was a Governor of North Carolina during the Federal period.

CARSON
Dinwiddie County

Following a wreck on the Atlantic Coast-line Railroad many years ago, the telegrapher sent the message, "Cars on." For some reason, the hamlet that developed near the telegrapher's station adopted the name, Carson. *See: Dundas*

CARTER HALL
Clarke County

This estate was built by a descendant of the wealthy Carter family. Nathaniel Burwell of Carter's Grove had a summer house erected prior to 1790 shortly after his second marriage to Lucy, the widow of George Baylor. At first the Burwells lived at Carter's Grove during the winter and at Carter Hall during the summer, but by 1804 they remained here for the full year. Edmund Randolph, Governor of Virginia and U.S. Secretary of State, died here. *See: Carter's Grove; Fairfield of Gloucester; Millwood of Clarke*

CARTER'S GROVE
James City County

When Robert "King" Carter purchased 1,400 acres of land in the old Martin Hundred area, he specified that the plantation should be "called by and go by the name of Carter's Grove." Income from the farm was assigned to his daughter, Elizabeth, for her lifetime and then ownership of the estate was to go to her second son, Carter Burwell, whom she had by her husband Nathaniel Burwell of Fairfield in Gloucester County. The designated second son married Lucy Grimes in 1737. They moved into one of the small plantation dependencies and settled down to raise a family. After a seemingly endless procession of girl babies, their first son was finally born in 1750. In celebration, work was begun almost immediately on a suitable house which is the center portion of the present mansion.

This celebrated son, Nathaniel Burwell II, the next owner, married his cousin, Susanna Grimes, by whom he had eight children, five of whom survived their mother. A year after Susanna died, Burwell married a widow, Lucy Page Baylor after a rather abrupt, business-like proposal. They had eight more children to add to the six which she brought to the union from her first marriage to George Baylor. With all these children, Burwell began work on Carter Hall in Clarke County to which he and his growing family moved in 1804. Carter's Grove was left in the charge of the eldest son, Carter Burwell III. The last of the line to maintain residence in this famous house was Philip Lewis Carter Burwell who sold it in 1838. *See: Belvoir; Black Swamp Quarter; Carter Hall; Ceeleys; Cownes; Fairfield of Gloucester; The Forrest; Trebells Landing; White House*

CARTERSVILLE
Cumberland County

This tiny settlement originally consisted of a tavern next to a wharf, a place for an overnight stop for James River boats during the eighteenth and nineteenth centuries. Obviously, it was named for (and probably by) a descendant of Robert "King" Carter. Both the wharf and tavern have disappeared.

CARYSBROOK
Fluvanna County

This land was acquired for Miles Cary, Jr. by his mother when he was underage. He built the house on it in 1725 and named it after Carisbrooke Castle in england. *See: Carrsbrooke; Ringneck*

CASTLE HILL
Albemarle County

Dr. Thomas Walker acquired 11,000 acres of the vast Nicholas Merriwether patent when, in 1741, he married Mildred Merriwether, the widow of the original landholder. When Dr. Walker finally got around to settling on the land and building a house twenty-four years later, he named it Castle Hill, a name closely connected to King Charles II who, though dead since 1685, was still remembered.

Thomas Walker, a physician by training, was a staunch Royalist until Revolutionary times. He was too advanced in age and weary from his many travels to take an active role in the fight for independence. As an agent for the Loyal Land Company during the days of the Hanoverian kings of England, he explored the Kentucky Territory in the Allegheny Mountains in what is now southwest Virginia. He discovered a river and traced it to its pass through the mountains, naming both the river and the gap for the Duke of Cumberland, a son of George II. Walker claimed 800,000 acres of land in that area which he surveyed and sold to the people who moved west through Cumberland Gap.

In 1765, wealthy and growing old, he built his home in Albemarle County and named it for the site of Charles II's only battle, an event that had taken place long before Walker was born.

When the young king gathered a rag-tag army in Scotland in 1651, he pressed southward in a futile attempt to regain his throne in England by military might, two years after his father had been beheaded by the Parliamentary forces of Oliver Cromwell. After a month of marching, hoping in vain to generate a huge host of Royalists, he reached Worcester without having been opposed. Cromwell was waiting for him, his army blocking the main road to London. Vastly outnumbered, King Charles prepared to defend himself within the city of Worcester. The key to the city, however, was a knoll outside the walls called, for centuries, Castle Hill. Charles personally led the attack to take this point but his forces were repulsed. He fled the scene with a few companions and wandered, a disguised fugitive, for seven weeks before reaching the safety of France. After he was restored to the English throne, Charles II loved to retell the story of the battle at Castle Hill. *See: Abingdon of Washington County; Blenheim; Boscobel; Cumberland Gap; Grace Church of Albemarle; Mount Walker; Walkerton*

CASTLEWOOD
Russell County

A portion of Russell County was known as Castle's Woods, named for an early settler. When he was joined by others, they looked to Hamlin's Fort for protection against the frequent raids by the Shawnee Indians. There were enough people living in Castle's Woods in 1782 to raise a company of thirty men for the militia to fight the Shawnees. Gradually, a few homes were built near the old fort which became the nucleus of the present village of Castlewood.

CATALPA
Culpeper County

Before the Barbour family built the mansion known as Barboursville, they lived a few miles away at a home called Catalpa. This building fell victim to fire forcing James Barbour to build again. Catalpa was named for the catalpa tree which is native to South Carolina. The botanist, Mark Catesby, sent samples of this tree to England in 1726. It did not do well in the English climate. However, Governor William Gooch had catalpa trees planted in Williamsburg in 1737 on the palace green. It produces a long bean-like fruit that is sometimes known as an Indian cigar. The tiny hamlet of Catalpa developed near this first Barbour residence and has kept the name. *See: Barboursville*

CATAWBA
Roanoke County

Catawba is a Choctaw Indian word meaning *separated*. These Indians lived in the mountains along the border between North and South Carolina but they probably lived in this area for a short time, long enough to leave the name which was adopted by this community.

CATLETT
Faquier County

An early land owner here was John Catlett.

CAT-TAIL CHURCH
King William County

Although most of the basic parts of this building date from 1751 when this church was built by the Anglicans, the present form is so strange that only an expert could identify it as colonial. It now has two steeples, buttresses against the north and south walls, green shingles on the roof, and stuccoed walls. After the Revolution, this church was acquired by an all-black group of freedmen who formed Mt. Sinai Baptist Church. The origin of the name Cat-Tail is unknown. Quite possibly it refers to the cattail plants that grow naturally in wet places, especially bogs or mires. There are both salt water and fresh water varieties.

CAWSONS
Chesterfield County

Theodoric Bland, the brother of Richard Bland II, and both from Jordan's Point on the James River, lived here during the eighteenth century with his wife, Frances Bolling. Here, in 1773, was born the controversial wag and future Congressman, John Randolph. He was the third son of John Randolph and his wife, Theodorick Bland. *See: Roanoke Plantation*

CEDAR BLUFF
Tazewell County

This was the location of the Cedar Bluff Woolen Mills, organized in 1832. It specialized in finely patterned coverlets. The mill burned in 1898 and again in 1922, but it was rebuilt each time.

CEDAR LEVEL
Prince George County

Robert Bolling moved from the original family home, Kippax, to the higher ground on the south bank of the Appomattox River. He built a modest home in the very early years of the eighteenth century. The new place was called Cedar Level for the abundant cedars that grew wild on the level ground. The house is a story and a half high with huge chimneys at either end. Years later, after the Bolling family moved again, the former dwelling was converted into a tavern called Halfway House because it was midway between City Point and Bollingbrook. *See: Bollingbrook; City Point; Kippax*

CEDAR SPRINGS
Smyth County

Virginia is littered with wild cedars that grow everywhere, planted by birds that eat the blue cedar berries but often cannot digest them. The berries pass on through and are naturally pre-fertilized when they hit the ground. Virginia is also blessed with an abundance of springs fed by runoff from the mountains. Separately, these two words, cedar and springs, appear in dozens of names. It was inevitable that they would be combined as Cedar Springs.

CEELEYS
Hampton   **Site**

Abraham Bush was the first owner of this tract. He patented it in 1624 and sold it a year later to Thomas Ceeley who owned it for sixty years and bestowed his name upon it. However, it was Major William Wilson who made the name Ceeleys rather well known. The Major, a successful Hampton merchant, bought 250 acres of the tract and built a handsome two-story house in 1705 near Salter's Creek overlooking Hampton Roads. His home became famous for his great entertainments, his fine collection of books and silver, and, more to the point, for his beautiful daughters. During his lifetime, Major Wilson added 2,000 neighboring acres to his estate and became an influential force in Hampton and Elizabeth City county politics. The Wilson and Cary families were related through marriage in the previous century and the custom continued. Thus, Colonel Wilson Miles Cary, the son of Wilson Cary of Richneck, married Mary Wilson, one of Major Wilson's daughters. Through this link Ceeleys came into the Cary family's collection of real estate on the Peninsula. Mary Cary, their daughter, was the young lady who refused George Washington's marriage proposal at Carter's Grove. Another daughter married George William Fairfax of Belvoir in 1748. This Sally Fairfax faithfully corresponded with George Washington during the Revolution after she and her husband moved to England prior to outbreak of hostilities. A third daughter married William Rostow, the Commissioner of Warwick County. Today, Ceeleys is nothing more than an old name in present day Hampton, known only to those residents who care for their historical heritage. The old house is long gone. *See: Belvoir; Fairfax; Richneck*

CENTER CROSS
Essex

Two main highways cross here near the center of Essex County. Originally this hamlet was called Center Crossroads.

CENTERVILLE
Mathews County

Thomas Smith built his home in the center of a number of other established farms shortly after receiving a grant of land in 1730. He called it Centerville. Two of his sons, Thomas II and Armistead Smith, were among the founders of Phi Beta Kappa, the honorary scholastic society. *See: Ville*

CENTREVILLE
Fairfax County

Located midway between Arlington and Warrenton, this was the site of the Eagle Tavern. At one time the settlement was called Newgate but it was renamed Centreville in 1792. Note the spelling uses "re" in the British fashion which has not been changed in all these years. The tiny hamlet was destroyed during the Civil War when the two Battles of Manassas were fought nearby. The stone Methodist church, untouched in the confusion of the first battle, was used as a temporary hospital. It was destroyed during the second battle which, although better fought by the Union forces, was another Confederate victory. *See: Middleburg; Newgate*

CHAIN BRIDGE
Potomac River

The first bridge built across the Potomac was a wooden structure erected just below Little Falls in 1797. It was replaced seven years later when a flood washed away the original. When another flood wrecked bridge number two in 1808, a suspension bridge was constructed using chains with iron links, each four-and-a-half feet long, anchored to stone piers. In 1852, after years of rust, the chains gave way and another wooden bridge was built using heavy crossbeams. This was standing during the Civil War and appears in many photographs. Since it was the only connection between Virginia and Washington during this conflict, the floor planks were removed for security and put down only as needed. In 1874 a steel bridge was built which collapsed during heavy rains in 1936. The present high cantilever structure was completed two years later. Although the old chain bridge has been gone for a century, the name Chain Bridge has been continued. *See: Woodbridge*

CHANCELLORSVILLE
Spotsylvania County **Site**

In 1816 George Chancellor announced in the *Virginia Herald* that he was then "living in his new Brick building, which is large and commodius for entertainment of travellers." The inn was known as Chancellorsville. During the Civil War, a battle was fought here between Lee and Union General Joseph Hooker in May 1863; Mrs. Sanford Chancellor, widow, and her family occupied the place. Hooker used the inn as his headquarters during the battle. Confederate artillery hit the structure and momentarily stunned Hooker during the engagement. The battle was known as "Lee's Masterpiece," and the action caused Hooker to retreat back across the Rappahannock River. Union losses in men killed, wounded and captured far exceeded the Confederate casualties even though Lee was outnumbered two to one. The Southern cause was dealt a mortal blow in this engagement, however, with the wounding and subsequent death of General Stonewall Jackson.

After the war one wing of the old Chancellor House was rebuilt. It burned in 1927 and the standing ruins fell down twenty years later. The foundations of Chancellorsville have been preserved by the National Park Service. A few miles away, in the direction of Fredericksburg, is a small, scattered community of recent vintage which calls itself Chancellor to perpetuate the name.

CHANTILLY
Fairfax County **Site**

Richard Bland Lee, one of the Lees of Virginia and a descendant of Richard Henry Lee, lived at his plantation Sully in Fairfax County. When he acquired an adjacent piece of real estate, he named it Chantilly in memory of the old homestead in Westmoreland County. This was about 1794. This land has been subdivided many times but the name lives on as a section of Fairfax County near Dulles Airport. *See: Tuleries*

CHANTILLY
Westmoreland County **Site**

Just east of Stratford is Chantilly, the home of Richard Henry Lee who organized the Westmoreland Association in 1766 to protest the Stamp Act. He presented the resolution for Independence to the Continental Congress in 1776. Born at the Lee homestead of Stafford, he moved to his own home Chantilly in 1764 and died there thirty years

RICHARD HENRY LEE
CHANTILLY, WESTMORELAND COUNTY

later. He was buried, according to his own request, between his two wives, Anne Aylette and Anne Gaskins Pinkard. Their remains are in the family plot at Machadoc in Burnt House Field.

Chantilly was named for a chateau in France, the home of the Duc de Bourbon, the head of the Bourbon Conde family who ran the French government for the fourteen-year-old Louis XV in 1722. This home in Westmoreland County was destroyed by fire many years ago. *See: Burnt House Field; Fairfield of King William; Langley; Leedstown; Machadoc; Menokin; Peckatone; Stratford; Sully*

CHARLES CITY
Charles City County

A town never developed here as was the case at other county seats. Today it is a very tiny settlement with little more than the courthouse, an annex and a school. Modest as it is, this was the focal point of much early activity, long before the present courthouse was erected in 1730 beside one of the oldest roads in English America (now Route 5). Known for its entire length from Williamsburg to Richmond as the Charles City Road, and not as the Richmond Road which also connects the two cities along a different route, it has probably seen more of the important figures of early American history than any other road in the nation. *See: Bermuda Hundred; Cape Charles; Charles City County*

CHARLES CITY COUNTY

One of the eight original shires formed in 1634, the history of this territory goes back to 1614 when the Four Ancient Boroughs were created. It was spread over both sides of the James River. When named, it honored Charles, Duke of York and heir to the throne of James I. In 1702 the land on the south bank of the river was formed into Appomattox, Prince George, and Henrico counties. Two Presidents were born in Charles City County— William Henry Harrison and his Vice President, who succeeded him into the White House, John Tyler. This duet was the famous "Tippicanoe and Tyler too." *See: Berkeley; Charles River County; Corporations; Sherwood Forest*

CHARLES RIVER COUNTY
Obsolete

When the eight original shires were formed in 1634, the lands surrounding the Charles River were formed into a county, the northern boundary being the Potomac. Both the county and the river were renamed York nine years later to eliminate confusion with Charles City County. *See: York County*

CHARLOTTE COUNTY

Formed in 1764 from a portion of Lunenburg, this county was named for Queen Charlotte of Mecklenburg, the wife of George III.

CHARLOTTE COURT HOUSE
Charlotte County   **Town**

In 1756 this storage depot and warehouse was called The Magazine. In 1759, the name was changed to Daltonsburgh, possibly for Catherine Dalton, the wife of Lieutenant Governor Francis Fauquier. The name was changed to Marysville in 1836, to Smithville in 1874, then to Charlotte Court House in 1901. It has been the county seat ever since the county was formed in 1764.

CHARLOTTESVILLE
Albemarle County   **City**

The site of this town on the Three Chopt Road was patented in 1737 by Williams Taylor. A settlement of homes was built on a low bluff overlooking the Rivanna River, and in 1762, when it was recognized as a town, it became the new county seat replacing Scottsville (or Scott's Ferry). Charlottesville was named for Charlotte of Mecklenburg, the Queen of King George III.

Burgoyne's army, captured at the battle of Saratoga in 1777, was quartered near here for two years until those who were left were moved to Frederick, Maryland in 1780. By then, many of the escaped Hessian and British soldiers had married Albemarle County girls and had been secretly assimilated into the population of the area. After the war, some of them migrated into town, but most chose to remain in the rural sections of the county where many of their descendants still live. British Colonel Tarleton camped in Charlottesville briefly on June 4, 1781 enroute to capture Governor Thomas Jefferson and the Virginia legislature, then at Monticello, and that was the town's excitement for that war.

During the War Between the States, the town was a supply center utilizing the railroad. Several hospitals were organized to care for Confederate wounded. General Phillip Sheridan and his mounted troops rode through late in the conflict but stayed only briefly, and burned the woolen mill. Since 1865 the city has flourished into a modern-day educational and medical complex due to the expansion of the University of Virginia. *See: Albemarle County; Cuckoo Tavern; Elk Hill; Glendower; Monticello; Scott's Ferry; University of Virginia*

CHASE CITY
Mecklenburg County   `   **Town**

It was Christiansville until 1873 when Northern post-Civil War settlers changed the name to honor Salmon P. Chase, Chief Justice of the U.S. Supreme Court, 1864-1873.

CHATHAM
Pittsylvania County   **Town**

William Pitt, the elder, argued successfully in the British House of Commons for the repeal of the Stamp Act. For this he became a hero in the American colonies. George III elevated him to the peerage in July 1766 when he became Prime Minister. The First Earl of Chatham served very ineffectually, for he was quite ill with gout and other assorted ailments, and spent most of his brief time as the head of government "taking the waters" at Bath. King George was relieved when he resigned. Since Pittsylvania County had been named for William Pitt, it was only natural that the county seat was named Chatham.

CHATHAM
Stafford County

William Fitzhugh, son of Henry Fitzhugh, was born at his father's estate Eagle's Nest in 1742. After being educated in England, he came to Virginia and settled near Fredericksburg. He married Anne Randolph, a daughter of Peter Randolph of Chatsworth, built his home here in 1765, and raised a large active family of five sons and several daughters. One of them, Mary, married George Washington Parke Custis and was the mother of General Robert E. Lee's wife.

William Fitzhugh II was a Burgess from 1772-75, a member of the Virginia Conventions of 1775 and 1776, and a delegate to the Continental Congress. The house here was designed by an English architect who was commissioned for the task by William Pitt (the younger), the Second Earl of Chatham, a classmate of William Fitzhugh at Eton and Oxford and a lifelong friend. The large brick house of two stories with balancing wings was finished in 1771 after three years of labor. The lands were worked by slaves and the estate was prosperous. Fortunately, it was untouched by the Revolution.

Because the tall house overlooked the Rappahannock River and commanded a full view of the town of Fredericksburg, it was occupied by Union officers during the battles for the town. Pressed into service as a hospital during the war, both Clara Barton, founder of the American Red Cross, and the poet Walt Whitman served the wounded for many months. Barton's personal comments of this place have been preserved in some of her letters. Federal soldiers ripped away much of the interior paneling for firewood, pencilled graffiti on exposed plaster walls, and left the beautiful home a wreck.

Chatham recovered its former elegance during Reconstruction through the determination of its owners and became one of the most noted mansions of nineteenth-century Virginia. Now under the administration of the National Park Service. *See: Bedford; Boscobel; Marmion; Ravensworth*

CHATSWORTH
Henrico County

This was the home of Colonel Peter Randolph, a member of the governor's Council who was the Receiver-General of Customs. His Virginia home was named for the famous estate of the Cavendish family in Derbyshire, England. During Colonel Randolph's lifetime, Chatsworth, in the mother country, was the seat of the Fourth Duke of Devonshire. The connection between the Duke and the Randolph family is not clear at this writing.

CHEATHAM ANNEX
York County

Cheatham Annex, a U.S. Navy facility, was named for Admiral Joseph Johnston Cheatham who, as the chief of the Navy's Bureau of Supplies and Accounts, modernized the system of supplying the fleet and established the Supply Center of Norfolk in 1930, which is known as the world's largest store. Admiral Cheatham, the son of a former Confederate general, was named for General Joseph E. Johnston, his father's friend.

This satellite establishment on the York River occupies land that once was the site of Utimara in the middle 1600s and was the location of a huge shell-loading plant during World War I. Cheatham Annex was formally commissioned in June 1943, as the principal assembly and shipping point for advance bases during World War II. All types of material were received, packed, and assembled in the many warehouses and transit sheds for loading directly aboard the ships.

The Annex now serves as a bulk and backup stock point for the Norfolk Naval Supply Center. Encompassing 2,360 acres, it is a complete community, except for churches and schools, with its own waterworks and railroad. Today it houses the largest government-owned refrigeration facility on the east coast. It has over 2.5 million gross square feet of heated warehouse space, a supply pier, and a fuel pier.

Other tasks include the fabrication of eyeglasses for Navy personnel, training seagoing stevedores, the maintenance of prepositioned emergency hospital equipment and supplies, disposal of surplus materials for emergency hospital equipment and supplies, disposal of surplus materials for all Department of Defense activities on the Peninsula, and the processing of personal effects of Navy personnel who desert, are missing in action, or die while at sea. *See: Defense General Supply Center; Penniman; Utimara*

CHECK
Floyd County

A post office was established in a local country store where the game of checkers was a constant attraction. The name Checkers was proposed to the postal authorities who turned it down for some unexplained reasons. On the second try, the name Check was offered. It was accepted.

CHELSEA
King William County

Colonel Augustine Moore came to Virginia about 1700 and obtained a patent for 8,600 acres between the Pamunkey and Mattaponi rivers. He named it for Chelsea, a borough of London on the north bank of the Thames. Colonel Moore was a direct descendant of Sir Thomas Moore, Lord Chancellor to King Henry VIII, who was beheaded for his refusal to sanction the king's divorce from Queen Catherine.

When Augustine Moore built his house in 1709, he hired Indians from the Mattaponi tribe to work. The old mansion, of fine brickwork using glazed headers alternating with dark stretchers in a checkerboard pattern, faces the river. A rear addition, of Dutch colonial design, was added by the builder in 1740. Governor Alexander Spotswood assembled some of his Knights of the Golden Horse Shoe at Chelsea in 1716 at the start of his journey of exploration. Colonel Moore was one of the gentlemen in the party. *See: Swift Run Gap*

CHERICOKE
King William County

Carter Braxton of Elsing Green owned this land and built the present house. He lived here in later life after moving from Delaware Town. He was a signer of the Declaration of Independence for Virginia, an honor he accepted reluctantly. By the time he moved here, his fortunes had declined badly and he was in financial difficulty, not because of his participation in the independence movement, but simply because he was not a good businessman. Chericoke is an obscure Indian word. *See: West Point*

CHERITON
Northampton County   **Town**

On the bay side of the lower Eastern Shore is Cherrystone Creek, an important waterway in the early days. The village of the "Laughing King of Accawmake," Chief Debedevon, probably was located at the upper, shallower end. In the nineteenth century, Dr. William S. Stockley owned the land on which the native village once stood. He named his farm Cheriton, possibly for the English village five miles from Denver. However, the name of the creek goes back to the early 17th Century when Thomas Savage settled there. It's possible Cherrystone is a corruption of Cheriton. *See: Cherry Grove of Northampton; Savage Neck*

CHEROKEE INDIANS

The Cherokee Nation, a group of related tribes, was spread all through the mountains of southwest Virginia, Tennessee, and North Carolina. They occupied towns on the banks of the Savannah, Yadkin, and Tennessee rivers. A highly organized and intelligent group who had a system of civil government, they were ruthless savages and excellent fighters who gave the early settlers of southwest Virginia a difficult time. Occasionally they aided the Americans, particularly during the French and Indian Wars. Their principal town, what may be called their capital, was Choto, remnants of which can be found about five miles from the ruins of Fort Loudoun in Tennessee. In 1735 it was estimated that they had at least sixty-four populous towns. In 1776 the Cherokees of southwest Virginia, living principally in the Holston Valley, could field over 2,400 warriors. Their ancient enemies were the Shawnees, a group of Indians that no natives liked. *See: Battle Knob*

CHERRY GROVE
King William County

Ambrose Edwards, who came to Virginia in 1745, built this house and lived in it until his death in 1810. His second wife was a rich widow who insisted on a prenuptial contract which stipulated that Ambrose could not interfere with the management of her property. In turn, she agreed to make no claim upon his. This foresighted lady's name was Barbara Finch.

CHERRY GROVE
Northampton County

Located near the tip of Savage Neck, due west from Eyre Hall, this is most likely the site of Ensign Thomas Savage's first home. He was the English lad who came over as a cabin boy for Captain Christopher Newport and was given as a peace hostage to the Indians during the early days of the Jamestown colony. The present house at Cherry

Grove dates from about 1737. It was built by Nathaniel Littleton Savage, a direct descendant of the brave lad whose contribution to the success of the first permanent English settlement in the New World has been overlooked. Cherry Grove lies on Cherrystone Creek. *See: Occahannock; Savage Neck; White Cliff*

CHESAPEAKE
City

The city of Chesapeake was formed in 1963 by consolidating the city of South Norfolk and Norfolk County. It has a total area of 361 square miles. It is the only major city to use the name of the famous bay.

CHESAPEAKE BAY

The first European to explore this bay was Lucas Vasquez d'Ayllon, a Spaniard who came in 1524. Claiming the area for his king, he called it Bahia de la Maria. Two years later, Jesuit missionaries were planted here to Christianize the natives while extracting from them the best route to the Western Ocean. Their camp, recorded as San Miguel, was not on the shore of the bay and is thought to have been well up the James. No trace has been found of this earliest settlement and it has been assumed that the men were soon murdered when the ship left for home. The Spanish never tried to settle here again.

The English mariner Bartholomew Gilbert came exploring in 1603 for King James I. He named the bay Chesupioc after the Indian word k'tchisipik, meaning "great water." When he was killed by the natives while ashore on a peace mission, his crew took home the news that they had found no evidence of Spanish attempts to colonize that far north. This fostered thoughts of colonizing this area with English settlers to cement a claim.

The bay is about 200 miles long and, at its widest, is about 30 miles across. Geologically, it is the drowned mouth of the Susquehannah River. Responding to tidal changes as far north as Baltimore, the water is brackish with seawater mixed with the outpourings of the Susquehannah, Potomac, Rappahannock, York, and James Rivers. *See: Cape Charles; Cape Henry; Hampton Roads*

CHESAPEAKE CITY
Hampton   **Obsolete**

Briefly, the suburb of Phoebus in Hampton was a separate town. Its first name was Chesapeake City since it was located at the extreme southern end of Chesapeake Bay. *See: Phoebus*

CHESTER
Chesterfield County

Joseph Snead and Charles Stebbins purchased land between Richmond and Petersburg on the R & P Railroad at the junction of the Clover Hill Railroad. In 1856 they laid out a town and advertised in a Richmond newspaper for buyers. Many people came, bought lots, and built homes. Chester was selected by the two developers as the name for no special reason except the land was in Chesterfield County. It was only a thirty minute train ride from the heart of Richmond. The advertisement suggested (as do modern ads) that by living in the county new residents could avoid city taxes. A plentiful supply of cheap coal for heating the homes was available from the nearby Midlothian Coal Mines. Those who bought lots when the offer was first made received a free pass, good for ten years, on the railroad. A hotel lured visitors. Shops for the two railroads provided work for those who had no business dealings in Richmond.

Chester was badly mauled at the end of the Civil War. Many homes were looted and burned. The railroad shops were utterly destroyed. Chester nearly died during Reconstruction but today it is a tiny, interesting village. *See: Midlothian*

CHESTERFIELD COUNTY

Formed from Henrico in 1748, this county was named for Philip Stanhope, the Fourth Earl of Chesterfield, a British statesman who is remembered today more for the parental letters he wrote to his son than for his accomplishments within the British government. The first courthouse was in a tavern near the center of the territory, but a proper building was soon erected. Since most of the citizens lived in Manchester, across the James River from Richmond, the court was moved there in 1871. However, this arrangement lasted for a mere five years when complaints from those who lived in the lower section of the county forced a return to the original site where it is today. The early courthouse was torn down and replaced by the present structure in 1917.

The name Chesterfield was known the world over in the first half of the twentieth century when a cigarette by that name was manufactured and popularized by aggressive advertising.

47

CHESTERVILLE
Langley Field, Hampton   **Site**

This was the early home of George Wythe, the first law professor in Virginia and the teacher, friend, and advisor of Thomas Jefferson. The land was patented originally by John Laydon of Jamestown. In 1692 Thomas Wythe, a Burgess of Elizabeth City County, bought the 204 acres and slowly expanded them into an estate of more than 750 acres on the northwest branch of Back River.

George Wythe was born here, although not in the manor house since he had it built in 1771, sixteen years after he inherited the estate from his brother. Wythe successfully worked the place as a plantation until 1792. He married the daughter of the most noted eighteenth century Virginia architect, Richard Taliaferro, who designed, built, and then gave as a wedding present to his daughter, the famous Wythe House of Williamsburg. It was only natural that Jefferson should be attracted to George Wythe who, primarily a lawyer, was interested in philosophy and the natural sciences. The elder man was a Burgess, the Attorney General of Virginia, s signer of the Declaration of Independence, a member of the Continental Congress, and, for many years, the Speaker of the Virginia House of Delegates. He moved to Richmond in 1791 to follow the new state government there.

When a very old man, Wythe was poisoned by his only sister's grandson, George Sweeney, who knew that he was to inherit the old man's estate and wanted to hasten the time of acquisition. Wythe found out who had poisoned him and managed to change his will before he died. The murderer was brought to trial but was acquitted because the only witness to the crime was a servant who, because she was a black woman, by law could not testify against a white man.

Chesterville was allowed to go to complete ruin through the neglect of the army which built Langley Field in 1917 partly on the Wythe lands. The remains of the old house, which burned in 1911, have been allowed to disappear through the indifference of NASA which now occupies part of this famous installation, although lately there has been some attempt to preserve what is left. A pile of stones and the remains of the basement, plus the old family burial plot, can be found near the NASA Langley Research Center. *See: Elmwood; Oares Plantation; St. Johns of Richmond*

CHESTNUT GROVE
New Kent County

Martha Dandridge was born here on June 21, 1731. She was the first of eight children born to Colonel John Dandridge and his wife Martha. He had moved from Hampton about ten years before and had sited his house not far from the Pamunkey River on his 1,700 acres. At eighteen, Martha Dandridge married Daniel Parke Custis in nearby St. Peter's Church. The ceremony was performed by the Reverend David Mossum and the couple is said to have left the church in a coach drawn by six white horses with six outriders dressed in white mounted on black chargers. They lived in White House, not far away, where they had two children before Daniel died suddenly in 1757. Two years later the Widow Custis married George Washington.

Chestnut Grove burned in 1926 shortly after it had been renovated. All that was left was one chimney and the front door key. The chimney was torn down in the 1950s and a new home was built on top of the old foundation. The original terraced gardens on the river side still remain, as does the Dandridge burial ground. *See: Arlington; Eltham; White House*

CHESTNUT HILL
Campbell County

This was the home of Charles Lynch, Sr., the father of John Lynch who founded the city of Lynchburg. He was an Irishman who served a term of indenture as a servant to a Louisa County Quaker family. He married Sarah Clark, an ardent member of the Society of Friends, the daughter of his master. A large Quaker settlement became the nucleus of Lynchburg, a town built primarily for the tobacco trade of the upper James River. Charles Lynch died in 1753 but his house here was known to have been built many years earlier although the exact date is questionable. *See: Lynchburg*

CHESTNUT RIDGE
Albemarle County

The long hill northeast of Charlottesville, part of the Southwest Mountains chain, was called Chestnut Ridge, probably for the abundance of chestnut trees that still grow there. In 1762 Thomas Garth lived in a small home near Buck Island Creek on a farm then known as Darby's Folly. He purchased land on the western slope of Chestnut Ridge, built a new house, and named his enlarged farm for the mountain that dominates the view from the front porch. Later Thomas Garth became one of the most affluent landholders in the county when he purchased the Lewis estate on Ivy Creek. He then owned land from the Three Chopt Road to the junction of Mechum's Creek and Morman's River. *See: Southwest Mountains*

CHICACOAN
Northumberland County   **Obsolete**

This Indian district of early colonial times was located on the lower Potomac River. It took its name from the dominant tribe of the same name. They were friendly with the settlers and willingly traded both corn and pelts. The first settler here was John Mottrom who came across the river from the Citie of St. Mary's of Maryland in 1640. He was attracted to the region because it had good farm land, the creek afforded an inlet for the deep water vessels that would call to pick up his tobacco, and the natives were friendly. Mottrom took no chances, however, for before settling down, he obtained permission by bribing the chief, Marshwap, with many gifts. The creek on which he and others settled was spelled Sekacawone on early maps, probably a close phonetic presentation of how the tribe actually pronounced its name. *See: Coan Hall*

CHICKAHOMINY INDIANS

These Indians laid claim to the land upon which the Jamestown settlers built their first village in 1607. They were always resentful of the intrusion and never made any sort of lasting peace with the colonists. Members of this tribe captured Captain John Smith in December 1607 and dutifully took him to Powhatan, the chief of the local Indian confederacy. According to Smith's account, written many years later, he was saved from execution by Pocahontas. The Chickahominy tribe gleefully took part in the massacres of 1622 and 1644 after having harassed the settlers for years with sudden attacks in the silent forests. Only a few of this tribe remain today. Although they were a part of Powhatan's confederacy, this was the only tribe that was not ruled by a *werowance* (chief) but was, instead, headed by a group of priests. Their mortal enemies were the Monacans. *See: Fort James; Purton; Smith's Fort Plantation*

CHICKAHOMINY RIVER

One of the few unspoiled major tributaries of the James, the mouth of this river is but a few miles upriver from Jamestown. It is navigable for small boats for about twenty beautiful miles through cypress stands and

flocks of waterfowl. It was named for the Indian tribe of the same name who had their village on the lower bank near the mouth of the James within easy walking distance of the first colony. The tributary, a sluggish and narrow brook, winds around the eastern boundary of modern Richmond. At that point it is called Chickahominy Creek. *See: Fort James*

CHILESBURG
Caroline County

The first owner of the land upon which this village stands, and the man for whom it was named, was Macajah Chiles who settled here about 1666. His son, Walter, was a protege of Robert Beverley. *See: Barn Elms*

CHILOWIE
Smyth County   **Town**

This town on the Holston River was established about 1748 by Colonel James Patton. The name is an Indian word meaning *valley of the deer.*

CHINCOTEAGUE
Accomack County   **Town**

An Indian word meaning *large inlet*, this long island on the ocean side of the Eastern Shore has been lived on by fishing families for three centuries. It was first deeded to Captain William Whittington in 1662 by Wachawampe, the "Emperor" of the Gingo Teague tribe. Chincoteague is pronounced *SHIN-ca-teeg.* The town of the same name, the only one on the island, is the center of activity each year for the sale of wild ponies brought over from Assateague Island.

CHIPPOKES
Surry County   **Site**

Captain William Powell, commander of the fort at Jamestown, was the first owner of this land. He named it for a friendly Indian by the name of Choupouke. Captain Powell patented 750 acres in 1612, two years after he came to Virginia with Sir Thomas Gates. When he was killed by Chickahominy Indians in 1623, his son, George, inherited the property and leased 300 acres of it to Stephen Webb in 1642. Webb promised to build a house which was to become a part of the estate. For the land he agreed to pay one capon a year as rent, due each St. Thomas Day. In 1643 George Powell died without heirs and the land reverted to the Crown.

Governor Sir William Berkeley gained control of Chippokes and the Powell house. After his death, his widow, Lady Frances Culpeper Stevens Berkeley, married, as her third husband, the governor's private secretary, Colonel A. Phillip Ludwell. Since there was no official home for the royal Governors, and with Jamestown destroyed by Bacon, the Ludwells lived at Chippokes and rented Green Spring to the Crown for the use of the governors. When the capital was moved to Williamsburg, the Ludwell family moved back to Green Spring and let this Surry County estate be managed by overseers. The property remained in the Ludwell family for four generations during which time the original Webb/Powell house suffered from neglect. Today there is some doubt about its location. The present eighteenth century house now standing vacant near the river possibly is on or near the site of the original house and could even have been built on the foundations since they are obviously much older than the existing nineteenth century brickwork.

The large manor house which now dominates the property was built in 1854, as were the various dependencies. In 1970 Chippokes was given to the Commonwealth of Virginia for a public park by Mrs. Victor Stewart as a memorial to her husband who had purchased it in 1918 and began the long process of restoring the lands after many years of abuse. Today it is still being operated as a working farm. *See: Green Spring; Richneck*

CHISCHIAK
York County   **Site**

After the Massacre of 1622, the colonists erected a palisade from the James to the Pamunkey (now the York) as a barrier between English land and Indian territory. At the eastern terminus lay the abandoned Indian village of Chischiak. At a meeting in October 1630, the Council decided it needed a garrison here to keep an eye on the Indians who lived across the river under the leadership of Chief Opechancanough, the successor to Powhatan. The Council offered fifty acres to every man who would settle here, a necessary inducement since this region was rather far away from Jamestown and, if attacked by Indians, the people could expect no immediate help.

Captains John West and John Utie volunteered. They collected small bands of men and moved here without their families. The two captains each received a bonus of 300 additional acres for their responsibilities of command. Utie settled on the north side of King's Creek and West occupied the south side. Soon they were joined by Captain Robert Felgate, a newcomer from London,

who built his modest home near Captain West on what is now known as Felgate's Creek. Another captain was Nicholas Martiau who occupied land down the river near the present village of Yorktown. The entire region was called Chischiak which, over the years, has been spelled a variety of ways including the more modern Cheesecake.

Captain Utie was a participant in the events which ousted Governor John Harvey and, while enroute to England to stand trial for treason, John Utie died aboard ship. Captain West, a brother of Lord Delaware, stayed out of this fracas, and was granted an additional 2,000 acres by the Council"...in the right of his son being the first born Christian at Chischiak." In 1650 Captain West sold his holdings to Edward Digges and moved up the York River to found West's Plantation at the fork of the Pamunkey and Mattaponi rivers. Shortly before this, John Utie's land was purchased by Henry Lee whose house, Kiskiak, is still standing. *See: Bellfield; E. D. Plantation; Kiskiak; Moore House; Penniman; West's Plantation; Utimara; Yorke*

CHOPAWAMSIC
Prince William County

Settlement began here in 1651 when Governor Samuel Mathews of Denbigh patented land far up the sparsely settled Potomac River. Chopawamsic is an Indian word meaning *by the outlet of the creek. See: Denbigh*

CHRIST CHURCH
Alexandria

Fairfax Parish was spread out over a lot of territory. The mother church was near Fairfax Hall, and a Chapel of Ease was near the future site of Alexandria. When the chapel became too small to take care of the expanding population, the vestry voted in 1765 to erect a larger building. John Alexander of Stafford County donated the land. A special tax, to be paid in tobacco, was levied against every family to pay for the new church. James Wren, possibly a descendant of Sir Christopher Wren, drew up the charming design and work was begun in 1767. It was five-and-a-half years before the structure was accepted by the vestry in February 1773.

CHRIST CHURCH
Lancaster County

Completed in 1732 on the site of an older building of 1669, this is the least modified of all colonial Virginia churches. It was built at the expense of Robert "King" Carter to serve Corotoman and other estates in the vicinity.

He reserved one quarter of the interior to seat his family, tenants, and servants. This building is considered the first Greek-cruciform colonial church building in America. Robert Carter is buried here with his two wives as is his father, John Carter, with his three wives and two daughters. An ambiguous inscription on John's tomb gave rise for many years to the notion that he had five wives. "King" Carter agreed to pay for the building in order to have a suitable monument over the vault of his parents who lie under the chancel.

Less than fifty years later, when the church was no longer supported by taxes, attendance here, as elsewhere, ceased. The new Commonwealth confiscated all of the buildings and glebe lands and sold them to help support the new government. When in 1802 the General Asembly enacted a law which declared that privately donated churches were no longer state property, this Christ Church again became a part of the Carter family's estate. In 1836 the family leased it to the Episcopal congregation of Lancaster. Without light or heat, services now are held here only during the summer months. *See: Corotoman*

CHRIST CHURCH
Middlesex County

This parish was established in October 1666 through a petition granted by the House of Burgesses. The first building, a replica of the church then standing at Middle Plantation, was begun immediately and was completed in 1668. This Christ Church was the mother church of the parish from 1666 until dis-establishment shortly after the Revolution. The building then fell into ruin through lack of use, as did so many other Anglican churches, during the post-war upsurge of the Methodists and Baptists, the latter being the more active. Fortunately, this structure was saved from complete ruin and restored in 1840. The other churches of the parish were the Upper Chapel at Church View, which burned in modern times, and the Lower Chapel, now called the Lower Methodist Church, which is still in use. In the quiet graveyard of Christ Church is buried the colonial governor, Sir Henry Chicheley, who died while staying at nearby Rosegill.

CHRISTIANSBURG
Montgomery County   **Town**

Founded in 1792 by Colonel James Craig, the settlement was first called Hans Meadow. Later it was renamed in honor of Colonel William Christian, an early explorer, Indian fighter, and the brother-in-law of Patrick Henry. The town is the seat of Montgomery County. *See: Fort Christian; Chase City*

CHRISTOPHER NEWPORT COLLEGE
Newport News

Authorized as a two year junior college in 1960, an extension of William and Mary, this institution expanded into a four year college in one decade and became independent of the mother organization. It was named for Captain Christopher Newport, the man who was in command of the three-ship flotilla that brought the original settlers to Jamestown in 1607.

CHUCKATUCK
Chesapeake

Chuckatuck is an Indian word meaning *crooked creek*. When the English came to this area in 1607, the Nansemond Indians had their village at the head of this creek which emptied into Hampton Roads. They were always unfriendly, refused to trade, and often killed settlers for pure pleasure. They took an active part in the terrible Massacre of 1622 but paid for their acts when Governor George Yeardley led a force of Virginians against them, defeated them soundly, burned their village, and forced the survivors to flee to the south. Later the colonists came back to stay. The hamlet of Chuckatuck today is proud of the unusual name. *See: Nansemond*

CHULA
Amelia County

This is a Choctaw Indian word meaning *red fox*.

CHURCH HILL
Gloucester County

The land grant of 1,174 acres given to Mordecai Cooke dates from 1650. The first known house here dates from 1658. Originally known as Mordecai's Mount, it was the happy home of Joan Constable, a lass of very humble beginnings who came to Virginia with the boatland of "suitable maidens" sent over by the London Company in 1621. She lived to see her son hob nob with the royal Governor, Sir William Berkeley. Her grandson, also named Mordecai, was the sheriff of Gloucester County in 1698 and was elected Burgess in 1696. Her granddaughter, Frances, married Gabriel Throckmorton in 1690 and they inherited the property. The ancient Throckmorton family was active in English politics during the reign of Henry VIII. Those who came to America during the

51

seventeenth century settled primarily in this county where many of them became socially and politically prominent. The old house of Church Hill burned in the 1700s and was rebuilt in the nineteenth century on the old foundations. *See: Airville; Isleham; Ware Church; Wareham*

CHURCHLAND
Chesapeake
Formerly in Norfolk County, a collection of churches was built here by various denominations on a site known as Sycamore Hill. Eventually everyone called the area Churchland, some with derision, some with pride. Although it is close to the city of Portsmouth, it is a village within the city of Chesapeake.

CHURCH VIEW
Middlesex County
In 1852 Joseph Perciful purchased 200 acres across from Hermitage Church on the old road to Urbanna from King and Queen courthouse. He built his house a year later and called his farm Churchville. When the property was purchased by William T. Richardson in 1886, he changed the name to Church View, added special touches to the house, and made it the show place of upper Middlesex County. Sadly, the frame two-story building was torn down in 1913 and replaced by another larger house.

CHURCHVILLE
Augusta County
One early log church served many different denominations in early times. When they could afford to, the congregations built their own churches in the locality since everyone was used to coming here for services. The location became known as Churchville.

CINQUOTECK
King William County   Site
When Captain John Smith was taken captive in December 1607, he was brought to this Indian village first. It was located on the tip of land at the confluence of the Mattapanient and Youghtanund rivers (Mattaponi and Pamunkey). Cinquoteck, one of the chief towns of Powhatan's confederacy, was the village of Opechancanough, the leader of the massacres of 1622 and 1644. John Smith came back here voluntarily in 1608 to successfully trade with these natives for food for Jamestown. Having been pardoned from execution by Powhatan, he was in no danger for he had the blessing of the great leader. Smith called this village

Pumunkey Town on his map of 1612. In 1691 a settlement established here was called Delaware Town. Later the name was changed to West Point. *See: Delaware Town; Purton*

CISMONT
Albemarle County
Nicholas Meriwether, owner of huge tracts of land in Albemarle County, built a house here about 1736. Much later, a descendant named the farm Cismont, a shortened version of *cismontane*, Latin for "on this side of the mountain," the mountain being Chestnut Ridge. During the late nineteenth century, a tiny hamlet called Bowlesville grew up around Bowles blacksmith shop and a local store. When Bowles died the hamlet became Brown's Store. When a tiny church was built, the region reverted to its original name of Cismont. Here, at the church each Thanksgiving Day, is held the traditional Blessing of the Hounds, a very old English custom. *See: Cloverfields of Albemarle; Grace Church of Albemarle*

CITY
The word *city* was used to define a territory in which civil and religious authorities were equal. Within a city the major economic, political, and religious factions were in balance, each exerting influence upon the people. Although there often were several towns in an English city, there was only one bishop, thus giving the church a slight edge in power. When the colony of Virginia became sufficiently populated to require political organization, it was envisioned that each of the four original boroughs would eventually have a bishop in his own cathedral, and so the colonists formed James City, Elizabeth City, Charles City, and the City of Henricus, each containing a collection of settlements which were expected to grow into towns. Cathedrals were not necessary since the Bishop of London, who was the ecclesiastical head of the Virginia colony, never authorized an American bishop but sent his own representative who bore the title Commissary which, by definition, means a person to whom some duty is given by an authority. (In the Soviet Union, the head of a government department is still called a commissar.)

In 1619 Virginia's Four Ancient Boroughs were reorganized into Four Incorporations containing twelve boroughs, each of which could elect two Burgesses. In 1634, when eight shires were established, later to be called counties, the old term was continued, such as James City County, although by then it was obvious that no bishops would be authorized by the Bishop of London anywhere in Anglican America. Instead, parishes were established which seldom crossed county lines. Frequently there were several parishes in a county.

In 1680 Charles II decided that the only way the colony would properly grow was to have established towns. He did not call for cities but instead ordered Governor Culpeper to require each county to purchase fifty acres to be laid out for a "towne." The king also required ports to be established on the major rivers "as soon as storehouses and conveniences can be provided to prohibit ships trading (in Virginia) to load or unload but at fixed places," thus beginning the enforcement of customs taxes.

After the Revolution, when the principal of separation of church and state was high on the list of priorities in the minds of the people, the word city was applied to large centers of population, ranking above town or village. In Virginia the word city remains connected to some of the very old counties as a footnote to the past. Thus, to the confusion and amusement of the uninformed, we still have James City County and Charles City County. Elizabeth City County disappeared when it was annexed by the city of Hampton after World War II.

In modern times, there are three types of communities in the Commonwealth: unincorporated villages, incorporated towns, or chartered cities. Both towns and cities have their own government. Unincorporated settlements are governed by the county. As of this printing there are forty-one cities in Virginia of various classes. *See: Borough; Burg; Corporation; Hundred, Shires; Town; Ville*

CITY POINT
Hopewell   **Site**

Long before the city of Hopewell was established during World War I, the land on which the city now stands was called Nether Bermuda Hundred. In 1619, when the Virginia colonists were permitted to select two representatives from each of twelve boroughs to serve in the first General Assembly, Nether Bermuda Hundred was attached to Charles City which then straddled the James River. When eight counties were established in 1634, the arrangement continued at a great inconvenience to those on the south bank of the James. When Prince George County was formed in 1702, the powerful Eppes family, who owned all of a large point of land that

stuck into the James, preferred to cross the river to the Charles City courthouse rather than travel over land by bad roads to Prince George courthouse. Therefore, a small bit of land was retained by Charles City. It was known as Charles City Point. Although eventually the Eppes land was put into Prince George County, the name City Point remained. When General Grant was besieging Petersburg in 1864, most of his supplies came up the James River and were put ashore at City Point and hauled to his army by rail. *See: Appomattox Manor; Bermuda Hundred; Charles City; Hopewell*

CLAIBORNE'S NECK
Newport News

This was the estate of Richard Kemp, an unpopular Secretary of the Colony under the despised and deposed Governor John Harvey. The neck of land on which it lies was named for Colonel William Claibourne. When Kemp died, he was not greatly mourned and his widow married shortly after the funeral. Her new husband was a scamp, Sir Thomas Lunsford, who once was described by the Earl of Dorset as "that young outlaw who fears neither God nor man." Lunsford's youthful escapade once landed him in London's Newgate Prison from which he escaped and fled to France. There he fought in several battles and a few duels before returning to England to fight with distinction for King Charles I against the Scots. So daring were his exploits during the English civil war that the Puritans hated him and taught their children to fear his very name. He came to Virginia in 1649 and was immediately appointed general of the militia by Governor William Berkeley. Later he was appointed to the Council. He had a daughter by the Widow Kemp, Katherine, who married Ralph Wormeley of Rosegill.

When Thomas Lunsford died, Claiborne's Neck was purchased by Thomas Ludwell, another member of the Council. His brother, Colonel Phillip Ludwell, came to Virginia about 1664 and became the private secretary to the Governor. When Governor Berkeley died, Phillip married Berkeley's widow and became her third husband. On the tombstone of Thomas Ludwell, which was removed to Bruton Parish Churchyard, is the statement that nearby lie the remains of Richard Kemp, Esq., and Sir Thomas Lunsford. The bodies of the latter two were not removed and they remain at Claiborne's Neck.

The estate was next owned by Miles Cary, Sr., who bought it about 1660. His son renamed the place Richneck. *See: Airville; Chippokes; Green Spring; Kempsville; New Kent County; Richneck*

CLAREMONT
Surry County   **Town**

One of the first Indian villages visited by the English in 1607 was Quioughcohanock. It lay directly across the James on the broad curve of the river which forms what is now known as Cobham Bay. This land was not patented until 1649 although there undoubtedly were early settlers here who were either killed or frightened away during the massacres of 1622 and 1644.

The patentee of the 12,000 acres was Arthur Allen who erected the first house here shortly after receiving title to the land. A runaway prince of the German House of Hanover, his real name was Allen Guelph. He and his brother, Eric, were rivals for the love of a highborn English lady. Eric was successful in his suit, but on his wedding night he was fatally stabbed by his jealous brother who then fled England. Using the name Arthur Allen, the choice of first name possibly prompted by the King Arthur legend of honor, he came to Tidewater and took up this Claremont tract which he secured by transporting in March of 1649 four settlers, one of whom became his wife. Clare (or Claire) is the Anglicized version of Clara. The house is one of a few that had a secret escape

GENERAL GEORGE ROGERS CLARK
CLARKE COUNTY

passage from the basement to the river. Arthur Allen also acquired the lands of what is now called Bacon's Castle and erected that interesting mansion. It is separated from its nearest neighbor, Brandon, by Chippokes Creek.

During the days of steamboats, the town of Claremont was an important landing. *See: Bacon's Castle, Tapahanna*

CLARKE COUNTY

Named for George Rogers Clark, the Conqueror of the Northwest Territory, this county was formed from parts of Frederick and Warren counties in 1836. The courthouse is located at Berryville. It is not known when the final "e" was added to General Clark's name.

CLARKSVILLE
Mecklenburg County   **Town**

The town was formed in 1818 and named for Clark Royster, who operated a ferry and owned the land when the town was established on the Roanoke River.

CLAY SPRING
Hanover County   **Site**

Here was born the famous statesman Henry Clay on April 12, 1777. He attended the log cabin school of the neighborhood, carried grain to the mill called The Slashes, studied law under George Wythe, and was admitted to the bar at the age of 20. Shortly thereafter, he moved to Kentucky where he became known as the "Mill Boy of the Slashes" and, later, the "Great Pacificator." *See: Chesterville; Slash Church*

CLEAR BROOK
Roanoke County

Too often a simple name such as this has a peculiar origin. Not so this time. The village was named for a clear brook that runs nearby.

CLEVE
King George County   **Site**

Built in 1729 for Charles Carter by his father Robert "King" Carter of Corotoman, this estate was inherited by Charles' son, Landon Carter. Lucy Landon Carter of Cleves married General John Minor, a Revolutionary leader who came from Hazel Hill near Fredericksburg. St. Leger Landon Carter sold the estate to the Lewis family in 1852.

Undoubtedly, this place took its name from the home of Anne of Cleve, known as the

Flemish Mare, one of the six wives of Henry VIII. She escaped execution and divorce when it was decided that their marriage was never consummated and was annulled. The Carters were fond of using names that recalled historical places or events. *See: Blenheim; Sabine Hall*

CLEVELAND
Russell County   **Town**

Grover Cleveland was President when this post office needed a name in 1890. Gradually the population grew and a small town came into being around the post office.

CLIFFORD
Amherest County   **Town**

This settlement, incorporated as Cabellsburg, in 1795, was named for Dr. William Cabell, physician, surveyor, and early settler. The name was changed to New Glasgow and then to Clifford.

CLIFTON
Accomack County

The original 1,200 acres were bought in 1663 by Colonel John Wise from Ekeeks, the king of the Onancock Indians. John, who died here in 1695, was followed by five more generations without a break. John VI was the half-brother of Governor Henry A. Wise who came from another branch of the family which settled at Onley. Clifton's original house was destroyed and was replaced by the present, comparatively younger dwelling. *See: Onancock; Onley; Wise County*

CLIFTON
Fluvanna County

This home of Carter Henry Harrison was built on land patented in 1723. As a member of the Cumberland Committee of Safety, Harrison wrote instructions for independence which were presented to the Virginia Convention of 1776. Apparently, this was the first such declaration publicly approved. The Convention voted for independence as a result of this motion. Clifton was named for the English spa in Gloucestershire.

CLIFTON FORGE
Alleghany County   **City**

A local blacksmith, James Clifton, operated his forge here in the latter part of the eighteenth century. Gradually he expanded his modest shop into the Clifton's Iron Works. However, by then everyone was used to calling the settlement Clifton's Forge. Through the years the population increased until the town of Clifton Forge was large enough to become chartered as a city of the Commonwealth.

CLIFTS
Westmoreland County   **Site**

These 1,300 acres were known as Clifts Plantation during the middle of the seventeenth century. They were patented about 1650 by Nathaniel Pope and became part of the Stratford estate when they were purchased by Thomas Lee in 1716. The land is now a part of Westmoreland State Park. *See: Mattox; Stratford*

CLINCHCO
Dickenson County

This is a shortened version of Clinchfield Coal Corporation. It was quickly adopted as the village name when the company suggested it.

CLINCHPORT
Scott County   **Town**

The Clinch River carried light supplies and people in shallow-draft vessels. This place was a landing at the uppermost point of good water. Further travel required a portage here around shallow rapids. Probably the name meant Clinch River portage. *See: Port*

CLINCH RIVER

This river, and its verdant valley, has been called Clinch since the late seventeenth century. The origin of the name can no longer be determined and some of the theories are just too wild to perpetuate. Most probably it was named for an early explorer. The Clinch and the Holston are major tributaries of the Tennessee River.

CLINTWOOD
Dickenson County   **Town**

Once known as Holly Creek, the town's name was changed to honor Senator Henry Clinton Wood of Scott County. It is the seat of Dickenson County. It could not have been named Dickensonville since that name already had been used in Russell County.

CLOVERDALE
Botetourt County

About 1787, Robert Harvey built an iron smelter which he named Cloverdale Furnace. It operated until well after the Revolution, the last owner being John Tayloe who bought it in 1810. Nearby was a farm of the same name (which came first, farm or furnace?) where John Cabell Breckenridge was born in 1821. He was the Vice President of the United States under James Buchanan (1857-1861) of War under Jefferson Davis. *See: Bristol Iron Works*

CLOVERFIELDS
Albemarle County

This plantation was the first to be cut from the giant Meriwether grant of 1727. Cloverfields was created by Nicholas Meriwether II for his son David. Nicholas III, the grandson of the patentee, built a house in 1760. From the Cloverfields tract were formed Cismont Manor and Clover Hill. The Cloverfields tract adjoined Shadwell.

CLOVERFIELDS
Charles City County

The property here was a grant of 10,000 acres to Colonel William Cole, Esq., of Bolthrope late in the seventeenth century. A native of Warwickshire, England, he was a member of the Council, and Secretary of the colony. The exact dates of the land grant and the original houses were lost in the destruction of the county records during the Civil War, but it is assumed that the first house was built by his son, William Cole II, about 1700. In 1714, William, then a member of the House of Burgesses, gave his bond to construct warehouses on this land in a section known as Swine Yards. There are indications that the first house was torn down and a larger dwelling built farther back from the river about 1725. The present building, possibly the second home, is of an early English type, low and rambling, with hand hewn clapboards, and full basement containing the kitchen and other work areas. In 1769, William Cole IV sold 4,000 acres of this land to William Byrd III who changed the name from Cloverfields to Riverview. Sometime during the latter part of the eighteenth century, the landing, once known as Swine Yards Landing, was named Wilcox Wharf. *See: Bolthrope; Eniscorthy*

CLUSTER SPRINGS
Halifax County

Within a three mile radius of this hamlet are nearly 100 springs. Many of them are thoroughly saturated with minerals of various sorts. This is one of the few instances where the plural springs actually refers to more than one.

COAN HALL
Northumberland County

Here along the Coan River were the first settlements in Northern Neck. The leader of this area was John Mottrom who, in 1640, established a colony of settlers who migrated from the city of St. Mary's in Maryland because of the heavy Catholic requirements of that colony. Colonel Mottrom went to Jamestown as a representative of this group for the first time in 1645, the same year his daughter was born. She later became the wife of Nicholas Spencer, President of the Council, and acting governor from May 1683 until February 1684. *See: Chicacoan*

COATESVILLE
Hanover County

The present hamlet took its name from a farm named Coatesville owned for generations by the Coates family.

COBB'S HALL
Chesterfield County

Ambrose Cobb was granted 350 acres on the Appomattox River in 1639 for bringing three new settlers when he immigrated with his wife and son. He built his home shortly after his arrival. The estate was sold to John Bolling, the great-grandson of John Rolfe and Pocahontas, an astute businessman who carried on extensive trade with the Indians and the other colonists. Bolling's descendants lived here for generations. Many members of the Bolling family lie buried at Cobb's Hall, the first of which appears to have been John himself who died in 1709 at the age of 33. His wife was Mary Kennon of nearby Brick House. *See: Bollingbrook; Brick House; Cedar Level; Kippax; Smith's Fort Plantation*

COBB'S HALL
Lancaster County

Cobb's Hall, near Ditchley, was acquired by Richard Lee some time before 1651. The progenitor of most of the Lees in Virginia, he was a Burgess, a member of the Council, and the Secretary of the colony. Loyal to the Crown during the Cromwellian hiatus, he chartered a Dutch vessel, sailed to Brussels, and there surrendered Sir William Berkeley's commission as Virginia's Governor to the exiled Prince Charles. The Prince gave Richard Lee a new commission for Berkeley who kept it secret during the years others served as governor. The present house here at Cobb's Hall is the fourth on this site. *See: Green Spring; Stratford*

COBHAM WHARF
Surry

Cobham Wharf was a landing for steamboats, beginning in the middle of the nineteenth century. This community was named for the village Cobham of Surrey, England.

COEBURN

Wise County   **Town**

At first this railroad junction was called Guest's Station for the station master, a Mr. Guest. When this town was incorporated in 1894, a better name was needed. Coeburn was devised to honor two leading citizens. One was W. W. Coe, the chief engineer of the N & W railroad. The other was Judge W. E. Burns, of nearby Lenanon, who "had connections." *See: Brookneal*

COLCHESTER

Prince William County   **Site**

Captain John Smith came here in 1608 where he found the "king's house" of the Doeg Indians, a fierce and unfriendly tribe. In 1729, Robert "King" Carter built a landing at the mouth of the Occoquan River which he named Colchester for the city in Essex, England. Carter planned to ship copper ore from a discovery in the foothills of the Blue Ridge. By the time the wharf was built, the ore had been assayed as green sandstone that did not contain any mineral. The wharf remained for public use when the wealthy man abandoned it.

The famous tavern, The Arms of Fairfax, was built at the landing by a Mr. Gordon who spent huge sums of money on its interior. A contemporary visitor wrote, "Every luxury that money can purchase is to be obtained at the first summons ... the richest viands cover the table . . . and ice cools the Madeira . . . Apartments are numerous and at times spacious . . . carpets of delicate texture cover the floors; and glasses are suspended from the walls in which a Goliath might survey himself." No mention was made of entertainment. Around this fabulous tavern the town of Colchester was established in 1753. It competed unsuccessfully for trade with Occoquan and then gradually disappeared. *See: Frying Pan Run; Occoquan*

COLD HARBOR

Hanover County   **Site**

The most reliable explanation of the unusual name (since there is no navigable river here to offer a harbor) centers on an open shelter erected on the road in which passengers could wait for the stagecoach. Located in many remote spots, these were called cold harbors since they had no means to provide heat. Similar shelters can be seen today on rural roads where children wait for the school bus. A discounted, but more colorful story tells of a sailor who came to visit the lady of his dreams. When she gave him the brush-off, he was said to have remarked, "Now that really was a cold harbor."

Near this tiny settlement, General Grant learned a lesson about the tenacity of the Confederate defenders of Richmond. Hurling his army against General Lee, Grant's army suffered 7,000 casualties in twenty minutes, enough to convince him that a frontal assault on the city would be expensive and futile. After Cold Harbor, Grant slipped his men south to Petersburg.

COLEMAN

Essex County

Richard Coleman planted an early settlement here and shortly thereafter opened a trading post in 1652 to deal with the Portobago Indians. Their principal town was just a few miles north. By 1660 a church was built nearby to which everyone was required to hasten with their arms for mutual protection against the Indians. The Portobagos had no intention of going on the warpath since they were happy as traders and had no desire to spoil a good thing. Either because of the settlers' defense plans or in deference to the local tribes' business arrangements, other Indians from the north left this area alone. *See: Portobago Indians*

COLES POINT

Westmoreland County

This point of land commands a view up and down the Potomac River and was a navigation landmark for boat traffic. It is mentioned frequently in early travel accounts, especially the Carter papers, as part of the land holdings of Robert Carter II. It was Cole's Point as early as 1726 but nothing has been unearthed about Mr. Cole. *See: Nomini Hall*

COLLE

Albemarle County

The house at Colle was built in 1770 by workmen who were also engaged in building Monticello a few miles away. Filippo Mazzei, a native of Italy and a friend of Jefferson, lived here for six years while attempting to make Albemarle county a land of wine, silk, and citrus. He arrived in Virginia in 1773 on board a ship chartered by the Grand Duke of Tuscany. With him were Italian vineyard workers, vine cuttings, olive and lemon trees, silkworms, and other baggage and equipment. He had been invited by Thomas Jefferson who, attracted by this wine merchant's experiments, reasoned that since Virginia was on a latitude equal to that of central Italy, such Mediterranean crops might do well here. Unfortunately, the Tuscany grapes did not thrive in the Albemarle clay, the European silkworms did not care for the American mulberry leaves, and the olive and lemon trees were killed by the severe cold of winter.

As the experiments were failing, Mazzei became infused with the cause of liberty for the colonies and wrote speeches and pamphlets which Jefferson translated. While enroute to Europe in 1779 as a financial agent for Virginia, he was captured by a British privateer and spent three months in prison. During his absence, Colle was occupied by Baron de Riedesel, a Hessian mercenary, who, with his countess, entourage, commander General Phillips, and an army of 4,000, had been taken prisoner at Saratoga. The Baron's horses, Jefferson wrote, "destroyed in one week the whole labor of three or four years." Thomas Mann Randolph lived here briefly after he married Jefferson's daughter Martha. *See: Barracks; Blenheim; Buckroe; Edgehill of Albemarle; Monticello*

COLLINGWOOD
Fairfax County
The mansion house was constructed in 1785 upon that portion of George Washington's estate known as the River Farm. It was named for British Admiral Collingwood who assumed command of the fleet during the Battle of Trafalgar upon the death of Admiral Lord Nelson. On it is a bounteous spring which the Indians called The Fountain. Sailing vessels filled their casks here before setting out to sea because the water was so crystal clear. Nearby was a duelling ground where the last reported duel on that spot was fought in 1805. *See: River Farm*

COLLINSVILLE
Henry County
In 1931 the Collins Company operated a plant to make flashlights. The name Collinsville was adopted when the post office was opened here in 1945.

COLONIAL BEACH
Westmoreland County   Town
On the Potomac River, this resort town has been a popular place since colonial times. The effect of the tides, felt as far up river as Alexandria, gives the water a moderate salinity. The inlet around which most of the activity is located is known as Monroe Bay since James Monroe's family lived not too far away. The name Colonial Beach is quite modern and simply highlights the colonial past of this place. *See: Monrovia*

COLONIAL HEIGHTS
Chesterfield County
During the Revolution, when General Benedict Arnold was spreading havoc on the south bank of the James River, he captured Petersburg and burned much tobacco and other supplies. To prevent him from moving northward to Richmond, a contingent of the Continental Army, under General Lafayette, occupied the high ground across the Appomattox River. The "colonials" held the "heights." *See: Petersburg*

COLUMBIA
Goochland County   Town
The Indians to the west of Powhatan's confederacy, his mortal enemies, were the Monacans. They lived in various villages on both sides of the James River above the fall line in what is now Goochland and Powhatan counties. Their principal town, Rassawek, was just below present-day Scottsville. They had a minor village about five miles up the James from William Byrd's trading post, in what is now Richmond, in order to keep in contact with the whites for trade. During the early Federal times, these Indians moved westward and lost their identity as they were assimilated by other tribes. Their principal town was sited too well to be ignored by settlers migrating westward. A group built a small hamlet at Rassawek after the Revolution and, in the spirit of the times, named it Columbia. *See: District of Columbia; Huguenots; Manakin Town; Rassawek*

COLUMBIA FURNACE
Shenandoah County
This town takes its name from an iron ore smelter built in the mid-third of the eighteenth century. Columbia Furnace was a major producer of pig iron during the Civil War. Three times the Union forces burned it, and each time it was repaired and put back into service. The main feature of such an operation is the furnace in which the ore is heated and, being built of stone, always escaped major damage from fire. Since the facility was made more efficient each time it was rebuilt, the Federal troops seldom accomplished their objective. Columbia Furnace operated for many years after the war. The village in which the workers lived has continued, keeping alive the name.

COMMONWEALTH

Any nation or state in which there is self-government is a *commonwealth*, meaning the political entity is organized for the common *weal*, a Middle English word meaning "well-being." When the first constitution for Virginia was written in 1776, the framers carefully chose the words "Commonwealth of Virginia" to establish its independence. The first elected governor was Patrick Henry who was followed by Thomas Jefferson.

Three other states call themselves Commonwealths. They are Kentucky, Massachusetts, and Pennsylvania. *See: Old Dominion*

CONCORD
Campbell County

The present community took its name from the three local Presbyterian churches: Old Concord, New Concord, and Little Concord. Obviously, these people of Scottish descent could not worship in Concord (with one accord). Here was Concord Furnace which supplied iron during the Revolution and the Civil War.

COPPER HILL
Floyd County

Copper ore is present in this county. Early prospectors included a Mr. Tony Crafty who opened a mine in Copper Valley. The town nearby was named Copper Hill. When Captain John Smith first traded with the Indians in eastern Virginia in 1607, he noted that copper was used as personal decoration and assumed they had gotten it from the Spanish. The metal is found in many places in small deposits.

CORBIN HALL
Accomack County

The land here was patented by Colonel Edmund Scarburgh of Occohannock in 1664 after he discovered it during his quixotic campaign against the friendly Assoteague Indians which fomented years of unnecessary warfare on the Eastern Shore. Colonel Scarburgh sold the 3,000 acres to Mrs. Ann Toft for 9,101 pounds of "Mevis sugar in Caske and 708 pounds of Indigo." She changed the name to Wolfridge.

The present house has been standing here, virtually unchanged, since it was built in 1725 by Samuel Welbourne. Shortly after the Revolution, the farmlands changed hands again. The new owner, George Corbin, renamed the place Corbin Hall and enjoyed

the magnificent view of Chincoteague Bay. *See: Earle's Nest; Laneville; Occahannock*

COROTOMAN
Lancaster County   **Site**

Little remains of old Corotoman, named for a small Indian tribe. The immigrant, John Carter, patented the huge tract before 1654, but the place did not become prominent until his son, Robert "King" Carter (1662-1732) made it the wellspring of a Virginia dynasty. Even though Robert had inherited a fair fortune from his father and from his first wife, Judith Armistead of Hesse, it was his second marriage, in 1700, to the widow of Richard Willis that gave his fortune the greatest boost. Elizabeth Willis brought to the marriage her inheritance of 3,000 pounds sterling, eighty-four head of cattle, six horses, miscellaneous servants and slaves, and a well-stocked wine cellar.

When Corotoman burned in 1729, it was not rebuilt since "King" Carter, then 67, did not feel equal to the trouble. He and his wife moved into one of the small dependencies of the destroyed manor house and withdrew from society and politics. His four sons and several daughters shared his accumulated wealth. Robert II established Nomini Hall; Landon's home was Sabine Hall; Charles built Cleve; John married Elizabeth Hill of Shirley, lived there, and inherited that estate when old Colonel Hill died. Carter's daughters also married well. Elizabeth married Nathaniel Burwell and her son inherited Carter's Grove; Lucy married William Fitzhugh, Jr., and lived at Eagle's Nest. *See: Colchester; Frying Pan Run; Hesse*

CORPORATIONS

Governor Sir George Yeardley announced shortly after his return to Virginia in April of 1619 that the colony would be reorganized. An assembly would be convened to permit the settlers to propose laws that were peculiar to the colony and would supplement English Common Law. The proposed laws would not be effective until they had been approved by the king's Privy Council and had been signed by the king. This was a radical departure from the martial Laws Divine and Moral under which the colony had been governed since 1610.

The existing four boroughs were changed to four corporations that were made up of eleven boroughs. The Corporations were Henricus, Charles City, James City, and Kecoughtan. Each of the new boroughs were entitled to send two representatives to the First Assembly that began its work during the last week of July, 1619. Fifteen years later, in 1634, the Four Corporations were divided into eight shires and the corporation arrangement was abandoned. The next year the term shires was changed to county, and the former boroughs became districts just as they are today. *See: Boroughs; City; Hundred; Shire*

COUNTY
In ancient times in England, the territory under the jurisdiction of a Count was a county. In time the term was changed to shire (such as Devonshire), the word adopted by the government of Virginia when, in 1634, the colony was sufficiently populated to require local courts for civil affairs. For some unknown reason, the House of Burgesses dropped shire a year later in favor of county. *See: Borough; Corporation; Hundred; Shire*

COURTLAND
Southampton County   **Town**
The early name for this county seat was Jerusalem. The name was changed to Court-land in 1788 and became an official town in 1791. Just to the north of this city was the Nottoway Indian reservation. William Byrd II visited this tribe in 1729 while he was running the boundary line between North Carolina and Virginia. The Nottoway tribe was in residence here as late as 1825 and then gradually disappeared through assimilation or migration. *See: Nottoway River*

COVESVILLE
Albemarle County
Nearby, Cove Presbyterian Church was established in 1769. A small community developed around it.

COVINGTON
Alleghany County   **City**
The Midland Trail entered the Alleghenies through a pass cut by Dunlop Creek. In 1746 it was protected at the foot of the mountains by Fort Young on land owned by Peter Wright. A settlement later grew around a Mr. Merry's store. In 1819 lots were laid out and the new town was named for Peter Covington, then the oldest inhabitant. However, land sales lagged and it was not until the 1890s that a settlement grew to any size, although Covington had been the county seat since 1832. Today it is a thriving city.

COWNES
King William County
This was a part of the original 5,000 acres patented in 1699 by Nathaniel Burwell of Fairfield in Gloucester County. In 1763 William Cowne, Gentleman, settled here. He was a successful merchant who turned his attention to farming and made Cownes famous for its excellent orchard. *See: Burlington; Carters Grove; Fairfield of Gloucester*

COWPASTURE RIVER
Beginning as a tiny brook in Highland County, the Cowpasture flows through choice pasturelands. When it joins the Bullpasture River in northern Bath County, it becomes a major stream. For all of its length it is clear and cold, excellent for sportfishing. Just below Iron Gate, it unites with the polluted Jackson River to form the James. *See: Bullpasture, Calfpasture, Jackson and James Rivers; Iron Gate*

CRADDOCKVILLE
Accomack County
This hamlet once was Teakle Farm. The land was patented by the Reverend Thomas Teakle, an early important character in the history of the Eastern Shore. He tended a scattered flock via canoe and horse until churches could be built and their pulpits filled by ordained preachers. The house on Teakle Farm, located on Nadua Creek, is built of brick with one side of the roof gambrel-roofed and the other side straight. The Reverend Teakle and Col. Edmund Scarburgh of Occahannock became involved in a law suit when the colonel accused the preacher of seducing Mrs. Scarburgh and attempting to poison him. Teakle denied the charge and asked for a trial to clear his name since his credibility as a man of the cloth had been severely damaged by the false charges. The Council found Teakle innocent and required the colonel to make a public retraction. After winning his case, the Reverend Teakle never had difficulty finding listeners since Colonel Scarburgh was not among the most popular people in this area. In fact, he was a bit of a nut. *See: Dale's Gift; Occahannock*

CRAIG COUNTY
Named for Robert Craig, a member of Congress at the time of its forming in 1851, this county was put together from parts of Botetourt, Giles, and Monroe counties. The courthouse is in the town of New Castle.

CRAIG'S MILL
Lunenburg County

Craig's Mill was owned and operated by the Reverend James Craig. It stood beside Flat Rock Creek and served the territory here. Much of the local corn crop was ground into meal and stored in the mill for shipment to the Continental Army during the Revolution. Colonel Banastre Tarleton burned the mill in July 1781 and confiscated the contents. The Reverend Craig is said to have been forced to help kill hogs for the troopers.

CRAIG SPRINGS
Craig County

A mineral spring was discovered here about 1750, but the region was too remote for development at that time. It was not until 1869 that Giles Smith established a spa which he called Yellow Sulpher Springs to compete with nearby White and Red Sulphur Springs. Martin Huffman, a wealthy Craig County landowner acquired control of the establishment about 1895 when he learned that the C & O Railroad was planning to build a spur line to New Castle, twelve miles away. With the completion of the spur, patrons found it easy to reach the location and business was good for many years. In 1909 the property was purchased by an investment group that formed the Craig Healing Springs Company. In addition to other improvements, a splendid hotel, the Merrimac, was built by the company.

Nathan S. Buck of Cincinnati, one of the investors, disagreed with the other partners and opened a competing resort, called Monte Vista. Buck's place was more elaborate with a golf course and bowling alley. Both places prospered until the Great Depression forced spas to close all over the country. However, J. W. Oulds of Lynchburg, a man who had weathered the crash of 1929 with most of his wealth intact, bought both places and combined them into Craig Healing Springs. The resort operated until 1960 when it was purchased by the Christian Churches (Disciples of Christ) and converted into a conference center. The town of Craig Springs retains the name of the old resort.

CRAIGSVILLE
Augusta County   **Town**

The early settlement here was called Marbledale for the local marble quarry. Nobody today remembers who Mr. Craig was or how he got his name used for the post office.

CREEK

An inlet below the fall line of a major river and under the influence of the tides is called a *creek*. Many of them in the Virginia Tidewater region were deep enough to accommodate sea-going vessels and many fine estates had private wharves on tidal creeks. If the creek is fed by a stream, it is actually a river and may be called by that name. For example, Hampton Creek does have a few small runs emptying into it and is now officially a river although in all past historical references it was known as Hampton Creek. Sometimes a creek is called a cove. A creek very definitely is not a brook, stream, or run, although in other parts of America, the term creek is applied to any small running stream. The famous Cripple Creek of the old song is not a true creek, but a brook or small river. *See: Run*

CREWE
Nottoway County   **Town**

Crewe was established when the Norfolk and Western Railroad built a roundhouse here in 1886. It was named for the English railroad center of the same name. Today Crewe has developed into a town with diversified interests.

CRICKET HILL
Mathews County

This is not a hill and it has never been occupied by anyone by the name Cricket. It gained its name when American forces under General Andrew Lewis forced Lord Dunmore to leave Virginia forever in July, 1776. After the last royal Governor had been defeated at Great Bridge, rebuffed at Norfolk, and ignored elsewhere, he took his fleet of nearly 100 vessels from the Portsmouth area and, on the first of June, 1776, set up a camp for his refugee followers on Gwynn's Island at the mouth of the Piankatank River. To defend his island against any attempt by the Virginians to take it by storming across the narrow part of Milford Haven separating the island from the mainland, he threw up a breastwork and manned it with Royal Marines and volunteers.

When informed that the colonials were across the way in growing numbers, Dunmore vowed to crush them like "so many crickets." While hunger and disease ran through his camp and struck others on board his ships, he waited for reinforcements from New York which never arrived. General Lewis set up two batteries of seven cannon of

GENERAL ANDREW LEWIS
CRICKET HILL

several sizes and set the stage for the final curtain.

On July 8, 1776, General Lewis touched the smouldering match to the first gun at 8:00 a.m. The Governor's flagship, the *Dunmore,* was hit by the second shot fired and soon became a favorite target. All of the armed ships were hit numerous times before they could be moved out of range. Many British were killed and the ships were heavily damaged. Lord Dunmore was struck in the leg by a flying splinter. When his personal china was smashed about him he cried, "Good God! That I should ever come to this!" After the guns cooled during lunch, the cannonading began again, this time against the camp and fortifications on the island. That night Dunmore sent in small boats to evacuate those who were still alive and then sat in the Chesapeake Bay for three weeks before finally giving up and sailing for home via New York.

John Murray, the fourth Earl of Dunmore, the last royal Governor of Virginia, was chased away from his colony by a small force

of determined "crickets." *See: Great Bridge; Gwynn's Island; Norfolk; Salem; Suffolk; Williamsburg*

CRIGLERSVILLE
Madison County

Jacob Crigler was among a band of German emigrants who left their homeland in 1717, bound for Pennyslvania. Provisions on the ship ran low; a storm blew them to Virginia. Upon landing, the passengers were sold as servants by the captain to pay for their transportation, an arrangement that probably had been previously agreed to since it was not an uncommon way to get to America. Alexander Spotswood bought their indentures and added them to his people at Germanna to work his iron mine and smelter. After serving the usual seven yers, these people had to go to court to gain their freedom. They moved westward into what is now Madison County and established their homes. Jacob Crigler settled on the Robinson River where he built the first tannery in the region. *See: Germanna; Hebron Church*

CRIMORA
Augusta County

In 1881 a local landowner gave property to the N & W Railroad for a station on the condition that he could name it. Tradition has it that he named it for his sweetheart. Possibly there is some truth to this and Crimora probably is a combination of two or more names. At any rate, the railroad made a lot of money hauling out manganese produced in this region and the village has prospered.

CRIPPLE CREEK
Wythe County

This busy stream has been called Cripple Creek for so long that nobody remembers why any more. The famous fast banjo tune *Cripple Creek* immortalizes the mountain run. One has to be a banjo artist of the highest degree to play it well. The Cripple Creek of the western silver mining region was named by fortune-seeking Virginians.

CRISS CROSS
New Kent County

This is a corruption of Christ's Cross, the shape of a house built shortly after 1675 by George Poindexter. In addition to the unusual design, the framing timbers are pegged together in the Tudor style, giving it exceptional strength. No wonder Criss Cross has lasted more then 300 years.

CROOKED RUN BAPTIST CHURCH
Culpeper County
This church was organized in 1772. Among its first pastors was Thomas Ammon, an outspoken preacher, who once was jailed just prior to the Revolution for speaking too freely about secular matters. The church's name comes from the twisting stream nearby, aptly named Crooked Run. *See: Run*

CROWS
Alleghany County
The first colonel of the Alleghany Militia was John Crow. With the eleven children that he sired, everyone knew where Colonel Crow's house was. In time the name was adopted for the local community without proper punctuation.

CROZET
Albemarle County
Colonel Claudius Crozet, a distinguished French army engineer, came to America after the final defeat of Napolean's forces at Waterloo. He spent many years as an instructor at West Point Academy in New York until he was hired by the Commonwealth of Virginia as the state engineer. Colonel Crozet was a cartographer, the author of several textbooks on mathematics, and an accomplished designer. He specialized in highways, railroads, and aqueducts for canals. The railroad tunnel under Afton Mountain is his masterpiece. When complete in 1856, it was the largest in the world, nearly a mile long. It permitted the commercial overland linkage of the Piedmont with the Shenandoah Valley. A little depot on the eastern side of the Blue Ridge was his base for supplies. After his death in 1864, the village was named in his honor. *See: Kanawha Canal*

CUB CREEK CHURCH
Charlotte County
About 1738 John Caldwell brought a colony of Scotch-Irish here and obtained permission to establish a Presbyterian church, the oldest church in this section. The neighborhood became known as the Caldwell Settlement. The founder was the grandfather of the famous John C. Calhoun of South Carolina.

CUCKOO
Louisa County
Cuckoo Tavern stood here late in colonial times, operated by the father of Jack Jouett.

This tiny hamlet retains the unusual name which should be better known. In June, 1781, when it appeared that the Revolution was a lost cause, Lt. Colonel Banastre Tarleton and his dragoons stopped at this tavern late in the afternoon. After a few heavy noggins of rum, one of Tarleton's men revealed that their mission was to capture Governor Thomas Jefferson and members of the General Assembly who were meeting at Monticello. General Benedict Arnold had seized Richmond, the capital of the Commonwealth of Virginia.

While the British were delayed by more servings of rum, Jack Jouett slipped away and rode cross-country to sound the alarm. He rode all night, stopping only at Castle Hill, on the road he knew Tarleton would take, to ask Colonel Thomas Walter to offer the cavalrymen breakfast as an additional delaying action. Walker complied. Jouett reached Monticello in plenty of time to allow the men governing Virginia to escape. In fact, legend has it that Jefferson had sufficient warning to supervise hiding his silver and to have his horse reshod. The members of the Assembly and the Governor met again two days later in Lynchburg. Because Jack Jouett rode at night on back roads and across fields, his face was badly cut by low hanging branches. He bore the scars for the rest of his life.

Not until well after the Revolution was he recognized for his gallant action when he was presented with an elegant sword. His ride was far more dangerous than Paul Revere's famous gallop six years previously and, what is more important, he finished his task successfully while Revere, using prepared roads, suffered nothing more than the indignity of being captured before his mission was completed. However, the Virginian, Jack Jouett, did not have a famous poet to sing his praises. *See: Castle Hill; Elk Hill; Warrenton*

CULPEPER COUNTY
Formed in 1748 from Orange, this county was named for Lord Culpeper, Governor of Virginia from July, 1677 to August, 1683. He resided briefly in Virginia (which most titular governors did not do) and was then represented in the colony by his deputy, Sir Henry Chicheley. Originally, the county seat was named Fairfax after the fifth Lord Fairfax who, with Lord Culpeper, was a proprietor of Northern Neck. The town's name was changed to Culpeper by an act of the General Assembly in 1870. *See: Christ Church of*

CULPEPER COUNTY

Middlesex; Chippokes; Fairfax; Green Spring; Northern Neck

CUMBERLAND
New Kent County

As a small but important shipping center not far from the county seat, this river port provided a warehouse and wharf on the Pamunkey River. It was on the edge of Richard Littlepage's land. When the Capitol building in Williamsburg burned in January, 1747, a committee was formed in the House of Burgesses to prepare a bill "for the removal of" the capital. Cumberland was one of the recommended sites. The pro-Williamsburg faction managed to kill the bill before it was presented to the House and succesfully offered a plan to repair and modify the old building in Williamsburg. *See: Newcastle*

CUMBERLAND COUNTY

Goochland County covered both sides of the James River south of Henrico. With the courthouse on the north bank, the people of the south bank had difficulty getting to it. Therefore, a new county was authorized in 1749, "for the Ease and Convenience of the Inhabitants." It was named in honor of Prince William Augustus, Duke of Cumberland, the third son of George II. It was he who led the British army against the Jacobite forces of "Bonnie Prince Charlie" in the battle of Culloden Moor in 1745. The victory crushed any future hopes of the Stuarts to regain the English throne. When Cumberland County was divided to create Powhatan in 1777, the courthouse was in the wrong county. A new village was laid out and named Effingham, probably for Thomas, Baron Howard of Effingham, a member of the House of Lords who spoke in opposition to the British government's policy toward the colonies. The name Effingham did not last since the people preferred Cumberland Courthouse, today shortened to Cumberland. *See: Prince William County*

CUMBERLAND GAP

Discovered by Dr. Thomas Walker on April 12, 1750, this is a natural passage through the Allegheny Mountains where the present states of Virginia, Tennessee, and Kentucky join. At the time of the discovery, all of this territory was part of Virginia. Dr. Walker named the gap in honor of the Duke of Cumberland, the son of King George II. Through this gap passed thousands of settlers into the western lands, many of them guided by Daniel Boone. The settlement of Kentucky brought on the severe Indian up-risings of Little Turtle and the Miami Indians of Ohio and Indiana about ten years after the Revolution. Kentucky had been declared off-limits to settlement as ancient Indian hunting grounds controlled by no particular tribe. Because of the numerous clashes between the

CUMBERLAND RIVER, CUMBERLAND GAP

64

two races Kentucky became known as the Bloody Ground. *See: Castle Hill*

CURLES
Henrico County

Between the mouth of the Appomattox and Varina Grove, the James River curls itself into a series of tight bends, some of them nearly a full circle. Edward Gourgany, of Argall's Gift, patented land on the north bank of the river in this region and named his new farm Longfield. Gourgany, a Burgess in the first General Assembly of 1619, died a year later. When Nathaniel Bacon, Jr., came to Virginia in 1674, his uncle, Nathaniel Bacon, Sr., a member of the Council, helped him acquire Longfield. The name was changed to Curles since it had been Mr. Curles' place.

The newcomer, rather quickly appointed a Councillor, was of a rebellious nature. He objected to the tight rule of Sir William Berkeley, especially the Governor's apparent willingness to allow the Susquehannock Indians to raid homes near Curles without fighting them. Bacon believed that the Governor was placing the value of his fur trade above the lives of Englishmen. A group of neighbors gathered a small army, elected Bacon their leader, and received reluctant permission from Berkeley to mount a limited offensive. Bacon's men, a band of about 300, defeated the Indians in skirmishes in New Kent and Charles City counties, and forced the natives to retire northward. When the Susquehannocks raided again in 1676, Bacon applied for a commission to renew the warfare. Again, he was given permission for a local campaign. This time, however, he and his men pressed the natives southward to the Roanoke River where the warriors and their families were totally annihilated at Occaneechee. Bacon returned to Jamestown triumphantly only to find that the Governor had branded him an outlaw and a traitor for exceeding his limited commission.

When the rebel was elected to the General Assembly by the people of Henrico, Berkeley pardoned him but secretly plotted to bring him to heel. Catching wind of the plot, Bacon seized Jamestown when the Governor was away and resisted the colonial militia's feeble attempts to retake the capital. After a stand-off of a few days, during which Bacon placed women and children of the town on the ramparts to thwart an attack, the rebels finally slipped away at night after setting fire to the town. That autumn, Nathaniel Bacon, Jr., died in Gloucester County; his body was disposed of secretly. With the collapse of the rebellion, Berkeley hanged forty men in revenge and, by so doing, lost the respect of the Virginians and the support of King Charles II.

During the Civil War Fredericksburg was fought over twice. After the battles the town was a total ruin. *See: Brompton; Ferry Farm; Frederick County; Germanna; Kenmore; King's Highway; Spottsylvania County*

CUTTAWOMAN
Accomack County

The name of this tribe has nothing to do with the disfigurement of women. Although the exact meaning is unknown, the Indian word *woman* appears to have something to do with a road. The Cuttawomans lived on both sides of Chesapeake Bay. *See: Assawoman; Mattawoman*

DAHLGREN
Prince George County

Admiral John A. Dahlgren, U.S. Navy, specialized in the design of cannons with rifled barrels and the shells they fired. A Dahlgren gun was a prized piece of ordnance during the Civil War. The present hamlet of Dahlgren is next to the Navy's Surface Weapons Laboratory, on the Potomac River, which was named for Admiral Dahlgren. Here big guns and shells are tested and new designs are proven.

DALE'S GIFT
Northampton County Site

In 1614 Governor Sir Thomas Dale sent twenty men, under the command of a Lieutenant Craddock, to the lower end of the Eastern Shore to boil salt from sea water and to catch and salt fish for the colonists of Virginia. These men settled along what is known as Old Plantation Creek (which memorializes the "planting" of this party) at a camp known as Dale's Gift. Those assigned here at first thought they were being exiled, but they soon found that corn, fruit, and vegetables would grow abundantly in the fertile, warm, sandy soil. They were amazed at the huge schools of fish in the surrounding waters and the numerous wild fowl that covered the marshes. Other game was equally abundant, the Indians were most friendly, and the climate was delightful. Soon the so-called exiles were envied by those who lived in and around Jamestown where fevers and Indians were an equal threat. Dale's Gift was the first permanent settlement on the Eastern Shore. Gradually they were joined by others in what became the Plantation of Accawmacke. *See: Pungoteague; White Cluff*

DAMASCUS
Washington County Town

This small town close to the Tennessee border, was named for the capital of Syria. Biblical names were quite often used by the pioneers for village names. Saint Paul was converted to Christianity on the road to Damascus in the region of the Holy Land. *See: Fluvanna County; Palmyra*

DANCING POINT
Charles City County

Colonel Philip Lightfoot argued with the Devil about property the Colonel owned but which the Devil claimed. After much heated discussion, the two agreed to a solitary dancing contest to settle the dispute. They met at dusk on a point of land at the mouth of the Chickahominy River where they danced all night. At dawn, the Devil limped away and went to Surry County where some say he still lives. The site of the contest, called Dancing Point for nearly three hundred years, is a barren bit of ground where nothing grows although all adjoining land is quite productive. *See: Lightfoot*

DANTE
Russell County

This village began as a real estate development at the beginning of the twentieth century. The secretary of the corporation that began it all was W. J. Dante. Enough homes were sold by 1903 to require a post office.

DANVILLE
Pittsylvania County City

A major textile and tobacco center, Danville takes its present name from the Dan River which flows beside it. Originally known as Wynn's Falls, for a local ford that made settlement attractive, it became Danville when it was chartered in 1793 as a town.

Here, in 1858, was begun the "Danville System" of selling tobacco. Previously, the leaves were purchased, sight unseen, in

*TOBACCO IN HOGSHEAD
ROLLING TO MARKET
DANVILLE*

packed hogsheads and the buyers had to rely on the reputation of the farmer who grew it. At Neal's Warehouse, the tobacco leaves were placed in open, loose piles for inspection, and the batches were sold at auction. Since the buyers could examine the entire lot, this system was preferred and soon was adopted in all tobacco centers in other states.

Danville achieved modest, fleeting fame in April of 1865 when President Jefferson Davis met with his cabinet here for the last time. This, in effect, made the city the last capital of the Confederacy.

It was also the scene of a famous railroad wreck. On September 27, 1903, just a few miles out of town, the southbound express mail train of the Southern Railway left the tracks on a trestle and plunged into a ravine below. This was the wreck of the old 97, the subject of a familiar ballad. *See: Monroe; Wyndale*

DARVILLS
Dinwiddie County

The earliest known settler here was a wealthy Englishman, Colonel Joseph Buffington Darvills, who came to Virginia prior to 1749. It was said that Colonel Darvills left England and built his home in the semi-wilderness to get his daughter away from a suitor of whom he did not approve. Love triumphed, however. William Thompson followed his lost love, found her here, and, although the Colonel still objected, they were married. Thompson built his home nearby which he called Oak Grove.

DAVENPORT
Buchanan County

William Davenport was the first postmaster here, in 1885. When the post office needed a name, it was called Davenport.

DAYTON
Rockingham County   Town

At first the only habitation was a stone house that was surrounded by a palisade as protection against Indian attack. It probably was built by a member of the Harrison family. The date of this private fortress and the reason the name Dayton was applied has not been recorded. Dayton has been incorporated as a town since 1833. *See: Harrisonburg*

DEEP CREEK PLANTATION
Accomack County

In 1671, John West II, "in right of" his wife Matilda Scarburgh, the daughter of Colonel

Edmund Scarburgh of Occahannock, secured a patent for land on the south side of Deep Creek. The first house is thought to have been built by their great-grandson, Tully Robinson Wise, who inherited the property in 1745. His small home is believed to be the center section of the present dwelling. In the old detached kitchen is a curiously shaped oven that resembles a beehive. Three generations of men named Tully Robinson Wise have lived here.*See: Occahannock*

DEERFIELD
Augusta County

Deer are more plentiful now than in colonial times. With more cleared land providing excellent pastures, and with a limited hunting season, the deer herds have multiplied. Thought to be timid animals that fled from the habitations of man, they are still seen in the suburbs of large cities and frequently become a menace to aircraft at commercial airports and military fields. Every year several motorists collide with startled animals who attempt to dash across a road.

Strangely, this is the only community in the Commonwealth that uses the word deer in its name. It is on the Cowpasture River in a valley that is full of these graceful creatures. *See: Elk Creek; Elkton*

DEFENSE GENERAL SUPPLY CENTER
Chesterfield County

This installation occupies a tract of 638 acres of land formerly farmed by James Bellwood. First construction for the Richmond General Depot of the Army's Quartermaster Corps was completed a few weeks before the attack on Pearl Harbor in 1941. After the war, the Quartermaster Inventory Control Center was created on the reservation to provide national accountability for general supplies, non-perishable substances, petroleum products, clothing and equipment. In 1962 it became the support center for the entire Department of Defense. Here are more than five million square feet of covered storage space in twenty-seven warehouses served by thirty-one miles of internal railroad tracks and twenty-one miles of surfaced roads. The old Bellwood family residence forms the core of the Officers' Club.

DELAPLANE
Faquier County

Washington Delaplane operated a general store here many years ago.

DELAWARE INDIANS

No tribe of Indians called themselves by this name. Thomas West, the first Governor of Virginia, was Lord Delaware. His name was applied to the body of water known as Delaware Bay which he never saw and which was named in his memory. The Indians who lived on the banks of this bay were called the Delawares although they called themselves *Grandfathers,* boasting that they were the oldest tribe and that they knew the secret beginnings of the red man. When the white men from England, Holland, and Sweden occupied their lands, the Delawares migrated west and settled in central Ohio and Eastern Indiana where they took the name Miami from the Maumee River on which they established their capital. They fiercely resisted the invasion of the white settlers who crossed the Ohio River and built homes, forts, and small towns.

One of President George Washington's biggest problems during his first term was the conquest of the Indians of that region. Many tribes, mainly of the Miami and Shawnee nations, under the skillful leadership of their warchiefs Little Turtle and Blue Jacket, resisted attempts to subdue them and make the region of the Northwest safe for settlers. Washington sent out two armies against the Indians, both of which were soundly defeated. Finally, the Revolutionary hero General "Mad Anthony" Wayne succeeded in conquering the Miami confederacy. A remnant of the Miami Indians today live near Kokomo, Indiana.

DELAWARE TOWN

King William County   **Obsolete**

Although this name is obsolete, many of the old-timers who live here occasionally use it when looking back to the past. It did not begin as a town but as the only customs port for the upper York River basin. An act of the House of Burgesses in 1691 ordered land "set aside at West's Point in Pamunkey Neck" for the port. John West III gave fifty acres of his property for the landing; the residents of the county were forced to pay for the wharf and warehouse through a special tax on tobacco. In 1702 a fort was erected on the point to control the passage of vessels into the Pamunkey and Mattaponi rivers which join here to form the York.

Finally, four years later Harry Beverley surveyed the fifty acres given by John West and laid lots to form a village that was named Delaware Town in honor of the first

Governor of Virginia, Lord Delaware, from whom the grantee was a collateral descendant. Those who bought lots for 480 pounds of tobacco also had to pay an annual rent of one ounce of flax seed and two ounces of hemp seed. They also had to build a good house not less than twenty feet square within one year or lose the lot which the town trustees could resell. The name Delaware Town continued for the next 164 years. For some unknown reason, it was changed to West Point when it was incorporated in 1870. *See: Chischiack; Cinquoteck; West Point*

DELMARVA

The peninsula that extends between Delaware Bay and the Chesapeake Bay is divided among three states: Delaware, Maryland, and Virginia. The name, obviously, is a combination of these state names.

DELTAVILLE

Middlesex County

Once known as Unionville when two local churches combined into one congregation, the name was dropped during the days of secession when the local residents wanted no part of the Union. Since this little fishing community lies at the extreme eastern end of the county in the lowlands of the delta of the Rappahannock River, the new name was easy to come by.

DENBIGH

Newport News   **Site**

Samual Mathews, Sr., came to Virginia in 1622 and patented this land four years later. After building his home, Mathews' Manor, he married Frances Hinton West Piersey, the widow of the Cape Merchant, Abraham Piersey. Although this in itself did not make Sam Mathews wealthy, it gave his fortune a tremendous boost. The Widow Piersey's business connections enabled him to expand into the export-import trade while he improved his land holdings. He named his plantation for Denbigh Castle that has stood in the west-central region of England, near Liverpool, since the thirteenth century to control the people who lived in the northern end of the Cambrian Mountains.

Denbigh Plantation produced flax which was spun and woven into cloth for sale. The cattle were butchered for local use and some of the meat was salted and sold to ships that called at the private wharf. The hides were cured in Mathew's tannery and the leather was worked into shoes and other necessary products. The wheat, barley, and corn always brought a good price, as did the hogs and chickens raised on Denbigh Plantation. An inventory made in 1643 showed many valuable personal items as well as forty slaves.

The immigrant's son, Samuel Mathews, Jr., continued his father's business and became one of the wealthiest men in Virginia. He was elected Governor of the colony in 1656, during the days of Oliver Cromwell, and served Virginia for two years. The first courthouse of Warwick County was built on land donated by Mathews in 1690, and official business was conducted at Denbigh until the seat of the county was moved to Richneck on land donated by Miles Cary, Jr. *See: Bennett's Choice; Balthrope; Maryland; Mathews Manor; Warwick*

DENDRON
Surry   **Town**

A lumberyard and mill, established near the Blackwater River in the 1880s became the chief source of income for the residents of the area, either as suppliers of logs, lumberjacks, or employees of the yard and mill. When the resulting community needed a name, someone with a knowledge of Greek selected Dendron, a modified version of the word for tree, *dendreon*.

DEWITT
Dinwiddie County

At first just a railway message point and now a modest village, this community was named for a local resident, DeWitt Smith.

DICKENSON COUNTY

Formed from parts of Russell, Wise, and Buchanan counties in 1880, the name honors W. J. Dickenson, a locally prominent man of that era. The courthouse is at Clintwood.

DICKINSONVILLE
Russell County

This was a crossroads hamlet with only a few homes when Russell County was formed. When the site was selected as the new county seat, Henry Dickenson gave the land for the construction of the new courthouse which was a crude affair made of hewn logs. He furnished the small structure with proper seats and a bar—that is, the barrier between the judge and the contestants, the bar of justice. Dickenson hoped that his efforts would result in an important community bearing his name, but it was not to be. A proper courthouse was erected ten miles away at Lebanon and Dickensonville faded. *See: Clintwood*

DINKLETOWN
See: Bridgewater

DINWIDDIE COUNTY

Formed in 1752 from Prince George, this county was named for Lieutenant Governor Robert Dinwiddie who resided in Virginia as the deputy of the Earl of Albemarle who was the royal Governor. The earl never bothered to come to Virginia. Robert Dinwiddie served during the fretfull time of the French and Indian War in the middle of the eighteenth century. George Washington was a Major of the Virginia Militia who hoped to receive a commission in the British army from Dinwiddie. The Governor did not think it would be appropriate to have a native-born American be a commissioned officer in the king's army and refused Washington's request. During the war, an extension of the war that England was then waging against France, Washington served with distinction under General Edward Braddock who was killed during the expedition to seize Fort Pitt in 1755. The county seat is at Dinwiddie Courthouse, a name that today has been shortened to Dinwiddie.

DISMAL SWAMP
Suffolk

This large and beautiful swamp was known to seventeenth century settlers who avoided it. When William Byrd II was in charge of a party in 1728 to fix the boundary between Virginia and North Carolina, he remarked that it was a rather dismal place and he is credited with giving the region its name. It may be uninhabitable for humans, but it is far far from being a dismal area for it abounds in wildlife and is a section of southeastern Virginia that attracts many naturalists. The last owner, Paul D. Camp, a man who made his fortune in paper manufacture, gave the 103,000-acre reserve to the Commonwealth in 1973 for a wildlife refuge.

George Washington and a small group of men acquired 40,000 acres here in 1793, planned to drain the swamp, cut the cypress and oak trees, and open the rich land to farming. Fortunately, the plan was never carried out.

In the heart of the swamp is Lake Drummond, the largest natural lake in

Virginia. Nearly perfectly round, its size has been shrinking as the water table of this water-hungry area has been slowly lowered by constant pumping for municipal supplies. *See: Carolina; Lake Drummond*

DISPUTANTA
Prince George County

When the people here finally managed to get a post office authorized, they could not agree on a name. After endless arguments and disputes, a postal inspector named it Disputanta.

DISTRICT OF COLUMBIA

Columbia is a feminized version of Christopher Columbus' last name. It has been used since the early days of the Republic as a substitute for America in patriotic songs, poems, toasts, and slogans. Therefore, when a Federal City was planned as the capital of the United States, the land given for it by Maryland and Virginia was called the Territory of Columbia. It was a square mostly in Maryland, with the four corners oriented to the four cardinal points of the compass. The lines were marked with boundary stones, quarried at Aquia Creek, that were each one foot square, four feet long with a pyramidal top, and were set into the ground at exactly one mile intervals. Each bore the name of the state on one side and District of Columbia on the other. George

Washington set the first stone at Jones Point, where Hunting Creek enters the Potomac, on April 15, 1791. Few of the stones remain; most have been stolen or vandalized.

The Maryland portion of the District was Washington County; that in Virginia was Alexandria County. At first each county was under the jurisdiction of the state from which it had come, and the citizens retained the right to vote in presidential and congressional elections. In 1801, this was changed when the entire District was placed under the control of Congress, eliminating all connections with the two states.

In the 1840s, the residents of Alexandria, believing (quite correctly) that the District was favoring the commercial interests of Georgetown and the new Washington City, petitioned for a return of the Virginia portion that was unused. Retrocession finally was approved in 1846. The returned territory was renamed Arlington County to separate it from the city of Alexandria.

DITCHLEY
Lancaster County

Located near Kilmarnock on land patented in 1651 by Richard Lee, the first of the famous family to come to Virginia, the original house was built by Hancock Lee, the fifth son of the patentee. Ditchley was named for the Lee family home near Oxford,

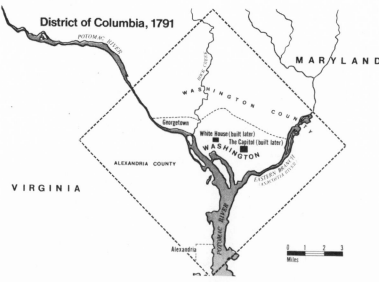

DISTRICT OF COLUMBIA

England. The first house of 1686 was replaced in 1752 by Kendall Lee, a grandson of Hancock Lee. *See: Cobbs Hall*

DOGHAM
Henrico County

Joseph Royall was granted 1,100 acres in 1635 for transporting twenty people to Virginia. Many of the newcomers were from well-known English families who added class (and some wealth) to the expanding colony. The name Dogham probably is a variation of D'Aughams, a small river in Normandy. Joseph Royall's widow married Henry Isham, and the estate remained in the Isham family for 280 years until it was acquired, through sale, by a member of the Harrison family in 1928. When Henry Isham, Jr., bequeathed the lands to his two sisters, Mrs. Mary Randolph and Mrs. Anne Isham, he described it in his will of 1678 as "my land on Turkey Creek and James River above Shirely Hundred, known as Doggams. ..." Next to this estate lies Riverview, once a part of the Royall grant. *See: Curles; Dungeness*

DOGUE INDIANS
Fairfax County

Dogue Creek, which empties into the Potomac, marked the northern boundary of the colony as late as 1675. Captain John Smith bumped into this tribe during his explorations of 1608. He reported them to be mean and surly. They were one of the tribes that joined the Senecas on the raids against the farms of the northeastern frontier. William Dudley, a lieutenant of Nathaniel Bacon, defeated the tribe, forced them to move south, and patented land near their former village. It is quite possible that this tribe's name was something else but they were called *dogues,* the French word for a fierce dog. When the early settlers in these parts said someone was as "mad as a dog," they meant "mad as a Dogue" since these Indians refused to trade or make peace. *See: Belmont of Stafford; Gunston Hall*

DONATION CHURCH
Virginia Beach

The restored building of red brick with a high-pitched roof was built in 1736 to replace an earlier structure that was then forty-four years old and in bad repair. That was the third church here; the first dated from 1640. Severe storms and erosion have caused considerable damage to the original site. The remains of the early cemetery have fallen into Lynnhaven River. Salvaged from the waters was the basin of the original baptismal font which is used in the present sanctuary.

In 1776 the Reverend Thomas Dickson left his personal farm in trust to the vestry to be added to the Glebe lands. The income from this farm was to be used to hire a teacher to instruct male orphans of the parish in Latin, Greek, and mathematics. This led to the church being called Dickson's Donation Church which was shortened in time to Donation Church. The 1736 building was gutted when a forest fire engulfed it in 1882. Only the walls were left standing. Restoration was begun in 1966. *See: Princess Anne County; Lynnhaven Bay*

DONCASTLE'S ORDINARY
New Kent County   Site

Unfortunately, no trace of this ordinary exists today. It played a minor part in the activities immediately preceeding the Revolution when Thomas Doncastle was the proprietor. He had leased the building from the estate of the late Speaker, John Robinson on a year-to-year basis. When Lord Dunmore seized the gunpowder from the Magazine in Williamsburg, Patrick Henry organized the Hanover Militia and had himself appointed the colonel. His intent was to confront the Governor with an armed force to require him either to return the powder, which belonged to the colony of Virginia, or pay for it. He marched his men as far as Doncastle's Ordinary where they halted while Colonel Henry reconsidered the operation. It was here that Patrick Henry, the lawyer, realized that the Hanover Militia was no match for British regulars and he decided to negotiate rather than fight. When Lord Dunmore signed a warrant for the cost of the gunpowder, at an inflated price set by lawyer Henry, the episode ended and the militiamen went home. Doncastle's Ordinary was located about one and one-half miles west of present day Barhamsville on the stage road from Williamsburg. *See: Laneville, Ordinary*

DOSWELL
Hanover County

Captain James Doswell, a soldier in the Revolution, came home from the war to run a farm that specialized in fine horses. He entertained his old friend Lafayette in his home in 1824. A descendant, Thomas Walker Doswell, who lived here in the nineteenth century, continued the family's tradition of breeding excellent race horses at the estate named

Bluefield. In the days when horse racing was legal in Virginia, Doswell's racetrack was always well attended. *See: Castle Hill; Hunting Quarter; New Market of Caroline County*

DOVER CHURCH SCHOOL
Henrico County   **Site**

About five miles from Tuckahoe, at Dover Church, the Reverend William Douglas conducted classes in a school in which he was the sole instructor. Thomas Jefferson was a student here for five years, boarding for eight or nine months and returning to the family home at Shadwell for the summer. Among his classmates were Thomas Randolph, Sr., of Tuckahoe and James Madison of Montpelier. The tuition and board came to sixteen pounds (money, not tobacco) per year. After this school, Tom Jefferson was sent to another boarding school, one that was operated by the Reverend James Maury in Albemarle County.

DRAGON RUN
Middlesex County

This tributary of the Piankatank River looks like a dragon on a map—if one has a vivid imagination. Many of the records of Middlesex County were hidden "in the Dragon" during the Civil War to save them from being destroyed by Union soldiers. Dragon Run forms the boundary between Middlesex and Gloucester counties for many miles.

DRANESVILLE
Fairfax County

This tiny hamlet was named for Drane's Tavern which prospered during the years between the formation of the Republic and the Civil War. Teamsters and pioneers, heading west along Leesville Pike for the lands on the other side of the Blue Ridge, stopped at the tavern for refreshment and supplies.

DRAPER
Pulaski County

The first settler here was John Draper who built his home about 1765 in this pleasant valley. He came from Draper's Meadow.

DRAPER'S MEADOW
Montgomery County   **Site**

Settled in 1745 by Colonel James Patton, this settlement was wiped out in a raid by the Shawnees in July 1755. John Draper, after whom the meadow was named, saw his wife carried off as a captive during the attack. He

searched for her for six years, finally found her, paid a ransom, and brought her home. When he left for a new home site in present Pulaski County, the land lay idle for a generation until it was reclaimed by William Black after the Revolution. What was once Draper's Meadow is now the location of the town of Blacksburg and the State University at Virginia Polytechnic Institute. Not far from here, at Radford on the New River, another woman was carried off by Indians. Mary Draper Ingles managed to escape and walked barefoot to her home. *See: Blacksburg; Radford*

DREWRY'S BLUFF
Henrico County   **Site**

Fortifications were constructed here on land owned by Captain A. H. Drewry during the Civil War. This battery enabled the Confederates to prevent the Union gunboats from getting close to Richmond. It remained in Confederate hands all through the conflict and was a vital part of Richmond's defenses.

DREWRYVILLE
Southampton County

Samuel Drewry owned much of the land in this vicinity. He lived from 1800 until 1862. A small village grew up around his farmhouse.

DUFFIELD
Scott County

Members of the Duff family were early settlers in this area. Duffield, the name of their family farm, was adopted as the name of the village that developed here.

DUGSPUR
Carroll County

Many years ago, a road was needed to connect a small community with the main highway on the other side of the mountain. The local residents got together and dug the road, which they called a spur, with picks and shovels and a lot of hard work. The road was well-used by wagoneers who called it the Good Spur Road. The villagers, proud of their accomplishment, named their community Dugspur. *See: Carson; Dundas*

DUMFRIES
Prince William County   **Town**

A tobacco warehouse was built here in 1730 next to a wharf on one of the streams which feeds Quantico Creek and gives access to the Potomac River. A town was formally established at this location in 1759 with

George Mason IV of Gunston Hall and John Taylor of Hazelwood among its founders. It was named for the city of Dumfries of southern Scotland.

An active group of merchants competed here, each one busily creating a great company while erecting a more impressive house than the last ones built. These merchants imported English finished goods and exported tobacco and grains. One of the leading firms was Jennifer and Hooe. The most noted home was attached to the side of the steep hill, overlooking the river, by Major Fouchee Tebbs. In 1774 the town of Dumfries elected one of the first Committees of Correspondence and the community was a hotbed for patriots who were hellbent for independence.

The town began to die when the harbor filled with silt from the upriver farms. It suffered when the county seat was moved from here to Brentsville. A devastating fire in 1833 crippled it, and when the railroads carried much of the freight that once had moved by water, Dumfries nearly died. It survived adversity and grew again as a charming, quaint community in Northern Virginia. *See: Brentsville; Colchester; Gunston Hall; Hazelwood; Woodbridge*

DUNDAS
Lunenburg County

When the Virginian Railroad was built in the nineteenth century, a local laboror was reported to have said with pride, when the first cars rolled over the track, "We dun dis!" This was accepted with local amusement and, when a station was erected here, the local name was, by then, Dundas. *See: Dugspur*

DUNGANNON
Scott County   **Town**

Dungannon is a tiny village in Ireland. Captain Patrick Hagan, an early settler, named his Virginia home for his home in the old country.

DUNGENESS
Goochland County   **Site**

This is a Welsh name which Isham Randolph gave to his home. He was the third son of William Randolph of Turkey Island. The old house stood where the Goochland County courthouse is now located. Isham Randolph's daughter, Jane, married Peter Jefferson and was the mother of Thomas Jefferson. Although Jefferson was proud of his English father, he was more proud of his Welsh heritage. *See: Dogham; Shadwell; Snowden*

DUNLAP PASS
Rockbridge County

The Maury River cuts through the mountains here to form a pass that was named for Alexander Dunlap, an early explorer. It is believed that John Lederer was the first white man to cross through here in 1669. During Dunmore's War of 1774 against the Indians, General Andrew Lewis marched his men through Dunlap Pass enroute to Point Pleasant, where the Kanawha River joins the Ohio. There Lewis defeated a large conglomerate force of Indians led by Cornstalk. *See: Maury River; Salem*

DUTCH GAP
Chesterfield County

Sir Thomas Dale served for many years as a soldier in the Netherlands for his king, James I. Dale came to Virginia in 1610 with Lord Delaware and, as the second ranking soldier (behind Sir Thomas Gates) was the High Marshall of Virginia whose task was to keep the colonists in line by rigidly enforcing martial law. He was sent up the James River by Lord Delaware to find a new town which was to be the base for exploration for gold which the Governor was certain came from mines worked by the Indians. After all, the Spanish had found gold among the natives of Central Amercia and the English assumed the precious metal could be found in Virginia, too.

The new town was situated on a teardrop-shaped neck of land that was nearly completely surrounded by a great loop of the James. To make the settlement completely enclosed by a natural moat, Dale had his men dig a ditch across the narrow end of the land. Many men said the idea came from Dale's service in the Netherlands where water barriers protect many of the ancient cities. The colonists called the ditch Dutch Gap. When Henricus was abandoned after the Massacre of 1622, no one lived here for generations. The frequent floods filled in the ditch and the river contined to meander, lazily, around what became known as Farrar's Island.

During the Civil War, a plan was devised of constructing a canal at Dutch Gap which would permit Federal gunboats to go up the river and attack Chafin's and Drewry's Bluffs.

Peter S. Michie was placed in charge of the project, which began on August 10, 1864.

Working under fire of enemy batteries, the digging was done mostly by colored troops.

The canal was finished in April, 1965, but was not completed soon enough to be used by the Federals for its intended military purpose.

During the twentieth century, using modern dredging equipment, the Civil War cut was cleared and deepened to make it possible for ocean vessels of moderate size to deliver products to Richmond's deep water port. All through the years the name Dutch Gap has been retained although few know of its origin or history. *See: Farrar's Island, Henricus*

EAGLE ROCK
Botetourt County

Overlooking this community is a huge rock resembling an eagle. At least, that's what the local residents say.

EARLYSVILLE
Albemarle County

An early settler in this part of the county was John Richard Early. Near his former home Albemarle County built the small, but busy airport that serves the county and the city of Charlottesville. When it was constructed shortly after World War II, many local people were amazed that such a facility was needed. They thought that flying airplanes was a wartime fad that would soon end. Until the airport was constructed, local flying machines had to use the muddy fields of old Milton: *See: Milton*

EASTERN MENNONITE COLLEGE
Harrisonburg

Begun in 1917 under the auspices of the Virginia Mennonite Conference, this school was accredited as a junior college in 1930. At first it conferred only degrees in theology, but today's academic program covers subjects that lead the student to the traditional degree in arts and sciences.

EASTERN SHORE

The lower portion of the Delmarva Peninsula was, from the very beginning of the colony of Virginia, known as *Accawmacke,* an Indian word meaning land beyond the water. The water in this case is the Chesapeake Bay which, in the Virginia portion, is so broad that only on exceptionally clear days can those who live on the Western Shore make out the bayside bluffs of brilliantly white sand. This peninsula is bounded on the east by a series of barrier islands that keep the Atlantic Ocean away and deny access to boats with a draft of more than three feet. On the bay side, numerous creeks and inlets stay naturally deep enough for moderately-sized pleasure craft and fishing boats.

The Chesapeake Bay is actually the drowned Susquehanna River, and the current that flows steadily down the eastern side of the bay sucks silt from these creeks and keep them constantly open. One of these

creeks, at the town of Onancock, once was a port of call for bay steamers until the pre-Depresion era. At the town of Cape Charles, about fifteen miles north of the tip of this land mass, a ferry landed on regular schedules to meet the southern extremity of the Pennsylvania Railroad that was built down the center of the Eastern Shore in the latter part of the nineteenth century. The old ferry slip is still used as a transfer point for railroad cars barged over from Norfolk, but the passenger ferry was made obsolete when the Chesapeake Bay Bridge Tunnel was completed.

The first settlers arrived in 1614, sent by Governor Sir Thomas Dale to make salt from sea water at Dale's Gift. The first permanent settler of note was Ensign Thomas Savage who built his home on Cherrystone Creek. A large percentage of the original settlers of the Eastern Shore were Scots who farmed the fertile, sandy soil and enjoyed the moderate climate. During the seventeenth century, messages sent by the government were addressed: "To our faithful subjects of Ye Colonie of Virginia and Ye Kingdom of Accawmacke."

The main industry has always been agriculture. Second in importance is fishing and harvesting the plentiful Chesapeake Bay crabs and the succulent sea-tag oysters that grow abundantly in the inlets of the Atlantic. *See: Arlington of Northampton; Cheriton; Dale's Gift; Eastville; Occohannock; Oyster; Savage Neck*

EASTERN SHORE CHAPEL
Virginia Beach

Lynnhaven Parish was organized about 1640. The first church was built on the western shore of Lynnhaven Bay on the site now occupied by Old Donation Church. For the convenience of the people on the opposite side of Lynnhaven Bay, the Chapel of Ease was erected about 1657. It was called the Eastern Shore Chapel. The present building, the congregation's third, dates from 1953. The communion service, still in use, bears the inscribed date 1759. *See: Donation Church*

EASTOVER
Surry County

Opposite the mouth of the Chickahominy, on the south bank of the James River, Colonel Henry Browne patented a tract in 1637. He sold part of it later to Colonel George Jordan who was the Crown's first Attorney-General for Virginia. Another part of Browne's tract was sold to Colonel John Flood in 1638. Because both Jordan and Flood were involved in Bacon's Rebellion, these lands were confiscated by Governor William Berkeley and were sold to Benjamin Harrison III, then the Attorney-General and Treasurer of the colony whose home was across the river at Berkeley. He named this combined tract Eastover in obvious competition with Westover, the home of the Byrd family.

Not far from the present house, which was built about 1790, is an old cemetery where there is a slab of stone inscribed: "Here lyeth buried Alyce Myles, daughter of John Myles of Branton neer Herreford, Gent.: and late wife of Mr. George Jordan in Virginia, who departed this life the 7th of January 1650. She touched the soil of Virginia with her little foot and the wilderness became a home." Her grave is in Major Browne's orchard on the old Four Mile Tree Plantation. This small portion of the Brandon lands, in the Pace's Paines section, was occupied by the Cocke family for many generations. *See: Berkeley; Brandon; Four Mile Tree Plantation; Jordan's Point; Mount Pleasant; Pace's Paines; Westover*

EASTVILLE
Northampton County   **Town**

When the Eastern Shore was divided into two counties in 1663, the lower half was named Northampton and a courthouse (of a sort) was built at Townfields the next year. This proved to be too inconvenient for many people and the county seat was moved to the Hornes (forks) of Hungars Creek where a proper courthouse was put up in 1690. At this time the new settlement was called Eastville because it was east of the old site of the first courthouse and was the easternmost county seat in Virginia. It has been the site of the Northampton County courthouse ever since.

Either because the salt air was too harsh or the courthouse builders used poor materials and poorly skilled labor, the courthouse has been replaced many times, in 1716, 1730, 1795 (the first one of brick that was next to a convenient tavern), and 1899. The last one erected is still in use and the little, rather quaint courthouse of 1730 remains as a clerk's office and the only colonial courthouse in the Eastern Shore. Records here date back to 1632, the oldest continuous court records in America.

From the front steps of this little building, on August 13, 1776, the Declaration of Independence was read to the assembled citizens. County militiamen were quartered here during the Revolution, but there was no fighting and no destruction of either town, building, or public records. For a short time, Eastville was known as Peachburg.

Christ Church, in the tiny town, owns a communion cup made by John Coney of Boston some time before 1705. It was presented to the church by Governor Francis Nicholson. The congregation also cherishes a silver chalice on which is engraved "The Gift of John Custis, Esq. of WmBurgh to the Lower Church of Hungars Parish 1741." *See: Arlington of Northampton; Peachburg; Townfields*

EAST VIRGINIA

No part of the Commonwealth is officially East Virginia, but sometimes the expression is used in exasperation. There are times when people from other parts of the country ignorantly confuse the Old Dominion with the relatively new state that was formed during the Civil War. When told by a Virginian that home is in Virginia, the addled reply often is, "Oh, yes. How nice. West Virginia." The emphatic answer is politely stated through gritted teeth, "No! *East By God Virginia!" See: Southwest Virginia; West Virginia*

EDGEHILL
Albemarle County

The land here was first owned by William Randolph of Tuckahoe as early as 1735. He was the brother of Thomas Jefferson's mother. His son, Thomas Mann Randolph, occupied the family property in 1767 when he came of age. He named it Edgehill in honor of the field on which the Cavaliers of King Charles I and the Roundheads of Oliver Cromwell first joined in battle in 1641 to open the active phase of England's civil war. This estate was inherited by Thomas Mann Randolph, Jr., who married Thomas Jefferson's daughter, Martha. Some said this young Randolph was not capable of managing so large a farm and was forced to move to Varina Grove, somewhat smaller, which he had also inherited. However, in his defense, because Edgehill adjoined the property of Monticello and Jefferson was prone to play the part of the head of the family, it was possible that his son-in-law and Martha decided it would be prudent to put some distance between them and the Sage of

MARTHA JEFFERSON RANDOLPH
EDGEHILL OF ALBEMARLE COUNTY

Monticello. Note that Edgehill is always spelled as one word. *See: Eppington; Monticello; Tuckahoe; Tufton*

EDGEHILL
King George County

Here lived Samuel Schooler, the best educated man of his generation in Caroline County. Graduating at the top of his class at the University of Virginia in 1846, he taught school at two academies before opening his own school here. His textbook *Descriptive Geometry* was used by the University for many decades. The origin of the name here is the same as Edgehill of Albemarle County.

EDINBURG
Shenandoah County   Town

One would be inclined to guess that this town was named for the capital of Scotland since so many Scots settled in the Valley of Virginia. That is not the case. It is a matter of poor spelling. The first settlers called their new home Eden for the Biblical Garden of Eden. No one knows who changed Edenburg to Edinburg but that was the way it was spelled when the town was incorporated in 1852. *See: Glasgow*

EDMUNDSBURY
Caroline County

The home of Edmund Pendleton became the center of activity during the years immediately prior to the Revolution. Pendleton built his brick and frame house on high ground above Maracossic Run, a tiny stream that is dry half of the year. The house had eight rooms, each heated by a corner fireplace served by one enormous chimney that is fifteen feet square at the base. Edmund's second wife was Sarah Pollard of Bowling Green whom he married seven months after his first wife died in childbirth. The couple were mildly criticized for not waiting the normal year of mourning, the only tinge of scandal to touch Pendleton's life which began in 1721 and extended to 1803.

Pendleton's career of public service was mingled with his vocation of lawyer. An excellent courtroom attorney, he was elected a Burgess for his district and was a delegate to the Continental Congress. He did not like serving outside his state and returned to be the chairman of the Virginia Committee of Safety for two years. In May of 1776, he presided over the Virginia Convention that wrote the constitution to create the Commonwealth of Virginia, a document that was written, discussed and adopted in less than two months, becoming effective on July 1, 1776.

After Patrick Henry was elected the first Governor of the Commonwealth, Pendleton retired to Edmundsbury, coming back into the limelight to serve as the president of the Virginia Convention that ratified the U.S. Constitution in 1788. On many occasions George Washington pleaded with Pendleton to be an official of the Federal Government, but the Virginia squire always refused, insisting that any public service he performed would be only for Virginia. (He would have been a fine Confederate.)

Edmund Pendleton was buried on his beloved estate in Caroline County. His remains later were removed to Williamsburg. *See: Bowling Green; Bury; Piscataway*

EGGLESTON
Giles County

An early settler in this region, Adam Harmon, established a resort on his property about 1849. Although the official name was Hygeian Springs, it became known as Gunpowder Springs because the water had a highly sulphurous taste and smell. A Dr. Chapman took over the spa in 1853, added a few buildings, changed the name to Chapman's Springs, and then decided to call it New River White Sulpher Springs. Business continued throughout the Civil War, but during the postwar years few people could afford to come. During this time Captain William Eggleston acquired the property and erected an elegant hotel.

When the Norfolk and Western Railway built a branch line along New River in 1883, guests could reach the place with little difficulty and business boomed. However, several years later the Virginian Railroad laid its tracks so close to the resort that the peaceful setting was spoiled and the enterprise began its fatal decline. Operations ceased in the 1930s, killed off by the Depression. The buildings were torn down, the land was divided into lots, and the village of Eggleston grew on the site.

ELIZABETH CITY COUNTY
Obsolete

One of the original eight shires formed in Virginia in 1634, this area has been continuously inhabited by English-speaking people since 1610. It was called Kecoughtan at first, for the tribe whose village was located where the older part of Hampton now stands. When the House of Burgesses decided to eliminate all "heathen" names, the county was named in honor of Elizabeth, the only daughter of King James I. The princess was married to Prince Frederick, the Elector of Palatine who, through ineptitude, managed to be the king of Bohemia for only a brief time—one winter, to be exact. Elizabeth was thereafter known as the Winter Queen. After World War II, the city of Hampton annexed all of this old county and Elizabeth City County is no more. *See: City; Hampton: Kecoughtan*

ELIZABETH RIVER

This rather short river empties into the south side of Hampton Roads. It has three branches which join just a few miles from its mouth. The Elizabeth River separates the cities of Norfolk and Portsmouth. Freighters, tankers, colliers, and navy ships move up and down the last five miles or so, all adding to the pollution from industrial complexes on the shore. Pleasure boats must ply through the oily waters to get to the northern beginning of the Inland Waterway. The river was named for Princess Elizabeth, daughter of James I.

ELK CREEK
Grayson County

ELK GARDEN
Russell County

ELKTON
Rockingham County   Town

Elk were plentiful in Virginia before the first colonists arrived. Although the herds have been nearly depleted by continuous hunting, some of these great animals still roam in the mountainous area of western Virginia, appearing infrequently in the open pastures to graze with cattle. Of the three communities of this entry, Elkton is the largest and the only incorporated town.

ELK HILL
Goochland County

This rather small estate near the north bank of the James River was inherited by Thomas Jefferson from his father-in-law, John Wayles. Martha Jefferson and her children were staying here in May 1781 when they were warned of the approach of British troops under General Benedict Arnold. She hurried to Monticello but was sent on to Poplar Forest by her husband since the Jefferson home was also vulnerable to a raid. General Arnold stayed at Elk Hill while waiting for Lieutenant Colonel Tarleton to dash to Monticello to capture Jefferson and members of the Virginia legislature who were known to be meeting there. When Tarleton and his dragoons returned to Elk Hill without prisoners, Arnold moved his men to Petersburg. He left the house thoroughly pillaged and vandalized, killed or took with him the livestock, and emptied the storage buildings of anything that could be of use or value. Among the loot were the slaves who had worked the estate. *See: Charlottesville; Cuckoo*

ELLERSLIE
Brunswick County

Near the present town of Lawrenceville, overlooking the Meherrin River, stands Ellerslie, the home of the Hartwell family. Prior to the Revolution, this was one of the westernmost estates in Virginia. Not far from here was Fort Christanna, built in 1714 by Governor Alexander Spotswood. *See: Fort Christanna*

ELLERSLIE
Stafford County

Michael Wallace was indentured to a physician in Charles City, Maryland. As he neared the end of his six-year apprenticeship, he fell in love. At the age of twenty-one, he eloped with one of his master's daughters in a classic elopment with a ladder to a second-story window late at night. At first his new father-in-law was upset, as could be expected, but having nine daughters, he assumed a practical attitude and made no effort to recover his daughter or his indentured servant. He knew that his apprentice had learned his lessons well. The newlyweds settled first in Falmouth where Michael adopted the title Dr. Wallace and set up his practice. He quickly made money, invested in land, and built Ellerslie in 1748 for his wife and family. Dr. Wallace also applied his skill in the healing art to many patients in Culpeper, Fauqier, and Loudoun counties for numerous successful years.

ELLERSON
Hanover County

Andrew R. Ellerson, a Confederate soldier, ran the family mill on Beaverdam Creek before the war. The establishment was known as Ellerson's Mill when a sharp Civil War battle was fought nearby. Ellerson was assigned elsewhere at the time but came back when the fighting was ended at Appomattox.

ELLISTON
Montgomery County

First known as Big Springs, this community became a steel center during the boom times of the 1880s. After the financial crash of 1888, the village lay dormant with little to offer the residents for an income. A Major Ellis, who had married one of the daughters of President John Tyler, breathed new life into the community, organized businesses, and had the post office named for him near the turn of the century.

ELMINGTON
Gloucester County

The first patentee was Edmund Dawber of London, the son-in-law of Sir Thomas Gates. Although this tract had been "seated," and thus became a valid claim, it was unoccupied in 1649. William Deynes re-registered the land in his name but, in the civil suit that followed, he lost his title to the tract. Richard Young managed to gain control in 1665 through a grant issued by Governor William Berkeley. Young solidified his holdings well enough to have the land inherited by his grandson without contest. In 1705, the tract was divided into four parcels.

The house site, plus 950 acres, was purchased by Henry Whiting who built the core of the present dwelling. His son, Henry, Jr., expanded the house to its present size. His son, Colonel Beverley Whiting, was a Burgess from Gloucester for fifteen years. A lawyer of ability and modest fame, the Colonel was George Washington's godfather. The last Whiting to own Elmington was Major Peter Beverley who sold the estate to Benjamin Dabney in 1804 after his family had lived there for a century. *See: Exchange; Isleham; Toddsbury; White Marsh; Whiting's Mount*

ELMWOOD
Essex County

Built about 1774 by Muscoe Garnett, the materials for the house were brought by water from Baltimore. Elmwood was situated on an elevation about two miles away from the Rappahannock River to avoid the malarial marshes. It was inherited by the builder's son, James Mercer Garnett, a politician, educator, and agriculturist. The brickwork of this house is similar to that of Blandfield, ten miles away, and the structure is in the style of Mount Vernon.

ELMWOOD
Langley Field   **Site**

Owned by the Cary family in the early eighteenth century, three generations of that family lived here, all direct descendants of Thomas Miles Cary. The land was purchased by the Federal Government in 1917 as part of the acquisitions for Langley Field. The NASA Langley Research Center now occupies the Elmwood property. No trace of the Cary home remains. *See: Chesterville*

ELSING GREEN
King William County

This estate was founded by William and John Dandridge soon after they arrived in Virginia in 1716. Two Braxton brothers, George and Carter, both of Newington, purchased the land of Elsing Green in 1750. While Carter Braxton was abroad on business, his brother, George, supervised the construction of a house which caught fire and was utterly destroyed just prior to its completion. It was rebuilt in time for Carter Braxton to move in and enjoy the view of the Pamunkey River, a short distance away.

Carter Braxton, a Burgess for this district, was a member of the Virginia Conventions of 1774 through 1776, and was a signer of the Declaration of Independence to which he attached his signature reluctantly. He was not in favor of independence but signed only to insure that the Virginia delegation appeared to be in unanimous agreement since the measure had been proposed by one Virginian and had been written by another. The Braxton brothers were the sons of George Braxton and Mary Carter. *See: Chantilly of Westmoreland; Chericoke; Newington; White House*

ELTHAM
New Kent County   **Site**

Members of the Bassett family moved here from Bassettaire to locate a new home at Machot, an abandoned Indian village. The house was erected in 1730 for Colonel William Bassett who named it for Eltham Lodge of Kent, England. The fourth generation of the family in America, Burwell Bassett, was born here in 1734. The owner of Eltham during Revolutionary times, he was the husband of Anna Maria Dandridge, Martha Washington's sister. George Washington was a frequent visitor here when he travelled from Mount Vernon to Williamsburg. He was at the side of his stepson, John Parke Custis, when the young man died at Eltham in November 1781, after contracting camp fever at Yorktown. This was one of the largest and finest homes in Virginia at the time of its destruction by fire in 1875. The foundations remain but the old house has never been reconstructed. *See Arlington; Bassettaire; Mount Vernon; White House*

EMORY AND HENRY COLLEGE
Washington County

Founded in 1836 by the Methodist church, this institution was named for Bishop John Emory and the "Firebrand of the Revolution," Patrick Henry. It was consolidated with Martha Washington College in 1918 to become coeducational.

EMPORIA
Greensville County   **City**

The first settler here was Captain Robert Hix, an Indian trader, who had his post on Fort Road where it crossed the Meherrin River. A small settlement, named Hicksford, gathered around his establishment. Some years later, another hamlet developed on the opposite side of the river which was called Belfield. When Greensville County was organized in 1780, it was decided that the best place for the county seat was at Hicksford which eventually merged with Belfield to

create a new town that was named Emporia. Whoever suggested the name knew Latin. An *emporium* is a trading place; *emporia* is the plural form of the word. Since there were many trading places (stores and shops) in the consolidated county seat, Emporia is most correct—and probably easier to say.

ENDVIEW
York County

The land here was granted to a member of the Harwood family in 1632, but it was not utilized for many years. It was purchased from a descendant of the first owner in 1720 by Daniel P. Curtis who built the present house. His heirs still own it. Troops enroute to Yorktown refreshed themselves at the farm's spring in 1781. During the War of 1812, and the Civil War, the fields were covered with tents for a brief time as troops camped. When the road from Lee Hall to Yorktown was rerouted many years ago, it passed the house at the side end rather than at the front, giving the visitor an "end view." *See: Queen's Hith*

ENNISCORTHY
Albemarle County

Shortly after John Coles came to Virginia about 1730, he became interested in the Green Mountain section of Goochland County (later cut off and formed into Albemarle). Some time shortly after 1747, Coles built a lodge which he called Enniscorthy for the family home in County Leinster, Ireland. John Coles II inherited this estate and added to his father's 3,000 acres until his tract was nearly double the original size. He served as the commandant of the prisoner of war camp that had been established during the Revolution by John Harvie, Jr. It was to Enniscorthy that Governor Thomas Jefferson first came for refuge in 1781 after he fled from Monticello to escape capture by Tarleton's dragoons. *See: Augusta Parish; Barracks; Belmont of Albemarle; Colle; Cuckoo*

EPPING FOREST
Lancaster County

The house at Epping Forest was built in 1680 by Colonel Joseph Ball who named his home after the Ball family estate in England. He married Elizabeth Romney and raised a son and four daughters. Widowed at the age of 58, he gave the farm property and house to his son, Joseph, Jr., and divided his personal property among all five children. The Colonel reserved the right to live in the manor until his death. It was a wise precaution since he married shortly thereafter.

His new wife, Mary Montague Johnson, bore him another daughter who was named Mary. When Mary Ball was still quite young, her father died. Her mother soon married Captain Richard Hawes who took his bride and stepdaughter to his home on Cherry Point in Northumberland County. When Mary's mother died in 1721, she was sent to live with her guardian, Colonel George Eskridge, at Sandy Point where she remained until she married Augustine Washington in 1731. Her first child, whom she named George for her guardian, was the famous general and the first president. *See: Bewdley; Ferry Farm; Sandy Point; Wakefield of Westmoreland*

EPPINGTON
Prince George County

About a decade after the founding of Jamestown, Francis Eppes came to the colony and lived in James City (probably at Jamestown). He was a member of the Assembly of 1619 and later, in 1635, he was appointed to the Council. He received a grant of 1,700 acres on the south bank of the James River (then still a part of Charles City County) for his "personal adventure" and an additional 650 acres for bringing with him his three sons and thirty servants. His home, which he named Eppington, was located at the point of land where the Appomattox River flows into the James. It commanded a view as magnificent as that at Mount Vernon and for miles one could watch the commerce of the rivers.

The early home was pulled down and replaced by the present one in 1751 by another Francis Eppes whose son, John Wayles Eppes, married Thomas Jefferson's younger daughter, Mary. She lived here for only a few years and died of breast cancer at the young age of 25. Her husband later became a Congressman for this district of Virginia and lived in the Executive Mansion in Washington, D.C., while Jefferson was President. Eppington's gardens were trampled to ruin by British forces during the action around Petersburg in the summer of 1781.

The father of the Congressman and Jefferson were brothers-in-law, of a sort, since their wives were half-sisters, both the daughters of John Wayles of the estate named The Forest across the James from Eppington. Jefferson said that Francis Eppes, Sr., was "not only the finest horticulturalist in America but a man of the soundest practical judgement on all practical subjects." In later years, Eppington's house was known as Appomattox Manor. *See Albemarle County; the Forest of Charles City; Hopewell; Monticello; Tuckahoe; Virginia Grove; Weston*

ESSEX
Northampton County

Arthur Upshur and his brother, Abel, ran away from their home in England in 1637 and came to Virginia. Arthur settled on the Eastern shore and laid claim to a point of land now called Neville's Neck where he built a home that he called Warwick. His son, Arthur Upshur, Jr., inherited the lower tip of the neck and built his own home, Essex. Both Warwick and Essex were areas of England that were associated with the family's background. Across the wide Machipongo Creek that washed the edge of Essex was Brownsville. Arthur, Jr., met his wife Sarah Brown there. *See: Vaucluse; Warwick of Northampton*

ESSEX COUNTY

Formed in 1691 from Old Rappahannock County, Essex was named for the ancient shire in England. Many of the landed gentry of Essex County were loyal Tories during the Revolution. In fact, the area was often berated by patriots as being a "sink-hole of Toryism." The county seat is Tappahannock. *See: Blandfield*

ETTRICK
Chesterfield County

Local tradition says the early settlers came from Scotland and named their village for their home town. For many years, the community was called Ettricks Banks, possibly a Scottish name, but that proved too much for more modern residents. The name was shortened to Ettricks and then to Ettrick.

EVELYNTON
Henrico County

William Byrd II detached this tract from Westover and gave it to his wife, Lucy Parke. It was named for his daughter, Evelyn, who, it is said, died of a broken heart when her father rejected the man she had fallen in love with while she was in England. He was the Catholic nephew of the dissolute Earl of Peterborough, a notorious rake. Whether William Byrd turned thumbs down on the young man because of his uncle's unsavory reputation or because he was a Catholic is a

81

matter of conjecture. At any rate, Evelyn Byrd was terribly unhappy with life in rural Virginia after her return to Westover and she died a disconsolate and bitter spinster at the age of twenty-eight. Most likely she died of tuberculosis contracted in England rather than of a broken heart. *See: Westover*

EVERGREEN
Accomack County

Dr. George Hack, a German surgeon, came to the Eastern Shore in 1652 and bought a tract of land from Tepitiason, the king of the Nuswattock Indians. To doubly insure his right to the land, he patented what he had "purchased" with the Virginia government. As dated by an old insurance inventory, Dr. Hack's house was built prior to 1655. One hundred years later the estate passed into the Muir family when a female descendant of the surgeon married Adam Muir in 1766. Evergreen is located at the water's edge about a mile southwest of Harborton.

EVINGTON
Campbell County

The Southern Railway established a station on land owned by Miss Evie Smith. The station was named for her. There is some evidence that the first settler in this area was Colonel Jeremiah Early who moved from Culpeper about 1755. He built his home, a mill, and a tavern, and was the partner of James Callaway in the Washington Iron Mine. Colonel Early died in 1779 when he was forty-nine years old. Evie Smith was not related. *See Callaway; Earlysville; Leesville of Campbell County*

EXCHANGE
Gloucester County

Located on the North River of Mobjack Bay, just up from Elmington, this is one of the oldest homes in Tidewater. Much of the original house, built about 1720, has been replaced by the various owners. In all the years, five families have lived here, beginning with the Andersons, followed by the Tabbs, Buckners, Dabneys, and the Gleysteens. The unusual name is thought to have been applied after the Andersons and the Buckners ex-changed property. The land was part of a large tract patented by Henry Whiting in 1692. *See: Elmington*

EXETER
Loudoun County

Dr. Wilson Cary Selden settled here and built his house in the last decade of the eighteenth century. He made his home, Exeter, the social center of Loudoun County during the early days of the republic. Dr. Selden obviously had roots in the lower Peninsula. All three of his names were those of families that were prominent in Elizabeth City and Warwick counties beginning in the middle of the seventeenth century. Exeter was named for the old city in Devonshire, England. *See: Buckroe; Ceeley's; Richneck of Newport News*

EXMORE
Northampton County   **Town**

Tradition has it that this once was the eleventh stop on the rail line from the Virginia-Maryland border. Written in Roman numerals, the northbound train crew had "X" more stops to make before reaching Maryland. A more likely source of the name might be the old village of Exmore in England.

EYRE HALL
Northampton County

Littleton Eyre built his home on a spit of land across from Savage Neck. The date was approximately 1740. The land had been granted to three brothers, John, Thomas, and Daniel Eyre in 1662 by Governor William Berkeley. There is a possibility that an earlier dwelling was located on the site, but evidence is lacking. An interesting feature of the house garden is the brick wall which, it is said, was made of bricks dropped off as ballast by the vessels that called at the private wharf. However, it is possible that the imported bricks served as ballast by the ship that brought them. Some people are certain that they had been taken from the remains of the first house. Severn Lyre, a Burgess from the county, lived here when the estate's land extended all the way across the spit. *See: Savage Neck; Winona*

FAIRFAX
Fairfax County   City

When Alexandria was in the territory that was given by Virginia to form the District of Columbia, the citizens of Fairfax County moved their county seat to a third location. A new courthouse was erected in 1799 on two acres of land donated by Richard Ratcliffe at the intersection of Little River Turnpike and Ox Road. In 1805 the General Assembly authorized a new town, named Providence at Fairfax Court House. The name Providence was dropped in 1874 when the town of Fairfax was incorporated. It was chartered as a city in 1961. *See: Alexandria; Fairfax County; Springfield*

FAIRFAX COUNTY

This county was formed from Prince William in 1742. It was named for the dominant personage of this region, Thomas, sixth Lord Fairfax, Baron of Cameron, the last Proprietor of the Northern Neck. The same act of the House of Burgesses that created the county also specified that the courthouse was to be built at a place called "Spring Field" situated between New Church Road and Ox Road, about a half-mile south of present day Tyson's Corner. Six acres of land for the court building and jail were given by Colonel William Fairfax.

This site was abandoned in 1752 when businessmen in Alexandria offered a courthouse within their town, Spring Field being too inconvenient for them. Alexandria was within the land given to the republic in 1791 to form the District of Columbia. Fairfax County residents did not want their courthouse in the Federal District so, after nearly a decade of discussion, the county seat was moved to another place—once more in the center of the territory which had been changed in shape by a re-alignment of the Loudoun County boundary. The present brick building was erected in 1799. Over the many years of use it was altered, modified, and added to until it was a hodge podge of mixed design. It was restored to a more colonial style in 1966. *See: District of Columbia; Greenway Court; Springfield*

FAIRFAX HALL
Farirfax County

William and George William Fairfax, brothers, were the sons of Colonel William Fairfax and the grandsons of the Proprietor of Northern Neck. The elder of the two men, William, lived here while his brother preferred Belvoir. In 1771 Fairfax Hall was sold to Robert Adam, the founder of the Masonic Lodge in Alexandria. *See: Belvoir; Greenway Court; Shuter's Hill*

FAIRFIELD
Accomack County

This was the home of Charles Scarburgh, one of the more stable members of a rather active family. He was a member of the Council in 1694. *See: Craddock; Occhannock*

FAIRFIELD
Clarke County

Warner Washington purchased land from Colonel William Fairfax in 1749. His first house was of modest size which he replaced, on another site, about 1774 using plans drawn by the noted American architect, John Arris. The early name of this estate was Fairfield but, when the new home was completed, the name was changed to Audley. Warner Washington was George Washington's first cousin. He married Hannah Fairfax and they lived quietly in this lower portion of the Shenandoah Valley near other relatives, also gentlemen farmers. Because they could not ship their products by water to eastern markets, since the Shenandoah River is shallow at Harper's Ferry and the Potomac is blocked by the falls above Georgetown, George Washington and his Valley relatives became interested in developing canals around these barriers. They organized the Patowmack Canal Company. The lands of Fairfield, under its new name, were purchased by Lawrence Lewis when he married Nelly Custis. *See: Audley; Belvoir; Fairfax Hall; Patowmack Canal*

FAIRFIELD
Gloucester County

This was the home of Lewis Burwell II, III, and IV. The first house here was erected by Lewis II prior to 1692 which his son, Nathaniel razed to make room for the present structure. He had plenty of capital since his wife was the daughter of Robert "King" Carter of Corotoman. Their first son, Lewis III, lived his whole life at Fairfield except for a few years he spent in England at Cambridge University. He was a member of the Council and, now and then, was the acting governor. His daughter was Thomas Jefferson's "Fair Belinda" who refused his offer of marriage in favor of Jacquelin Amber of Jamestown. "Belinda's" brother, Lewis Burwell IV, was the last of the family to live at Fairfield. Sometimes this estate is referred to as the House on Carter's Creek for the stream that runs through the property on its way to the York River. *See: Carter's Grove; Ringneck*

FAIRFIELD
King William County

Owned for generations by members of the Aylett family, Fairfield was a large and successful tobacco plantation during the late colonial period. The leaves, packed in hogsheads, were shipped from Todd's Wharf down the Mattaponi River and then to larger vessels that tied up at the customs house wharf at Delaware Town. George Washington periodically stopped here enroute between Northern Virginia and Williamsburg since he was on friendly terms with the Ayletts. Philip Aylett married Elizabeth Henry, one of the daughters of Patrick Henry. They soon abandoned the old house at Fairfield and moved to a new home site on higher, healthier ground. Their new house was called Montville. Old Fairfield was razed. *See: Aylett; Chantilly; Delaware Town; King's Highway; Scotchtown; Todd's Wharf*

FAIRY STONE STATE PARK
Henry and Patrick Counties

Large crystals of stone found here have the natural shape of crosses: St. Andrew's, Roman, and Maltese. When polished, the fairy stones are worn as charms. No one seems to know who first gave them their fanciful name, but it has been perpetuated commercially and is, of course, the name of this state park where they lie in abundance.

FALL HILL
Stafford County

Shortly after Francis Thornton arrived from Yorkshire, England in 1673 he patented land at the falls of the Rappahannock River. His home was sited on a high knoll near the Village of Falmouth. It was completed in 1680. His son, Francis, Jr., married Frances Gregory, the daughter of Roger Gregory and Mildred Washington. Francis Thornton II, a cousin of the first president, was a Justice, a Burgess, and was a Lieutenant Colonel in the county militia. The name of the home was naturally derived, being on a hill and overlooking the falls of the river below.

FALLING CREEK FURNACE
Chesterfield County   Site

The first attempt to process iron ore began here in 1619. The smelter, known in those days as a furnace, was destroyed by the Indians during the Massacre of 1622 which took the lives of all of the men who lived here. They were dangerously exposed, far from the nearest settlement at Henricus, and lived and worked about fifteen miles south of the present city of Richmond. No attempt was made to reconstruct the furnace and continue operations. Because the ore in the local area was of a very low grade and the furnace consumed huge quantites of charcoal, the project was considered a failure. The creek was named for its many falls as it tumbles down to the James River. Actually, this stream is not a creek in the true sense and the project of 1619 did not go by its present name. It was called, rather simply and factually, The Furnace because it was the only one in Virginia at the time. *See: Wilderness*

FALLING SPRING
Alleghany County

This little community was named for a nearby spring that normally produces 7,000 gallons of water per minute which falls some 200 feet into a valley. Falling Spring is a tributary of the Jackson River.

FALLS CHURCH
Fairfax County   City

This city is named for an early church that was erected at the intersection of Wilderness Road and the road to the Little Falls of the Potomac. The first structure of 1665 was the mother church of Fairfax Parish. It was replaced by the present building in 1734. With easy access to Washington, D.C., Falls Church became a bedroom community for Federal employees. What was once a small village outgrew its township status and became chartered as a city after World War II.

FALMOUTH
Stafford County

Named for the seaport of Falmouth in Cornwall, England, this village was founded in 1727 as a trading center to serve the upper portion of the Northern Neck. It is the seat of Stafford County. Hunter's Iron Works, located nearby, was the objective of the

British army in the early summer of 1781. *See: Belmont of Stafford*

FARMINGTON
Albemarle County
The land here was patented in 1735 by Michael Holland who sold it to Charles Lewis. Francis Jerdone, the noted Tory, purchased the tract in 1758. He was a shrewd Scot who made a modest fortune in New Kent and Hanover counties before moving to Albemarle just prior to the Revolution. He decided to live on his fortune as a country squire, a custom still prevalent today. During the Revolution, Jerdone's property was confiscated by the new Commonwealth, but an adjustment was reached somehow which permitted him to regain possession. Thomas Jefferson designed a manor house for him, but the Sage of Monticello became annoyed with the changes made to his plans during construction and he washed his hands of it. Jerdone sold Farmington to George Divers in 1785 who went back to Jefferson for advice on remodeling. The place was enlarged, the entrance re-oriented, and the present white columns added. The Jeffersonian portion still remains as part of the main clubhouse of Farmington Country Club. *See: Jerdone's Castle; Mount Stirling; Providence Forge*

FARMVILLE
Prince Edward County   Town
During colonial times, this was a distributing and trading point for flat-bottomed boats and barges that worked the Appomattox River above the fall line. When Prince Edward County was formed in 1753, Rutledge Ford was selected as the county seat, although, oddly, the first courthouse and the necessary jail were erected at King's Tavern, about five miles to the south two years after the county's organization. Years later, Rutledge Ford became the county seat when the town was officially recognized in 1798. Many years later, the name was changed to Farmville. *See: King's Tavern; Longwood College; Prince Edward County*

FARNHAM
Richmond County
For many years the principal structure of this village was Farnham Church, the mother church of the parish that served this region. The name is identified with Farnham Castle of Surrey, England, which has been the seat of the bishops of Guildford for hundreds of years. Cyrus Griffin was born about four miles away in 1748. Educated in England, he served Virginia as a Burgess and was the President of the Continental Congress in 1788.

FARRAR'S ISLAND
Chesterfield County
When Sir Thomas Dale founded the Citie of Henricus in 1611, on land that was nearly completely surrounded by the James River, he had his men cut Dutch Gap to create an island that could be more easily defended. The town was abandoned after the Massacre of 1622; subsequent floods washed away all traces of the early habitations. It lay idle and unclaimed until about 1638 when it was granted to "William Farrar, sonne and heir of William Farrar, Esquire, deceased, 2,000 acres for transportation of 40 persons at his own expense." The elder Farrar had come to Virginia in 1618 indentured to Samuel Jordan who made him the overseer of Jordan's Journey. In 1626, the year after his bond of seven years service to Jordan was satisfactorily completed, William Farrar was appointed to the Council by the King upon the recommendation of Governor Francis Wyatt, a position of high prestige he held until his death in 1637. This illustrates the point that those who came to Virginia as indentured servants could rise to gentleman status without prejudice.

William, the elder, was a respondent in the first breach of promise suit in the colony when the widow of his former master, Cecily Bayly Jordan, promised to marry Farrar and another man, a minister. When the case was settled, Cecily became the wife of William Farrar, the Councillor. As a result of the suit, the Assembly passed a law that forbade any woman to promise herself to two men at the same time. The name Farrar is pronounced with the accent on the first syllable, using a flat "a" (as in farrier). *See: Dutch Gap; Henricus; Jordan's Point; Powhite*

FAUQUIER COUNTY
When this county was formed in 1759 from a part of Prince William, it was named to honor Francis Fauquier, the Governor of Virginia who had died the previous year. Fauquier's father, a Protestant, had fled France to escape religious persecution. In England he married Elizabeth Chamberlayne and became a successful businessman. Their son, Francis, gained a sound business background from his father. He published a pamphlet on taxation that was well received

in England. The notoriety led to his appointment as Governor of Virginia. He replaced General Amherst, the military commander of British America, who never had time to visit the colony he was supposed to govern. When Thomas Jefferson wrote his book, *Notes on the State of Virginia,* after the Revolution, he described Francis Fauquier as "the ablest man who ever filled the chair of government here." The courthouse of Fauquier County is located at Warrenton. *See: Amherst County; Huguenots*

FEDERAL HILL
Fredericksburg

The house of Federal Hill is reported to have been built by orders of Queen Anne during the time that Alexander Spotswood was the Governor of the colony. The original brick exterior has been covered by clapboard of tulip wood. Inside are exquisitely carved wooden wall panels and a unique staircase. In the early days of the Republic, Virginia's Governor, Robert Brook, bought this house and renamed it Federal Hill after the Federalist party of which he was a founder. There is no record of its colonial name. It is said that the ghost of Alexander Spotswood can be seen now and then standing by the sideboard where he helps himself to a touch of liquor (spirits?). Those who claim to have seen him say he raises his glass in a silent toast and then disappears. *See: Germanna*

FERRUM
Franklin County

When the N & W Railroad built a line through this section of the county, the officials were interested in a local iron mine and scheduled a stop here. They gave the station the name Ferrum, the Latin word for iron. Prior to this time, 1889, the collection of houses and hovels had no formal name.

FERRY FARM
Stafford County   Site

George Washington's parents, Augustine and Mary, were forced to leave their home on Little Hunting Creek (later known as Mount Vernon) when fire destroyed their simple dwelling in 1738. This being the second time they were burned out, they decided to live closer to a settled community. Augustine Washington bought "the little place where Mr. William Strother lately lived" which was described as being "about two miles below the falls of the Rappahannock, close on the riverside and with a ferry belonging to it." This

FERRY FARM

farm, more or less opposite Fredericksburg, was for thirty-seven years the Washington family's home.

George Washington lived here for sixteen years. When he was 22, he moved back to Little Hunting Creek with his half brother, Lawrence, where they built a cabin. Augustine Washington worked the 600 acre Ferry Farm, received a little income from the ferry operation, and had a full-time job late in his life in an iron foundary at Massaponnox to which he went every day on his own ferry. When Augustine died, George's mother remained on the homestead until her eldest son convinced her to live in Fredericksburg in a house he bought for her near her daughter's home, Kenmore, that was just up the hill. George inherited Ferry Farm and sold it in 1772 to Dr. Hugh Mercer of Fredericksburg.

It was at this home that, according to the ficticious tale, the first president was supposed to have chopped down his father's cherry tree and tossed a Spanish dollar across the Rappahannock. Prior to becoming the Washington family's residence, the farm was known as Pine Grove, a name that seldom appears in the records of this famous family's history. *See: Bel Air; Mount Vernon; Wakefield of Westmoreland*

FIELDALE
Henry County

Here, in a beautiful valley, Marshall Field and Company, of Chicago, built a textile plant shortly after World War I. The company also erected a number of dwellings for the employees which developed into a village that took its name from Fieldcrest Mills.

FIGSBORO
Henry County

The G. W. Lester Tobacco Factory, outside of Martinsville, made a pressed plug of chewing tobacco, named Lester's Fig, that resembled a small carton of pressed figs in shape and color. Licorice and peach juice were added to the plug for flavoring. This suburb of Martinsville, once a separate community gathered around the factory, still retains the name Figsboro.

FINCASTLE
Botetourt County   **Town**

A short-lived county bore the name Fincastle from 1772-1776. It embraced all of southwest Virginia, including Kentucky. The county courthouse was built on land donated by Israel Christian. The tiny hamlet that was the county seat was named Fincastle. Both the county and the hamlet were named for George, Lord Fincastle, the eldest son of John Murray, Lord Dunmore, the last Royal Governor of Virginia. The name itself had something to do with the county's demise, but its gigantic size required that it be carved into smaller divisions. The settlement at the courthouse retained its name. Fincastle is now the seat of Botetourt County, and is the only place in Virginia that bears any reference to the despised last Royal Governor. *See: New Castle of Craig*

FINDOWRIE
Albemarle County

In 1733, Thomas Darsie patented 2,000 acres in the rolling foothills of Albemarle County near Southwest Mountain. He called his homesite Aspen Grove. Although aspens are generally associated with the Rocky Mountains, a variety of the tree grows well in Virginia. The date of the first house here is thought to be 1734. Possibly the present house is the original. During the Federal period the name Aspen Grove was changed to Findowrie, a name of Scottish origin. *See: Southwest Mountains*

FISHERMAN ISLAND
Northampton County

This island did not exist when the colonists first came to the Eastern Shore in the seventeenth century. According to records in the Navy Real Estate Office on the Norfolk Naval Station, the island began to form over 150 years ago as accumulation of sand around a ship that had sunk in the shoal water off Cape Charles. Every year the land mass grows larger until, eventually, it will become attached to the Delmarva Peninsula. When first acquired by the Treasury Department in 1891, to be used as a quarantine station for sailors with communicable diseases, the island was "twenty-five acres, more or less." When it was transferred to the War Department in 1919, it measured 225 acres. In 1973 the Navy gave 625 acres of Fisherman Island to the Department of Interior for a Wildlife Refuge and retained twenty-five for possible military use. An aerial photograph, taken in 1976 at low tide, show nearly 1,000 acres of sand and salt marsh. It is still growing, formed of sand from the barrier islands on the ocean side of the Eastern shore and from Virginia Beach. *See: Smith Island*

FIVE FORKS
Prince George County   **Site**

Here was fought one of the last significant engagements of the Civil War. General Phillip

FIVE FORKS

Sheridan's cavalry and Warren's Fifth Corps infantry defeated Pickett's Confederate troops that were assigned to shield the rear of Lee's army defending Petersburg. As a result of this action, in April 1865, the door was now open for the fall of Richmond and the capture of the Confederate Army of Northern Virginia. In a masterful maneuver, General Lee disengaged his troops from the network of trenches and bunkers around Petersburg and slipped away. He hoped to reach the railroad at Danville to join General Joseph E. Johnston, who was retreating from the beating inflicted by General Sherman coming up from Georgia. Twenty-five miles short of Lynchburg, Lee's men were cut off by the converging arms of Grant's Federal Army which forced the Southern surrender at Appomattox Court House. *See: Brandy Station*

FLINT HILL
Rappahannock County

A good supply of white flint was found on a hill here that was excellent for flintlock muskets and other firearms. When the village developed it took the name of the hill.

FLOWERDEW HUNDRED
Prince George County

Sir George Yeardley, Governor and Captain-General of Virginia, patented the land here in 1619. He named it for his wife, Temperance Flowerdew. This tract has been actively producing ever since, although the original grant has been cut into smaller parcels over the years. Governor Yeardley spent little time on this plantation, preferring to live in Jamestown, the colony's capital, while the work was supervised by a trusted overseer. Flowerdew Hundred was protected from Indian raids by a stone barricade which recent archeological digs prove to have been at least 4,000 feet long. Behind it were at least twelve buildings, including the manor house that was erected in 1620 upon foundations made of sandstone imported from England. The other structures included the usual outbuildings and dependencies, three barns, and at least four tobacco warehouses. Although struck during the Indian attacks in 1622 and 1644, the inhabitants of Flowerdew Hundred were spared during the first massacre by being warned in time, and by being on the alert during the second.

The first windmill in America was constructed on this land in 1621 for Sir George. Although no documents have been found to describe this mill, it probably looked very much like the reconstructed mill now at Flowerdew Hundred that was built in the 1970s by the current owner of this historic place. *See: The Forest; Hundred; Martin's Hundred; Mill; Mulberry Island; Windmill Point*

FLOYD COUNTY

Formed from parts of Montgomery and Franklin counties in 1831, this county was named for James Floyd, then the Governor of the Commonwealth. The first courthouse was a log cabin in the village of Jacksonville which was renamed Floyd Court House. It grew into an incorporated town now known simply as Floyd. The primitive structure was replaced by a proper courthouse of brick and stone in 1845.

FLUVANNA COUNTY

Formed in 1777 from Albemarle, this county bears the contrived name by which the upper James River was known until the Civil War. Fluvanna is a Latinized combination of *fluvia* meaning "river," and Anne, the queen whose name was used so often in Virginia. The design of the courthouse is attributed to John Cocke of Bremo who probably had help from Thomas Jefferson. The county seat, Palmyra, most likely was named by Jefferson who was fond of ancient and historic places. *See: Glendower; Palmyra*

FLUVANNA RIVER

Early in the English colonization of Virginia the James River ended at the falls. Above the falls the river was known by a variety of names for the Indian tribes discovered living on its banks. When Queen Anne came to the throne after the death of William III, Virginians applied her name to the western portion. The upper James was the Fluvanna on all maps until after the Civil War. It was not until Claudius Crozet supervised the publication of a newly-authorized official map of the Commonwealth late in the nineteenth century that the entire river bore the same name. *See: Crozet; Fluvanna County; James River; Rapidan River; Rivanna River*

FLYING POINT
Surry County

William Rookings patented land on the south bank of the James River in 1636 and established a modest plantation. His son, William, Jr., was one of the leaders of Bacon's Rebellion in 1676 and, as a result, his family lost title to the tract. The origin of the name is unknown. *See: Bacon's Castle*

FOLLY CASTLE
Petersburg

This was the home of Peter Jones who had it built in 1763. His neighbors derisively called it Folly Castle when it was completed since Jones was then childless and they could see no need for a man and his wife to have such a large home. They did not count on the many children who were born here who filled the place. This Peter Jones was an ancestor of the Peter Jones for whom Petersburg was named. *See: Fort Henry; Petersburg*

FORD
Dinwiddie County

A depot was built at this place many years ago by the Norfolk and Western Railway. Fred Ford was the first agent at what the railroad called Ford's Depot.

THE FOREST
Charles City County

This was the home of John Wayles whose daughter, Martha, lived here with her first husband, Bathurst Skelton. When she became a widow after a short married life with Skelton, Thomas Jefferson came courting. He and Martha were married at The Forest on January 1, 1772, in the house which is sited not far from the bank of the James River. John Wayles had another daughter, Maria, who married Jefferson's good friend Francis Eppes of Eppington. Wayles also had an illegitimate daughter by a mulatto slave. She grew up to achieve notoriety as "Dusky Sally" who served Jefferson as a house servant. Sally Hennings, reportedly an attractive quadroon, was Martha's much younger half sister. Because she was one-fourth black and her mother was a slave, she was considered a Negro and was legally a slave under the statutes of the Common-wealth. Jefferson did not want to free her since under the laws of manumission she would have been required to leave the state within one year or be eligible to be sold at public auction. Neither her master nor Martha Jefferson wanted her to be forced to leave Virginia. *See: Eppington; Poplar Forest*

THE FOREST
Newport News **Site**

Miles Cary, Sr., purchased this land from Zachary Cripps about 1657. It adjoined the Cary plantation called Magpie Swamp and was known, at the time of the purchase, as Claiborne's Neck. The Forest was inherited by Henry Cary (who built the first Capitol in Williamsburg), the second son of Miles Cary, Sr. Cary built the courthouse for York County and the fort on the York River at Pamunkey Neck. His son, Henry Cary, Jr., moved to Williamsburg in 1776 when his father died. In 1730 the land of The Forest was "docked" and sold to Colonel Wilson Cary of Richneck. *See: Magpie Swamp*

FORESTVILLE
Shenandoah County

For many years this village was known as Hesse-Cassel, named for the largest house in the little community. It was owned by Henry Hess, the wealthiest man in the vicinity, the owner of the only store, and the founder of this settlement. Obviously he was of German extraction since the duchy of Hesse-Cassle in Germany was the seat of the Hanoverian kings of England. Hess' home was close to George Brock's mill that had begun operation before 1749. When the miller's lands were platted and sold as lots to form a village, Hess suggested the name Forestville rather than the longer name of his home. Since he was the first postmaster, his suggestion was accepted. This area of Shenandoah County, thickly timbered, had long been known as The Forest. Other hamlets nearby were named Timberville, Pine Woods, and Woodlawn.

FORK UNION
Fluvanna County

A church was built in 1824 at the confluence of the Rivanna River with a fork of the James by three (possibly four) denominations. It was a unified effort from which the name Fork Union developed. Located here is the famed Fork Union Military Academy, one of the most respected prep schools in the country. It was organized in 1898 as a community school and then expanded. Military training, a requirement, was begun in 1902.

FORT ALGERNOURNE
Fort Monroe **Site**

This was the first fort at Point Comfort, but exactly where it was sited nobody knows. It was constructed in 1609 under the leadership of Captain John Radcliffe of local materials—logs, planks, and sand. There were a few dwellings inside the palisade plus a magazine for stores. Primarily designed as a refuge for colonists in case of Indian attack, it also served as a lookout for ships entering Chesapeake Bay, especially Spanish ships since the Englishmen were acutely aware of Spain's claim to the New World. Its few iron cannons would have had little effect upon an armed ship that dared to sail past enroute to the James River.

The first test came in 1611 when a Spanish caravel, probably sent to spy on the colony, anchored off Point Comfort and sent three men ashore to talk with the Englishmen. The colonists held the three men captive and sent one of their own men out to the ship to inform the captain that he was not welcome. When the warship unlimbered its guns and made ready to fire, the commander of Fort Algernourne told him to "go to the devil" and made his own guns ready. That was enough for the Spanish captain who decided not to fight and sailed away with the fort's best cook. Two of the Spaniards died in captivity but the third man, a grandee, survived nearly two years of confinement at Jamestown and eventually was sent home. In his report to his king, Senor de Molina wrote that the fort at Point Comfort was "a weak structure of boards 10 hands high with 25 soldiers and four iron pieces" (cannons).

The government at Jamestown had difficulty supporting the garrison since the soldiers refused to farm or hunt and spent their time trying to keep their fort from being washed away by the tides. Many terrified colonists fled to the safety of this fort after the Massacre of 1622, over-taxing the crude facilities, but the Indians never attacked this lonely post. When a Dutch man-of-war raised havoc among the ships in Hampton Roads in 1667, the guns of Fort Algernourne proved ineffective. Although improvements were immediately begun, a hurricane that autumn washed everything away. Another Dutch vessel sailed past the ruins in 1673 and destroyed a number of ships in the James River without opposition, but this did not spur the colonists to refortify Point Comfort.

In 1699 the Governor of the colony recommended permitting all of Virginia's many forts to fall into decay since he did not have the funds to keep them up and was not worried about Indian or foreign attacks. In 1727, because of the danger from pirates, a replacement fort, Fort George, was built. It, too, was destroyed by a hurricane twenty-two years later. *See: Fort George; Fort Monroe*

FORT A. P. HILL
Caroline County

Covering 76,981 acres of scrub land, this army reservation was named for Confederate General Ambrose Powell Hill who was killed late in the Civil War during the siege of Petersburg. In the summer of 1981 the Boy Scouts held a huge international jamboree here that was such a success that it will be repeated in the future. *See: Powell River*

FORT BELVOIR
Fairfax County

The major home of the powerful Fairfax family was Belvoir on the Potomac River south of Alexandria. Colonel William Fairfax received a huge tract of land from his uncle, sixth Lord Fairfax, and built his mansion about 1741. This magnificent home was abandoned at the outbreak of the Revolution when most of the Fairfax family returned to England. Only Lord Fairfax remained during the troubled times but he lived in seclusion at Greenway Court in Clarke County. The land of Belvoir was confiscated by the Commonwealth and was left unattended. The house was destroyed by fire in 1783 while it was occupied by squatters. After the war the family unsuccessfully sued to regain title to this plantation and other properties. The state ruled that only those properties actually occupied by Lord Fairfax and his relatives would be released.

For about a century and a half, the fields and woodlands of Belvoir lay idle. The tract was deeded to the Federal Government in 1918 for use by the expanded Army Corps of Engineers. It has been the headquarters of the Corps ever since. The engineers had been tasked with creating and maintaining inland waterways during the nineteenth century, plus making a stab at flood control. Robert E. Lee was commissioned in the Corps of Engineers following his graduation from West Point. Among his assignments was the repair of the Mississippi River levee at New Orleans. The Corps has worked hard to control flooding in the interior of the nation by building dams, canals, and locks. In some instances the natural courses of rivers have been changed. *See: Belvoir of Fairfax*

FORT BLACKMORE
Scott County

Under the leadership of Captain John Blackmore a rude fort was built in 1774 on the Clinch River near the mouth of Stony Creek. It was erected to provide protection for the local settlers who were in constant danger of attack by Shawnees. The name has been continued by the village that occupies the site of the old fort.

FORT BOWMAN
See: Harmony Hall

FORT CHARLES
Hampton **Site**

In the late fall of 1609, George Percy, the acting governor of the colony, ordered two forts built between Kecoughtan Town and Point Comfort to serve as temporary quarters for newcomers while they were "seasoned" to the climate before mingling with those who had been in Virginia for a longer period of time. One post was named Fort Charles and the other Fort Henry, named for the sons of King James I. Because no new people came that winter, construction was delayed until after Lord Delaware's arrival in the spring of 1610. Hampton University occupies the site of Fort Charles; the Veterans Administration covers the site of Fort Henry. Neither of these two camps were forts in the military sense. They had no armaments and afforded scant shelter. The few guards assigned to them were taken away by Lord Delaware and sent up the James River in search of gold. The two places were permitted to fall to pieces. *See: Elizabeth City; Henricus; Richmond*

FORT CHISWELL
Wythe County

Today's community of this name occupies the site of Fort Chiswell, built in the autumn of 1760 under the supervision of William Byrd III. Settling down for the winter on the farm of Alexander Sayers, Byrd's men reinforced the pioneer farmer's cabin and added a powder magazine next to it. When the troops left in the spring, John McGavock gambled on future westward migration which he was certain would pass this point and built an ordinary and a trading post. Within a few years he added a mill and shops for a blacksmith and a carpenter, both vital to the maintenance of wagons that passed on the public road to Cumberland Gap. Fort Chiswell was named during the Revolution for John Chiswell, the first owner of the nearby lead mine that produced much metal for the Continental Army during the war and for the postwar surge of settlers who headed for Tennessee and Kentucky. *See: Austinville; Scotchtown*

FORT CHISTANNA
Brunswick County **Site**

This fort was built on the banks of the Meherrin River as a refuge for local settlers and friendly Indians from the marauding Iroquois. It was begun in 1714 and was slowly expanded. Under the sponsorship of Governor Alexander Spotswood, a school was established here for the benefit of the Nottoway and Saponi Indian children, the first successful attempt to integrate the two races through a common language (English) and Christianity. The school did not last long since the Indian elders realized their children were being taught the white's culture and were being weaned from the old traditional ways. When settlements spread beyond here to the west, the fort and school were abandoned. The site has been located in modern times and has been marked. The name is a direct combination of Christ and Anna (the queen) under whom Spotswood served. *See: Assamoosick Swamp; Ellerslie; Nottoway County; Saponi Indians*

FORT CHRISTIAN
Montgomery County **Site**

This important fort was erected in 1774 by Daniel Smith, a surveyor, engineer, and captain of the local militia company. It was named in honor of Colonel William Christian, the head of the Virginia militia in the Clinch Valley who also was Patrick Henry's brother-in-law. *See: Christianburg.*

FORT DEFIANCE
Augusta County

This name has been used in several locations by different generations. It is typically American. Each time the meaning was clear whether the enemy was Indian, British, French, Spanish, German, or Japanese. When the original fort here in Augusta County was taken and destroyed in 1755, during the French and Indian War, the Americans rebuilt a stronger fortification after the Indians left and defied them to try again. The Indians wisely did not try a second time. When the railroad came through here in 1874, a stop was scheduled at the village that retained the fort's name. It was Fort Defiance to the railroad, to the post office, and to the people who lived here.

FORT EUSTIS
Newport News

Named in honor of Brevet Brigadier General Abraham Eustis, who served as an outstanding artillery officer from 1808 to 1843, Camp Eustis was established in 1918 as an artillery base on Mulberry Island, a part of the Peninsula that was quite empty and uninhabited. In 1946, as Fort Eustis, it became the principal post for the new Army Transportation Corps. Today it is the Army's Transportation Center where officers and enlisted personnel are trained in all phases of movement of men and supplies whether it be by helicopters, trucks, railroads, or ships. Its ten square miles of land once supported several farms. An unusual activity here is the Army's fleet of small craft which operates from the Third Port. During the Depression, between World Wars I and II, the reservation was used as a training site for civilians where young men were taught automotive repair skills. *See: Fort Story; Mulberry Island; Queen's Hith; Stanley Hundred*

FORT GEORGE

Fort Monroe **Site**

When a hurricane washed away Fort Algernourne in 1667, no military barrier guarded the entrance to Hampton Roads and the vital James River for the next sixty years. Finally, Governor William Gooch, a man with an understanding of military preparedness, received the necessary funds to build another fort. Construction began in 1727. When complete, the installation was named Fort George in honor of King George II who ascended the English throne that year. No details of its design or strength exist today. It is thought to have been located about where the Chamberlin Hotel now stands. Twenty-two years after its completion, in 1749, another hurricane struck the Virginia coast and this fort also was washed away when heavy waves undercut the foundations.

The caretaker of the ruins, John Dames of Hampton, erected and maintained a small light tower to aid ships coming from the Atlantic that had to make a sharp left turn off Point Comfort to enter Hampton Roads. Dames' light was replaced in 1802 by a stone tower, still standing, that has been flashing a warning light to mariners ever since. However, from 1749 until Fortress Monroe was erected in 1819, no military establishment guarded the throat of Hampton Roads. *See: Fort Algernourne; Fort Monroe; Hampton; Old Point Comfort*

FORT HENRY

Dinwiddie County **Site**

Built in 1645 at the falls of the Appomattox River, this fort was garrisoned with forty-five men under Captain Abraham Wood. It was named for Prince Henry, son of executed Charles I. Some years later the House of Burgesses granted all of the land around the fort to Captain Wood who lived here for thirty years, long enough to see the old barricade evolve into a trading center of major importance. Wood's successor was Captain Peter Jones. *See: Fort Charles; Gloucester County; Ingle's Ferry; Petersburg*

FORT HUNT

Fairfax County

Established in 1897 as part of the defenses of Washington, D.C., for the expected war with Spain, this fortification was named in honor of General Henry Hunt, the chief of the Union artillery at the battles of Fredericksburg and Gettysburg. It is now the headquarters for the National Capital Park Police.

FORT JAMES

New Kent County **Site**

After the second massacre shocked the residents of southeastern Virginia in 1644, a few forts were erected along a palisade that stretched from the James River to the York. Other outposts were located at strategic points. One such outpost was built on the upper portion of the Chickahominy River (near the present hamlet of Lanexa) to keep an eye on the remnants of the Chickahominy tribe whose town was Maysonec. These Indians had pledged peace, but the English settlers wanted to make sure. The military camp was named Fort James in honor of James, Duke of York, the second son of King Charles I, who was then fighting for his father against the forces of Oliver Cromwell. (Virginia remained loyal to the Crown, in subtle ways, during the English Commonwealth.)

The first commander here was Thomas Rolfe, the son of Pocahontas and John Rolfe, both of whom were long dead by this time. Rolfe had come to Virginia three years previously to claim lands willed to him by his father. Governor William Berkeley appointed Thomas Rolfe a lieutenant of militia and sent him to this post since the young man was not suited to be a farmer. A restless halfbreed, he did not fit into Virginia's white society and had not been accepted by his Indian relatives who twice had tried to kill all of the English. Rolfe's duty in this remote site gave him the opportunity to prove his loyalty as an

Englishman for, having been snubbed by his kinsmen, he had decided to turn his back on them and forget his Indian heritage. For his duty at Fort George, Rolfe was granted 600 acres of land near the stronghold which he learned to farm successfully. Twelve years later he was granted an additional 300 acres which adjoined his farm. Fort James is called Fort Chickahominy in some old records.

Thomas Rolfe married Jane Poythress by whom he had one child, a daughter. She eventually married Robert Bolling. Thousands of people today claim direct kin to Pocahontas through this marriage which also produced one child, a son. *See: Kippax; Lee Hall of Lancaster County*

FORT LEE
Prince George County

Named for General Robert E. Lee, this installation was opened as Camp Lee during World War I. From 1927 to 1940 the reservation was under the control of the Commonwealth of Virginia which converted it to a wildlife reserve. Situated in rolling, wooded country, near the site of the Battle of the Crater of the Civil War, the untended land was opened at various times to hunters, hence the name reserve rather than preserve. The many acres were reoccupied by Federal armed forces for World War II and the installation was not closed completely at the end of that conflict: It became Fort Lee in 1950.

Here are located the U.S. Army Quartermaster Center and the Army Logistic Center, both mutually dependent and necessary for today's modern ground forces. Training takes place at Fort Lee for both officers and enlisted personnel.

FORT LEWIS
Bath County   Site

A fort was erected here in 1756 by a group of men under the command of Lieutenant Charles Lewis, the brother of General Andrew Lewis. This was one of a series of strong points built from Winchester to southwest Virginia to protect the settlers from Indians who were on the warpath as mercenaries, hired by the French during the French and Indian War. In this region the Indians were primarily Shawnees who loved to kill. Charles Lewis was a casualty in 1774 at the Battle of Point Pleasant during Dunmore's War. His brother, Andrew, was in command of the Virginia militia who were attacked by a host of Indians well led by Cornstalk. The Virginians were victorious

after a day-long fight. Charles Lewis was buried at the site of the battle. *See: Cricket Hill*

FORT LOUDOUN
Winchester   Site

After General Edward Braddock's defeat and death at Fort Pitt in 1755, Lieutenant Colonel George Washington assumed command and brought the surviving troops back to Winchester. There he found panic and confusion among the civilian populace which he quieted by his calm actions. He built a fort and manned it with 450 men armed with twenty-four cannons. It was named Fort Loudoun for the Earl of Loudoun, then commander-in-chief of all colonial forces in America. The Earl enjoyed the rank and title but did not come to the New World. This fort was never attacked and its many heavy guns were never fired against an enemy. But, since the French and their Indian allies were led to believe that it was impregnable, it served its purpose and kept that part of Virginia at peace during the rest of the international conflict. *See: Loudoun County; Winchester*

FORT MAYO
Patrick County   Site

This outpost was the southernmost fort in a line of stockades built in 1756 under orders of Governor Dinwiddie as frontier defenses. George Washington was in charge of its location, design, and construction. The first commander was Captain Samuel Harris.

FORT MONROE
Near Hampton

Named Fortress Monroe for President James Monroe who was in office at the time of construction, this moated stronghold guarding the entrance to Hampton Roads is the third fortification built here. Fort Algernourne was the first (1609) and Fort George the second (1727). Both fell victim to hurricanes. Work began on Fortress Monroe in 1819 and continued for many years. Made of granite, it was thoroughly engineered and perfectly designed. Robert E. Lee, who served here as a lieutenant shortly after graduating from West Point, spent his time supervising the construction of the moat.

This important fort remained in Federal hands all through the Civil War. General George McClellan began his Peninsula campaign to take Richmond from Fortress Monroe in the summer of 1862, and through this major base men and supplies were funneled to support his failed operation. For the rest of the War Between the States, no major campaign was begun here although it remained an important headquarters. After 1865, Jefferson Davis was held in a casemate in the outer wall for two years. His eventual release was brought about by the efforts of his wife Varina, newspaper editor Horace Greeley and countless others.

When the Spanish American War began in 1898 and Chesapeake Bay lay exposed to the unlocated "phantom fleet" of the Spanish, huge guns were installed outside the moat in concrete batteries. The Coast Artillery guns, with an exceptionally long range, could hurl a shell as far as the Capes, about 15 miles away. These guns rose up over the wall to fire and then settled back for reloading. Although they were never used except for practice, they served as the model for the sixteen-inch guns of the American battleships of World War II. During both World Wars, Fortress Monroe was the control point for electrically-operated underwater mines that protected the entrance to Hampton Roads.

Fort Monroe is still actively garrisoned but without firepower. The Army's Training and Doctrine Command uses the old brick and stone buildings of the only moated fort in America still on active duty. *See: Fisherman Island; Ft. Algernourne; Ft. George; Ft. Wool*

FORT MYER
Arlington County

On a part of the Custis-Lee property called Arlington Heights, General Amiel W. Whipple sent up a manned observation balloon on August 28, 1861, to spy on the Confederates surrounding the western approaches to Washington. When he was killed at Chancellorsville, Arlington Heights was named Fort Whipple. At first primarily an artillery and infantry post, it became the headquarters of the new Signal Service in 1869. When the first commander of that service, General Albert J. Myer, died in 1880 Fort Whipple was renamed Fort Myer, a name that has continued.

Shortly after 1880, the Signal Corps began making regular weather observations at the post which led to the founding of the U.S. Weather Bureau. By 1902, Fort Myer was used as a cavalry post which shared space with the Signal Corps. When the army decided to test the Wright brothers' flying machine, many flights were made from the north drill field. Since this was then a cavalry post, by order of the commanding general army officers who flew the machines had to wear spurs. In 1913 the U.S. Navy erected three steel towers at Fort Myer for its radio station, called Radio Virginia, to broadcast national and international news.

Since the early 1900s Quarters Number One here has been the official residence of the army's Chief of Staff. A unit from Fort Myer furnishes the honor guards for the Tomb of the Unknown Soldiers at Arlington Cemetery and provides military honors for all state funerals. As a remnant of its days as a cavalry post, the horses for the funeral caissons are kept here.

FORT NELSON
Portsmouth   **Site**

Fort Nelson, erected early in the Revolution as part of the defenses of Norfolk, was named for the Nelsons of York County. In May 1779 British troops commanded by General Edward Matthews stormed and easily captured the fort which was quickly evacuated by the outnumbered and timid garrison. The British then destroyed ships, naval stores, and tobacco and sailed from here to Suffolk on the Nansemond River where they burned that village. After these successful raids, the British retired to New York where they reported their activities to General Clinton. This was a delayed revenge for the Americans' stunning defeat of the last royal Governor, Lord Dunmore. *See: York Hall*

FORT STORY
Virginia Beach

This is the site of the first landing by the Jamestown settlers who touched Virginia soil on April 29, 1607, after a long voyage from England in three small ships. Later this hump of land, at the mouth of Chesapeake Bay, was named Cape Henry for the Prince of Wales. No attempt was made to settle here for centuries because it was too exposed to storms coming from the north over Chesapeake Bay or from the east over the Atlantic.

The first structure erected, Cape Henry lighthouse, dates from 1791. The original brick tower still stands although it no longer flashes its light since it has been replaced by a more modern structure. At the end of the nineteenth century, the Federal government established an army camp at the base of the lighthouse which was named for Major John Patton Story, an officer of the Coast Artillery. Today Fort Story is a satellite station of Fort Eustis. *See: Fort George*

FORT WITTEN

Tazewell County **Site**

About 1767 Thomas Witten settled his family on a tract then known as Big Crab Apple Orchard. He built his solidly-constructed house in the upper Clinch River Valley. Since it was a private dwelling, it was never officially recognized or garrisoned by the colony. *See: Battle Knob*

FORT WOOL

Hampton Roads

Just across the main shipping channel from Fort Monroe is Fort Wool, constructed on an artificial island. Authorized in 1825, the small fortress was not built until 1844 during the war with Mexico, a rather strange time to improve the defenses of Hampton Roads but probably as good a time as any to get Congress to appropriate the money. When it was completed, it was named Fort Calhoun for John C. Calhoun who twice had been vice president. At the outbreak of the Civil War, it was occupied by Union forces and its name was changed since John C. Calhoun was a Southerner. It was renamed Fort Wool for Major General John E. Wool who occupied Norfolk on May 10, 1862, and who, shortly thereafter, was the commander of Fortress Monroe. Last fitted with active guns during World War II, it is now owned by the city of Hampton.

FOTHERINGAY

Montgomery County

This house, built in the late years of the eighteenth century for George Hancock, was one of the first major homes to display the new Federal style of architecture that calls for a boxy shape, tall windows with flat arches above the lintles, and steep roofs. The name recalls the sad fate of Mary, Queen of Scots, who was beheaded at Fotheringay Castle in 1587 on orders of her cousin, Queen Elizabeth I.

FOUR MILE TREE PLANTATION

Surry County **Site**

Just across the James River from Jamestown, near Smith's Fort, lay 150 acres that were patented in 1624 by John Burrows. He called his place Burrow's Hill. On the land was a huge tree that marked the western boundary of the limits of the James City Corporation, giving rise to the name Four Mile Tree. In 1628 Burrows sold the land to John Smith (not *the* Captain John Smith who

had returned to England in October 1609) who changed the name of the farm to Smith's Mount. Sometime after 1637, Major Henry Browne bought Smith's holdings. A part of this tract was sold to Colonel George Jordan, the colony's Attorney General, at the same time that Jordan was acquiring the lands he called Eastover. The balance of the property remained in the Browne family until the end of the nineteenth century. Colonel Jordan's wife was buried on this tract in 1650 and, at his request, he was buried beside her "in Major Browne's orchard." *See: Eastover; Mount*

FOXCROFT

Loudoun County

Between the Blue Ridge Mountains and the Bull Run Hills is the first brick house constructed in Loudoun County. It was built in 1733 for Robert Kyle, a lawyer who had come from England just a short while before. He married Jane Ball who, soon after bearing him a daughter, lost her mind. She was chained in the garret to keep her out of sight, a common practice in those days, since the insane were either thrown into jail or confined in some horrible asylum if there was one organized for those thought to be lunatics.

One day when Kyle was away on business, his wife slipped her chains and made a mad dash for freedom. She was fatally injured when she tripped and fell down the stairs. Reportedly, her ghost haunts this old house. In 1925 when foundations for a new house were being dug in the old orchard, the skeletons of a man and a woman were found. Presumed to be the bones of Kyle and his wife, they were reburied under the apple trees of their orchard. *See: La Grange*

FOXHALL'S MILL

Westmoreland County **Site**

On property owned by a Major Underwood in 1670, a vein of iron ore was discovered about 1720 which led to the establishment of the Bristol Iron Works a year later. Nothing is known about the old mill. *See: Bristol Iron Works*

FRANKLIN

Southampton County **City**

Originally this community was called Southampton for the Earl of Southampton for whom the county was named. However, confusion existed between this place and Southampton Court House (which was at Jerusalem). When the county seat's name was

*BENJAMIN FRANKLIN,
FRANKLIN COUNTY*

changed to Courtland, the people here decided to change the name of their town too, and they called it Franklin in honor of the man from Pennsylvania, Benjamin Franklin. This was about 1788.

FRANKLIN COUNTY

Formed in 1785 from parts of Henry and Bedford counties, and later added to from a bit of Patrick, this county honors Benjamin Franklin. The name appeared in the enactment bill without explanation. The courthouse is at Rocky Mount.

FRANKTOWN
Northampton County

In 1764 the settlement here was called New Towne, one of several throughout Virginia to bear that name. When Frank Andrews operated a general store, those who depended upon his establishment for staples said they went to Frank's, and when a tiny community developed around his place, the residents decided to call it Frank's Town since he was the leading figure—and probably owned much of the property.

FRASCATI
See: Barboursville

FREDERICK COUNTY

Formed from Orange in 1738, this county was named for Frederick, Prince of Wales. He was the son of King George II and, at the time the county was organized and named, he was expected to become the king of England after his father died. Most likely he would have been Frederick I, a new name for an English monarch. However, George II fooled everyone and lived to the ripe age of seventy-seven, outliving his eldest son. When he died, the crown went to his grandson who became George III. By coincidence this county was formed the same year the future king was born. The county seat originally was called Frederick Town, but the name was changed to Winchester in 1752 for the cathedral city in England.

FREDERICKSBURG
Spotsylvania County   **City**

Captain John Smith sailed up the Rappahannock River to its falls in 1608 and there met some rather unfriendly Indians. Just who was the pioneer to first make his home here is not a matter of record, but there are indications that a settlement was attempted about 1617. The first official recognition occured in May 1671 when Governor William Berkeley granted to Thomas Royston and John Buckner a section of land that now lies within the old part of Fredericksburg. The land grant was described as adjoining the lands of Captain Lawrence Smith, who also was an early settler. Smith was the commander of the fort that was built three years later for protection against the Indians. The fort was named Fort Frederick in honor of the Prince of Wales.

In 1727 a community was laid out on property known as Leaselands and was incorporated as a town which took the name of the fort. Fredericksburg became an important trading center for the region. The county courthouse was located here in 1732 but was later moved to an isolated spot some ten miles away, closer to the center of the county.

During the Civil War, Fredericksburg was the scene of a major battle on December 13, 1862 which ended in a barren Southern victory for General Lee.

Federal troops under General Ambrose Burnside crossed the Rappahannock River and stormed the Southern-held heights overlooking the town.

The battle ended in a repulse with heavy loss for the Federals.

Today the battlefield and other related areas are maintained and preserved by the National Park Service. *See: Brompton; Chatham of Stafford; Ferry Farm; Frederick County; Germanna; Kenmore; King's Highway; Spotsylvania County*

FREDERICK'S HALL
Louisa County

The first president of the Louisa Railroad was Frederick Overton Harris. He had a station built near his home, Frederick's Hall. A small community developed around it.

FREEDOM HILL
Fairfax County

When Fairfax County was formed in 1742, the first courthouse was built on land known as Spring Field. When the county seat was moved to Alexandria in 1752 the old site slowly withered away. (Today it is the bustling commercial center of Tyson's Corner.) Old Spring Field was later known as Freedom Hill, possibly because freed slaves gathered here in great numbers enroute to the District of Columbia where they expected the Federal Government to take care of them. The hill is merely a rise in the terrain.

FRENCH ORDINARY
York County   **Site**

A tavern was built about 1680 on the road from Williamsburg to Yorktown near the intersection of the road from Martin's Hundred. The tavern served as the courthouse of York County from 1681 until 1697. The site of the ordinary lies on a ridge of ground between the head of King's Creek and the western branch of Felgate's Creek. Nearby was Kiskiak Church.

French physicians practiced in York County in the middle of the seventeenth century. Those who are known were Dr. Giles Mode (changed to Moody), Dr. John Peteet (which became Pettit), and Dr. Peter Plovier (or Plouvier). There is no evidence to link this ordinary with any of these men, but it is a matter of record that French settlers lived in York County in the late seventeenth century and there was a settlement called Frenchtown near Delaware Town in the early eighteenth century. It is not known if these people were Huguenots or people of French extraction who had come from England. However, the fact that there were three physicians living near the ordinary, and a church was built here too, indicates that the intersection of these two roads was a place of major importance in days gone by. The site lies within the reservation of the Yorktown Naval Weapons Station and can be visited only through special arrangements. *See Kistack; Ordinary; Penniman; York County*

FRENCHTOWN
King William County   **Obsolete**

Runaway slaves often were captured and detained by landowners until their ownership could be determined. Often there was a reward for their return. In 1724 several runaways were caught "40 miles from ye frenchetown where said slaves" belonged. Five French families were known to be living in the Pamunkey Neck region at a very early date. *See: Delaware Town; Huguenots*

FRONT ROYAL
Warren County   **Town**

The early name for this community was Lehewtown for Peter Lehew on whose land the town was platted. A giant oak, which the locals called The Royal Oak for its size and solidity, stood in the square. British troops quartered here before and during the Revolution always formed ranks aligned with the tree in response to the command by their sergeant, "Dress the front rank on the Royal Oak!" Gradually this was shortened to "Front on the Royal!" By 1788 the name Lehewtown had slipped into oblivion and Front Royal was the accepted name of the town. *See: Boscobel*

FRYING PAN RUN
Prince William County   **Site**

The name of this stream continues in general use, but the origin of the name is anyone's guess. In 1728 deposits of what was thought to be copper were discovered here. Robert "King" Carter founded a mining company to work the land that he had acquired "in the Frying Pan region." When Thomas Lee refused to let him cross his land to bring the ore to the Potomac, Carter cut a new road to the Occoquan River and erected a warehouse and wharf at Colchester. This road, named Ox Road, is presently covered by State Highway 123 which runs south from the city of Fairfax. All this preparation was in vain, however, since the copper ore turned out to be nothing more than green sandstone. On the other hand, the construction of Ox Road led to the future development of the interior lands of Fairfax and Loudoun counts. *See: Colchester; Goldvien; Run; Springfield*

FURNACE

To extract metal from ore, tremendous heat is required which must be concentrated in a stone or brick furnace. The actual process begins with the reduction of the ore to small pieces and then heating the rubble in an enclosed cylinder or cone. Primitive furnaces permitted the melted metal to collect on the ground; later a crucible was placed in the bottom which had a spout from which the liquid metal could drain into molds to form "pigs." The modern term *smelting* did not come into use until the middle of the nineteenth century when coal was used for the fuel.

The first Furnace at Falling Creek, built in 1619, used charcoal, a fuel that was used in many Virginia furnaces until as late as the Civil War. In any case, whether coal or charcoal was used, the iron was actually a mild grade of steel since the fuel added carbon to the iron during the melting process. It has been estimated that in the thirty years between 1826 and 1855, fifty charcoal furnaces were at scattered locations throughout Virginia from the Potomac River to Smyth County in the far southwestern corner of the Commonwealth. At the end of this period it was discovered that Pennsylvania anthracite coal produced a good grade of iron more efficiently than charcoal and the primitive process was discarded.

The Civil War forced the resumption of the charcoal furnaces to provide supplies for the Tredegar Iron Works of Richmond when the supply of anthracite from Pennsylvania was cut off. It was not until 1864 that the Union army thought to destroy the sources of iron supply to the Confederacy and then, in most cases, the destructive efforts were half-hearted. The heart of the system, the stone towers, seldom were pulled down so that the Southerners could quickly make repairs to the supporting equipment and get back into production. The last two iron smelters in Virginia ceased operation in 1888. *See: Wilderness*

GAINSBORO
Frederick County

This old village was laid out in 1798 under the name of Pughtown. The origin of the present name is obscure. It could have been in honor of the famous English painter, Thomas Gainesborough, who died in 1788, but this is only a guess. More than likely it was named for a local resident.

GAINES MILL
Hanover County   **Site**

A mill stood beside Powhite Creek prior to the Civil War. It was owned by a local physician, a Dr. Gaines, whose home was on a bluff overlooking Richmond.

During the Seven Day Battles of the Civil War, the Union Army defended a strong position in the vicinity of Gaines Mill.

Taking place on June 27, 1862, the entrenched Federals were attacked by poorly coordinated Southern commanders.

The Confederates took a heavy toll, but encouraged personally by General Lee, General John Bell Hood's Texans led an attack which succeeded in breaking through the Union line and saved the day for the boys in gray. *See: Powhite Creek*

GAINESVILLE
Prince William County

When the railroad acquired a right-of-way through his land in 1850, Thomas Gaines insisted that the company schedule a stop here for the convenience of himself and his neighbors. The railroad complied and named the depot Gainesville. Eventually a village grew around the flag stop.

GALAX
Carroll and Grayson Counties   **City**

This city was named for the galax plant which grows naturally and abundantly on the sides of the nearby mountains. The leaves are shipped to florists all over the United States for use as fillers in floral arrangements. Galax is most noted for its annual Old Fiddlers' Convention which was begun in 1935 under the sponsorship of the local Moose Lodge. The event is dedicated to "keeping alive the memories and sentiments of days gone by." The county line divides this city in half. The original name was Bonaparte which was changed to Galax in 1906 when the town was incorporated.

GATE CITY
Scott County   **Town**

Near the Tennessee border, this village calls itself the "Gate-way to the Smokey Mountains." Not yet a city but an incorporated town, it is the county seat.

GEORGE MASON UNIVERSITY
Fairfax

Opened in 1957 as an extension of the University of Virginia, this institution was named in honor of George Mason IV, the patriot who lived in the county at Gunston Hall. First a community college, it expanded to a four-year college ten years after its founding. It was upgraded to university status in 1977.

GEORGES TAVERN
Powhatan County

In colonial times, George's Tavern stood here on the Three Chopt Road. It was an important stage stop some forty miles west of Richmond. When a post office was established to serve the small community that grew near the old tavern, the obvious name was George's Tavern. *See: Three Chopt Road*

GEORGE WASHINGTON NATIONAL FOREST

Made up of three separate sections along the Blue Ridge, Massanutten, and Shenandoah mountains, this park contains more than one million acres. It encompasses the area supervised by Lieutenant Colonel George Washington who was ordered by Governor Dinwiddie, in 1756, to build a series of protective forts along the frontier. During special seasons, public hunting under strict supervision is permitted by the National Park Service.

GERMANNA
Orange County

Swiss Baron von Graffenried brought a group of miners from the German Palatinate in 1713 to work a vein of silver in Massanutten Mountain in the Shenandoah Valley. When the vein played out rather quickly, the Baron leased his miners to Alexander

Spotswood to work his newly-opened iron mine on the Rapidan River. Twenty more families came from the Rhine valley three years later to join Spotswood's work force. He called the settlement (and the mine) Germanna, a combination of *German* and *Anna*, his queen, for whom the river was also named (the Rapidan). At the end of their terms of indenture, the miners left, some going north into Faquier County where they grouped together on farms in a settlement called Germantown, and others going south to the Robinson River in what was later to become the heart of Madison County.

When the Germans left, Spotswood put blacks to work in his mine and at his furnace and production dropped. It was during this time (1716) that the Governor led his expedition into the Shenandoah Valley with his Knights of the Golden Horseshoe. In 1722, while he was in northern New York to negotiate a treaty with the Six Nations of Indians, he was relieved of his governorship. Undaunted by this reversal of his status within the government, (others who had lost the post of governor had returned to England) Alexander Spotswood moved to Germanna to supervise his mining-smelter-ing venture and to take a good look at the land that he had deeded to himself while the chief executive of the colony.

About 1726 he began the construction of his home. Little is known of this structure, but contemporary writers who visited there told of terraced gardens, marble fountains, and many spacious rooms. William Byrd II, that constant traveller, visited Spotswood in 1732 and wrote in his diary about the "Enchanted Castle" and, of course, about the ironworks.

At the time of his death in 1740, Alexander Spotswood owned 85,000 acres. His widow, Anne, lived for many years after him. She came to a strange end at La Grange in 1775. *See: Criglersville; Federal Hill; Hebron Church; La Grange; Massaponnox; Swift Run Gap*

GERMANTOWN
Fauquier County   **Obsolete**
Some twenty-five miles north of German-na, Alexander Spotswood's former inden-tured miners resettled on a collection of farms which became known as Germantown, even though no town was ever established. There is some evidence that their Lutheran clergyman, who had come with them from the German Palatinate in 1613, had en-couraged them to leave the employ of Spotswood as soon as their terms of indenture had been completed. In their Fauquier County commune, twelve families pooled their talents and their profits for their mutual benefit. They organized a church which was their own form of Evangelical Reformed Lutheranism. Two years after they arrived they harvested a bumper crop of tobacco and slaughtered some of the fattest beef in all of Virginia.

Germantown was so spread out that it never resembled a village. By 1746 the homes of their descendants were so dispersed by the addition of more cropland that Germantown ceased to exist as a separate entity and was more a district of the county. In this region Thomas Marshall, a surveyor who acquired land on Licking Run in 1754, built his home. The first of his nine children was John Marshall, the famed Chief Justice. *See: Hebron Church; Midland; Oak Hill of Fauqier*

GILES COUNTY
Parts of Montgomery, Tazewell, and Mon-roe counties were joined in 1806 to form Giles County. It was named for William B. Giles, a U.S. Senator from Virginia at the time. He was a native of this region. Giles became the Governor of the Commonwealth in 1827. The courthouse of this county is at Pearisburg.

GINGASKIN INDIANS
Northampton County   **Site**
Three miles east of the present town of Eastville was the main village of the Gingaskin Indians, one of the largest tribes on the Eastern Shore. Remnants of this tribe lived here until as late as 1860. By then they had been absorbed by marriage with the white populace and all trace of their culture has been lost. From their first contact with the early settlers, this tribe was always friendly. *See: Cheriton; Dale's Gift*

GLAD SPRING
Smyth County   **Town**
Named by Captain James Byars, who had a farm here in the early 1700s, the first hamlet adopted the name of a spring that fed water into the Middle Fork of the Holston River. Possibly Captain Byars's farm was called Glade Spring.

GLADYS
Campbell County
When this was the site of a relay station for

the mail carried by riders, Connelly's Tavern was the main structure. Later the old tavern was called Pigeon Run for the many wild pigeons that roosted everywhere. The creek that supplied water for the residents was named Big Glades using the Old English word *glade* which means a bright, smooth place. In the old manner, the people pronounced it GLAYD-ess. By 1856 the tiny village was Glad-es-ville. When the post office was established, the name Gladesville was too similar to Gladeville, a town in West Virginia. Therefore, the new name was Gladys, a feminine name which retained the former pronunciation. *See: Saxis*

GLASGOW
Rockbridge County   **Town**

Joseph Glasgow built a fine brick home here in 1810. After his death, the house was allowed to go to ruin. In 1890 a company headed by the former Confederate General Fitzhugh Lee attempted to build a large hotel, power plant, and local industries on the Glasgow property. After remodeling the old house, the company ran out of funds and the project ended. A modest town grew around the remains of the venture which today is a corporate entity. Novelist Ellen Glasgow, who was born in 1874 and was a descendant of the original owner of the property on which the town flourished, often spent time here. *See: Edinburgh*

GLASS
Gloucester County

Although the surname Glass is more commonly associated with Senator Carter Glass of the Shenandoah Valley, a local merchant of the same last name was the first postmaster for this little community.

GLEBE

Any house or land that was owned by a parish for the use of the rector was called the glebe. Thus, the word was seldom used by itself but was coupled with the name of the parish. A glebe house was the rectory, the home provided for the rector. In some of the wealthier parishes, the glebe lands were more than the minister needed and the congregation owned black slaves to work the fields. The profits from the sale of the tobacco, or whatever crop was raised, were used to support orphans and those in need.

In some parishes it was necessary for the parson to work part of the glebe to raise food to feed his family. By law during colonial times the vestry of each parish was required to purchase at least two hundred acres for the glebe. They had to build a convenient house, kitchen, barn, dairy, meathouse, and cornhouse and fence in a garden plot. The rector's salary was supposed to be 1,600 pounds of tobacco per year, but only the wealthier congregations ever managed to pay that much and often the tobacco was of the poorest grade.

Parishes were identified by clergymen for the strain of tobacco used to pay their annual salaries. "Sweet-Scented" was more popular with smokers and brought a better price than the harsher "Oronoco." In the early 1700s, the Parson of a Sweet-Scented Parish could count on receiving about £120 when his leaves were sold. A man serving an Oronoco Parish had to be content with £80. The 16,000-pound allowance was reduced by mid-century, and, when the price of the best tobacco fell to two pence per pound, most clergymen were nearly destitute. They fed their families on what they could raise on the glebe land's expanded garden plot.

GLEBE CHURCH
Old Nansemond County

It is unusual for a church to be called Glebe Church since all churches had glebe lands attached to them. When this building was erected in 1738 it was Bennett's Creek Church, named for the creek that bore the name of the principal family of the region. This is one of the few churches in Virginia that has managed to retain its original glebe lands. The 300 acres, on the east side of the Nansemond River, yield an income that is shared by this church and St. John's of Chuckatuck.

GLEN ALLEN
Henrico County

A resort was built here in the 1870s by Benjamin B. Allen. It attracted young people from Richmond and it resounded with activity for many years. After the turn of the century, when the resort had lost its popularity, the land was divided into small parcels and was sold for home sites.

GLENDOWER
Albemarle County

This is a typical Scottish name which most likely was the old country family home of Edward Scott who patented 550 acres "on the north side of the Fluvanna (now the upper

James) at a place called Totier." The house still stands in the Green Mountain District of Albemarle between the Rockfish and Hardware Rivers that empty into the James River upstream from Scottsville. In this small house, built about 1735, the county of Albemarle was organized. Samuel Scott, the son of the original landowner, gave his bond that year, 1745, to build a public warehouse by the river on land owned by his brother Daniel. *See: Albemarle County; Scottsville.*

GLEN LYN
Giles County

This village has had a variety of names, each with a different flair. When John Toney settled here in 1750 he called his home *Montreal*, the French word for "royal mountain." *Glenn Lynn*, which is Scottish for "lovely glen," was adopted by the local residents in 1883. When the workmen came through the region while building the N & W Railroad, they blew off enough steam in the local taverns to give the name Hell's Gate to the community. However, when the Appalachian Power Company's plant was built in 1919 the more sedate Glen Lyn (with one "n" this time) was adopted as the official name of the post office.

GLOUCESTER COUNTY

Formed in 1651 from York, this county was named in honor of Prince Henry, Duke of Gloucester, the third son of Charles I. For many years there was no town in the entire county and the seat of county government had little more than the courthouse, a clerk's office, a jail, and a tavern or two. It was not until 1769 that the House of Burgesses ordered a town to be laid out at Gloucester Court House. In the enabling act, the name Botetourt was given to this new town to honor the current Governor, Norbourne Berkeley, Baron de Botetourt. This was the same year that Botetourt County had been organized in the upper part of the Shenandoah Valley, causing all sorts of confusion when Gloucester County affairs were recorded as having been conducted in Botetourt Town. After a few years of this confusion, the name Botetourt was dropped and the county seat reverted to Gloucester Court House. Many years later, a hotel was built next to the small town square. It resurrected the old name when it was called the Botetourt Hotel. This is now the courthouse annex. Gloucester is pronounced *GLOSS-ter* in New England, but in Virginia it's *GLAW-ster* in the English tradition. *See: Fort Henry; Long Bridge Ordinary; Poplar Spring Church*

GLOUCESTER POINT
Gloucester County

Known as Tyndall's Point in colonial times, this lower end of the county that guards the northern side of the mouth of the York River, just across from Yorktown, has been a strategic point in two conflicts. A fort of earthworks was thrown up by British marines when Lord Cornwallis occupied Yorktown in the late summer of 1781 to give him control of the river. When the English were surrounded by American and French troops in September of that year, Allied marines swooped down upon the Gloucester Point outpost and carried the redoubt after a sharp, brief attack cutting off Cornwallis's avenue of retreat. The capture of Gloucester Point was equally as important to the eventual surrender of the besieged British as was the taking of two redoubts outside of Yorktown.

During the Civil War the Confederates rebuilt the earthworks in an attempt to control traffic entering or leaving the York but they were evicted in 1862. Union troops occupied and held the point for the rest of the war.

The region of Gloucester Point was sparsely settled until the middle of the twentieth century when a high drawbridge was built to replace the ferry. After the bridge gave quick access from the Peninsula to the lower section of Gloucester County, homes and business places sprouted. At Gloucester Point is located the Virginia Institute of Marine Sciences, a research organization that looks into the lives and habits of sea creatures that are harvested by the seafood industry. *See: Little England of Gloucester; Sarah Creek; Timberneck Hall; Tyndall's Point*

GOLANSVILLE
Caroline County

In the 1750s when Quakerism reached its zenith in Virginia, the Society of Friends had a meeting house here. Known as Golan's Meeting House for many years, the name was changed to Golansville about a hundred years ago. No place in Virginia today uses *meeting house* in its name although there were a number of such names prior to the Civil War.

GOLDBOND
Giles County

When the National Gypsum Company

came here in 1945 and opened a plant, the previous name of Olean (by which the tiny hamlet had been known for many years) was changed to Goldbond, one of the company's trade names.

GOLD MINES

The great motivating force behind the establishment of a colony in the New World by the English was the desire to find gold in amounts equal to that which Spain had been stealing from Central and South America since the years immediately following Columbus' landing at Santo Domingo in 1492. Most of the gentlemen who came to Virginia in the Jamestown group of 1607 felt certain that they would become rich when they found the mother lodes, the mythical Indian gold mines. Captain John Smith had his hands full to keep his men working on the necessities of life—food and shelter—when they preferred to dash off into the wilderness to find riches. The fact that the local Indians did not wear gold ornaments, but fancied copper instead, did not deter the searchers, many of whom were killed by the Indians who objected to strangers running around in their forest.

No gold was found until the late seventeenth century when a few nuggets were panned from the streams of the Allegheny Mountains. It was not until 1830 that a significant vein was found. The Morrow Mine in Buckingham County, near Dillwyn, was moderately successful. Once the news was noised abroad, Buckingham County saw a modest gold rush and a few other mines were opened, but the amounts of gold recovered in the underground digs was insignificant. All of the old mines have been closed as commercially unworkable. *See: Mineral*

GOOCHLAND COUNTY

Formed in 1727 from Henrico, this county was named for the man who became the Governor of Virginia that year, William Gooch. This county was a huge territory from which many other counties were later formed. During the twenty-two years that Governor Gooch served, much of the western portion of the colony was settled, particularly in the Piedmont. The Jeffersonian-styled courthouse, at Goochland Court House, was erected in 1826 by Dabney Cosby and Valentine Parrish, the master builders who constructed many of the original buildings at the University of Virginia. *See: Albemarle County*

GOOSE CREEK
Loudoun County

That portion of the Potomac River above the Great Falls was, for countless centuries, a gathering place for geese during the spring and autumn migrations. The Indians called this region *Cohingarooton*, which means Goose River. The lower portion was called *Patawokmeke*, the River of Swans. Eventually the entire river was known as the Potomac, but one of the tributary streams kept the name Goose Creek.

In 1736 a Chapel of Ease was erected on Goose Creek, the first church of any sort in Loudoun County. It was served, infrequently, by the rector of Pohick Church which was a long distance away. Not far from the chapel was Goose Creek Meeting House, a Quaker center. The old stone meeting house, now used as a cottage, was built before the Revolution.

GORDONSDALE
Faquier County

The Reverend Alexander Scott came to Virginia from Scotland in 1711. While serving as the rector of Overwharton Parish, he received a grant of land. When he died his brother, the Reverend James Scott, inherited the property and let it lie unused. James's son, John, was sent to Scotland at the age of eighteen after taking part in a duel. There he attended King's College in Aberdeen and, like his father and his uncle, was ordained by the Church of England. Prior to being sent to Maryland in 1768 to be the Anglican chaplain of Sir Robert Eden, the royal Governor of that colony, he married Elizabeth Gordon.

After a brief stay in Maryland, the Reverend John Scott was ordered to leave because he involved himself too deeply in politics. Upon reaching Virginia, he was ordered to live no closer than 100 miles of Point Comfort since his reputation as a political meddler was already known by the government. He settled on his father's land in Fauquier County, built a log cabin, and named his estate Gordonsdale for his wife. He lived here rather peacefully until his death in 1785. *See: Aquia Church*

GORDONSVILLE
Orange County

Nathaniel Gordon operated an inn on the stage line prior to 1787. His establishment became famous for its chicken dinners, an item that was continued by his children and their children for many years. In 1855

103

Gordonsville was the terminus of the Louisa Railroad where passengers enjoyed the food at Gordon's Inn before continuing their journeys by stage coach or any other means available to them. When the Louisa Railroad was extended, the trains no longer stopped long enough for the passengers to patronize the old inn, so the townsfolk peddled the chicken at the cars through the opened windows. Later, the Orange and Alexandria Railroad terminated at Gordonsville to bring more people.

In the late nineteenth century, when George Pullman's sleeping cars created a need for dining cars, the railroads stocked up on dressed chickens at Gordonsville and used the name on the menu. The famous inn was razed after World War II despite a cry of public outrage.

GORE
Frederick County

Originally Cross Junction, where two roads from the mountains joined, the name was changed to Gore when the first post office was established. Although the Gore family was among several in the neighborhood, Mrs. S. S. Gore was a particularly active churchwoman and civic leader. The post office was named for her.

GOSHEN
Gloucester County

Built upland from the Ware River some time between 1750 and 1760, Goshen was the first seat of the Tompkies family. Over the years, the family name was changed to Tompkins, probably because that was the way the original name was pronounced.

VENDORS AT TRAIN, GORDONSVILLE

"Captain Sally" Tompkins, of Poplar Grove, was the only woman to have been an official member of the Confederate Army.

GOSHEN
Rockbridge County **Town**

Goshen was the Biblical "land of milk and honey." Early settlers thought this region fit the description and the resulting town was named Goshen. *See: Edinburg*

GOSPORT
Portsmouth **Obsolete**

When Colonel William Crawford made such a success of his land development in the founding of Portsmouth, a Scot by the name of Andrew Sprowle acquired land a short distance up the Elizabeth River and built a shipyard in 1767. The enterprise quickly made money for him, especially when the Royal Navy adopted the shipyard as its base and commissioned Sprowle as the agent. A small village grew up around the yard for the workers which the proud Scot named Gosport after the shipyard at Gosport, England, which is adjacent to the city of Portsmouth, for centuries the headquarters of the Royal Navy. Sprowle's shipyard remained under British authority until May 1776 when the last Royal Governor, Lord Dunmore, was forced to leave a camp near Portsmouth for the false safety of Gwynn's Island. Sprowle and his family left with the Governor and died on a ship in the Chesapeake Bay a short time later.

The navy yard became a base for the Virginia navy until it was raided in 1779 by Sir George Collier who destroyed the works and nine large warships that either were under construction or in for repairs. The shipyard was repaired and the new vessels were used during the last years of the Revolution. It became a U.S. Navy shipyard in 1794 and was seized by the Confederates at the beginning of the Civil War.

It was here that the USS Merrimac was clad with iron plates below the waterline to create the CSS Virginia, which fought the USS Monitor in Hampton Roads in the first Battle of the Ironclads. The battle was a draw with neither ship doing major damage to the other. When the Union forces occupied Norfolk, the Confederates blew up the Merrimac, burned the shipyard and left. The works were repaired and the yard has been in operation ever since.

Today it is known as the Norfolk Naval Shipyard although it is located in Portsmouth.

Gosport was annexed by its larger neighbor and that name is no longer used.

GOVERNOR'S LAND
James City County **Obsolete**

The Charter of 1618 authorized the first division of land among those who had been in the colony since "before the going away of Sir Thomas Dale" in 1616. Instructions with the Charter called for the establishment of farms to support a proposed college at Henrico and to provide food or income for the various officers, soldiers, and officials of the colonial government. One special parcel was laid out near Jamestown for the particular benefit of the Governor. Fifty new colonists were scheduled to work this land (few arrived). One half of the profits would belong to the farmers, the other half would be for the Governor as part of his salary.

In 1649, during his first term, Governor Sir William Berkeley founded his estate Green Spring adjacent to the Governor's Land. His primary lieutenant, William Drummond, was permitted to build his house on the edge of the Governor's Land and work a portion of it for his own benefit. It was Drummond's appointment as the Governor of Carolina that gave him this special remuneration, and it caused the assigned farmers to rebel and run away since their shares were greatly decreased.

During Berkeley's second term, after King Charles II was restored to the throne of England, Drummond and Berkeley argued over the use of the Governor's Land bringing on a severe break in their relationship. Drummond joined Nathaniel Bacon in the rebellion of 1676 for which he was hanged when captured at Brickhouse in Gloucester County. The vengeful Governor confiscated all of William Drummond's estate, leaving Drummond's widow without support for herself and her young children. She petitioned the king for redress and won her case. That portion of the Governor's Land that her husband had farmed became hers, and from then on it was no longer available to those who succeeded Berkeley.

Another tract, on the Eastern shore, which also was called the Governor's Land, was better managed. It provided an income for the soldiers who guarded "Ye Plantacione of Accawmacke." *See: Brickhouse; Green Spring*

GRACE CHURCH
Albemarle County

This little church in Cismont is the second

to stand here. The first was known as Walker's Church since the land upon which it was built was given by the Walker family of Castle Hill in 1745. At that time it was designated the Middle Church of Fredericksville Parish which had been created three years earlier and lay entirely within Louisa County until 1761. One of the first rectors was a former Jesuit priest, the Reverend Anthony Gavin. The Reverend James Fontaine Maury served Walker's Church from 1751 to 1769 and he was followed by his son, the Reverend Matthew Maury.

Of particular interest here at Grace Church, its current name, is the annual Blessing of the Hounds, an ancient custom that began in England. This part of Albemarle County is still "hunt country" although long cross-country chases are difficult to stage. Local farmers are reluctant to permit a pack of hounds and a troop of horses to trample their fields. *See: Castle Hill; Cismont; Maury's School*

GRACE CHURCH
Yorktown

The first two churches of this parish (once called Charles River Parish when the York River was the Charles) were built outside of the limits of Yorktown in accordance with an edict from an early governor who wanted all church property to be completely outside any town. The first church, built in 1642, was replaced in 1667 on a site that now lies within the Yorktown Coast Guard Reserve Training Center. When the building of 1667 had to be replaced, the third church was constructed within the village of Yorktown since the old "out of town" edict had been revoked. Governor Francis Nicholson subscribed twenty pounds of his own money for the small building, erected in 1697, using marl for the outer walls. Marl is a mixture of decomposing shells and clay that is somewhat moist when freshly cut, and, therefore, easy to shape, but which becomes nearly rock hard after exposure to the air.

During the disestablishment of the church during the Revolution, this building, like so many others in Virginia, was abandoned. When the British burned Yorktown in 1814 the old house of worship was destroyed, too. It was restored in 1848 by using what was left of the original walls and adding new marl as needed. During this period, the name was changed from York Parish to Grace Church.

In the quiet graveyard next to this historic edifice is the tomb of Thomas Nelson, Jr., a signer of the Declaration of Independence for Virginia and a Governor of the Commonwealth. *See: Charles River County; York Hall*

GRAFTON
York County

Once known by the delightful name Cockletown, the name of this village was changed to Grafton for the only church in the immediate neighborhood. It had been organized by a preacher who came to Virginia from Grafton, Massachusetts, in 1783. For those who knew, the name Grafton was not much better than Cockletown since the Massachusetts town had been named for the Dukes of Grafton, members of the FitzRoy family. The first Duke of Grafton was the bastard son of Charles II by his mistress Lady Castlemaine. The origin of the name Cockletown is obscure. Was it a garbled pronunciation of Kiccowtan? The hamlet lay astride the old road from Yorktown to Kiccowtan (Hampton).

GRAY
Sussex County

A school for black children was established in 1878 in Elam Church. The site was inconvenient for the majority of the pupils so it was moved to Piney Grove. A benefactor, and the first teacher, was Joseph N. Gray whose home was near Piney Grove. It was for him that this tiny community was named. In later years a lumberyard was established at Gray which provided employment for the local residents. When the Southern Railroad built a siding for the lumber products, the end of the spur was formally recognized as Gray.

GRAYSON COUNTY

In 1792 Wythe County was divided to form Grayson. It was named for William Grayson, one of the two men who were Virginia's first U.S. Senators. Old Town, about three miles from present Galax, was the first county seat. When Grayson County itself was divided in 1842 to form Carroll, the courthouse was rebuilt in a centralized location after a lengthy squabble. The new county seat was named Independence. *See: Independence*

GRAY'S POINT
Middlesex County

As far back as 1648 this point of land on the Piankatank River, a few miles east of Urbana, was known as Troublesome Point for reasons unrecorded. The original owner sold it to

William Gray in 1709 who bestowed his name upon it. Now no longer troublesome, it is the anchor of the southern end of a modern bridge that connects the Middle Peninsula with Northern Neck.

GREAT BRIDGE
Chesapeake

A small stockade was built in 1775 by British forces to command a causeway and bridge over swampy lands south of Norfolk. Virginia militamen slipped into a warehouse at the other end of the bridge. Lord Dunmore ordered his troops to attack. The resulting fight was a slaughter. Most of the British Regulars and accompanying Loyal Virginia Volunteers were mowed down as they attempted to cross the narrow wooden span. Not one of the defenders was hurt. After a futile second assault, in which more brave men were needlessly killed or wounded, the British withdrew to Norfolk where they were berated by the enraged Governor Dunmore who had been certain of success. This battle, fought on December 9, 1775, was the first of several that were won by the determined Virginians with a little help from North Carolinians. *See: Cricket Hill; Gwynn's Island; Norfolk; Windsor of Caroline County*

GREENBACKVILLE
Accomack County   Site

United States paper money has been printed with black ink on one side and green on the other for a long time. Bills, therefore, were once known as greenbacks. During the days of Reconstruction, when Confederate money was worthless, Southerners struggled to earn greenbacks to pay their living expenses. A group of watermen established a community on the upper end of Virginia's Eastern Shore, near the Maryland line, which they used as their base for a very successful fishing venture. They harvested great quantities of fish and dug mountains of oysters which they sold in markets in Baltimore, New York, and Boston. They were so successful, reaping stacks of greenbacks, that they named their community Greenbackville. Unfortunately, a series of devastating hurricanes in the first quarter of the twentieth century, wiped out the homes, packing shed, and boats ending the community. Today Greenbackville is a ghost town where little remains beyond a few pilings in the marsh and the skeletons of the fishermen's boats.

GREEN BAY
Prince Edward County

Two ordinaries competed for trade here in 1797, one operated by John Queensberry and the other by Mackness Rowlett. The names of the taverns are not in the history books, but since this hamlet has been known as Green Bay for nearly two hundred years and there is no bay within 125 air miles of the locality, undoubtedly the more popular tavern bore that name.

GREENE COUNTY

In 1838 Orange County was divided to form a new county. It was named for General Nathaniel Greene, the commander of the Army of the South during the Revolution. Unfortunately, the exploits of this wing of the Continental Army have been shoved into obscurity by the more famous activities of General Washington. It was General Greene's men, however, who pressed Lord Cornwallis all the way north from Georgia, depleting his men and supplies. Although the British managed to win nearly every battle, Cornwallis was heard to exclaim that if he continued to win any more battles (and lose more men) he surely would lose the war. He was ordered to Portsmouth for the winter of 1781-82 but disobeyed his instructions and took his troops to Yorktown. Nathaniel Greene and his veterans were on hand to see

GENERAL NATHANIEL GREENE
GREENE COUNTY

107

the British surrender in October 1781. The courthouse of Greene County is at Stanardsville. *See: Stanardsville*

GREENFIELD
Charlotte County

About a half-mile north of the present town of Charlotte Court House is a farm called Greenfield. It was first settled by Isaac Reed. He was a Burgess from 1769 to 1771 and attended the Virginia Conventions of 1774 and 1775. An officer in the Revolutionary army, he died of wounds in 1777.

GREEN SPRING
James City County   **Site**

On land between Powhatan Swamp and the James River, not far from Jamestown, once stood the magnificent manor house of Governor William Berkeley. It is thought likely that he moved into his home in 1649 where he remained a private gentleman during Cromwell's Commonwealth. He maintained contact with the exiled Prince Charles through the efforts of Richard Lee of Cobbs Hall. When Charles II came to the English throne at the Restoration in 1665, a different William Berkeley resumed the Governor's chair. Whereas during his first term he had managed to get along fairly well with the House of Burgesses, this time he quarreled with them, with the Council, with his neighbors, and with his lieutenant and colleague, William Drummond. No one seems to be able to explain his change in personality. It could be partly attributed to his younger and rather domineering wife, Lady Frances, and quite possibly to a mild stroke.

When Bacon's Rebellion in 1667 finally collapsed and the leaders were captured, Berkeley hanged forty men and confiscated the land and property of anyone who was thought to have been in sympathy with the rebels. For this heavy-handed vengence, he was recalled by Charles II who is reported to have said, "That old fool has hanged more men in that naked country than I did for the murder of my father." Berkeley's replacement was Baron Culpeper of Thoresway, one of the proprietors of Northern Neck.

William Berkeley's widow married her husband's former secretary, Colonel A. Phillip Ludwell, when the disgraced Governor died in England while waiting for an audience with the king to defend his suppression of the revolt. Lady Francis Berkeley and Colonel Ludwell moved across the James to Chippokes and rented Green Spring to subsequent governors since the official residence had been burned when Bacon put Jamestown to the torch.

Green Spring was impressive enough to have been a small palace. The foundations, uncovered some years ago, measured 160 by 52 feet. According to contemporary descriptions, the salons of the first floor were connected by a long gallery, ten feet wide, that stretched for the entire length of the house. The lower walls were thirty inches thick. The upper two stories contained thirty bedrooms and miscellaneous rooms. The mansion had been sited close by a "fine green spring whose waters are so cold that 'tis dangerous drinking thereof in the summer time." Green Spring had its own jail and gibbet along with numerous small dependencies. Lord Culpeper was quite happy to live here as was his successor, Lord Effingham.

Regretably, the manor house was demolished as unsafe in 1806 before the advent of photography. The only sketch available was made by the distinguished architect Benjamin Latrobe, who designed many of the public buildings in Washington, D.C. during Jefferson's presidency. *See: Chippokes; Cobb's Hall; Governor's Land; Jamestown; Old Dominion*

GREENSVILLE COUNTY

Formed in 1780 from Brunswick, this county probably was named for Sir Richard Grenville, the leader of the settlement of Roanoke Island in 1585. This county and Buckingham are the only two whose names cannot be traced with any certainty. If it was named for Grenville, nobody knows why the spelling includes the double "e." The county seat was once Hicksford, now Emporia.

GREEN VALLEY
Arlington County   **Site**

The Army-Navy Club of the Washington, D.C. area occupies the land of James Green, an early settler who named the farm for himself. The tract was leased to Daniel Frazer who, in 1821, built Green Valley Manor which was destroyed by fire in 1924. The present clubhouse is on the site of the original manor. The family cemetery, carefully isolated behind the golf course's twenty-sixth green, is guarded by an iron fence where many an iron shot has been made.

GREENVILLE
Augusta County

This village was named in honor of the

Revolutionary general, Nathaniel Greene.
See: Greene County

GREENWAY
Charles City County

About two miles west of Charles City Court House is Greenway, the first home of John Tyler, Sr. He moved here from Williamsburg shortly after marrying Mary Armistead. A close friend of Thomas Jefferson and Patrick Henry, the senior John Tyler was a member of the Virginia Committee of Safety in 1774. He was with Patrick Henry's group of volunteers at Doncastle's Ordinary during the gunpowder incident. Appointed one of the judges of the High Court of Admiralty for Virginia in 1776, he was elected a member of the General Assembly the following year. He was the vice president of the Virginia Convention of 1788 when the state constitution was adopted. Elected Governor of the Commonwealth in 1808, he died in 1813 and was buried at Greenway.

His son and namesake was born at this family estate in March 1790. John Tyler, Jr., who also served as Governor of Virginia, was the tenth President of the United States following the sudden death in office of William Henry Harrison, who was born just a short distance away at Berkeley. Although neither Harrison nor Tyler are especially well-remembered, they are well remembered for their campaign slogan, Tippicanoe and Tyler too. President Harrison served only a few weeks. He died of pneumonia which began as a cold he caught while delivering his inaugural address on the cold, wind-swept day of March 15, 1841.

President John Tyler sold Greenway in 1829. He bought Sherwood Forest while President and retired there with his second wife Julia Gardner after his one term in the White House. *See: Sherwood Forest*

GREENWAY COURT
Clarke County

Greenway Court was the last permanent residence of Thomas, sixth Lord Fairfax, Baron of Cameron, the Proprietor of Northern Neck. Born in Leeds Castle, England, in 1693, he settled in Virginia in 1747 when he inherited the huge Virginia tract. He moved to the lower (northern) end of the Shenandoah Valley in 1751 and spent the rest of his life at Greenway Court.

Lord Thomas Fairfax, the last Proprietor, inherited Northern Neck from his mother, a daughter of Thomas, Lord Culpeper, who had bought out the other Proprietors of this wilderness and reaped the rewards of countless quit-rents from those who lived on the land. Rich and financially secure as the sixth Lord Fairfax was, he seldom was happy. To begin with, he had come to Virginia an embittered man after losing an affair of the heart when his fiance suddenly married someone else. As a consequence, he became something of a woman hater and admitted no ladies to his parties. He always had difficulty finding honest men to collect his rents and was constantly required to go to court to make the renters pay.

He was a Tory during the Revolution, but, unlike his nephews and their wives, he chose to remain in Virginia during the entire conflict. Because of his early association with Lord Fairfax as one of his many surveyors, General George Washington permitted the reclusive lord to live unmolested. Although Fairfax was a landlord, he had no serious enemies and was one of the few acknowledged Tories who was not troubled by brigands or over zealous patriots. When the news came to him of Lord Cornwallis's surrender at Yorktown in October 1781, the old man took to his bed, turned his face to the wall, and murmured that it was time to die. Slightly more than a month later, in December of that fateful year, he did. *See: Belvoir; Fairfax County; Northern Neck; Winchester*

GREENWOOD
Albemarle County

An early eighteenth century settler Isaac Hardin named his home Greendwood. Notice that the original spelling contained an interior "d." Nothing is known of Hardin or his farm.

GREENYARD
Sussex

Hugh Belsches came to Virginia with his brothers Patrick and James about 1765. They were descendants of John Belsches, Baron Stritchel of Scotland. Soon after settling in the colony, Hugh married Martha Avery, the daughter of Colonel Richard Avery of Surry County. Together the newlyweds planned their house which was built of the finest materials and the best workmanship. They named their home Greenyard for the family home in Scotland.

GRETNA
Pittsylvania County   Town

In the years prior to the Civil War the major

establishment here was Sulphur Springs, the home of John Ward who freed all of his slaves in his will of 1826. A small community developed during the late nineteenth century on the Ward property which had a brief spell as a vacation spa where people could subject themselves to the waters that had a high sulphur content and a bad smell. This locality is linked with Gretna Green, a border village of southeastern Scotland to which many English couples eloped to be married under more relaxed Scottish laws.

GROTTOES
Rockingham County   **Town**

Named for the many coves in the hills nearby, this town began life as Shendun when it was incorporated in 1890. At that time it was alive with industry, predominently the Mount Vernon Forge which produced iron products from the locally mined ore. The boom became a bust by the turn of the century. To begin again, the town trustees reorganized the bankrupt town and reincorporated in 1912 as Grottoes.

GROVE
James City County

A section of the Carter's Grove plantation was called Black Swamp Quarter. Here many of the plantation slaves had their cabins. After the Civil War many former slaves decided to remain where they had been born rather than wander around looking for work. As many of the Carter's Grove field hands stayed here in their familiar cabins, the area for awhile was called Grove Quarter. The small collection of homes is now, simply, Grove. *See: Carter's Grove; Quarter*

GRUNDY
Buchanan County   **Town**

This town was named for Felix Grundy, a statesman who lived his adult life in Tennessee. The town of Grundy was incorporated in 1858.

GUILFORD
Accomack County

Guilford Quaker Meeting House stood in this vicinity for about fifty years. The local Quakers purchased a small piece of property from Edmund Scarburgh in 1686. The trustees confirmed the purchase in a document that read in part, "That the People of God Comonly called Quakers shall have

the right and priviledge from time to time to meet upon said ground . . . (in a) meeting house and there at pleasure to meet and bury their dead." By 1728 the Quaker movement in Virginia had died and the abandoned meeting house was left to fall down. *See: Hedra Cottage*

GUINEA
Caroline County

The name originally was spelled Guiney for the family that lived in this locality. This is the strawberry center of the county. In the home of Thomas Chandler, near Guinea, General Stonewall Jackson died of complications following the amputation of an arm that had been shattered by a shot fired by one of his own men. He died on Sunday, May 9, 1863.

GUINEA NECK
Gloucester County

You can take your pick of the possibilities about the origin of this name. It goes back to very early colonial times and no one is certain any more. Be certain, however, that the good people who live here now, on the extreme southeastern portion of the county, can trace their ancestry to very old Anglo-Saxon families. They do not care much for those who speculate about how this territory was named. Make your selection quietly: (1) Land here was rented to farmers at the rate of one guinea per year. A guinea is an obsolete English coin, last minted in 1813, that was worth one pound, one shilling in the old system. (2) Men who lived here hired themselves as farmers or laborers for one guinea for a set period of service. (3) The first settlers were sailors who (a) were shipwrecked after a voyage from Guinea in West Africa or (b) jumped ship and hid in the forest behind the marshes to avoid serving on a slaver bound for Guinea, a favorite place to buy slaves. (4) The first landowner's name was Guiney, or some variety of the name that was corrupted to Guinea.

GUM SPRING
Louisa County

On the old Three Chopt Road, about thirty miles northwest of Richmond, a fine, clear spring was marked by a huge gum tree. Long before taverns were established along this road, travellers refreshed themselves and their horses under the shade of the gum tree at the spring.

GUNSTON HALL
Fairfax County

Richard Turney patented land on Dogue's Neck in 1651. Turney's land was confiscated by Governor William Berkeley after he was hanged for taking part in Bacon's Rebellion. In 1696, George Mason II acquired Turney's land and passed it on to his heir. The present house was erected between 1755 and 1758 by George Mason II under the direction of the noted English architect William Buckland who had been brought to Virginia to work for George's brother. The estate was named Gunston Hall for the Staffordshire, England, residence of the ancestors of the Virginia lines of the Mason family.

George Mason was the author of the Declaration of the Rights of Man which he presented to the General Assembly on June 12, 1776. Adopted unanimously, it served as a model for the first ten amendments to the new U.S. Constitution, the Bill of Rights, which Virginia insisted upon as a condition for ratification.

Patrick Henry called George Mason the greatest statesman he had ever known. Thomas Jefferson said he was the wisest man of his generation. *See: Aquia Creek; Dogue Indians; Marlborough; Pohick Church; Woodbridge*

GWYNN'S ISLAND
Mathews County

Two royal Governors sailed from this island in the face of armed uprisings: Sir William Berkeley in 1676 during Bacon's Rebellion, and Lord Dunmore in 1776 at the beginning of the Revolution. Berkeley went to the Eastern Shore and managed to crush the rebellion. Lord Dunmore went to New York and never returned to Virginia.

Gwynn's island is about 2,000 acres in size, some of it barely three feet above sea level. It was named for Hugh Gwynn, a Burgess from what was, in his day, Gloucester County. It is said that he was given the island by Chief Powhatan for saving the life of Pocahontas when he pulled her from the Piankatank River across which she had tried to swim. If the story is true, she must have tried her crossing farther up river, for the Piankatank is at its widest here at its mouth where it enters Chesapeake Bay.

Between Gwynn's Island and the mainland of Mathews County is a strip of water called Milford Haven where the U.S. Coast Guard has an important station. The large marina on the Milford Haven side of the island is a favorite harbor for pleasure craft. *See: Cricket Hill; Gosport; Great Bridge; Milford Haven; Norfolk; Richfield; Stratton Manor*

H

HADENSVILLE
Goochland County

A colonial tavern stood here on the Three Chopt Road, operated by the Haden family. The tavern is long gone, but it is remembered in the name of a present day hamlet called Hadensville.

HALF WAY HOUSE
Chesterfield County

There were many taverns in colonial times which marked half-way points. Usually they had some other name as did this one, built in 1760 by William Hatcher and probably known as Hatcher's Tavern. Located half-way between Richmond and Petersburg, it gave shelter to many distinguished visitors. Among them were Washington, Lafayette, Patrick Henry, and Thomas Jefferson. *See: Cedar Level*

HALIFAX COUNTY

Formed in 1752 from Lunenburg, this county was named for George Montague, the second Earl of Halifax. Many historians call him the Father of the Colonies for his work as the president of the Board of Trade and Plantations from 1747 to 1761 during the reign of George II. Through his efforts, American commerce was greatly expanded. The port of Halifax, Nova Scotia, established in 1748, was named for him, as were counties in Virginia and North Carolina. The courthouse for this Virginia county was erected at a little town called Banister, named after the major stream in the region but that name disappeared when the county seat was incorporated as a town called Halifax Court House. *See: Banister River*

HALLWOOD
Accomack County   **Town**

Henry Hall married Mary Shaw in 1769. Her father gave the happy couple a tract of land as the bride's dowry. The resulting farm, known as Hallwood, gave its name to the present town.

HAMILTON
Loudoun County   **Town**

This town was named for James Hamilton, one of the first landholders here. He was born in 1720 and died in 1775.

HAMPDEN-SYDNEY COLLEGE
Prince Edward County

Formed in 1776 just six months before the adoption of the Declaration of Independence, the college was named for two English patriots: John Hampden and Algernon Sydney. Among those on the first board of trustees were Patrick Henry and James Madison. President William Henry Harrison was a member of the class of 1791. This college, one of the leading institutions of the Presbyterian Church, is located near Farmville.

HAMPSTEAD
New Kent County

Situated high on a bluff overlooking the Pamunkey River, this was the home of George Webb, Treasurer of the colony for many years. Hampstead is a borough of London. Various members of the Webb family were prominent in the social and political life of Virginia. They lie buried in the family plot near the site of the original house. The present mansion was built by Colonel Conrad Webb in 1820. Many of the huge boxwoods and trees on the old terraced gardens date from colonial times. After the Civil War, Colonel W. W. Gordon, of the Stone Wall Brigade, made his home here. *See: Manassas*

HAMPTON
City

After being attacked by Indians at Cape Henry when they first set foot upon Virginia's soil, the original Jamestown settlers came here four days later, April 30, 1607. They landed on the bank of a creek that, to their delight, was covered with wild strawberries. The friendly natives, the Kecoughtans, entertained them with a great feast and much ceremonial dancing. They assumed that the Englishmen were gods who had returned. They had been told that God would come to earth again by Spanish Jesuits who had been here briefly in 1525.

In 1609 the President of the Council, Sir George Percy, ordered Ft. Algernourne built about a mile away from the Indian village where it was to guard the entrance to the James River. The two dozen men of the garrison had nothing to fear from the friendly Kecoughtans who never attacked or molested them. In the spring of 1610, after the Starving Time which was forced upon the Jamestowners by Powhatan who forbade all trade with the newcomers in an attempt to starve them into submission, the Governor, Lord Delaware, adopted a policy of enmity between the English and all Indians within a fifty mile radius of Jamestown. When a member of Fort Algernourne's garrison was killed far from the Kecoughtan village, Sir Thomas Gates, Lord Delaware's Captain-General, used the incident to attack and occupy this peaceful village while the men were out on a hunt for game. Sir Thomas later wrote of his disappointment in the "few peas" and other minor booty he found. However, the local natives did not attempt to retake their homes but drifted off to parts unknown, under the leadership of their chief, Pochin.

The English occupation of the Kecoughtan village was the beginning of a town that is the oldest continuous English-speaking community in America. The first church here was erected in 1613. In 1619, when this region of the colony was formed into the Incorporation of Elizabeth City (one of four), the little town was well organized. The inlet on which it lay was named Hampton Creek honoring Henry Wriothesly, the Earl of Southampton, a leader of the Virginia Company in England. When the eight counties of the colony were formed in 1634, this village adopted the name Hampton. Four years prior to that time, William Claiborne had established his trading post as the first businessman; a public warehouse was erected in 1633 for the inspection, grading, and storage of export tobacco; and the first free school in America was established here in 1635. A Dutch fleet entered Hampton Roads in 1667, caught many tobacco ships ready to sail, burned five, captured eight, unsuccessfully attempted to raid the town.

By an Act of 1680, the village of Hampton was made the official customs port for the lower James River. The first battle of the Revolution in Virginia was fought here in October 1775 when Lord Dunmore sent in Royal Marines with orders to burn the town. Their landing was repulsed with heavy British losses and no casualties among the defenders. Except for occasional pirate raids, which were ended by a Hamptonian who killed Blackbeard and stuck his head on a pole at the entrance of the creek, Hampton was untouched by war until Admiral Cockburn pillaged it in 1813.

The last calamity struck in 1861 when Confederate radicals needlessly burned their town to keep Union forces from using it. *See: Ceeley's; City; Elizabeth City County; Ft. Algernourne; Kecoughtan; New Kent County*

HAMPTON UNIVERSITY
Hampton

Brevet Brigadier General Samuel Chapman, a twenty-seven-year-old officer assigned to the local Freedman's Bureau, began classes for Negro children in 1868 under a huge tree that still stands. It is revered as Emancipation Oak. With the help of Northern philanthropists and the Bureau, Chapman managed to gain funds to have the first building erected three years later. Since Federal money was involved, Indian children from the Pamunkey and Mattaponi reservations were later admitted, an arrangement that continued until 1912 when the Indians were sent elsewhere and the institute became an all-black school.

Bachelor degrees were authorized in 1922, at which time all elementary and secondary courses were dropped. Graduate studies were begun in 1928. The name was changed to Hampton University in 1985.

HAMPTON ROADS

In 1610 the creek which led to the Kecoughtan Indian village was named for the third Earl of Southampton. He was the Treasurer of the Virginia Company who took a lively interest in the colony. The great natural harbor at the mouth of the James River was named Southampton Roads since, by definition, a "roadstead" is a sheltered area of water near a shore in which vessels may ride safely at anchor.

Officially, Hampton Roads is that body of water formed by the collective confluence of the James, Elizabeth and Nansemond rivers. Ships enter when they pass between Port Comfort and Willoughby Spit, inbound from Chesapeake Bay. They may proceed to piers at Norfolk, Portsmouth, and Newport News, or enter the James River enroute to Hopewell and Richmond.

The first battle of ironclad ships was fought in this body of water on March 9, 1862. The CSS Virginia (formerly the USS Merrimac) exchanged shots with the USS Monitor. The fight was a draw, but neither ship fought again. The Virginia was later destroyed when the Confederates abandoned the area. The

Monitor sank off Cape Hatteras in a storm.
See: Tidewater

HANOVER COUNTY

Formed in 1720 from New Kent during the reign of King George I, this county was named for the Electorate of Hanover, Germany, the seat of the man who gained the English throne in 1714 upon the death of Queen Anne who left no heirs. George I's claim was traced through Princess Elizabeth, the daughter of King James I, who had married a German prince who attempted to become the king of Bohemia. She was known as the Winter Queen because she reigned for such a short time.

The town of Hanover Court House was established in 1735 near Hanover Wharf when a permanent court building was erected. *See: Cold Harbor; Gaines Mill; Scotchtown*

HANOVER TOWN
Hanover County

For many years most county activity centered about Page's Warehouse on the Pamunkey River. The town was laid out in 1762 when the General Assembly ordered 100 acres set aside for lots and streets. It was named Hanover Town for the county in which it lay. An old tavern here, built about 1723, which had been acquired in 1760 by Patrick Henry's father-in-law, John Shelton, was the major building, aside from the warehouse. Patrick Henry lived here when he made his first big splash in law and politics giving the winning summary for the Parson's Cause. The most important event in the town's history occured when the newly formed Committee of Safety met in Hanover Tavern in 1775 to issue commissions to the officers of the growing Army of Virginia, to plan for the raising of additional troops, and to find the means to obtain arms, ammunition and supplies for them.

When thought was given to moving the capital of the new Commonwealth away from Williamsburg, serious consideration was given to Hanover Town as the new capital, but instead, Richmond was selected. Today Hanover Town no longer exists, not even the wharf. *See: Jerdone's Castle; Pine Slash Farm*

HARBORTON
Accomack County

Before 1893 this was Hoffman's Wharf, an important steamer landing on the bay side of the Eastern Shore. When Hoffman's Wharf changed hands, the little community near it called itself Harborton. *See: Evergreen*

HARMONY HALL
Shenandoah County

A stone house, the main keep of Fort Bowman, was built here in 1753. It was enclosed inside a stockade by the builder, George Bowman, during the French and Indian War. He had four distinguished sons by his two wives, Anna Maria and Mary Hite. They were John Jacob, later prominent in Kentucky affairs; Abraham, a colonel during the Revolution; and Joseph and Isaac, both members of the Lewis and Clark Expedition in which Major Joseph Bowman was second in command. In later, peaceful times, this house was named Harmony Hall.

HARPER'S FERRY
West Virginia

This was within Virginia until the Civil War when several northwestern counties were formed into West Virginia. The settlement was first known as Peter's Hole. In 1747 Robert Harper was granted permission to operate a ferry here at the confluence of the Shenandoah and Potomac rivers between Virginia and Maryland and his name has been fixed in history. A Federal arsenal was located at Harper's Ferry which the abolitionist John Brown attempted to seize. He was captured by troops under the command of Colonel Robert E. Lee, U.S. Army, in 1860.

HARRISONBURG
Rockingham County   **City**

In 1779 Thomas Harrison laid out a town at the intersection of the Valley's Indian Road and Spotswood Trail which came through Swift Run Gap. His new settlement was called Harrisonburg. Harrison and his wife had been settlers here since 1739 and he was instrumental in getting an act passed by the General Assembly which authorized the establishment of the new town. Those who objected to having the county seat named for Harrison called it Rocktown, a name that appears on early maps. *See: Indian Road; Keesletown; Swift Run Gap*

HARRISON'S LANDING
Charles City County   **Site**

For many years the wharf at the riverfront warehouse here was known as Harrison's Landing after its owner, Benjamin Harrison III of Berkeley, who operated a shipyard in addition to handling imported or exported freight. He owned or hired about 100 slaves at this place, many of them skilled shipwrights. The last vessel completed at his shipyard slid down the ways in 1772. It was a double-decked merchantman of 100 tons displacement which could carry 380 hogsheads of tobacco.

Harrison's son, Benjamin IV, employed the shipwrights to build his house at Berkeley for his wife Anne Carter. They used boat-building techniques to make the mansion as sturdy as any fine vessel. When he sold the property to Nathaniel Burwell II of Carter's Grove, the wharf became known as Burwell's Landing. Not only did it continue to handle freight but for many years it was an important slave-trading point for this section of the James River. *See: Trebell's Landing*

HARROP

James City County   **Site**

Dr. John Pott, "a Master of Arts ... and well practiced in chirurgerie and physique and expert also in the distilling of waters ..." came to Virginia in 1621. He settled at the head of Archer's Hope Creek (now College Creek) about seven miles from Jamestown at a plantation he called Harrop Hundred. An astute politician, Dr. Pott soon was the leader of a devoted group. Shortly after his arrival in Virginia, he was appointed to the Council but was removed from it, briefly, at the request of Sir Robert Rich, the Earl of Warwick, for using poisons against the Indians in retaliation for the Massacre of 1622. In and out of court many times for various nefarious offenses, he was popular enough to get reappointed to the Council.

In March 1629 Dr. Pott was elected acting governor to serve until Captain John Harvey arrived in the spring of 1630. Governor Harvey governed with an iron hand and became so unpopular that Dr. Pott led an uprising against him with the help of Samuel Mathews, John West, John Utie, William Peirce, and George Menefie. They deposed Harvey and sent him back to England in the spring of 1635. Although Harvey managed to get himself returned to Virginia as Governor, he was deposed a second time. By then Dr. John Pott had departed the political scene and lived quietly. A portion of Harrop was acquired from his heirs to create Middle Plantation.

HARTWOOD

Stafford County

The male of the European red deer is a hart.

However, any stag with a good rack of horns was called a hart in America. For many years this region was thickly infested with deer in the woodlands. Hartwood, is a coined word combining hart and wood.

HARWOOD'S MILL

York County   **Site**

Thomas Harwood was in Virginia by 1623 since he patented land that year on the lower portion of Mulberry Island where he "planted" a few settlers. Although Queen's Hith did not thrive and soon was abandoned, Harwood turned to other means by which to make money. One of his better investments was a grist mill that he built east of Denbigh. He dammed a small stream, created a pond to feed a millrace, and used an undershot wheel to turn the grindstone. Harwood's Mill is now covered by one of the reservoirs that serve Newport News and Hampton. *See: Queen's Hith; Weyanoke*

HAT CREEK PRESBYTERIAN CHURCH

Campbell County

Established in 1742 this is Campbell County's oldest congregation. The church, located near the town of Brookneal, took its name for the brook that runs close by. Nobody today admits knowing the origin of the name Hat Creek, but it is thought to echo some long ago incident when a local settler lost his hat and saw it washed away. About eight miles from here is Red Hill, the last home and burial site of Patrick Henry, who died in 1799. *See: Brookneal; Temperanceville*

HAW BRANCH

Amelia County

This old plantation was established in 1745 by Colonel Thomas Tabb who built the present manor house which he sited in an unusual manmade depression. The house at Haw Branch was enlarged to its present Georgian style in the 1790s by John Tabb, Thomas's only son. John was a delegate to the Virginia Conventions of 1774 and 1775 and was a member of the Virginia Committee of Safety during the Revolution. The *haw* in the name refers to a wild hedge called a hawthorn, the berries of which are called haws.

HAYFIELD

Frederick County

Shortly after the French and Indian War (about 1760) three men were mowing a field when they were attacked and murdered by

Indians. Local residents believe there is a connection between the site of this massacre and the choice of the name for the post office.

HAYMARKET
Prince William County   **Town**

William Skinner bought the Red House Tavern after the Revolution when he came into some money. He laid out a town on the property next to his establishment and called it Haymarket. The tavern was a popular meeting place and it is possible that some of the local farmers traded their surplus hay and other items here, although the actual reason Haymarket was selected for the name is unclear. The tavern was destroyed, along with the entire village, when it fell under a heavy Federal artillery barrage during the Civil War. Rebuilt, it grew into a town.

HAYNESVILLE
Richmond County

Corbin Haynes, whose residence was Haynesville House, was the principal citizen of the locality. When the post office was established in 1890 the proper name to select was obvious.

HAYSI
Dickenson County   **Town**

Years ago two men ran a local general store. They have been identified as Charles Hayter and a Mr. Sypher. When the store was accepted as the new post office, the two names were combined for official use. Sometimes the name is spelled Haysy in Commonwealth documents.

HAZELWOOD
Caroline County

This was the home of John Taylor of Caroline, Thomas Jefferson's chief political lieutenant and a leading advocate of States Rights. He lived at and is buried at Hazelwood on the Rappahannock River in Caroline County. The colonial home was burned during the Civil War and the 2,200 acre farm was divided and sold in 1922 by John Taylor's granddaughter Dallie Penn Taylor Turner. *See Dumfries, Tayloe's Furnace*

HEAD WATERS
Highland County

This tiny settlement lies at the headwaters of Calfpasture River.

HEALING SPRINGS
Bath County

The water from a local spring is a constant

77.2 degrees. In the heyday of spas operating near mineral springs, this one advertised with directness.

HEATHSVILLE
Northumberland County

In 1706 this settlement became the seat of Northumberland County. It took its name from its principal attraction, the store owned by John Heath. At times this village was called Heath's Store. *See: Northumberland House*

HEBRON CHURCH
Madison County

This is the oldest Lutheran congregation in Virginia, established in 1717 by miners at Germanna who were working off their seven year indenture in Governor Spotswood's iron mines. One communion service bears the date May 13, 1727; another one dates from March 28, 1737. The present frame building, erected in 1740, houses a fine German-made organ, installed in 1802. The members of Hebron Church established the first school in this rural area in 1735. *See: Germanna; King George Parish*

HEDRA COTTAGE
Accomack County

Originally called Occohannock House, the land here was purchased by Edmund Scarburgh in 1649 from Okiawampe, "the great King of the Eastern Shore." The estate passed through many generations where the spelling of the family name on the deeds varies from Scarburgh to Scarborough. In 1756 William Scarburgh adopted the name Hedra Cottage for his dwelling, which was more modest than he was. *See: Occohannock*

HELLTOWN
Accomack County

Young people of past centuries were no less wild, immoral, or irreverent than some of them are today. The drovers and wagoneers of the eighteenth century were a hard bunch who whooped it up whenever they could. The track gangs of the nineteenth century, laying rail through unsettled regions, enjoyed drinking and wenching during their infrequent days off near taverns. In upper Accomack County a small center of vice and unlawful behavior developed at a tavern that served the Pennsylvania Railroad gangs. Known as Helltown, it was only a mile away from Modest Town which had a quieter reputation. Helltown was shut down as quickly as the gangs moved on along the center of the Eastern Shore. *See: Broadway; Rosslyn*

HENRICO COUNTY

One of the original 1634 shires, this county traces its history to much earlier times. It was named in memory of the lost town of Henrico which did not recover from the Massacre of 1622. The first church of Henrico Parish was at Varina where the parson often complained to the Bishop of London that his parishoners were "not so observant of Devout Postures as could be wished." At one time Henrico County was a Quaker stronghold. Richmond, the capital of Virginia, also serves as the county seat.

While Richmond was the capital of the Confederacy, a large number of battles and actions were fought in the county. *See: Henricus; Varina Grove*

HENRICUS
Chesterfield County   **Site**

Four years after the founding of Jamestown a third town was attempted. It was located on what is now known as Farrar's Island, in the curles of the James River, about fifteen miles downstream from the falls. The town was sited on a teardrop-shaped neck of land, about seven acres in size, that could easily be defended since the river formed a natural moat around it. The leader of the new settlement was Sir Thomas Dale, a soldier, and the High Marshall of Virginia under Governor Thomas Gates.

Naming the town The City of Henricus (sometimes spelled Henrico) in honor of the Prince of Wales, the settlers, all men at first, erected houses on three short streets. With them was the Reverend Alexander Whittaker, who supervised the building of a small church in the center of town.

On the north bank of the James, in a section called The Main (because it was on the mainland) the settlers established a farm, protected by a low palisade, which an early writer boasted was large enough to grow all the corn needed to feed the entire colony of Virginia. Following that project, the settlers built a long palisade on the south bank of the James that stretched in a wide bow all the way to the next settlement, Bermuda Hundred, at the mouth of the Appomattox River. At five equidistant points along this barrier were five forts, or watchtowers, that seldom were manned because of an acute shortage of soldiers. Within this second "impaling," was

established Mount Malado, a sort of hospital where sick people and newcomers were kept in isolation. During the following eight years about 350 people were assigned to Henricus but, with death from sicknesses and Indian murders, the population seldom reached 100 at any one time.

The highlight of Henricus' history occurred in 1614 when Pocahontas was sent here for safety after being captured by Captain Samuel Argall, the master of the ship *Treasurer*. Much to her disgust, her father, Chief Powhatan, made no attempt to rescue or ransom his daughter. However, she was treated kindly and she enjoyed being with the English people. After becoming conversationally fluent in the English language, she accepted Christianity, was baptised Lady Rebecca (at Jamestown, it is assumed), married John Rolfe, and gave birth to a son, Thomas Rolfe. When Pocahontas died in England in 1617, the informal treaty that resulted from her marriage slowly dissolved.

When Sir George Yeardley returned to Virginia in 1619 with a new charter, lands were set aside on The Main and near Mount Malado for a university where young Englishmen would be trained for the ministry and for a college where Indian children would be taught Christianity. These plans never fully materialized. Henricus was brutally mauled in the Massacre of 1622 by reason of its complacency, its isolation, and its connection with the capture and conversion of Pocahontas. The local Indians, always permitted to enter the town at will, fell upon the inhabitants on Good Friday, murdering all within the town. No amount of persuasion could get volunteers to go back to Henricus to rebuild the town which lay on the island as a burned ruin.

Periodic floods eventually washed away all traces of the town. Centuries of farming on both banks of the James eliminated all traces of the palisades. Today all that remains is the name, now Henrico, the county in which the city of Richmond lies. *See: Argall's Gift; Bermuda Hundred; Farrar's Island; Hampton; Hog Island; Potomac Creek; Varina Grove*

HENRY
Franklin County

This village, astride the line between Henry and Franklin counties, formerly was called Alumine. Although the post office was situated in Franklin County, the N & W Railroad elected to build its depot in Henry County. Since Patrick Henry was more beloved in Virginia than Benjamin Franklin, the railroad named its station Henry. In this rare instance, the post office was forced to yield to the power of the N & W.

HENRY COUNTY

Formed in 1776 from Pittsylvania, this county was named for Patrick Henry, the first Governor of the Commonwealth of Virginia. In 1790 it was divided and the other half was named Patrick County. Thus the Revolutionary firebrand has two counties named after him, the only man so honored in Virginia where great men abounded during the late eighteenth century. Martinsville is the county seat. *See: Hanover Town*

THE HERMITAGE
Northampton County

This house was built by Edward Bayly some time after 1775 at the head of Craddock Creek. Generally referred to rather ambiguously as a "mansion-cottage," it combines the elegance and charm of both styles. Wallpaper originally found in the parlor has been copied by Colonial Williamsburg. Quite possibly the name came from Hermitage Castle of Scotland, an old stronghold of the Douglas family where Mary, Queen of Scots lived for a time. The Eastern Shore was

PATRICK HENRY, HENRY COUNTY

thickly populated by Scots. Bayly was one of them. *See: Craddock*

HERNDON
Fairfax County   Town

This town was named in memory of Captain William Herndon who was lost at sea in 1857.

HESSE
Mathews County

William Armistead patented 500 acres on the Piankatank River in 1659, about fourteen years after coming to Virginia from Yorkshire, England. He built the first house here and began to acquire adjoining lands. The mother of Lord Culpeper, who was the governor of Virginia at this time, was Margaret van Hesse. It is assumed that this estate was named for her rather than for the Hesse region of Germany.

William's son, John, inherited the place. Aghast at the ousting of James II in 1688, he resigned his seat on the Council rather than take the oath of loyalty to William and Mary. It was he who built the present Georgian mansion to house the many children he sired. Several married into the leading families of Virginia. One daughter, Judith, married Robert "King" Carter of Corotoman; another, Elizabeth, married Ralph Wormeley of Rosegill.

The son and heir, John Armistead II, married Martha Burwell of Fairfield (Gloucester) much to the rage and disappointment of Governor Francis Nicholson who wanted Martha for himself. Nicholson threatened to shoot the bridegroom and the rector who performed the ceremony but never carried out his threat. John's daughters also married well. Lucy was the wife of Secretary Thomas Nelson of Yorktown, and Martha became the wife of Dudley Digges of E. D. Plantation in York County.

The great-grandson of the founder of this estate, Charles Carter Armistead, was the last of the family by that name to occupy Hesse. When he died in 1797 without a male heir, the 3,900-acre farm passed out of the well-connected family. Neglected for over 150 years, its present owners are attempting to restore Hesse to its original glory. *See: Cleve; Corotoman; E.D. Plantation; Fairfield of Gloucester; Westover*

HEWICK
Middlesex County

The first of this line of the Robinson family to come to Virginia was the brother of the

Bishop of London. Christopher Robinson came over in 1666 and established his seat at Hewick soon after his arrival. Appointed to the Council in 1691, he was named Secretary of the colony the next year. His eldest son, Christopher II, was a naval officer and a Burgess. His second son, John, settled at Piscataway in Essex County and also served on the Council. A third son, Benjamin, settled at Moon's Mount where he became the "master" of young Edmund Pendleton. John Robinson II, born here at Hewick, was the owner of Piscataway when he became the Speaker of the House and the Treasurer of the colony. His well-meaning but illegal handling of colony funds caused quite a scandal. *See: Edmundsbury; Moon's Mount; Piscataway; Wellington*

HICKORY NECK CHURCH
James City County

This church was built in 1740 on the road between Williamsburg and Providence Forge. Nearby are the stone foundations of a home that possibly dates from about 1650.

HIGHLAND COUNTY

Formed in 1847 from Bath and Pendleton counties, this county got its name from its high elevation in the Allegheny Mountains. Pendleton County was in Virginia at the time but it was one of those western counties that broke away during the Civil War to create West Virginia. The seat of Highland County is Monterey.

HILL'S FARM
Accomack County

Richard Hill, a very early settler on the Eastern Shore, owned vast acreage on the bay side. His first patent in 1632 was for what has always been known as Hill's Farm. Richard Hill wisely invested in more land until he owned almost all of Drake's Neck, named for his wife Mary Drake. The Hill's had one child, a daughter also named Mary who married into the Drummond family. Because Hill believed that only male heirs should inherit his land, he willed his holdings to his two grandsons. Richard Drummond got the home site parcel, encircled by Hunting Creek, where he built the present house in 1697, one of the first brick houses on the Eastern Shore. It was modernized in 1768 and repaired or restored many times since.

As this Hunting Creek tract also included Half Moon Island, some old records intermix Hunting Creek, Half Moon, and Hill's Farm as three different places. To further complicate matters, the Indians called it Newteske.

In 1683 Richard Hill sold a piece of the plantation to William Willet, who built a grist mill and was the county miller. The old mill pond, quiet and stagnant today, is called Drummond's Pond, a name that was applied sometime after 1840. The last generation of Drummonds lived here as late as the twentieth century.

HILLSVILLE
Carroll County   **Town**

An interesting event that took place in this town in 1912 does not shed any light on the selection of the name, but it does give proof of its connection with the people who live in the hills of the region. Floyd Allen, a mountain man of Scottish descent, got in trouble with the law when he tried to free two younger members of his clan who had been arrested for disturbing a church service. After Judge Thornton Massie pronounced a one year sentence in jail, Floyd stood up and shouted "I aint a-goin'!" His relatives instantly produced guns and shot up the courtroom. The judge, the Commonwealth attorney, the sheriff, the jury foreman, and a witness for the prosecution all died. The six gunmen were eventually arrested. Two were condemned to death and the other four were sent to prison for long terms. The two condemned men were never executed and, in time, all six were pardoned. However, Floyd Allen served his year despite his protest and the support of his clansmen.

HILTONS
Scott County

This small village along the Southern Railway was named in honor of the Hilton family. E. B. Hilton was one of those who went to California in 1849 to search for gold. He returned rich in stories but with little metal. Later he had wilder experiences in the Civil War which he managed to live through.

HIWASSEE
Pulaski County

This is an Indian word meaning a grassland or meadow.

HOBB'S HOLE
Essex County

For many years the settlement here was called Hobbs His Hole by Jacob Hobbs. In 1682 a port was established at this point on the Rappahannock River and named New

Plymouth. Today it is the town of Tappahannock. *See: Naylor's Hole; Tappahannock*

HOG ISLAND
Surry County
Across the James from Jamestown, and about five miles down river, lie a collection of low islands close to the shore. The settlers of 1607, when resupplied by Christopher Newport the next year, placed their hogs on one of the islands and left them to forage for themselves. Although hogs can swim, they do so only under the highest provocation and, by placing them on an island, the settlers saved themselves the bother of erecting and maintaining fences. Knowing also that chickens cannot fly far, they deposited their surplus fowl on Hog Island and let nature take her course. In the spring of 1609 the settlers were pleased to find that the original three sows had, in one year alone, produced "60 odd pigs; and near 500 chickens brought themselves up." That winter, when the Indians refused to bring in food and murdered those who ventured out of Jamestown's palisade to hunt, the colonists retrieved and ate all of the livestock on Hog Island. Before that winter was over, food supplies ran out causing the Starving Time in which 90 percent of the people died of starvation, disease, and Indian attacks.

Lord Delaware's timely arrival in May 1610 prevented the abandonment of the English colony. With the coming of more people during the next few years, and especially during the Peace of Pocahontas from 1614 until the Massacre of 1622, homes were established in this area that continued the inglorious name of Hog Island, a name that continues today. John Rolfe settled here when he came back from England after the death of his wife, Pocahontas, and willed his property to his son Thomas. In the census of 1623, thirty-one persons were listed as residents of Hog Island in what was to become Surry County.

Today it is the site of a nuclear power plant owned by the Virginia Power and Electric Company. There is another Hog Island in Virginia, uninhabited, on the Eastern Shore. It probably earned its name the same way. *See: Bull Island; Surry County; Ultimara*

HOLLAND
Suffolk
This small village was named for Z. T. Holland who opened the first store here. The Ruritan Club, now organized all over the country, was formed in Holland on May 21, 1928. At least fifty percent of its members must be farmers. The club strives to make rural communities better places through service, fellowship, and good will.

HOLLINS COLLEGE
Roanoke County
The first chartered college for women in Virginia was founded in 1842 as the Valley Union Seminary. It was located on the estate of an early successful settler, William Carvin, who came here prior to 1746. The school was renamed Hollins Institute for early benefactors, Mr. and Mrs. John Hollins. It became a college in 1910.

HOLLYBROOK
Bland County
The land for this farm was purchased in 1760 by Henry Harman, pioneer and Indian fighter, who lived to the ripe old age of 95 (and that says something about his abilities as a warrior). It received its name from the luxuriant growths of wild holly trees beside a clear, busy brook. The present village keeps the name alive.

HOLSTON
Washington County
This hamlet on the north fork of the Holston River was named for the river. *See: Holston River*

HOLSTON RIVER
Washington County
An early explorer and settler in southwest Virginia, Stephen Holstein built a cabin near Burke's Fort on the headspring of the middle fork of the Indian River about 1748. In later years, when other settlers came to join him, they named the river Holston, spelling it as they pronounced Holstein's name. It is a major waterway in southwest Virginia.

HONAKER
Russell County   Town
The Norfolk and Western Railway named many stations for local residents who were associated with the railroad. In this instance, it honored Harve Honaker, the local postmaster, when a depot and mail drop was established. The village had been New Garden when the post office was begun in 1849, but that didn't bother the N & W. When it chose a name, the postal authorities had to step aside.

HOPE

Hope is an obscure seventeenth century Scottish word meaning a small bay or inlet. It was used by Gabriel Archer to name his tract below Jamestown at the mouth of a creek where the James River has a slight inward bulge, hence Archer's Hope. Another archaic use of the word hope is as a verb meaning to trust, as in the name of the ship *Merchant's Hope*. *See: Hopewell; Littletown; Merchant's Hope Plantation*

HOPE FERRY
Buckingham County   **Site**

Near Snowden on the upper James River was a ferry crossing in colonial times. Depending upon which family held the charter, it had several names and was known as Waugh's Ferry in the mid eighteenth century. As late as 1970 a free ferry operated here for cars traveling on a secondary state road. Thomas Jefferson crossed at this place with his daughter Martha, who reported that she only saw her father lose his temper twice in her lifetime. One incident concerned a slave's unauthorized use of a carriage. The other happened during a crossing on this ferry. The boatman became so engaged in idle gossip with another man that he allowed the ferry to drift downstream. Jefferson shouted that if he didn't row for their lives he'd toss him into the river. The ferryman got back to work in a hurry. *See: Scott's Ferry; Snowden*

HOPEMONT
Mathews County

Located on the Piankatank River, nine miles up from the bay, the house was built in 1750 by the Fritchett family. In 1799 the estate's name was changed to Howlett Hall, and then, years later, to Hopemont. *See: King's Tavern*

HOPEWELL
Prince George County   **City**

In 1635 Francis Eppes patented a large tract of land along the mouth of the Appomattox River. He named his home Eppington and his land Hopewell Farm after the ship *Hopewell* which had brought him to Virginia. In 1911 the DuPont Chemical Company purchased a portion of Hopewell Farm from Richard Eppes, a descendant of the immigrant, and built a small plant to manufacture dynamite. Three years later, with the outbreak of World War I in Europe, DuPont expanded the facility to produce gun-cotton, a major component of smokeless powder used in artillery ammunition. By late 1915 the area surrounding the sprawling industrial maze was populated by nearly forty thousand people who lived in a variety of temporary houses. Included were foreign workers who spoke little or no English, dependents, merchants, gamblers, saloon-keepers, and a horde of prostitutes. Hopewell was a wide open town that neither the local government nor the state government could control.

In the early morning hours of December 9, 1915, a fire in a restaurant got out of hand and spread throughout the tar paper shanties. Most of the town was destroyed. Destruction only slowed the rate of illegal activity and the settlement was rebuilt.

Everything came to an abrupt halt with the armistice in November 1918. DuPont hastily closed the plant and the population dropped to less than 2,000. Hopewell got a second chance during World War II when DuPont reopened the factory and other major chemical plants were established. This time the influx of workers was better controlled and a permanent city developed.

Hopewell made international news in the 1970s when a small company dumped its waste into the city sewers. The insecticide *kepone* contaminated the James River all the way to Hampton Roads, utterly destroying commercial and sport fishing and oyster harvesting in the James and its many tributaries. Kepone contamination is still a major problem, one that possibly will continue for decades. *See: Bermuda Hundred; Cheatham Annex; City Point; Eppington; Penniman*

HORNTOWN
Accomack County

Long a trading point on the mainland for the people of Chincoteague Island, local tradition says the name was derived from the horns the fishmongers blew to advertise that they were ready to sell or trade their catch.

HORSEPEN
Tazewell County

This name is so obvious that some folks search for a unique explanation when there is none. Many years ago a corral was located here in which horses were penned. Horsepen Road, in the city of Richmond, continues the odd name.

HORSEY
Accomack County

This name has nothing to do with horses. It was named for the postmaster, a Mr. Horsey, who tended the mail here in the 1890s. Members of the Horsey family can be found all over the Eastern Shore. This settlement is so small that only a sharp bend in the road makes a motorist take any notice of it.

HOSKINS CREEK
Essex County
This water way just outside of old Tappanhannock was named for Bartholomew Hoskins, the first person to own land along the creek. Although rather short, Hoskins Creek is an important inlet of the Rappahannock River.

HOT SPRINGS
Bath County
These delightful, naturally hot springs were known to the Indians for countless generations. When the colonists finally dared, they ventured forth to enjoy the pleasant waters. A hotel was first erected here in 1766 to cash in on the tourist trade. Water comes from the ground naturally heated between 90 and 104 degrees. Here is located the famous Homestead Hotel, a haven for golfers and skiers.

HOWARDSVILLE
Albemarle County
The town was laid out in the eighteenth century on land patented in 1730 by Allen Howard. The settlement attempted to become an important trading point on the James River, but it was eclipsed by Scottsville on the great bend a few miles downstream. Howardsville is at the mouth of the Rockfish River which had very little traffic because of its rocky, shallow bed. See: Norfolk; Rockfish Gap; Weyanoke Indians

HUDDLESTON
Bedford County
The name honors Henry Huddleston Rogers, a financier of the Norfolk & Western Railway.

HUGUENOTS
Protestants of Calvinist beliefs who left the Catholic Church in France were called Huguenots (and other things not necessary to record here). For generations these French Protestants were severely persecuted by both the Catholic Church and the king. In 1598 Henry IV of France issued the Edict of Nantes which gave these people political equality with other Frenchmen and the right to worship as they chose.

When the edict was revoked in 1685 by another French king, the Huguenots fled after enduring torture and other horrors. Many of them came to Virginia in separate family groups during the following fifteen years, settling in Goochland County through the good offices of William Byrd. In 1700 the House of Burgesses collected them all together and settled them at an abandoned Monacan Indian village on the north bank of the James River, a few miles above Richmond. They were allowed to purchase land on both sides of the James at the rate of fifty acres for each adult.

Within a short space of time, with added immigration and the maturity of their children, they had acquired 10,000 acres of good farmland. The General Assembly established a Huguenot parish for them but stipulated that they had to use the Anglican Book of Common Prayer, had to hold their services in English, and had to teach their children the Catechism in the language of Virginia. They were not required to pay their ministers a fixed fee in tobacco as in other parishes in the colony, but were allowed to decide their rector's salary according to their means and customs. It was unusual open-mindedness but it was worth it. The Huguenots quickly adapted to the Anglican services, and their children spoke English as well as French. These highly-intelligent people became teachers, scientists, and writers who contributed much to Virginia's culture and learning. Noteworthy among them were the Macon and the Maury families, although there were many others who advanced through the political and social structure of the colony. See: Fauquier County; Glebe; Manakin Town; Maury River

HUMPBACK BRIDGE
Alleghany County
This is the oldest remaining covered bridge in Virginia and is the sole survivor of its type. Built on a wooden arch in 1835, it was part of the James River and Kanawha Valley Turnpike.

HUNDRED
A hundred was a territorial division adopted in England by the Norman conquerors as an administrative district. Each had its own court to deal with private disputes among the locals according to custom and Common Law. The hundred court punished wrong-doers and settled questions of taxation. Possibly the idea of dividing the county this way had

Roman origins since legions were composed of companies of 100 soldiers under a centurion. It is uncertain now if the Normans collected a hundred people, a hundred families, or applied it to a hundred acres (or whatever land measurement was then in use).

In Virginia, hundred was first connected to the provisions of Particular Plantations, early entities that were each led by a "governor," either the person who held the patent or his deputy. These governors established their own rules and laws to suit the times and conditions. When the first General Assembly was organized in 1619, the colony was divided into eleven boroughs, sometimes containing more than one settlement, and all plantations, towns, and settlements were required to observe English Common Law. The word hundred continued in use as part of a place name. *See: Bermuda Hundred; Bury; City; Corporations; Martin's Hundred; Particular Plantation; Plantations; Shires*

HUNGRY MOTHER STATE PARK
Wythe County

The officially accepted origin of this name goes back to colonial times when the Shawnee Indians of this region often kidnapped white women and children. The story in this instance relates the escape by a captive who had a very young child. While wandering in the vicinity of Molly's Knob, the mother collapsed from fatigue. The young child wisely followed a shallow creek and found a settler's cabin. Repeating in near panic "Hungry! Mother! Hungry! Mother!" she directed the rescuers up the stream. Both principals survived.

HUNTING QUARTER
Sussex County

Not far from the Nottoway River is the old home of Captain Henry Harrison who was famous for his stable of fine blooded racing horses. At one time he owned thirty blooded mares, some of the them imported. His stallion Jolly Roger was said to have been the first horse to give distinction to the racing stock of Virginia, and his Silver Heels was also quite well known. Captain Harrison served under Braddock after he won a commission in the Virginia regiment commanded by Major George Washington. After his death in 1773, his sons received a grant of 3,000 acres "due their father on account of services in the French and Indian War."

Hunting Quarter was first owned by Benjamin Harrison III who had the house built about 1710. When Benjamin Harrison III died, his widow, in settling the estate, sold 1,600 acres of the Hunting Quarter tract, the Rattle Hill Plantation of 2,100 acres, and the Goodrich Plantation of 1,700 acres—all along the Nottoway River. Evidently the house site was not sold since Captain Henry Harrison lived there in 1753, having inherited it from his father, Benjamin Harrison IV. *See: Berkeley; Brandon; Doswell; New Market of Caroline; Wakefield of Surry County*

HURLEY
Buchanan County

Here S.B. Hurley founded the Mountain Mission Home for underprivileged and orphaned children.

HURT
Pittsylvania County   **Town**

John L. Hurt, Jr. purchased a tract of land and developed it into a small community. He had a good eye for location. Enough people came to Hurt to make it grow into a town.

INDEPENDENCE
Grayson County   **Town**

When Carroll County was formed from Grayson in 1842, the courthouse of the former jurisdiction was in the center of the populated area at Old Town about three miles from Galax. This was an inconvenient site for the people who lived in the southern districts and there was agitation to move the courthouse to a new place. Naturally, the citizens of Old Town campaigned to retain the county seat. Another faction, some twelve miles away to the north and west, argued that their village would be better. Neither of the proposed sites was located conveniently for the people in the south of the county. The dispute went on for years until, in desperation, a commission was formed to make the final decision. When the citizens of the southern half of Carroll County were asked their opinion, they refused to enter the argument, preferring, they said, to remain independent. The commission selected a centrally located site and, in respect for the southerns, named it Independence. No one could argue about that name in America. Independence has been the county seat since 1850, and all who argued about its location are now forever silent.

INDIAN ROAD
Shenandoah Valley

The Indians had many trails throughout Virginia but this one was the ancient war path of the Catawba and Delaware Indians through the entire length of the Shenandoah Valley. During the migrations of the late eighteenth century, it was known as the Great Wilderness Road or the Valley Road. Some time after 1840 it assumed its present name, the Valley Turnpike. U.S. Highway 11 follows this old road fairly closely, but its has been supplanted by Interstate 81. The old Indian Road crossed the mountains at Cumberland Gap. *See: Iroquois Trail*

IRON GATE
Alleghany County   **Town**

This town was one of the centers of the iron industry in western Virginia in the nineteenth century. Settlement began here long before the town was incorporated in 1890. Just east of the settlement is a gap that was cut through Waite Mountain by the

Jackson River. The pass was named Iron Gate many years ago for the iron deposits seen in the outcroppings of rock. The town took its name from the water gap. *See: Clifton Forge*

IROQUOIS TRAIL

An ancient trail wound through Virginia along the eastern slopes of the Southwest Mountains. U.S. Highway 15, from Frederick, Maryland, to Clarksville, Virginia, fairly well follows the original route. In the northern part it was called the Carolina Road. After the Piedmont section began to be populated and the Indians were gone, this old trail developed into an important freight highway for wagons that rolled from the Potomac to northern Carolina. After crossing the Rappahannock River at Norman's Ford, it intersected the Three Chopt Road at Zion Church, one of the major crossroads in the interior portion of the colony.

The name came from the Iroquois Indians of Pennsylvania who followed this trail when they went on raids or went to trade with other tribes at Ocaneechee. When Governor Spotswood of Virginia and Governor Burnet of New York concluded a treaty with the northern tribes in 1722, the Indians were forbidden to use this trail. Instead, they traveled south through the Shenandoah Valley on what became known as the Indian Road. Many settlers heading for the Ohio River rode their wagons down the Iroquois Trail to the Three Chopt Road where they then headed west. Later the pioneers sent back droves of horses, cattle, hogs, and sheep along the same route. Because there were so many highwaymen lying in ambush to rob the travellers during the latter part of the eighteenth century, this trail became known as Rogue's Road. *See: Indian Road; Three Chopt Road*

IRVINGTON
Lancaster County   **Town**

In the nineteenth century, this part of Carter's Creek was settled by the Irving family. In 1891 it was officially named Irvington when a plant was built to extract oil from menhaden. The remains of the fish were ground into fertilizer. This is a well known haven for pleasure boats next to the Irvington Inn. *See: Reedville*

ISLEHAM
Gloucester County

Sir John Peyton, an English baronet, came to Virginia in the mid-1700s to occupy a tract of 2,000 acres that had been patented by his ancestor about 1650. Although there was a house of a sort on the property, Sir John built a more suitable manor. It was destroyed by fire in 1780. Another house was erected at a different site about 1800. Traces of the wide, impressive driveway that brought carriages to the first house can still be seen.

ISLE OF WIGHT COUNTY

This was one of the original eight shires formed in 1634. First known as Warrascoyak, after the Indians of the area, the name was changed in 1637 to Isle of Wight for the island in the English Channel near Portsmouth.

IVANHOE
Wythe County
IVOR
Southampton County

Both of these villages started life as flag stops of the N & W Railway. They were named by the wife of the president of the railroad who chose the titles of novels by one of her favorite authors, Sir Walter Scott. *See: Waverly of Sussex; Zuni*

IVY
Albemarle County

The Three Chopt Road crosses Ivy Creek at a shallow ford some seven miles west of Charlottesville. At one time there was a small settlement around a tavern called Woodville named for the Wood family that owned much property here. The ivy along the banks of this stream is the native evergreen Kalmia, often mistaken for ivy. *See: Farmington; Locust Hill; Terrell's Ordinary*

JACKSON RIVER

Rising in Highland County, where the elevation is about 3,000 feet above sea level, the Jackson River fills Lake Moomaw behind the Gathright Dam. From there it runs freely, clear and cold, through pleasant country until it reaches Covington, where it is captured by a huge paper mill. When it exits the plant, the Westvaco Mill owners have worked hard to ensure a relatively clean effluence from the plant. However the color of the Jackson is still much darker than the pristine Cowpasture River with which it merges, near Iron Gate, to form the James. *See: Bull Pasture; Calfpasture; James River*

JAMES CITY COUNTY

When Jamestown was founded in 1607, the colonists named their first settlement in honor of their king, James I. By 1612, when it was obvious that the English had been successful in permanently locating a colony in the New World, those who wrote home often referred to their town as James City, not so much to puff up its importance but because the master plan called for the establishment of See Cities, as in England. When the colony was divided into eleven boroughs in preparation for the First Assembly, the region around Jamestown was James City Borough. In 1634 when eight shires were organized, and redesignated as counties a year later, the territory on the north bank of the James River surrounding the capital of the colony was named James City County. *See: City; Shires*

JAMES RIVER

The longest river in Virginia is the James. It begins in Botetourt County with the confluence of the Cowpasture and Jackson Rivers near Iron Gate, and flows, in a winding way, 340 miles to Hampton Roads. For a while, ocean vessels stopped at City Point if they could not negotiate the looping bends that begin just above the mouth of the Appomattox. Today, with Dutch Gap cutting off one of the more severe curls, and with the main channel dredged, ocean vessels can get to the port of Richmond just below the falls. In the nineteenth century, a system of locks on a canal bypassed that barrier. The very early settlers called this river the Powhatan for the great chief of the local Indian confederacy. When it was discovered that Powhatan's main village was on another river, the colonists named this river the James in honor of their king, James I.

Above the falls the river went by several Indian names until the days of Queen Anne, and then the upper part was officially the Fluvanna until military maps were drawn during the Civil War. After 1865 the entire length of this important waterway was known as the James.

Although English custom uses the word "river" before the name, as the River Thames, the early colonists reversed this custom and labeled all the rivers as they are known today. *See: Fluvanna River; Kanawha Canal; Werowocomoco*

JAMESTOWN

James City County   **Site**

England's efforts to establish a colony in the New World which began during the reign of Queen Elizabeth I, failed miserably. One settlement in Maine was abandoned because of the severe climate. Two others, on the Outer Banks of North Carolina, also were failures. The first of these two ended when the settlers went home with Sir Francis Drake who had stopped by and offered to take them to England. The second, the famed Lost Colony, simply disappeared. In all three cases, a combination of climate, unfriendly Indians, disease, and a lack of supplies doomed the ventures.

A fourth try, authorized by King James I in the winter of 1606-07, sent 105 men and boys out in three small ships. They departed England in January under the leadership of Captain Christopher Newport, their "admiral." After four storm-tossed months at sea, the three ships, the *Susan Constant, Godspeed,* and the *Discovery,* arrived at the mouth of the Chesapeake Bay. A group of selected men went ashore at Cape Henry on April 26, 1607, to claim the territory for their king. After being attacked by the Chesapeake Indians, they sailed to another village where they were warmly greeted by the friendly Kecoughtans at present day Hampton. The colonists explored the James River for two weeks in search of a spot that matched the specifications in their written orders. Armed with the knowledge of the previous failures, the men sought a place that was away from the coast (so the Spanish could not easily find them), that provided a healthy environment, and that offered a close mooring for their vessels.

On May 13, 1607, the Englishmen chose Jamestown Island which met all of the conditions except the one concerning health—and this error did not become evident until after the first fort had been built. The land was infested with insects from a swampy, shallow body of water separating the island from the mainland, It was a poor place to dig wells since the brackish James River seeped through the sandy soil which also allowed human wastes to contaminate the water. More colonists died of disease than from any other cause, although the Indians took their toll for they objected to the desecration of their holy place on which the newcomers had unwittingly decided to live.

The first President of the Council, Edward Maria Wingfield, was a weak man who could not maintain the necessary discipline regarding the sharing of work and the division of food. Too many of the colonists were gentlemen who refused to do manual labor but went out in search of gold. Wingfield was deposed during the first winter by Captain John Smith whose leadership kept the colony from splintering and ending in death. When Smith was forced to leave Virginia in October 1609 to return to England after being badly burned in an accident, the Jamestowners slipped into a lazy, indolent way of life, ate all of their food by Christmas, and died during the Starving Time. By the next spring, 440 men and women, of the 500 people that Smith had left behind, were dead. Most of those who survived were those who had moved from Jamestown to other locations.

In May 1610 "all save John Martin" voted to return home. Their plans were thwarted at the last moment by the timely arrival of Thomas West, Lord Delaware, the new Governor, who brought supplies and more people. He was determined that the colony would continue. Under his successors, Sir Thomas Gates and Sir Thomas Dale, who ruled the colony under martial law, Jamestown developed into a modest "citie" with "two faire rows of howses, a street, and a church." By 1614 settlers were building their homes outside Jamestown's fort in New Towne to occupy and farm most of the island that was two and one-half miles long and, at its widest, about a mile across.

On July 30, 1619, six months before the Pilgrims struggled ashore in New England, the first General Assembly met in the Jamestown church to draft laws that were necessary to supplement English Common Law. Martial law had been lifted, under Governor Sir George Yeardley, by a new charter.

Fire was a constant plague in a settlement of wooden houses and thatched roofs. The town was put to the torch by Nathaniel Bacon, Jr., during his rebellion in 1676, but most of the homes and public buildings were rebuilt. When the fourth statehouse caught fire in 1699 the capital was moved to Williamsburg, a much healthier site. Jamestown was abandoned. The island was eroded by the constant action of the James River during the next century. The remains of the original fort, the wharf and landing, the early rude dwellings, and the last statehouse were washed away as Virginians ignored this historic island.

In the first part of the twentieth century, the U.S. Army Corps of Engineers halted the erosion of the land and the Association for the Preservation of Virginia Antiquities took steps to save the ruins of the old brick church. What remains of old Jamestown is now a National Historic Park. *See: City; Green Spring; Hampton; Hog Island; Kecoughtan; Mulberry Island; Old Towne; Pace's Paines; Varina Grove; Williamsburg*

JARRATT
Greensville County   **Town**

The Jarratt family came to this area in 1652. About two hundred years later a descendant of the original pioneers, William Nicholas Jarratt, gave the right of way through his property to the Petersburg and Weldon Railroad. In 1939 the Johns-Manville Corporation opened the world's largest plant to manufacture insulating panels.

JEFFERSON NATIONAL FOREST

Extending from the James River, near Natural Bridge, southwest to the tip of Virginia, this reserve contains about 600,000 acres. It is under the control of the National Park Service.

JEFFERSONTON
Culpeper County

Authorized by an Act of the General Assembly, this town was platted in 1798 as "Ye anciente towne of Jefferson." Adjacent to it was the hamlet of Wealsborough which, when the post office was opened in 1807, disappeared by name. The combined settlements were named Jeffersonton by the postal authorities.

JERDONE'S CASTLE
New Kent County   **Site**

Francis Jerdone came from Scotland in 1750, married Sarah Macon of New Kent County, and built a rather impressive house next to his trading center on the Pamunkey River which he called his castle. He supplied the local planters with imported necessities and took, in exchange, their corn, wheat, tobacco, and other farm products which he shipped to England and the Continent. Using the wharves at Hanover Town and Fredericksburg, he accumulated a considerable fortune.

About 1770 he became the partner of Charles Smith, a fellow Scot and a Presbyterian minister, and William Holt, a man experienced in ironwork. The three men operated a forge near Providence Church at what today is known as Providence Forge. Jerdone lived a mile or so away from the operation in a handsome house on an estate called Mount Stirling. He then moved to Albemarle County to Farmington which he had owned since 1758. He was a noted Tory who was punished for his loyalty to the Crown by confiscation of his properties by the Commonwealth during the Revolution. *See: Farmington; Hanover Town; Mount Stirling; Providence Forge*

JERUSALEM
Southampton County   **Obsolete**

It is a pity that this Biblical name is no longer used. Think of all the people who would like to go to Jerusalem before they die. The name was changed to Courtland in 1788.

JETERSVILLE
Amelia County

This hamlet was named for the first postmaster, Thomas E. Jeter. When General Lee pulled his troops away from the Richmond-Petersburg defenses in April 1865, he intended to go to Danville to join General Joseph E. Johnston's forces.

Lee found the road blocked here by the Federal troops of General Philip Sheridan. Instead of attacking, Lee made a decision to change his original plan. He turned west and headed to Lynchburg via Farmville.

JONESVILLE
Lee County   **Town**

Frederick Jones donated the land for the Lee County courthouse when the county was formed in 1792. Located near the Powell River, Jonesville is the most western county seat in the present Commonwealth. *See: Lee County*

JORDAN MINES
Alleghany County

There were several iron mines in this region—Low Moore, Rich Patch, and Iron Gate. This mine was named for a Mr. Jordan whose identity is not recorded. The community near the digs was named for Jordan's Mine. *See: Low Moor*

JORDAN'S POINT
Prince George County

Samuel Jordan established his home here in 1619 and built his house on a point of land that jutted into the James River. He called his home Jordan's Journey, although there are some references to the place as Beggar's Bush. Jordan was one of the representatives to the First Assembly of 1619, taking his seat as a member from Charles City which then covered both banks of the James. After his death in 1623 two men courted his widow, Cecily. One was William Farrar of Henricus, and the other was the Reverend Greville Pooley of Varina. So successfully did Cecily practice her feminine wiles that both men were convinced that they would be her next husband. She married Farrar. Upon learning that he had been jilted, the Reverend Mr. Pooley sued the widow for breach of promise. The Council heard the complaint but did not reach a verdict since, in their opinion, the matter was already settled. However, to prevent such an incident from happening again, the Governor issued a proclamation that made it unlawful for any woman to promise herself in marriage "to several men at the same time."

During the onset of Bacon's Rebellion, the settlers of this region met at Jordan's Journey to select their leader. They chose Nathaniel Bacon, Jr., whose home was across the river and who "just happened to be present." Because the owner of this estate, a descendant of William Farrar, was involved in the rebellion, the land was confiscated by Governor William Berkeley. For many years it belonged to the colony and was unworked. In the eighteenth century, it was purchased by Richard Bland, the Revolutionary figure. In Virginia, many members of the Jordan family pronounce the name JER-dun. *See: Curles; Eastover; Farrar's Island; Sully*

JOYLES NECK
Mulberry Island   **Site**

At the southern tip of Mulberry Island lie the ruins of a very old jail which either date to colonial times or are the ruins of a more recent jail built on the old site. In the middle of the seventeenth century, as early as 1665, Joyles Neck appeared on charts and the building was a landmark for vessels turning into the Warwick River. Miles Cary, Sr. owned the land in 1660 when it was called Joyles Neck. The jail was called Saxon's Gaol.

See: Mulberry Island

K

KANAWHA CANAL

The most ambitious canal ever attempted in Virginia was never completed. It was to have linked the James River with the Ohio, via the Kanawha River, to open the Midwest by a waterway. When finished, the people of the inland region would not have to rely on the port of New Orleans, using the Mississippi, but would have access to Hampton Roads and the Atlantic.

Beginning with the by-pass of the falls at Richmond, built in the 1790s, the newly organized stock venture, the James River and Kanawha Canal Company, started digging in 1835. Within three years the canal reached Maiden's Venture in Goochland County and was extended to Lynchburg by 1840. This was relatively easy work. It required another eleven years before the barrier of Balcony Falls had been overcome to make Buchanan the western terminus since revenues were less than expected and maintenance costs were high. Finally, in 1853, the next section was begun with Covington as the target.

At the height of this phase, more than 3,000 laborers struggled to dig and blast through heavy rock. Numerous viaducts crossed streams and swamps, at two spots arching over the James itself. Two tunnels were required to cut through the mountains, only one of which was completed. Hundreds of workers died from accidents, while disease carried off the men and their families. Hundreds were buried near Snowden in a cemetery that is now lost and forgotten. Although the canal was dug as far as Eagle Rock, where the lock was never completed, the blocked tunnel prevented the passage of vessels. Meanwhile, the company improved the Kanawha River and cleared a road through the last pass to Covington and had much of the towpath ready as far as the Ohio. However, the money ran out and all work ceased a few years prior to the outbreak of the Civil War.

In the sections completed, the standard width was thirty feet at the bottom with sloping sides that opened to fifty feet to enable the canalboats to pass. Under normal conditions, the water was five feet deep. Mules towed the freight barges and horses pulled the passenger packets from the towpath about twelve feet wide, moving at a steady six miles an hour in either direction. At dusk all watercraft tied up to a convenient bank for the night and the passengers slept on board in separate accommodations for men and women. The

KANAWHA CANAL

daily food was reported to have been coarse and rather spartan.

As the terrain rose in elevation, locks lifted the boats. These stone chambers were fifteen feet wide and one hundred feet long, enough to lift or lower one boat at a time. Small houses were provided for the lock-keepers who opened and shut and sluice gates, collected the fees from non-company users, and let the crews move the vessels their own ways. As a sideline, the lock-keepers made a few extra dollars by selling fodder for the privately owned animals.

The final section never opened west of Buchanan. Although some portions were used west of Buchanan to the uncompleted tunnels, revenues remained low and no profits were made. Competition from the railroads reduced utilization. Constant repairs to the banks and viaducts drained resources. Then, when Union troops wrecked long portions by blasting holes in the sides to let out the water, the end of the venture was near. Repairs were made after the war, but severe floods from heavy rain washed away the repairs. By 1888 the company was bankrupt.

The right of way was sold to the Richmond and Allegheny Railroad. Within a year, that company was forced to sell its assets to the Chesapeake and Ohio Railroad. The C&O laid track on the towpath and let the canal fall apart. Most of the rail traffic these days rumbles over or beside the old James River and Kanawha Canal, hauling coal from the western mountains to Newport News piers. Short sections of the canal can still be seen at Richmond with a preserved lock at Battery Creek Park in Bedford County. *See: Patowmack Canal*

KECOUGHTAN

Hampton   **Site**

The first friendly Indians that the settlers of 1607 encountered lived in a modest village on Hampton Creek. They welcomed the newcomers with strange gestures, made odd markings on the earth, and gave a feast during which they entertained the settlers with wild dances and weird songs. When asked who they were, the Indians said their village was Kiccowtan, as Captain John Smith spelled it in his book published in 1612. Actually, these people were not the original inhabitants but were members of the Pamunkey tribe placed there by Powhatan after he had expelled the original Kecoughtans to a river far to the north during his

conquest of the scattered tribes that made up his kingdom.

At the time of the Jamestowners, the chief was Pochin, reportedly one of Powhatan's many sons. Although these people remained on friendly terms with the English, Sir Thomas Gates, the Captain-General of the colony, believed they were a threat to the safety of Fort Algernourne. In the spring of 1610 he attacked the village while the men were out on a hunt. The women and children were chased off and the lodges were ransacked for whatever food was left after the hard winter. For some strange reason the Indians did not counter the attack, nor did they ever attempt to regain their village. An English town was established across the narrow waterway of what was then called Southampton Creek in the vicinity of today's Hampton University.

William Claiborne was the first man to occupy the old Indian site when he built a warehouse in 1623 to store the furs that he bought from other Indians in exchange for iron tools, cooking pots, and trinkets. By 1623 the entire lower portion of the Peninsula was called Kecoughtan, and the English town was Elizabeth City. In 1634 the name Kecoughtan was dropped and the entire region was Elizabeth City. *See: Fort Algernourne; Hampton; Shires*

KEESLETOWN

Rockbridge County

Established about 1790 shortly after Thomas Harrison laid out Harrisonburg, this village was organized by George Keisell, a local resident. Seeking to have the courthouse built near his home, Keisell began a campaign among the local leaders. When a decision could not be reached between Keezletown and Harrisonburg, Keisell and Harrison agreed to let the site of the county seat be decided by a race between horses. Each man entered his own horse. Mr. Harrison was the easy winner. *See: Harrisonburg*

KELLER

Accomack County   **Town**

John Harmon was the first landowner here. His patent was granted in 1779. In 1894 the farmers of the region organized The Eastern Shore Agricultural Fair Association, Incorporated. It sponsored an annual event that gave the local farmers and their wives an opportunity to show their prize animals and their handiwork at a typical county fair. In

1917 the association bought four acres of land from the Harmon heirs and built a fair ground with permanent facilities. They called it Keller Fairgrounds, either for the nearby town or for the organizer of the project. The fair ground has been cleared but the town of Keller remains.

KEMPSVILLE

Virginia Beach   **Site**

The settlement at the head of the north fork of the Elizabeth River was known as Kemp's Landing for the wharf established there by members of the Kemp family. Richard Kemp was the Secretary of the colony under Governor John Harvey in the second and third decades of the seventeeth century. This landing was an important port for those who settled near Dismal Swamp and used Norfolk as their deep water port. From 1778 to 1884 Kempsville was the county seat of Princess Anne County. The county was annexed by the city of Virginia Beach after World War II and the little town has lost its identity. *See: Claiborne's Neck; New Town*

KENBRIDGE

Lunenburg County   **Town**

Land for the town was once owned by the Kennedy and Bridgeforth families. The two names were combined when the post office needed a name. It was originally called Tinkling before 1908. *See: Brookneal; Coeburn*

KENMORE

Fredericksburg

Fielding Lewis built this fine home for his seventeen-year-old bride, Betty, the only sister of George Washington. Completed in 1752, the house had no specific name. It was the manor house of an 863 acre farm called Millbrook.

When the colony prepared itself for the War of Independence, the Virginia Convention sought to arm the expanding militia. In 1775 Colonel Fielding Lewis was granted a contract to produce muskets. By the spring of the following year, his Manufactory of Small Arms, built on Millbrook beside Hazel Run, was in full productions. Quality pieces were turned out in impressive numbers all through the Revolution. The Commonwealth government, however, failed to provide additional money when the initial 12,500 pounds ran out. Colonel Lewis, a dedicated patriot, supported his manufactory with his own funds and then mortgaged his property when

he had to borrow money. Deep in debt by 1781, the land of Millbrook was lost when his creditors foreclosed and the Commonwealth did not come to his aid. When he petitioned the Virginia government for rescue, an attempt was made in the General Assembly to discredit Colonel Lewis with the claim that the guns he produced were of inferior quality. An impartial commission found that the weapons were all equal to or better than the required specifications.

Although petitions were circulated on his behalf, Lewis died penniless and broken-hearted in 1782. His widow, Betty Lewis, continued to live in the house until she was forced to sell the home and its interior furnishings in 1796. Those who lived there later reported seeing the ghost of Colonel Lewis seated at his desk, shuffling through papers, trying to figure out how to pay the bills.

In the nineteenth century, the home was purchased by members of the Gordon family who changed the name to Kenmore, by which it is known today. Kenmore is a small village in Scotland, northwest of Perth on Loch Tay. *See: Brompton; Marmion; Warner Hall*

KENTS STORE

Fluvanna County

James M. Kent owned the local store in 1845 when it was selected as the location of the post office.

KENTUCKY COUNTY

                                       Obsolete

Although the king of England proclaimed, in 1763, that the lands west of the Ohio River were reserved for the Indians and were off limits to settlers, 30,000 people ignored the proclamation during the next five years. When the Indians objected to this migration and declared war, Lord Dunmore, the Governor of Virginia, led a force of about 3,000 men to settle the disputes. The treaties he made in 1774 were favorable to the settlers. The king chastised Dunmore for breaking the "royal word." Still, the region had been opened for new settlement.

Daniel Boone encouraged a great number of families to move to the Kentucky Territory which was a part of Virginia. William and James Harrod founded the town of Harrodsburg. Soon there was another town called Boonesboro. Other settlements quickly sprang up.

George Rogers Clark and John Gabriel Jones were sent to Williamsburg with the petition for county status. Although some Virginians opposed this idea, the General Assembly voted to accept this vast territory as Kentucky County in the summer of 1776, thus strengthening Virginia's claims against the British, French, and Spanish. Harrodsburg was made the county seat. First the settlers had to contend with the angry Shawnees who renewed their attacks against the settlers. Then they had to defend themselves against the British who came from Detroit under the command of Lieutenant Colonel Henry Hamilton, the notorious "Hair Buyer" who paid the Indians for scalps.

General George Rogers Clark's beautiful campaign against Hamilton saved the entire Northwest Territory (which included Kentucky) for the fledgling United Colonies. By 1792 enough people lived in Kentucky to qualify for admission into the Union as the fifteenth state. *See: Cumberland Gap; Washington County*

KEOKEE
Lee County

A coal mine was opened here in 1905 by the Keokee Coal and Coke Company. The wife of one of the company founders, Keokee Perrin, was of Indian descent. The mine was named for her and the village near it took the name of the mine.

KERR RESERVOIR
Southside

Lying in Virginia and North Carolina, this reservoir covers 83,000 acres with 800 miles of shoreline. Sometimes called Buggs Island Lake, for a small island within the flooded land, the reservoir was named for Congressman John H. Kerr who served North Carolina from 1923 to 1949. He was the father of the Roanoke River Flood Control and Power Project which was formally dedicated in 1953. Under the water lies Occaneechee, the scene of Nathaniel Bacon's slaughter and extermination of the Susquehannock, Occaneechee and Totem Indian tribes. Below the John H. Kerr dam, in Virginia, is another huge lake that is nearly entirely in North Carolina, backed up by a dam at Roanoke Rapids. *See: Occaneechee*

KESWICK
Albemarle County

Originally part of Peter Jefferson's Shadwell land, the name Keswick was brought up from Chesterfield County by Colonel James

Clark when he moved to Albemarle. He was the father of George Rogers Clark, who was born in the new home. Keswick is a village in northwestern England in the beautiful Cumbrian Mountains on Derwent Water.

KESWICK
Chesterfield County

Located across the James River from Tuckahoe, the land was patented in the seventeenth century but no trace remains of the first occupants. In the first quarter of the eighteenth century, Charles Clark acquired 1,500 acres, most of which extended along the river. In 1732 he built his home, Manor House. The interior and exterior walls were of solid brick, and the doors to all rooms opened only to the outside much like a modern motel. This native of Surrey, England was worried about fire and provided exits for everyone. In 1750 the house was expanded on either end to give it the final "H" floor plan.

A grandson, Colonel James Clark III, lived here during the Revolution. His son, Major James Clark IV, who was born in 1776, established an iron foundry for casting cannons near his home in 1814. He was instrumental in getting the Commonwealth to build Bellona Arsenal next to his land. Although Major Clark's cannons blew apart now and then during test-firing by U.S. government inspectors, the Union Army continued to purchase them until 1834. *See: Bellona Arsenal; Keswick of Albemarle*

KEY'S GAP
Frederick County

Originally known as Vestal's Gap, this pass through the mountains carried a road from Winchester to Charles Town, West Virginia. John Vestal operated the ferry across the Shenandoah River. The current name honors Francis Scott Key who wrote the words to the national anthem during the War of 1812.

KEYSVILLE
Charlotte County   **Town**

An early tavern keeper, John Keys, gave his name to this town. Every year a Dixieland festival is held in Keysville in late July or early August. The festivities are in conjunction with the Dixie Limited train excursions sponsored annually by the Old Dominion Chapter of the National Railroad Historical Society.

KILMARNOC
Lancaster County   **Town**

This town was named for the city of

Kilmarnoc in Ayreshire, Scotland, a locality closely associated with the poet Robert Burns.

KIMBALLTON
Giles County
In 1881 E. J. Kimballton, the president of the Norfolk and Western Railway Company, visited this part of Virginia to look into the possibility of extending a branch of the railroad to the coal fields. The terminus of the new line was a village that was named Kimballton.

KING AND QUEEN COUNTY
When King James II was deposed for his repression of Protestantism and his heavy-handed support of the Roman Catholic Church, the English Parliament looked for a Protestant sovereign. The obvious successor was the king's daughter, Mary. She was married to a Dutchman, William, Prince of Orange of the House of Nassau who also had a claim to the throne as a direct descendant of Charles I. Parliament offered the throne to them as co-rulers. They accepted. King William III and Queen Mary II were the renowned William and Mary for whom this county was named when it was organized in 1691. Queen Mary II died five years after they were crowned in 1689. William III remained as the king of England for another eight years. He was followed on the throne by Mary's sister, Queen Anne. *See: King William County*

KING GEORGE COUNTY
Formed in 1720 from Westmoreland during the reign of King George I, this county was named for the monarch who could speak no English. Except for a brief visit to England for his coronation, George I remained in Hanover, Germany all his life while his kingdom was governed by his ministers. The first of the Hanoverian kings, George I's claim to the throne was traced back to Princess Elizabeth, the only daughter of James I, who had married the Elector of the Palatinate. (Elizabeth City and the Elizabeth River were named for her.) Giving the crown to a German prince was made necessary when Queen Anne, the last of the Stuarts, died without a living male heir. George I was the absent king of England from 1714 until his death in 1727. *See: Prince George County; Prince William County*

KINGSVILLE
Prince Edward County
During late colonial times, King's Tavern was a popular stop on the old Iroquois Trail. The name was dropped rather suddenly when the Declaration of Independence was adopted and was read at every public point throughout Virginia. The tavern sign was pulled down with great glee and the owner's name was substituted. For many years the stage stop was called Worsham. Here was Prince Edward County's first courthouse and jail, both built about 1755. At some unrecorded time, the name Worsham was dropped and the little settlement that had grown up around the former King's Tavern was called Kingsville, a name that continued to modern times. *See: Anderson's Tavern; Prince Edward County; Rutledge Ford*

KING WILLIAM COUNTY
Formed in 1701 from King and Queen, this county was named for King William III who reigned as co-sovereign with Queen Mary. It is an odd quirk of fate that there is a King William County but no Queen Mary County. *See: King and Queen County; Prince William County*

KINSALE
Westmoreland County
Kinsale was established in 1705 as a port on the Yeocomico River, on the Northern Neck, near the mouth of the Potomac. Without explanation or official elaboration, the name of the port was selected by the House of Burgesses. It honors a moment of history during the exile of young King Charles II when a squadron of the Parliament Navy mutinied and sailed to Kinsale, a tiny harbor on the southern tip of Ireland. The crewmen scattered in fear for their lives. Prince Rupert of Holland, Charles II's cousin, attempted to recruit new sailors in Ireland by having Mass said in the Irish seaports in direct violation of Oliver Cromwell's orders, which made unlawful any Catholic worship. Prince Rupert's efforts were mainly unsuccessful. He collected one crew and managed to sail out of Kinsale to the safety of Holland. In cruel retribution for this modest Irish support, Cromwell personally led an army to Dublin in 1650 and made the Irish pay dearly in blood and pain for their religion and their modest support of the mutineers who were successfully hidden.

Many Irish people migrated to Virginia after Cromwell's bloodbath, some of them settling in the old Chicacoan Indian district on Northern Neck where they worked for the royalist Cavaliers who had carved out huge farms in this region. The tiny port of Kinsale,

Virginia, served this territory for two centuries. It was a port of call for the Chesapeake Bay steamers until the early 1930s. *See: Boscobel; Chicacoan; Lancaster County*

KIPPAX
Prince George County   **Site**

On the north bank of the Appomattox River, across from present day Hopewell and near the old Bermuda Hundred settlement, stood the home of Robert Bolling. He married Jane Rolfe, the granddaughter of Pocahontas. They had one child, a son born in 1676, whom they named John for his grandfather, John Rolfe. Kippax was the site of a former Indian village of the Appomattox tribe. *See: Cedar Level; Cobbs Hall of Chesterfield; Fort James*

KIPTOPEKE
Northampton County

Kiptopeke was an Indian chief who lived in the seventeenth century. He was the coruler of "Ye Kingdom of Accawmacke" with Debedeavon, the Laughing King. *See: Cheriton*

KISKIACK
York County   **Site**

The northern part of York County, between King's Creek and Queen's Creek, was inhabited by a tribe of Indians known as the Chischiaks. Their name was spelled various ways including Kiskyacke and, in more modern times, Cheesecake. After being settled by Captain John West in 1630, an unused parcel was granted to Henry Lee in 1647 under the "Head Rights" provision of the colony's laws for his importation of a number of settlers. Henry had come to Virginia about 1625 with Richard Lee who was either his brother or his cousin. The relationship is not clear. Both served as justices for York County. Both also served as

a Burgess from York, Richard in 1647 and Henry in 1652.

Richard Lee received a grant of land in the Northern Neck region (then known as Chicacoan) and moved away. Henry remained on his 247 acres at Chischiak, built his small home in 1641 and, given the non-standard spelling of the day, called it Kiskiack. His farm was between land owned by John West on one side and Edward Digges on the other. Henry Lee, a physician of some renown in the local region, died in 1657. His home was destroyed and was replaced by another, probably of similar design, in 1680. It was lived in continuously until 1918 when the land was acquired by the Federal government for a shell loading plant.

Today the property of Kiskiack is on the reservation of the Yorktown Naval Weapons Station. The house of 1680 was burned accidentally in 1915. It was reconstructed almost immediately by William Harrison Lee, a descendant, who was the resident at the time of the fire. The exterior walls of the original brick laid in Flemish bond were reused. Flemish bond of alternating stretchers and headers was rarely used prior to 1680. The Garden Club of the Naval Weapons Station maintains this old house as a shrine. It is accessible only through special arrangement with the station's commanding officer. *See: Cheatham Annex; Chischiak; Lee Hall of Lancaster; Machodoc; Penniman*

KNOB

A knob is a rounded protuberance on a surface, according to the *American Heritage Dictionary.* When applied geographically, a knob is a rounded, isolated hill, or the rounded portion near the top of a mountain. It is commonly applied to the tops of mountains in the Blue Ridge and Allegheny mountains. A good example is Beamer Knob, near Galax, that is 3,361 feet high. *See: Peak*

L

LACEY SPRING
Rockingham County

The colonial name for what is now called Lacey Spring was Big Spring. A Mr. Lacey was a later owner. John Koontz built the first house near the spring in the early eighteenth century and was soon joined by members of the Lincoln family. They all either worked at Isaac Hite's tannery, or in a sawmill powered by the rushing water. Big Spring (or Lacey's Spring) flows with a tremendous gush into Smith Creek at the estimated rate of 4,000 gallons a minute. The village of Lacey Spring is close by.

LA GRANGE
Orange County

Parson John Thompson built a majestic square, brick house a few years before he married Anne, the widow of Alexander Spotswood, in 1742. Filled with furniture, some of his and some of hers from Spotswood's "enchanted castle" at Germanna, La Grange was a showplace of the region. One day in 1775, worried about the coming war that seemed inevitable, Parson Thomas rode to the five churches he served, collected the communion silver for safekeeping, and took it all to La Grange. Upon arrival at his home, he was immediately called away to comfort some soldiers who had been wounded in a skirmish with British troops near Fredericksburg. The good parson was killed while on this mission.

No one ever saw his wife or the silver again. Subsequent owners of La Grange reported seeing the ghost of an elderly woman who would silently sweep through the lower rooms of the old house and then disappear through a wall of the drawing room. Not too many years ago, when the apparition appeared and then disappeared through the usual spot, the wall was carefully inspected. A moveable panel was discovered which, when opened, revealed a secret passage. At the bottom of a steep stairway lay a pile of heavily tarnished communion silver and a skeleton. Tests of the bones proved it to be that of an elderly woman. Was this Anne?
See: Federal Hill; Foxcroft; Germanna

LAHORE
Orange County

This settlement grew up with the name Woolfolk. However, in 1881, the local residents requested the post office change the name to Lahore for some unrecorded reason. It might have been for a prominent resident or the postmaster. It might have been for the capital of Pakistan.

LAKE ANNA
Spotsylvania County

This manmade lake was formed when a power dam was built at Dike to hold back the Anna River. The river was either named for Queen Anne or for Anne, the wife of Alexander Spotswood. *See: La Grange; Rapidan River*

LAKE CHESDIN

This reservoir serves Petersburg and Colonial Heights with water. Since the manmade lake lies in both Chesterfield and Dinwiddie counties. Chesdin is a coined name combining the first part of both county names.

LAKE DRUMMOND
Suffolk

Lake Drummond lies within Dismal Swamp. It is the largest of the two bodies of fresh water in Virginia, the other being Mountain Lake. This lake was named for William Drummond who was appointed the first governor of Carolina in 1664 by Sir William Berkeley. Unfortunately, Drummond was hanged by Berkeley for taking part in the rebellion of 1676.

The land surrounding Lake Drummond is about twenty feet above sea level. The water is not stagnant but is supplied by several streams that flow into it from various directions. Averaging six feet in depth, the lake covers about 3,000 acres and has a circumference of nearly three miles. It is sparcely inhabited by fish since the water is quite acidic, made so by the numerous cypress trees that stand on its banks and in the swamp that surrounds it. With increased pumping from wells for municipalities on the south side of Hampton Roads, lowering the water table, Lake Drummond is slowly contracting and growing smaller each year.

Its nearly round shape cannot be explained. One theory holds that it was formed by the impact of a meteorite, but this is discounted by the absence of a surrounding wall of earth that normally follows such an impact. Those who subscribe to the meteorite theory say the

136

soggy, water-laden earth of the swamp would not have been mounded. On the other hand, there are those who say that a meteorite probably would have struck the earth at an angle to create an elongated scar rather than a circular depression.

It is possible that Lake Drummond was formed from a fire that burned away the peat as it spread in all directions over many years. This theory can be supported by an Indian legend of a firebird whose smoke rose from this area in a mysterious fashion. *See: Brick House; Carolina; Dismal Swamp; Mountain Lake*

LAMBSBURG
Carroll County

The first settler here was Wilmot Lamb for whom this community was named.

LANCASTER COUNTY

The entire eastern end of Northern Neck was first known as the Chicacoan Indian District. In 1648 it was formed into one large county, Northumberland, which, in 1652, was divided to form Lancaster County on the north bank of the Rappahannock River. It was named for the county of England from which many Cavaliers emigrated to the colony during Cromwell's Commonwealth. The county seat is Lancaster Court House.

LANEVILLE
King and Queen County   **Site**

Richard Corbin, the Receiver General of the Virginia colony at the outbreak of the Revolution, maintained his home at Laneville. The house, built in 1758, was 194 feet long but only twenty-seven feet wide. After Lord Dunmore seized the public gunpowder in Williamsburg in 1775, Patrick Henry, then a colonel of the Hanover militia at Doncastle's Ordinary, sent a small detachment of men to Laneville to request Corbin to write a warrant for payment of the powder. The Receiver-General was not at home, so Mrs. Corbin said, and the troops left without molesting the place.

It is possible that Corbin was at home but his wife either did not know or did not care to become involved in her husband's business. Richard Corbin and his wife were estranged. He lived in his apartment at one end of the long house and she lived in hers at the other end. The connecting doors were blocked. Once a year, on New Year's Day, Richard Corbin would pay his wife a formal call. He would ride in his coach from his end of the great house, around the circular driveway, to

her entrance. After tea and polite conversation (or so it is assumed—they took their tea alone) he would re-enter his coach and return to his quarters in silent dignity. Corbin was a strong Tory who left Virginia in August 1775 and remained in England until his death. *See: Doncastle's Ordinary*

LANGLEY
Fairfax County   **Site**

Richard Bland Lee of Sully owned an additional parcel of land near his home. When he sold Sully to his cousin, "Lighthorse Harry" Lee, he moved to his other farm and built a house which he called Langley for the ancestral home of the Lee family in England. His son, Thomas Lee, was the last to live here. The land passed through several hands during the next century. When the Central Intelligence Agency was organized after World War II, the land of Langley was acquired by the Federal government for its headquarters. *See: Sully*

LANGLEY FIELD
Hampton

Samuel Pierpont Langley, while superintendent of the Smithsonian Institution, became interested in powered flight about the same time the Wright brothers were experimenting with gliders. Langley, too, began with gliders and then attempted to add power. With great fanfare, he seated himself in his craft and made ready to be the first man to fly. The test was an embarassing failure. The machine waddled down its launching ramp and promptly fell into the Potomac River in full view of photographers. However, since he was one of the pioneers of aviation and some of his ideas were later used by other aircraft builders, he was honored when a flying field was established by the Army near Hampton in 1917.

Langley Field is the oldest continuously used military airfield in the country. Billy Mitchell flew World War I bombers from its runway to demonstrate the vulnerability of ships to air attack. Since he sank "unsinkable" German warships, captured at the end of the Great War and which the U.S. Navy brass said couldn't be sunk, he originated much of the interservice rivalry between the Navy and the Air Force that continues, in muted style, today.

From one remote portion of Langley Field, the Army experimented with dirigibles in the late 1920s. That part of the Federal reservation, still known as the LTH Area (Lighter

137

Than Air), is now occupied by the NASA Langley Research Center. Prior to the organization of NASA, the National Advisory Committee for Aeronautics (NACA) provided many engineering advances in its wind tunnels during the upsurge in aviation between the two World Wars.

Today, the headquarters for the USAF Tactical Air Command is at Langley Field.

LAUREL
Henrico County

Laurel grows abundantly all over Virginia, particularly in the mountains. One variety, the cherry laurel, contains a deadly poison. The name Laurel has been used in various combinations for the names of creeks and farms. The tiny community Laurel Fork in Carroll County takes its name from a fork of Laurel Creek. The hamlet Laurel of Henrico County was named for the non-poisonous flowering shrub.

LAWNE'S PLANTATION
Isle of Wight County   Site

Captain Christopher Lawne led a group of settlers to Virginia in the summer of 1619. He was granted a large tract of land "on the Surry-side, over across the water from Jamestown." Enough people were at Lawne's to qualify the plantation as a borough that year, and Captain Lawne appointed himself one of the two representatives from Warrascoyack in the First Assembly held in August 1619. The people of Lawne's Plantation were hit hard by the Warrascoyak Indians in the Massacre of 1622, but the Captain escaped with his life. Instead of fleeing in terror, the brave men here immediately launched a counterattack, killed all of the Indians in the nearest village, and erected a fort on the site. Captain Roger Smith was placed in command of the small garrison.

The fort became a major trading post which, years later, was called Old Towne in belated memory of the Indians who were all dead or gone. At a church in Old Towne, the men of the territory met in 1680 to protest being taxed by officers of the Governor without having a voice in the matter, a very early complaint about taxation without representation. *See: Old Towne; Richneck of Isle of Wight; Smith's Fort Plantation; Isle of Wight County*

LAWRENCEVILLE
Brunswick County   Town

Colonel James Rice gave the land for the town in 1814 next to the courthouse complex. All he asked in return was the privilege of deciding the name. The local citizens were startled when he named it for his favorite horse. Today Lawrenceville is the seat of Brunswick County.

LEAD MINES

Lead is not plentiful in Virginia but a few good pockets have been worked. Usually the metal is mixed with silver, another scarce mineral in the Commonwealth. An important source of lead was discovered in 1756 by Colonel John Chiswell in southwestern Virginia. The mine supplied lead for the Continental Army of the Revolution and for the pioneers who moved through the Cumberland Gap into Tennessee and Kentucky. *See: Austinville; Fort Chiswell; Shot Tower*

LEBANON
Russell County   Town

The cedars of Lebanon were used in the construction of Solomon's temple in ancient Jerusalem. Because wild cedars grow in abundance here, as in most parts of the Commonwealth, the county seat of Russell County was named Lebanon when the first permanent courthouse was erected in 1816. That building was destroyed by fire in 1872 but the thrifty citizens salvaged much of the rubble and used it in the construction of the present courthouse. *See: Dickensonville*

LEBANON CHURCH
Shenandoah County

Early in its history, this village was known as Cottontown for the locally prominent Cotton family. A church was built that was called Lebanon, a name that is associated with Solomon's Temple. When a community grew to a size that warranted a post office it was named for the church.

LEE COUNTY

Virginia would not be complete without a county honoring the Lee family that produced so many leaders in three centuries, beginning with the seventeenth. This county, formed in 1792 from a part of Russell, was named for Henry (Light-Horse Harry) Lee who was Governor of Virginia when this county was formed. His nickname came from the military organization he commanded during the Revolution. In essence, his unit was really mounted infantry. The men travelled light, rode fast horses, and dragged only a few small-bore field pieces. They served under General Nathaniel Greene and clashed with Lord Cornwallis as he moved north from Savannah to Yorktown.

Henry Lee was a good soldier but an extremely poor businessman. He was thrown into a debtor's jail cell in the 1820s. During the long days of his incarceration, he wrote his memoirs in which he was critical of Thomas Jefferson's actions as the wartime Governor of the new Commonwealth. His account of the Revolution has been discounted by some historians as more fiction and personal aggrandizement than fact. *See: Langley; Leesylvania; Jonesville*

LEEDSTOWN
Westmoreland County

Leeds was the family castle of Thomas, Lord Culpeper, the royal governor of Virginia from 1677 to 1683. Although he lived in the colony for a brief period, he returned home and sent deputies. The sixth Lord Fairfax, the last proprietor of Northern Neck, was a direct descendant. Settlement in Westmoreland County, a portion of Northern Neck, began about 1681. Most of the people lived on the large estates of the major landholders but a few merchants had their shops in the hamlet that was recognized as the Towne of Leeds in 1742.

Here at Leedstown, on February 27, 1766, a group of county residents formed themselves into the Westmoreland Association. They adopted a resolution against the Stamp Act. Drafted by Richard Henry Lee of Chantilly, this "resolve" was one of the first written protests against that tax. It influenced public opinion in several other colonies by its directness and daring. It had much to do with motivating the rowdies of Boston to stage the Tea Party. *See: Chantilly; Greenway Court*

LEE HALL
Lancaster County

Built in 1720 by Thomas Lee for his brother Henry, this Lee Hall is best known as the home of Henry's second son, Richard, who was always called Squire Lee. The squire remained a bachelor for fifty-nine years. At last he married his cousin Sally Poythress, sired three daughters in quick succession, and died in 1795, disappointed because he did not have a son. After Squire Lee died, Sally married Willoughby Newton of Linden. *See: Fort James; Kiskiack*

LEE HALL
Newport News

Lee Hall, located on the old highway between Elizabeth City and Williamsburg, has been a landmark for travellers since the decade before the War Between the States. The present house was erected between 1848 and 1859 by Richard Decator Lee to replace an earlier home on the former Cary family, Oak Grove farm. Once a major estate, the lands have been sold off until only a small portion of the original tract now surrounds the manor. Lee Hall is the only major nineteenth century antebellum plantation house still in use on the lower Peninsula. The little hamlet near the house was brought into being when a special rail line was laid from this point to Yorktown for the 1881 centennial celebration of the surrender of Lord Cornwallis. Although trains seldom stop at Lee Hall for passengers any more, the old station was spruced up for the 1981 bicentennial surrender ceremonies. *See: Merrie Oaks*

LEESBURG
Loudoun County   Town

There was a settlement here long before the county was formed in 1757. Originally it was called Georgetown, probably for King George II. When a town was formally laid out for the county seat, the name was changed to Leesburg to honor Francis Lightfoot Lee and Philip Ludwell Lee, local land owners who were among the town's first trustees. The early settlement was surrounded by a stockade which fell into disrepair and disappeared. On June 14, 1766, the "Loudon Resolves" were adopted in the county courthouse to protest the Stamp Act. *See: Leedstown*

LEESVILLE
Campbell County

The first known settler here was Captain Jacob Early, the son of Colonel Jeremiah Early. The land was purchased by John Lee in 1794. Although the name Lee is sacred in Virginia, this Mr. Lee was not of the Stratford Hall branch of Westmoreland County. John Lee conceived the idea of a town in 1818, laid off lots, and made a bit of money. While he was at it, he named his new town Leesville. *See: Evington*

LEESYLVANIA
Prince William County

Here in 1756 was born Henry "Light-Horse

Harry" Lee. A graduate of Princeton in 1773, he was an officer during the Revolution where he earned his nickname for the Light Horse Cavalry he commanded. After the hostilities, he married Anne Hill Carter of Shirley and they moved to the old Lee homestead at Stratford where Anne gave birth to a son, Robert Edward Lee, who became the famous Confederate general. "Light-Horse Harry" served as the Governor of the Commonwealth during the early Federal period. *See: Lee County; Shirley; Stratford*

LEETON FOREST
Fauquier County

Thomas Lee of Stratford patented this tract in 1718. It was inherited by his son, Richard Henry Lee, who in turn left it to his daughter Anne. She married a kinsman, Charles Lee, the Attorney General in Washington's and John Adams' cabinets while they were president.

LEVEL GREEN
Gloucester County

A level green was sometimes the name applied to a grassy place, kept closely cropped, for playing at bowls in which opponents roll white balls to see who can get the closest to a red ball, or some variation of this idea. John Robins was the first settler here in 1642, but it is not certain if he gave the estate the name. The present house, the third to stand here, dates from 1692. Over the years the occupants have added to or otherwise modified the small house that once was situated on 2,000 acres of choice waterfront property. It is not know if any owner actually had a bowling green.

LEXINGTON
Rockbridge County

When Rockbridge County was formed in 1778, the courthouse was erected near the junction of the Valley Pike and the road that headed west to the mountains and the Kanawha River. Tradition says that the little town that grew near the courthouse was named by Thomas Jefferson to honor the battle fought near Lexington, Massachusetts, at the beginning of the Revolution. In Lexington are two renowned schools, Virginia Military Institute and Washington and Lee University. Two great heroes of the Confederacy lie buried here: General Thomas Jonathan (Stonewall) Jackson who, before the Civil War, was an instructor of mathematics at V.M.I.; and General Robert Edward Lee

who was the president of Washington College from 1865 until his death in 1870. *See: Virginia Military Institute; Washington and Lee University*

LIBERIA
Prince William County

The land of this farm was owned originally by Robert "King" Carter who gave it to his son, Robert II. A descendant married William J. Weir who built the present house in 1825. Known first as the Weir Place, and then as The Brick House, the current name dates to Reconstruction. Located about a mile-and-a-half from the town of Manassas, this house once sheltered the presidents of both the Union and the Confederacy. When General Beauregard used it as his headquarters, President Jefferson Davis came for a conference on strategy. A few years later, when Federal General McDowell lay wounded in this house, he was visited by President Abraham Lincoln. *See: Freedom Hill; Monrovia*

LIBERTY HALL ACADEMY
Rockbridge County

Founded in 1749 as Augusta Academy, this school was re-established north of Lexington in May 1776 as Liberty Hall Academy. Six years later it was moved to the town of Lexington where it was chartered as a college. When George Washington endowed it in 1796, the college was named for him. After the War Between the States, General Robert E. Lee was invited to become its president. After his death in 1870, his name was incorporated into the title as Washington and Lee College. *See: Washington and Lee University*

LIGHTFOOT
James City County

John Lightfoot, one of the very early settlers in Virginia, owned property on Jamestown Island at Goose Hill Marsh. The name Lightfoot appears on the roll of the Council all during the seventeenth century but disappears in the middle of the eighteenth. John Lightfoot, Esq., served on the Council with the Reverend James Blair and Robert Carter during the dispute in 1705 which forced Governor Nicholson from office. A communion service owned by Westover Church is inscribed, "The Gift of Colonel Francis Lightfoot Anno 1727."

Philip Lightfoot augmented his income from his law practice with the profits from a trading post about ten miles north of Williamsburg where the village of Lightfoot now stands. Philip called his home Tedington which he built about 1717. *See: Dancing Point; Menokin; Westover Church*

LIGNUM
Culpeper County

The post office was established in a wooded area of the county in 1880. The Reverend Frank Robertson, a local cleric, suggested the name *Lignum*, the Latin word for "wood."

LILIAN
Northumberland County

Lillian Cockrell was the wife of George Reed. He suggested her name for the new post office in 1885. Much to her disgust, the postal clerk left out one "l" in the official spelling. It was impossible to get the postal authorities to admit or correct the mistake.

LITTLE ENGLAND
Gloucester County

Situated on Sarah Creek, an inlet near the mouth of the York River, Little England is opposite Yorktown. The first house was constructed prior to 1680 by Captain John Perrin who had been granted 400 acres by Governor Berkeley in 1651 for transporting himself and several others to Virginia. The main house, said to be built according to plans by Christopher Wren, was completed in 1716 by Thomas Perrin, the grandson of the immigrant. Originally the waterway serving the house was Perrin's Creek, but it was later named Sarah's Creek for Sarah Churchill, the first Duchess of Marlborough. An adjacent inlet today is called Perrin Creek. During the Revolution, this house was referred to as the Sarah's Creek House when it was used as a spy point by patriots to keep watch over ships entering or leaving the York River. *See: Marlborough*

LITTLE ENGLAND
Hampton   Site

William Capp was one of the early residents of the little town of Kecoughtan where he was the respected leader of the community. He was a delegate to the first Assembly in 1619. When King James I revoked the charter of the London Company in 1624, Capp was sent to England by the Assembly to deliver a petition asking the king to allow the colonists to continue writing local laws. While awaiting his turn for an audience, James I died and Mr. Capp had to redirect the petition to Charles I. The request was granted.

In 1634, William Capp patented a section of land adjoining the town. Called Little England,

the site lay in the portion of modern Hampton bounded on the south by Sunset Creek in the vicinity of the Yacht Club. An entrepreneur in a modest way, he was granted permission to build a saltworks in the Buckroe area where he evaporated water from the Chesapeake Bay using the heat of the sun. The product was not popular since it was too caustic for curing meat and fish; some complained it was not salty enough. The little stone house at the saltworks still stands, but nothing remains of Little England except the name. *See: Buckroe*

LITTLE HUNTING CREEK
Fairfax County   Site

About five miles south of present Alexandria is Little Hunting Creek. Margaret Brent, once the secretary to Lord Baltimore in Maryland—and a woman far ahead of her time in more ways than one—patented a tract of land in 1663. The sister of Giles Brent, she was the first woman in America to campaign for the right to vote since she was a land owner and qualified in every way except by sex. Although she was not successful, she made a lot of noise about the issue and was none too popular. She always signed her name "Margaret Brent, Gent."

Augustine Washington lived not far from Margaret Brent's old home from 1734 to 1739. George Washington returned to his father's property on Little Hunting Creek, called Wakefield, after his marriage to the Widow Custis and created his estate Mount Vernon. *See: Aquia Creek; Pecatone; Richlands; Wakefield of Westmoreland*

LITTLE SCOTLAND
Hampton   Site

This tract in old Elizabeth City County was located on the east side of Hampton Creek on land now occupied by Hampton University. It was bounded on the east by Bull Bay (now John's Creek) and on the north by glebe land of the local parish. In 1813 it was listed as belonging to Captain Spencer Drummond, a Scot, who possibly was related to the Drummonds of the Eastern Shore and might have been a descendant of William Drummond. This farm was known to have been called Little Scotland before the Revolution. Some local historians are convinced that the name goes back even earlier. *See: Accomac; Governor's Land; Hill's Farm; Metomkin*

LITTLE SURRY
Obsolete

That portion of Surry County that lies

south of the Blackwater River was known as Little Surry. No one today remembers why.

LITTLETON
Sussex County

Littleton Academy was established at Laurel Grove in 1722. The choice of name is clouded in the mysteries of time since the history of the academy has not been written. About 1850 the school was moved to the farm of Augustus Stephenson, close by Jerusalem Plank Road, and classes were held for the neighborhood children. After the Civil War, it was a school for black children for about a decade. The building was razed in 1879 and nothing remains save the name Littleton which was applied to a small hamlet that developed near the site of the old school. *See: Jerusalem*

LITTLETOWN
James City County   Site

This land was claimed by Captain Gabriel Archer from whom it got its more common name, Archer's Hope. One of the first settlers in Jamestown in 1607, Archer and Edward Maria Wingfield attempted to steal one of the three ships to return to England. When their plan was discovered, Wingfield was stripped of his authority as the President of the Council by John Smith, who assumed command. The next spring Wingfield and Archer were sent home on a returning supply ship.

When George Menefie came to the colony in 1620, he settled at Archer's Hope, named his place Littletown, and created an important farm on which he grew herbs and spices. He had an orchard that had the first serious planting of peach, apple, pear, and cherry trees in Virginia. In addition to land husbandry, Menefie was the business agent for several mercantile firms in England. While a member of the Council, he and Dr. John Pott engineered the revolt that sent Governor John Harvey home. For his part in this, George Menefie spent a number of expensive years in London clearing himself of treason charges. When he finally returned to Virginia, he relocated farther up the James River at a farm called Buckland.

During World War II, Camp Wallace was established at Littletown. The Army obliterated all traces of Menefie's orchards. Of course, by then the trees had died of old age, but the organization was still there. *See: Buckland; Harrop; Jamestown; Utimara*

LOCUST DALE
Madison County

A private school named Locust Dale operated successfully from 1858 until 1911. It was founded by Andrew James Gordon, (how's that for a true Scottish name?) a native of Vermont who fell in love with Virginia. A fire that began in the laundry, quickly spread by a brisk wind, destroyed every building. The school was forced to close and never reopened. The little village in which most of the instructors lived with their families was named for Locust Dale School.

LOCUST GROVE
Orange County

Robinson's Tavern once stood here at a major crossroads. The tavern, built prior to 1785, was owned by Dr. George Robinson. It is claimed he was a member of Alexander Spotswood's expedition to the Shenandoah Valley in 1716 and, if that claim is true, Dr. Robinson would have been a very old man in 1785, probably close to ninety. More than likely he was the son of one of the Knights of the Golden Horseshoe. The present hamlet of Locust Grove undoubtedly took its name from a local farm. *See: Germanna*

LOCUST HILL
Albemarle County

Robert Lewis of Belvoir occupied this tract in 1740 as one of the early settlers in this region. It is thought his grandson, Meriwether Lewis, was born here in 1744 although the records are unclear. All that can be said for certain is that his mother, Lucy Lewis, was living here while her husband was away on military duty. When she was widowed, Lucy married Captain John Marks who moved his new family to Georgia. Lucy's son, named for Nicholas Meriwether, probably her father, returned to Locust Hill in 1792 when he inherited the estate.

Meriwether Lewis was the co-leader with Captain William Clark of the famed expedition that travelled all the way to the Pacific in the Oregon Territory in 1803. This was the Lewis and Clark Expedition that was sent out by President Jefferson. Both of the men were natives of Albemarle County. *See: Belvoir of Albemarle*

LOCUSTVILLE
Accomack County

The first post office was opened here in 1835. Since locust trees grow abundantly in Virginia and many farms and estates used the name, it is assumed that the post office was named for a local establishment.

LONDON BRIDGE
Virginia Beach   **Site**

A crude bridge built over one of the tributary streams of the Lynnhaven River was one of the earliest spans in this area. In jest, and with a touch of nostalgia, it was named London Bridge. A small settlement grew near it and adopted the name. Near it was the first courthouse of old Princess Anne County. When the county seat was relocated at Kempsville, the hamlet of London Bridge languished in neglect. This is one of the few places in Virginia that has London in its name, a rather strange fact since many other places were named for sites in or near the English capital. *See: New London*

LONG BRANCH
Clarke County

This house, in American classical style, was begun in 1811 by Robert Carter Burwell. It is one of the four surviving homes known to have been designed, at least in part, by Benjamin Latrobe, America's first professional architect. A *branch* in Virginia, is a tributary of a stream or river. *See: Branch; Carter Hall; Green Spring*

LONG BRIDGE ORDINARY
Gloucester County

Probably built in 1727, this was a popular tavern and an important stage and post stop on the road from Fredericksburg. A poster which now hangs in the Rising Sun Tavern of that city, dated 1736, announces the morning departure of the daily stage. It stopped here for passengers having business at Gloucester Court House about a mile away. The two-story brick structure of this ordinary has double thick door panels, one board has its grain running vertically and the other on a diagonal. This layering made it difficult to cut through with a hatchet or axe and is said to have been designed to make it Indian-proof. Many such double paneled doors are found in remote colonial dwellings. The name of the ordinary comes from a long trestle and causeway over a sluggish stream through a low, muddy bottom. *See: Ordinary*

LONG ISLAND
Campbell County

Named for a long narrow island in the upper James River that once was the site of a fortified Indian village, the farm on the bank took its name from the island, as did the present tiny community nearby. Patrick Henry owned Long Island Farm for two years, beginning in 1794, before he settled at his last home, Red Hill.

LONGWOOD
Prince Edward County

Near Farmville, this was the birthplace of Peter Johnston, a lieutenant in "Light-Horse Harry" Lee's Legion during the Revolution. His son, Joseph E. Johnston, also born here, was a full Confederate general during the Civil War. He was the highest ranking former U.S. officer to join the Confederacy.

General Johnston commanded the Southern forces at the beginning of the Seven Days Battles around Richmond. He was wounded during the battle, being replaced by General Robert E. Lee.

Johnston returned to duty after his wound healed. He commanded in the lower-South theater of the war.

He was relieved during the Atlanta campaign by John B. Hood.

Later, Johnston was restored to command. After he surrendered his army at Appomattox, Johnston surrendered his forces to General William Sherman at Bennett Place near Durham Station, N.C. *See: Cheatham Annex*

LONGWOOD COLLEGE
Farmville

When first opened in 1884 under the guidance of William H. Ruffner, this was the State Female Normal School. In 1924, the name was changed to State Teacher's College. However, in 1949 it became Longwood College, named for the nearby estate. *See: Longwood*

LOUDOUN COUNTY

Formed in 1757 from Fairfax, this county was named for John Campbell, the Earl of Loudoun, the titular governor of Virginia for three years beginning in 1756. Although the Earl also was the head of all British armed forces in America, Campbell never came to this country but was represented by Robert Dinwiddie and Francis Fauquier who bore the title Lieutenant Governor. Beginning about 1720, Quakers came from Pennsylvania to take up farms in this region. They were followed by German Lutherans who built their homes in the isolated northwestern portion of what was to be Loudoun County, but they kept themselves apart from the other settlers and retained their own language and customs. The English, meanwhile, established large estates along the Potomac. The courthouse was erected in Leesburg in 1758 and has been there ever since.

Early in the Civil War, in October 1861, a battle was fought at Ball's Bluff two miles from Leesburg. It was a disaster for the Federal troops. The Confederates lost only 150 men, killed and wounded, while more than 750 Union soldiers died, either killed during the action or drowned in the Potomac River while attempting to escape. During the last two years of the war, Mosby's Rangers roamed throughout this region at will.

Today Loudoun County is horse country where many famous race horses have been bred and schooled. *See: Waterford*

LOUISA COUNTY

Formed in 1742 from Hanover, this county was named for Louisa, Queen of Denmark, the daughter of George II. The first courthouse was built on the Talley farm on Beaver Creek (now Tanyard Branch) about a mile from the present courthouse complex. For many years the settlement around the courthouse was modest. As more people moved closer to the commercial center and the various stores, Louisa Court House became large enough to be incorporated as a town with its own government. The county seat is now called Louisa.

LOVETTSVILLE
Loudoun County   Town

Land for the hamlet was laid out into lots in 1820 by David Lovett who called his planned community New Town. Prior to that, the settlement was known as Thrasher's Store. When it was incorporated, the name Lovettsville was adopted to avoid confusion with New Town of Princess Anne County.

LOVINGSTON
Nelson County

The seat of Nelson County, Lovingston, was named for James Loving, Sr., who donated the land on which the courthouse was built in 1808. Just a year before, the hamlet was incorporated as a town. In 1938 the citizens succeeded in having Lovingston de-incorporated, one of the few instances where this has been accomplished in Virginia. *See: Town*

LOWLAND COTTAGE
Gloucester County

This early colonial home was built beside the Ware River about 1690, probably by a member of the Warner family. Intermingled with its pre-federal history are the names Throckmorton, Jones, and Taliaferro. This small house, truly a cottage, is one of the oldest, yet least known homes in Gloucester County. *See: Warner Hall*

LOWESVILLE
Amherst County

The first postmaster here was Lowe Fulcher. Since everyone knew him by his first name, the local hamlet and the post office was named Lowesville rather than Fulcherville.

LOW MOOR
Alleghany County

Augustus Low, of New York, and his chief engineer whose last name was Moor, organized the Low-Moor Iron Company in the nineteenth century. They processed the local low grade ore in their furnace. The tiny community near the site of the Low-Moor operations retains the unusual name. Today spelled as two separated words, it gives the impression that there is a low moor nearby. A moor, typically British in nature, is a tract of open land usually covered with heather, especially in Scotland. Although there is a variety of heather that grows wild in Virginia, and there are many open tracts, no place in the Commonwealth is known as a moor. Rather, they are called meadows. *See: Jordan Mines*

LUCKETTS
Loudoun County

In years past, this settlement was known as Goresville, named for the local farmer, Thomas Gore. He was an early landowner who served in the militia in 1757. The name was changed to Lucketts after 1865 when the leading citizen was elected sheriff and he ruled the region as if it was his own fief. More correctly, this should be spelled Luckett's.

LUNENBURG COUNTY

Formed from Brunswick in 1746, this county was named for King George II who, while he ruled England, retained the German title of Duke of Brunswick-Lunenburg. The county seat is Lunenburg.

LURAY
Page County   Town

This town was laid out by William Staige Marye in 1812. He was the son of Peter Marye who built the first toll road across the

Blue Ridge from Culpeper to the Shenandoah Valley. The seat of the Marye family is Luray, France. *See: Brompton*

LYNCHBURG
Campbell County   **City**

John Lynch of Chestnut Hill operated the first ferry across the James River at this location. Although a large Quaker settlement had long existed near the public tobacco warehouse, nobody cared much about crossing the river until Lynch provided the means in 1756. The stubborn Quakers did not bother with the conveyance, since they were smart enough to have been on the proper side of the James when the warehouse was built. Lynch's ferry enabled other farmers to bring their products to the little town and there to purchase needed staples and supplies that were brought up the Fluvanna River. When Campbell County was organized in 1781, the hamlet next to Lynch's Warehouse was designated the county seat and was named Campbell Court House.

By preference and local custom, the name was changed to Lynchburg when it was incorporated as a town in 1786. Although this city has taken a bum rap for many years as being the place where the "Lynch Law" began, an extra-legal method of exacting quick, fatal justice, the practice of lynching developed in other Southern states. A frontier court was established at Alta Vista by Colonel Charles Lynch, the ferryman's brother, along with two other prominent men, before the county was organized. *See: Alta Vista; Chestnut Hill; Fluvanna River*

LYNCHBURG COLLEGE
Lynchburg

Begun in 1903 as Virginia Christian College, under the sponsorship of the Disciples of Christ Church, this liberal arts, coeducational school was named for the city in which it was located in 1919.

LYNDHURST
Augusta County

The name of this village honors an Englishman, George C. Milne, Lord Lyndhurst.

LYNNHAVEN BAY
Virginia Beach

This beautiful stretch of water enters Chesapeake Bay through a narrow opening just inside Cape Henry. The first man to settle on its bank was Adam Thoroughgood who located his home on the western branch sometime between 1636 and 1640. His house, still standing and open to the public, is now known as the Thoroughgood House although in older writings it is called Old Lynnhaven. The builder named his place, and the body of water that lapped the edge of his land, for his home in Lynn, England, a small town in Norfolkshire. Before pollution became a disgraceful problem, Lynnhaven oysters

LYNNHAVEN BAY

were famous all along the eastern seaboard. The oysters have begun to purge themselves of harmful bacteria. Local residents report the bay is loaded with oysters; few dare to eat them yet. Efforts are under way to eliminate the hundreds of septic tanks that caused the pollution by connecting the homes to the municipal sewer system. *See: Donation Church; Glen Lyn*

LYNNWOOD
Rockingham County

Three miles north of Port Republic, on the south bank of the Shenandoah River, Thomas Lewis built a modest frame house in 1756. He was a pioneer surveyor of the county who had worked at his trade with George Washington when they both were employed by Lord Fairfax. The general visited his old friend in 1784, and this is one place that can truthfully say, "George Washington slept here." Quite possibly, Thomas Lewis had ancestral roots in Lynn, England.

MACHODOC

Westmoreland County   **Site**

Thomas Lee leased this place from his brother, Richard Lee III, and lived here with his family while Stratford Hall was built. Thomas was the magistrate for the county who ordered the arrest of "a pernicious crew of transported felons" to safeguard the peace. This was in 1729 when English judges often sent convicted felons to exile in Virginia rather than to prison. Before the men could be seized by the Westmoreland sheriff, they set fire to the house at Machodoc late at night. Lee, his wife, and three children escaped by climbing out of a window clad in "nothing but their shifts and the shirts on their backs which was all they saved not two minutes before the house fell in," according to a newspaper story of the incident. The Lee family moved into the incompleted Stratford Hall not far away.

Since others of the family had lived and died here in previous decades, the family burial plot remained in Burnt House Field. Some years later George Lee, only son of Richard III, inherited the Machodoc property, built a new house, and changed the name to Mount Pleasant. The old name, from a local Indian tribal village in the vicinity, is pronounced Ma-SHO-dock. *See: Burnt House Field; Chantilly; Pecatone; Stratford Hall*

MACON

Powhatan County   **Site**

A Huguenot family by the name of Macon, settling here in 1753, established a tavern, a livery stable, a gristmill, a saw mill, and a store. Parts of the early buildings are still in use. *See: Grist Mill; Manakin Town*

MADISON COUNTY

When Culpeper County became too populated to be served from one court center, it was divided to create Madison County in 1792. It was named for James Madison, the "Father of the Constitution" who later became the fourth President. Court was held in a temporary building for many years until the present structure in the town of Madison was erected in 1828. *See: Montpelier of Orange; Page County*

MADISON HEIGHTS

Amherst County

Madison's tobacco warehouse was located on the James River on the Amherst County side. Later a small town grew on the high ground behind it, safely above flood level. Because the river here is rather shallow, the hogsheads of tobacco were transported downstream on rafts supported by dugout canoes.

MADISON MILLS

Madison County

Francis Madison obtained permission to erect a water grist mill on the Rapidan River in 1793. At that time the location was in Orange County. The name was then Madison's Mill.

MADISON UNIVERSITY

Harrisonburg

Established in 1908 as the State Normal School for Women, its name was modified after World War I when it became the State Teacher's College. Realizing there was no great monument to James Madison in Virginia beyond the name of a county, the General Assembly authorized the school to be renamed Madison College just prior to World War II. It became a coeducational institution in 1967 and was upgraded to James Madison University ten years later.

MAGPIE SWAMP

Newport News   **Site**

Originally patented by John Baynham in 1624, this tract was thought to contain 350 acres, but a later survey found 688—much to everyone's surprise. In 1657 Captain Thomas Taylor owned it. His son-in-law, Miles Cary, Sr., inherited the land and began his acquisition of quantities of real estate. Magpie Swamp was described in Taylor's will as adjoining the lands of Captain Samuel Mathews and William Claiborne (two of the leading men of the colony at that time) and three miles up the main creek between Saxon's Gaol and Blunt Point. The creek is now known as the Warwick River; the gaol was at the tip of Mulberry Island. Major Thomas Cary, the son of Miles Cary, inherited Magpie Swamp along with Windmill Point Plantation and added other lands to the family estate. *See: The Forest; Richneck*

MAIDENS
Goochland County
A farm here years ago was called Maiden's Adventure. It was named for a local legend of a young girl who crossed the James River to warn her sweetheart of an imminent Indian attack. Just which portion of her trip involved her adventure is not known but it does fuel the imagination. The present village retains the quaint name.

MAIDSTOWN
Site
A group of stockholders of the Virginia Company planned to organize a Particular Plantation using mostly women as settlers. They were to be selected from among "worthy young women" who would become the wives of the existing bachelor colonists. The town, in the center of the tract, was to be called Maidstown. The plan was approved by the company and a charter was issued in 1622. However, before the new settlement could materialize, the company fell into difficulties from which it never recovered. When the Virginia Company was dissolved in 1624, the plans for Maidstown died with it. *See: Particular Plantation; Virginia Company*

MALVERN HILLS
Henrico County   Site
Thomas Cocke came from Worcestershire, England, in 1630. Here in Virginia he built one of the best examples of Colonial architecture, famous for its beauty, which was named Malvern Hills after the low hills in northeastern Wales near Worcester. James Powell Cocke was the last of his family to live here. Shortly after the Revolution, he sold the plantation and moved to Albemarle County where he built a new house named Edgemont in 1796. The dwelling at Malvern Hills was demolished during the Civil War during a severe battle at the end of the 1862 Peninsula campaign. *See: Bremo*

MANAKIN
Goochland County
This was the site of a Monacan Indian village. Powhatan called them his enemies because he could never exact tribute from them, but there are no reports of warfare and the two Indian nations remained apart. After the Massacre of 1644, in which the Monacans apparently did not participate, they migrated to other locations, probably westward. When a group of Huguenots came to Virginia in 1700, under the leadership of the Marquis de la Muce, they were settled in this abandoned village by the General Assembly. Here the newcomers prospered and multiplied. They were intelligent, well-educated people. Many of them became teachers, school masters, and college professors. *See: Columbia; Frenchtown; Huguenots; Menokin*

MANASSAS
Prince William County   City
Here were fought two severe battles of the Civil War, both Confederate victories. The armies fought to control two rail lines that joined at Manassas Junction in what some call the Battles of Bull Run. On July 21, 1861, in the first full-scale battle of that war, the new inexperienced armies clashed. During the battle, General Barnard Bee is credited with the famous saying about Thomas Jackson, "There stands Jackson like a stone wall! Rally behind the Virginians!" The ensuing Union defeat became a rout.

The second engagement was fought August 28-30, 1862. After McClellan's failure to capture Richmond, the Union forces covering Washington were consolidated into an army under General Pope.

General Lee, in a daring move, divided his army and sent Jackson on a flank march to Manassas. Jackson seized the Union supply depot which set the stage for the battle.

Pope concentrated his men in the vicinity of Manassas and attacked Jackson on the 29th.

Reinforced by Longstreet, the Confederates delivered a defeat to Pope's forces.

Today the battlefield is under the direction of the National Park Service.

In 1911 a Jubilee of Peace was held here by veterans of both armies to celebrate the fiftieth anniversary of the first battle. Men of each army formed two lines, marched across an open field toward each other and met to clasp hands in a token gesture of peace.

Manassas is the seat of Prince William County. *See: Run*

MANASSAS GAP
This is the lowest pass through the Blue Ridge at an elevation of only 950 feet. John Lederer discovered it about 1670. George Washington and Abraham Wood surveyed it for a possible road in 1761. It is flanked by High Knob, 2,385 feet. The Manassas Gap Railroad, organized in March 1850 was authorized to be a line "from some convenient

RETREAT OF UNION FORCES AFTER BATTLE OF SECOND MANASSAS, MANASSAS

point on the Orange and Alexandria Railroad, through Manassas Gap, passing near the town of Strasburg, to the town of Harrisonburg, in the county of Rockingham."

MANASSAS PARK
Prince William County   **City**

After World War II, a real estate development was begun just outside the city limits of Manassas. Named Manassas Park, it quickly grew to become one of the forty-one cities in the Commonwealth.

MANCHESTER
City of Richmond

William Byrd owned great quantities of land on both sides of the James at the falls. His son, William II, quickened the settlement of Richmond by selling off parcels of land and seeing to it that they were subdivided into lots with streets between them. William III, a compulsive gambler, sold the land which he had inherited on the south bank of the river to cover his many debts. A small hamlet, later called Manchester, after the city in England, was established at Rocky Ridge, just across the Shoccoes Hill. Connected by Mayo's toll bridge during the early nineteenth century, it was annexed by Richmond in the twentieth century. Because Manchester streets

remained unpaved for so long, it was often called Mudchester. *See: Richmond; Stone House*

MANNSFIELD
Spotsylvania County

After Mann Page II nearly went broke completing Rosewell in Gloucester County and paying off his father's huge debts, he moved to the vicinity of Fredericksburg to try to recover from the financial strain. There he built a home which he named Mannsfield. Although not nearly as pretentious as his father's dream house, it was magnificent in a more refined and restrained way. Completed in 1775, Mann Page II lived out his life here with his wife Ann Corbin Tayloe of Mount Airy.

Their son, Mann Page III, inherited Mannsfield and lived here with his wife (and cousin) Mary Tayloe, also of Mount Airy. It was he who rode to Williamsburg and back (200 miles) in twenty-four hours to find out what was going on in the capital immediately after Lord Dunmore stole the gunpowder from the Magazine. When he came back with the news that Peyton Randolph advised that the Fredericksburg militia should not ride south to attack the Palace, the troopers voted not to begin a military action at that time, although the decision carried by only one

149

vote.

Mannsfield was famed for its avenue and grove of magnificent chestnut trees. It was burned by Union troops shortly after the surrender of 1865. *See: Laneville; Menokin; Mt. Airy; Pecatone; Shelly; Rosewell*

MANOR MANSION
Augusta County

William Beverley built his mansion in the far western frontier on land granted to him in 1736 by Governor Gooch. The grant, "in consideration for inducing a large number of settlers to this community," was for 118,491 acres. In what is now the city of Staunton, William Beverley built his large mansion in 1739. It was the first house of that size and refinement in the Shenandoah Valley. Although Beverley was content to live out his years in the Valley, his eldest son, Colonel Robert Beverley, preferred the old family lands along the Rappahannock River.

Manor Mansion was bought by Daniel Shelley in 1805. When he died, his widow and daughters converted the house into a school for young ladies and renamed it Kalorama about 1830. *See: Blandfield; Staunton*

MAPPSVILLE
Accomack County

Samuel Mapp owned a store here many years ago. Members of this family now live all over southeastern Virginia.

MARIE'S MOUNT
Newport News

In 1621 Sir William Newce, who was the Marshall of Virginia, settled on the north shore of Hampton Roads with his brother, Captain Thomas Newce and Daniel Gookin. All three came from Newcetown, Ireland. They selected a bit of flatland watered by a fresh stream at the mouth of the James River. This tip of land was called Point Hope by the early settlers because by the time they reached this point they had but a short way to sail to reach Jamestown. Sir William died shortly after settling in Virginia; Captain Thomas, a seafaring man, traveled on. Daniel Gookin remained, established a plantation here by importing settlers, and headed a small, but thriving settlement which he named Marie's Mount in honor of his wife who remained in England. *See: Mount; Newport News*

MARION
Smyth County   **Town**

Founded in 1831, this town honors Francis Marion, the famed Swamp Fox who led a group of irregulars in South Carolina during the Revolution.

MARKHAM
Fauquier County

The Washington and Old Dominion Railroad's president bought an estate in this county in 1854. James Markham Marshall gallantly bestowed the name Markham to what previously had been called The Hollow. A small village developed around the depot.

MARKHAM
Pittsylvania County   **Site**

This was the home of Colonel John Donelson who, over a thirty-five year period, served as a county militia officer, surveyor, justice, vestryman, Burgess, and emmissary to the Indian tribes along the Banister River and to the south along the Carolina border. Here was born Rachel Donelson, the youngest of his eleven children. In 1779, when Rachel was but 17, John Donelson disposed of all his Virginia holdings and led 120 women and children and forty men into the Kentucky-Tennessee frontier. There the sparkling Rachel became the belle of the border and married Lewis Robards in 1785. For some reason, Robards began divorce proceedings against his wife and left her.

Ignorant of the law and the time interval required for an official termination of her marriage, she married Andrew Jackson before the final decree was handed down by the distant court. Because she married before she was officially divorced, she was guilty of bigamy. This scandal followed Jackson for much of his public and private life. The old Donelson place in Virginia is gone and the site of Markham is barely marked.

MARLBORO
Frederick County

South of Winchester, Izaac Zane owned 21,000 acres. A member of the *American Society for Promoting Useful Knowledge,* he had a personal library of 400 books at the outbreak of the Revolution. In 1778 he purchased from Mary Willing Byrd the famous Westover library of nearly 4,000 volumes for which he paid the then fantastic sum of 2,000 pounds sterling.

MARLBOROUGH
Stafford County   **Site**

Settled in 1647 by Giles Brent, who came from Maryland, the land at the mouth of Potomac Creek was not laid out as a port village until 1705. Named for John Churchill, the first Duke of Marlborough, this was supposed to be the principal city of Stafford County. Ships found the site inconvenient, and when the courthouse burned down the whole project was abandoned within twenty years.

John Mercer, a lawyer and partner in a successful Potomac River shipping firm, acquired the land and established a plantation in 1725, the same year that he married Catherine, the sister of George Mason III of Gunston Hall. It was not until 1748 that the mansion was begun, styled after a Venetian villa. The library at Marlborough contained nearly 500 books, more than half of them dealing with law, which were read and studied by Mercer's nephew, George Mason IV, the author of the Virginia Bill of Rights and of the Commonwealth's first constitution. John Mercer's legal work was so controversial that he twice was disbarred by the General Assembly. Still, he was an astute businessman who made a modest fortune.

His eldest son, George Mercer, sent to England to be the business agent of his father's company, was foolish enough to return to his homeland in 1765 as the Collector of Stamps for Virginia. He quickly resigned the post when a mob, directed by Richard Henry Lee, burned him in effigy and prompted him to leave for England in haste. George's brother, James, fought a duel with Arthur Lee about this, but neither man was injured.

John Mercer gave up the practice of law at this time and, although deeply in debt, built a brewery and cooperage and purchased more slaves to grow barley on his farm. Andrew Monroe, the grandfather of the future president, was engaged as overseer of this project but the resulting brew was of such poor quality that no one drank it. When the elder Mercer died in 1768, nearly bankrupt, the oldest son, George, the "Collector," fell heir to Marlborough. Rather than risk returning to America. George gave the estate to James who worked hard to lift the debts. However, by 1819 the Mercer family abandoned the estate completely. When excavations were made in 1930, the foundations of the fabulous mansion were barely discernable under the weeds and rubble. The house apparently had burned while empty.

Although James Mercer was not successful as a plantation manager, he was a better lawyer than his father and was a patriot, unlike his brother. A Burgess and a member of the Continental Congress, toward the end of his life he was appointed a judge. Having worked hard to establish the Commonwealth of Virginia, Mercer joined Patrick Henry in opposing ratification of the Federal Constitution as written, fearing a loss of state's rights. *See: Aquia Church; Berry Hill; Brentville; Bristow; Chantilly; Gunston Hall; Little England of Gloucester; Monrovia*

MARLFIELD
Gloucester County

John Buckner, clerk of the Gloucester County court, made his home at Marlfield, named for the marl found on the York River banks. He imported the first printing press to Virginia, and in the spirit of public service, printed the laws of 1680. However, he had neglected to obtain a license for printing and found himself at the wrong end of the law. Governor Culpeper reprimanded him and in 1682 shut down his printing plant for a period of time. Freedom of the press would not arrive for another hundred years. *See: Grace Church of Yorktown*

MARMION
King George County

Named in honor of Lord Marmion, this is believed to have been the site of the first homestead selected about 1674 by the immigrant, William Fitzhugh. The lands of Marmion were inherited by his youngest son, John, who built the large house and quite possibly incorporated the old man's original house into the new dwelling. In 1785 Philip Fitzhugh sold Marmion to George Washington's nephew, Major George Lewis of Kenmore. William Fitzhugh, a frugal Scot, moved to Ravensworth about 1695 to get away from too many free-loading travelers. Marmion was located on the King's Highway, a major artery. *See: Chatham; Kenmore; Lamb's Creek Church; Ravensworth*

MARSHALL
Fauquier County

Incorporated in 1796 as the village of Salem, the name was changed in 1882 to honor Chief Justice John Marshall. *See: Germantown; Oak Hill of Fauquier*

MARTIN'S BRANDON
Prince George County   Site

John Martin came to Virginia with the first settlers in 1607. In the spring of 1610, after the terrible Starving Time, all of the survivors "save only John Martin" voted to

151

abandon Jamestown and go home. He was delighted to see Lord Delaware's ship arrive just in the nick of time to prevent the end of the English settlement in the New World. A hothead who quarreled frequently with Lord Delaware, Martin and a few followers were banished from Jamestown that summer. They settled on the opposite side of the James River about five miles up stream and, instead of perishing as was expected, they prospered independently.

In 1617 Martin went back to England to receive a grant for 7,000 acres and a charter for a Particular Plantation which exempted him from the "Laws of Jamestown." Using his own money, he built houses and imported settlers. He refused to pledge loyalty to any governor in the colony, especially not Jamestown's, and for that reason his representatives were excluded from the first General Assembly of 1619.

About a decade later a contagious conflagration wiped out his houses and other buildings. The losses forced John Martin into a debtor's cell in England when he stubbornly refused to declare himself bankrupt. In 1630 he successfully petitioned King Charles I "for the space of six months to go freely about" to collect money owed him, but he was only partially successful before he died in Virginia in 1632. His body was buried in an unmarked grave at Brandon.

Five years later, Martin's holdings were purchased by the owners of the ship *Merchant's Hope.* They were John Sadler and Richard Quiney, both merchants, and a mariner (possibly the captain) William Barber. These three partners built new houses farther from the river's edge, imported more settlers, and successfully farmed the land. *See: Brandon; Merchant's Hope Plantation; Particular Plantation*

MARTIN'S HUNDRED
James City County   **Site**

Sir Richard Martin acquired 80,000 acres of land on the north bank of the James in 1617. The tract was located about seven miles below Jamestown. The first people were "planted" the next year and more followed. When insufficient housing was available for some of the newcomers, Governor Samuel Argall sent them to his own tract, Argall's Guift, which did not endear him to the proprietor of the grant. By 1619 there were enough people at Martin's Hundred to entitle them to representation at the First Assembly. In 1621 a group of Englishmen formed the

"Society of Martin's Hundred" and began to acquire additional property until their tract stretched from the James River all the way across the Peninsula to Chischiak on the York. They also bought a part of John Martin's land on the Surry side of the James which they named Merchant's Hope Plantation. The Massacre of 1622 struck hard at Martin's Hundred with seventy-eight people killed, including the two Burgesses. All of this land was too much for society to control properly, and the tract was slowly broken up and sold to others. *See: Bellfield; Carter's Grove; Merchant's Hope Plantation*

MARTINSVILLE
Henry County   **City**

Martinsville is the county seat of Henry County. It was named for General Joseph Martin who settled here. Born in Albemarle County in 1740, he ran away from home at seventeen to seek adventure. He found plenty as an Indian fighter, Indian agent, and land supervisor. Described as a brawny, picturesque man of six feet, he always wore buckled knee breeches and sported a long beard which he braided and wore tucked into his shirt. For his services he was appointed Brigadier General of the state militia in 1793. By then he had fathered eighteen children. He was quite a man. *See: Figsboro*

MARY BALDWIN COLLEGE
Staunton

The oldest senior college for women of the Presbyterian Church of the United States, classes began in 1842. Known for many years as the Augusta Female Academy, for the county in which it is located, the name was changed in 1895 to honor Mary Julia Baldwin, longtime headmistress and principal. During her lifetime the school offered only a two year curriculum. It expanded to a four year college in 1923.

MARYLAND

The original negotiations for the grant of this territory were begun by Lord Baltimore as a refuge for himself and his Roman Catholic friends. Dying before the grant was made, his son, Cecelius Calvert, inherited his father's "lands, plans, obligations, and hopes." It was to this new Lord Baltimore that the Maryland charter was issued on June 30, 1632. Clearly, the lands lay within the boundary of Virginia, and the disturbed Virginia Council sent William Claiborne to England to oppose the grant. However, the

Catholic-minded King Charles I informed the troubled Virginians that he had, indeed, given Lord Baltimore a large portion of their territory and that he would not even consider changing his mind.

When two ships arrived at Point Comfort in February 1634, under the leadership of Cecelius' brother, Leonard Calvert, with instructions from the king for the Virginians to give all possible aid to the new settlers, Captain Samuel Mathews of Denbigh threw his hat to the ground, stamped on it, and cried in a fury of frustration, "A pox upon Maryland!" There followed a lengthy dispute about the exact location of the boundary, especially on the Eastern Shore. Lord Baltimore, as the governor of Maryland, and Virginia's governor, Sir William Berkeley, finally worked out an agreeable line which has remained until the present time despite the efforts of Colonel Edmund Scarburg to change it to his liking in 1659.

Usually, when a river divides two states, the border runs down the center. In this case, however, Virginia's border stops at the western bank. Maryland controls the entire Potomac River. *See: Carolina; Denbigh; Occohannock; New Kent County; Richlands; Virginia*

MARY WASHINGTON COLLEGE
Fredericksburg

Doors opened here for the first time in 1911 as another of Virginia's State Normal Schools to train women for teaching jobs in the public schools. It was given its present name in 1838 in honor of Mary Ball Washington, the mother of the first president, whose last home was in Fredericksburg.

MASSANUTTEN MOUNTAIN

This is technically a short mountain range about fifty miles long that stands in the lower Shenandoah Valley. The name has two possible meanings, both Indian: *potato ground* or *basket*. The early English name was Peaked Mountain for its many summits, especially at the southeastern end where its stone capping has been revealed by erosion. Peaked was pronounced peak-ed. *See: McGaheysville; Shenandoah Valley*

MASSAPONNOX
Spotsylvania County   Site

The stream along which the Massaponnox tribe lived empties into the Rappahannock River just below Fredericksburg. When Alexander Spotswood operated his Tubal Furnace at Germanna, the resulting pigs of iron were moved by barge down Massaponnox Run for loading onto deepwater vessels anchored off its mouth. Movement of the heavy loads down this run often was hampered by low water making connections with the ships difficult since their arrival was seldom known in advance. When his Germans deserted him at the end of their indentures and he was forced to use blacks to keep his ironworks going, Spotswood closed Tubal Furnace, built a new one closer to the Rappahannock, and moved the ore and charcoal to it in wagons. Massaponnox Furnace ceased operation with his death in Annapolis in 1740. *See: Bristol Iron Works; Germanna; Tubal Furnace; Wilderness*

MASSIES MILL
Nelson County

A grist mill was built in 1801 by Major Thomas Massie near his home Level Green. He served on Washington's staff. The present community retained the old name which was originally Massie's Mill.

MASSINACAK
Powhatan County   Site

Captain Christopher Newport found this Indian village in 1608 on his journey of exploration up the James River with 120 selected men. He was searching for the main village of the Monacans of whom he had received good reports. Later Newport wrote, "the people neither used us well nor ill, yet for our securities we tooke one of their petty kings, and led him bound to conduct us on our way." In 1670 John Lederer visited Massinacak while enroute to explore the land west of the Blue Ridge. It was he who accurately located this village on his map. Now pronounced MASS-na-cack. *See: Columbia; Rassawek*

MATHEWS COUNTY

Gloucester Court House was too far away for the people who lived between the Rappahannock and Potomac rivers on the eastern end of the Middle Peninsula. Therefore, a new county was formed in 1790. It was named for Colonel Thomas Mathews, a local Revolutionary soldier. The village of Mathews Court House is the largest community in the county. *See: Gwynn's Island*

MATILDAVILLE
Fairfax County   Site

About three miles below the Great Falls of the Potomac, locks were built for the

Patowmack Canal by a company in which George Washington had a major interest. Lined with huge blocks of sandstone, each lock was 100 feet long and fourteen feet deep. Near these locks the town of Matildaville was established in 1790. It was named for the first wife of "Light-Horse Harry" Lee, also an investor in the company. It was hoped that the surplus water of the river would provide power for a great industrial center here on the canal, but the project was unsuccessful. The only residents of the new town were the lockmaster and his family. The railroads put the canal out of business in the early nineteenth century and Matildaville died by 1830. *See: Fairfield of Clarke*

MATOACA
Chesterfield County

The Indian woman everyone knows as Pocahontas had a secret clan name, one that was selected at birth for some special sign revealed to her mother or father. This private name, Matoaca, has never been given an English meaning. This small village, and a lake near Williamsburg, are the only two spots in Virginia that go by this name. It is pronounced Ma-TOW-a-ka.

MATRIMONY CREEK
Henry County

When William Byrd II headed the Virginia Commission to establish the Virginia-North Carolina border in 1728, his group camped beside this stream. He wrote in his diary that the creek was "called so by an unfortunate marry'd man because it was exceedingly noisy and impetuous. However, tho the stream was clamorous, like those women who make themselves plainest heard, it was perfectly clear and unsully'd." *See: Rocketts of Henrico*

MATTAPONI INDIANS
King William County

These Indians were part of the Powhatan confederacy when the colonists came in 1607. Their present reservation lies in King William County about ten miles up the Mattaponi River from West Point. Very early in Virginia's history, this tribe made peace with the settlers and provided not only food and supplies but women for wives and servants. They sent braves for joint military campaigns against other tribes. After the Massacre of 1644, in which they took no part, they moved farther up the river to the Piscataway Swamp to avoid contact with the settlers who did not differentiate between friendly and hostile

Indians but rather murdered them all in an indiscriminate war against all natives.

After two generations of peace, the Mattaponi tribe convinced the Virginia government they were peaceful and were allowed to return to their original village. The treaty granting them permission to return to the land of their fathers, where their descendants live today, required payment of an annual tribute of one fresh-killed deer and some grain to be delivered to the Governor. *See: Delaware Town; King and Queen County; Pamunkey*

MATTAPONI RIVER

Now a shallow, meandering stream with encroaching banks, the Mattaponi River takes its name from the Indian tribe that lived near its junction with the Pamunkey River at West Point. The Mattaponi, the true headwaters of the York, once was navigable as far upstream as Aylett in Prince William County. Now badly silted, only small pleasure boats play upon its lower portion. Three minor streams, the Matta, the Po, and the Ni are the tributaries. Crossed by Interstate 95 between Ashland and Fredericksburg, each is appropriately marked at the bridge carrying the speeding traffic. Before these streams were given their present amusing names, the Ni River was the Lewis River named after the family that settled along its banks. The other streams probably had family names, too.

MATTAWOMAN
Northampton County   **Site**

The Mattawoman Indian tribe was a peaceful group that lived under the dominion of Debedeavon, the Laughing King of Accawmacke. The name derives from an Indian word meaning "on the road coming down from the north." Another tribe with a similar name, Cuttawoman, lived to the north. When Debedeavon gave Sir George Yeardley a 3,700-acre tract in 1625, Yeardley requested these Indians move elsewhere. About twenty-five years later, this tract was occupied by Argoll Yeardley, Sir George's only son, and was named Old Town. *See: Assawoman; Oak Grove of Northampton; Peachburg*

MAUPIN'S TAVERN
Albemarle County   **Site**

An early tavern stood here on the Three Chopt Road. It was west of Ivy Tavern, about half-way to Yancey's Mill. It was owned by members of the Maupin family who sold it to a Mr. White. *See: White Hall of Albemarle*

MAURERTOWN
Shenandoah County

The people who live here call their village Morry Town. The early settlers were of the Maurer family whose name was spelled a variety of ways in old records—Mowray, Maury, Mowery—depending upon the whim of the writer.

MAURY RIVER
Rockbridge County

Matthew Fontaine Maury, the Pathfinder of the Seas, became extremely fond of the scenery along this river, especially at Dunlap Pass, when he was teaching in Lexington. On his deathbed he requested his body be taken through the pass enroute to Richmond for burial. Shortly after his death in 1873, the North River was renamed the Maury River in his honor.

Born near Fredericksburg in 1806, Maury was a career naval officer who studied the wind and currents of the Atlantic Ocean. His charts enabled mariners to reduce sailing times on many routes. His book, *Physical Geography of the Sea*, published in 1855, was the beginning of modern oceanography. From 1844 until his retirement in 1861, Maury was the director of the U.S. Naval Observatory. While retired, to add spice to his teaching jobs in Lexington, he roamed the countryside along the North River. Many years later, a statue was raised in his honor in Richmond.

MAURY'S SCHOOL
Albemarle County   **Site**

On the road to Gordonsville from Charlottesville was a classical school conducted by the Reverend James Maury, rector of Fredericksburg Parish from 1754 to 1769. He was a descendant of the Huguenots of Goochland County. This was a boarding school that was in session for nine months of the year. Among the students were Thomas Jefferson and Dabney Carr. The rector's famous grandson was Matthew Fontaine Maury, the Pathfinder of the Seas, who charted the major ocean currents of the Atlantic. *See: Bear Castle; Huguenots*

MAUZY
Rockingham County

Thomas Mauzy came from Fauquier County prior to 1805 and settled near McGaheysville. His brothers joined him. In time they branched out on their own to the good farm land north of Harrisonburg. Enough people of the name Mauzy required a post office of their own.

MAX MEADOWS
Wythe County

An early settler in this region was William Mack. Originally Mack's Meadows, the spelling was changed to Max in later, more careless years.

MAYCOCK'S PLANTATION
Prince George County   **Site**

On the south bank of the James River were many large plantations. This one was patented in 1618 by Samuel Maycock, a former don of Oxford. Although he was slain in the Massacre of 1622, his name was continued as a tribute to him by a later occupant, George Pace, who purchased the land after his marriage in 1637. A convenient place for a ferry, since the river here is relatively narrow, several notable crossings took place at this point during the later part of the Revolution. Cornwallis crossed here on May 24, 1781, on his way to cause havoc in Williamsburg during his summer of terror. "Mad Anthony" Wayne crossed here in September to pressure the British into a defensive encampment, coming ashore near Westover at Harrison's Landing. When all this was taking place, Maycock's belonged to David Meade who had purchased it in 1774. The name is sometimes spelled Maycox. *See: Pace's Paines; Westover*

MAYMONT
City of Richmond

Major James Dooley, a Confederate veteran, read law after the war and practiced law in Richmond. With money scarce during the Reconstruction, he accepted stocks, bonds, and real estate for his services. By the 1880s, he was one of the 400 millionaires of the country. In the style of the times, to show his wealth, he purchased a former dairy farm on the north bank of the James, not far from Hollywood Cemetery, and there he built a mansion of red granite. The place was named for his wife, the former Sally May, who loved swans. Likenesses of the graceful birds were incorporated into furnishings; the most sumptuous was her bed in the form of a huge swan. Below the house, she had Swan Lake created, where the creatures were kept as pets.

Maymont was the first house in Virginia to have electric wiring installed during construction. Because the supply of current was not dependable, all of the ceiling and wall fixtures incorporated both wires and gas lines. First

155

occupied in 1893, the mansion was the scene of many gala social events. When both of the Dooleys died childless, their wills gave the property to the City of Richmond without providing funds to maintain it. A few decades ago, a private association began to maintain it through private donations and opened it to the public. *See: Swannanoa*

McCLURE
Dickenson County

An early local settler, whose last name was McClure, was killed by Indians near here in April 1774 while in pursuit of Chief Logan. Stumbling into an ambush, he was slain. Days later his body was found next to a stream. The village of McClure still memorializes the victim.

MCGAHEYSVILLE
Rockingham County

Located about eleven miles east of Harrisonburg, this little village was settled in the late eighteenth century by a group of Irishmen. Through the heart of the town meanders a stream which the locals call The Kettle, an old name for Massanutten Mountain which is the source of the rivulet. When the first post office was opened in 1801, Tobias McGahey was appointed the postmaster. With typical Irish modesty, he named the town for himself. Born in Dover, Delaware his first years were miserable and poor. As a young man, he migrated to this community where he married a rich local widow. The luck of the Irish?

MCGUIRE MEDICAL CENTER
Chesterfield County

This huge Veterans Administration hospital was named for Dr. Hunter Holmes McGuire, the chief medical officer of Stonewall Jackson's Army of the Shenandoah Valley.

MCKENNEY
Dinwiddie County   **Town**

William R. McKinney, a lawyer for the Seaboard Air Line Railroad, purchased several large tracts of land in this vicinity. Some of it was laid out to form a town which bears his name. It is not known when, or by whom, the spelling of McKinney's name was changed to the present McKenney.

MCLEAN
Fairfax County

John McLean was one of the two Justices of the U.S. Supreme Court to dissent in the famed Dred Scott case of 1857. He and Justice Benjamin Curtis disagreed with the majority decision, written by Chief Justice Roger B. Taney, that said slaves were property even when they accompanied their masters to border states which, though not slave states, had laws recognizing the institution of slavery elsewhere. The slave Dred Scott had gone with his master to Missouri. After living there for some time, he considered himself free and brought suit to legalize his status when his master took him back to a slave state. Many historians have said that Taney's decision made the Civil War inevitable.

Justice McClean owned a house a few miles from the District of Columbia to which he went whenever the Court was not in session. He died in his Virginia home. Although this bedroom community is thoroughly populated with homes, it has yet to be incorporated as a town.

MEADOWS OF DAN
Patrick County

The meadows along the Dan River offered a pleasant place for homes.

MECHANICSVILLE
Hanover County

Here on the stage road from Richmond to Fredericksburg, a few miles east of Richmond, was a collection of repair shops where coaches, wagons, and farm machinery could be repaired by blacksmiths and mechanics. It was also the gathering place for farmers and their families who sold or traded their produce while having things repaired by the mechanics. Naturally, several taverns were handy to slake the thirst of the visitors during Virginia's hot summer days.

MECKLENBURG COUNTY

Formed in 1764 from Lunenburg, this county was named for Princess Charlotte of Mecklenburg, the wife of George III. Near the present town of Clarksburg, Nathaniel Bacon, Jr. defeated an alliance of Indians at Occaneechee in 1676. This removed an obstacle along the Iroquois Trail and opened the way for settlement of the interior portions of northern Carolina. The county seat is Boydton. *See: Boydton; Occaneechee; Susquehannock Indians*

MEHERRIN RIVER

In 1669 about 200 Meherrin Indians were living in this region of Prince Edward County.

They belonged to the Iroquoian family. Earlier they had lived on the banks of the Nottoway River, in the Assamoosic Swamp region, but they had moved westward to escape the settlers. The present hamlet of Meherrin possibly occupies the site of the old Indian village. The river is a long, shallow stream that rises in Charlotte County and flows southeasterly into North Carolina where it eventually meets salt water.

MELFA
Accomack County **Town**

Named for an official of the Pennsylvania Railroad who supervised the construction of this vital transportation system down the spine of the Eastern Shore, the original spelling possibly was Melfer. The Navy established an auxiliary field here during World War II as part of the defenses of Hampton Roads. The strip is used now only for general aviation. The county has recently established an industrial park next to it and provides minor maintenance.

MENOKIN
Richmond County

Francis Lightfoot Lee built this house about 1769 for his bride Rebecca, daughter of John Tayloe of Mount Airy. Francis Lightfoot Lee, born at Stratford Hall, was a signer of the Declaration of Independence and a member of the Continental Congress from 1775 through 1779. He died here in 1797. The name of his home is Indian in origin. *See: Chantilly; Lightfoot; Manakin; Mannsfield; Mount Airy; Stratford Hall*

MERCHANT'S HOPE CHURCH
Prince George County

This church, built about 1657, is one of the oldest church buildings in English America still in use. Originally it was within the Parish of Martin's Brandon which, for a short while, encompassed land on both sides of the James River. In 1635, when "The Society of Martin's Hundred" purchased much of Martin's Brandon and named it Merchant's Hope Plantation, a new parish was established bearing the same name as the plantation.

The church's Bible, with its title page missing, is thought to be the "great Bible" given to the parish in 1658 by a London merchant, John Westhorpe, who also gave 1,000 pounds of tobacco to purchase a "Communion Cuppe," now located at Brandon Church. The Bible appears to be a combination of Westhorpe's New Testament

and an Old Testament of 1640. Little about the church building has changed over the centuries, including the land surrounding it. Standing off the beaten track, isolated and hidden, it retains its very early colonial charm. *See: Charles City County; Martin's Brandon; Martin's Hundred*

MERCHANT'S HOPE PLANTATION
Prince George County **Site**

A number of merchants formed the Society of Martin's Hundred in 1621 and began to acquire lands on both sides of the James River. They first expanded eastward to the York River and eventually controlled more than 100,000 acres from the present vicinity of Carter's Grove to Yorktown. In 1635 they acquired a large chunk of John Martin's plantation on the south bank of the James which they named for a ship they owned, the *Merchant's Hope*. In 1720 Nathaniel Harrison of Brandon purchased these 1,973 acres and added them to his estate. When his son attempted to sell this tract in 1765 to raise money to buy more slaves, he had to petition the General Assembly for special legislation to iron out the many overlapping entails which had accumulated over the years.

The property was finally purchased by Colonel Richard Kidder Meade, the officer detailed by General Washington to supervise the execution of the famous British spy, Major Andre. Some time during the latter part of the eighteenth century, this parcel of land became known as Coggins Point. It was the nineteenth century home of Edmund Ruffin. *See: Brandon; Hope; Martin's Hundred; Richneck of Surry; Westover Church*

MERRIE OAKS
Newport News

This was a portion of the Oak Hall tract from which Merrie Oaks and Lee Hall were formed, all holdings of the Cary family. *See: Lee Hall of Newport News*

MERRY POINT
Lancaster County

Settled by Daniel Gookin, Jr. before 1630, this parcel of land was first called Mary's Mount. The name was changed to Merry Point in 1748. *See: Marie's Mount*

METOMKIN
Accomack County

Colonel Edmund Scarburgh and Edward Ravell each thought they owned this tract which stretched across the Eastern Shore from Metomkin Bay on the east to the Chesapeake Bay on the west. In one of his more amiable moments, Colonel Scarburgh settled the dispute by dividing the land with Ravell. Scarburgh worked his portion for a while but then sold it and remained at Occahannock. These fertile fields, when acquired by the Custis family of Arlington and Hungars Plantation, were referred to as the Great Metomkin Bay Plantation. A portion of the plantation was later purchased for the new county seat of Accomack County which was called, for many years, Metomkin. The name, Indian in origin, means "to enter into a house." *See: Accomac; Accomack County; Arlington of Northampton; Hungars Plantation; Mount Custis; Ravenswood*

MICHIE TAVERN
Albemarle County
John Henry, the father of the famous patriot, patented 1,250 acres in what was then the western part of Goochland County. He sold the land to John Michie who probably was the builder of the first part of the tavern about 1730. Operated by his son, it was located on Buck Mountain road about 25 miles from its present location. In 1763 additions were made to the original structure. In 1927 Michie Tavern (pronounced Mickey) was uprooted and moved to a new site halfway up Monticello Mountain. *See: Mount Brilliant*

MIDDLEBROOK
Augusta County
Near the center of this village is a small stream which flows across Main Street. When the post office was established prior to 1840 and a name had to be chosen, some clever person selected Middlebrook. Fortunately that person knew the difference between a brook and a creek.

MIDDLEBURG
Loundon County   Town
Aptly named, this town is midway between Alexandria ·and Winchester on the old colonial road now rather faithfully followed by US 50. Since Lord Fairfax used Winchester as his western headquarters when he was Proprietor of Northern Neck (while he lived at Greenway Court in what is now Clarke County) many people passed through here in colonial times. At one time the settlement was known as Chinn's Crossroads after an early tavern keeper. The Red Fox Tavern, still standing in Middleburg, is reported to be the oldest tavern in the United States. *See: Centreville; Snicker's Gap*

MIDDLE PENINSULA
That portion of land between the York and Rappahannock rivers is known as Middle Peninsula. To the north, on the other side of the Rappahannock, is Northern Neck. To the south, across the York, is the Peninsula. Middle Peninsula is occupied by the counties of Mathews, Gloucester, Middlesex, and a portion of King and Queen.

MIDDLE PLANTATION
James City County
The word *plantation* refers to the posting (planting) of men to guard the middle point of a barricade built by settlers after the Massacre of 1622. Probably more symbolic than defensive, the palisade created a line separating the English from the Indians who were not permitted to be south of the barrier without a pass on pain of death. Starting at Archer's Hope Creek (on the James) to the head of Queen's Creek (east of present Williamsburg), the line was under constant surveillance by men who were conscripted for specific periods of duty under professional soldiers. The Keepers of the Guard made their headquarters in the center, on the highest ground that was better drained and less infested with mosquitoes. The conscripts were required to raise their own food, bag their own game, and otherwise take care of themselves. As could be expected, the permanent soldiers were soon joined by wives in the little cluster of houses.

Middle Plantation slowly grew into a small hamlet which required a church, named Bruton. The Reverend James Blair selected this site for the College of William and Mary. When Governor Francis Nicholson received permission to move the colonial capital away from miasmic Jamestown, he planned a proper town whose main streets were laid out in the form of a "W" and an "M," for William and Mary, his sovereigns. This, of course, became Williamsburg. *See: Fort James; Harrop; Jamestown; Williamsburg*

MIDDLESEX COUNTY
Formed in 1673 from Lancaster, which then occupied both sides of the Rappahannock River, this county was named for the English shire of the same name. It is separated from Mathews County by the Piankatank River. The suffix "sex," which also forms the ending of Sussex and Essex, is

an old Norman word meaning a camp or military headquarters. Thus, Essex was the east camp, Sussex the south, and Middlesex the center. The present county seat, Saluda, replaced Urbanna in 1852. *See: Christ Church of Middlesex; Hewick; Rosegill; Saluda; Urbanna*

MIDDLETOWN
Frederick County   **Town**

As early as 1766, this village was widely known for its excellent clockmakers. The leading citizen was Dr. Peter Senseny who was instrumental in getting the town chartered. Modestly he insisted that it be called Middletown although for years it was unofficially called Senseny Town. The community of clockmakers then lay in the middle of Frederick County which was much larger than now, hence the choice of name. Elaborately patterned eight-day clocks were created by the early settlers who also fashioned watches and surveying instruments of high quality. One citizen, Jacob Danner, who specialized in making compasses, worked with such precision that his reputation endures today. *See: Belle Grove of Frederick; Shenandoah County*

MIDLAND
Fauquier County

The origin of the name is obscure, but it probably was the name of a major farm here.

*CHIEF JUSTICE JOHN MARSHALL
MIDLAND, FAUQUIER COUNTY*

Midland earned its small niche in history as the birthplace of John Marshall, Revolutionary soldier, Congressman, Secretary of State, and Chief Justice of the U.S. Supreme Court who presided over many of the landmark decisions that gave the Constitution strength and meaning. He was born on September 24, 1755, and died in Philadelphia July 6, 1835. *See: Germantown; Oak Hill of Fauquier*

MIDLOTHIAN
Chesterfield County

Midlothian is the county in southeastern Scotland in which Edinburgh is located. Many of the people who owned or worked the coal mines here came from Midlothian, Scotland where there are ancient coal mines that once competed with those in Wales. It was not until two Scottish miners were employed by a Mr. Heth for his Black Heath Mine, about 1788, that coal mining in this locality became profitable. Credit must also be given to the development of the steam engine which created enough power to pump the water out of the deep shafts.

In the 1840s eight mines operated in what the U.S. Geologic Survey called the Black Heath Basin. In time all of the privately-owned mines were acquired by one corporation, the Midlothian Mining Company. Carving into seams fifty feet thick at depths of over 800 feet from the surface, huge quantities of soft (bituminous) coal were sent to the Tredegar Iron Works in Richmond during the Civil War. The frenzied mining by hundreds of men emptied the veins by the 1880s forcing the closing of all shafts. A feeble attempt was made in 1912 to rework the region but the small amounts of coal made it unprofitable. All of the shafts were permanently sealed. Today, only those who live in the village of Midlothian know of the past history of mining. *See: Bellona Arsenal; Pocahontas*

MIDLOTHIAN
Gloucester County

Northeast of Gloucester courthouse is an old home facing the North River of Mobjack Bay. Known as Middleway when built by the Iverson family long before the Revolution, the exact date of construction cannot be determined. It is claimed that two ghosts haunt the gardens, the spirit of the builder's eldest son and his sweetheart who came from a family of more humble circumstances. When they were denied permission to marry, they both died rather suddenly "of broken hearts." When the next owners, members of the Marable family, purchased Middleway, they changed the name to Midlothian after a region of Scotland.

MILFORD
Caroline County
This hamlet is all that is left of a port on the Mattaponi River created by order of an Act of the General Assembly in 1792 "To establish a town and inspection of tobacco on the lands of John Hoomes in the County of Caroline." Milford once was at the head of navigation of this river which today had been made shallow by generations of silting. At the time of the Act, the Marquis of Milford Haven,active in English government, was favorably inclined to accept the formation of the new country, the United States. *See: Bowling Green*

MILFORD HAVEN
Mathews County
The narrow stretch of water between the mainland of Mathews County and Gwynns Island was named for the seaport in southwestern Wales. From its station here the U.S. Coast Guard tends the middle portion of Chesapeake Bay.

MILL
The most common mill in colonial times was the grist mill that used granite stones to grind various grains into flour. It was operated by a miller. The usual power source was moving water in a millrace that either fell over a paddlewheel or moved under it. The lower stone was stationary while the upper stone moved in a circular fashion. A variety of the water mill was the tidemill that stored water behind a dike as the tide rose and let it move under the wheel after the tide had fallen. A tidemill sometimes had a gearshift to take advantage of the motion of the water in both directions. Generally, the mill operated only when the water moved in one direction.

Other mills used wind (which permitted their operation inland), animals walking either in a circle or on a treadmill, or, by the nineteenth century, a steam engine. Two other variations were used to process the grain: a pound mill in which a heavy pestal was raised and allowed to fall into a stone mortar, and a rolling mill which operated much like the old-fashioned clothes wringer. Mills, of course, were used to make other things besides flour. Sheets of metal had been rolled as far back as the fourteenth century.

Wood was shaped into moldings or turned into cylinders from the power of a mill.

As an interesting side note, practically all of the places in Virginia that refer to a person's mill have been changed in spelling, probably for ease of pronunciation. The final "s" from the owner's name has been moved to the end of the word mill. Thus, Yancey's Mill is now Yancey Mills. The same thing has happened to the word spring. Craig's Spring is now Craig Springs. *See: Flowerdew Hundred; Pound*

MILLBORO
Bath County
In 1829 the Lowman family built a rolling mill to grind local wheat and corn. When a post office was established years later, it was named Millborough.

MILLBROOK
Fredericksburg   **Site**
A "Manufactory of Small Arms" was established by Colonel Fielding Lewis on his estate during the Revolution. At that time his farm was called Millbrook for the stream that ran through one quarter of it. The name was changed in the nineteenth century to Kenmore. *See: Kenmore*

MILLER SCHOOL
Albemarle County
Samuel Miller, a native of Albemarle County who died a bachelor, decided to establish a boarding school for boys who otherwise might not be able to get a basic education. In his will of 1869 he left a bequest of approximately one million dollars to fund his plan. Chartered by the General Assembly as a non-profit, charitable corporation, his school began classes in 1878 and has since offered vocational training and college prep programs from grades five through high school. For seventy-five years, this was Miller's School, a name that gave full recognition to its founder. Samuel Miller began his business career as a clerk in a retail store. With a partner, he opened his own establishment and, when the business was a success, invested his profits wisely.

MILLWOOD
Clarke County
This tiny community takes its name from an old mill that began operating in 1785. It was last used commercially in 1943. Jointly owned by General Daniel Morgan of Saratoga and Nathaniel Burwell II of Carter Hall, this mill had two pairs of French buhr grindstones

moved by wooden gears powered by an overshot wheel. One stone was for wheat, the other for corn. Although no longer in operation, the old mill has been restored.

MILLWOOD
Powhatan County
Built in the second quarter of the eighteenth century by John Harris, this structure originally was two separate homes which sat side by side. They were both of frame construction with brick veneer, an uncommon building method in those days. Later the two units were connected by a single one story room to give the present house its angled form. The builder was a descendant of Major William Harris, an explorer and scout for Governor William Berkeley.

MILTON
Albemarle County   Site
Once the main shipping point for central Albemarle, Milton is now nothing more than an open field, a ghost of a metropolis that died too young. Located on the south bank of the Rivanna River at the head of navigation, it came into prominence when water freight began to boom during the last quarter of the eighteenth century. Much of the produce from the great estates, such as Monticello, was shipped down the Rivanna from here and, indeed, much of the imported stone for Thomas Jefferson's home came up this same river through Milton where the Rivanna Navigation Company had its headquarters.

The growth of Charlottesville and the establishment of Scotsville were the chief cause of Milton's decline, although heavy silting of the river made it difficult for the boats to manage. As late as 1835 this little town still had a large stone warehouse and a population of sixty whites and ten blacks. The emergence of the railroads finally killed it. Today no one remembers its heyday. The site became an airfield for the University of Virginia. An aerial photograph taken in the 1930s shows clearly the outline of the old streets of Milton.

The origin of the name is obscure. However, Milton Abbey near Bristol, England, is a famous landmark. *See: Rivanna River*

MINERAL
Louisa County   Town
This settlement was once a shipping point for minerals—iron, mica, sulphur, and a bit of gold—all mined in the vicinity. In 1848 Robert and James Hart, brothers, had a smelter here, which they named Rough and Ready in honor of Zachary Taylor, a general during the war with Mexico. After the Civil War, the local sulphur supply was exhausted; however, iron pyrites found nearby continued to supply the Rough and Ready Furnace until about 1900. *See: Big Stone Gap*

MINE RUN
Orange County
This tiny settlement takes its name from a small stream that passed near Alexander Spotswood's iron mine of 1714. *See: Germanna*

MIRADOR
Albemarle County
This was the estate of Chiswell (Chilly) Langhorne, the father of two famous women. Both beautiful, they easily attracted a host of admirers. Irene married Charles Dana Gibson, the artist. She was the model for his renowned Gibson Girls of the 1920s. Nancy married an Englishman and, as Lady Astor, became the first woman elected to the British House of Commons. The Astor home in England was Cliveden and those who attached themselves to lady Astor became known, worldwide, as the Cliveden Set. During World War II, an emergency radio that was held between the legs while being cranked was called the Gibson Girl Radio for its hourglass shape which Charles Dana Gibson had made famous.

MOBJACK BAY
Gloucester County
The confluence of the North, Ware, and Severn rivers form Mobjack Bay, a rather shallow reach of water which separates most of Gloucester County from Mathews County. Opening into the Chesapeake Bay, it is a body of water rich in history. The origin of the name is murky. On most eighteenth century maps it is called Mockjack Bay. One story, quite common though probably incorrect, suggests that because the foliage along the banks once was rather dense, voices would be reflected back to the ships to "mock" the sailors (known as Jack Tars because they served under the Union Jack and often tarred their pigtailed hair.) However, seldom does a mass of trees and brush reflect sound; rather, it absorbs.

A more plausible explanation lies in the shallowness of the bay. A most inviting stretch of water that runs for miles and on

which were located many large and prosperous plantations, this bay mocked all
attempts to bring in a ship of any size. The
products of the land had to be hauled via road
closer to the York River for shipment to
markets. At low tide, the exposed mud flats
extend for hundreds of yards from both
banks to the rather shallow natural channel.
Definitions of the word mock include imitate,
deceive, defy, and make futile—all of which
apply here.

MODEST TOWN
Accomack County
Local lore says this village was named for
the reputation of two modest ladies who
operated a very strict and proper boarding
house that was also a stage stop. Their
establishment was named Sunderland Hall.
Those who did not care to live quietly could
visit Helltown about a mile away.

MONACAN
Powhatan County
The original owner Peter Chastain, a
Huguenot, built his modest home on the site
of the former Monacan Indian village. He had
come to Virginia at the end of the seventeenth
century. The date of construction is uncertain, however a recorded deed of sale shows
that Chastain sold Monacan to a Mr. Scott in
1729. The only original outbuilding still
standing is the log corn crib. See: Huguenot;
Manakin Town; Rassawek

MONETA
Bedford County
Tradition says the town was named in 1882
for its first postmaster. One must assume his
name was Moneta.

MONROE
Amherst County
When the first post office was established
here in 1897, it was named Potts. However, in
February 1905, when James Monroe Watts
was postmaster, the name was changed to
Monroe. For many years it was an important
railroad service point on the Southern
Railway. Casey Jones, the engineer of the
famous ballad The Wreck of the 97, received his
orders in Monroe and was told, "You're 'way
behind time." Running at full throttle, his
engine went off the tracks on a trestle outside
of Danville. See: Danville

MONROVIA
Westmoreland County   Site
Andrew Monroe came to Virginia from
Scotland in 1647 and settled on the Virginia
bank of the Potomac. The next year he
returned to Scotland and fought in the Battle
of Preston where he was captured and
sentenced to banishment. He rather willingly
came back to Virginia and, in 1650, patented
the tract where he had previously settled.

On April 28, 1758, James Monroe, the fifth
President, was born at Monrovia, the son of
Spence Monroe and Elizabeth Jones Monroe.
He was great-great-grandson of the immigrant, Andrew Monroe. James Monroe was
instrumental in helping freed slaves return to
Africa where they established their own
country, Liberia. In honor of the man who
helped them get to Africa, they named the
capital of their new country Monrovia. The
area around the old Monroe homestead is
now the city of Colonial Beach. See: Ash Lawn;
Marlborough; Monticello

MONTEBELLO
Orange County
The lands here were granted to Benjamin
Cave by King George II in 1728. Signed by
Governor William Gooch, the colonial
Governor, the patent is proudly preserved by
the present owners. Benjamin Cave, a
member of the House of Burgesses, was the
Colonel of the local militia in 1739. The six-
room house was built about 1740 by slaves
using only local materials, and the kitchen
garden was designed by Elizabeth Cave in
1760. For a time, Montebello was owned by
the Taylor family. Here, on November 24,
1784, was born Zachary Taylor, the twelfth
President. Montebello is Italian for "beautiful
mountain." Just when the name was applied is
unclear, but it follows the custom, begun by
Thomas Jefferson, of using Italian words as
names for estates.

MONTEREY
Highland County
The seat of Highland County was first
settled in 1774 by Samuel Black who built a
cabin here. When the country courthouse
was built in 1847, the village was still tiny
with only a few homes on the turnpike that
crossed the Alleghany Mountains. When
Zachary Taylor was elected the twelfth
President in 1849, the local residents named
their village Monterey to honor General
Taylor's victory in the battle fought near
Monterey, Mexico, just a few years previously.
Monterey is Spanish for "king's mountain."

MONTGOMERY COUNTY

Originally this region was a part of the huge county of Fincastle, formed by Lord Dunmore and named for his son. During the early days of the Revolution, Fincastle County was dismantled and several others formed from it. This one, dating from 1776, was named for General Richard Montgomery who was killed at Quebec, Canada the previous year. The county seat is at Christiansburg.

MONTICELLO
Albemarle County

This section of land which Thomas Jefferson inherited from his father, Peter Jefferson, always held a special attraction for young Tom, probably because it was the highest point of the Shadwell estate. From boyhood, according to the story, he was determined to build upon it the best and most unique home in Virginia. After years of research and travel, he drew four complete plans for his house before commissioning work to begin in 1770.

The first stage was lowering the top of the low mountain (hence the name *Monticello* which means "little mountain" in Italian) to provide a large level area for his main building and the proposed attached pavillions. At first it was a modest six-room house with numerous unconnected dependencies and it did not take on its present beautiful form until after Jefferson retired from public life in the early 1800s.

Jefferson was forced to occupy his new home prematurely when the family homestead at Shadwell burned in 1770 and he more or less camped in the shell of his new mansion. In January 1772, again before the manor house was ready for occupancy, he brought his bride, Martha Wayles Skelton, to Monticello and set up housekeeping in one of the two small pavillions which flank the main structure. They lived in what is still known as Honeymoon Lodge until the big house was ready in 1775.

After the untimely death of his wife in September 1782, Jefferson began to occupy his time by enlarging and remodeling his home, a project which kept him busy until 1809 when he finally decided it was finished. By then it had grown into the mansion of its present form with thirty rooms and numerous dependencies attached by underground passages. Monticello was a radical departure from the common practice of the times of building a home adjacent to a major river

THOMAS JEFFERSON, MONTICELLO

upon which the produce of the farm could be shipped. Jefferson was completely dependent upon horse-drawn conveyances to ship his commodities.

Monticello became the true social, political, and cultural center of Virginia when the royal Governor's court was abruptly ended by the Revolution. When this estate was in its prime, Williamsburg was moribund, Alexandria was mired in commerce, and Richmond was a small town just emerging as the new capital of the new state. *See: Colle; Cuckoo Tavern; Eppington; The Forest; Milton; Monrovia; Shadwell; Snowden; Tuckahoe*

MONTPELIER
Orange County

Four miles southwest of Orange is Montpelier, the home of Colonel James Madison. More than likely his estate after the retirement home of Sir Edwin Hyde, the first Earl of Clarendon, confidant of King Charles II and grandfather of Queen Mary II and Queen Anne. At Montpelier, England, Hyde began the history of his times which for many years was the accepted version of the exile of King Charles II and of his reign after the Restoration.

Colonel Madison built the original portion of his house here in 1741. Of modest size, it was enlarged by his son James Madison, the fourth President, who added wings, a second story, and a portico of pure Jeffersonian design. Montpelier meant as much to "Jamie" Madison as Monticello did to his close friend, Thomas Jefferson, under whom he served as Secretary of State and from whom he inherited the mess with England that led to the War of 1812. During the many years that Madison and his energetic wife, Dolley, lived in Washington City, they kept a close eye on this estate, supervising it from afar and always making plans to live here in retirement.

When the Madisons came to Montpelier at the end of his two terms, in 1817, they entertained lavishly and frequently. Dinner parties for ninety guests were not unusual. But, as was the case with Jefferson and Monroe, the expenses of grand living and open hospitality had to be paid by those who lived on after his death at the age of eighty-five. Dolley was forced to sell Montpelier and moved to a smaller house on Lafayette Square in Washington after the Father of the Constitution died in 1836.

For nearly a century, Montpelier was neglected and in danger of disappearing. It was saved from possible destruction and restored in this century by William DuPont. *See: Oak Hill of Loudon; Port Conway; Scotchtown*

MONTPELIER
Surry County
Benjamin Harrison, the first of the line, acquired a huge tract of land on the Surry side of the James River in 1632. This parcel went to his son, Benjamin II, about 1657 who built a modest home. If there was a name for this estate in that year it is unrecorded. He probably adopted the name Montpelier after 1667 since that was the year that Sir Edwin Hyde, the Earl of Clarendon, retired to his new home Montpelier near London, after his many years of service to King Charles II.

Benjamin Harrison II is buried in the churchyard near Cabin Point. His tombstone, which was later removed to Brandon, reads, "Here lyeth the body of the Hon. Benjamin Harrison, Esq., Member of the Council of Virginia who did Justice, loved Mercy, and walked humbly with his God, was always loyal to his Prince and a great benefactor of his Country. He was born in this Parish the 20th day of Sept. 1646, and departed this life the 30th of Jan. 1713." *See: Berkeley; Brandon; Surry County; Wakefield of Surry*

MONTROSS
Westmoreland County   Town
The year before the founding of the county

and the selection of this hamlet as the site for the courthouse, William Black purchased 100 acres for his own use. He had been sent to Virginia as the factor of a Scottish company store in the village of Currioman. In 1752 Black built a store near the courthouse which he called Montross for a ship that he owned named *Montross of Ireland,* after the town of his birth. He managed both emporiums, giving more emphasis to his own establishment, of course. In time, the people of the area said they were going to Montross rather than to Westmoreland Court House. Within a few years, the name was fixed and appeared on the Fry-Jefferson map of 1755. The store at Currioman soon failed and no village grew around it.

MONTVILLE
King William County
At times this name was applied to the little hamlet of Aylett since Montville was the name of the new home of the family that owned and controlled the town. Philip Aylett, who married one of Patrick Henry's daughters, pulled down the old homestead that stood near the Mattaponi River and built a new house on higher ground to escape the insects of the lower land. The old name, Fairfield, was replaced with Montville which means a villa on a high rise of terrain. *See: Aylett; Chantilly; Mount Todd's Wharf; Scotchtown; Ville*

MOON'S MOUNT
Caroline County
Benjamin Robinson, the youngest son of Christopher Robinson the immigrant, inherited 1,200 acres from his father, added 900 more from an adjoining tract, and established an estate called Moon's Mount. Politically powerful all through his life, his first accomplishment was to lead the struggle to establish Caroline County from the western ends of Essex, King and Queen, and King William counties in 1728. Benjamin Robinson was elected sheriff and later clerk of the court. Edmund Pendleton spent his boyhood here as an apprentice attached to "Master Robinson." Moon's Mount was bounded on the southeast by Moon Swamp beyond which lay the Stanhope lands. About four miles away was John Roy's warehouse. *See: Hewick; Mount; Port Royal*

MOORE HOUSE
York County
Sir John Harvey, Governor of Virginia,

received a grant of land on the York River which he called Yorke. A part of this Harvey grant was later sold to George Ludlow. Situated just downriver from the present village of Yorktown, this tract adjoined that of Nicholas Martiau. Ludlow, a prominent person in the colony, was made a member of the Council. His nephew, Colonel Thomas Ludlow, inherited the estate. Thomas's widow married the Reverend Peter Temple who worked the land which became known as Temple's Farm despite the other more prominent men who previously had owned it. Lawrence Smith, the next owner, left it to his grandson, Robert Smith, who, in turn, sold it to his sister's husband, Augustine Moore. It was Moore who built the house which bears his name, and it was in this house that the British and American commissioners met to draft the Articles of Capitulation after the surrender of Cornwallis at Yorktown. *See: Chischiak; Yorke*

MOORMAN'S RIVER
Albemarle County

This river of extremely pure water rises in the Blue Ridge Mountains. Named for a Quaker, Charles Moorman, who settled on its banks in 1735, for years it was the sole source of water for Charlottesville.

MORATTICO
Northumberland

The mother Baptist church of Northern Neck was organized here in 1778 under the leadership of the Reverend Lewis Lunsford. The present structure was built in 1856. Both the church and the village which developed near it echo an old Indian name, probably a local tribe. *See: Nomini Hall; Peckatone*

MOSLEY
Powhatan County

Arthur Mosley patented 1,200 acres in this region in 1730, settled down as a farmer, and raised, besides good crops, a host of children. The Mosley family has been active in county and state affairs. Arthur and his brother, William, were county magistrates. William, Jr. rose to the rank of general and served with distinction in the fourth Regiment of the Virginia Cavalry in the War Between the States.

MOUNT

Although this word today is used as a shortened form of mountain, as in Mount Rogers of Grayson County (elev. 5,729 ft.),

the old meaning had military significance. A mount was a fortification, a place of prepared defense, or the location of a battery of guns. Of course, mount also referred to an elevation from which the surrounding territory could be viewed. By the seventeenth century, it also meant a man's home, estate, or castle which he would defend by any means. During the late eighteenth century, the Italian word *mont* was used as in Monticello, meaning Little Mountain. *See: Church Hill; Marie's Mount; Moon's Mount*

MOUNTAIN LAKE
Giles County

This lake, high in the mountains, was discovered in 1751 by Christopher Gist. The legend that it was formed by cattle trampling over the outlet of a stream has been thoroughly discredited by geologists and historians. Referred to on early maps as Salt Pond, its waters are clears and free of minerals. In fact, no natural salt deposits have ever been found in the vicinity. This has been a popular resort since the first hotel was built about 1852. At normal level, the lake's surface is 3,934 feet above the sea. *See: Lake Drummond*

MOUNT AIRY
Richmond County

The first house here was neither on a mount (a rise of ground) nor was it built in an airy location. Built by William Tayloe, the first of that family in Virginia, who emigrated from England prior to 1670, his house was sited on a low flat field close to the Rappahannock River. In 1747, a descendant, Colonel John Tayloe, wealthy from inheritance and his own business ventures, replaced the old house with the present dwelling on higher ground, about a mile from the original home. To prepare the site, six acres on the crest of a hill were leveled and the slope was restrained by five sets of walled terraces. The spacious manor, made of locally cut brown sandstone and trimmed with white stone quarried at Aquia, was completed in 1758. Colonel John Tayloe named his new place Mount Airy for its excellent location. *See: Hazelwood; Mannsfield; Menokin; Mount; Roswell*

MOUNT AIRY
Wythe County

Settled late in the eighteenth century by Germans, the settlement was named for the home of their employer, John Tayloe of Mount Airy in Richmond County.

MOUNT BRILLIANT
Hanover County   **Site**

John Henry purchased this tract while living at Studley. In 1750 Henry moved his family to this site on the South Anna River about twenty miles west of Studley. Here was built a house sufficiently large to house a family of eleven children (nine of whom were girls). Patrick, the elder of the two sons, and fourteen years old when they moved here, remained at Mount Brilliant only three years before going off on his own. Both John Henry and his wife Sarah died here. Like Studley, Mount Brilliant has long disappeared and the lands have been divided among other owners.

Tradition says the house was one-and-one-half stories of frame construction on brick foundations. The frame was of oak, not nailed but held together by wooden pins. It was sited on one of the highest points of land in Hanover County which provided it with good drainage and welcome breezes in the hot summer. The lands were cleared and tilled all the way down to the South Anna River. The house was torn down in 1807 and the timbers used to make a barn. The site of the house is still evident although it is now in the middle of a cultivated field. While at Mount Brilliant, the Henry family went to church at Allen's Creek, or at Fork Church, or occasionally at St. Pauls which was known as the Slash Church for many years. *See: Michie Tavern; Mount; Scotchtown; Slash Church; Studley*

MOUNT CRAWFORD
Rockingham County   **Town**

This town has had three names—Mt. Pleasant, Mt. Stevens, and Mt. Crawford. The present name has stuck since 1825.

MOUNT CUSTIS
Accomack County   **Site**

John McKeel (or Michael, as it was later written) migrated to Virginia by way of Holland in 1640. This adventurous Scot came to the New World with his companion John Custis I and eventually married John's daughter. He built his unnamed home overlooking the broad waters of Metomkin Bay. Through McKeel's wife the property passed into the Custis family. The name Mount Custis was applied to the property when Lieutenant Colonel Henry Custis built the west end of the present house in 1710. This was often called the Great Metomkin

Bay Plantation. *See: Arlington; Metomkin; Mount; Wilsonia*

MOUNT JACKSON
Shenandoah County   **Town**

A group of homes and shops were built here on the Valley Pike during the latter portion of the eighteenth century. Calling their little town Mount Pleasant, the people changed the name to Mount Jackson after the news was received of Andrew Jackson's victory in the Battle of New Orleans shortly after the official end of the War of 1812. *See: Mt. Crawford*

MOUNT MALADO
Henrico   **Site**

This name, which does not exist today in Virginia, used *malado* in its ancient meaning, an unwholesome place. It was an isolation camp of a few long houses built on high ground outside the town of Henricus to which sick people were confined until they either recovered or died. Mount Malado also served as a quarantine point for newcomers who often arrived on "pestered ships" that carried immigrants suffering from all sorts of communicable diseases. Unfortunately, many who arrived healthy were infected at Mount Malado while waiting out their period of "seasoning," designed to get them used to the climate. When Henricus was abandoned after being hit very hard in the Massacre of 1622, Mount Malado ceased to function and no traces have been found of the encampment. This could be called the first hospital in America although there were no physicians and the inmates nursed each other as best they could. *See: Henricus*

MOUNT PISGAH
King William County

This large brick house stands in a grove of trees and lets the lawn sweep down to the river. The thick walls, wide floor boards, and a basement kitchen here are typical of the later half of the eighteenth century. A fireplace brick bears the date 1760 which may be the date of the house or the date of the fireplace repair. Mount Pisgah was built by Henry Robinson, a brother of "Speaker" John Robinson. The name is of Biblical origin. Mount Pisgah is a ridge east of the north end of the Dead Sea. From the summit, Mount Nebo, Moses was given a glimpse of the Promised Land. *See: Hewick; Mount; Piscataway*

MOUNT PLEASANT
Surry County

John Hartwell, sheriff of James City, owned a parcel of land on the James River which he bought from the heirs of Colonel Thomas Swann of Swann's Point and Richard Pace of Pace's Paines. It came into the Cocke family when Elizabeth Hartwell married Richard Cocke in the middle of the eighteenth century. A fine brick home was built here in 1750, probably by Richard Cocke IV who was a Burgess from Surry County from 1744 to 1748. The house commands a good view of the James with long frontage on the river within sight of Jamestown. After it burned, the central part was rebuilt on the same sturdy walls of Flemish bond. The west wing was destroyed during the Revolution and the east wing during the Civil War. Some authorities think there was a tunnel to the river here similar to the tunnels at the Warren House on Gray's Creek and at Claremont. *See: Bremo; Eastover; Pace's Paines; Richneck of Surry County; Smith's Fort Plantation; Swann's Point*

MOUNT ROGERS
Grayson County

This is the highest mountain in Virginia. Its summit is 5,729 feet above sea level. It was named for William B. Rogers, the Commonwealth's first state geologist.

MOUNT SIDNEY
Augusta County

This mountain was named by Samuel Curry for Sir Philip Sidney, a sixteenth century English soldier, courtier, and poet.

MOUNT SOLON
Augusta County

Samuel Curry named this mountain for the Greek philosopher Solon who framed the ancient democratic laws of Athens.

MOUNT STIRLING
Charles City County

Between Charles City Court House and Providence Forge stands an early eighteenth century house built by the descendants of Henry Soane who patented the land in 1662. His granddaughter Elizabeth Soane married the Reverend David Mossom, the clergyman who twice performed the marriage ceremony for Martha Dandridge: in 1749 uniting her with Daniel Parke Custis, and in 1759 with George Washington. Mossom is buried here with his wife, but the graveyard is no longer a

part of Mount Stirling. In 1771 Francis Jerdone acquired the Stirling Plantation, as it was called then, and the estate remained in the Jerdone family for 169 years. Not far from the old house is Soane's Bridge which crosses the Chickahominy River. *See: Chestnut Grove; Jerdone's Castle; Mount; White House*

MOUNT VERNON
Fairfax County

John Washington built a small simple house here before his son George was born. After a few years, John returned with his family to Wakefield. Lawrence Washington, George's half brother, inherited the tract and expanded the original tiny house into an eight-room home in 1743. George inherited the property in 1752 from Lawrence, who had named it Mount Vernon in honor of his hero Admiral Edward Vernon, the captor of Porto Bello.

The future first president did not make a serious effort to run the plantation or improve the house until his marriage seven years later to the Widow Custis, one of the wealthiest women in Virginia. Eventually, George and Martha and her two children, Jack and Patsy, moved to Mount Vernon. During the following forty years, Washington expanded the estate from 2,700 acres to nearly 8,000 and became intimately involved in every detail of running the place. When he was forced to be absent for six years during the Revolution and again during his eight years as President, he kept in touch with his estate through a steady stream of letters which have given an interesting insight into the intri-

MOUNT VERNON

cacies of running a vast plantation in those times.

After both George and Martha died and were buried at Mount Vernon, the place was inherited by his nephew Bushrod Washington. From Bushrod it reverted to John Augustine Washington whose wife sold it to the Mount Vernon Ladies Association for its preservation as a national shrine. *See: Arlington; Belvoir; Bushfield; Epping Forest; Fairfax; Kenmore; Mount; Pohick Church; Queen's Creek Plantation; Rippon Lodge; River Farm; Wakefield; White House*

MOUNT WALKER

A long series of mountains that extends in a southeasterly direction from Blacksburg, Virginia to Kingsport, Tennessee. The barrier to westward migration was named for Dr. Thomas Walker, the explorer from Albemarle County, who ranged this region in the mid 1700s. To the west of Walker Mountains are the Clinch and the Cumberland mountain chains. The major pass through Walker Mountain is west of Abingdon.

When an interstate highway was constructed to connect I-88 with the West Virginia Turnpike, the roadway was thrust through the range at Big Walker. It is the longest tunnel through any mountain in Virginia and is one of the longest in the world. *See: Castle Hill*

MOUNT WALLA
Albemarle County

At the top of the hill overlooking the James River at Scotsville is Mount Walla, built in 1770 by John Scott, one of the founders of the town. He moved back away from the river's edge shortly after the county seat was moved from Scotsville to Charlottesville in 1762. There he lived the life of a farmer rather than a ferryman and freight handler, his former occupations. Walla possibly is a version of Wallace, a Scottish national hero who led the clans against the English King Edward I in the late thirteenth century. *See: Mount; Scott's Ferry*

MOUNT WHARTON
Accomack County

The house here was built by George Thomas prior to 1772. It is situated on Bogue's Bay where, on a clear day, one can see the sparkling Atlantic. Better still, on a clear night a light from the house can be seen from the sea. Mount Wharton is believed to have been the headquarters of John Wharton, the noted smuggler of the Revolution. He did not live here but used it as his coastal collecting point while he kept up appearances in his great home farther inland on Assawoman Creek. After Wharton's death, the place was purchased by Dr. James Core. *See: Assawoman Creek; Mount*

MOUNT ZION
Tazewell County

This was the home of the Reverend Charles Thruston, the Fighting Parson. Ordained an Anglican priest, he raised a company of troops and fought with them in the Revolution. Mount Zion's house dates to about 1771. Many churches have been called Zion for the hill in Jerusalem on which Solomon's temple was built. *See: Zion Crossroads*

MOUTH OF WILSON
Grayson County

Wilson Creek joins New River here close to the North Carolina border. The mouth of a river, its end, generally is the widest part. What an unusual name for a village! *See: Wilsons*

MULBERRY ISLAND
Fort Eustis

This peninsula in the lower James River shields the mouth of the Warrick River at its tip. The first attempt to settle here was made by people sent by the Stanley family who were stockholders in the Virginia Company. The original patent for 1,000 acres was managed by Sir George Yeardley when he returned to Virginia in 1619 as the Governor. John Rolfe owned land here which he willed to his third wife, Joane Pierce, whom he had married three years after the death of his second wife, Pocahontas.

The peninsula never was an island but, in early colonial days, any neck of land was often called an island. The name came from the abundance of wild mulberry trees which later were used in a silkworm venture that failed. Thomas Harwood sponsored a plantation here. He settled his people on the lower end in 1623 in what was called Queen's Hith. The plantation did not last very long.

From 1650 onward for about a century, the lower tip was identified as Joyle's Neck and/or Saxon's Gaol on charts used by mariners who took their ships up the Warwick River to service Denbigh Plantation or to take on fresh water. Many ships with cargo for Williamsburg in the eighteenth century were ordered to go "no farther than the point of Mulberry" to make certain that they reached the wharves at the end of the road from the colonial capital.

In 1749, Carter Crafford built a home on the lower end near the old gaol and operated a ferry from Mulberry Island to Isle of Wight across the James. *See: Buckroe; Ft. Eustis; Queen's Hith; Stanley Hundred; Trebell's Landing; Windmill Point*

N

NANSEMOND COUNTY
NATURAL BRIDGE

NANSEMOND COUNTY
Obsolete
This county formed in 1637 from Norfolk County, was first called Upper Norfolk County since it was to the west, farther away from Cape Henry and the Atlantic Ocean. In 1642 the name was changed to Nansemond, either for the Nansemond River that runs through the heart of the territory or for the Indian tribe that gave its name to the river. For many years the town of Suffolk was the county seat. Nansemond County no longer exists, having been combined with Suffolk to form one large city. *See: Chuckatuck; Suffolk*

NANSEMOND INDIANS
The main village of the Nansemond Indians was on Chuckatuck Creek. It was found by the English settlers who went there to trade. As the newcomers approached, the Indians came out in their canoes to attack but when the English fired their muskets to protect themselves, the Indians jumped into the water and swam to shore in panic. The hungry colonists gathered the native craft, took them to the village, and sold them back for corn. The next time the English came over to trade, the Nansemonds were no longer afraid of the guns and drove the settlers off, inflicting many casualties. One of those to die was Captain Radcliffe, the commander of Fort Algernourne, whose body was found with the mouth filled with corn as a gesture of defiance. Of course, all attempts to trade with these fierce people came to an abrupt end. The Nansemonds remained unfriendly, to say the least, and gleefully took part in the Massacre of 1622. In the war of retaliation that followed, Sir George Yeardley led the troops that attacked them, forced the warriors to flee, and destroyed their villages. Although this ended the Indian menace, many years elapsed before settlement was attempted in this locality. *See: Chuckatuck; Suffolk*

NARROWS
Giles County   Town
Through a deep gorge cut by the New River, a railroad and a major highway pass through the mountains into West Virginia. The hills here rise up steeply leaving a very narrow gap. Discovered in the late seventeenth century, a settlement grew here when pioneers travelled through this cut to find new places to live. It was always called The Narrows and the resulting town perpetuates the name.

NARUNA
Campbell County
Naruna is said to be an Indian name, but its meaning has not been recorded. Here, in 1923, was organized the Smith-Hughes Agricultural School.

NASSAWADOX
Northampton County   Town
The present town of Nassawadox owes its name to the first church organized on the Eastern Shore. Nuswattocks Parish, named for a local Indian tribe, was organized in 1623. For many years the congregation held services in different private homes until, in 1646, a church was erected on the bay side at the head of Hungars Creek. This building was used until the Custis family donated land in 1676 for a new house of worship. The parish's name was then changed to Hungars. Today the only hospital on Virginia's Eastern Shore is at Nassawadox. *See: Evergreen*

NATURAL BRIDGE
Rockbridge County
On July 5, 1774, Thomas Jefferson bought the rights to this natural wonder that had been surveyed by George Washington many years before. On the walls of this naturally formed arch is carved G. W., although there is no explanation how G. W. managed to scale the vertical wall and carve a bit of graffiti. But then, the young Washington was a remarkable man, rather tall by the standards of the day. Jefferson was most enthusiastic about the place and took visitors there whenever he could get them to ride with him the many miles from Poplar Forest, his retreat in Bedford County. He wrote in his book *Notes on the Present State of Virginia*, "So beautiful an arch, so elevated, so light, and springing up as it were to heaven. The rapture of the spectator is really indescribable! This Bridge is in the County of Rockbridge, to which it has given its name, and affords a public and commodius passage over a valley which cannot be crossed elsewhere for a considerable distance." *See: Lexington; Poplar Forest*

NATURAL BRIDGE

NAXERA
Gloucester County

When the post office was established here, the local residents wanted a name that was completely different from any other place in any state. After much thought and debate, they coined Naxera. *See: Alberta; Bacova*

NAYLOR'S HOLE
Richmond County   **Obsolete**

Colonel Moore Fauntleroy settled here in 1651 and established a shipping point for the family's export business. He was the Virginia resident agent while other members of the family tended to business in the more civilized environs of England. About 100 years later, Naylor's Hole was the home of George Washington's mysterious "lowland beauty" to whom he unsuccessfully proposed marriage. Elizabeth Fauntleroy turned him down in 1752 because (as she later confessed) she couldn't stand the sight of the smallpox scars on his face. Undaunted by her refusal, Washington wrote to her father, Colonel William Fauntleroy, that he hoped to

continue "to wait on Miss Betsy in hopes of a revocation of the former cruel sentence and see if I can meet with any alteration in my favor." *See: Tappahannock*

NELLYSFORD
Nelson County

Local tradition holds that a girl named Nelly drowned while crossing the local ford of the river. Even if untrue, the sad tale makes a nice, brief story and provides a colorful, unusual name for a community.

NELSON COUNTY

In 1807 Augusta County was reduced in size to form Nelson, one of many reductions for the originally huge Augusta. The new county was named for General Thomas Nelson, the third person elected Governor of the new Commonwealth of Virginia. He was the first to serve after the surrender at Yorktown and was faced with the enormous problem of the war debt. The courthouse is at Lovingston. *See: York Hall*

NEVILLE'S NECK
Accomack County

Simon Fosque and his wife Ann purchased this tract in 1718 from Captain William Whittington who had patented much land in 1685. Whittington discovered that hundreds of acres had not been "proved" by former owners and could be claimed by the first man to step up and record them in his name. The Fosque family lived on a portion of this estate for generations.

NEW BALTIMORE
Fauquier County

The date of the settlement and the choice of the name are obscure. The first group of houses was built around a Mr. Ball's store and that is how the hamlet was known until New Baltimore was authorized for the name of the post office in 1822. Near here is Vint Hill Farms Army Station, tucked away in a remote section of the county. Its mission is classified.

NEW BOHEMIA
Prince George County

At the beginning of the twentieth century a group of Bohemians and Slovaks came to Virginia from the industrial and mining sections of western Pennsylvania and eastern Ohio. Purchasing land at ridiculously low prices (because it had been worn out by one-crop planting for decades) they amazed local farmers by rehabilitating the soil and producing exceptionally large crops. These successful farmers sent money to relatives to come join them from Bohemia, Poland, and Lithuania. After awhile, those locals who boasted of an English heritage and called themselves true Virginia farmers, quietly adopted the newcomer's conservation and rehabilitation methods.

NEW CANTON
Buckingham County

William Cannon owned the land upon which the first post office was located in 1802. The name suggested was New Cannon. Much to the disgust of the local residents, the approved name was New Canton. No amount of argument could get the postal authorities to admit the error or make a correction. After awhile, because the name caused comment, the locals thought that New Canton was a pretty fine name after all.

NEW CASTLE
Craig County

One of Governor Dinwiddie's many frontier forts was sited here in 1756. As the small community grew into a recognized unincorporated town, the people adopted the name New Fincastle about 1774 in honor of Lord Fincastle, the eldest son of the royal Governor, Lord Dunmore. This caused some confusion since the town of Fincastle was in the area. To make the delivery of mail easier and to delete any reference to the deposed Governor, during the Revolution the people dropped the "Fin" from the name and called their village New Castle. It is now the seat of Craig County.

NEWCASTLE
Hanover County   **Site**

When a severe fire damaged the Capitol at Williamsburg in 1747, a committee of four was formed to search for a possible new site. High on the list was Newcastle, an excellent choice, so it was said, close "to the Bulk of the People ... seated on a fresh River, the Chief Branch of the York, a dry and healthy soil, fine Air, and excellent water, on a River that affords sufficient Navigation for all the Necessities of Life, the greatest Plenty, and likely to be so to the latest Generation." Even with all these attributes, the House of Burgesses decided not to relocate but to repair the damaged old building in Williamsburg. Today the site of Newcastle is difficult to find. It lies in a cornfield beside a shallow river so badly silted that only during high water after a few days of rain can a rowboat make its way. *See: Cumberland; Hanover Town*

NEW CHURCH
Accomack County

The first town one reaches when entering Virginia from Maryland on the Eastern Shore is the village of New Church. There is no mystery to the origin of this name. The Reverend Francis Makemie organized a new church here about 1705. For a short while he was the minister, but in time he managed to import a clergyman from Scotland to conduct the services and care for the small flock. *See: Temperanceville*

NEW GARDEN
See: Honaker

NEWGATE
Fairfax County

This was the early name for the present village of Centreville. Newgate is a common name in old England, generally referring to a new opening in a city wall. The most famous use of the name, of course, is in London. Near a new gate in the city's wall is Newgate Prison, still in use. Many people convicted of petty crimes during the seventeenth and early eighteenth century were taken from the prison and transported to Virginia to serve their sentences as indentured servants in exile. Those who bought these felons had to pay for their transportation and for that modest sum had a servant for seven years. It did not take much to be a convicted felon in England in those days. The list of felonies contained hundreds of offenses, some as simple as stealing a few pennies' worth of food.

The Newgate of Fairfax County, however, had nothing to do with a prison. This tiny settlement called itself the gateway to the west. It lay astride a road constructed by General Edward Braddock on his way to Fort Pitt in 1755. *See: Gate City*

NEW HOPE
Augusta County

Believe this if you want to. In 1772 John Kerr tried to make a living on 400 acres of poor land. His wife, tired of the hard scrabble existence, begged him to give up and try elsewhere. He put in one crop which, he said, would be his last attempt. The yield was gratifying. It gave him new hope for better times. A small community developed near his farm which, of course, he named New Hope. *See: Hopewell*

NEWINGTON
King and Queen County

Colonel Jacob Lumpkin lived at Newington during Bacon's Rebellion in 1676. A strong supporter of Governor William Berkeley, the colonel's home was in constant danger from the rebels but it was never touched. Newington next became the home of the Braxton family. George Braxton married Mary Carter, the fourth daughter of Robert "King" Carter. Here at Newington, on the bank of the Mattaponi River, was born their son Carter Braxton, a signer of the Declaration of Independence for Virginia. *See: Corotoman; Elsing Green*

NEW KENT COUNTY

Formed in 1654 from York, this county was named for Kent Island, a large patch of good land that is located in the upper Chesapeake Bay near Annapolis. William Claiborne and a number of other settlers lived on the island for many years where they had a very

successful trading post. They traded for furs with the Delaware tribes of the region, farmed the fertile land, and had an excellent, lucrative business arrangement.

Lord Baltimore, of Maryland, coveted the island since it was such an important point for the fur trade. Baltimore's grant gave him the territory of Maryland but it excluded any land that was already occupied by Virginians. Despite this exclusion, William Claiborne and his fellow settlers were evicted by force. Claiborne went to England to protest and received another writ from King Charles I acknowledging his claim and ordering Lord Baltimore to give the island back to its rightful owner. The greedy Marylanders ignored this writ and occupied the settlement in defiance of their king.

Claiborne and about 100 of his people moved to a new tract of land in 1639 between the Chickahominy and Pamunkey rivers which Claiborne had found many years previously when he led a company of the Virginia militia against the Indians in retaliation for the Massacre of 1622. This new tract was named New Kent. By the time New Kent County was formed, William Claiborne had established himself on his plantation named Romancoke which now lies in King William County. *See: Hampton; Romancoke; Sweet Hall*

NEW LONDON
Bedford County   Obsolete

With all of the Englishmen who came to Virginia during the hundreds of years of migration, it is odd that no city, town, village, or hamlet today bears the name London. There was a settlement in Princess Anne County known as London Bridge, but that is now a precinct of Virginia Beach. New London of Bedford County is an obsolete name, no longer used and barely remembered.

When Bedford County was organized in 1753 the courthouse was erected in a tiny hamlet called New London which was a health spa beside a naturally warm spring. The spa never developed into a major attraction and the settlement withered away. *See: Bedford County; London Bridge*

NEWMANS
Hanover County

The Newman family farm never got a fancy name. It was known, simply, as Newman's Farm. The present hamlet continues the name. Very few places in Virginia today bother with the "apostrophe s" in the name.

The postal authorities are so busy with numbers that proper punctuation is ignored.

NEW MARKET
Caroline County

Colonel John Baylor owned the plantation that adjoined Edmundsbury, the home of his good friend Edmund Pendleton. When Baylor specialized in the breeding of fine horses, it was only natural that he call his place New Market for the famous race course in England. The Colonel was forced to give up horses when he found the expenses too great and the financial return too uncertain. Since he had many acres of fine pasture land, he turned to breeding cattle and became a pioneer in the art and science of selective mating. Advocating better care of the animals during the cold of winter, his ideas about careful and humane treatment of cattle had a profound influence upon his friends and neighbors. Although he made money in this new industry, he did not give up his stallion Fearnaught which, he claimed, was "by far the finest in this part of the world" and for which he said he would not take a thousand guineas. *See: Edmundsbury; Hunting Quarter*

NEW MARKET
Shenandoah County   Town

This town was established in the late eighteenth century as a new market for the farmers of the area. It had nothing to do with race horses, as the name New Market of England would seem to suggest, although the local people did not hesitate to have a good race now and then.

This town was the scene of a famous battle of the Civil War, fought on May 15, 1864, in which Corps of Cadets from VMI distinguished themselves with valor and added another chapter to that school's colorful history. Confederate General John C. Breckinridge, a former Vice President of the United States, was defending the Shenandoah Valley. Union General Franz Sigel's troops were attempting to gain control of the great "Bread Basket of the Confederacy." When the Commandant of VMI learned of the thinness of the Southern line, he marched the cadets down the valley to join in the battle. Sigel was defeated and was forced to retreat. *See: Virginia Military Institute*

NEW PLYMOUTH
See: Tappahannock

NEW POINT
Mathews County

At the extreme eastern tip of Mathews County, where Mobjack Bay and the Chesapeake join, the shoals near the shore have snagged many vessels. In 1805 the U.S. Government erected a lighthouse at the point which was a twin to the one built at Old Point Comfort three years earlier. This spot was given its name by the early sailors when the original Point Comfort was ancient enough to be called Old Point. The New Point tower was abandoned in 1963 when the U.S. Coast Guard modernized its navigational aids in the bay and put up automated lights on more accessible steel towers. The little hamlet near the old stone tower calls itself New Point. *See: Fort George; Old Point Comfort*

NEWPORT
Giles County

During the days of westward migration, travel this far was relatively easy over flat or rolling terrain. From here the pioneers entered the wild frontier where supplies were scarce. This hamlet developed on the road leading to the mountains where sutlers sold items to those moving west. They called it Newport, the new portal to the west. *See: Gate City*

NEWPORT
Isle of Wight County   Obsolete

First called Patersville, the name of this eighteenth century settlement next to Smithfield was changed to Newport after the Revolution when a wharf was built to encourage ships to call. During the years between Patersville and Newport, the hamlet was known as Old Towne for an ancient Indian village. It lay on Pagan Creek, also named for the pagan Indians. Today it is known as Battery. *See: Battery; Old Towne*

NEWPORT NEWS
City

Here at Point Hope, many sailing ships took on water before sailing for foreign ports. According to a writer in 1633, "A fine spring lies inside the shore of the river convenient for taking water from. All ships come here to take in water on their way home." (Later, better fresh water was found in the springs that feed the Warwick River at Mulberry Island.) Daniel Gookin's plantation, called Marie's Mount, was established here about 1621. Many refugees came from up river locations after the Massacre of 1622 and many were the praises for Gookin's kind treatment.

The original settlement was occupied by the Newce brothers who had come from Newcetown, Ireland and who might have called their plantation New Newcetown. (There is no evidence of this name and all that can be said with certainty is that the Newce brothers lived here in the very early seventeenth century.) When they left, the land was unclaimed and those who lived there made no effort to record a patent.

A town developed in the late nineteenth century when the railroad magnate, Collis B. Huntington, pushed a line to the water's edge to piers especially designed to handle the dumping of coal onto colliers. When the Newport News Shipyard was organized about the same time, the city's population exploded.

The origin of the name Newport News cannot be fixed. it most probably was named for Captain Christopher Newport who brought the Jamestown settlers to the New World in three small ships in 1607. He made several more voyages with supplies and additional colonists. It is said that when his ship passed Point Hope, the news was quickly spread that he had arrived with news of England. Bearing out this theory is the fact that the official spelling of this city's name was Newport's News until as late as 1909. *See: Marie's Mount*

NEW POST
Spotsylvania
This was the location of a new post office established in 1730 when the former Governor of Virginia, Alexander Spotswood, was named the deputy Postmaster General for the colony. *See: Germanna; Post Oak; White Post*

NEW RIVER
When Peter Jefferson and Joshua Fry drew their rather accurate map of Virginia, published in 1755, they labeled a river west of the Cumberland Mountains "Wood's River or New River." Abraham Wood had discovered the river many years previously and had named it for himself. Therefore, the double name was not necessary. When a road was being built to Abingdon from Richmond in the early part of the nineteenth century, the surveyors encountered a stream of major size that was not on the map that they were using. This they called the New River, a name that was officially fixed when Claudius Crozet

drew the next map of Virginia in 1848. The New River is one of the few that traverses the mountains. It rises in Tennessee, flows north through the western triangle of the Commonwealth of Virginia, and pours through a gap in the mountains near Pearisburg. Many miles beyond, it joins the Elk. Both rivers then lose their identity and become the Kanawha which flows into the Ohio at Point Pleasant. *See: Cumberland Gap; Petersburg; Wood's Gap*

NEW TOWN
Virginia Beach   Site
This town was platted into lots in 1697 by speculators from Norfolk, It was pleasantly situated on the Eastern Branch of the Elizabeth River, giving it access to deep water. When Princess Anne County was organized in 1753, New Town was selected as the county seat and a temporary courthouse was erected. When Norfolk was burned in January and February 1776 New Town was a place of refuge for many citizens who overburdened its resources. When the county seat was moved to Kempsville in 1778, New Town was crippled. By 1781 it was nearly empty as the refugees left. When they came five years previously, they brought salvaged bricks from their burned houses and places of business. When they returned to Norfolk, they tore down their temporary homes and carted the bricks with them to rebuild that city. Recently the site of New Town has been brought back to life, albeit modestly and with commercial intent, as a housing development.

NOKESVILLE
Prince William County
This was the center of Dunkard activity in this part of Virginia. As recently as forty years ago, Nokesville was described as a "loosely assembled village" on a plain of good grazing land. The name Nokes is a variation of the German name Notz. In 1909 the Church of the Brethren founded an academy here to prepare young people for Bridgewater College.

NOMINI HALL
Westmoreland County   Site
Nomini Hall was built about 1730 by Robert Carter II, the son of "King" Carter of Corotman. It was altered by Robert "Councillor" Carter about 1770 at which time the famous avenue of poplar trees was planted. They are still in evidence, a silent symbol of independence that many landowners adopted after the Stamp Act fiasco. The lands

associated with this estate extended for five miles along the Potomac, from Coles Point to Sandy Point and inland for about the same distance. The house itself was located at Nomini Creek, named for an Indian tribe that lived nearby on the Coan River. This was in the Chicacoan Indian district.

Councillor Carter was, perhaps, the most accomplished man of this important family. He believed in exploring different religious and political views. Nomini Hall was opened to those who wished to discuss the new Baptist doctrines. Robert Carter III was the first of any prominent Virginia family to embrace the faith that had been brought from New England when a shortage of Anglican ministers forced the government to relax its stringent religious laws.

Nomini Hall was seventy-six feet long, forty-four feet wide, and two stories high. At each corner of the main house, about 100 yards away, stood four identical dependencies, each one-and-one-half stories high and measuring forty-five by twenty-seven feet— larger than many homes elsewhere in the colony. Used as a schoolhouse, a laundry, a stable, and a coachhouse, they formed a perfect square with the manor house in the center. Between the main dwelling and the dependencies were smaller buildings for the kitchen, storehouses and bakery. The avenue of poplars that Councillor Carter planted flanked a lane leading to the Richmond Road, so called because it led to Richmond Court House to the south.

This Northern Neck estate passed into the Arnest family when a daughter of Robert Carter II married, as her second husband, a Mr. J. Arnest. Nomini Hall burned in 1850 and was never rebuilt. *See: Blandensfield; Coles Point; Coratoman; Northern Neck; Pecatone*

NORA
Dickenson County

First called Mouth of Open Fork, and then Ervinton, this village was named for Nora Dorton, the first postmistress. The Old Buffalo School, organized in 1880 by Alexander Skeen, was the first free school in the county. It held classes for twenty-five years.

NORFOLK
City

Captain Thomas Willoughby settled on the Elizabeth River in 1636, building the first habitation on the site of one of Virginia's important modern cities. Norfolk dates from the 1680 Act of Cohabitation in which the House of Burgesses directed that "on the Eastern Branch of the Elizabeth River at the entrance of the branch" fifty acres should be "measured about, layd out and appointed for a towne." The land was finally purchased in 1682 for "tenn thousand pounds of tobacco and caske." Surveyors marked off streets and the new port was named Norfolk for the shire in England. The Howard family, the hereditary Dukes of Norfolk, had long been powerful in the affairs of the kingdom; using the name was a political gesture. It proved to be a wise choise since the next Governor of Virginia, who took office in 1683, was Francis Howard, Baron of Effingham, undoubtedly a relative of the Duke of Norfolk.

Settlement in the new town was slow and did not increase until a number of Scots recognized the potential of the site with its abundant anchorages in the Elizabeth River and its proximity to Hampton Roads. By 1740 Norfolk had a population of about 1,000, quite high for a city at that time. The dominant inhabitants were the Scots who were canny traders, merchants, ship-owners, and brokers in the export-import trade. Dependent upon peace, they were ultra-conservative Royalists. In recognition of their loyalty, and because so much money was raised here in customs duties, Governor Robert Dinwiddie presented a mace to the town as a symbol of good will. Having been the king's Collector of Customs during the years before he was appointed Governor, Dinwiddie knew and respected these busy, relatively honorable men.

Although the merchants of Norfolk joined in the protest against the Stamp Act and the Townsend Duties, they did so not because of any revolt against taxation without representation but because the Acts effected business and cost the merchants and shippers a lot of money. The drive for independence found little support in Norfolk. When the last royal Governor, Lord Dunmore, came to town for refuge among his fellow Scots after he was forced to leave Williamsburg, he was given a lukewarm welcome because his presence most probably would bring trouble and unrest. The Governor's lack of cash and his tendency to confiscate what he needed "in the name of King George" soon soured the people of Norfolk who viewed the world through their ledgers and not through any great loyalty to their Governor. Even so, most of the merchants were Tories.

ELIZABETH RIVER, NORFOLK

When patriots kept Dunmore and his men prisoners on board their ships by shooting at any head that was raised above a ship's railing, Dunmore, in a fit of anger and frustration, bombarded Norfolk on New Year's Day 1776. His men set fire to the warehouses along the waterfront that had shielded the snipers. The cannonballs from the warships knocked down many of the expensive homes and set more fires. Most of the inhabitants fled. The Tories scrambled for protection on the river in their own ships or in those of the Governor. The other inhabitants of patriotic or neutral persuasion, simply abandoned the town. Before the patriots pulled away, they set fire to the remaining buildings under orders from the Virginia Committee of Safety in Williamsburg to deny the British use of this excellent port. When the fires had burned out, only the Borough Church (now Saint Paul's) remained. For the rest of the Revolution, Norfolk was a field of cold ashes, unoccupied until the peace treaty was signed in 1783.

By the time the Commonwealth joined the Union in 1790, the population had climbed to more than 3,000. Recognized early for its strategic importance by the Northern commanders, Norfolk was occupied by Union forces on May 10, 1862 and it remained lost to the Confederates for the balance of the war. The city came back to life during Reconstruction and, as an important commercial center, it competed with Richmond for power. In the past few decades, the population of Norfolk has been declining and it has been eclipsed by other major cities in the Commonwealth in population. Today it remains a vital center for banks and foreign shipping. *See: Great Bridge; New Town; Ocean View; Portsmouth; Willoughby Spit*

NORFOLK COUNTY
Obsolete
Formed in 1637 during the period of

political reorganization in the colony, Norfolk County was soon divided into Upper and Lower Norfolk counties. In 1742, Lower Norfolk was that portion dominated by the town of Norfolk. Upper Norfolk became Nansemond County. Lower Norfolk was divided in half in 1691 to form Norfolk County and Princess Anne. All of these jurisdictions disappeared during the decade immediately following World War II. To avoid the duplication of services by both a city and a county government, new, superlarge cities were created, notably Virginia Beach and Suffolk.

NORFOLK STATE UNIVERSITY
Norfolk
Starting life as the Norfolk Division of Virginia State College (of Chesterfield County), this school is now independent. It achieved university status in 1977.

NORGE
James City County
Many farmers who settled in this part of Virginia had ties with Norway. They had migrated from Wisconsin to live in a milder climate.

NORTHAMPTON COUNTY
When the colony of Virginia organized itself into eight shires in 1634, the entire Eastern Shore was Accomac County. Nine years later, the name was changed to Northampton in honor of the Earl of Northampton, an early member of the Virginia Company. This was during the period of reform when the General Assembly decided to get rid of all heathen names. A few years later it was acknowledged that the territory was too large for one county and Northampton was divided in half. The northern portion became Accomack. The southern half continued as Northampton. The county seat, Eastville, is one of the oldest

towns in the Commonwealth. *See: Accomack County; Townfields; Arlington; Eastville*

NORTHERN NECK

Before he managed to regain the English throne, the young exiled King Charles II had little money to give to his followers. To curry a bit of favor and to retain their support, he gave away a huge chunk of Virginia much the way his father, Charles I, had given away Maryland to Lord Baltimore. At the time of the gift, Charles II was not officially the king of England since he had been crowned at Scone only as the king of Scotland. Those receiving his largess were John, Lord Culpeper, Thomas Culpeper, and five other "right trusty and well beloved companions." The land, called The Proprietary from then on, lay between the Potomac and Rappahannock rivers in the territory now occupied by the counties of Prince George, Westmoreland, Northumberland, Richmond, Lancaster, and a part of Stafford. (Later, the lines were extended in a fan shape to the western mountains to include all of Stafford, Prince William, Culpeper, Fauquier, Warren, and Frederick, plus parts of today's Loudoun, Fairfax, Clarke, and Shenandoah counties.) Only that portion between the two rivers, however, is the Northern Neck.

By the time of the Restoration in 1660, Lord Thomas Culpeper had managed to gain control of six of the seven shares. The remaining share belonged to the Fairfax family, but not for long. When Lord Culpeper's granddaughter married Thomas, fifth Lord Fairfax, she combined her huge legacy with her husband's smaller one and Lord Fairfax became the sole Proprietor. In return for the right to collect an annual rent, the Proprietor paid the king an annual tribute of slightly less than seven pounds sterling. Since one shilling was collected for each hundred acres occupied by a tenant, the income was considerable. Expenses were mainly for his agents who collected the quit rents and for his band of surveyors who continually mapped and platted his holdings as it was divided into farms. However, Lord Fairfax was constantly in court to protect his claims. George Washington, as a youth, was one of the surveyors, employed by Thomas, sixth Lord Fairfax.

When Virginia gained its independence from England, Lord Fairfax lost almost everything. His heirs managed to reclaim only those small portions on which they had lived or had supervised as working farms. *See: Belvoir; Carolina; Greenway Court; Maryland*

NORTHUMBERLAND COUNTY

The Indian district of Chicacoan occupied this territory near the mouth of the Potomac River. When William Claiborne was unlawfully ejected from Kent Island by the greedy Lord Baltimore, some of his people sailed down the Potomac and settled on the Coan River among the friendly Indians. This was in 1639. Two years later, when the civil war in England came to its climax with the execution of Charles I, many Cavaliers left their homes and estates and patented great plantations in Chicacoan. By 1648 there were enough people in the region to warrant the organization of a new county. It was named Northumberland, a county in England from which many of the settlers had originated. Many of them were surprised, if not actually shocked, to learn that Charles II gave away this territory to a group of favorites and an annual quit rent would be collected by the proprietor. *See: Chicacoan; Lancaster County; Northern Neck*

NORTON

Wise County **City**

A trading and shipping center, hemmed in by the steep slopes of the encroaching mountains, Norton is in the coal mining section of the Commonwealth. This town originally was called Prince's Flats for William Prince who settled here in 1787. The name was later changed to Norton for Eckstein Norton, the president of the Louisville and Nashville Railroad. Norton was incorporated as a town in 1894 and became a chartered city after World War II.

NORWOOD

Nelson County

A forested portion in the northern section of Nelson County for many years was called the North Woods. In time, the name was contracted to Norwood, a typically English pronunciation. This little hamlet adopted the name when a post office was authorized.

NOTTOWAY COUNTY

This was the home of the Nottoway Indians who were peaceful most of the time. An attempt was made by Gov. Alexander Spotswood to create a school for the children of the Nottoway and Saponi tribes at Fort Christanna in 1714, but the project was a failure when the older Indians became suspicious. For many years this part of the colony was unsettled. It was not until 1788 that the population was sufficiently large to require the organization of a county. A portion was cut off from Amelia and was named for the Indian tribe that called this area their home. A town never developed around the courthouse and its dependencies, and today Nottoway Court House is a quaint settlement that retains the look of county seats of a bygone era. Fort Pickett, near Blackstone, occupies a large portion of the southeastern corner of the county.

NOTTOWAY RIVER
Named for the tribe that lived along its banks, this river is an unnavigable shallow stream. With the Nottoways were the Saponi and Meherrin Indians who gradually migrated west to escape the press of settlers. The Nottoway River twists and winds through Nottoway, Dinwiddie, Brunswick, Sussex, and Southampton counties.

NUTTSVILLE
Lancaster County
This village grew around a farm once owned by Colonel William O. Nutt.

O

OAK GROVE
Northampton County
At the eastern end of a fingered cove, called Mattawoman Creek, is a white clapboard house with varying roof lines. Sited on what is now called Old Town Neck, the home was built in 1735 by John and Sarah Haggoman on land that was titled in 1625 by Sir George Yeardley. He had been given the 3,700-acre tract by Debedeavon, the Laughing King. The Old Town refers to the Mattawoman village on the property that was vacated on Yeardley's request when he took title to the land. *See: Assawoman; Mattawoman; Peachburg*

OAK GROVE
Westmoreland County
While living at Wakefield, George Washington and his younger brother Charles went to school here from 1744-46. Nearby is the site of the old Bristol Iron Works. *See: Bristol Iron Works; Wakefield of Westmoreland*

OAK HALL
Accomack County
Henry Smith patented 1,700 acres in the upper portion of Accomack County in 1666. Five years later, he sold out to Colonel William Kendall. In the deed, Smith's land was identified as the "Plantation knowne by the name Oake Hall." The name is preserved by the village which today sits astride the main highway that forms the spinal cord of the Eastern Shore.

OAK HILL
Fauquier County
Thomas Marshall purchased a small tract near here in 1773 not far from the county seat. He and his eighteen-year-old son John, with some neighbors to help, erected a seven-room house on the old Winchester-Fredericksburg road. From this house both father and son went to join the Continental Army, father Thomas as a major and young John as a lieutenant.

John Marshall returned to Oak Hill after the Revolution, practiced law for a while at Fauquier County Court House and eventually was appointed Chief Justice of the U.S. Supreme Court. He led the Court to many important decisions which set the Federal Government above the separate states. He also presided at the trial of Aaron Burr who killed Alexander Hamilton in a duel. Fauquier Court House was renamed Warrenton in 1790. *See: Fauquier County; Midland; Warrenton*

OAK HILL
Loudoun County
Built over a span of three years by James Monroe, he retired to Oak Hill in 1825 at the end of his second term as the fifth President. The name came from sapling oaks sent to Monroe as gifts from each state, and the trees were planted under his personal supervision. Monroe lived here as a country squire, cash poor as many squires were and hounded by his creditors.

When his wife died in 1830, lonely and in ill health, he moved to New York City to live with his daughter. Oak Hill was put up for sale. He had already disposed of Ash Lawn in Albemarle County and the proceeds from Oak Hill were his only hope of settling his debts. He died in New York on the 4th of July, 1831, the third President to die on Independence Day (Jefferson and John Adams were the other two; they died on the same day in 1825), and his body was buried in Richmond's Hollywood Cemetery beside his wife.

Oak Hill was designed by Monroe's close friend Thomas Jefferson. The south porch,

JAMES MONROE, OAKHILL, LOUDOUN COUNTY

overlooking the gardens, has a portico supported by five columns, an unusual number, to provide an unobstructed straight-away view from the windows of the two first-floor drawing rooms and the upper chambers. Oak Hill was not sold until twenty-one years after James Monroe's death. Later owners added complimentary wings on either side of the original house. *See: Ash Lawn; University of Virginia*

THE OAKS
Amelia County

About twenty miles from the present Amelia County courthouse was an old home, built about 1745 by Benjamin Harrison IV of Berkeley. In the middle of the twentieth century, this fine colonial home was dismantled for Miss Lizzie Boyd and was re-erected on Windsor Farms in the city of Richmond. *See: Berkeley*

OARES PLANTATION
Langley Research Center   Site

One of the original Jamestown settlers, John Laydon, a carpenter, married Ann Burras in 1608. It was the first wedding in the new colony. Their daughter Virginia, born the next year, was the first child born of English parents in the successful Jamestown settlement. By 1623 Laydon and his family were living in Elizabeth City but the exact place is not known since the entire lower portion of the Peninsula went by that name. In 1636 Laydon was granted 500 acres on the upper reaches of Back River, about five miles from Kiccowtan Town, on what is now known as Brick Kiln Creek.

The tract was purchased by Thomas Wythe who called it Oares Plantation, possibly for an intervening owner. Thomas Wythe's great-grandson, George Wythe, was born here in 1726. Many years later, when George inherited the property from his brother, he built a small house which he called Chesterville. *See: Chesterville; Chischiak*

OATLANDS
Loudoun County

George Carter, the great-grandson of Robert "King" Carter, built this mansion on an estate of 3,400 acres in 1800. All of the bricks and lumber were produced on the place. Greek revival ornaments grace the interior which is distinguished by lofty ceilings of molded plaster, carved woodwork, an octagonal drawing room, and flanking staircases that descend to the formal entry foyer. The terraced gardens, planned by George Carter, are among the finest of early Virginia landscape design. The Corinthian columns at the front portico were added in 1827.

Confederate troops, billeted in the old house during the Civil War, caused minor damage and their scratchings in the plaster can still be seen. In 1903 Oatlands was purchased by Cocoran Eustis of Washington, D.C. His daughters gave the property to the National Trust for Historic Preservation in 1965. It is open to the public.

Oatlands most probably was named for Oatlands Palace, near Weybridge in Surrey, England and built for Henry VIII. At its zenith, the king's Oatlands Palace covered nine acres and had extensive gardens which were the envy of many gentlemen of the kingdom. The palace was demolished during the days of the English Commonwealth. Its contents and the building materials were sold to raise money to pay Cromwell's soldiers. *See: Carter Hall*

OCCANEECHEE
Mecklenburg County   Site

At the confluence of the Dan and Staunton rivers lived the Occaneechee Indians. Their villages, astride the main north-south trail from Virginia to the heartland of Carolina, effectively blocked any expansion of settlement or trade by settlers. The Occaneechee stronghold was a fortified island (later called Blandina) which was large enough to contain the entire tribe and its livestock. Nearby was a smaller island occupied by the Totem tribe.

In April 1676 the people of Charles City and Henrico counties decided to do something about the raids by the Susquehannocks from the upper portion of the Potomac River. About 300 men led by young Nathaniel Bacon, Jr. mounted an expedition against these Indians. After many skirmishes, the natives retreated south, pressed hard by Bacon's men. Granted safety by the Occaneechees, the Susquehannocks entered the fortified island. By then Bacon and his men considered all Indians their enemies and began to attack the local villages. The people quickly left their lodges and joined the Susquehannocks on the island. After two days of battle, Bacon's men were victorious. Sweeping over the native fortress, they killed every inhabitant—braves, old men, women and children—completely wiping out every trace of the Susquehannocks, the Occaneechees, and the Totems. The southern trail was opened to the settlers. The island now lies under the waters of the reservoir backed up by the Kerr Dam. *See: Iroquois Trail; Kerr Reservoir; Susquehannock Indians*

OCCOHANNOCK
Accomack County

This was the home of Colonel Edmund Scarburgh II, the Surveyor General of the Virginia colony, who purchased land on Occohannock Creek in 1649 from Okiawampe, "the great king of the Eastern Shore." The first dwelling was called Occohannock House, and it was from here that Colonel Scarburgh sailed forth on his many quixotic adventures. First he tried to relocate the Virginia-Maryland border on the Eastern Shore after it had been carefully negotiated by Virginia's Governor William Berkeley and Maryland's Lord Baltimore. Although he was admonished for this by Berkeley, in 1659 Scarburgh organized "300 men and 60 horses, with sloops and all other things necessary for a campaign" and led his small force against the peaceful Assateague Indians. This raid sent the defeated and bewildered Indians on the warpath for several years, the only sustained Indian troubles suffered by the residents of the Eastern Shore.

To end the troubles he had caused, Colonel Scarburgh called a council of the leading chiefs and promised that the Great Spirit would talk to them. Seating them close together in a ditch, the "Great Spirit" was a concealed cannon that "spoke" with deadly effect, murdering them all. For this, Governor Berkeley ordered Scarburgh's arrest and trial. In October 1670 it was the "unanimous Judgement of the Governor and Burgesses" that he was guilty of the horrible act and it was "accordingly ordered that the said Collonel Edmund Scarburgh shall henceforth stand suspended from all offices as well military as civill until his future obedience and fidelity It shall please the Right Honorable the Governor to restore him." During the next seven months, when he died of natural causes, the name Edmund Scarburgh completely disappeared from all local records. He was a non-person just as though he did not exist. Governor Berkeley noted in a letter of May 23, 1671 with some apparent relief, "The said Scarburgh is Deade."

His son, Charles Scarburgh, gained notoriety of his own in 1688 when he objected in public to King James II's placing so many Roman Catholics in positions of authority in government. Scarburgh said, "that his Majesty, King James, would wear out the Church of England, for that, when there was any vacant office, he supplied them with men of different persuasion." For speaking against the king, Governor Howard brought the Colonel before the Council where, after a brief interrogation, he was deprived of all of his offices and rank. Scarburgh was guilty of being too outspoken, of voicing the complaints of many others in England and Virginia.

The same year that the younger Scarburgh was punished, 1688, King James II was forced from the English throne for his pro-Catholic tendencies and was sent into permanent exile in France. He was succeeded by his son-in-law and daughter, William and Mary. Although Virginia was a Protestant colony, controlled by the Anglican Church, neither Governor Howard nor the Council could permit anyone, especially a member of the House of Burgesses, to speak against the king. *See: Chincoteague; Craddockville; Hedra Cottage; Pamunkey Indians*

OCCOQUAN
Prince William County   **Town**

Here Captain John Smith found, in 1608, the "King's House" of the Dogue Indians. They were a wild, fierce warrior tribe and Smith was lucky to have been able to visit and leave without incident. When the settlers began to homestead this frontier region many decades later, the Dogues resisted the invasion with bold attacks which many people described as madly suicidal. The town of Occoquan was formally established in 1734 when the General Assembly ordered a tobacco warehouse built on the south side of the Occoquan River. The name is an Indian word meaning "at the end of the water." *See: Colchester; Corotoman; Dogue Indians; Rockledge; Woodbridge*

OCEANA
Virginia Beach

This hamlet was known as Tunis for many years. It was the next-to-the-last stop before the oceanside resort of Virginia Beach on the old Norfolk Southern Railway. The collection of homes was renamed Oceana in 1891. At present most of the land is occupied by the Oceana Naval Air Station.

OCEAN VIEW
Norfolk

All of this section of Norfolk overlooks the

lower end of the Chesapeake Bay. At one time the houses at the eastern end of the strip could see the Atlantic Ocean beyond Cape Henry. Today that eastern section is occupied by the Little Creek Amphibious Base and the houses were forced back in the direction of Willoughby Spit. On a very clear day the Atlantic can be seen from Ocean View.

OILVILLE
Goochland County
The oil referred to in this name is sassafras oil. Late in the nineteenth century, a press was set up to crush the roots and stems of the sassafras shrub for the pungent oil that was used in medicinal rubs. The enterprise did not last long. Many people think Oilville was named for an oil field. The only petroleum ever pumped from the ground in Virginia was found in Lee County. *See: Ben Hur*

OLD DOMINION
King James I claimed sovereignty over four dominions, England, Scotland, Ireland, and France. Since the colony of Virginia did not have an heraldic symbol, the king did not include it in his royal arms but, even so, he called it his Fifth Dominion. When a coat of arms finally was authorized for the colony many years later, toward the end of the seventeenth century, the motto under the shield was, in Latin, "And Virginia makes the fifth." When England and Scotland were united in 1707, the motto was changed to say Virginia was the fourth dominion.

Throughout the Cromwellian hiatus (1645-1660), many of the leading citizens of Virginia remained quietly loyal to the "Prince Over the Water," meaning Charles, the exiled heir to the throne who had been forced to live on the Continent. When the Commonwealth ended, the former governor of the colony, Sir William Berkeley, hastened to send an emissary to the Prince to proclaim him king, even before he had been crowned in London. This so delighted the young king Charles II that he blessed his "Old Dominion," but he never got around to reappointing Berkeley as governor. *See: Carolina; Green Spring*

OLD POINT COMFORT
Hampton
That portion of the Peninsula which marks the extreme southwestern end of Chesapeake Bay was named Point Comfort by Captain John Smith during his exploratory trips in 1608. He reported that he and his companions felt much comfort when that piece of land came into view because they knew they were again in friendly and familiar territory. It is the first bit of the mainland that can be seen off the bow when a ship enters from the Atlantic and it is still a comfort to sailors and passengers to know that a long voyage is nearly over. A lighthouse has been operating at Old Point Comfort since 1750 and the name has been used affectionately for well over 350 years. *See: Fort George; Hampton; New Point; Thimble Light*

OLD TOWNE
Isle of Wight County   Site
The Warrascoyak Indians were the dominant tribe on the land across the James from the Jamestown fort. At first they traded with the newcomers but, under orders from Powhatan in the autumn of 1609, they refused to sell their surplus corn and became quite hostile. They went on the warpath during the Massacre of 1622 and, in reprisal, the English killed the entire tribe and built a fort on the site of their destroyed village. Many years later a trading post was erected near the old fort and, when a few people built their homes nearby, they created the hamlet called Old Towne in belated memory of the late Indians. This settlement was overshadowed by Smithfield and soon disappeared. *See: Isle of Wight County; New Port*

ONANCOCK
Accomack County   Town
Onancock is an Indian word meaning *foggy place*. This site was occupied by a native village until about 1670. When the settlers began to outnumber the Indians in this delightful place at the head of a broad creek, a tidal tributary of the Chesapeake on the bay side of the Eastern Shore, the Indians left to live with others of their kind elsewhere. Onancock was made an official port in 1680, the same year that the courthouse for Accomack County was built in Onancock. It remained the county seat until the courthouse was relocated at Metomkin. The famous Presbyterian preacher, Francis Makemie, lived in Onancock for many years and then moved farther north to Temperanceville. When the county court was moved from this village, it continued to be an important port for freight boats that connected the Eastern Shore with the Western Shore. *See: Accomack County; Clifton; Temperanceville*

ONLEY

Accomack County   **Town**

This town is named for the home of the Wise family that is situated on the north side of Onancock Creek. The family has long been active in Virginia affairs. Henry A. Wise was elected the Governor of the Commonwealth in 1856. In the election, he did not carry his home district, something that the oldtimers here still chortle about. The accepted pronunciation of Onley is OWN-ly. *See: Clifton; Wise County*

OPAL

Fauquier County

First incorporated as Fayettesville in 1798, this village was later renamed New Brighton for the English seaside resort. The origin of Opal is unknown.

ORANGE COUNTY

Formed in 1734 from Spotsylvania, this county was named for the Dutch Prince of Orange, who in that year married Princess Anne, the daughter of King George II. When the county was established, the House of Burgesses set the boundary at the "utmost limits of Virginia." This included all of western Virginia and the territory on the other side of the Allegheny Mountains from which were created the states of West Virginia, Kentucky, Ohio, Indiana, and Illinois. The county seat is the town of Orange. *See: King William County; Princess Anne County*

ORDINARY

This word had two meanings in colonial times. An ordinary was a tavern or an inn that served food and drink to ordinary people. Anyone who could afford to pay was made welcome. All of the rooms were open to the public except those used by the man who owned the place and who might have lived there. Occasionally an ordinary would have a private room where gentlemen could dine alone for an extra fee.

The Ordinary was the head of a diocese, usually the Bishop, but sometimes a delegated representative who was called the Commissary. When a person was required to appear before the Ordinary, he had to answer for crimes against the church. *See: Tavern; Varina Grove*

ORAPAX

New Kent County   **Site**

When the English first arrived in 1607 Chief Powhatan's main village was on the York River, possibly at Purton near the location of Rosewell. Powhatan had a lodge on the upper portion of the Chickahominy River which was identified in seventeenth century writings as Orapax. Some historians believe this was his place of birth. Whenever something annoyed him or he wanted to be alone before making a major decision, he retreated to Orapax with a few trusted warriors who always accompanied him as a private guard. In the eighteenth century, when the Three Chopt Road was blazed west across the wilderness, it began at a tavern here and ended in Staunton. *See: Purton; Three Chopt Road*

ORISKANY

Botetourt County

The Continental Army won a rare victory over the British on August 6, 1777, near the village of Oriskany, New York. Quite possibly a veteran of that battle settled here after the war and preserved the name. It is also possible the name was given by Thomas Jefferson. During the Civil War iron ore was mined locally. Called Oriskany ore, it was shipped to Richmond as pig iron after being processed in the furnace near the mine. Some say the iron from this mine was used on the hull of the Confederate ironclad, the CSS Virginia (more commonly known as the Merimac), but this may be stretching pride a bit too far. *See: Furnace; Lexington*

ORKNEY SPRINGS

Shenandoah County   **Town**

The village of Orkney Springs is located near a group of seven mineral springs that were known to local settlers long before the Revolution. The village was incorporated in the 1830s, just a few years before a resort was established. The first hotel, the Maryland House, was erected in 1850 with members of the Lee family of Westmoreland County among the investors. A second hotel, the Virginia House, was opened to the public in 1873.

The Orkney Springs resort operated until 1960. That year the Maryland House was taken over by the American Symphony Orchestra League for its annual summer Shenandoah Valley Music Festival. The Virginia House was acquired by the Episcopal Diocese of Virginia for use as a religious retreat.

OYSTER
Northampton County

This little fishing hamlet on the Atlantic side of the Eastern Shore is known for its yearly harvest of oysters and soft-shell crabs.

Oysters tonged from beds flushed by the tides coming directly from the ocean, called sea-tags, are often preferred by connoisseurs for their saltier flavor.

PACE'S PAINES
Surry County   **Site**

In December 1620 Richard Pace settled on the south bank of the James River between Four Mile Tree and Mount Pleasant. He had been granted 100 acres for his own personal "Adventure" and 400 more for transporting four people to the colony at his own expense. Why he called his place Paines has not been recorded, but living in the wilderness in the seventeenth century was a pain with frequent distress or suffering caused by great anxiety, grief, or disappointment. Pace did not give up, however, and remained in Virginia for the balance of his life.

It was at Pace's Paines that Chanco, an Indian friend, was told of the uprising against the English planned for the very next day. Quietly slipping away, Chanco revealed the plot to Richard Pace who had befriended him on numerous occasions, thus risking his own life as an informer and betrayer of a secret. According to the records of the Virginia Company, "Pace, upon this discovery, secured his house (and) before day rowed over the river to James City, in that place near three miles in breadth, and gave notice thereof to the Governor, by which news they were presented there, and at such plantations as was possible for a timely intelligence to be given, for when they saw us standing upon our guard, at the sight of a Piece, they all ran away." The uprising began at noon on Good Friday 1622.

Richard Pace remained at Jamestown for the rest of that year. During the winter, he received permission from the Governor to return "to fortify and strengthen the place with a company of able men." When Pace died at his home in 1628, Pace's Paines was divided between his widow and his son. The widow, Isabella Pace, married Captain William Perry who had been in Virginia since 1611.

Captain Perry, a Burgess for all of the territory on the south bank from Pace's Paines to Lawne's Creek, was appointed to the Council in 1637. His tombstone can still be read in the old burying ground at the site of the first Westover Church. Benjamin Harrison II, of Brandon, gained control of Pace's Paines in 1663 which he added to adjacent tracts to form Eastover. *See: Brandon; Eastover; Four Mile Tree Plantation; Maycocks; Old Towne*

PAGAN CREEK
Isle of Wight County

This inlet of the James River was named for the Warrascoyak Indians who lived here in the early 1600s. Of course, they were the pagans for whom the creek was named. *See: Old Towne*

PAGE COUNTY

Parts of Shenandoah and Rockingham were put together in 1831 to form Page County. It was named for John Page, the Governor of the Commonwealth from 1802 to 1805. The land underneath this county is honeycombed by caverns, the most well known being the Caverns of Luray. The town of Luray is the county seat.

PAINT BANK
Craig County

A mineral used in the manufacture of paint was mined from the bank of a stream here during World War II. The resulting settlement adopted the unusual name.

PALMER SPRINGS
Mecklenburg County

Amasa Palmer a local resident, decided to bottle and sell water from his spring. He was modestly successful. Originally this was Palmer's Spring.

PALMYRA
Fluvanna County

This is the seat of Fluvanna County. The hamlet was named for the old city of Palmyra in Syria near Damascus. During colonial times, when the Rivanna River was navigable for barges and low draft boats, Palmyra was a minor river port for the produce of the local farms. *See: Fluvanna County; Rivanna River*

PAMUNKEY INDIANS
King and Queen County

Just why these Indians were called the Pamunkey by the early English colonists is a mystery. Several tribes lived along the upper portion of the York River (primarily the Warranuncock and the Youghtanund) which John Smith located on his map of 1612. Not long after the settlers made contact with these people, they called them all Pamunkey which was some Indian word that was mistaken for the tribal name.

Their chief was Opechancanough, a kinsman of Powhatan, either a brother or his nephew. Opechancanough was the power behind the two massacres. The first, in 1622, nearly wiped out the English as planned. The second attempt, in 1644, was a failure although many settlers were killed. Opechancanough was captured and, while a prisoner in a cage, was shot to death by his guard. After this, the Pamunkeys wandered north with the Mattaponi and other tribes but eventually drifted back to their old villages.

In 1656 these Indians were sufficiently friendly to offer 100 warriors to help the Henrico militia in a campaign against the Senecas. The expedition was badly led by Colonel Edward Hill of Shirley. All of the Pamunkey warriors, including their warchief Totopotomoi, were killed.

In 1676, remembering the injustices done them, this tribe joined the Senecas and Susquehannocks in raids against homes and barns. In a separate action, they were defeated. Those who survived made peace and promised to pay an annual tribute that is still offered to the Governor of the Commonwealth. By the treaty, they were confined to a reservation which still is owned by the descendants of this proud tribe. *See: Council; Mattaponi; New Kent County; Occahannock; Occaneechee; Susquehannock Indians*

PAMUNKEY RIVER

This shallow river joins the Mattaponi at West Point to form the York. It is generally agreed by geographers that the Pamunkey is the source of the York, although this is hardly important since both rivers lie in Virginia and neither are important to water traffic. On John Smith's map of 1612, he named it the Youghtanund for the tribe living along its banks. *See: Charles River*

PARIS
Fauquier County

This community was formally named in 1819 in honor of the Marquis de Lafayette. Why the residents chose the capital city of France instead of the nobleman's name is not known. Although there have been several Lafayette Taverns, no settlement in Virginia honors this Frenchman directly.

PARRAMORE ISLAND
Accomack County

For many years legend declared that the pirate Blackbeard buried his surplus treasure on this island. Blackbeard's real name was Edward Drummond and probably he began life in this part of the Eastern Shore. Although he was a bloody pirate, he still had family pride and called himself Edward Teach to protect his relatives. Nobody has ever found any of his treasure. This barrier island, due east of Exmore, was called Teach's Island for many years. It was renamed Cedar Island when it was owned by the Parramore family in the early eighteenth century. Thomas Parramore was a successful dealer in skins and hides who died about 1725. When a hurricane in 1857 swept it clean of all vegetation, the island was renamed Parramore Island. The U.S. Coast Guard has an important station here.

PARTICULAR PLANTATION

After the news of the Starving Time during the winter of 1609-1610 reached England and was noised about, the London Company found it difficult to attract new settlers. As an inducement, huge tracts of land were granted to men who had the funds to transport people to Virginia. To sweeten the offer, these new "plantations" would be independent of whatever laws were formulated for Jamestown and other prior settlements. The man in charge, called a governor, could make any rule he felt necessary to ensure proper order. The only exception was the requirement to furnish men to the Governor of Virginia for a common defense of the colony.

When Governor Sir Thomas Dale began to enforce the *Laws Divine, Morral, and Martiall*, written by the Company in 1612, the governors of the Particular Plantations objected, citing the peculiarities of their grants. While Dale observed these exemptions, they caused friction elsewhere and divided the colony into small fiefs. When the Company's charter was revoked by James I in 1624, all of Virginia was placed under English Common Law and the exceptions ended. *See: Martin's Brandon; Plantation*

PASPAHEGH INDIANS
Charles City County   **Site**

The tribe of Indians living closest to Jamestown was the Paspahegh. Their main village, on the Chickahominy River was but a few miles away. It is thought by some historians that the land upon which the English built their first fort was sacred to these Indians and that is why they attacked so often. When Lord Delaware took command of the colony in the spring of 1610, he sent a company of men to eliminate this tribe. Under the leadership of Captain Sir George Percy, the colonists surprised the sleeping Indians at dawn, killed or captured most of the braves, burned the village, and cut down their corn. Among those taken captive was the wife of the old chief whom the English called the queen. Before she was taken to Jamestown, where Lord Delaware ordered her "put to the sword," her children were tossed into the Chickahominy and were callously slaughtered when the men used them as floating targets for their muskets. This was the first of many English atrocities that did not end until all Indians were swept away from the vicinity of Jamestown. The empty Paspahegh village was occupied in 1617 by Captain Samuel Argall who had houses built for his settlers in a town that he called Argall's Gift. *See: Argall's Gift; Old Towne*

PATOWMACK CANAL
Fairfax County   Obsolete

The rapids of the Potomac River presented a serious obstacle to river traffic. If they could be circumvented, barges and other shallow draft vessels could then carry freight as far upstream as Harper's Ferry. And, if the shallow rapids there could be bypassed by another canal, the way would be clear for landowners in the Shenandoah Valley to ship their farm products by water directly to Chesapeake Bay. The first stage of the project was begun in 1785 by the Patowmack Company. George Washington was a major investor and was the company's first president. A series of locks around the Great Falls of the Potomac were built, but the work had to be halted when funds ran out. The remains of the canal, the footpath, and the stone-lined locks are still visible and have been preserved in a park northwest of Washington, D.C. The Chesapeake and Ohio Company picked up the idea during the early part of the nineteenth century and, until the railroads were able to connect the Shenandoah Valley with the eastern seaboard, the C & O Canal operated with moderate success. *See: Kanawha Canal; Matildaville*

PATRICK COUNTY

In 1790 Henry County was divided in half to form Patrick County. The famous orator, the Firebrand of the Revolution, is the only Virginian for whom two counties were named. Patrick Henry must share the double honor with the Duke of Cumberland, Prince William Augustus, who also has two counties named for him. The seat of Patrick County was originally Taylorsville. After the Civil War, it was renamed Stuart to honor the colorful Confederate general Jeb Stuart who was born in this part of Virginia. *See: Cumberland County; Prince William County; Stuart*

PATRICK SPRINGS
Patrick County

Many years ago a summer resort developed around a mineral spring. A huge Victorian hotel catered to the visitors. Although the hotel was destroyed by fire and "taking the waters" fell out of fashion, those who worked at the hotel remained to make this their permanent place of residence. Originally, the resort was known as Patrick's Spring.

PEACHBURG
Northampton County   Obsolete

This is an old, forgotten name for Eastville, the county seat of Northampton and one of the oldest towns in America. When Sir George Yeardley patented land here in 1625, the king of the local Indians required the natives to relocate their village elsewhere. This they did unwillingly, of course, and some sort of peaceful arrangement was worked out, most likely with gifts for the village leaders. When Sir George's only son, Argoll Yeardley, made his home here about two decades later, the old peace treaty was remembered and some called his farm Peaceburg. The pronunciation was changed from *peace* to *peach*, a rather common happening in some parts of Virginia. Even today the city of Portsmouth is Porchmuth to some people, while the Peninsula is often called the Peninchula. *See: Cheriton*

PEAK

Geographically speaking, the top of a mountain is its peak, a nautical term that means the top of a mast. More correctly, the highest part of a mountain is its summit. If the summit is pointed, it is called a peak. If it is rounded, it's a knob. In some instances an entire mountain is called a peak.

The word also was the name given to Indian beads made from shells that had been rubbed into small cylinders. If the peak was black or purple in color, it was *wampum;* if white, it was *rhoanoke* and was worth half as much. The wampum on display in many museums today is often misnamed since it was made from bits of porcupine or feather quills, a practice of the Plains Indians.

PEAKS OF OTTER
Bedford County

The Otter River winds from the Blue Ridge Mountains through Bedford County. Prominent near the stream are several mountain peaks which reminded the early Scottish settlers of a place in their homeland known as Otter. The word *Otteri* in the Cherokee language means "high hill." The Otter River might have been named for the hills or for the animal while the Peaks of Otter may have been named for the river or a place in Scotland.

PEARISBURG
Giles County   **Town**

This town, near the West Virginia border, was named for Captain Richard Pearis who commanded a band of friendly Cherokee Indians during the siege of Fort Pitt during the French and Indian War. Pearisburg is the county seat of Giles County. It is an old settlement that appeared on the Fry-Jefferson map of 1755, slightly misspelled as Pearsburg.

PEARTREE HALL
Newport News   **Site**

The third and fourth generation of the Cary family lived here during the eighteenth century. Peartree Hall was built to overlook Potash Creek, not far from Windmill Point on the Warwick River. The last of the Cary family to live here was Judge Richard Cary who was in residence when the structure caught fire and burned to the ground shortly after the Revolution. He was a member of the committee that framed the Declaration of Rights and drew up the first constitution for the new Commonwealth of Virginia in 1776. *See: Magpie Swamp*

PECKATONE
Westmoreland County

Named for an Indian chief of this region, Peckatone is one of the landmarks of this county of many famous homes. When Hannah Lee, the daughter of Thomas Lee of Stratford, married Gawen Corbin in 1748, she moved twenty miles away from her childhood home to become the mistress of Peckatone. One of Corbin's ancestors had patented the land on the Yeocomico River in 1664 and built the house which is believed to have been the first brick house erected on

Northern Neck. Gawen Corbin was a member of the Council during the tenure of Lord Dunmore. When he died, his will did not please his widow and she felt that her late husband had insulted all womanhood. Hannah inherited Peckatone but could keep it only if she remained unmarried.

She abided by the provisions of the will in her own way. When she fell in love with Dr. Richard Hall, a man of great integrity and understanding, they were married by a Baptist preacher. Since such a wedding was not legally valid and was not recorded in a parish register by a rector of the Church of England, they were officially not married. All the rest of her life she signed herself Hannah Corbin, Widow. The two children she had by Dr. Hall also bore the name Corbin. During the eighteen years of their life together, which ended with Hall's death in 1778, they never lost the respect and affection of the rest of the Lee family. *See: Bushfield; Stratford*

PEDLAR MILLS
Amherst County

A grist mill on the Pedlar River operated for many years during the nineteenth century. The mill's owner and the miller, who might have been the same person, have passed into obscurity. Known as the Mill on the Pedlar, few remains can be found of this important facility. The origin of the name of the stream is also unknown but most likely it was named for its discoverer or an early settler named Pedlar. The community of Pedlar Mills retains the memory of the Mill on the Pedlar with a slightly different spelling. There was only one mill.

PEMBROKE
Giles County

The earliest residents here were members of the Lybrooks family. It should come as no surprise that the first four postmasters were Lybrooks. One of them was Pem Lybrooks whose first name most likely was Pembroke.

PEMBROKE MANOR
Virginia Beach

Built in 1764 by Jonathan Saunders, this fine Georgian home closely resembles the Wythe House in Williamsburg. It probably was named for Pembrokeshire, a county in Wales. An entire section of present-day Virginia Beach is called Pembroke after this former estate.

THE PENINSULA

The land between the York and the James rivers is, without doubt, the most historic territory in all of the United States. It was settled and formed into an organized government years before the Pilgrims made their way to New England in 1620.

Permanent settlement at the lower tip began in 1610 and has continued, without interruption, ever since. From the Peninsula people moved to the Middle Peninsula between the York and the Rappahannock, to the Norfolk region just inside Cape Henry, and to the Eastern Shore.

At its tip is Point Comfort where Fortress Monroe was built to control the entrance to Hampton Roads. From that landing, General McClellan began his Peninsula campaign in the summer of 1862, intending to march right up to Richmond and take it quickly to end the Civil War. McClellan's troops, those that survived the Seven Days Battle, were transported north by ship from Harrison's Landing August 14-16, 1862.

Today the lower portion of the Peninsula is thickly populated by Hampton, Newport News, and York County. *See: Cape; Hampton; Jamestown; Middle Plantation; Newport News; Old Point Comfort*

PENNIMAN

York County   **Site**

Prior to the outbreak of World War I, the DuPont Company purchased 4,000 acres of land on the York River for a new dynamite plant. The land had once been the farm of Captain John Utie who settled at Chischiak in 1630. In the eighteenth century, the land was owned by Major Lewis Burwell and, until the DuPont Company got to work, this was a quiet waterfront area where nothing of significance transpired. Along with the new chemical plant, the company built housing for the workers and their families to create a town of about 15,000 people which was named Penniman. It honored the inventor of ammonia dynamite, Russel S. Penniman. Before any material was made, the Federal government took over the facility for a shell loading plant for the military forces then engaged in the Great War.

During the height of activity, 10,000 people worked at the Federal plant, most of them living in Penniman. Thousands more came by train on three runs a day from Williamsburg and the lower Peninsula. When World War I ended, the government quickly ceased all activity at the shell loading plant and the town of Penniman was emptied. The name disappeared except for Penniman Road that still winds from Williamsburg to Cheatham Annex.

During World War II, the site of the old plant was reactivated by the creation of the U.S. Naval Mine Depot which today is known as the Yorktown Naval Weapons Station. Cheatham Annex, where the town of Penniman once stood, is now a huge supply point, a complimentary facility of the Naval Supply Center of Norfolk. *See: Cheatham Annex; Chischiak; Hopewell; Utimara*

PENN LAIRD

Rockingham County

According to the *Oxford Dictionary of Place Names, Penn* means "the place on a hill." The early settlers of this region of Massanutten Mountain were of the Laird family. *Laird* is the Scottish word for "lord," a nobleman. Taken literally, Penn Laird is a lord's place on a hill.

PENOLA

Caroline County

This village originally was called Polecate from Polecate Creek that runs nearby. It was renamed to honor John Penn, a signer of the Declaration of Independence who represented North Carolina. He was born near Port Royal, VA., in 1741 and died in his home in Granville County, N.C., in 1788. *See: Port Royal*

PEN PARK

Charlottesville   **Site**

Originally in Albemarle County, the first house was erected by Charles Lynch whose relatives moved west to found Lynchburg. Owned prior to 1774 by John Harvie, Sr. of Belmont, he sold it to George Gilmer in 1777 who lived at Pen Park for the remainder of his life. Gilmer was a county magistrate and the sheriff of Albemarle County. When the town of Charlottesville was founded, he was one of the civic leaders. The origin of the name Pen Park has been lost. *See: Albemarle County; Belmont of Albemarle; Charlottesville; Lynchburg*

PENTAGON

Arlington County

Penta is the Greek word for the number five. This structure, the world's largest office building covering forty-two acres, is in the shape of a pentagon. It has five sides and is five stories high. Within this gigantic concrete structure are seventeen-and-one-half miles of corridors and numerous crooks and crannies that serve as offices for many who rank below colonel. Perhaps the world's largest center for shuffling papers, couriers ride tricycles from one office to another in a constant movement of reports, plans, manuals, interoffice memos, and an occasional decision or original idea. It is the headquarters for the Department of Defense and is known the world over as the seat of military power for the United States. *See: Rosslyn*

PETERSBURG

Prince George County   **City**

In 1645 Abraham Wood established Fort Henry fifteen miles up the Appomattox River. Wood was the first commander of the garrison. He was succeeded by Peter Jones in 1675 who had married Wood's daughter. By then Fort Henry, only a name and not a fortification, was a thriving trading post managed by Captain Peter Jones himself. Before long, the little settlement became known as Peter's Point, a name it retained until after William Byrd II paid a visit in 1732 and suggested it be called Petersburg. With typical Virginia vigor, a town was laid out fifteen years later in 1747. It was not officially recognized as a town until 1850 and was chartered as a city immediately thereafter.

Twice the town was caught in wartime activity. In 1781, General Benedict Arnold moved into town, burned 4,000 hogsheads of tobacco in the local warehouses, and wondered how to cross the Appomattox River to clash with General Lafayette who held the high ground now known as Colonial Heights. During a skirmish, Arnold's second-in-command, General William Phillips, was wounded. Already ill from some undisclosed disease, General Phillips died and was buried in the Blandford Churchyard on a hill a few miles from the heart of Petersburg.

In the summer of 1864, Petersburg became the victim of its own prosperity. Being the rail hub of supply for the Confederates, Grant shifted his army to surprise and capture Petersburg.

Almost overnight 150,000 troops faced each other in what became a siege and the last major battle of the Civil War.

Today the interpretation and preservation of the battle areas are in the charge of the National Park Service.

After the Civil War, Petersburg turned to textiles to get away from its dependence on tobacco. The mills operated for several decades but went bankrupt in the financial panic of 1888. Today, tobacco is king again. *See: Blandford Church; Colonial Heights; Shirley*

PETERS MOUNTAIN

Giles-Craig Counties

Peter Wright settled near here in 1746. At 4,035 elevation, Peters Mountain, near Covington, is one of Virginia's highest hills.

PEYTONSBURG

Pittsylvania County   **Site**

This settlement was established before Halifax County was organized in 1752. It became a town in 1759 and was within Pittsylvania when the new county was organized in 1767. Supplies, mainly canteens, were made here for General Nathaniel Greene's army in 1780. Then, when people migrated elsewhere or moved to Chatham, about fifteen miles to the west, the town fell apart and slowly disappeared.

PHENIX

Charlotte County   **Town**

The phoenix is the legendary bird that rose from its own ashes and flew away. The name of this town, spelled Phenix as early as 1906, was suggested by a railroad superintendent. The fire or fires that prompted the name have been forgotten, but the town and the name have survived.

PHOEBUS

Hampton

During the Civil War, Fortress Monroe was overcrowded with troops. A tent city, erected on the lands of Roseland Farm between the fort and Hampton, was called Camp Hamilton. When Union soldiers were mustered out after 1865, the tent city remained as a temporary home for freed slaves who had flocked to the safety of Fortress Monroe after running away from their former owners. When Camp Hamilton was closed in 1871, the land of Roseland Farm, no longer fit for agriculture, was divided into lots to form Chesapeake City. Located just outside the military reservation, the new town quickly became a collection of saloons and brothels which was an embarrassment to the Army and to the good citizens of Hampton, about two miles away. A reform group under the leadership of Harrison Phoebus tried hard to eliminate the vice and seedy places and by 1900 they were moderately successful.

191

Chesapeake City was renamed Phoebus, was incorporated as a town, and Harrison Phoebus was elected the first mayor. During Prohibition the saloons were closed and the numerous bordellos slowly faded away. The Old Soldier's Home, established on Roseland Farm, became a Veterans Administration Hospital in the early 1930s to give some stability to the population. After World War II, when Hampton consolidated with Elizabeth City County to form one large city, Phoebus was annexed and ceased to be an independent town. *See: Fort Monroe; Hampton*

PIANKATANK RIVER
The shortest of the five rivers that flow into the Chesapeake Bay, the Piankatank separates the Middle Peninsula counties of Gloucester and Mathews from Middlesex. Its source, Dragon Run, is about twenty-five miles from its mouth where Gwynn's Island lies as a misplaced plug. The Piankatank's tidal water and the pristine scenery along its banks is rivaled only by the Chickahominy for cleanliness and natural beauty. *See: Gwynn's Island*

PIEDMONT
This name comes from the Latin words *pedis* and *montis*, foot and mountain. The rolling region lies between the Blue Ridge Mountains and the sea and is, literally, at the foot of the mountains. Although the word piedmont is used in other locations in other states, the Piedmont section of Virginia yields to none other for pleasant views and its place in history. Settlement began just prior to 1730 as the colonists moved west away from the coastal plain.

PINE GROVE
See: Ferry Farm

PINE SLASH FARM
Hanover County   **Site**
Cut off from Rural Plains in 1745 by John Shelton, this 300-acre farm was given to Patrick Henry and his bride Sarah Shelton as a wedding gift. Perhaps it would be more accurate to say it was Sarah's dowery. Included in the gift were six slaves to work the land. In the spring of 1757, the house and all of its contents were destroyed by fire. The young couple, with their first child Martha, moved into the former overseer's cabin for the summer. That fall, not wanting to winter in such primitive quarters, they moved to the Hanover Inn which was then run by John Shelton. The Henry's lived at the Inn for several years where Patrick took his turn as

barkeep between appearances in court as a lawyer. *See: Roundabout; Rural Plains; Scotchtown; Studley*

PINEY RIVER
Nelson County
The pines that grow luxuriously in this section of Virginia give their name to this active river. Flowing through Piney Woods, the Piney River has been sung about for years.

PISCATAWAY
Essex County
John Robinson, a member of the Council, made his home here. He was the acting governor of the colony while Governor Alexander Spotswood was off on his trek with the Knights of the Golden Horseshoe. His son, John Robinson II, was the more famous of the two men who lived here. He was called "Speaker John" since he was the Speaker of the House of Burgesses for twenty-seven years. He was also the Treasurer of the colony at the same time since, by custom, the two positions went together. After Speaker John's death, however, the two posts were legally separated.

During a depression that gripped Virginia in the middle of the eighteenth century, John Robinson lent large sums of public money to his friends in unsecured and unrecorded loans to keep them from bankruptcy. When he died, these unpaid debts were discovered during an audit. Although Speaker John did not personally benefit from this misuse of public funds, the many private arrangements caused quite a scandal and sullied his otherwise good name. Edmund Pendleton, the executor of Robinson's estate, spent nearly two decades of devoted labor to clear up the mess. *See: Edmundsbury; Wellington*

PISCATAWAY INDIANS
This tribe originally lived in Maryland where they were known by the tribal name Conoy. They allied themselves with the colonists against the hostile Susquehannocks, Sennecas, and other Iroquois tribes in the unrest of 1676. After the first campaign by Bacon's Virginians and a few Marylanders, the Conoy tribe was thanked by being confined to a tiny reservation in 1679. Persecuted by the bold unconquered Iroquois and ignored by the settlers, they fell into miserably poor conditions and dropped into despair. Feeling rather certain that the Marylanders intended their complete anni-

hilation, they looked to the friendly Virginians across the Potomac.

Giles Brent, who had been expelled from Maryland for marrying a princess of the tribe, helped them settle on vacant lands near Aquia Creek on a stream that bears their name today. Two years later they moved away from Piscataway Creek to an island in the Potomac called Heater's Island. There they built a large fort with eighteen cabins within the enclosure and nine outside. It is not known why they had changed their name from Conoy to Piscataway or what the name means. Their security within the fort was false. About 1705 an epidemic of smallpox struck the island and the entire tribe was wiped out. *See: Aquia Creek; Mattaponi Indians; Wellington*

PITTSYLVANIA COUNTY

Formed in 1766 from Halifax, the organization of the new county coincided with the appointment of William Pitt (the elder) as England's Prime Minister. Pitt was opposed to the Stamp Act, enacted a year earlier, and was the chief spokesman in the House of Commons for its repeal. In place of the Stamp Act, however, Parliament placed heavy duties of many of the necessities imported by Americans. The Townsend Duties were designed to force the colonies to pay for British army and navy units on duty in the New World. William Pitt was too ill to oppose the imposition of the new duties in 1767 and, although he was the Prime Minister, he was ineffective and was replaced in six months. Even so, his vocal support of the colonies made him a hero. For his services to his king, he was made the first Earl of Chatham. Therefore, the seat of Pittsylvania County was named Chatham. *See: Chatham of Stafford*

PLANTATION

In the very early days of Virginia, during the first two decades of colonization, the word "plantation" meant the settlement of people in places where they were to take root and remain permanently. Those who sent these people, usually paying for their transportation and supplies, were called "planters" or "Adventurers," since they ventured their money to populate the virgin land. Those who were living in Virginia at the time of the departure of Sir Thomas Dale were called "Ancient Planters" because of their tenure as planted people, and for this they were given larger sections of land in the first division in 1619.

The Adventurers themselves gained huge tracts for having risked their capital.

In order for these new owners to retain the titles to the tracts, they had to "prove" their lands by erecting a modest dwelling and by having a portion worked as a farm. Then, if they paid the annual quit-rents, they could either sell what they had been granted or pass it on to their heirs. "Prove" was a shortened form of "improve," and the improvements often were most moderate or faked entirely.

In time, as the English language changed, any large farm was called a plantation, referring to the crops, not the inhabitants. The word still evokes memories of antebellum houses beside broad fields worked by slaves. While there were a number of such places in Virginia, few of the owners used the word "plantation" in the formal names. A very early exception dates to about 1623 for a garrisoned post in the center of a long palisade. Middle Plantation belonged to the colony and was not intended to be a farm. The garden plots tended by the militiamen and their families had no bearing on the choice of the name and no plantation, in the modern sense, ever was created. *See: Middle Plantation; Particular Plantation; Sabine Hall; Williamsburg*

PLEASANT POINT
Surry County   Obsolete

William Edwards patented land along the south bank of the James in 1657 and built his home there. He was the clerk of the General Court for many years and served also in the House of Burgesses. One of the oldest houses in the county, Pleasant Point is situated on 490 acres of farmland, marsh, and swamp. It remained in the Edwards family until 1812. The present name for Pleasant Point is Scotland Wharf. It is the southern terminus of the only public ferry line still operating in Virginia.

POCAHONTAS
Tazewell County   Town

This town was named for the famed Pocahontas Coal Mine located nearby. Jordan Nelson, a blacksmith, found an exposed seam of coal in a mountain behind his forge, packed it in by mule, and used it to heat his iron. When Thomas Graham of Philadelphia was extending his New River Railroad from Radford to Hinton, his chief engineering officer heard about the coal that Nelson had found. Sending a sample east for analysis, it proved an excellent grade, suitable for locomotives. Financed by the railroad, the mine opened in 1883 in Powell's Bottom and produced more coal than the railroad needed. The surplus was shipped to Norfolk for export. Until it was closed in 1955, the Pocahontas Coal Mine produced over 44 million tons during the seventy-two years of digging. Today a portion of the old mine is open to the public. The town of Pocahontas was incorporated in 1884, the year after the mine was opened. *See: Midlothian*

POCAHONTAS STATE PARK
Chesterfield County

This park of over 7,000 acres was known as the Swift Creek Recreational Area when it was acquired by the Federal government in 1934. The Virginia Conservation Commission accepted it as a state park in 1946 and changed its name to Pocahontas. It is very unlikely that the Indian princess ever set foot here since in her day, this territory was controlled by the Monacans, bitter enemies of her father Powhatan.

POHICK CHURCH
Fairfax County

The present building is the third Lower Church of Truro Parish that was established in 1732 to serve the estates in the vicinity. The previous churches were located about two miles to the south. George Mason, George Washington, and George William Fairfax were all members of the building committee. Mason wanted to build a mile away on Pohick Creek, but Washington and Fairfax outvoted him. As a compromise, it was named Pohick Church. Work began in 1769 but was not ended until 1744. The selected spot had some historic significance, although it had no bearing on the choice of the site. In 1722 a treaty was signed here with the local Indians who promised to deliver to the authorities all run-away slaves they managed to capture. *See: Gunston Hall; Powhite*

POINT

A tapering piece of land that projects into a major waterway is called a point, from the shape and from the rather obvious fact that it points into the water. Some major points have lighthouses or other markers to aid mariners. The most noted of those in Chesapeake Bay are Point Lookout on the tip of Maryland at the mouth of the Potomac, Windmill Point at the mouth of the Rappahannock, New Point in Mathews County at the entrance to Mobjack Bay, Gloucester Point just inside the York River, and Old Point Comfort where Hampton Roads joins the bay. There are other points within the major rivers that are too numerous to mention here. *See: Cape; Spit*

POINT HOPE
Newport News

On John Smith's map of 1612, the present site of lower Newport News, at the extreme end of the James River, was marked Point Hope. As a traveller sailed through Hampton Roads and turned into the mighty river, the hope of reaching Jamestown was about to be realized within an hour or two of sailing. *See: Hope; Marie's Mount; Newport News*

POPE'S CREEK
Westmoreland County

Colonel Nathaniel Pope was a very early settler in this section of Northern Neck. He had a private wharf on the creek that bears his name to which ships could moor to unload items from England or other countries and take on farm products, mainly tobacco and grain.

In 1657 the English merchantman *Seahorse*, out of London, foundered in the Potomac shortly after departing a neighboring wharf. It settled to the bottom in salvagable condition. When it was refloated and brought into Mattox Creek for repairs, the ship's second officer, John Washington, was temporarily quartered with Colonel Pope. By the time the *Seahorse* was ready to sail again, Washington had decided to remain in Virginia in order to be near his host's daughter Anne. They were married in 1658. As a wedding gift, Colonel Pope gave the couple a 700-acre tract on Bridge Creek. John Washington prospered, was elected a Burgess, and became actively involved in the affairs of the county.

His grandson, Augustine, was born in the Bridge Creek house in 1694. When he was twenty-four years old, he purchased 200 acres on Pope's Creek, built a house, and called his farm Wakefield. Here George Washington was born.

On the other side of Pope's Creek was Machodoc, the home of the Lee family. Just a few miles up the Potomac was Monrovia, the home and birthplace of James Monroe. *See: Epping Forest; Wakefield of Westmoreland*

POPLAR FOREST
Bedford County

This plantation of over 4,000 acres was

inherited by Martha Skelton Jefferson from her father John Wayles. Her husband, Thomas Jefferson, designed the house to fit into the rolling landscape in such a way that, from the front approach, it appears to be a one story building although it is actually two stories with a basement. The poplar tree had been adopted by many patriots in the mid-1700s as a silent symbol of independence and Jefferson planted many of them around the place. To connect this country retreat with his wife's former home, he named it Poplar Forest. He spent time on this remote estate with his family whenever he wanted to get away from the political and social pressures of Monticello. It was here that he wrote his book, *Notes on the State of Virginia* after serving two terms as President. Poplar Forest was inherited by Francis Eppes, a son of Jefferson's daughter Maria. *See: Elk Hill; Eppington; The Forest of Charles City; Natural Bridge*

POPLAR GROVE
Accomack County

This land was patented by Richard Hill of Hill's Farm in 1671. It lay on the north side of Gingoteague Creek. In his will of 1694 Hill left his lands equally divided between his two grandsons, Richard and John Drummond. John's portion was the Poplar Grove tract, although at the time it did not have the name. John's youngest daughter, Tabitha, married George Douglas, the seventh and youngest son of William Douglas, Lord of Baads of Midlothian, Scotland. George Douglas had migrated to Virginia about 1715 and had located on the Eastern Shore. A good lawyer and an outstanding leader, he was elected a Burgess for this region for thirty-two consecutive years. About 1856, Douglas Hall was renamed Poplar Grove.

POPLAR GROVE
Mathews County

John Patterson purchased this tract about 1750, built the oldest part of the present dwelling about 1750, and planted the poplar trees for which this farm was named. He used the trees as a symbol of independence. He fought with the Continental Army and was breveted to general by Washington after the Battle of Monmouth in New Jersey. He was rather surprised to be in the army. Washington had recommended him for a commission in the navy. During the latter part of the eighteenth century, one of the few tide mills in Virginia operated at Poplar Grove. *See: Mill*

POPLAR GROVE
New Kent County

Richard Chamberlayne kept his house here not far from Williams Ferry which crossed the Pamunkey River. In 1758, while George Washington was his guest enroute to Williamsburg for a session of the House of Burgesses, Chamberlayne introduced the bachelor to a charming widow who lived nearby at White House. Washington was late for that session of the House and, on his return trip, he stopped to see the Widow Custis at her home. After a most proper courtship, the two were married in 1759. *See: Naylor's Hole; White House*

POPLAR HALL
Norfolk

In the remote country on Broad Creek before Norfolk was laid out into lots, Thomas Hoggard built his home about 1650. A red brick structure of simple design, the house has massive end chimneys. A small porch at the front door is not consistent with the design of that period and probably was added in the nineteenth century. The dwelling has never been sold but has been passed from generation to generation through inheritance. The grounds have diminished in size through the years and the great grove of poplars has been replaced by a stand of pecan trees.

POPLAR SPRING CHURCH
Gloucester County

Two church buildings have occupied this site, both of which are gone. Here ended the life of the rebel, Nathaniel Bacon, Jr. in late 1676. He was reportedly buried under the floor of Petworth Church (commonly known as Poplar Spring Church for the stream that trickles close by) by his followers shortly after his unexpected death. At the time, Bacon was a fugitive who was sought by Governor William Berkeley. The rebel had defied the government, set fire to Jamestown, and had led the first serious rebellion against colonial authorities. When it was learned that he was dead, the casket was dug up in order to hang the corpse, as was the custom. It would be left dangling until it rotted as an example to others who might be inclined to stage another treasonous affair. When opened, the casket was full of stones. Bacon's remains were never found. It was thought that his followers had sunk his body in the deep waters of the York River to prevent the public shame, but there were those who felt the rebels had had a falling out and that one of them had murdered Bacon and had hidden the body to conceal the deed. Since the body was never recovered and those who were with him at the end never spoke of his death, Nathaniel Bacon's demise remains a mystery. *See: Bacon's Castle; Curles; Jamestown; Occaneechee*

POQUOSON

York County   **City**

The first settlement here occupied an abandoned Indian village about two miles south of the present business district. Hardy colonists began building their homes and clearing the land for farms about 1631 in the area the natives called *Po-co-son,* meaning "marshy place." Despite the swarms of fierce mosquitoes that still breed abundantly in the salt marshes, the English families remained. The land is well suited to agriculture; the shallow waters of Back River provided fish, crabs, and oysters. Since Poquoson is within easy reach of Chesapeake Bay, the watermen sailed all over the Tidewater region, making frequent contact with the settlers on the Eastern Shore. The farmers raised corn and other Indian vegetables which they sold in Elizabeth City and elsewhere. The residents of Poquoson also used the system of placing hogs and cattle on isolated islands where the animals could forage or graze unmolested and reproduce without supervision.

It is said that the forerunner of modern football was played here as early as 1635, probably copied from an Indian sport. The ball was a hog stomach filled with seaweed and was carried by the players from one goal to another. The rules were never formalized or recorded, but the game was popular. As late as 1820 Cedar Creek, one of the many streams that thread through the marshes, was known as Football Quarter Creek.

No colonial homes remain in modern Poquoson. The last one was razed as a nuisance in the careless days of the early twentieth century. The people who lived here during the Revolution were mostly Tories who depended upon trade with England for their income. When these Tories were evicted, much of the land was purchased or claimed by squatters, mainly Scots from the Eastern Shore. The settlement languished in obscurity for nearly two hundred years and then began to expand in the 1960s. Within a decade it became an incorporated town and then quickly became a city. The name is pronounced Pa-CO-son.

POROPOTANK

King and Queen County

No one knows what Poropotank means. *Tank* is the Indian word for "little." The name of the creek appears in journals as early as 1640 and John Lewis appears to have been the first settler. In 1663 a band of indentured servants from Gloucester County, weary of their hard life, met at the head of this creek and plotted an insurrection. Before their rebellion became a reality, the plot was betrayed by a servant who lived at Purton. For his timely information, which probably prevented a massacre, he was given his freedom and a present of tobacco. John Lewis, Jr., living here when the followers of Nathaniel Bacon camped nearby toward the end of that rebellion, suffered at the hands of the outlaws for his strident pro-government views.

Edward Porteus, who had come to Virginia after Bacon's Rebellion had been quelled, built a house on the east side of the creek within view of the York River and named it Poropotank. In 1693 he was appointed to the Governor's Council because he was a "Gentleman of estate and standing suitable for appointment." *See: Purton*

PORT

The word "port" dates from the 10th century when it was used by the Anglo-Saxons to identify a marketplace. All buying and selling was monitored by an agent of the local ruler who cared little about the honesty of the deals but was most interested in who had money to buy in large quantities and who had what to sell. The open field where the trading took place was called a port. The roadway leading to it was the portway. Port Meadow is still a section of Oxford, England, although it no longer is used for that purpose. When trade expanded to other countries via ships, the largest ports quite naturally developed on the rivers that reached the sea. This led to the imposition of customs duties, a fine source of income for the king. In Virginia, as in other colonies, many market towns on the interior rivers included the word "port" in their names. *See: Port Republic*

PORT CONWAY

King George County

James Madison, the fourth President, was born here on March 16, 1761, while his mother, the former Eleanor Rose Conway, was visiting her parents. The birth was

JAMES MADISON, PORT CONWAY

unexpectedly early for it had been planned that the child would be born at Montpelier, the Madison estate in Orange County. The father, James Sr., who had remained at Montpelier to attend to business matters, was pleased and rather surprised to have his wife return from an otherwise routine visit with their son. Port Conway, as the river estate was called, was across the Rappahannock River from Port Royal with which it competed. The wharves provided the last unloading point for larger vessels since from here the river becomes shallower with each mile to Fredericksburg. Port Conway's commercial activities were eclipsed by Port Royal as there were more homes and farms on the Caroline County side of the river.

Today, neither Port Conway nor Port Royal serve commercial vessels. Both wharves have rotted away. While Port Conway continued as a private estate, Port Royal matured into a small community. A modern bridge now connects King George and Caroline counties at this point. *See: Montpelier; Port Royal*

PORTOBAGO INDIANS
Essex County   **Site**
These Indians survived the intrusion of settlers longer than most tribes. They managed to maintain their tribal identity and

customs until the end of the seventeenth century when they then gradually drifted away. As late as 1669 their village here had sixty lodges. They were primitive farmers and traders who occupied the rich lands along the south bank of the Rappahannock River. Possibly there is some connection between the name of this tribe and two small tobacco trading centers, both called Port Tobacco. The one in Virginia, near here, has disappeared. The hamlet in Maryland continues the name. *See: Rose Hill*

PORTO BELLO
Cheatham Annex   **Site**
Just above Capitol Landing on the York River was a farm whose most famous owner was Lord Dunmore, the last royal Governor. When he purchased the place, which included a rustic lodge, it already bore the name Porto Bello for the naval engagement won by Admiral Edward Vernon during the siege of Cartagena. It is a curious quirk of history that Lord Dunmore and George Washington, early friends but later bitter enemies, each owned a plantation that was connected by name to the same man, although neither had selected the names Mount Vernon or Porto Bello. When Dunmore purchased this farm in 1773, he was advised by Washington about various aspects of management.

The small estate was seized by the new Commonwealth in the summer of 1775, when Dunmore was forced to flee Williamsburg, and was sold at auction. After the Revolution, the proceeds from the sale were sent by the Commonwealth to the former governor. Nothing remains of the old lodge. The land is now within the restricted reservation of Camp Peary. *See: Camp Peary; Mount Vernon*

PORT REPUBLIC
Rockingham County
In colonial times this hamlet was the county seat. Situated on a fork of the Shenandoah River, Port Republic was a shipping point for agricultural products that were brought in by boat and transferred to wagons or carts for overland travel to the east. When the village was officially established as a town in 1802, only twelve years after the founding of the republic, patriotic enthusiasm led to the adoption of the name. *See: Port*

PORT RICHMOND
King William County   **Site**
In 1924 the Southern Railway pushed a

spur down to the junction of the Pamunkey and York rivers just outside West Point. A major river port was planned but the venture did not succeed. Now a part of the town of West Point, the docks mainly serve small freighters that bring pulpwood to the Chesapeake Corporation to be converted into paper products. *See: West Point*

PORT ROYAL
Caroline County   **Town**

Thomas Roy established a warehouse and wharf on the south bank of the Rappahannock in 1742. It handled the tobacco and other farm products for the people south of Fredericksburg. His son, John, sponsored financially by Edmund Pendleton whose home is nearby, received a license to operate a ferry and an ordinary at the wharf. The Roy family maintained these enterprises for many generations and it was for them that the place was given its original name, Port Roy. It is not known when the more important-sounding Port Royal was adopted, but no doubt it did not hurt business at the ordinary. *See: Port Conway*

PORTSMOUTH
City

Captain William Carver, a mariner, settled here in 1659. Five years later he acquired a grant of land along the western branch of the brackish Elizabeth River that empties into Hampton Roads and gives direct access to the sea. Captain Carver participated actively in Bacon's Rebellion and paid for his work dearly. He led the force of rebels who attempted to capture Governor William Berkeley which was, in the Governor's mind, the greatest sin of all the many sins committed during this rebellion. When Captain Carver was captured, he was quickly hanged and his land was confiscated.

Forty years later, in 1716, Colonel William Crawford was granted title to Carver's land but it took thirty-four more years before he did anything with it. Colonel Crawford laid out "one hundred and twenty-two lots, commodious streets, places for a courthouse, market, and public buildings for a towne..." in 1750 and offered to sell homesites to "divers persons desirous to settle and build theron speedily." He named his development Portsmouth for the English port of the same name, the home of the Royal Navy. Two years after the lots were first put up for sale, the House of Burgesses voted to formally recognize the new town.

At the outbreak of the Revolution, Portsmouth was a hotbed of Tory traders who competed with the Tory merchants of Norfolk directly across the Elizabeth River. When Norfolk was burned, some of the refugees were given aid and comfort in Portsmouth. In 1776 Washington ordered General Charles Lee, the commander of this military district, to clear the "notorious traitors" from the area. General Lee burned the homes of the most influential, ordered the erection of Fort Nelson at the river's edge, and felt quite satisfied with his work. In May 1779 a British flotilla under the command of Sir George Collier entered the river and landed 2,000 marines. General Edward Matthews's men quickly captured Fort Nelson, burned the shipyard at Gosport, set fire to the warehouses bulging with tobacco and other supplies, and carted off much booty.

Benedict Arnold wintered here in January 1781, occupied Patrick Robinson's house as his headquarters, and used the old sugar house on Crawford Street as a barracks and prison. His presence brought back the surviving Tory families who, by then, were convinced the Revolution was lost. They welcomed Lord Cornwallis in July 1781 and invited him to make Portsmouth his winter quarters. He decided to winter in Yorktown instead where he was boxed in and forced to surrender.

In 1784 the patriot citizens of Portsmouth told "those execrable miscreants called Tories," as one person described them, to "leave this township immediately" or "measures" would be taken. The banished Tories moved across the river to ruined Norfolk and helped rebuild that city. Portsmouth and the shipyard at Gosport recovered nicely from the war.

In 1830 the site of old Fort Nelson was selected by the U.S. Navy for a military hospital. Still operating and enjoying a fine reputation for modern medical service, it is the oldest Naval hospital in the country. *See: Gosport; Norfolk; Peachburg; Suffolk*

POST OAK
Spotsylvania County

The first post office in this region was located in a grove of post oak trees. When it opened in 1855 John A.B. Gordon, of Post Oak Farm, was named the first postmaster.

POTOMAC CREEK

Near the mouth of this inlet of the Potomac

River stood the village of the Patowomeke Indians. Since their name has been spelled so many different ways, it is impossible to know how this tribe's name should be pronounced. Of course, today it is Potomac.

In 1647 Giles Brent built his home on Potomac Creek after he had been expelled from Maryland. About 1665 he helped his fellow Catholics create the town of Brentsville when King James II created a "refuge for people of all religions" in this portion of Virginia. When the first Catholic congregation was organized in Brentsville, the government of the colony left it alone since the people were too far away from the major centers of population to cause any problems among the Protestant Anglicans.

In the nineteenth century, this creek was the main point of contact between the river boats and the railroad that supplied the Union Army of the Potomac during the Civil War. After that conflict, Potomac Creek was a quiet region of the important river, eclipsed by the activities at Aquia Creek and Occoquan, Dumfries and Colchester. *See: Aquia Creek; Argall's Gift; Brentsville; Marlborough*

POTOMAC RIVER

The Indians had two names for this river. Above the falls they called it *Cohongarooton,* meaning "goose river." Below the falls it was *Patawomke,* "the river of swans." The upper region was once on the major north-south route for migrating geese, ducks and, swans that covered the waterway each spring and autumn in countless numbers. Because of the growth in urbanization and the severe pollution of the Potomac, the birds now fly closer to the coast in their migrations. English cartographers used the names Goose River and Potomac on their maps as late as 1730, but by the time of the Civil War, the entire river was called the Potomac. A tributary retains the name Goose Creek.

When the boundary between Maryland and Virginia was formalized, Virginia's territory ended on the south bank of the Potomac. Today, the entire river is under the control of Maryland. *See: Patowmack Canal*

POUND

Wise County   Town

A pounding mill was built here about 1815 by James Mullins. This type of mill employs a huge mortar and pestle to pound grain into a coarse flour. The pestle was raised by a water-powered mechanism and then allowed to fall. Especially good for grains with a tough

husk, a pounding mill does not have the capacity to make the fine flour that comes from mills using a rotating stone. The process is also somewhat slower. Native Americans made their flour by the pounding process, as do primitive people today in many parts of the world. The modern offspring of a pound mill is the drop forge used to shape hot metal. Another hamlet, Pounding Mill in Tazewell County, was named for a similar mill. *See: Mill*

POUND RIVER
Wise and Dickenson Counties

This short river near the West Virginia border was named for the pounding mill that it powered many years ago. The river was named long before its waters were impounded by several dams, the largest of which creates the John W. Flannagan Reservoir in the mountains of Dickenson County. *See: Pound*

POWELL'S CREEK
Prince George County

Captain Nathaniel Powell patented a tract along the south bank of the James River in 1619. As the commander of the garrison at Jamestown, and a senior member of the Council, he was the acting governor for a brief time between the speedy departure of Samuel Argall and the arrival of Sir George Yeardley. When he left the confines and confusion of Jamestown, he found peace and happiness in this quiet wilderness. Several years after building his home, he sold out to the group that created Merchant's Hope Plantation. During Revolutionary times, Bland's Mill stood here. Later it was known as Cocke's Mill. *See: Bremo*

POWHATAN
James City County

Richard Eggleston patented 1,173 acres of land near Jamestown in 1634, eight years after his arrival from England. The last great house on the Powhatan tract was built about 1730 by the noted architect Richard Taliaferro for his own use. He was one of the three active designers of note during the middle of the eighteenth century. The other two were John Arris of Fairfield and Thomas Jefferson of Monticello.

On the southwestern edge of the lands of this estate lies Powhatan Swamp, named for the famous Indian chief of the region. It is said that the natives built a formidable fort on the edge of the swamp in response to the one constructed by the settlers at Jamestown. Portions of this defensive position can still be seen if one knows where to look and exercises an imagination. An Indian fort is a rarity since the natives preferred to remain free to maneuver individuallly and fight man to man. On the other side of Powhatan Swamp lie the covered remains of Green Spring, once the home of Governor William Berkeley. *See: Battle Knob; Green Spring*

POWHATAN COUNTY

Formed in 1777 from Cumberland and Chesterfield, this county was named for the great chief Powhatan, the powerful leader of a confederacy of thirty-two tribes along the James, York, and Rappahannock rivers when the first English settlers came in 1607. His influence was felt among the tribes of the Potomac and the Eastern Shore, but since he ruled by cruelty and force, the farther the tribes were from Werowocomoco, Powhatan's headquarters on the York River, the less they obeyed his demands for annual tribute of food, warriors, and women.

This county, on the south bank of the James River, across from Goochland, was never under Powhatan's control. It was occupied by the Monacans, his bitter enemies, whose main village was at Rassawek. When a name had to be selected by the colonists who were then 170 years removed from the days of this great chief, his memory was honored. The major settlers of newly-formed Powhatan County were the descendants of the Huguenots who had come to Virginia in great numbers from France after the Edict of Nantes was revoked in 1685.

The county seat, originally Powhatan Court House, was renamed after the Revolution for a local war hero, General Charles Scott. As there already was a Scottsville, just a few miles up the James River at Scott's Ferry, the new name was dropped to avoid needless confusion. Today, Powhatan Court House is, simply, Powhatan. *See: Columbia; Manakin; Rassawek; Scottsville; Werowocomoco*

POWHATAN'S CHIMNEY
Gloucester County   **Site**

As a gesture of peace, the English colonists built a house for Powhatan near his main village of Werowocomoco. He was the only Indian to have a house with a fireplace and chimney, an invention that amazed the natives since they built their fires in the center of their lodges and allowed the smoke to escape through a hole in the roof. The door was another strange idea (Indians used a flap

of animal skin), but the most marvelous gadget was the brass door lock that so intrigued the chief that he turned the key back and forth incessantly. The house itself was of wattle and daub with a thatched roof. It fell down and rotted away within decades. The marl chimney was more durable and stood, as a silent memorial, for about 300 years on the bank of the York River. Through neglect, it, too, fell down and was washed away by the yearly rains. *See: Purton; Werowocomoco*

POWHITE PLANTATION
Hanover County

Originally pronounced Po-white Plantation for the creek on the land, the pronunciation was changed by the Commonwealth Highway Department in the 1970s, probably to avoid offending anyone. Powhite was owned prior to the Civil War by a Dr. Gaines whose home was on a bluff that overlooked Richmond. He was a physician who had a large and lucrative practice in the neighborhood. He also owned a mill on his plantation that was powered by Powhite Creek. Two Civil War battles fought here wrecked the house and mill as the Confederates taught the Union soldiers a lesson in defense. After the war the plantation was purchased by the Garthright family who sold it to Franklin Floyd Farrar. Descendants of Farrar who visited the farm in the early years of the twentieth century remember vividly that he called his place Po-white Farm.

PRESTWOULD
Mecklenburg County

Sir Peyton Skipwith, an American-born baronet acquired the nucleus of his Roanoke River lands by winning a gambling game he played with William Byrd III who put up his father's Blue Stone Castle lands as his wager. Sir Peyton added to the Byrd property by purchasing an adjacent tract from Joseph Royster in 1773 to give him control of 10,000 acres. Sir Peyton was descended from Sir Grey Skipwith, an English Cavalier who had come to Virginia during the rule of Oliver Cromwell.

A baronet is the lowest hereditary British title, ranking below a baron and above a knight. A baronet is addressed as "Sir," and usually adds "Bart" after his signature, such as Sir Peyton Skipwith, Bart.

The manor house was built of stone quarried on a high knoll overlooking Occaneechee Island which lay at the junction of the Dan and Roanoke rivers. Completed in 1795, Prestwould House is in a fine state of preservation. Many of the wooden outbuildings have been reconstructed. *See: Blue Stone Castle; Westover*

PRINCE EDWARD COUNTY

Formed in 1753 from Amelia, this county was named for Prince Edward, Duke of York, the son of Frederick, Prince of Wales, the younger brother of King George III. The courthouse was first erected at King's Tavern but was moved to present day Farmville in 1871. Confederate General Joseph E. Johnston was born in this county at Longwood. *See: King's Tavern; Longwood*

PRINCE GEORGE COUNTY

Formed in 1702 from a part of Charles City County, this territory was named for George, Prince of Denmark, the consort of Queen Anne. The last of the Stuart monarchs, she came to the throne of England in 1702 following the death of her brother-in-law, William III.

When Charles City was formed in 1634, it extended to both sides of the James River. With the courthouse on the north bank at Charles City, the inhabitants of the south bank were unhappy to have to cross the river to conduct court business, especially those who had to pay a ferryman. This discontent led to the formation of Prince George County. One tip of land, owned by the Eppes family at the mouth of the Appomattox River, was excluded from the new county and was called Charles City Point, later shortened to City Point.

The county courthouse has occupied four different sites. First it was located near Merchant's Hope Church. It was moved to Frog Hole near the present site of Hopewell. Then it moved to Blandford, a small village near Petersburg. All three of these locations were inconvenient for the people of the southern and western portions of Prince George County so a new center was constructed at the present site, near the center of the county.

In the beginning, Prince George stretched west from the James River to the Blue Ridge Mountains and south to the Carolina border. From it were formed Brunswick (1720), Amelia (1734), Dinwiddie (1752), and then Lunenburg, Greensville, Nottoway, Prince Edward, Halifax, Bedford, Charlotte, Mecklenburg, Pittsylvania, Henry, Patrick, Campbell, and Franklin counties. Within this

territory was Bristol Parish, an experiment in combining civil courts with the parish vestry that did not succeed.

Prince George County was devastated by the Civil War when it was overrun by federal troops during the long siege of Petersburg in the winter of 1864-65. Its most famous relic of the seige is the crater formed when Union troops tunneled under the Southern earthworks to blow a huge hole through which an attacking force could flow. The Battle of the Crater, the last great Confederate victory, was won not so much by Southern courage as by Northern blunders after the great explosion rocked the morning calm.

Crater Battlefield today is under the direction of the National Park Service and is part of the Petersburg Battlefield complex. *See: Blandford Church; Bristol Parish; City Point; Merchant Hope Church*

PRINCESS ANNE COUNTY
Obsolete

Formed in 1691 by the division of Lower Norfolk County into Norfolk and Princess Anne counties, this area was named for Princess Anne, second daughter of King James II, who eventually became Queen Anne. The name Anne or Anna is common throughout Virginia, applied mainly by Alexander Spotswood while he was governor during her reign. Soon after Princess Anne County was formed, a courthouse was erected near Donation Church (which at that time was the church of Lynnhaven Parish; it received its unusual name after 1776). The site was described as being "in Jno. Kneeling's field by London Bridge." When the courthouse was finally erected in 1696, it was put upon land belonging to "the Brick Church." This was the scene of the trial of Grace Sherwood who was accused of being a witch and was ducked in Lynnhaven Bay at Witchduck Point.

The county seat was moved to Kempsville in 1778 where it remained until 1884. It was then moved to a new hamlet called Princess Anne Court House where it remained until the county ceased to exist following its annexation by the city of Virginia Beach in 1963. *See: Donation Church; Kempsville; Orange County; Newtown; Prince George County; Witchduck Point*

PRINCE WILLIAM COUNTY

Formed in 1730 from Stafford, this county was named for Prince William Augustus, Duke of Cumberland, the son of George II who was disappointed when his nephew was given the crown. The Duke was in command of the English army that defeated Bonnie Prince Charlie's vain attempt to regain the throne for the Stuarts in 1745. For his merciless execution of prisoners taken in the battle and for his ruthless destruction of villages that were suspected of harboring either the Prince or Jacobite soldiers, the Duke of Cumberland earned the lasting enmity of the Scots and the disgust of many of the English lords. Advanced in age when his father George II died, and with a reputation for cruelty, he was not even considered for the throne which went to the young son of the dead Prince of Wales, the Duke's elder brother.

The first courthouse of Prince William County was erected at Dumfries. In 1822 the county seat was relocated at Brentsville, at Aquia Creek, where it remained until after the Civil War. By then the citizens of the other parts of the county wanted their court center located near the middle of the county and began a long campaign to have Manassas Junction named the county seat. Naturally, the people of Brentsville objected and delayed the movement until a referendum in 1892 authorized a new courthouse at the site of two great Confederate victories in the Civil War. Manassas has been the seat of Prince William County ever since. *See: Brentsville; Cumberland County*

PROVIDENCE CHURCH
Augusta County

Many Presbyterian churches use this name, even today. The congregation here, organized by John Blair, first met in a log meeting house in 1746. The second minister was Samuel Brown who married Mary Moore, the woman known as the "Captive of Abb's Valley." Kidnapped as a young girl by the Indians, she had to be "re-civilized" when she returned to her own people.

The Presbyterian Synod of Virginia was organized here in 1788 as a result of the work of the Reverend Francis Makenie of the Eastern Shore. The original log meeting house was replaced in 1793 by a stone church, still standing. However, in 1859 the congregation moved about five miles away from the first location to erect a brick church. *See: Temperanceville*

PROVIDENCE CHURCH
Louisa County

Probably built in 1747, this is one of the few

frame churches of colonial times to survive the neglect of the twentieth century. First erected as a reading house under the direction of Samuel Morris, a noted dissenter of the Church of England's monopoly, it soon became a Presbyterian house of worship and was recognized as a church after independence and the adoption of the Commonwealth's Statute for Religious Freedom. In 1769 the congregation accepted a gift of two communion cups, each of which holds a quart of wine. Although the old building was wired for electricity after World War II, it is heated on wintry Sunday mornings by two wood stoves connected to a single chimney. Quite possibly, both James Madison and James Monroe worshipped here as boys while attending the nearby boarding school. *See: Maury's School; Montpelier; Monrovia*

PROVIDENCE FORGE
New Kent County

Here, about 1770, the Reverend Charles Smith, a Presbyterian minister, settled with his congregation. In partnership with William Holt and Francis Jerdone, he built and operated a blacksmith shop to make and repair iron implements. The forge was destroyed by Lieutenant Colonel Bonastre Tarleton's dragoons in 1781 after General Benedict Arnold had finished using the minister's house as his temporary headquarters. Fortunately, the house was not burned.

It passed through a variety of owners and was marked for destruction by the Virginia State Highway Commission in 1947 to clear the way for a major improvement of Highway 60. The old Manse was rescued by Mrs. Braithwaite Houghwout who bought it, had the dwelling carefully disassembled, and re-erected in Williamsburg where it is now known as Providence Hall.

The unincorporated village of Providence Forge keeps the old name alive. There is, unfortunately, no forge there today. In fact, the art of blacksmithing, the creation of useful objects from iron by hand with a hammer on an anvil, is a dying art kept alive by strong men who love the ring of the hammer, the curl of hot iron, and the ability to create objects beside a hot fire. *See: Jerdone's Castle; Mount Stirling*

PULASKI COUNTY

Count Casimir Pulaski, an experienced soldier from Poland, volunteered to help George Washington train the Continental Army. He was killed in the Battle of Savannah in 1779. When this county was formed in 1839 from parts of Wythe and Montgomery, it was named for him. The county seat, once Pulaski Court House, but now shortened to Pulaski, is one of two communities in Virginia with a Polish name. *See: Warsaw*

PUNGOTEAGUE
Accomack County

This is an Indian word meaning either *place of fine sand* or *sand fly river*. For many years the tiny community here was little more than two taverns, one run by Anthony Hoskins and the other by Thomas Fowkes. Although the county of Accomack was organized in 1634, it had no courthouse for years. From 1663 until 1708 court sessions were held in one of these two taverns.

It was here that the trial was held to decide if the play *Ye Bare and Ye Cubb* ws unfit for the public to view. A local busybody had lodged a complaint about it and the promoter, cast, and crew were hauled into court to answer a charge of performing an immoral play. In defense, the play was performed. The judge found the company not guilty, but this free performance ruined business since everybody around had come to see the free performance. Unfortunately, the script to this play has been lost, but if ever found and played again, no doubt there would be someone ready to object.

During the War of 1812, British Admiral Sir George Cockburn landed on the shore of Pungoteague Creek with 500 Royal Marines. This action was considered so objectionable that the local men staged an attack. The Admiral was nearly captured. Wisely, he retreated to his ships and took himself and his surviving men to Tangier Island. The fight occurred on May 30, 1814. This was the only place where the British were effectively resisted. A week later, Sir George sailed up the Potomac, raided Federal City, and set the Executive Mansion afire. James Madison and his fearless wife Dolley were in residence at the time. She braved the flames to rescue a portrait of George Washington. *See: Metomkin; Occahannock*

PURCELLVILLE
Loudoun County   **Town**

The first settler here was Valentine Purcell who came to this part of Virginia about 1764. For years his descendants operated Purcell's Store in which was located the first post office in 1832. Today this community continues the name.

PURDY
Greensville County

An owner of a great amount of land in this region was William Purdy. When the N & W Railway came through during the latter part of the nineteenth century, a depot was named for him.

PURTON
Gloucester County   **Site**

Two theories exist about the origin of this name. The least likely holds that Purton is a contraction of Put In Bay since the York River is idented here. If that was the case, it would have been called Put In Hope or something similar. The more likely supposition is that Purton is a slurred pronunciation of Powhatan for here was located the great chief's house, built for him by the English, near his headquarters at Werowocomoco. It would be natural for the early settlers to call this Powhatan's which probably degenerated into Purton. Later, this was the waterfront of Rosewell. *See: Cinquoteck; Hope; Poropotank; Powhatan's Chimney; Rosewell; Werowocomoco*

QUANTICO

The site of an Indian village in the seventeenth century, Quantico takes its name from an Algonquin word meaning *by the long stream*. It was first used by the military as a minor naval base during the Revolution to serve the ships of the Potomac Navy. When the U.S. entered World War I in 1917, the Marine Corps selected this tract of 57,512 acres as a training camp and maneuver area, making it a permanent installation a year later. Quantico has been synonymous with the Marine Corps ever since. Thousands of young men went through a very tough ninety days of training here during World War II and emerged as Second Lieutenants whose life-expectancy in battle was brief because of the exposed leadership they gave with great valor.

Today it is the headquarters of the Marine Corps Development and Education Command. In a remote corner of the reservation is the FBI Academy where new agents are carefully trained. In the latter part of the 1970s, when Arlington Cemetery was declared filled, an annex to the National Cemetery was created in another section of the huge Marine Base which spreads into parts of three counties, Prince William, Stafford, and Fauquier. Just outside the main Marine base is the town of Quantico which so closely adjoins the Federal reservation that it is difficult to know where its official boundary ends.

QUARTER

While we today generally think of this word to mean a fourth part of something, it also means a lodging for troops or employees. An older meaning is a district or a section of a city, such as the Latin Quarter. In early colonial days it was a section of land; during the days of slavery, it meant the area of a farm where the slaves lived. They lived in the slave quarters—in the quarter. *See: Grove*

QUEEN'S CREEK
York County

There are several creeks by this name. Perhaps the most historic and well known is the one which flows from a pond north of Williamsburg to the York River at Cheatham. It once was a major commercial artery for passenger and light freight traffic to and from the old capital. Originally it was called Queen

Mary's Creek, named for Queen Mary II. Today, unfortuantely, it is shallow and unnavigable. Most of the broad creek that was the scene of so much colonial traffic is choked with reeds and marsh grasses which have grown in the silt washed down from the farms along its banks. *See: Capitol Landing; King and Queen County; Porto Bello*

QUEEN'S CREEK PLANTATION
James City County   Site

John Custis IV inherited this plantation in 1714 from his grandfather, John II of Arlington. The death of a number of close relatives (grandfather, father, and mother) made John IV one of the wealthiest men in Virginia, owning much land with 15,000 acres under successful cultivation. He and his wife, the former Frances Parke, lived alternately between Arlington and this plantation, although they preferred living here rather than on the Eastern Shore. In fact, John IV, known as John Custis of Williamsburg, was an active member of Bruton Parish. This estate contained 3,330 acres just outside the colonial capital which was reached by Capitol Landing Road. On the Frenchman's map of 1781 are shown a collection of eighteen buildings plus a grist mill.

The original patentee of the land was Daniel Parke I, a lawyer, physician, member of the Council, and Secretary of the Colony. He was the grandfather of Frances Parke, John IV's wife. The property was inherited by Martha Dandridge Custis who had married Daniel Parke Custis, the son of John IV, and, of course, the plantation then came under the control of George Washington when the widow married the country squire from Mount Vernon. Martha and George sold the property to her grandson, George Washington Parke Custis many years after the Revolution, and he, in turn, sold it to a Mr. Waller.

Few traces remain of this important estate which now is part of Camp Peary. Not far from the site of the old mill are the remains of the family cemetery, but the tombstones now are of rather recent vintage. John IV is buried at old Arlington where he boasted on his tombstone that he enjoyed life only after his wife died. *See: Arlington; Mount Vernon; White House*

QUEEN'S HITH

Fort Eustis   **Site**

On the River Thames in London just below St. Paul's Cathedral, is a landing bearing the name Queenshith. *Hith* is an old English word meaning place, and this London landing once was reserved for the queen.

In 1623 Thomas Harwood established a plantation of settlers on the lower end of Mulberry Island which he called Queen's Hith. He had received a patent for the land through the "head rights" provision of the New Charter since he had brought the people over at his own expense. Queen's Hith did not prosper and the land was sold to others. *See: Harwood's Mill; Mulberry Island; Stanley Hundred*

QUINBY

Accomack County

On Upshur's Neck, a local attorney, Mr. Quinby, inherited land from his mother who was a descendant of the original owner. This community honors the Quinby name.

R

RADFORD
Pulaski County   **City**

Originating in 1856 as a railroad town, this city once was known as Central. When it was incorporated in 1887, it was named for a prominent citizen, Dr. John B. Radford. Here is located a munitions plant, owned by the Federal government, known as the Radford Arsenal.

Of local historic interest is Mary Draper Ingles, the wife of a pioneer settler, who was captured in an Indian raid in 1755 and taken to Chillicothe, Ohio by the Shawnees. She managed to escape and walked, barefoot, back to her home, guided purely by instinct and kept alive by her own wits. *See: Bellona Arsenal; Blacksburg*

RADFORD COLLEGE
Montgomery County

Opened in 1913 as State Normal and Industrial School for Women, for many years this was an extension of V.P.I. Along with similar colleges at Farmville and Harrisonburg, also state supported, the name was shortened to State Teachers College in 1924. Twenty years later, the name was changed to Radford College. Made an independent school with its own board of visitors in 1964, it now confers graduate degrees and is coeducational.

RANDOLPH MACON COLLEGE
Ashland and Lynchburg

Incorporated as the oldest Methodist college in America, this institution began in Boydton in 1832. Named for John Randolph, a Virginia Congressman and ambassador to the court of Catherine the Great of Russia, and Nathaniel Macon, a North Carolinian with Virginia ancestors. The college was moved to Ashland in 1868. A branch for women was established in Lynchburg in 1891. *See: Huguenots; Roanoke Plantation*

RAPIDAN RIVER

This busy, rapid river begins in the Blue Ridge Mountains and joins the Rappahannock about eight miles from Fredericksburg. The name is a contraction of Rapid Anne, a description of the current and an honor to Queen Anne. When Alexander Spotswood had an iron foundary and forge at Germanna, the stream then was able to power a twenty-six-foot water wheel that worked the bellows. *See: Fluvanna River; Germanna; Tubal Furnace*

RAPPAHANNOCK ACADEMY
Caroline County   **Site**

When Mount Church, built about 1750, was sold in 1808 along with its glebe lands, the proceeds were used to establish a school in the old church building. Once one of the most noted schools in Virginia, it is no more. A tiny settlement continues the name.

RAPPAHANNOCK COUNTY

The territory along both sides of the Rappahannock River was formed into a county in 1665. The courthouse was erected about ten miles north of New Plymouth. In 1691 Rappahannock County was broken into Essex and Richmond counties and for the next forty years the name Rappahannock applied only to the river. Then, in 1833, the name reappeared when a portion of Culpeper County was broken off to form a new political entity. The county seat is the town of Washington. *See: Essex County; Richmond County; Tappahannock; Washington*

RAPPAHANNOCK RIVER

One of the major waterways of Virginia, this river separates the Northern Neck from the Middle Peninsula. Many large estates were established along its banks during the latter part of the seventeenth century, quite a few of them served by private wharves. Merchant ships could sail about seventy-five miles up this river from the Chesapeake Bay to Port Royal and Port Conway, the end of deep water. Smaller vessels could get up as far as the fall line at Fredericksburg.

The name Rappahannock is an Indian word meaning *rise and fall of water*, which, of course, is the same as "tidewater." Tidal action is felt in all of Virginia's major rivers up to the fall line. *See: Port Conway; Port Royal; Tappahannock*

RASSAWEK
Fluvanna County   **Site**

This was the capital of the Monacan Indians, a Siouan tribe with several towns along the north bank of the James above the fall line. They were constantly harassed by bands of roving Iroquois, especially the Susquehannocks. Pressed by their ancient enemies and by the white settlers, the tribe gathered together and migrated west beyond the mountains. When colonists occupied abandoned Rassawek, they renamed it Point of Fork since it was located at the confluence of the James and Rivanna rivers. In 1788, this collection of houses became the town of Columbia. *See: Massinacak*

RAVENSWOOD
Accomack County
Patented in 1622 by Colonel Edmund Scarburgh of Occohannock, this tract was first called the Great Metomkin Plantation. Edward Ravell contested the patent since he thought he held the patent rights. The settlement was uncharacteristically amiable (for Colonel Scarburgh) since the two men peacefully divided the lands. On his piece Edward Ravell build Ravenswood early in the eighteenth century. It was inherited by his daughter, Rachell, the wife of Henry Custis of Arlington. *See: Bedford; Boscobel; Chatham; Great Metomkin Plantation; Marmion; Occohannock*

RAVENSWORTH
Fairfax County   **Site**
This was the second home of William Fitzhugh of Bedford. He built it in 1695 to get away from the many travelers who were constantly dropping by his house to enjoy a few days of rest—and free food. Offering travelers hospitality was a necessity in those days and no gentleman could refuse. The inns and taverns were little more than crude watering holes where the main beverage was beer or cider, the food unpalatable, and the sleeping accommodations were completely unseparated—definitely not places for women and children. Of course, traveling gentlemen avoided taverns whenever possible.

When the frugal William Fitzhugh found that too many people found Bedford very convenient and comfortable, he pulled up stakes and moved off the beaten path. The name of this estate is a thinly-veiled reference to the ravens of the Bible, known to be always ravenous (hence the word) and of little worth to society. Here William Fitzhugh enjoyed what what the "ravens" left him. Reference to ravens was not an original idea with this old man. The Fitzhugh family had lived in the vicinity of Ravensden, Bedfordshire, England since the sixteenth century. The site of this old home is now completely covered by the Braddock Road Shopping Center on Inter-

state 495 in Virginia near Washington, D.C. *See: Bedford*

RAWLEY SPRINGS
Rockingham County
Jospeph Hicks built a resort in 1825 near a mineral spring named for a local farmer. By 1880 the hotel and cabins of Rawley Springs could accomodate 800 guests. Fires destroyed everything over the years and the spa closed in 1915.

RECTORTOWN
Fauquier County
A small village established here in 1772 was named Maidstone for a Fairfax estate in England. The few people who settled here drifted off and the village disappeared. The sole remaining inhabitant was John Rector, the chief trustee. After the Revolution when newcomers built homes on the old site, it was named Rectortown.

RED ASH
Tazwell County
A particular type of coal mined in this area leaves a red ash when burned. This is caused by a contaminant, ferrous oxide. A small community developed near the mine which called itself Red Ash for the type of coal produced.

RED FOX TAVERN
This is reported to be the oldest tavern in the United States. It is located midway between Fairfax Court House and Winchester. *See: Middleburg*

RED HILL
Charlotte County
Patrick Henry had a number of homes during his lifetime, most of them in the vicinity of his birthplace in Hanover County. Toward the end of his life, when he had many children to support, he purchased this farm in 1796 and spent more time looking after its production than in practicing law or politics. Shortly before Patrick Henry's death on June 6, 1799, he was elected a U.S. Congressman for the rural district surrounding Red Hill although he did not campaign and really did not want the position. He was too ill to travel to the District of Columbia and never took his seat. *See: Marlborough*

RED OAK
Charlotte County
The local residents were proud of twelve huge red oak trees growing in a grove. When the last one died a few years ago it was said to

have been the largest red oak on U.S. Route 15 between New York and Florida.

REEDVILLE
Northumberland County

Elijah Reed came from Maine in 1875 to organize a company to catch menhaden, a fish rich in oil used in cosmetics and paint. The oil is exported to Europe for cooking and for making margarine. These fish, also known as ale-wives, are caught in huge numbers, pressed for their oil, and then ground into fertilizer. Their flavor is too strong for most palates and they are not used for food. *See: Irvington*

REMINGTON
Fauquier County   **Town**

No one really knows why the present name has lasted so long. Its name was Millview until 1850 and Bowenville until 1853. The railroad changed it to Rappahannock Station, and somebody, now unidentified, began calling it Remington in 1890.

REMLIK
Middlesex County

Remlik is Kilmer spelled backwards. Here Willis S. Kilmer had a training stable for race horses. *See: Doswell; New Market of Caroline*

RESCUE
Isle of Wight County

An early name for this settlement was Smith's Neck, for William Smith who received a grant for the land in 1645. There are several peculiar ideas for the origin of the current name. The most probable comes from a Methodist church founded here more than a hundred years ago that attempted to rescue the local watermen from their sins.

RESTON
Fairfax County

Reston is a modern settlement that was conceived and developed by Robert E. Simon who put his initials into the name. A bedroom community for Washington, D.C., everything was planned before a single house or street was constructed. Within convenient walking distance of most homes are schools, playgrounds, lakes, golf courses, swimming pools, tennis courts, and a large stable for horses.

RETREAT
Hanover County

This was the home of Robert Carter

Nicholas, Treasurer of the Colony from 1766 to 1779. Strongly conservative during the early discussions of independence, he tried to mediate the disputes between the hotheaded members of the House of Burgesses and the Governor. It was Patrick Henry's inflammatory speech on March 20, 1775, in Richmond's St. John's church about liberty or death that turned Nicholas firmly to the patriot cause. It was he who offered a resolution to authorize a standing army of 10,000 men for the duration of the conflict then just beginning. Had it carried, the manpower problems for the Virginia levy to the Continental Army would have been solved, but the convention did not want to go that far that soon.

RICE
Prince Edward County

Rice Meeting House was built here about 1775 by William Rice for those who preferred to worship in their own way rather than follow the Anglican service. The meeting house is gone but the small hamlet continues the name.

RICHARDSVILLE
Culpeper County

Richard's Ferry crossed the Rappahannock River here. The name Richardsville goes back at least two centuries.

RICH CREEK
Giles County   **Town**

Five large springs near here produce unusually cold water with a high mineral content. The water from one spring was bottled and sold for its medicinal benefits, bringing the bottler a good income. It was, indeed, a rich creek. The town that developed beside it took the name.

RICHFIELD
Roanoke County

This was the home of General Andrew Lewis who fought the Battle of Point Pleasant during Dunmore's War on October 10, 1774. He was a seasoned fighter who had served with General Braddock and George Washington during the French and Indian War. During the march toward revolution, he sided with his fellow Virginians and was in command of the Americans at the battle of Gwynn's Island on July 8, 1776, which forced Lord Dunmore to leave Virginia forever. Andrew Lewis served throughout the Revolution. He died enroute to his home from Yorktown after he had witnessed the surrender of British troops in October 1781. *See: Cricket Hill*

RICHLANDS
Tazewell County   **Town**

Kentuckians, driving their cattle to the market at Lynchburg, gave this land its name because of the fine pastures that grew naturally. Coal mining and brick making caused the town to grow.

RICHMOND
Henrico County   **City**

Christopher Newport sailed up the James River to the falls a week after the settlers began their fort at Jamestown. He and his party set up a cross on a small island near the foot of present Ninth Street to claim the region. Various attempts to place men in this area, who were to search for gold, failed because of the hostility of the Indians. In 1637 Thomas Stegge opened a trading post on the river at the falls and did a brisk business trading with the Indians and selling supplies to other settlers who worked small farms nearby. Business was so good that Stegge

needed help. He wrote to his sister in England who sent her son, William Byrd.

When Thomas Stegge died suddenly in 1670, William Byrd inherited the business. To expand trade he offered "certain privileges" to those who would settle near his trading post. An old building, erected after the Massacre of 1644 and named Fort Charles, became Byrd's Warehouse or Shocco. When a severe flood in 1684 washed away everything except the stone house in which he lived, William Byrd moved to higher ground and built a new home which he called Belvedere where he lived until his death.

His son, William Byrd II, living at Westover, became a successful speculator of the lands he had inherited, competing with Major William Mayo who owned a hillside opposite Shocco on the same side of the James. Mayo had marked off thirty-two lots on Church Hill into a small town which he called Richmond after an old city near London. By 1742, when Mayo's venture was a modest success, the General Assembly proclaimed it a town. The population was then about 250. William Byrd II laid out his land "at Shoccoes" (where the state Capitol now stands) and competed for settlers. Within a generation the two villages

RICHMOND

merged into one entity giving Richmond a population of over 500.

The church of Henrico Parish was erected on Mayo's portion of the city on Church Hill. Called St. John's prior to the Revolution, it was the scene of Patrick Henry's "Liberty or Death" speech in March 1775 during the Second Virginia Convention. At the Third Convention, also held in St. John's, Virginia created the Committee of Safety and made plans to finance the war. When Williamsburg was abandoned in 1780, Richmond was made the capital of the Commonwealth of Virginia. Governor Thomas Jefferson moved into a rented house and began drawing plans for the Capitol building which, when erected on Shocco Hill, dominated the scene as a temple to freedom.

During the Civil War, Richmond was made the second capital of the Confederacy when the government was moved from Montgomery, Alabama. The city was the object of General McClellan's unsuccessful 1862 Peninsula Campaign and several other aborted attempts. It was bypassed by Grant whose main objective was the destruction of Lee's Army. When Petersburg fell in April 1865, the Confederate government fled to Danville. Supplies of cotton, tobacco, munitions, and food were set afire by the retreating military. The conflagration, begun at the riverfront, quickly spread to other parts of Richmond, burning most of the downtown as well as the Tredegar Iron Works and the naval shipyard. The mayor of Richmond, a Mr. Mayo, a descendant of the founder, had already surrendered the helpless city to Union forces across the river at Manchester. Although for years the Yankees were accused of burning Richmond, the fire, needlessly kindled by the Confederates, was controlled and extinguished by Union troops as their first occupation task. Abraham Lincoln arrived a few days later, sat in Jefferson Davis' presidential office, and quietly rejoiced that the war was finally over.

Richmond recovered from the shock, slowly rebuilt, and, over the following century, expanded in all directions to become a huge metropolis. There are few people in this country today who have not heard of Richmond. The name has been applied to cities and towns in most of the fifty states. *See: Belvedere; Jamestown; Manchester; St. John's Church; Westover, Williamsburg*

RICHMOND COUNTY

When this county was formed in 1692 from the portion of Old Rappahannock County that lay on the north bank of Rappahannock River, it was named Richmond County for the small city of Surrey, England, a few miles up the River Thames from London. That English city had long been the seat of the Dukes of Richmond who were always deeply involved in the affairs of the old country. These dukes derived most of their income from estates in Ireland and some of the Cavaliers who had settled in this portion of Northern Neck were of Irish ancestry. The county seat was called, naturally, Richmond Court House. This led to confusion when the city of Richmond in Henrico County grew to prominence as the capital of the Commonwealth. Therefore, in 1846, the name of the county seat was changed to Warsaw to honor the many people of Poland who served in the Continental Army during the Revolution. *See: Pulaski County*

RICHNECK

Newport News

Although Miles Cary bought this land in 1660, the history of the place goes back many years. Called Claiborne's Neck, it was the home of Richard Kemp, Thomas Lunsford, Thomas Ludwell, and Phillip Ludwell, all of whom were associated with Governor William Berkeley. Miles Cary, a bit younger than all of them, expanded his real estate holdings. He added Claiborne's Neck to The Forest and Magpie Swamp and retained the names of each piece. When he was killed at Point Comfort fighting the Dutch invaders in 1667, the lands were divided among his sons. Major Thomas Cary inherited Windmill Point and Magpie Swamp; Captain Henry Cary, the builder of the Capitol in Williamsburg, got The Forest.

Miles Cary, Jr. inherited Claiborne's Neck which he renamed Richneck for Sir Robert Rich, the second earl of Warwick, for whom also the shire, county, river, and town of Warwick were named. Miles Cary, Jr., a justice of Warwick, was a charter trustee of William and Mary College.

On Richneck grew Charter Elm, by tradition the site of an early Warwick County courthouse where court was held until 1793. This tree has been commemorated in the seal of the City of Newport News. Today a huge hackberry tree still marks the spot, and it now shades the graves of Miles Cary, Jr., and his wife Mary Milner Cary, along with four generations of the family. The original property is now bisected by the N & W Railroad line from Richmond. The last owner of the tract was Colonel Wilson Miles Cary, a great-grandson of Miles Cary I. He sold Richneck and settled at Ceeley's, the old Wilson place. *See: Airville; Carysbrook; Ceeley's; Chippokes; Claiborne's Neck; Denbigh; Green Spring; The Forest; Magpie Swamp; Tuckahoe; Windmill Point*

RICHNECK
Surry County

Robert Ruffin built this small house about 1685 on a grant of land some 2,200 acres in size. He was the son of William Ruffin, the first settler in Isle of Wight County. There is a tradition that the Ruffin name once was spelled Ruthvin, and that the Ruffin family of Virginia descended from William Ruthvin, fourth Earl of Gowie, Scotland who was executed for his enmity toward Mary, Queen of Scots. Supposedly, the Earl's son William reached Virginia after the Edict of Nantes was revoked and changed his name from Ruthvin to Ruffin. Edmund Ruffin, a fiery Secessionist, fired the first shot at Fort Sumter to begin the Civil War. When the South lost the conflict, he could not take defeat and shot himself rather than live within the restored Union. *See: Huguenots; Lawne's Plantation; Manakin Town; Merchant's Hope Plantation; Mount Pleasant of Surry*

RIDGEWAY
Henry County   **Town**

For a few decades prior to the Civil War, this was a busy tobacco market. The land, on a slight ridge, makes excellent home sites. Today it is a bedroom community of Danville. Four miles south is Matrimony Creek.

RINER
Montgomery County

This village was named for an early settler, David Riner, who came here about 1800.

RINGFIELD
York County   **Site**

Jospeh Ring's house was built on a bluff at the mouth of King's Creek on the York River between 1693 and 1698. The site commands a view down the river to Gloucester Point. In addition to exporting the products of his farm, Joseph Ring also operated a store which carried a full line of necessities for his neighbors who lived between Williamsburg and Yorktown. Two hundred acres of the plantation lands were set aside some time about 1700 as glebe lands on which was built a church and parsonage. A second church stood here until the Civil War when it was torn down for its bricks. Joseph Ring was a leading citizen of York County during the latter part of the seventeenth century. For twenty years he was a member of the Council and had a hand in the application for the royal charter for the College of William and Mary. He also was enthusiastic about port towns for Virginia and was instrumental in getting the port established at Yorktown about the same time he was building his house. When he died at the age of fifty-seven in 1703, he was buried in the garden at Ringfield which is now a picnic area on the Colonial Parkway.

His widow, much younger, married Joseph Walker of Yorktown by whom she had several children. Their daughter Elizabeth married John Wormeley of Rosegill. Upon inheriting Ringfield, she sold it to James Pride who, in turn, sold it to Dr. William Pasteur, the mayor of Williamsburg who lived here from 1778 to 1781. When Pasteur sold it, he advertised Ringfield as a farm of 630 acres on King's Creek with an elegant two story brick house of nine rooms and ten closets. The house was destroyed by fire in 1920, and since then the smith shop, granary, stable, and kitchen have also disappeared. *See: Rosegill; Tyndall's Point; Yorktown*

RINGSNECK
Gloucester County

Located next to Fairfield, the estate of Lewis Burwell, this place was developed by Landon Carter, the fourth son of Robert "King" Carter of Corotoman. He held the original patent to the land surrounding Carter's Creek. *See: Carters Creek; Corotoman; Fairfield; Ripon Hall*

RIPON HALL
Camp Peary   **Site**

As far as can be determined, the first residence on the present Federal reservation of Camp Peary was built by Edmund Jenings on property he purchased from John West II from the Chischiak grant. It is thought to have been located on Poplar Neck, a bit of land that is bordered by the York River. Nothing is known of the dates and particulars of the dwelling. The building has disappeared. Jenings (sometimes spelled Jennings) was a son of a member of Parliament who represented Ripon, England. He came to Virginia late in the seventeenth century and established his estate here through a loan from Robert "King" Carter. When the loan came due and could not be paid, Carter foreclosed, gave Jenings what it then was worth, and took title to the farm. Mr. Jenings, a member of the Council (as was Carter) moved to Williamsburg and was elected the President of the Council. When Governor Nott died in office in August 1706 Edmund Jenings was the acting governor until the arrival of Alexander Spotswood in 1710. Work on the Governor's Palace was begun while Jenings held the reins of government. At various times he was the Secretary of the Colony, the Director of Building in Williamsburg, an officer in the militia, and a commissioner of the College of William and Mary. Ripon Hall became one of the homes of Landon Carter, Robert Carter's fourth son.

The original Jenings house was replaced just before 1800 by local people. It also was named Ripon Hall. During the Civil War it was used as hospital after the Battle of Williamsburg in 1862. When it was torn down by the Federal government in 1961, several inscriptions were found in the attic written by two Yankees and two Confederates. The Northern soldier who did not sign his name, wrote defiantly, "Down with the Traitor and the Star; up with the Stripes and peace forever." *See Corotoman; Rippon Lodge; Sabine Hall*

RIPPLEMEAD
Giles County

Located high in the mountains, 1,600 feet above sea level, the New River ripples by pleasant meadows. Someone with a poetic nature coined the name for this community.

RIPPON LODGE
Fairfax County

The house here was built about 1725 by Colonel Richard Blackburn who came from the cathedral town of Ripon, England. He was a Burgess, an architect of some note, and a rather quiet gentleman. The one story house originally had only five rooms over a full basement from which led a long, mysterious tunnel, then end of which has been blocked.

The builder's son, Colonel Thomas Blackburn, was a member of various patriotic committees and a delegate to the Second Virginia Convention in 1775. He earned the right to be there by being an activist who planted tea bushes on his lawn in an attempt to raise his own leaves in protest to the tea tax. He voluntarily quartered Continental troops at his home at his own expense during the Revolution.

One of his daughters married Justice Bushrod Washington; the other married John Augustine Washington. Each, in turn, became the mistress of Mount Vernon and both are buried there. Across the Rippon Lodge can be seen traces of the old King's Highway. *See: Bushfield; Falls Church; King's Highway; Ripon Hall*

RIVANNA RIVER
Albemarle County

The River Anna was one of the many streams named in honor of "Good Queen Anne." This relatively shallow tributary of the James once was a major waterway for freight from Albemarle County's estates such as Monticello, Castle Hill, Belmont, and the town of Charlottesville. Freight was transferred from James River riverboats to barges which were poled up the gentle current to the town of Milton, the shipping terminus. Since heavy freight loads had to wait until a good rain provided an increased flow of water, the movement of goods was directly dependent upon the vagaries of the weather. When floating downstream after a rain, the rivermen had to have a high degree of dexterity and an intimate knowledge of the river to guide their ungainly batteaux in the rushing torrent. A breed of watermen soon developed who thrived on this hard work until the railroad killed water traffic about 1835. For 100 years, the Rivanna was a major waterway. The corporate headquarters of the Rivanna Navigation Company was at Milton. This company chartered the flat bottom boats, provided the workers, kept the river channel clear of snags and debris, erected dams at shoal places, and even built levees to raise or lower the boats to different levels. In some early writings, the Rivanna River is called Mountain Falls Creek. *See: Fluvanna River; Milton; Rapidan River; Rassawek*

RIVER FARM
Fairfax County

These 1,207 acres, now known as Wellington, were a part of George Washington's land holdings which he preferred to lease to others rather than farm himself. River Farm was advertised as comprising 879 acres with seven fields for farming, 212 acres in fine pasture, an orchard, and a comfortable dwelling for the overseer. *See: Collingwood; Mount Vernon; Wellington*

RIVER LAWN
See: Argyle

RIVER ROAD

Two main roads headed west from Richmond to the upper counties of the Piedmont region. One was the Three Chopt Road, now replaced by Interstate 64 on a much more direct line. The other was the River Road which followed the north bank of the James River west until it turned north at Rassawek to intersect the Three Chopt Road at Boyd's Tavern. Virginia Route 6 through Manakin, Crozier, Goochland, and George's Tavern to Rassawek fairly well follows the old River Road. Its northward portion is now covered by US Highway 15 to Zion's Crossroad. Both the River Road and the Three Chopt Road were the main arteries taken by those who were heading for Wood's Gap, the best passage across the Blue Ridge Mountains. *See: Boyd's Tavern; Three Chopt Road; Wood's Gap; Zion Tavern*

RIVERVIEW

See: Cloverfields of Charles City; Dogham

RIXEYVILLE

Culpeper County

The Rixey family settled in this part of the county about 1804. The hamlet was named for them.

ROANOKE

Roanoke County

A marsh in southwest Virginia was known to Indians and early explorers as a natural attraction for all sorts of animals who felt drawn to the salt deposits. When the first settlers came here in the colonial period, the site was known equally as Big Lick or Totero Town for the Indian tribe which lived nearby. The name Big Lick persisted, however, after the Indians were defeated and forced to move away. The town of Big Lick was incorporated in 1874. The name was changed to Roanoke in 1882. It calls itself Star City. *See: Carolina*

ROANOKE BRIDGE

Charlotte County

Land here was patented in 1746 and was settled a few years later. It was the homestead of Joseph Morton, one of the leading pioneers of this section and one of the founders of Old Briery Presbyterian Church, organized in 1755. Roanoke Bridge does not cross the Roanoke River but crosses a branch of the Meherrin. Possibly the name is associated with shells found here from which the Indians made rhoanoke. *See: Roanoke County*

ROANOKE COLLEGE

Salem

Founded in 1842 in Augusta County as the Virginia Institute, a liberal arts school of higher learning for men and women, the establishment was moved to Salem five years after is founding. Shortly thereafter, it was chartered as Roanoke College for the county in which it is located. One of the few colleges that managed to remain in operation during the Civil War, the men of the student body formed themselves into a company and reported to the Confederate Army in September 1864.

ROANOKE COUNTY

The county was formed in 1838 from parts of Botetourt and Montgomery Counties. The name possibly is a reminder of the Lost Colony of Roanoke that ended mysteriously about 1585. Another source of the name might be the medium of trade used by the Indians, called rhoanoke, made of bits of polished shells. The county seat is Salem. *See: Carolina; Peak*

ROANOKE PLANTATION

Charlotte County   **Site**

John Randolph, Jr., born at Cawsons in 1773, was the son of John Randolph of Curles and Theodorick Bland of Blandfield. During Lord Cornwallis' invasion of Virginia in 1781, the Randolph family evacuated their endangered home on the James River and moved to Bizarre for safety. After the Revolution, John Jr. remained at Bizarre with his brother until a scandal and murder trial, involving Robert Randolph and Miss Nancy Randolph, not only shocked the region but caused both brothers great mental anguish. In 1782, full of hatred for his brother's sister-in-law (who was the principal in the trial) John removed himself from Bizarre and established a modest bachelor's home on other family property about forty miles up the river in the wilds of Charlotte County. He had earlier named this place Roanoke Plantation after the river which flowed past its only partially-tended fields.

Randolph became an active participant in the government of Jefferson's presidency. He was not a farmer, not a family man (fortunately he never married), and not much of a lawyer. For a brief time he was the Envoy Extraordinary to the Russian court. Moody and unpredictable, with a grotesquely-shaped body, he had a keen, almost mad mind which gave quick vent to his frequent bursts of anger through a glib and acid tongue. This John Randolph contributed nothing of lasting value to his patient Commonwealth of Virginia. He died in Philadelphia in May 1833 and was buried there, although later his remains were removed to Richmond. *See Bizarre; Cawsons; Curles*

ROANOKE RIVER

This river drains a large portion of Southside Virginia, from the interior of the Commonwealth in Campbell County all the way to the Virginia-North Carolina border. It empties into Albemarle Sound. A short portion, between Brookneal and Clarksville, is called the Staunton River, for some odd reason. Many immigrants, particularly Scots who first settled in the New Bern and Bath area, traveled up the Roanoke River to new homes in the interior of Virginia where they could live unmolested by government. Later they sent the products of their farms back to the seaports along the same waterway.

ROBINSON RIVER

This minor stream, a tributary of the Rappahannock, joins the Rapidan in Madison County. Too shallow for water traffic and too slow to power mills, it was a source of clear water and fish in early times, as it is today. In old records, references to "the forks of the Rappahannock" meant the junction of the Robinson and the Rapidan. Most probably the name honored John Robinson, the Speaker of the House of Burgesses at the time of settlement along its banks. *See: Criglersville; Germanna*

ROCHELLE
Madison County

Known as Jack's Shop when the post office was established here in 1854, the early name of this village was La Rochelle. The postal authorities did not care for Jack's enterprise and could not understand the "La." Therefore, the name adopted was Rochelle.

ROCKBRIDGE COUNTY

The outstanding geographic feature of this area is the Natural Bridge that was cut by a persistent stream eons ago. When a new county was formed in 1778 from Augusta and Botetourt, the name to select was obvious although there is an excellent possibility that Thomas Jefferson influenced the choice. He was an enthusiastic observer of the Rock Bridge and reportedly suggested the name

Lexington for the county seat. Sam Houston, the first President of the Republic of Texas, was born in this county, as was Cyrus McCormick, the inventor of the first practical reaper. *See: Natural Bridge*

ROCK CASTLE
Goochland County

The house was built in 1750 for Tarleton Fleming who had the unpleasant experience of seeing his home plundered in 1781 by a distant cousin, Lt. Col. Banastre Tarleton of the British Dragoons. Tarleton was then enroute to Monticello to capture Governor Thomas Jefferson and members of the General Assembly. The little community here was named, of course, for Fleming's home. *See: Cuckoo*

ROCKETTS
Henrico County   Site

Early in the eighteenth century, the Rockett family established a ferry a few miles south of Richmond just below the rocky falls of the James. In 1731 Robert and Charles Rockett were the ferrymen. William Byrd II wrote "the stream murmured loud enough to drown (out) a scolding wife." This section of present-day Richmond serves the deep water port facility at the height of navigation of the James. Here was located a shipyard operated by the Confederate government and burned in the evacuation of 1865. President Lincoln landed at Rocketts at the end of the Civil War and walked to the Capitol through throngs of former slaves who hailed him as their savior. *See: Matrimony Creek*

ROCKETT'S MILL
Hanover County   Site

One of the earliest iron foundaries to take up where Alexander Spotswood left off was established in Hanover County. Charles Chiswell of Scotchtown had a financial interst in the foundary since pig iron bars were unearthed a few years ago at this site bearing the stamp "CC 1737." The millwheel, moved by the South Anna River, powered the bellows to provide the necessary air to create fires hot enough to melt the iron from the ore. When the smelting company died because the ore was of a poor grade, a member of the Rockett family of Richmond used the wheel to rotate his grindstone to make flour. *See: Germanna; Scotchtown*

ROCKFISH GAP

This gap in the Blue Ridge Mountains, southwest of Wood's Gap, was one of the earliest passes to be traversed on horseback. It was cut eons ago by the Rockfish River, a tributary of the James. When wagons were needed, a road was cut through the easier gap to the north making Wood's Gap the major entry point into the upper Shenandoah Valley. Rockfish Gap has been lowered by modern engineering and now carries Interstate 64 from Charlottesville to Waynesboro. *See: Howardsville; Swift Run Gap; Wood's Gap*

ROCK HILL

Hanover County **Site**

Colonel John Syme II, halfbrother of Patrick Henry, Jr., built his house on the South Anna River about 1750 duplicating a house elsewhere which his wife had seen and liked. Construction of the home was one of her prerequisites to marrige. Colonel Syme, born at Studley, was seven years older than Henry. Sometimes the name of this place is written Rocky Hills. *See: Studley*

ROCKINGHAM COUNTY

This county was formed in 1778 from a portion of Augusta. It was named for the Marquess of Rockingham, English Prime Minister under George III who, in 1765, replaced Lord Grenville in the government shake up following the American colonies' response to the Stamp Act. Grenville had sponsored the act to raise money to pay England's subsidy to Frederick, King of Prussia. The new Prime Minister's ancestral home was Rockingham Castle of Northamptonshire, built by William the Conqueror. This county's seat was established in a new hamlet first known as Rocktown. Later the name was changed to Harrisonburg.

ROCKLEDGE

Prince William County

Built in 1759 by John Ballendine, the house was designed by William Buckland, the architect of Gunston Hall. Ballendine was a highly successful Colchester importer-exporter who lived in this two story rock structure for many years. Ballendine was an early industrialist, map maker, and the founder of the little town of Occoquan. The house, fastened to the steep edge of the hill above his town, is being renovated. *See: Colchester: Occoquan*

ROCKTOWN

See: Harrisonburg

ROCKY MOUNT

Franklin County **Town**

Booker T. Washington, the famous educator of his people, was born a slave in 1856 on a plantation near here that was worked by the Burroughs family. He lived on the scrubby farm with the rest of his family, worked the fields, and harbored a passion to learn to read. So often did he wish to know what was in books that he was given the nickname "Booker" which he adopted as his first name when he was freed at then end of the Civil War. Penniless, he walked to a nearby school for whites and was allowed to learn and read. The plantation, restored by the National Park Service to appear as it did in the 1850s, is open to visitors. The town of Rocky Mount is the seat of Franklin County.

ROKEBY

Loudoun County

The name Rokeby goes far back into English history. Even there its fame is modest and nearly forgotten. When young Charles Stuart was crowned king of Scotland in the Cathedral of Scone in January 1651, all of England, Ireland, Wales, and southern Scotland were under the domination of Oliver Cromwell's Commonwealth. The only town in England brave enough (or perhaps foolish enough) to proclaim Charles king of England was Rokeby, a market town near the Scottish border.

Just why Charles Binn used the name Rokeby when he built his house in 1754 in Virginia is unknown. Either his family's ancient home was there or he was a thorough student of history. At any rate, Binn was the first clerk of Loudoun County when it was formed in 1757. Since the courthouse was not built until three years later, he kept the county records at his home.

During the War of 1812, when the capital city of Washington was threatened by British raiders, Rokeby was selected as the secret hiding place for the original copies of the Declaration of Independence and the Constitution. The valuable documents, sent there by President James Madison, were cared for by Charles Binn, Jr. who, like his father, was also the clerk of the Loudoun County Court.

ROMANCOKE

King William County

William Claiborne, Secretary of the colony,

patented 5,000 acres here in 1653. He was granted this tract for having quelled an Indian uprising during the Massacre of 1644. Claiborne had come to Virginia as a twenty-one-year-old Surveyor General in 1621, hired by the London Company to straighten out the conflicting land claims by older settlers. In his travels throughout the colony, he made many friends among the Indians, and soon realized that a fortune could be made from furs. He settled on Kent Island, far up the Chesapeake Bay near the mouth of the Susquehannock River. There he built a sturdy house and warehouse. Others joined him in a new settlement.

Four years later, Lord Baltimore was given a huge tract of land, known as Maryland, with the stipulation that he could claim title to all lands "not yet planted." Even though Kent Island clearly was not eligible to be under Lord Baltimore's rule, he saw it as the key to the lucrative fur trade which he coveted for himself. When Lord Baltimore took the island, Claiborne went to England and received a judgement from the king that specifically exempted Kent Island from Maryland, but Lord Baltimore ignored the judgement, sent an invading force, and evicted Claiborne and his settlers since they refused to recognize Lord Baltimore's authority.

The Kent Islanders moved with Claiborne to new lands between the Pamunkey and the Mattaponi rivers and established New Kent County. When King William County was formed many years later, the section where Claiborne's home, Romancoke, was located was broken away from New Kent County, almost as though William Claiborne's travails at Kent Island were destined to be ignored by history.

Of Romancoke itself, nothing remains except the old graveyard about 1,000 yards off the old King William Road, about a mile northwest of the present Ephesus Church. In 1770 Romancoke was purchased by George Washington who referred to it in his diary as "my quarter." Much later, the land was owned by George Washington Parke Custis through inheritance. The present house was built by Capt. Robert E. Lee, Jr. about 1870.
See: King William County; New Kent County

ROOSEVELT ISLAND
Potomac River
This island, about a mile-and-a-half long, lies in the Potomac River between Key Bridge and Memorial Bridge. It was the early home of the Necostin Indians. Maps of 1670 identify it Anacostia Isle. Previously, since it was within the territory claimed by Lord Baltimore's Maryland, it was known as My Lord's Island. In 1735 George Mason IV of Gunston Hall inherited the island from his father who had somehow managed to own it. From then on, it was known as Mason's Island.

The first home there, of stone, was built in 1792 by John Mason, Brigadier General of the District of Columbia Militia and president of the Bank of Columbia. He built a causeway to the Virginia shore and operated a ferry to Georgetown on the District shore. As this was the only crossing of the river, the Federal government took over the ferry and maintenance of the causeway in 1807. General Mason went bankrupt in 1833. All of his assets were taken over by his major creditor, the Bank of the U.S., which let the house go to ruin. The remains were washed away in a major flood.

For nearly 100 years, the island was a wilderness. In 1931 it was given to the Theodore Roosevelt Association which made it a living monument to the man who was so interested in preserving America's wilderness.

ROSEDALE
Russell County
About 1819 a post office was established at Rosedale Plantation for the people in this northeastern section of Russell county. Local politics had the name changed to Elway in 1897, but tradition finally conquered in 1941 when Rosedale was readopted.

ROSEGILL
Middlesex County
In 1650 Ralph Wormeley moved from York County and built his home on Nimcock Creek, a quiet inlet of the Rappahannock River. Rosegill became a favorite summer retreat for colonial governors, especially Sir Henry Chichley and Lord Howard Effingham. In 1776 the resident was Ralph Wormeley V who was kept under surveillance because of his family's past hospitality to these men. The Wormeley family were not Tories, although they were suspected. They were Royalists who loved Virginia but refused to take a part in the movement toward independence. Since they divorced themselves from politics, bothered no one, and remained on their self-contained estate in

private exile from society, they were not molested by the patriots. Ironically, the only damage Rosegill suffered during the Revolution came at the hands of a British privateer who plundered the home shortly before the surrender at Yorktown. *See: Christ Church of Middlesex; Ringfield; Rosewell; Sabine Hall; Tazewell Hall; Urbanna*

ROSELAND
Nelson County

An evangelist, Robert Rose, once owned a tract of land in Nelson County which he named Rose's Land. When a small community developed nearby, the two words were combined into Roseland.

ROSEWELL
Gloucester County   **Site**

Matthew Page and his wife, Mary Mann of Timberneck Hall, moved to the site of Rosewell some time before 1703 and lived in a small, rather modest house. Their son, Mann Page I, conceived the grandiose idea of an elaborate manor house from having watched, rather enviously, the building of the Governor's Palace in Williamsburg. Not only did Mann Page inherit considerable money from his parents, but twice he married wealthy ladies. His first wife was Judith Wormeley of Rosegill; his second was Judith Carter of Corotoman. Construction of Rosewell began in 1725 and was still incomplete when he died five years later

His son, Mann Page II, continued the building and completed the great complex according to his father's plan. It became a great three story pile of stonework and brick which sat high above an English basement. From the twin cupolas, about sixty feet above ground level, there was a magnificent view of the York River. In order to pay for the cost of construction and his father's other debts, Page had to sell some of the land. Finally, with poor crops and a glutted tobacco market, he gave up farming here and moved to Fredericksburg.

His son, John Page, who later became Governor of the Commonwealth, took over the management of Rosewell in 1771 and worked hard to save the family investment. However, the estate was too encumbered to make a profit and it slowly slid into bankruptcy.

The house was bought by Thomas Booth in 1838 who gutted it to salvage the treasure of carved panels, mouldings, mantles, chandeliers, and other decorations. The empty, ravaged house caught fire on March 16, 1916, and all that now remains are a few fire-blackened walls hidden by vines and undergrowth. Gaudy and tasteless as it was, Rosewell was one of the most expensive homes ever built in colonial Virginia. At its prime, it was the largest in the entire colony. *See: Bizarre; Carter's Grove; Corotoman; Mannsfield; Nelson House; Rosegill; Shelley; Timberneck; Warner Hall; Werowocomoco*

ROSSLYN
Arlington County   **Site**

In 1860 this vacant land along the Potomac was purchased by Joseph Lambden who deeded the property to his daughter Carolyn when she married William H. Ross. William and Carolyn developed the tract into a working plantation which they named ROSS-LYNN Farm, a combination of their two names. The idea was not original. Rosslyn Castle, a few miles south of Edinburgh, Scotland has borne that name since the fourteenth century. Many years later, while they were living in France, the couple sold the land to the Rosslyn Development Corporation.

Accessible to Georgetown via the Aqueduct Bridge, numerous saloons, gambling houses, and bordellos sprang up here becoming a wide open center of vice that became the object of a campaign by the Good Citizen's League of Washington. After fifteen years of struggle, the league managed to get everything closed down by 1904. The abandoned racetrack became Hoover Airport in the 1910s. It was later flooded to become the Pentagon Lagoon. When correctly pronounced, this section of Arlington County is Ross-Lynn, with equal accents on both names.

ROUNDABOUT
Louisa County   **Site**

About eight miles southwest of Louisa Courthouse was Roundabout Plantation where Patrick Henry lived while he represented this county in the House of Burgesses. Here he began his political career. The land had been purchased by his father, John Henry, in 1733 for two shillings from Nicholas Meriwether. Although John Henry never lived here, he had a portion of it farmed by a tenant. The tract was about 1,200 acres, most of it good farmland. When the elder Henry became strapped for money in 1765, his son Patrick purchased the land on Roundabout Creek.

In December of that year, he began building a modest home of one-and-one-half stories with three rooms on the first floor and one above. The house, constructed of hand hewn lumber, had a rough finish. John Anderson did much of the masonry, including subsequent additions and improvements, for which he was paid in cash, corn, fodder, and rum. Henry and his family moved in during the early summer of 1766. Shortly after the birth of their second daughter, Henry became disenchanted with the place and began to shop around for a new home. He purchased Scotchtown in 1771. The house built here by this early patriot stood until 1920 when it was destroyed by fire. In England, a traffic circle is called a round-about. *See: Pine Slash Farm; Red Hill; Studley*

ROUND HILL
Loudoun County **Town**
A large, round hill projecting from the nearby Blue Ridge was an easy landmark for early travelers. First settled in 1735, growth of this town was slow. The post office was not established until 1868.

RUCKERSVILLE
Greene County
At one time the only people living in this vicinity were all members of the Rucker family.

RUN
The word run is a shortened form of run-off, meaning any ditch or natural gully that carries water to a stream which eventually feeds into a river. The term creek (often pronounced "crick") is popularly mis-applied to runs and brooks and small streams. *See: Creek*

RURAL POINT
Hanover County
This brick residence, constructed late in the seventeenth century, is a story-and-a-half with four front and five rear dormers. All of the lower windows are protected by iron bars. The whole house was sturdily built, almost as

a fortress, with massive maple doors inside and out that have large and formidable English locks. It belonged to John Shelton whose daughter, Sarah, married Patrick Henry in 1754. A portion of this land was cut off and given to the newlyweds as a gift. They called their place Pine Slash Farm. When Patrick Henry's house burned in 1757, he and his young family lived temporarily at Rural Plains with his father-in-law and then moved into Hanover Tavern (sometimes called The Inn) which was owned by Shelton. Eight generations of the Shelton family have lived here. Today Rural Plains is known as Rural Point. *See: Pine Slash Farm; Scotchdown; Slash Church; Studley*

RURAL RETREAT
Wythe County **Town**
In stagecoach days, a tavern stood here with this unique name. Previously it was Mount Airy but that title apparently was too fancy for a rustic stage stop. Although the old tavern and stage stop is gone, a community developed nearby which grew into a town.

RUSSELL COUNTY
Formed in 1786 from Washington County, this county was named for General William Russell, a pioneer and soldier of the Revolution. The courthouse at Lebanon was erected in 1799. Still in use, it is one of the oldest public buildings in southwest Virginia.

RUSTBURG
Campbell County
Two years after Campbell County was organized in 1781, Jeremiah Rust donated a parcel of land for the courthouse and other public buildings. In his honor, the county seat was named Rustburg. The original courthouse fell victim to fire and was replaced in 1848 by the present red brick structure. *See: Campbell County*

RUTHER GLEN
Carroll County
Once called Chesterfield Station, a stop on

the Richmond, Fredericksburg and Potomac Railway, the name was changed to Ruther Glen by a Major Meyers, superintendent of the railroad's mail department. At Ruther Glen, on Scotland's River Clyde, stand the remains of an ancient castle of this name. It was taken from the English by Robert Bruce in 1313.

SABINE HALL
Richmond County

Built in 1730 by Landon Carter, a son of Robert "King" Carter. The brick house has four imposing white columns that support a front portico. Although definitely of colonial origin, the exterior of Sabine Hall helped set the style for many nineteenth century antebellum plantation houses in other states.

Landon Carter lived here with his second wife Elizabeth Wormeley of Rosegill. A strong Patriot, he made his views known during the Stamp Act crisis. Throughout the Revolution he corresponded with General Washington, offering advice and pledges of support.

Sabine Hall has remained in the family. It is now occupied by Carter Wellford, a descendent of Landon's daughter Elizabeth who married Dr. Armistead Wellford. *See: Blandfield; Corotoman; Farnham Church; Ripon Hall*

SAINT CHARLES
Lee County   Town

Charles Bondurant, an early coal mine operator and local businessman, selected this name for the post office. Possibly Saint Charles was his patron saint. The name Bondurant is French.

SAINT JOHN'S CHURCH
Hampton

When the Indian village of Kiccowtan was occupied by the English in 1610, one of the first needs was a church, the same as at Jamestown. While the congregation dates its founding to that year, there was a brief delay before a house of worship could be erected. It was not located in the town itself but was about a mile to the west on a small inlet of the James that became known as Church Creek. The people from all over the lower Peninsula

could get to it rather easily by water, a safety precaution as well as a convenience. The first rector, the Reverend William Mease, however, resided in the town as no rectory was added.

A second church was erected in 1624 on the east bank of Hampton Creek, about three miles away from the first one, since Church Creek was too shallow for the pinnaces and shallops commonly used. The foundations of this second church have been discovered near Hampton University. Although no sketches or descriptions of either of these two buildings exist, the second is thought to have been made of brick. Judging from the dimensions of the foundations, it was of modest size.

Some time prior to 1667, a third church was constructed of wood, this time not on a waterway but on the road heading westward from Hampton. The glebe land, adjoining the town, formerly was Pembroke Farm. The members of Elizabeth City Parish worshiped here for sixty years.

The fourth church was erected on the edge of the town in 1727. Made of brick, its exterior walls were laid in Flemish bond with alternating glazed headers. It was a major edifice that could be seen above the treetops from all directions. At this time the present churchyard was laid out and in it are graves that date back to the days of the consecration of the new, permanent structure. This one, however, was severely damaged twice by the ravages of war.

During the Battle of Hampton in October 1775, it was hit by naval gunfire. In 1812 it was pillaged by Admiral Sir George Cockburne's marines. When it was repaired and reconsecrated in 1825, the name was changed to Saint John's. It was gutted by fire early in the Civil War when the residents of Hampton put their town to the torch to deny its use by Union troops and runaway slaves that overflowed from nearby Fortress Monroe. When it was repaired again during the Reconstruction, the surviving walls were used but no attempt was made to restore the interior to its former colonial appearance. What is seen today resembles the church of 1727.

While other congregations elsewhere in English America may worship in older buildings, the history of Saint John's predates them all, going back to 1610 in a continuous line. *See: Camp Hamilton; Hampton; Phoebus*

SAINT JOHN'S CHURCH
Richmond

When Patrick Henry made his famous Liberty or Death speech in this building in March 1775, this structure was known as the Church of Henrico Parish. It was the only church in Richmond. Built in 1741, it had no steeple and had a different orientation.

Among the graves in its churchyard is that of George Wythe, the first professor of law in America (at the College of William and Mary) and a signer of the Declaration of Independence. Tucked away in an old section of Richmond, on Church Hill, this historic building is as much a shrine to independence as any other building in other states. *See: Chesterville; Henricus; Varina Grove*

SAINT LUKE'S CHURCH
Isle of Wight County

This church is thought to have been established in 1632 and there are some who believe that part of the present building dates from that time. More than likely, the earliest correct date of construction is 1682, although there is good reason to suspect that the date may have been seventeen years earler. At any rate, authorities agree that this Saint Lukes is the only original colonial Gothic building left in the country. Its exterior is much the same as it was two hundred years ago. Little of the original interior woodwork remains. The exterior conforms closely to what experts think the first brick church at Jamestown looked like.

SAINT MARGARET'S SCHOOL
Essex County

This excellent Episcopal school for girls was probably named for Saint Margaret, a Scottish queen whose principal chapel is in Edinburg, Scotland. Saint Margaret's of London is the Parish church of Westminster Abbey. This school is served by Saint John's of Tappahannock.

SAINT MARY'S WHITE CHAPEL
Lancaster County

A church was erected here as early as 1669. The tablets in the present church date from that year. The present church was erected in 1741 and was later improved. Noteworthy in the churchyard are the graves of the Ball family, all ancestors or relatives of George Washington's mother. *See: Bewdley; Epping Forest; Ferry Farm*

SAINT PAUL
Russell County   **Town**

This was the location of Moore's Fort that guarded Wheeler's Ford on the Clinch River in the 1770s. When the Carolina, Clinchfield and Ohio Railway Company made plans to lay track past this place in the last decade of the nineteenth century, a group of speculators bought the land on both sides of the river. They intended to found twin cities to be named Minneapolis and Saint Paul. The project was abandoned when the new railroad company could not be financed. Finally, in 1904, the rail line was constructed through this region. By then, the land speculators had managed to found one small town which they called Saint Paul.

SAINT PAUL COLLEGE
Lawrenceville

Founded by the Reverend James S. Russell, born a slave and educated at Hampton Institute, this is the third oldest Negro College in the United States. Organized in 1888, it is sponsored by the Episcopal Church.

SAINT PETER'S CHURCH
New Kent County

A church was erected here about 1703. For forty years, the rector was Reverend David Mossum who twice performed the marriage ceremonies for Martha Dandridge. When she married Daniel Parke Custis at the church in 1749, the couple left in grand style in a coach drawn by six white horses. Her second marriage was to George Washington in 1759, two years after she was left a widow with two small children. The heir to the great Custis fortune, Martha was one of the wealthiest women in Virginia at the time. Local tradition says that Martha and George were married in this church, but most historians discount this idea since the date, January 6th, makes it highly unlikely. Colonial churches were unheated and the roads from the local residences would have been muddy and nearly impassable at that time of the year. In all likelihood, the couple was married at Martha's own house, White House, and the event was then dutifully recorded in the parish register by the Reverend Mr. Mossum. Saint Peter's competed seriously for good preachers with Saint John's just across the Pamunkey River. *See: Arlington of Northampton; Queen's Creek Plantation; White House*

SALEM
Roanoke County   **City**

Salem, a city often mentioned in the Old

Testament, was a name used by settlers in many of the original thirteen colonies. This city was founded in 1802 by James Simpson, a real estate developer, on sixteen acres purchased from the estate of General Andrew Lewis who had a home nearby called Richfield. At first, Salem contained more taverns than houses: Old Time Tavern, The Bull's Eye, The Indian Queen, The Globe, and the Mermaid. At the latter place, run by Simpson's brother-in-law Griffin Lumpkin, cock fights were the main attraction. When the county was formed in 1838, Salem was selected for the site of the courthouse, possibly because of the abundance of taverns within which judges, lawyers, clerks, plaintiffs, and defendants could refresh themselves. Now a modern city of substantial size, Salem is the location of a large Veterans Administration Medical Center. *See: Cricket Hill; Marshall; Roanoke*

SALISBURY
Chesterfield County   **Site**

Two miles north of Midlothian, not far from the James River, was Salisbury. In the very early days of the settlement of Virginia, the territory on the south side of the James River was called the Salisbury Side for the Earl of Salisbury, an important member of the Virginia Company. Very quickly, the Salisbury Side became known as the Surry Side, since the land on the opposite side of the River Thames in London was Surrey, and all references to the Earl were dropped. The house here was built in the eighteenth century as a hunting lodge and was given its fancy name. During Patrick Henry's years as Governor of the Commonwealth, from 1784 to 1786, he used the lodge as a home. *See: Midlothian of Chesterfield*

SALTVILLE
Wythe County   **Town**

First called Preston's Salines, after General Francis Preston who had a salt works here in 1748, the name was changed to Buffalo Lick. The big animals roamed this region in the eighteenth century and came to lick the natural salt that was scattered all about. General William Russell came here from Aspenvale in 1788 to rework the deposits that

SALTVILLE ca. 1863

lie below large, marshy flats, giving the name Saltville to the community that grew nearby. Until the salt works were destroyed by the Union army in December of 1864, more than 200,000 bushels of the vital mineral had been refined. Brine is still pumped from underground and is used by present industries.

SALUDA
Middlesex County

When Middlesex County was formed from Lancaster in 1673, the courthouse was located at Urbanna on Nimcock Creek. The county seat was moved to a new location in 1852 and the tiny hamlet around the court complex was named Saluda. The name apparently is a corruption of an Indian Tribe that had lived here for a while after they came from Carolina. By the time the site was selected for the new county seat, the Indians had migrated to Pennsylvania. There are some who believe Saluda derives from *salubrious*, meaning "healthy." Although this is unlikely, it is possible. No one really knows the true origin of the name anymore.

SANDY POINT
Westmoreland County

At Sandy Point Mary Ball spent many years in the home of her guardian, Colonial George Eskridge. Here she married Augustine Washington in March 1731. It is generally accepted that she named her first son, George, for her guardian. *See: Epping Forest; Nomini Hall; Pecatone*

SAPONI INDIANS

This minor tribe, one of Powhatan's confederacy, lived along the James River at the falls, not far from Orapax. When the English settlers declared war on the Indians after the Massacre of 1644, the Saponi moved to the northwest, settling for a brief time in Albemarle County, near Charlottesville. Feeling too exposed and separated from other tribes, they moved south and settled on the Roanoke River. They were among the tribes that Governor Alexander Spotswood attempted to convert to Christianity at Fort Chrisanna. Saponey Church, built in 1728, retains their name, although it is spelled differently. In fact, this tribe's name has suffered through many different spellings by colonial writers. It is pronounced Sapo-NIE.

SARAH CREEK
Gloucester County

Until a few years ago, this was spelled Sarah's Creek. An inlet of the York River near its mouth just at Gloucester Point, the creek was named for Sarah Churchill, the wife of the first Duke of Marlborough. He gained fame as the general who led Queen Anne's army in the great victory at Blenheim in 1704. The Duchess was a close confidant of the queen until some unrecorded happening broke them apart. Sarah Churchill was never told why she was banished from the queen's presence and the mystery has never been resolved. *See: Blenheim*

SARATOGA
Clarke County

One of the best preserved of the larger pre-Revolutionary homes in this region, the dwelling was built about 1781 for General Daniel Morgan who named it for the historic Battle of Saratoga fought in New York. It was the Continental Army's first major victory. General "Gentleman Johnny" Burgoyne was defeated by Horatio Gates on October 17, 1771, in a British military disaster brought about by conflicting orders from London. Burgoyne was to have linked up with another force in this region and, with vastly superior numbers, would have easily defeated the colonials. However, the other British troops marched south leaving "Gentleman Johnny" helpless. Over 4,000 British and Hessian troops were made captive, including Burgoyne's second-in-command, General William Phillips. Later, Saratoga was the home of two noted authors, Philip R. and John E. Cooke. *See: Barracks; Blenheim; Millwood of Clarke*

SAVAGE NECK
Northampton County

This neck of land on the bay side of the Eastern Shore was given to Thomas Savage by Debedeavon, the chief, in 1619. Savage had come to Virginia with Captain Christopher Newport in one of the supply voyages of 1608, reportedly as a cabin boy. Then in his early teens, a strong and plucky youth, he was well liked by the crusty captain. Savage was given to the Indians as a hostage in exchange for Namontack, a trusted servant of Powhatan who was described as having a "shrewed, subtle capacity." To sweeten the exchange, Newport hinted that Tom Savage was his son, giving rise to the error that they were related directly. Namontack went to England and was killed by a fellow Indian in Bermuda on the return voyage. Savage quickly adapted to the Indian ways, learned

SARATOGA

the language and customs, and became a skilled interpreter for the colony when he was allowed to return to Jamestown. He did more to insure the success of the English settlement as an ambassador of good will and a skillful mediator of disputes than history has given him credit.

He first went to live on the Eastern Shore in 1618, possibly sent there by the Governor, Sir George Yeardley, who was eager to cement the friendship of Debedeavon, the major chieftan there. Although Savage was used as a messenger and interpreter in other parts of the colony when required, he retained his love for the Eastern Shore and made his home there. He married Hannah Tyng in 1619 after she had arrived in the colony on the *Sea Flower,* and received as a gift from the Indian king, 9,000 acres of good land which occupied most of a neck of land at Cherrystone Creek.

One child was born to Thomas and Hannah, a son. The lad was but four years old when his father died of an arrow wound in 1627. The circumstances of Ensign Thomas Savage's death have not been recorded. Many generations later, a direct descendant served as a member of the Revolutionary Convention of 1776. The name Thomas Savage still lives in the present generation. *See: Cherry Grove of Northampton; White Cliff*

SAXIS
Accomack County   **Town**

Originally patented in 1666 by Robert Sikes for his own use, the land here supports a thriving fishing village. The name was changed to Sykes by a careless postal clerk in 1896. That was minor compared to what followed by evolution. In the southern manner, the "i" sound is pronounced with a flat "a" in this part of the Eastern Shore. Therefore, the present spelling reflects the local pronounciation. This was Sikes's town. Today it is Saxis. *See: Gladys*

SCHUYLER
Nelson County

Many years ago a grist mill was operated here by Schuyler Walker who was called by his first name by everyone. Today the community's primary industry is quarrying soapstone, named Alberene. The stone's name is a combination of Albemarle and James Serene, the man who promoted the local material in 1870.

SCOTCHTOWN
Hanover County

This was a summer residence for Charles Chiswell of Williamsburg. The house dates from 1719. It was built by Chiswell who planned a new town to be inhabited only by fellow Scots. After building the present structure, he erected a mill and a tannery and then began work on a castle. The foundations were laid for his baronial manor just before disaster struck. Disease killed several workmen, the others became either ill or frightened, and the castle was never completed. Charles Chiswell, a man of violent temper, would have been a terrible master and if the illness had not frightened off his workers, his temper surely would have.

Accused of murder, which he stoutly denied having committed, he killed himself rather than stand trial. His son, John Chiswell, moved into the summer house soon after his marriage to Elizabeth Randolph of Turkey Island, but he was never able to erase the stigma of his father's suicide.

In 1771 Patrick Henry purchased the large frame house that appeared much as we see it today. By acquiring Scotchtown, then one of the largest houses in Virginia, he showed his increased prosperity. Henry sold Scotchtown to Wilson Cary after living in it for six years. Cary sold it in 1781 to Quaker John Payne, the father of Dolley Madison who spent much of her childhood here. Now owned by the Association for the Preservation of Virginia Antiquities, Scotchtown is open to the public. *See: Fairfield of King William; Montpelier of Orange; Rocketts Mill; Roundabout*

SCOTLAND
Surry County

The complete name of this tiny hamlet above the Jamestown-Surry ferry landing is Scotland Wharf. The origin of the name is unknown. For over 150 years the land here was part of a large farm known as Pleasant Point, owned by the Edwards family from 1657 until 1812. Nearby is Smith's Fort Plantation.

SCOTT COUNTY

Formed in 1814 from parts of Lee, Russell, and Washington, this county was named for Capt. Winfield Scott who had served with distinction during the War of 1812. Those who chose to honor a local hero must have been blessed with a vision of the future. Captain Scott rose to be the commanding general of the U.S. forces in Mexico during the war with that country in 1846-48. It was he who led the victory parade into Mexico City. During his army career, he earned the nickname Old Fuss and Feathers for his strict adherence to military rules and protocol. He was considered as a presidential candidate but did not receive the nomination in the Democratic convention of 1863. When the Civil War began two years before, he wisely admitted his age and resigned and let younger men direct the Union efforts. He died in 1866 at the age of 80. The courthouse of Scott county is in Gate City. *See: Buena Vista; Monterey*

GENERAL WINFIELD SCOTT
SCOTT COUNTY

SCOTTSBURG
Halifax County   **Town**

This town was named in honor of John Baytop Scott who is buried nearby. Scott was the first vice president of the Society of the Cincinnati, formed in 1783 by former officers of the Continental Army. George Washington was the Society's first president.

SCOTTSVILLE
Albemarle County   **Town**

On a wide bend of the upper James lived five tribes of Monacan Indians. Not until they migrated west in the late seventeenth century was any successful attempt made to create an English town here. It was a natural place for a port, one of a few openings in the bluffs that line the north bank of the river. From this landing, freight could be taken from barges and shipped to the north on a road that was cut through the wilderness to join Three Chopt Road.

When Albemarle County was organized here in Daniel Scott's house, he received a license to operate a ferry from the new county seat to the opposite shore. Scott also was granted a permit to operate a tavern in partnership with John Lewis. Even after the county seat was moved upland to Charlottesville in 1762, Scott continued to operate his ferry and tavern. Much freight passed through the tiny village which was incorporated in 1818 as Scottsville just before the railroads began to carry passengers and supplies through the heartland of the Piedmont. Losing both the courthouse and the important river traffic doomed Scottsville to obscurity. *See: Glendower; Mount Walla; Powhatan County*

SEAFORD
York County

Years ago, this tiny community was known as Crab Neck since crabbing was the major industry. In more recent times, it was renamed by E. E. Slaight for a shallow link between the York River and Back River that can be forded at low tide. Although Seaford is rather far from the sea, the name has a pleasant sound to it.

SECRETARY'S FORD
Albemarle County

A shallow crossing of the Rivanna River, just east of Charlottesville, this ford was named for John Carter, the Secretary of the colony, who owned land on both sides and who charged a toll for crossing. When another ford was found upstream by the frugal travellers, "Secretary" Carter countered by building a bridge. For a fee, a dry crossing could be made in all weather. His bridge was replaced 100 years later by the Commonwealth when a better highway was constructed between Charlottesville and Richmond. Finally, in 1934, because Federal money was used to repace the rickety span, a modern bridge was erected across the Rivanna River which was named Free Bridge. This toll free crossing helped join the Keswick section of Albemarle with the county seat.

SENECA INDIANS

This warrior tribe was not native to the region now known as Virginia. Its main village was far up the Chesapeake Bay. They were, however, the major cause of Bacon's Rebellion. Raiding Virginia settlements and farms between the James and the Rappahannock, they stirred the colonists to organize a force to wipe them out. The Senecas were too slippery for this badly led militia and disappeared into the forest. Without bothering to make certain identification, the Virginians attacked a Susquehannock village and brought that otherwise peaceful tribe onto the warpath. The Susquehannocks vowed to kill ten settlers for every one of their tribe murdered. The fight between them and the English continued until the Susquehannocks were completely wiped out in the battle at Occaneechee. The wily Senecas carefully stayed out of the fray and lived to molest the settlers of Pennsylvania. Today, as in the past, the two tribes are often confused.

SEVEN PINES
Henrico County

This settlement takes its name from a bitter Civil War battle that raged here for two days during General George McClellan's attempt to capture Richmond. The action here at Seven Pines was part of the Seven Days Battle. On May 31, 1862, the Union army received an attack from the Southern forces of General Joseph E. Johnston. The Confederates, in a series of failures, did not move at appointed times which spoiled the effectiveness of the attack. On the second day of this battle, General Robert E. Lee was given command of the Army of Northern Virginia, replacing General Joseph E. Johnston who was wounded. Today, seven pines grow at the Confederate cemetery in silent sentinel.

SEVEN SPRINGS
King William County

Dabney's Ferry was established in 1720 to carry travellers across the Pamunkey River to Hanover Town. The Dabney family owned this land and lived on it until 1827. Their home, called Seven Springs, was built about 1732. It was located about five miles from the ferry. *See: Hanover Town*

SEVERN
Gloucester County

One of the three short rivers that join to form Mobjack Bay, the Severn was named for the river in central Wales that flows past the English city of Bristol. This hamlet, sited on the edge of the Severn River, takes its name from the Virginia stream.

SEWELL'S POINT
Norfolk

Henry Sewell was a landowner in this stretch of land near the mouth of the Elizabeth River. He came to Virginia prior to 1640. When ships pass Sewell's Point on an outbound voyage, they enter into the great natural anchorage of Hampton Roads.

SHADWELL
Albemarle County   **Site**

Peter Jefferson, a third generation Virginian, was one of the first settlers in the section of the Piedmont that would become Albemarle County. His son, Thomas, wrote that Peter Jefferson was the "third or fourth settler, about the year 1737." Soon after the elder Jefferson married Jane Randolph, a daughter of Isham Randolph of Dungeness in Goochland County, he patented 2,000 acres adjoining those owned by his wife's cousin, William Randolph of Tuckahoe. The only good location for a homesite lay on the Randolph property which Randolph willingly sold to Jefferson. They sealed the bargain over a bowl of Henry Weatherburn's good Arrack punch in Williamsburg. (Later, a portion of this section was cut off as Punchbowl Farm.)

The name Shadwell came from the English parish in which Jane Randolph had been christened when her father was the colonial agent for Virginia in England. Peter Jefferson built a modest home where five of the six children were born, including Thomas, Randolph, and Martha, the three we know most about. Colonel Jefferson was a tall, extraordinarily strong man of sound intelligence and culture. He was a natural leader, a quietly sociable man, whose home beside the Three Chopt Road was a magnet to all travellers.

With Joshua Fry, he surveyed the colony in the early 1750s and produced an accurate map of Virginia, the first new one since Smith's map of 1612. The Fry-Jefferson map was the official depiction of the terrain until the next one was drawn in 1848 by Claudius Crozet.

Peter Jefferson died on August 17, 1757 leaving a widow, four daughters, and two sons. Jane Randolph Jefferson lived on at Shadwell until the house burned to the ground in 1770. She moved in with relatives until her death in 1776 after an illness of a few hours. At the time of the fire at Shadwell, Thomas was living in a cottage at Monticello where he was supervising the construction of his new home. Destroyed with the house were Peter Jefferson's library and his invaluable collection of notes and personal papers. All that was rescued from the fire was Tom's fiddle. *See: Albemarle County; Bear Castle; Dungeness; Edgehill; Keswick; Monticello; Snowden; Tuckahoe*

SHARPS
Richmond County

During the days of steamboats on the Chesapeake, this settlement was Sharp's Wharf, named for the manager of the landing, a Mr. Sharp. Both he and his nephew owned most of the land around here. This was a major shipping point on the Rappahannock River for many generations, beginning back in late colonial times. The wharf is gone and so is part of the name.

SHAWNEE INDIANS

A wandering tribe, the Shawnee lived primarily in the Ohio Territory. Their principal town was Piquo, the birthplace of their most famous warrior, Tecumseh, who sided with the British during the War of 1812. He died in a battle in Canada, wearing a British red jacket, forewarned of his death by a vision. The Shawnee were natural fighters who loved to raid, steal, fight, and murder others not of their tribe. They often slipped through the Cumberland Gap and attacked pioneers in the Clinch and Holston River valleys. William Henry Harrison subdued them after winning the battle of Tippicanoe which catapulted him into the presidencey. The Shawnee were among those tribes condemned to arid western reservations in 1817 when President Andrew Jackson moved the Cherokee and the Miami nations out of the excellent land coveted by settlers. Had Jackson had his way, he would have killed them all following a policy of genocide. Old Hickory detested all Indians. *See: Battle Knob; Kentucky County; Winchester*

SHAWSVILLE
Montgomery County

This village occupies the site of Fort Vause, built in 1754 by Captain Ephraim Vause at his own expense. When it was attacked by Indians, the captain, his wife and two daughters were taken prisoner and the fort, barn and all outbuildings were set afire. A council, held in the Augusta County courthouse, ordered the fort rebuilt. It was never attacked again. When the Norfolk and Western Railway was built through here, a station was located near the old site. It was named for a Mr. Shaw who was one of the construction engineers. Captain Vause was overlooked when Shawsville was named.

SHELLY
Gloucester County   **Site**

Adjoining Rosewell was the more modest home of Mann Page III who married into the Nelson family of Yorktown. The original dwelling, built in the eighteenth century, was destroyed by fire after the Civil War. The

226

name was derived from the huge pile of oyster shells found here, dumped by generations of Indians. Nearby was the site of Werowocomoco, Powhatan's main village. *See: Mannsfield; Rosewell; Timberneck Hall; Werowocomoco*

SHENANDOAH
Page County   **Town**

This town, in the shadow of the southern end of Massanutten Mountain, is on the south fork of the Shenandoah River.

SHENANDOAH COUNTY

Formed in 1772 out of Frederick County, the territory's name first was Dunmore County for the last royal Governor. In 1778, in the midst of the Revolution, the name was changed to Shenandoah. The courthouse at Woodstock, dating from 1791, is the oldest court building still in use west of the Blue Ridge. Of a rare Baroque design, complete with German cupola, it reflects the European heritage of the people. *See: Woodstock*

SHANANDOAH NATIONAL PARK

Created during the Depression of the 1930s, this forested park encloses about 300 square miles of ridges, valleys, hills, and hollows of the Blue Ridge Mountains. The renown Skyline Drive, constructed by the Civilian Conservation Corps (CCC) which gave young men worthwhile jobs, runs along the spine of the mountains for 105 miles to give scenic views of the piedmont to the east and the great Shenandoah Valley to the west. This drive connects with the Blue Ridge Parkway at Rockfish Gap near Waynesboro. One of the mountains is Pollock Knob, 3,580 feet high, named for George Freeman Pollock, one of the founders of the park. *See: Knob*

SHENANDOAH VALLEY

This valley was leveled by the action of the Shenandoah River which today has receded into two main branches, the North and the South, both of which are rather shallow rivers, full of eddies. When the river was first seen by the Knights of the Golden Horseshoe, led by Governor Alexander Spotswood, it was called the Euphrates. The fancy name did not last long and it became the Shenandoah, an Indian word meaning "Daughter of the Stars."

Although Spotswood thought he was the first white man to see this valley, it had been explored in the previous century by others who preferred to keep the beautiful region secret and undefiled. The Valley was populated during the first third of the eighteenth century, after Spotswood raved about it. Many of the pioneers came from Pennsylvania where they competed for the best location with those who came from the east. The German Lutherans and Scottish Presbyterians lived in peace once their land claims were acknowledged.

Since the Shenandoah Valley floor rises as it stretches to the southwest, a traveller goes up the Valley when heading south down the old Valley Pike (U.S. 11) or down Interstate 81. *See: Germanna; Staunton; Strasburg; Swift Run Gap; Winchester; Woodstock*

SHERANDO
Augusta County

This tiny community is on the fringe of the Lake Sherando Recreational Area. The name is a variation of Shenandoah. The man-made lake, southwest of Rockfish Gap, is a favorite spot for the people of four counties.

SHERWOOD FOREST
Charles City County

When John Tyler left the White House in 1845, he brought his bride of eight months, Julia Gardner, to his new estate in Charles City County. This new home was about three miles from the place of his birth. Tyler had purchased the house and farmland in preparation for his retirement from active politics. His becoming President had been a shock. He had not wanted to be the vice presidential candidate with General William Henry Harrison in the election of 1840 but had accepted the nomination only because he was certain that as Vice President he would have little to do other than preside over the Senate upon occasion.

When President Harrison died a few weeks after his inauguration, John Tyler became the tenth President of the United States. His first pronouncement after being sworn in was his immediate decision not to seek re-election at the end of the term. He sought legislation to enact some of the first national social programs. Since these laws took from the rich and gave to the poor, he was called Robin Hood in the press. Therefore, when he returned to Virginia, he named his home Sherwood Forest.

When his native state left the Union, he allowed himself to be elected to the Confederate Congress at the age of seventy-two.

JOHN TYLER, SHERWOOD FOREST

John Tyler died in Richmond in 1862 and was buried in that city's Hollywood Cemetery near the grave of James Monroe. The house of Sherwood Forest survived the Civil War, although Federal troops mutilated the interior and destroyed most of the furnishings. *See: Berkeley; Greenway*

SHIRE

The rapid increase in population in Virginia during the second decade of the colony's existence required a change in the political organization. The Four Ancient Corporations of 1619 were divided into eight shires in 1634. Listed alphabetically, they were: Accomack, Charles City, Charles River, Elizabeth City, James City, Northampton, Warrascoyak, and Warwick. The old English term *shire* was changed to *county* the next year. The "heathen name" Warrascoyak was changed to Isle of Wight in 1637. Charles River County was changed to York County in 1643. In England, when counties were called shires, the man in charge of keeping the peace was the *reeve*. Since shire was pronounced "sher," the shire reeve became known as the sheriff. Although the title reeve was not used in Virginia, the chief law enforcement officer in each county was called a sheriff. *See: Hundred*

SHIRLEY
Charles City County

The first Governor of the colony of Virginia was Thomas West, Lord Delaware. With his two brothers, he patented this tract in 1611. It was named West and Shirley Hundred, combining the last names of his Lordship's and his wife's family. Lady Delaware, who never came to the New World, was Cessallye, the daughter of Sir Thomas Sherley. Early settlement was interrupted by the Massacre of 1622, but Sir Francis West, "ye foresaid admiral," was reported living here in 1624.

Colonel Edward Hill purchased the land in 1653 and managed to complete his home seven years later. Edward Hill III built the present house in 1723, tore down his grandfather's home, and saved the bricks which were later used to construct Upper Shirley. Elizabeth Hill, the daughter of the builder, inherited the estate shortly after she married John "Secretary" Carter of Corotoman. Her son, Charles Carter, inherited the place and enlarged the house about 1769. At the same time, he remodeled the four outbuildings to accommodate his huge family of twenty-three children. One of his daughters, Anne Hill Carter, married "Light Horse Harry" Lee of Stratford and was the mother of General Robert E. Lee.

Shirley is the tallest house of the James River plantations, rising a full three stories. Carved pineapples, the symbol of hospitality, appear frequently. A large one is visible from the river on the peak of the roof. *See: Corotoman; Totopotomoi Creek*

SHORT PUMP
Goochland County

On the Three Chopt Road west of Richmond, about halfway to Gum Spring, stood a busy colonial tavern. At one time the well was in the yard near to the door. When the tavern was enlarged, a new porch extended over the well, making it difficult to get a full stroke on the pump handle to draw water. It was easier to shorten the handle than to dig a new well, and this gave rise to a new name for the tavern. Travellers spoke of staying "at the tavern with the short pump handle" which, naturally, became Short Pump Tavern. *See: Gum Spring*

SHOT TOWER
Wythe County

Near the lead mines outside Austinville, a shot tower was built about 1820 by Thomas

Jackson. Still standing, the hollow stone shaft is seventy-five feet high and seventeen feet square inside. Shot was produced by pouring molten lead onto a sheet of iron that had been pierced with holes of the desired diameter. The liquid lead assumed a globular shape that became nearly a perfect ball by the time it fell into the water at the bottom of the tower. In the receiving water tank was a sloping floor down which the shot rolled into collecting boxes. The rejects, of unacceptable shape, rolled off to one side where they were collected for remelting. The diameter of the balls could be changed by using differently pierced iron sheets. Every size, from tiny birdshot to musket balls, could be made more quickly in a tower than by the laborious molding process.

SHUTER'S HILL
Alexandria

Once the site of the home of Ludwell Lee, son of Richard Henry Lee, this is now the location of the Masonic Memorial in Alexandria. At one time, Shuter's Hill was under consideration as the site of the new Capitol building. In 1799, Ludwell Lee sold the land to Benjamin Dulaney and moved his residence to a more elegant house, Belmont, in Loudoun County.

SILVER BEACH
Northampton County

The sands of the beaches on the lower bay side of the Eastern Shore gleam silvery white. This settlement developed as a summer resort. While many of the cottages are for summer use only, there are year-round residences that give a permanence to the village of Silver Beach. At this point, Chesapeake Bay narrows to about sixteen miles in width and, on a clear day, the pines of Gwynn's Island can be seen from here.

SINGERS GLEN
Rockingham County

The man who became known as the "Father of Song in Northern Virginia," Joseph Funk, began teaching vocal music in the nineteenth century. His conservatory for advanced studies in music was established in 1868 with the appropriate name Singers' Glen School.

SINKING CREEK
Craig County

It is not unusual for streams to disappear into the limestone strata of the Great Valley of Virginia. Several places have had this name.

SIX MILE ORDINARY
James City County   Site

Allen's Ordinary was on the old road from Williamsburg to Doncastle's Ordinary (near present Barhamsville). It was approximately six miles from the Capitol, a convenient distance for a first stop to tighten the saddle or check the harness. An early Quaker settlement was a few miles away to the east. *See: Skimino Meeting House*

SKIFFE'S CREEK
Newport News

This creek ran through the glebe lands of Martin's Hundred Parish whose rector was the Reverend George Keith. Although he did not own the land, Keith was identified with it and the creek was known as Keith's Creek. Over the years, the name was slurred into Skiffe's Creek. In the vernacular of the region, a "th" sound was often changed to an "f." Thus, when asked, "Whose creek is this?" The answer would be " 'Tis Kiff's." It is not known how the "e" became attached to the spelling. Of course, in old English, it was common to add it to the end of a word, as in "towne." *See: Martin's Hundred*

SKIMINO MEETING HOUSE
York County

In York County's Upper Bruton district, a few miles northeast of Williamsburg, a group of Quakers made their homes. They held their first recorded meeting in December 1698. The English Quaker missionary, Thomas Storey, held the first gathering in the home of John Bates of Skimino Hundred, at which time Bates and the members of his family admitted their conversion. The group expanded into a full Society of Friends which included members of such old Virginia families as Ratcliffe, Harrison, Jordan, Crewes, Driver, Robinson, and Winston. They held their secret meetings in various places until they finally decided that it was safe to announce their Society in public.

As far as can be determined, the first meeting house was built about 1774 on property donated by William Ratcliffe Heathan. It was still standing as late as 1808. Membership in the Society began to decline as the eighteenth century ended, and Quaker activity in the area was entirely over by 1827. In that. year, the last of the members sold their York County property and joined other

Quakers in Ohio. The only present indication of this group's quiet stay in this area is Meeting House Road which is still in use. The Girl Scouts have a large campsite on Skimino Creek. The origin of the name is not known.

SKIPPERS
Greensville County

Unprovable, but quite likely, Skippers is a corruption of the family name Skipwith. *See: Prestwould, Tasley*

SLASH CHURCH
Hanover County   **Site**

This is the oldest existing frame church in America. It was built in 1729 as the mother church of Saint Paul's Parish. Early rectors complained of the size of the parish territory that stretched indefinitely westward into Louisa County and beyond. The rector from 1737 until 1777 was the Reverend Patrick Henry, Sr., who was not sure he approved of his nephew, the lawyer and orator, Patrick Henry, Jr., who argued against the clergy in the Parson's Cause trial in Hanovertown in 1763.

The Reverend Patrick Henry had come to Virginia a few years before being assigned to this church. His home had been in Aberdene, Scotland, where he and his brother, John, had spent their youth. Parson Henry, ordained in the Scottish Episcopal Church, was sent to Virginia to be the rector of Saint George's Parish in Spotsylvania County. He was delighted to receive a call from Saint Paul's, a church in which his brother was quite active and who, no doubt, arranged the transfer.

This old church was more commonly known as Slash Church from the slashes, a common pine that grows in wild abundance here in the rather swampy ground. At the time the building caught fire, it was the Slashes Christian Church, having been purchased by that denomination in 1952. *See: Ashland; Clay Spring; Rural Plains*

SLATE HILL
Prince Edward County

This was the home of one branch of the Venable family which became prominent in the early nineteenth century. Prior to the Revolution, Nathaniel Venable lived here. He was a charter trustee of Hampden-Sydney College, and was a member of the Prince Edward Committee of Safety. Slate, used as a roofing material for many years, can be quarried here.

SMITHFIELD
Isle of Wight County   **Town**

This town, laid out on land owned by Colonel Arthur Smith, was formally recognized by the House of Burgesses in 1752. Settlers had been living along Pagan Creek for at least 100 years before there was a need for a town. In very early days, this site was occupied by the Mokete Indian tribe and the name Pagan refers to the heathanism of the natives, not of the English settlers.

The Smithfield region has been connected with pork since the days of the Jamestown colonists. Just a few miles down the James River, they kept their swine on Hog Island. However, Smithfield's fame for hams and other cured pork products dates from the nineteenth century. Only a ham made here may be called a Smithfield ham. For a brief time, the county seat of Isle of Wight was located in this old town. When it was moved, the courthouse was abandoned and used for various purposes. Today it houses a museum. *See: Hog Island; Wrenn's Mill*

SMITHFIELD PLANTATION
Montgomery County

King George II granted 120,000 acres to Colonel James Patton in 1745. He and his nephew, William Preston, had come to Virginia nine years before. They first had settled near Staunton and then moved up the Valley to help found the Draper's Meadow settlement (near Blacksburg). Colonel Patton died in an Indian attack in 1755, but Preston escaped. Seventeen years later, Colonel Preston occupied 19,000 acres of his late uncle's original grant and built a home as the center piece of his plantation. The house was designed for defense against Indian attack with a stockade, secret escape tunnel, and chimney lookout niche. He named his farm for his wife, Susanna Smith.

Colonel Preston, a Burgess for this region, was well acquainted with fellow Burgesses George Washington, Thomas Jefferson, and Patrick Henry. In command of the county militia at the outbreak of the Revolution, he saved this part of Virginia for the patriot cause since there were many Tory families living in the Great Valley of Virginia. His sons did well for their native state: two became generals, one became the Treasurer of the Commonwealth, and James Patton Preston was elected Governor. *See: Draper's Meadow*

SMITH MOUNTAIN LAKE
Bedford County

The mountain beside which this lake is

located was owned in the eighteenth century by Gideon Smith who, with his brother, hunted and trapped on their own private reserve. The present lake was created by a dam built by the Appalachian Power Company on the Roanoke River. The lake is forty miles long, and with its many fingers, has a 500 mile shoreline. Containing the purest water of any impoundment in Virginia, the "mountain sea" is stocked with millions of game fish.

SMITH POINT
Northumberland County

Named by Captain John Smith for himself during his explorations in 1608, this point projects into Chesapeake Bay. The main ship channel to Baltimore passes between Smith Point and Tangier Island. *See: Stingray Point*

SMITH'S ISLAND
Northampton County

This isn't much of an island but rather a mud flat with high places for marsh grasses. When Captain John Smith first saw it and named it for himself, it had a different shape and quite possibly was connected to the island on which the Cape Charles lighthouse was built. The action of the Atlantic is slowly eroding it with the sand deposited at Fisherman Island. Barrier islands change constantly.

SMITH'S FORT PLANTATION
Surry County   Site

In 1609 Captain John Smith ordered a fort constructed on the other side of the James River from the main settlement. Called the New Fort, this was to be used as a haven in case the Indians forced an evacuation of Jamestown. All during the next two centuries the county records call this region Smith's Fort Plantation. Powhatan gave the land to John Rolfe in 1614 as a wedding gift when he married Pocahontas. It was inherited by Pocahontas' only child, Thomas Rolfe, who came to Virginia in 1635 to claim it.

Thomas Warren came to Virginia in 1640 and, three years later, purchased Rolfe's land which adjoined that which he had already acquired. In 1653, Warren began construction of a brick house fifty feet long which he managed to have completed by the time he married the daughter of an Ancient Planter, William Spencer. The house was known as the Fifty Foot House. Although this early dwelling has disappeared, the site has been established with some slight doubt.

The present building here was restored in 1935 by John D. Rockefeller while he was busy bringing Williamsburg back to life. Sited about a half-mile from Gray's Creek, the house probably was built by a descendant of Thomas Gray who owned a large adjoining tract in 1635 and for whom Gray's Creek was named. *See: Bacon's Castle; Plantation; Warescoyak*

SMYTH COUNTY

Organized in 1832 and named for General Alexander Smyth, a member of Congress for many years, this county was formed from parts of Washington and Wythe. The courthouse is located at Marion.

SMYTHE'S HUNDRED
Charles City County   Site

This was the second Particular Plantation in Virginia, the first being Martin's Brandon. Sir Thomas Smythe, a wealthy London merchant who was the Treasurer of the London Company of Virginia, acquired land in 1618 through the "head rights" provision of the New Charter by transporting a number of colonists. Smythe's Hundred was located at Dancing Point, a few miles up the James River from Jamestown. Sir Thomas was ousted as the Treasurer because he was more interested in profits than he was in people. He was replaced by Sir Edwyn Sandys who lasted but a year before King James managed to get rid of him in favor of the Earl of Southampton. Smythe's Hundred Plantation did not prosper. Today is is known as Sandy Point, possibly a connection with the name Sandys which was pronounced Sands. *See: Hundred; Particular Plantation*

SNICKERS GAP
Frederick County

This mountain pass first was known as Williams' Gap for an early settler who squatted on Lord Fairfax's land about 1730. When the road was cut through Winchester to the Blue Ridge, Williams received permission to operate the ferry across the Shenandoah River. He sold his license to Edward Snickers about 1760. So many pioneers crossed here that they eventually renamed the gap for the friendly ferryman. Relatively low, this pass is 1,150 feet above sea level. *See: Bluemont; Middleburg; Winchester*

SNOWDEN
Buckingham County

On the south side of the James River, across from Scottsville, was Snowden, the home of Thomas Jefferson's forgotten younger brother, Randolph. He was married to Anne Jefferson Lewis, a distant cousin, who came from Albemarle County. The Jefferson family's roots were deep in Virginia by Revolutionary times. The first Thomas Jefferson came to the colony in 1612. He was a member of the Assembly in 1619. This estate was named for the highest mountain in Wales, Mount Snowdon.

SOMERSET
Orange County

Somerset is a county in southwestern England on the Bristol Channel. Many colonists came from that region. The name was used by James Madison's sister for the home she built not far from Montpelier. The present hamlet took its name from the estate, not from the English shire.

SOUTHAMPTON COUNTY

Formed from parts of Isle of Wight and Nansemond in 1748, this county was named for the Earl of Southampton, Henry Wriothesly, for whom the town of Hampton and Hampton Roads were also named. When this county was formed, the courthouse was

HENRY WRIOTHESLY
THIRD EARL OF SOUTHAMPTON
SOUTHAMPTON COUNTY

built in a tiny community named Jerusalem. Forty years later, the name Jerusalem was dropped in favor of Courtland.

Nat Turner, a slave, led an uprising in August of 1831 that terrorized this county for two days. The wave of killings began near Cross Keys and swept eastward to the county seat. Before the insurrection was quelled, sixty whites had been brutally murdered. *See: Smythe's Hundred*

SOUTH BOSTON
Halifax County   **City**

For many years there were two settlements in Virginia named Boston, both honoring the port city in Massachusetts. When Boston was closed by the British in response to the famed Tea Party, Virginians passed resolutions of support for their New England compatriots. This support from the gentry of the oldest, largest, and the richest of the thirteen colonies gave encouragement to the people of the northern regions and probably had a lot to do with their acceptance of the idea of independence which was first proposed by a Virginian. When this city was chartered as a town in 1796, it was named South Boston to avoid confusion with the other village of Boston in Culpeper County. *See: Boston*

SOUTH HILL
Mecklenburg County   **Town**

True hills in this part of Virginia are hard to find. However, the land is rolling and there are high rises of the terrain which the local people call hills. At the beginning of the nineteenth century, a church and a school were established near the highest elevation, a well known landmark. To give directions to those who sought the church, the members said it was "south of the hill," and soon South Hill was the accepted name for the church and the school. In 1814, a post office was established near the church which was given the familiar name. When the post office was moved many miles away, in 1867, to be closer to the stage stop at an inn on the Boydton-Petersburg Road, the name South Hill went with it.

SOUTH RIVER

This is a tributary of the South Fork of the Shenandoah River. It runs briskly through the city of Waynesboro.

SOUTHSIDE VIRGINIA

The James River flows more or less in a west to east direction from the Blue Ridge

Mountains to Hampton Roads. As one floats down the waterway, the bank on the right is the south bank no matter what direction the river might take as it swirls and loops and bends through the heartland of the Commonwealth. Originally, all of the land on the southern side of the James was called the Surry Side (Surrey is on the south bank of the River Thames), but eventually it became known as South Side. When the boundary between Virginia and Carolina was drawn in 1728, the Appomattox River was the upper limit to Southside Virginia. As settlements grew, Southside contracted to the Blackwater River and then to the Meherrin. Now only those counties that border on North Carolina make up the region known as Southside Virginia.

To add a bit of confusion and to cling to an old term (as Virginians are so fond of doing) the people of Petersburg and Hopewell, on the south bank of the Appomattox River, still call their territory Southside Virginia.

Somewhere, about halfway to Tennessee, the lower counties of the Commonwealth are no longer Southside but are better known as Southwest Virginia. *See: Carolina; East Virginia; Northern Neck; Surry County*

SOUTHWEST MOUNTAINS

These mountains form the first ridges that must be crossed when moving westward from Chesapeake Bay. They were so named because they extend in a southwesterly direction from the upper Rappahannock to the James. Beyond the Southwest Mountains lie the Blue Ridge.

SPARTA
Caroline County

The people who first made their homes here felt the need to advertise their rough life by naming their village for the famous Sparta of ancient Greece.

SPEEDWELL
Wythe County

An iron smelter on Cripple Creek was called Speedwell Furnace for some unrecorded reason. Many people who lived here were associated with the furnace and kept the name for their community.

SPENCER
Henry County

D. H. Spencer owned a tobacco processing plant here in the days before the present century. His sons, James and John, added a sideline to the company to make the boxes in which the tobacco products (mainly chew) were shipped. When the brothers took over the active management of the company, renamed Spencer Bros., the best sellers were two brands of plug and twist. One was Old Crow, possibly for a popular whiskey. The other, Calhoun, was named after the two men had a chance meeting with the famous John C. Calhoun, the ardent Southerner.

SPIT

A long and very narrow piece of land that pokes into a body of water is called a spit because it resembles the slender rod upon which meat is impaled for broiling. *See: Cape; Willoughby Spit*

SPOTSYLVANIA COUNTY

Formed in December 1720, from parts of Essex, King and Queen, and King William, this county was named for Alexander Spotswood, the Governor of Virginia from 1710-1722. Since Spotswood owned 45,000 acres in this area, he was pleased to have the new county named for him, although being a landowner did not have much bearing on the matter. It was customary to honor the Governor this way, and he was neither the first nor the last to be so honored. Ironically, Spotswood's great home was in that part of Spotsylvania County that was cut off in 1734 to form Orange County. Many Civil War battles were fought in this region at Fredericksburg, Chancellorsville, The Wilderness, and Spotsylvania Court House. *See: Germanna*

SPRINGDALE
Frederick County

Springdale was the home of Colonel John Hite, the son of Joist Hite who led the pioneers into this territory about 1734. Not far away are the ruins of Hite's Fort. Springdale was built about 1753.

SPRINGFIELD
Fairfax County

When Fairfax County was organized in 1742, the county seat was first located at a place called Spring Field. It was situated between New Church Road (now Route 7) and Ox Road (now Route 123). The site was on the main highway that ran from Hunting Creek on the Potomac to the Blue Ridge Mountains. The six acres of land were donated by William Fairfax. After less than a decade the courthouse was moved to Alexandria. In 1952 the name was revived when a new community was founded many miles away. *See: Fairfax County*

SPRING HILL
Frederick County

This parcel was granted to Isaac Parkins by Governor William Gooch in 1735. It was purchased in 1764 by Frederick Koonrad who had come down from Pennsylvania. He first built a log cabin for his family and then erected a stone house that still stands. Frederick Koonrad was the progenitor of the large Conrad family of Virginia.

SPRING VALLEY
Albemarle County

In the southwestern portion of Albemarle County, in the section known as Wakefield Entry, was a large tract purchased in 1768 by Charles Massie. Among his many crops were apples. Massie was credited with the development and perfection of the Albemarle Pippin, reportedly the favorite apple of Queen Victoria.

STAFFORD COUNTY

Formed in 1664 from Westmoreland and originally a part of the Northern Neck Proprietary of Lord Fairfax, this county was named for Staffordshire, England. The first courthouse, at Marlborough Point, was replaced by a new one near the present boundary between King George and Stafford counties at a site still known as Courthouse Spring. When the present community of Stafford was created in 1715, it became the new county seat. The current courthouse dates from 1922. For many years, Stafford County was dominated by the many members of the influential Fitzhugh family. *See: Bedford and Chatham, both of Stafford*

STANARDSVILLE
Greene County   **Town**

When the courthouse was built for Greene County, Robert Stanards donated the land. In appreciation, the county seat was named for him.

STANLEY
Page County   **Town**

Stanley McNider was the son of the president of a company that located a factory here in the late nineteenth century. The collection of houses, built by the company for the workers, was named for Stanley. The town was incorporated in 1900.

STANLEY HUNDRED
Mulberry Island   **Site**

When Sir George Yeardley returned to Virginia in 1618 as the Governor, he claimed 1,000 acres on Mulberry Island where he hoped to establish a town. He named it Stanley Hundred for the rich family of England who had put up the funds for the transportation of colonists. Yeardley's mother-in-law was from this family. Yeardley's brother-in-law was Stanley Flowerdew who had come to Virginia in 1609 with his sister, Temperance. Both had taken one look at the colony and had immediately returned to England. However, when Sir George was named Governor, Lady Temperance came with him. She was the first Governor's wife to reside in the colony. Stanley Hundred did not prosper and soon was abandoned.

John Rolfe purchased some of this land, farmed it for a while, and then moved to Hog Island. Rolfe willed it to his third wife, Joan Pierce. The remainder of Stanley Hundred was purchased by Captain Thomas Flint who sold the land, at a good profit, to John Brewer in 1628. Miles Cary, Sr., acquired these 850 acres and passed them on to his son. Today all of the land is within the federal reservation of Fort Eustis. *See: Flowerdew Hundred; Fort Eustis; Magpie Swamp; Mulberry Island; Queen's Hith; Warwick River; Windmill Point*

STANLEYTOWN
Henry County

Thomas B. Stanley founded a furniture factory here to compete with the company at Bassett, a few miles away. Stanley also built homes for his employees and gave his name to the community when a post office was authorized.

STAUNTON
Augusta County   **City**

The first settler here was John Lewis who came from Ireland about 1732. He was the father of the Revolutionary War general Andrew Lewis. When Augusta County was reduced in size and reorganized in 1738, William Beverley, the richest man in these parts, donated twenty-five acres of land next to his mill for the new courthouse and jail, marking off lots for a properly laid out town. When there were sufficient people living here, they petitioned Governor Gooch to recognize it as a town. Gooch attempted to do so since the people had named it Staunton in honor of the Governor's wife, Lady Rebecca Staunton. For some reason, recognition was delayed for twenty years. The original pronunciation was STAWN-ton, and no one today knows why the local residents rather firmly insist that it be pronounced STAN-ton (as in Stanley).

Within sight of the preset city are two hills named Betsy Bell and Mary Gray. They were two girls who died of the plague near Perth, Scotland, in 1645, and were the main characters in a sad ballad which the Scots brought with them when they settled in with the Irish.

President Woodrow Wilson, was born in the Presbyterian manse in 1856. He was the son of the Reverend Joseph Wilson and his wife, Jessie. The manse, now a shrine, is open to the public. *See: Augusta County; Blandfield; Manor Manion; Three Chopt Road*

STAUNTON RIVER

The section of the Roanoke River between Brookneal and Clarksville has been called the Staunton River for many years. No one seems to know why. Below the John H. Kerr Dam, which creates Buggs Island Lake, the river resumes its correct name all the way across northwestern North Carolina to Albemarle Sound. Even map makers these days are uncertain about applying the name Staunton to the section of the river. It usually is shown as "(Staunton)". The Roanoke River was named for the old Indian medium of exchange, called *rhoanoke. See: Peake, Roanoke*

STEELE'S TAVERN
Augusta County

Known for a brief time as Midway, the colonial tavern was named for (and possibly by) Daniel Steele, a Revolutionary War veteran.

STEPHENS CITY
Frederick County   **Town**

This town was laid out in 1758 on land owned by Peter Stephens. Since it was close to the older town of Winchester, an early name was Newtown. This caused confusion with the Newtown near Norfolk, and the present name was adopted when the post office was established. *See: Newtown; Winchester*

STERLING
Loudoun County

Early residents here called their village

Guilford for the Revolutionary War Battle at Guilford Court House in North Carolina. Too many other towns adopted the name Guilford so another one had to be selected. The largest estate here was Sterling Farm which provided an obvious choice.

STEVENSBURG
Culpeper County

The oldest village in Culpeper County, this community was called York long before the county was organized in 1748. Because the name York was in such common use throughout Virginia, the citizens renamed their settlement for General Edward Stevens who was a local hero of the Revolution. The general died in 1820.

STEWARTSVILLE
Bedford County

Once known by the simpler name Crossroads, the principal property owners here gave their name when the post office was opened. They were the Stewart brothers.

STINGRAY POINT
Middlesex County

In June of 1608, while returning from an exploratory trip up the Chesapeake Bay, Capt. John Smith speared a strange fish-like creature with his sword. Unaware of the poison dart at the end of the tail, he was badly stung on the arm as he unskewered the writhing creature. According to Walter Russel, a member of the party who co-authored an account of the trip, "...no blood or wound was seen, but a little blue spot; but the torment was instantly so extreme that in four hours had so swollen his hand, arm and shoulder, we all with much sorrow...prepared his grave inland on an island (near) by, as himself directed; yet it pleased God by precious oil Doctor Russel at first applied to it when he sounded it with a probe, ere night his tormenting pain so well assuaged that he (ate of the flesh) of the fish (for) his supper, which gave us no less joy and content to us than ease to himself. For which we called the (place) Stingray Isle after the name of the fish."

Rays are still occasionally seen in the Chesapeake Bay. They can have a wing span of up to six feet and may have a five inch double-barbed stinger at the end of a four foot long tail. They have powerful jaws and can crack open oysters which make them the enemy of watermen. They do not attack humans but can swim close by and whip their tails in defense. It was not reported how large the ray was that stung John Smith, but from his reaction and the fact that it had a stinger two or three inches long, it probably had a wing-span of about three feet. Marine biologists and medical experts say that John Smith was lucky to survive.

STONEGA
Wise County

To be different, when the post office here needed a name, Stone Gap was combined into one word with the final letter omitted. *See: Naxera*

STONE HOUSE
Henrico County   **Site**

The exact location of the stone house that William Byrd built near the present city of Richmond cannot be determined. So often has the James River flooded that all traces of the house have been washed away. It is thought to have been located on the south bank. William Byrd had come to Virginia to help his uncle, Thomas Stegge, manage a trading post. When Stegge died suddenly, the business was inherited by the young nephew who slowly accumulated a modest fortune. He was forced to move to higher ground in 1685 after a terrible flood nearly wiped out his assets. He built a house on the Richmond side of the river, on Shoccoe Hill, which he named Belvedere. *See: Belle Aire; Richmond; Westover*

STONY CREEK
Sussex County   **Town**

The nearby creek, shallow and full of stones, is aptly named. A warehouse to hold the products of the local farms, built near its course, was called Stony Creek Warehouse when the railroad built a line through this region.

STRASBURG
Shenandoah County   **Town**

Peter Stover purchased land here in 1749 and sent word to his friend, Josiah Hite, that there was good land available for settlement. Hite came to Virginia with a group of people who named their new village Strasburg for the city in Alsace from which many of them had come. Although sometimes called Staufferstadt (that is, Stover's town) it became officially Strasburg in 1761. In times past, this was also known as Funk's Mill and Funkstown, for a local miller.

STRATFORD HALL
Westmoreland County

About 1725, Thomas Lee of Machodoc, then the President of the Council, completed this great house. The H-shaped building, marked by two massive chimney turrets with four flues each, has none of the curves and gracefully flowing lines of other manor houses of the period. Of the same vintage as Rosewell, and equally solid, Stratford Hall commands a magnificent view of the Poto-

STRATFORD HALL

mac. The main floor is high above a basement that is level with the ground. Between the two chimney stacks is an open promenade where, it is said, Phillip Ludwell Lee often employed musicians to play for the pleasure of his daughters and their visiting swains.

Phillip Ludwell Lee had studied law at the Inner Temple of London and, upon inheriting the estate, involved himself with county affairs. His daughter Matilda married a cousin, Henry "Light Horse Harry" Lee, by whom she had a son, also named Henry, who was known as "Black Horse Harry" to distinguish him from his father. When Matilda died, "Light Horse Harry" Lee married Anne Hill Carter of Shirley. Her son, born at Stratford Hall, was the famous Robert E. Lee, the great Confederate general.

Also born in this mansion house were Robert's uncles, Richard Henry Lee and Francis Lightfoot Lee, both signers of the Declaration of Independence. The last of the Lee family to live here was Major Henry Lee, the son of Francis Lightfoot, who died in 1822. *See: Belmont of Loudoun; Berry Hill; Burnt House Field; Chantilly; Clifts; Cobbs Hall of Lancaster; Ditchley; Kiskiak; Langley; Lee County; Machodoc; Menokin; Peckatone; Sully*

STRATTON MANOR
Northampton County

Near the present town of Cape Charles, on the bay side of the Eastern Shore, is Stratton Manor. Built by Thomas Stratton about 1657, it was modernized in 1764. During Bacon's Rebellion, Governor William Berkeley took refuge here as an uninvited guest. He commandeered one of Stratton's vessels which was wrecked through poor seamanship. The Governor did not compensate his host for the loss. Berkeley's haughty attitude lost him the loyalty of many Virginians who were rather glad to see him leave for England to explain his conduct to King Charles II in 1676. Sometimes Stratton Manor was called Old Castle, but just why is not clear. Perhaps the original owner applied it in memory of an old castle near the town of his birth in England. Possibly it was named in derision by the locals. *See: Arlington of Northampton; Bacon's Castle; Savage Neck*

STRAWBERRY BANK
Hampton

Nobody today really knows exactly where the newly-arrived Englishmen found a bank covered with wild strawberries when they first visited the Indian village of Kiccowtan on April 30, 1607. Most probably it was in the vicinity of the present motel of the same name near the ruins of the old manor house that burned a few years ago.

In 1707, Bertrand Servant gave to his son-in-law Francis Ballard the "plantation that Sam Selden called Strawberry Banks." In 1647 Sam Selden bought the 600 acre tract from Colonel William Clairborne.

A curious sidelight of the name is that it appears in New England, undoubtedly transported there by Captain John Smith who explored and mapped the upper region of America in 1614 and gave it its name, New England. His observation of the terrain, plus the advice that he had written to would-be colonists based on his own two years in Virginia, helped the Pilgrims avoid many errors that had been made by the Jamestowners. Without question, John Smith must be recognized as the father of the two major colonies that led the Revolution: Virginia and Massachusetts. *See: Buckroe; Hampton; New Kent County*

STUART
Patrick County   **Town**

First known as Taylorsville, the town's name was changed in 1884 to honor the dashing Confederate general, Jeb Stuart, who was born near here on February 6, 1833. He was mortally wounded while leading his cavalrymen in a minor action at Yellow Tavern just before the War Between the States ended. Lee called Jeb Stuart the "Eyes of the Army." When he died in Richmond, the people of the city knew the end of the conflict was near, for without their heroes, Stonewall Jackson and Stuart, the army could not fight as well.

STUART'S DRAFT
Augusta County

The first settlers here were related to Colonel William Preston of Smithfield Plantation in Montgomery County. This name is one of the great mysteries of this collection. Stuart's Draft has been known for many generations, yet no one seems to know the origin, especially the word draft. In some parts of West Virginia and the Midwest, a draft is a shallow part of a river where a crossing can be made (a ford). Since this small community is near the South River, that definition may well apply. However, others insist that a draft is an open field where the air is in constant motion, and the land here certainly is open and steadily cooled by air that tumbles down from the mountains not too far away. Draft also is a measure of liquid, and a method of brewing beer; it describes a workhorse (draft horse); it is the first version of something written; it is a promise of payment such as a mortgage or a check. The word draft does not appear anywhere else in Virginia in connection with a place name.

STUDLEY
Hanover County

John Henry came to Virginia in the early eighteenth century. He lived with a fellow Scot, John Syme, on a large farm, called Studley, about seven miles southeast of Hanover Court House. When Colonel Syme died suddenly in 1731, John Henry purchased 1,200 acres of the farm from the widow and moved to his own modest house for the sake of propriety. Two years later, he married the Widow Syme and moved back into her house. At Studley, the new Mrs. Henry's second son was born on May 19, 1736. He was named for his uncle, the Reverend Patrick Henry, and for that reason the great orator always signed his name Patrick Henry, Jr. When John Syme II came of age, John Henry moved his family back to his own land which he had named Mount Brilliant.

The foundations for Studley, named for a small hamlet in Scotland, were uncovered in 1936. An insurance policy, dated 1796, mentions a two-story brick dwelling with an outside nursery, kitchen, storehouse, dairy, and the other usual necessary dependencies. *See: Red Hill; Scotchtown*

SUFFOLK
City

First settlement was attempted here about ten years after the founding of Jamestown, but the Massacre of 1622 frightened the English away for many years. The Nansemond Indians of the region always had been unfriendly and it was not until they were wiped out in the war of revenge in the years following the massacre that settlement was tried again. By 1637 enough brave Englishmen were living on the Nansemond River to qualify as a county. Although the courthouse was located at the end of deep water, there were so few homes near it that the town of Suffolk was not recognized until 1742. It was named for the English shire of East Anglia which adjoins Norfolkshire.

The little village was pillaged and burned to the ground in 1779 by British General Edward Matthews, but it was rebuilt after the Revolution. For many years it slumbered peacefully as the county seat of Nansemond and became the peanut capital of Virginia during the post-Civil War period when that crop was given prominence by the internationally known Planters Peanuts Company, headquartered in Suffolk.

In 1974 the city merged with Nansemond County to form the largest city in the Commonwealth (in area) and the fifth largest in the United States. Its area is 430 square miles, mostly rural. *See: Fort Nelson; Nansemond County*

SUGAR GROVE
Smyth County

This village was named for a large grove of sugar maple trees that grow nearby. Virginia is a major producer of maple syrup that is shipped to New England for marketing.

SULLY
Fairfax County

Richard Bland Lee, one of the Westmoreland Lees, built his home here in 1794 on land that his grandfather had acquired nearly seventy years before. As was the case of Chantilly, the estate of Richard Henry Lee, Sully was named for a French chateau, the home of the Bourbon king of France. Richard Bland Lee married the daughter of a wealthy Quaker of Philadelphia. He furnished his home with many fine pieces made in eastern Pennsylvania, purchased thirty slaves to work his land and serve within the house, and produced great harvests of fruit and grain.

In 1842, Sully passed out of the Lee family when it was purchased by a New York Quaker, Jacob Haight. When the Civil War exploded in violence, most of the Haight family sought safety in Alexandria behind Union lines. Two brave women, Maria Barlow and Phoebe Haight, although Quakers and pacifists, courageously stayed at Sully to protect it from both Northern and Southern foragers whom roamed the region. The women managed to save the house, but were helpless to prevent the foragers stealing the horses and cattle and stripping the fields. Sully plantation never recovered from these losses and it went into a severe decline during Reconstruction.

The house was rescued from collapse by the Federal government in 1962. The interior has been refurnished with antiques of the early Federal period by the Fairfax County Park Authority. *See: Chantilly; Jordan's Point; Langley*

SUMMER HILL
Arlington County   **Site**

Between the northern Abingdon and the mouth of Four Mile Creek lay 150 acres of good bottomland that had been claimed prior to 1687 by John Pimmitt. He sold the land to John Alexander, the surveyor and founder of Alexandria, who sold it to Thomas Pearson in 1732. Pearson passed it on to his daughter, Constantia, in his will. When she married Nathaniel Chapman, they decided to build a home on the land overlooking the Potomac River. They named their place Summer Hill.

It remained in the Chapman family until it was purchased by the Federal government in 1940. The buildings were razed, the land leveled, and Summer Hill became Washington's National Airport. *See: Abingdon of Arlington*

SUNSET HILLS
Fairfax County

Whoever named this little village was poetically inclined. When the sun sets behind the Bull Run Mountains, it produces a spectacular sight.

SURRY COUNTY

In the beginning of the Virginia colony, the south side of the James River, opposite Jamestown, was the Indian territory of Tappahannah, named for the chief. Within a few years, the Indian name was replaced with Surry in remembrance of the county in England on the south bank of the River Thames across from London. The mildly homesick colonists often used familiar names, with the exception of the name London itself. The first person to permanently settle on the "Surrey Side" was John Martin, the renegade, who established Martin's Brandon in the autumn of 1610 and had it declared a Particular Plantation in 1617. Others who followed Martin were Samuel Maycock in 1618, and Richard Pace in 1620.

Until 1652, all of this territory was a part of James City County because the population was rather thin and was clustered primarily along the river. When the county was formed, it was named Surry County, spelled without the "e" through some clerical error which no one has bothered to correct down through the years. The county seat of Surry was established in a new town a few miles inland rather than at the water's edge, reflecting the growth of home and farms in the interior made possible when the Indians were either dead or had moved away. *See:*

Flowerdew Hundred; Hog Island; James City County; Maycocks; Pace's Paines; Southside Virginia; Sussex County; Tappahanna

SUSQUEHANNOCK INDIANS

This tribe of Iroquoian stock lived in a collection of fortified towns on the Maryland side of upper Chesapeake Bay. During the seventeenth century, they numbered about 600 warriors, and were strong enough to resist paying tribute to Powhatan. A large group of them migrated to the Virginia side, in the region of Colchester, where they became peaceful fur traders with the colonists. They were described as tall, handsome people of great strength and fortitude. Unfortunately, they were mistakenly attacked by a group of Virginians and Marylanders who were out to punish the Senecas. This outrage put the Susquennocks on the warpath for two years. They were pressed southward by Nathaniel Bacon's men and, in 1676, were completely wiped out in the attack at Occaneechee. *See: Curles; Occaneechee; Piscataway Indians*

SUSSEX COUNTY

Broken off from Surry in 1753, this county is situated in the Hunting Quarter Creek section of the Nottoway River basin. It was named for the English shire that lies directly south of Surrey and borders on the English Channel. The courthouse, in the village of Sussex, is in the center of the County. *See: Middlesex*

SUTHERLAND
Dinwiddie County

Fendall Charles Sutherland built his home about 1803 near the fork of Namozine and Cox roads. At a tavern where the two roads join, stagecoach passengers refreshed themselves, sometimes remaining overnight. By the time of the Civil War, Smith's Ordinary had been expanded to fourteen rooms. It was used as a temporary military hospital after the Battle of Five Forks in the early spring of 1865 and then slowly fell apart when travel throughout Virginia was halted for several decades in the severe economic times of Reconstruction. A small community developed near the old tavern, called Fork Inn, when the first post office was established. The name was changed to Sutherland to honor the early family. By coincidence, at the time of the name change, the postmaster was Winston Sutherland.

SWANNANOA
Augusta County

Built of Georgian marble and matching stone, this mansion was named by the wife of the man who owned it, Sally May Dooley. She was overly fond of swans, collecting figurines of the graceful creatures, inserting them into furnishings wherever possible. Her bed, in the winter home near Richmond, called Maymont, was in the shape of a huge swan and, in the lake near Maymont, which, of course, was called Swan Lake, she had a small flock. Her husband, Major James Dooley, one of America's millionaires, had this place erected atop Afton Mountain overlooking the western edge of Virginia's Piedmont on one side and the Shenandoah Valley on the other. The Dooleys called it their summer place. With terraced gardens all about, it simulates the Villa Medici of Rome. Within are Tiffany windows, works of art, magnificent wall panels, gold plumbing fixtures over marble tubs and sinks, and gigantic rooms on the lower floor. Three hundred artisans spent eight years completing it, and it was first occupied in 1912. After all the work and expense, it was used only for a few years. After standing empty during the Great Depression, it was leased in 1949 by Dr. Walter Russell, a noted artist, sculptor and writer. He made it the headquarters for his "University of Science and Philosophy." Swannanoa is now open to the public as a curiosity of a bygone age of affluence. *See: Maymont*

SWANN'S POINT
Surry County   **Site**

The first settler in this locality was Francis Chapman who patented land here in 1620. It was next owned by his father-in-law, William Perry, and for many years thereafter this estate was called Perryes Point. In 1635, William Swann, the Collector of Royal Customs, acquired 1,200 acres for transporting twenty-four people to the colony. They settled on his land which became known as Swann's Point.

A son, Colonel Thomas Swann, born in Jamestown in 1616, occupied his father's land about 1645. He served as a Burgess for the district and was appointed to the Council in 1660. He broke with Governor William Berekeley during Bacon's Rebellion but did not actively side with the rebels. The English commissioners who were sent over by the Crown in 1677 to investigate the rebellion stayed with Colonel Swann when Berkeley refused to receive them at his home, Green Spring. The commissioners, Sir John Berry

and Francis Moryson, invited the general populace to make known any grievances they might have against the Governor, especially his manner of provoking and then suppressing Bacon's Rebellion. The complaints were numerous.

The original house at Swann's Point was shelled several times by Union gunboats during the Civil War and, because it was so badly damaged, had to be torn down. The only trace of the Swann family today is a stone marking the grave of Colonel Thomas Swann dated "ye 16th day of September in Ye Yeare of our Lord God 1680." Swann was the sheriff of Surry County, a justice of the peace, and a Burgess. For many years the Jamestown ferry docked here until the ship was abandoned and a new one was built at Scotland Wharf. *See: Green Spring*

SWEET BRIAR COLLEGE
Amherst County

Established under the will of Indiana Fletcher Williams as a memorial to her only daughter, this liberal arts college for women opened its doors in 1906. It is located on a 2,800-acre tract once owned by Elijah Fletcher, a Vermont scholar who came to Virginia in 1810 to make his fortune in tobacco and real estate. He called his home Sweet Briar for the profusion of wild roses that grow here.

SWEET HALL
King William County

Thomas Claiborne, a descendant of William Claiborne of Kent Island, built his home here about 1720. There was no particular reason for the name Sweet Hall; that is, none has been recorded. A portion of this estate, directly on the Pamunkey River, was called Tuckacommon, obviously an Indian word but undefined. Thomas Claiborne's son, Augustine, built his home at Windsor Shades about a mile away in 1750. *See: New Kent County; Romancoke; Tuckahoe*

SWIFT RUN GAP

One of the few passes through the Blue Ridge Mountains, this gap was cut by Swift Run thousands of years ago. On September 5, 1715, Governor Alexander Spotswood and a party of thirteen gentlemen explorers (accompanied by many servants, much food, and a good supply of wines) passed through this gap enroute to the Shenandoah Valley. As they did on all special occasions, which occurred daily, they celebrated their passage with a series of toasts. Spotswood gave each gentleman of the party a golden horseshoe after their return as a memento of the journey. They were dubbed The Knights of the Golden Horseshoe. *See: Germanna; Rocktown; Rockfish Gap; Run; Shenandoah Valley; Wood's Gap*

SYCAMORE TAVERN
Hanover County

This old tavern, still standing, was identified by a huge sycamore tree close by. It was the fourth stop between Charlottesville and Richmond on the old Three Chopt Road.

SYLVATUS
Carroll County

Sylvatus Smith was a local character when the post office was established near the local mines. In good humor—but possibly as a sly jest—the hamlet was named for good old Sylvatus.

SYRIA
Madison County

Names of places mentioned in the Bible, particularly the Old Testament, were popular during colonial days. This hamlet is in the center of peach and apple production for this region. No one remembers who suggested the name Syria for the collection of homes. The early settlers were of German origin. *See: Fluvanna County*

T

TABB
York County

Miss Sally Tabb, a local resident, was active in community affairs. When the post office was opened here, the residents named it for her. *See: Haw Branch; Toddsbury*

TALLEYSVILLE
New Kent County

This hamlet was the seat of one branch of the Talley family prior to the Civil War. When a Confederate Army engineer prepared a map of the vicinity, he showed a small collection of homes where the stage road between Richmond and Williamsburg crossed the road to White House. The crossroads was marked Talley'sville. When the Tally family moved away, the name remained.

TANGIER ISLAND
Chesapeake Bay   **Town**

This island in the Chesapeake Bay, about midway up Virginia's portion, was discovered by Captain John Smith in 1608 during his exploratory trip in search of a western passage to the "far ocean." He found natives making pottery and learned that the Indian word for pottery was *tanja*. Whether he or others who came later changed it to Tangier is unknown.

In 1670 Ambrose White laid claim to the island which the people of the Eastern Shore called the Western Isle. It was not until 1686 that a group from Cornwall, England settled here. John Crockett and his sons' families were the first settlers to make their homes in the insect-infested island which has changed shape for hundreds of years as storms silt in the channel and wash away the other side. Efforts are being made today to build stone barriers to keep the island from disappearing.

In 1814 Tangier Island was temporarily occupied by British Admiral Sir George Cockburn after he had pillaged Norfolk, Suffolk, and Hampton. From here he moved up the bay to burn a portion of Washington, D.C. and attack Baltimore. *See: Pungoteague*

TAPPAHANNOCK
Essex County   **Town**

A warehouse and trading post were established here in the mid-1600s by Jacob Hobbs. He had no designs to create a town and thought so little of the location that he called it Hobbs His Hole. A small community gradually developed after all and became a port in 1680 where customs were collected. Its name then was New Plymouth. A map of 1705 shows it as Tappanhannocke Towne, named for the chief Tappahanna. The river on which it is situated, the Rappahannock, is also an Indian word meaning "rise and fall of water." *See: Essex County; Rappahannock*

TASLEY
Accomack County

The Tazewell family owned much land on the Eastern Shore. Careless spelling corrupted the name from Tazewell to Tasley during the nineteenth century.

TAVERN

The terms tavern, inn, and ordinary were interchangeably used in colonial Virginia. In England there was a distinction: a tavern was a place where alcoholic beverages were sold; an inn afforded overnight lodging; an ordinary was the common dining room of an inn where the ordinary people could be served (as opposed to a private dining room). One could not be certain in the colonies which term applied. As a general rule, however, a tavern or an ordinary in the hinterlands along a major road offered some sort of food and lodging although it was not unusual to have to share a bed with several others. The traveler provided his own blanket which came from under his saddle. The bed often was nothing more than a straw pallet held off the floor by ropes. The food was simple, often atrocious; the beverages were beer, ale, hard cider, or rum. *See: Ordinary*

TAYLOE'S FURNACE
Stafford County   **Site**

Iron was mined near the courthouse as early as 1728. John Tayloe had a smelter here on the stream. As was the case with most iron mines and allied metal operations in Virginia, the enterprise began with high hopes but ended after a few years when the small supply of ore was exhausted. *See: Bristol Iron Works; Furnace; Germanna; Hazlewood; Wilderness*

TAZEWELL COUNTY

Parts of Russell and Wythe were separated to form this county in 1799. It was named for Henry Tazewell, U.S. Senator from Virginia from 1794-1799. The county seat, an incorporated town, bears the same name. *See: Pocahontas Coal Mine*

TEDINGTON
See: Lightfoot

TEMPERANCEVILLE
Accomack County

Settled by Quakers in the middle of the seventeenth century, this town was named for a Mr. Temperance on whose farm the meeting house was built. Most of these Quakers moved north into Delaware and Pennsylvania when Virginia passed laws against their form of worship in 1657. About twenty-five years later, the Reverend Francis Makemie, a Presbyterian, came to the Eastern Shore with a license to preach as long as he used the Anglican *Book of Common Prayer*. He settled first in Onancock where he married the daughter of a wealthy merchant. After organizing a church in Onancock, he received permission to establish another church farther up the Eastern Shore. Choosing Temperanceville, where he built his home, Francis Makemie imported two more Presbyterian ministers. Moving to Pennsylvania where worship laws were not so strict, he formed the first Presbyterian Synod in 1706. Makemie is called the father of Presbyterianism in America. Upon his retirement, he returned to Temperanceville where he lived in peace and is buried near his home. Both the grave and house site are marked but no trace of his dwelling remains. *See: Accomack County; Onancock; New Church*

TEMPLEMAN
Westmoreland County

Until the postal authorities got sloppy about proper punctuation, this crossroads hamlet was Templeman's, a reminder that many years ago Templeman's Store served the neighborhood with general merchandise and food staples.

TERRELL'S ORDINARY
Albemarle County   **Site**

On the Three Chopt Road, about eight miles west of Swan Tavern in Charlottesville, stood one of the few taverns which provided overnight lodging. Most of the others were only way stations providing food and drink. Of course, Terrell's is not to be compared to a modern motel (or even the roadside tourist cabins which dotted the countryside some fifty years ago) for the beds were shared and often were nothing more than a straw ticking on a rope frame without blankets or pillow. This ordinary, owned and run by the Lewis family for many years, competed for trade with Ivy Tavern not too far away. *See: Ivy Tavern; Ordinary; Tavern*

THIMBLE LIGHT

At the lower end of Chesapeake Bay, mariners are careful to avoid the Horseshoe, a long shoal that stretches out from Buckroe to the Capes. The lighthouse at Point Comfort is an aid, but ships still run aground while trying to keep within the natural channel that bends to the southwest into Hampton Roads. When the channel was deepened by dredging to accommodate the giant vessels of the twentieth century, a caisson-styled marker was erected which, because it resembled a huge, inverted thimble, was dubbed Thimble Light. For many years, members of the Coast Guard lived within the steel cylinder. It was a noisy existence. Today, Thimble Light is automated. Even so, ships still run afoul of the shoal. The most celebrated case was the battleship *Missouri* which was stuck for a week when it cut too close to the Horseshoe.

THOROUGHFARE GAP

At the northern end of the Shenandoah Valley is a gap through the Bull Run Mountains with a relatively low elevation of 399 feet. A road was opened through it in 1812. Later the Manassas Railroad used this pass heading for Covington.

THOROUGHGOOD HOUSE
Virginia Beach

Adam Thoroughgood came from Lynn, England, in 1621 and settled first at Kecoughtan. He received a patent for land in 1634 and built his modest home a few years later on the western side of Lynnhaven Bay. Thoroughgood died in 1640, a relatively wealthy man although he believed in living modestly. His house is reported to be the oldest brick house in English America. It suffered periods of decay but was restored some years ago and now is an excellent example of a seventeenth century home. In some early writing, the merchant's name is spelled Thorowgood, with his home called Old Lynnhaven. *See: Belle Air of Charles City; Lynnhaven Bay*

THREE CHOPT ROAD

The origins of this old road are lost in the mist of early Virginia legends. It began at

AMERICAN STAGEWAGON, THREE CHOPT ROAD

Powhatan's village of Orapax southeast of Richmond and ended in the Valley at Staunton. An early pioneer blazed the trail by marking trees along the way with three chops of an axe, one above the other, hence, the name. The trail, well-planned, required the crossing of only one major stream, that being the Rivanna just east of the village of Charlottesville at Secretary's Ford. The Blue Ridge Mountains were crossed at Wood's Gap (now called Jarman's Gap). A series of taverns paced the distance, usually separated by about ten miles. Beginning at Richmond, the road passed Willis' Tavern, Short Pump, Poore's, Trevillian's, Sampson's, Parish, Phillip's, Haden's, Jennings', Zion, Boswell's, and the Swan Tavern at Charlottesville. From there to the west were fewer places— Ivy Creek, Terrell's, Wood's, and Yancey's Mill. The Three Chopt Road is sometimes spelled Three Chopped, Three Chop, or Three Notch. Other roads were marked with different blazes cut into the trunks of trees. Some were arranged into triangles or squares, some used a combination of chops and cross marks. Those who cut the bark away to the lighter wood were careful not to

ring the tree to make certain it did not die. Travelers removed low hanging branches or other growths that obscured the markers. *See: Charlottesville; Iroquois Trail; Orapax; Secretary's Ford; River Road*

TIDEWATER

The entire coastal plain of the Chesapeake Bay and its tributaries is the true Tidewater region of Virginia. Tidal action in the Potomac, Rappahannock, Piankatank, York, James, Nansemond, and Appomattox rivers extends all the way to the fall line. A tremendous flood of water twice a day flows in and out through the Capes. Therefore, to be accurate, Tidewater Virginia extends up the James as far as Richmond and up the Potomac as far as Washington. Historically, the Tidewater region has been limited to the southeastern part of the Commonwealth including all of the Peninsula and the eastern end of the Middle Peninsula. Modern residents tend to limit Tidewater to the area of Hampton Roads. A disturbing trend is being set by "come-heres" to limit Tidewater to Norfolk, Virginia Beach, and Portsmouth, especially TV newscasters, real estate developers and untutored hucksters. These cities are more properly South Hampton Roads, a part of Tidewater.

TIMBERNECK HALL
Gloucester County   **Site**

Located at the York River, not far from Powhatan's Chimney, this was the late seventeenth century home of John Mann, progenitor of the large and active Virginia family. His descendants were the builders of Rosewell, Mannsfield, and a host of other fine homes. The present frame house here, built about 1776 by John Catlett, was occupied through the fifth generation of the Mann family. There is evidence that at least two other houses were built earlier on this site. Just prior to the Civil War, Bishop Meade visited the place and reported finding tombstones lying near the stable yard, the earliest of which was dated 1693. John Mann I and his wife are buried here. He died in 1694. The land originally had been granted in 1639 to George Menefie, Esq., by Governor Sir Francis Wyatt. The 3,000 acres extended along "Timber Necke Creek." Not far from here, on Tydall's Neck, a fort was constructed by Governor Berkeley in 1667 to protect the mouth of the York River. *See: Mannsfield; Rosewell; Tyndall's Neck; Yorktown*

TIMBER RIDGE CHURCH
Rockbridge County

Founded in 1746 by the Scotch-Irish Presbyterians who settled in this section of the Shenandoah Valley, the old stone church has been standing since 1756. Sam Houston, the first president of Texas and a descendant of these settlers, was born not far from the church in 1793.

TIMBERVILLE
Rockingham County   **Town**

This small town in the heavily-wooded northern section of the county has had a variety of names: Williamsport, Thompson's Store, and Riddle's Tavern. For some reason, when the post office was established in 1827, none of these names were used but Timberville was officially recorded.

TINKER MOUNTAIN
Botetourt County

Deserters from both British and American armies hid in the secret glens of this mountain until the war was over. During their selfimposed exile, they supported themselves as itinerant tinkers, repairing

household items or farm equipment for women who were left behind by their more patriotic husbands. Although a person who makes tinware is called a tinker, a tinker also is anyone who can do odd jobs. The expression "tinker with" is still used today.

TOANO
James City County

Although there is no proof, local lore insists that Toano was an Indian who lived here many years ago.

TODDSBURY
Gloucester County

Toddsbury stands on the edge of Mobjack Bay's North River as "The Jewel of Tidewater." The oldest part of the house was built in 1658 by Thomas Todd, the first of the family to come to Virginia. He was the great-grandson of Sir Edwin Sandys, Archbishop of York. Thomas Todd II, born at Toddsbury in 1660, produced a son, Thomas III, who was one of the planners of the city of Baltimore. After four generations of Todds, the family name changed when Mary Todd married her cousin Phillip Tabb. These young people inherited the estate from their uncle, Christopher Todd, who had made numerous improvements to the house in 1722. Other modernizations to Toddsbury were made in 1784 and in the present century. *See: Haw Branch; Tabb*

TODDS TAVERN
Spotsylvania County

At the western end of this county, on the road from Orange Court House to Germanna, William Todd settled on a grant of 4,673 acres in 1726. Either he or a descendant of the same name operated a tavern around which this village grew.

TODD'S WHARF
King William County   **Site**

An important shipping point was located here in the mid-eighteenth century. During the 1750s, William Todd owned the bridge, warehouse, and wharf at the head of navigation on the Mattaponi River. He handled the tobacco grown at Fairfield, Bassetaire, and other farms in the region. During Washington's time, Todd's Wharf was a fair-sized settlement. William Todd's home, located on a high spot of ground nearby, was called The Mount.

TOMS BROOK
Shenandoah County   **Town**

Some time in the dim decades before the Civil War, a drifter named Tom received permission to build a cabin on a creek that ran through Donovan's farm. Nothing is known of either Tom or Donovan. However, the cabin builder must have made an impression upon the local residents for they soon called the stream Tom's Creek. The name later was corrected to Tom's Brook when a few more dwellings were erected along its banks. By 1842, enough Lutherans had settled nearby to build a church (now called Old Brook Union.) Although loyalties ran both ways in the Valley at the outbreak of the Civil War, the men of Tom's Brook organized themselves into an infantry company which was accepted as part of the famed Stonewall Brigade. The residents here claim there is no other Toms Brook in the U.S. Postal Register. However, there is a hamlet by the name of Toms Creek in Dickenson County, Virginia.

TOTERO
This was the Indian name for Big Lick salt marsh which is now covered by the city of Roanoke. *See: Big Lick; Occaneechee; Roanoke*

TOTOPOTOMOI CREEK
Hanover County

This minor stream honors an Indian chief of the Pamunkey tribe. In 1656, Totopotomoi and 100 of his faithful braves placed themselves under the leadership of Colonel Edward Hill of Shirley, to fight the Senecas who had come down from the Delaware Bay area to raid, steal, and murder. Colonel Hill had an equal number of settlers of the Henrico militia. He was such a bad military leader that his combined forces were mauled in the fray. Totopotomoi and all of his warriors were killed. Hill and a few militiamen straggled home in disgrace.

For his mishandling of the affair, Colonel Hill was found "guilty of crimes and weakness" by a unanimous vote of both the House of Burgesses and the Council. Governor William Berkeley was so outraged at the disaster that he struck Colonel Hill full in the mouth with the head of his walking stick, knocking out many teeth. For his guilt, the master of Shirley was suspended from all civil and military offices, and was ordered to pay the costs of the followup campaign. The queen of the Pamunkey tribe unsuccessfully pleaded for reparations which neither the government of Virginia nor Edward Hill

granted. A second expedition, better led by Colonel Abraham Wood, chased the Senecas back to their homes where they remained until 1665.

Patrick Henry's birthplace, Studley, is located on this creek. *See: Petersburg; Shirley; Susquehannock Indians*

TOWN
In the Commonwealth of Virginia, communities are of three types: unincorporated towns, incorporated towns, or chartered cities. Presently, there are 188 incorporated towns in Virginia which have their own local government, usually a town council. If a community does not wish to incorporate, its affairs are under the management of the County Board of Supervisors. *See: City*

TOWNFIELDS
Northampton County   **Site**

A port town was to be established here on the bay side of the lower portion of the Eastern Shore. A portion of Governor's Land was laid out in lots near a courthouse and jail. However, since the residents all lived rather contentedly on their farms, no one bought a lot. Court was held in a local tavern until 1664 when a courthouse finally was erected, but the location was unpopular. The little town of Eastville developed of its own accord about five miles inland and, in 1677, a new courthouse was erected. The site of the original town reverted to farmland. *See: Belle Vue; Eastville; Governor's Land*

TRABUE'S TAVERN
Chesterfield County

Members of the Trabue family were the proprietors of one of the eight Midlothian coal mines. For the benefit of the miners who commuted from miles away, a tavern was built on the edge of the Trabue plantation beside the Buckingham Road. *See: Midlothian*

TREBELL'S LANDING
James City County   **Site**

Adjoining Carter's Grove, upriver from the manor house at Burwell's Wharf or Burwell's Landing, was a warehouse and the necessary pier to receive freight from the ships. The 107 acres here were purchased in 1768 by William Trebell, a successful Williamsburg merchant. He had owned the Raleigh Tavern for five years before selling and reinvesting his money in this venture. Trebell imported coffee, tea, sugar, rum, and a few slaves and exported great quantities of meat and corn. By the time of the Revolution, the lands of this area had been depleted by tobacco and little of the leaf was shipped from the James side of the Peninsula. During the Revolution, William Trebell provided many senior Continental Army officers with comfortable quarters and wholesome food on their way to Yorktown in October 1781. When he and his wife, Sarah, both died in 1789, the property was acquired by Carter Burwell II. Occasionally this place was called Grove Landing. *See: Capitol Landing; Carters Grove; Mulberry Island*

TREVILLIANS
Goochland County

Trevillian's tavern first was located on the Richmond to Rocktown road. By the time of the Civil War, the family had moved to the Three Chopt Road where a new wayside inn was established. Near here, on June 12, 1864, Union General Phillip Sheridan unsuccessfully attacked the entrenched Confederates under Wade Hampton. The fierce battle that followed, as the Confederate forces banged away at the Union troopers, produced many casualties. When the battle was broken off, the Federals had been repulsed with loss and Sheridan pulled back and rejoined Grant on the James. *See: Five Forks; Rocktown*

TRIANGLE
Prince William County

When U.S. Highway 1 was constructed to touch near an entrance to the Quantico Marine Base, it intersected two county roads to form an attractive triangle of land. With heavy motor traffic heading for Washington, D.C., this became an obvious spot for filling stations and beaneries to cater to the public. Although U.S. 1 has been nearly deserted for parallel Interstate 95, Triangle's major industry is still filling stations, motels, and restaurants.

TROUTDALE
Grayson County   Town

Lying under the shadow of Mt. Rogers, this town on Fox Creek is a haven for trout fishermen. The hills and dales of the region add the second half of this name.

TROUTVILLE
Botetourt County   Town

A German family by the name of Trout settled on Peter's Creek prior to the Revolution. The town of Troutville recalls the family name.

TUBAL FURNACE
Orange County   Site

In 1716 Alexander Spotswood began

CAVALRY CLASH, TREVILLIANS

producing pig iron from ore mined near Germanna. At Tubal Furnace (a smelter), located a few miles below the junction of the Rapidan and Rappahannock rivers, he worked about 100 people, mostly black slaves and a few white indentured servants, producing pigs of iron which he shipped to England. A twenty-six-foot waterwheel powered the bellows to give air to the burning charcoal to create the high temperatures required. His export production reached the rate of 23 tons per year by 1723. Not content with merely making iron blocks, Spotswood built a forge nearby in which firebacks and andirons were cast. Soon he was making strap iron from which blacksmiths created wagon parts and farm implements for Virginia markets. The name Tubal is Biblical in origin. Tubalcain, a worker in brass and iron, is mentioned in Genesis 4:22. *See: Bristol Iron Works; Furnace; Germanna; Massaponnox; Rapidan River; Wilderness*

TUCKAHOE
Henrico County

The first settlers on these lands died in 1689, according to an old burial vault which gives evidence of a dwelling that vanished long ago. The tract was acquired in 1695 by William Randolph of Turkey Island who gave it to his son, Thomas. It was he who built the present house and vault and preserved the remains of the early settlers. Tuckahoe is the only one of five Randolph brothers' houses still standing.

In 1735, the son of Thomas, William Randolph III, expanded his land holdings by patenting an additional 2,400 acres along Chestnut Ridge in old Albemarle County. Although he never lived on these western lands, William was a firm friend of Peter Jefferson and, in fact, sold Thomas Jefferson's father the land on which the house at Shadwell was built. After William Randolph, a widower, died suddenly in 1747 and Peter was appointed the guardian of the orphaned Randolph children, the Jefferson family lived at Tuckahoe for seven years.

Since Thomas Jefferson and Thomas Mann Randolph had grown up together and had attended school at Tuckahoe, the two families continued to be close. Thomas Jefferson's daughter, Martha, married Thomas Mann Randolph, Jr. During the Revolution, the Randolph family entertained officers of both armies here at Tuckahoe. One British officer wrote, "We found many gentlemen of this province very liberal and hospitable to British

officers, among whom I may mention Messers Randolph of Tuckahoe, Goode of Chesterfield, and Cary of Warwick."

A *tuckahoe* is an edible water plant. The name is Indian. Tidewater residents for generations called all those who lived in the Piedmont region tuckahoes. The appellation has been lost by the present generation. *See: Edgehill; Monticello; Shadwell; Varina Grove*

TUFTON
Albemarle County

Peter Jefferson patented 2,000 acres south of the Rivanna River in 1737. Although his house was at Shadwell, he built an overseer's cabin here, along with stables and barns, and shelter for the slaves. The land produced wheat, rye, and some oats which were used primarily to feed the family's fine blooded horses. When Martha Jefferson married Thomas Mann Randolph, Jr., the bride's father built a small cottage on this land for use until they could afford a suitable home elsewhere. Martha named it for her friend Lady Tufton, a niece of the Duke of Dorset, who had been her close friend when she lived in France with her father after the Revolution. Here Thomas Jefferson Randolph, the President's first grandson, was born. *See: Edgehill; Varina Grove*

TULERIES
Clarke County

Joseph Tuley, Jr. built his home on a large estate about 1833. He graced his private park with formal gardens to create a splendid establishment. The name is a play on Tuileries, a famous French royal palace in Paris. At the time that Tuley named his estate, the French had just created another Republic after the death of Louis Napolean. Later, Louis Napolean II, elected President of the Republic, proclaimed himself emperor and reclaimed Tuileries. The French palace burned in 1871. Tuleries of Clarke County lives on. *See: Belle Vue; Chantilly; Sully*

TURBEVILLE
Halifax County

The first postmistress was Mrs. Eugene C. Turbeville. She was appointed in 1867.

TURKEY ISLAND
Henrico County

This plantation was named for a neck of land which juts into the curling James River. Discovered by Captain Christopher Newport in 1607, he named it for a great flock of wild turkeys roosting there. In 1676 it was owned by James Crews, a neighbor of Nathaniel Bacon, Jr., who lived at Curles. For his part in Bacon's Rebellion, Crews was hanged and his lands were confiscated by Governor Berkeley. Two years later it was acquired by William Randolph of Morton Hall, Warwickshire, England, the immigrant who founded the enormous Randolph family of Virginia.

Turkey Island farm was purchased in 1814 by George Pickett. His son, General George E. Pickett, led the last Confederate charge in the battle of Gettysburg in 1863. The next year, Pickett and General P. G. T. Beauregard cornered Union General Ben Butler in Bermuda Hundred from which there was but one small avenue of escape. When the Confederates blocked the escape route, Beauregard proudly reported to President Jefferson Davis that he had "put the stopper into the bottle." Butler was embarrassed and enraged. Often called The Beast for his callous treatment of property and civilians, he ordered Pickett's home destroyed to vent his frustration. In the conflagration, the original seventeenth century buildings, erected by the Randolphs, were also put to the torch. After the war, General George Pickett wrote to a friend, "Everything has been swept clean by the ruthless war ..."

TURNERS
Caroline County

On a Crown grant of 2,765 acres on the Mattaponi River, Richard Johnson built his home in 1711. His kinsman, Thomas Johnson (probably his son) operated a tavern in the old house as late as 1747. He sold it to Lewis Turner in 1756 with the lawyer Edmund Pendleton acting as the agent. During the following years, the little community became known as Turner's Store Post Office, one of the first in the county. After 1800, it was purchased by the Wright family who discarded the earlier names and called it Green Fall.

TYE RIVER
Nelson County

This pretty stream was discovered in 1735 by Allen Tye.

TYNDALL'S POINT
Gloucester County

This tip of land at the mouth of the York River was first sketched onto a map drawn by Robert Tyndall in 1608. It bore this name for about 100 years. It was not until well after Gloucester County was organized that it became known as Gloucester Point, but both names were used interchangeably.

The first owner of the land at Tyndall's Point was Sir George Yeardley who patented it in 1620. Neither he nor anyone else bothered to farm it. It was occupied by the British prior to the siege of Yorktown but when it was taken by American troops, they prevented Lord Cornwallis from escaping Yorktown in 1781. During the Civil War the Confederates erected an earthen fort but they were evicted by the Union army and it remained in Northern hands for the last three years of the war. *See: Gloucester Point; Little England; Timberneck Hall; Ringfield*

UNION HILL
Nelson County

This was the birthplace of William Cabell, born on March 30, 1730. A Burgess from this region, he attended the Virginia Conventions, was a signer of the Articles of Association (sometimes called the Articles of Confederation), and was a member of the Virginia Convention which ratified the new Federal Constitution in 1788. He died in 1798. The name Union Hill most probably is post-Revolutionary.

UNIVERSITY OF RICHMOND

The Virginia Baptist Education Society established a school of theology on Dunlora Plantation, Powhatan County in 1830. Two years later Dunlora Academy was moved to Henrico County and then into the city of Richmond where it became Richmond College. By 1840, it was the second university in the Commonwealth. A school for women, adjoining the all-male campus of the university, was established in 1914 as Westhampton College.

UNIVERSITY OF VIRGINIA
Charlottesville

Founded by Thomas Jefferson, the cornerstone of the first building was laid in the presence of three former Presidents: Thomas Jefferson, James Madison, and James Monroe. When chartered in 1819 by the General Assembly, it was the "capstone of education" in the Commonwealth, to use Jefferson's words. The plan was a traditional quadrangle with the famed Rotunda at one end and faculty houses and classrooms on either side of a long sweep of lawn. Since Jefferson was an architect of some note, he designed all of the first buildings, each one of a different architectural style which the students could study.

It was not until the beginning of the twentieth century that women were accepted as students, and today the University is open to all races and both sexes. Its various departments rank with the best universities in the country.

UPPER NORFOLK COUNTY
Obsolete

There were three precincts in this large county: East Parish, West Parish, and South Parish. They extended indefinitely south into Carolina until the border was established between the two colonies. Each of these precincts could elect one Burgess. *See: Nansemond County; Norfolk County*

UPPERVILLE
Fauquier County

Originally, this settlement was known as

UNIVERSITY OF VIRGINIA

Carr Town. The name was changed to Upperville in 1819 for some unknown reason. Perhaps it was so named because it was in the highlands near Ashby Gap on the road from Middleburg to Winchester.

URBANNA
Middlesex County   **Town**

When Middlesex County was formed, the courthouse erected was convenient to those who traveled by water but very inconvenient for those whose homes were up the peninsula. In 1680, the Port on Nimcock Creek was designated an official landing and customs point. It was not until 1705 that this village was given a name. Combining urban and Queen Anne, the government of Virginia created Urbanna, the *queen's city.*

When the new courthouse for the county was built some miles away, Urbanna lost glory. When bay steamers stopped calling, it went into abrupt decline. Now a quaint, little town that is home port to many pleasure craft, it competes with Irvington across the Rappahannock in Lancaster County. Every fall, usually in early November, the people of Urbanna put on an Oyster Festival which is growing in popularity. *See: Rosegill; Saluda*

UTIMARA
York County   **Site**

Ensign John Utie was listed in the 1623 census as a resident of Hog Island. In 1630, he was appointed one of the military commanders of the new settlement on the York River at Chischiak. Granted 6,000 acres for his service, he named his farm Utimara for his wife Mary. In 1631 he was elected to the Council where he joined others attempting to curb Governor John Harvey. At one meeting of the Council, George Menefie spoke against Harvey. The Governor struck him on the shoulder and shouted, "I arrest you for treason!" John Utie took hold of the enraged Governor and exclaimed, "And we the like to you, sir!" Utie, Menefie, Captain William Peirce, and a few others who also opposed the Governor, were all sent to England to answer charges of treason. Enroute, John Utie died.

His son, John II, who inherited Utimara, sold it and his other inherited land at Hog Island to William Tayloe. The transfer of the properties was delayed, however, because he, too, died suddenly. His widow wasted no time in remarrying. In December 1642, the County Court of Lower Norfolk ordered Richard Foster to settle the transfer of Utie lands to Tayloe and to "pay unto Mrs. Marian Utie, now the wife of Richard Bennett, Esq., 114 lbs of tobacco." Later Utimara came into the possession of Nathaniel Bacon, Sr., a loyal member of the Council during Bacon's Rebellion.

Utimara is now the site of Cheatham Annex, a part of the Naval Supply Center of Norfolk. *See: Bennett's Choice; Cheatham Annex; Chischiak; Curles; Middle Plantation; Penniman*

V

VANDERPOOL
Highland County

The first white man to have bragged about using the nearby pass through the mountains was a Mr. Vanderpool. Nothing else is known about him. This community either was named directly for him or for a descendant.

VANSANT
Buchanan County

A lumber company, Vansant Kitchen, which specialized in buying yellow poplar, was the principal reason that the N & W Railway scheduled a stop here. When a spur was added for the lumber company, it was named Vansant.

VARINA GROVE
Henrico County

This farm was named for the Varina strain of tobacco which John Rolfe developed into the first cash crop to be grown by the early settlers. He acquired the seeds secretly from a friendly ship captain and experimented with various growing techniques until he found one that was best suited to the Virginia soil and climate. When John Rolfe married Pocahontas in 1614, they lived at Varina, a few miles down river from Henricus. Here their only child, a son named Thomas, was born the next year. When Pocahontas died in England in 1616, Rolfe returned to Virginia, leaving his son with relatives, and took up residence at Hog Island. He died in Jamestown a few days after the Massacre of 1622, but since he had made his will and had it witnessed twelve days before the massacre, he probably was not a victim and died of an illness.

Varina was selected as the first seat of Henrico County when the shires were organized in 1634. Court was held here continuously until the county seat was moved to Richmond in 1752. A seventeenth century church, built close to the James River at Varina, served this region for many years. The Glebe House of the Reverend James Blair, Commissary of the Bishop of London, was at Varina, although he preferred to live in Williamsburg where he was the guiding force in the founding of the College of William and Mary and was a thorn in the side of three royal Governors, all of whom he managed to outmaneuver and have recalled. When the courthouse was moved to Richmond, Varina Grove went into a steep decline. Never well-populated, the region was mainly farmland, most of which originally belonged to the parish.

By the time that Thomas Mann Randolph, Jr. inherited the former glebe lands, there were few neighbors. Much to Thomas Jefferson's displeasure, young Randolph, who had married Jefferson's daughter, Martha, moved to Varina Grove from Edgehill in Albemarle with his family. When Randolph died, Martha and her children went to live at Monticello where she acted as her father's hostess since her mother, Martha Wayles Jefferson, had died. Varina Grove farm was sold.

During the Civil War, this was known as Aiken's Landing, most probably for the man who had purchased the farm from Randolph. The landing was used by both Union and Confederate troops as a major supply landing point. *See: Edgehill of Albemarle; Eppington; Hog Island; Tufton*

VAUCLUSE
Northampton County

Situated on Hungars Creek, about three miles in from the Chesapeake Bay, Vaucluse was the home of one branch of the Upshur family. The present house quite possibly is pre-Revolutionary. It was the home of Judge Abel P. Upshur, one of the many noted civil leaders of Virginia during the glory days of the Confederacy. Vaucluse was named for an old sixth century church in France that was built from the debris of an ancient pagan temple. The French church, now 1,400 years old, still stands. Today, the lands of Vaucluse have been subdivided into lots in a real estate development called Vaucluse Shores. *See: Essex; Warwick of Northampton*

VERONA
Augusta County

Someone who had the authority to name stations for the Chesapeake and Western Railroad liked Shakespeare's play *Two Gentlemen from Verona*. This name replaced an earlier name, Rolla. Since Rolla and Verona contain similar sounds, there might have been some sort of verbal purification to have Verona become the fixed name of the post office.

VERVILLE
Lancaster County

This brick house, built late in the seventeenth century, was the home of a Dr. Madison, a wealthy Scot, who might have been the builder. Verville long has been a familiar landmark in the southern portion of Northern Neck. The name, it is assumed, was derived from the Latin word *veritas*, meaning truth, something a man of science would have held in high esteem. *See: Ville*

VESUVIUS
Rockbridge County

A smelter for iron operated here in the 1830s. It was owned by the McCormick family to provide the metal from which the famous reapers were made. Showers of sparks, that always accompany the pouring of molten iron, reminded the workers of the volcano, Mount Vesuvius. *See: Walnut Grove*

VICTORIA
Lunenburg County **Town**

Local tradition says that this town was named for Queen Victoria. It's possible. The queen was on the British throne when this community was named. Alberta, in Brunswick County, is but twenty-five miles away. *See: Alberta*

VIENNA
Fairfax County **Town**

Yankees developed this community in the twentieth century and named it for a town in New York of the same name. For a while, only Northerners were welcomed here and, naturally, Southerners avoided it. Today it is a mixture of people from north and south, money being the great equalizer.

VIEWMONT
Albemarle County

Colonel Joshua Fry built his home in Albemarle County in 1744, the same year the county was organized. At first a modest dwelling, which suited the modest and intelligent Colonel Fry, later generations added to it. Its handsomely carved interior woodwork was well known. Sadly, the house was destroyed by fire in 1938.

Joshua Fry, a graduate of Oxford University, came to Virginia about 1720 to teach mathematics at the College of William and Mary. In 1745 he and Peter Jefferson surveyed and defined the western limits of Lord Fairfax's Northern Neck. After that project was finished, they set about to draw a new map of all Virginia east of the Allegheny Mountains. In their travels, the two men saw and surveyed with their relatively primitive instruments, nearly all of modern Virginia. They produced the first map of the Old Dominion since John Smith's rather good attempt of 1612. The Fry-Jefferson map was the standard reference for many decades, supplanted only by Claudius Crozet's map of 1848.

In 1754, after Colonel Fry had returned from the mapping expedition, he was sent out as the commander of the Virginia militia against the French and Indians in western Pennsylvania. His second in command, Major George Washington, carved the epitaph for his friend and leader when Colonel Fry died of wounds in the wilderness. "Under this oak lies the body of the good, the just, and the noble Fry." In his will, probated in August of 1754, Joshua Fry left his surveying instruments to Peter Jefferson. They were lost in the fire at Shadwell many years later. Mary Hill Fry, the colonel's widow, remained at Viewmont for thirty-two years. She sold the estate in 1786 to Governor Edmund Randolph just before she died. *See: Belle Grove; Shadwell*

VILLAGE
Richmond County

Originally this town was called Union Village. The first part of the name was dropped during the Civil War. Refusing to be "reconstructed" after the war, the citizens preferred the simpler name.

VINTON
Roanoke County **Town**

This name was coined in 1884 using the first part of Vinyard, the name of a prominent resident, and Preston, an early pioneer. Vinton, east of Roanoke, once was called Gish's Mill for a mill operated by David Gish as early as 1794.

VIRGILINA
Halifax County

The little community of Virgilina lies close to the border of Virginia and North Carolina. Obviously, the name is a combination of the two state names. If it had developed on the other side of the border, would it have been Carolinia?

VIRGINIA

In the sixteenth century, all of North America above Florida, east of the Mississippi, and north to Canada was called Virginia by the English. It was named, probably by Sir Walter Raleigh, in honor of Queen Elizabeth I, the Virgin Queen. By the time the English began to colonize this vast territory, it was no longer virgin. The Spaniards had been in the Chesapeake Bay region, had planted a few of their own, and had ravaged the local natives in their own cruel way. Spain made no effort to establish a permanent settlement since its exploratory party was principally interested in staking a claim to this northern region. The Jesuit priests who remained to convert the local Indians were to be retrieved at a later date. Their story of a god who one day would come from the East was the basis of a prophecy among the natives that one day a new nation would come to their land to kill them all. When the Spaniards returned for their priests, they discovered they all had been massacred.

When Sir Walter Raleigh attempted a settlement on the Outer Banks of Carolina in 1585, the Indians were very unfriendly and, after one year, the colonists gave up and went home with Sir Francis Drake who happened to stop by after his profitable adventures in the Carribean. A second English attempt on Roanoke Island, near the site of the first failure, ended when the people vanished without a trace, the famed Lost Colony. The English tried again at the mouth of the Kennebec River of Maine, to counter France's New World claims, but that, too, was abandoned because of the severe northern winter. Finally a permanent settlement was planted with the Jamestown group who arrived in April 1607.

The Pilgrims who landed in New England in 1620 were heading for Virginia, as all of the territory was still known, and there is some doubt if their real destination was the Chesapeake Bay or if they were planted at Cape Cod through the connivance of a rival company that wanted to begin a second settlement. It makes no difference now, for by 1620 the limits of the Virginia Company's jurisdiction had been narrowed to 200 miles north and south of Point Comfort and to all land, without limit, to the east and west. The eastern boundary included the island of Bermuda for a brief time but that was soon cut off with the organization of the Somers Isles Company. The indefinite western limits, however, continued for about 150 years.

King Charles I gave a huge chunk of Virginia to his Catholic friends to create Maryland (named for the queen). King Charles II gave Carolina to his Protestant friends (and named it for himself). By then the Mississippi River had been acknowledged as the western boundary. The northern border was angled to the Great Lakes (the Northwest Territory) while the southern border remained on a line of latitude roughly 200 miles south of Point Comfort. This Carolina border was moved northward in 1730 by a joint surveying party. Virginia's interests were represented by Colonel William Byrd II. However, the present line between Virginia and North Carolina was not agreed upon until as late as 1815.

After the Revolution, the Commonwealth relinquished its claim to the Northwest Territory, including the western portion of Pennsylvania. From this Northwest Territory eight states were created. During the Civil War, four large, poor, and remote counties were cut off to create a new slave-free state called West Virginia. With that reduction, the Old Dominion assumed its present shape.

From the original area of Virginia, nine states have their beginnings. Listed alphabetically they are: Illinois, Indiana, Kentucky, Maryland, North Carolina, Ohio, South Carolina, Tennessee, and West Virginia. Portions of Michigan, Minnesota, and Wisconsin also were a part of the Old Dominion.

VIRGINIA BEACH
City

For many years Virginia Beach was a quiet collection of summer cottages and a few hotels, supplemented by a sparce huddle of permanent residences, on the Atlantic oceanfront between Fort Story and Rudee Inlet. When the tide of population surged to the ocean area in the years following World War II, the growth was phenomenal. At one time Virginia Beach was the fastest growing city in the country. It became independent of Princess Anne County in 1952 and consolidated with the county in 1963 to become one of the largest cities in the U.S. with a land area of 291 square miles.

VIRGINIA COMMONWEALTH UNIVERSITY
Richmond

Richmond Professional Institute combined with the Medical College of Virginia in 1968 to create a new university. The former RPI section concentrates primarily on the arts. MCV is one of the three medical schools in Virginia. The name reflects the special organization of Virginia which became a

Commonwealth when it adopted a constitution during the Revolution. It is one of the few states in the Union to use the title Commonwealth. The others are Kentucky, Massachusetts, and Pennsylvania.

VIRGINIA INTERMONT COLLEGE
Bristol

Literally "in the mountains," this Baptist college was organized at Glade Spring in 1884. It was moved to Bristol seven years later. The present name was adopted in 1909. *See: Gladys*

VIRGINIA MILITARY INSTITUTE
Lexington

Founded in 1839 as a state military, engineering, and liberal arts college, this school is the West Point of the South. Graduates have assumed leadership roles in every action since the war with Mexico in 1846-48. The barracks, designed by Alexander Jackson Davis and completed in 1850, have served as a prototype for many of the nation's castellated military school buildings. VMI was burned in 1864 by Union troops under General Hunter, partly in revenge for the Corps of Cadets participation in the Battle of New Market, partly because so many excellent leaders were trained here, and partly for spite. The buildings were restored by 1873.

The most noted graduate of the present century was General George C. Marshall, the army Chief of Staff during World War II and later Secretary of State under President Harry Truman. The Marshall Plan speeded the physical and economic recovery of Germany after World War II.

VIRGINIA POLYTECHNIC INSTITUTE
Blacksburg

Established in 1872 as a land grant college, this school's founding marked the beginning of scientific agricultural and industrial instruction in Virginia. It now offers engineering, business, education, and liberal arts programs for men and women. Many agricultural experiment stations throughout the Commonwealth provide service and advice to the citizens. With its expanded programs, it adopted the unwieldly name Virginia Polytechnic Institute and State University. However, most everyone still calls it either V.P.I. or Virginia Tech.

VIRGINIA STATE UNIVERSITY
Chesterfield County

Established in 1882 as the Virginia Normal and Collegiate Institute, the name was changed in 1902 to Virginia State College for Negroes. Its 400 acres of farm land provides practical training in agriculture to complement its standard academic programs. The college was upgraded to university status in 1977 and has used the present name since then. Norfolk State University began as an extension of this school.

VIRGINIA WESLEYAN COLLEGE
Norfolk

One of the more recent Methodist colleges, Virginia Wesleyan began classes in 1966. Very quickly it established itself as a quality four year school offering degrees in a variety of fields. The name Wesleyan honors the founder of Methodism, the Reverend John Wesley, an Anglican clergyman who objected to the established church's method of conducting services and some of its teachings. His brother, the Reverend Charles Wesley, was the noted writer of hymns.

W

WACHAPREAGUE
Accomack County   **Town**

Behind the barrier dunes on the Atlantic side of the Eastern Shore and at the end of a tortuous, winding channel that only local boatmen can follow is the village of Wachapreague. Here the main industry is sport fishing where craft of all sizes may be chartered for deepwater trolling. This was the site of the Machipungo tribe of Indians who disappeared many, many years ago. The name is an Indian word that means "little city by the sea."

For decades the local landmark was the Wachapreague Hotel, a multi-story frame building with porches on each floor on which guests sat and rocked and swapped tall fish stories. It burned in 1976 and, because of the tremendous cost of building these days, could not be replaced. Its loss was mourned by fishermen from Virginia and Maryland and other places along the Atlantic seaboard.

Originally this village was Powellton, named for the Powell brothers who owned most of the land. When, in 1902, the town was incorporated, another name had to be selected to avoid duplication with Powellton of Brunswick County.

WAKEFIELD
King William County

Nathaniel Burwell patented 5,000 acres in Pamunkey Neck in 1699. He sold small parcels to William Cowne and Owen Gwathmey prior to 1776. The remaining portion, then known as Wakefield, was sold to the Gwathmey family in 1785. Although there is no certainty, more than likely the name was selected to honor the birthplace of George Washington. *See: Burlington; Carter's Grove; Cownes*

WAKEFIELD
Sussex County

Mrs. Billy Mahone, the wife of the president of Norfolk and Western Railway, was permitted to name several new flag stops along the railroads right-of-way. She named this stop for a book that she had enjoyed, *The Vicar of Wakefield* by Thomas Hardy. *See: Ivor*

WAKEFIELD
Surry County

Not far from the south bank of the James River, at Spring Grove, was the 1608 village of Pipsico, a local Indian chief. Benjamin Harrison I purchased the land from the chief's descendants and cleared much of it for farming. It was inherited by his son Nathaniel who is buried nearby in Sunken Meadow. His epitaph reads, "Here lieth the body of the Hon. Nathaniel Harrison, Esqr., son of the Hon. Benjamin Harrison Esqr. He was born in this Parish on the 8th day of August 1677. Appointed to the Governor's Council to succeed his father. Resided at Wakefield." Although Nathaniel's son, Benjamin II, acquired the Berkeley property across the river and moved his family there about the time of his father's death, the south-bank Harrisons retained Wakefield for many more generations. *See: Berkeley; Brandon; Montpelier of Surry*

WAKEFIELD
Westmoreland County

Wakefield was named for the city of Wakefield in Yorkshire, England. In 1718, Augustine Washington purchased 200 acres on Pope's Creek, about a mile from his father's place and he built a house sometime between 1722 and 1726. He selected the name Wakefield for his home. Augustine's first wife, Jane Butler, died in 1729, leaving him with three young children. He soon found another wife, Mary Ball, the ward of Colonel George Eskridge whose home was at Sandy Point, about twenty-five miles down the Potomac from Wakefield. The first of Mary's six children was George, born here on February 22, 1732. The child was named for her guardian whom she loved and greatly respected.

When George was about three-and-a-half years old, his father moved the family to another tract at Hunting Creek, some distance up the river. They stayed there for four years and then moved to a farm on the Rappahannock River near Fredericksburg, leaving the Wakefield property lie idle. It was inherited by Augustine Washington, Jr., one of George's half brothers. On Christmas Day of 1779, while General Washington was leading the Continental Army, his birthplace caught fire and was completely destroyed. William Augustine Washington, then the master of Wakefield, moved away.

The house was not rebuilt until recent times. For many years Wakefield was neglected until George Washington Parke Custis, Mary Washington's grandson, marked the spot with a stone tablet. Today a house stands beside the foundations of the original house. The new dwelling, erected by the National Park Service, followed a design common to the early eighteenth century since there was no record of what Washington's birthplace actually looked like. Now a National Monument, Wakefield is open to the public. *See: Epping Forest; Ferry Farm; Mount Vernon; Pope's Creek; Sandy Point*

WALKERTON
King and Queen County   **Town**

Located at the former head of navigation on the Mattaponi River, Walkerton was settled in 1663 by the Walker family. Dr. Thomas Walker of Castle Hill in Albemarle County was born here in 1715 when the family estate was known as Rye Field. The little town of Walkerton, formally created in 1709, had more public warehouses for tobacco storage than houses for inhabitants. It once was a major shipping point on the Mattaponi River. *See: Castle Hill; Grace Church*

WALLACE
Washington County

Once known as Wallace Switch, for a minor turnoff on the N & W Railway, this village honors the Reverend W. P. Wallace, the community's Presbyterian minister when the rail line was laid.

WALLOPS ISLAND
Accomack County

John Wallop, a successful trader who died in 1693, made his fortune by sending his own ships to the West Indies. During his lifetime, he owned thousands of acres of land in the northeastern area of the county near the present village of Wattsville. He is best remembered for having surveyed and supervised construction of a road that ran from above Accomack Court House to the Maryland line. This seventeenth century artery, long known as Wallop's Road, remained intact until 1918 when parts of it were straightened and relocated to form much of today's Highway 13. Although he owned Wallops Island, he never lived there and probably never saw it. Through the marriage of his daughter, much of the land was later owned by the Watt family but the name Wallops has remained along the coast. During World War II, the Navy purchased a huge tract on the mainland, opposite Chincoteague, for an Auxiliary Air Station. That, plus Wallop's Island, was conveyed to NASA in 1959. Today the island is used as a launching site for small research rockets into the upper atmosphere.

WALNUT GROVE
Augusta County

On this farm was born Cyrus Hall McCormick, the inventor of the first practical reaper. He revolutionized agriculture in 1831 at the age of 22 with a machine he fabricated

McCORMICK'S REAPER, WALNUT GROVE

to his own design in the farm's blacksmith shop. Before moving west sixteen years later, where he founded a factory that was the beginning of the International Harvester Company, nearly 100 of McCormick's reapers had been made here at Walnut Grove, most of them from iron that was mined and smelted nearby. *See: Vesuvius*

WALTERS
Isle of Wight County
A local resident, Walter Joyner, strove for many years to get the N & W Railway to establish a depot and flag stop here. When he finally was successful, the railroad made certain that his accomplishment was noted by naming the station Walter's since there already was a stop named Joyners.

WARD'S PLANTATION
Prince George County   **Site**
John Ward, granted land here in 1619, established a thriving community in quick order. It was represented as a borough in the First Assembly of that year, a part of the corporation of Charles City.

WARDTOWN
Northampton County
About 1820 Alexander W. Ward built his house near a crossroad. When a post office was authorized a few years later, Ward's name was chosen.

WARE CHURCH
Gloucester County
Ware Church is one of the oldest churches in Gloucester County. There is some uncertainty about the date of construction, but 1710 appears to be close. It was erected on land donated by the Throckmorton family whose farm, Mordecai's Mount, was nearby. Ware Parish had been established in 1653 and this was not the first church. The parish had been named for the Ware River, one of the fingers of Mobjack Bay. The River Ware in England flows through Hertford Shire and joins the Thames within the metropolitan area of greater London.

The first rector of this Virginia parish was the Reverend Alexander Murray who was with Charles II at the Battle of Worcester in 1652 and who remained the king's companion during his years of exile on the Continent. The Reverand Mr. Murray came to the colony twelve years after the Restoration, displeased and disgusted by his monarch's many mistresses. When he arrived, the church building was located on the opposite side of the Ware River. *See: Abingdon Church; Church Hill*

WAREHAM
Gloucester County
Patented in 1650 by Mordecai Cooke of Mordecai's Mount, this was the early home of the patentee's son, John Cooke. It was named for the small hamlet of Wareham in Dorset on England's south coast near Poole. When Governor William Berkeley was forced to flee from Jamestown during Bacon's Rebellion, he first went to Wareham for safety. From here he went to a more remote place of refuge on the Eastern Shore. The colonial house here no longer stands, and all that gives evidence of an early habitation are the tombstones of John's two wives who died in 1720 and 1724 and the grave of his son, Mordecai Cooke II, who died in 1751. *See: Church Hill; Stratton Manor*

WARESCOYAK
Isle of Wight County   Site
Captain Roger Smith came to Virginia in 1616. He returned to England three years later to complain he had been badly treated by the Governor, Sir George Yeardley, during the first division of land. In December 1620, he returned to the colony in command of fifty people who were to live as tenants on Company land at Warescoyak on the south side of the James. Making peace with Yeardley just before Sir George's first term expired, Smith was appointed to the Council in 1621 where he served for many years. After the Massacre of 1622, every twentieth man in the colony (nobody knows how they were selected) worked under "the command of Captain Roger Smith, who had served 12 or 13 years in the Wars in the Low Countries, to build a blockhouse upon the shore where it might as well command shipping and withall have a strong plantation, the ground being rich and good." Located where the James River was said to be "not a musket shot over," the blockhouse was completed in the summer of 1623. Six months later Captain Smith was paid 1,200 pounds of tobacco and twelve barrels of Indian corn by the Treasurer of the colony for his work.

The name Warescoyak (spelled a variety of ways in the old records) came from the Indian tribe that was living in this area when the Jamestowners arrived in 1607. Although they were chased away in the war of retaliation after the Massacre of 1622, their name was retained as one of the shires formed in 1634. The Indian name was changed to Isle of Wight County in 1637. *See: Bennet's Welcome; Isle of Wight County; Lawne's Plantation; Old Towne; Shires; Smith's Fort Plantation*

WARM SPRINGS
Bath County
The seat of Bath County, this community developed around a nineteenth century spa where one could take the waters at a warm spring that comes from the earth at a pleasant temperature. The famous spa at Bath, England, was built around a warm spring by the Romans. Englishmen had long believed that soaking in steaming mineral water was of great benefit for all sorts of ills. Today the springs are a curiosity and Warm Springs is better known for its golf course.

WARNER
Middlesex County
Virginia would not be complete without a post office named Warner since that family was directly linked to George Washington. The name was bestowed by the first postmaster here, Robert Warner Allsworth.

WARNER HALL
Gloucester County
Colonel Augustine Warner came to Virginia in 1628 and settled in York County where he was elected a justice. Most likely he was already on this side of the York River since Gloucester County was formed from York in 1651. He received his 340 acres here in 1657, but it was his son, Augustine Warner II, who built the house beside the Severn River of Mobjack Bay in 1674 and first applied the name Warner Hall to it. It was named for the family home in England.

Augustine II, the Speaker of the House of Burgesses during Bacon's Rebellion, had his house occupied by the rebels after they burned Jamestown. Unfortunately, all of his sons died young, but he was survived by three daughters. His sister married into the Ball family of Lancaster County and was one of the ancestors of Mary Ball, George Washington's mother. Thus, the original Colonel Augustine Warner was the great-great-grandfather of the first president.

The Warner Hall of 1674 was burned, but it was quickly replaced in 1740 by a house that resembled Rosewell on a much smaller and more tasteful scale. The second Warner Hall stood for over 100 years before it, too, was a victim of fire in 1845. The two wings that survived were connected with a third home that stands today. *See: Epping Forest; Lowlands Cottage; Wakefield of Westmoreland*

WARREN COUNTY
General Joseph Warren, a Virginian, was killed during the Battle of Bunker Hill in 1775. When this county was organized in 1836, from territory taken from Frederick and Shenandoah, it was named for him. The courthouse is at Front Royal. *See: Front Royal*

WARRENTON
Fauquier County   Town
Formerly Fauquier Court House, and not much of a town when it was selected as the county seat in 1760, the community grew when it was platted into lots and streets around the courthouse that sits atop a low hill. The dwellings cluster below it. Warrenton was named for Dr. Joseph Warren who helped Paul Revere begin his famous ride. Unfortunately, Dr. Warren was killed at the Battle of Bunker Hill. Many Virginians have long suspected that Paul Revere needed medical assistance to get on his horse. *See: Cuckoo*

WARSAW
Richmond County   Town
Richmond Court House, the seat of Richmond County of Northern Neck, often was confused with the capital city of the Commonwealth. In 1846 the name was changed to Warsaw to honor the many soldiers from Poland who served in the Continental Army. *See: Pulaski County*

WARWICK
Northampton County
The house overlooking Upshur's Bay was built about 1670 by Arthur and Rachel Upshur on land originally claimed by the builder's father. The elder Arthur Upshur had cannily conned the local Indian chief into giving him the land by making a present of four good coats. It was an excellent trade for several thousand acres. Rachel Upshur met a tragic end. Bitten by a rabid dog, she developed hydrophobia with all of the usual, horrible symptoms. To save her from continued suffering, she was smothered between two featherbeds. No one was charged with euthanasia. *See: Essex; Vaucluse*

WARWICK COUNTY
Obsolete
One of the original eight shires of 1634,

259

this was the most densely populated. It was named for Sir Robert Rich, the second Earl of Warwick, who was a shadey character, always involved in secret deals. When Samuel Argall raced home to England in 1619, after being the governor of the colony for two years and getting rich at the Virginia Company's expense, he was protected from charges of embezzlement by the Earl of Warwick (who quite possibly benefitted from Argall's rape of the colony). Also named for the Earl were a river and a town. The first courthouse of Warwick County was located at Denbigh on land donated by Samuel Mathews who was too independent to have been in the pay of Sir Robert Rich. The county disappeared after World War II when it was consolidated with the city of Newport News. Warwick is correctly pronounced WAR-ick. See: Denbigh; Richneck; Warwick Town

WARWICK TOWN
Newport News   **Site**

The Assembly of 1680 established a series of port towns to control the movement of exports. One authorized town was Warwick on the Warwick River. Samuel Mathews II donated fifty acres of his Denbigh plantation on a bluff near the mouth of the river just inside the tip of Mulberry Island. The land was divided into lots when a courthouse and jail were erected, and within a short time a public warehouse was also built at the wharf where tobacco would be inspected and graded. Although the warehouse and the court center were in full use during the eighteenth century, the proposed town did not grow as expected. Finally, in 1793 the obvious was accepted and the county seat was moved to a new location on land donated by Miles Cary II. The little settlement withered and disappeared. After that, the site was known as Town Point. See: Denbigh; Richneck; Warwick County

WARWICK RIVER

This very short waterway is more a creek than a river, although it does have a stream feeding it and is not completely dependent upon the tides. Named for the Earl of Warwick, it was a favorite anchorage for about 200 years where outbound ships filled their water kegs from a clear spring that trickles down the bank. Several large wharves were built near its mouth, at public expense, to handle the freight coming in for the neighboring plantations and to store the tobacco until shipping could be arranged. For

a time, most of the heavy stuff for Williamsburg was landed here. The Warwick River is now rather shallow and is used only for pleasure craft and small fishing boats. See: Bolthrope; Denbigh; Queen's Hith

WASHINGTON
Rappahannock County   **Town**

This is the only known community that was named for George Washington before he became a general and first president. He surveyed and platted the townsite in 1749 while working for Lord Fairfax who wanted to see new settlements at the foothills of the Blue Ridge. After the surveying task was completed, Fairfax named the townsite after his youthful employee. It became the seat of the new Rappahannock County when it was formed in 1833 from a portion of Culpeper. Aron's Mill, dating from 1765, was located nearby.

WASHINGTON AND LEE UNIVERSITY
Lexington

Founded in 1749 as Augusta Academy, this school was reorganized in 1776 as Liberty Hall Academy. Endowed by George Washington, who never went to college, this institution was named for him when it was moved to its present site within the town of Lexington. After the War Between the

GENERAL ROBERT E. LEE
WASHINGTON AND LEE UNIVERSITY

States, General Robert E. Lee accepted the appointment as president of the struggling college. He had spent his entire adult life as a soldier after his graduation from West Point and he badly needed an honorable occupation after the war. Lee served the college from 1865 until his death in 1870. When he was buried in the campus chapel, his name was added to that of another great Virginian. Washington and Lee University has proudly acclaimed its double name since 1871.

WASHINGTON COUNTY

Formed in 1776 when Fincastle County was eliminated, the territory was formed into three parts. Montgomery, Kentucky and Washington counties. The name honors George Washington who, at the time of the organization, was commander-in-chief of the Continental Army. In the beginning, this county covered the entire wedge-shaped triangle of the extreme southwesternportion of Virginia. From it were formed Buchanan, Dickenson, Lee, Russell, Scott and Wise counties during the next century. Court was first held in Black's Fort just outside of present day Abingdon, and the courthouse has been located in that town ever since the first proper one was built.

Unlike the rest of Virginia, the residents here opposed secession all through the early months of 1861. However, when the state convention voted to leave the Union, the county's voters ratified the decision and were more or less loyal to the Confederacy.

WATERFORD
Loudoun County

Settled in 1732, this village was first known as Milltown for the mill operated by the Quaker, Amos Janney, one of the surveyors of Lord Fairfax. The town was renamed by the local cobbler, Thomas Moore, in memory of his birthplace in Waterford, Ireland.

Acquaintances of Janney moved from Bucks County, Pennsylvania, and organized the Fairfax Society of Friends, erecting their Quaker meeting house in 1775. Good farmers, these people originated the Loudoun Method of rotating crops through a five-year cycle for better use of the land. The rotation system was praised by George Washington, a fellow farmer who was interested in better methods of agriculture.

Of course, these Quakers were pacifists during the Civil War yet, they were vocally pro-Union. They also believed in retribution, an eye for an eye, and did not hesitate to burn

the barns of those who aided the Confederate John Mosby and his Rangers. After the war ended, the local Quakers forgave those they had punished and helped with many barn raisings as a gesture of peace, although it is not recorded who paid for the materials.

Today Waterford comes to life for three days each October when the Waterford Foundation sponsors a fair dedicated to fostering (and selling) handcrafted items that range from primitive paintings to beautiful hand-forged iron products.

WATER VIEW
Middlesex County

Here, as at Ocean View, the view has been obstructed by buildings and trees but the old name remains. When the post office was first established, the community it served was near the Rappahannock River where most residents had an excellent view of the water. The town slowly moved away from the river to the main highway. The post office followed, taking with it the early name.

WAVERLY
Gloucester County

On the North River of Mobjack Bay stood a small house during colonial times where Dr. Richard Edwards reared a large family. The present house was built in 1812 by Captain Phillip Tabb of Toddsbury, a successful blockade runner during the War of 1812. *See: Toddsbury*

WAVERLY
Sussex County   Town

Mrs. Billy Mahone, the wife of the president of the N & W Railway, named this station after a novel by Sir Walter Scott.

WAYNESBORO
Augusta County   City

Settlement on the western side of Afton Mountain, on the Three Chopt Road to Staunton, began in the middle of the eighteenth century. For a while the small cluster of homes was known as Teesville for the local tavern run by the Tee brothers. Shortly after the Revolution, when more families built their homes along the South River, a village developed. It was named for General "Mad Anthony" Wayne.

Just outside of the town, an "oil boom" developed in 1895 where the liquid gold was thought to be underneath the pleasant land at the foot of Afton Mountain. Wells were drilled, land was leased by oil companies, and many folks expected to get rich. The drilled holes produced nothing but water. One hole was secretly filled with oil one night and the land around it was quickly sold for cash the next morning. By the time the trick had been discovered, the bogus oilman was long gone. *See: Basic City*

WEEMS
Lancaster County

Mason L. Weems and his brother George organized a steamboat company in 1817 to provide service between Baltimore and the Patuxent River area of Maryland. Gradually, the Weems Line acquired other companies and expanded service down the Chesapeake Bay to Point Comfort. Later it sent vessels up the Rappahannock as far as Port Royal. The people of Lancaster County, needing access to the steamboats to ship their farm products and to travel to Baltimore or Norfolk, requested service. The steamboat company said it would stop if there was a wharf so the locals built a landing, a warehouse, and a passenger shed. The first vessel to arrive was the company's flagship, the *Mason L. Weems*. The new stop was called Weems, a name that was adopted by the little hamlet that grew near the water's edge. In 1894, the Weems Line was purchased by a railroad company and was renamed the Baltimore and Virginia Steamboat Company. Regular service ended in 1932.

WELLINGTON
Fairfax

Captain Giles Brent of Richlands patented this tract in 1653 in the name of his infant son whose mother was a princess of the Piscataway Indians. Brent called his farm Piscataway Neck. It was inherited by George Brent, the Captain's nephew, and later was inherited by William Clifton who built the house here in 1757. Three years later he sold the plantation to George Washington who called it River Farm.

During the time that Colonel Tobias Lear leased River Farm the name Wellington was applied in honor of the Duke of Wellington, the victor at Waterloo in 1815. Colonel Lear was the military secretary to General Washington and was the private tutor of Martha Washington's children at Mount Vernon. He leased River Farm for fourteen years. By special provision of Washington's will, he was granted the use of the house and farm, rent free, until his death. Colonel Tobias Lear died in 1816 very shortly after he named the place Wellington. The estate was

inherited by two generations of the Washington family, the last occupant being Charles A. Washington who died in 1859. *See: Richlands; River Farm*

WEROWOCOMOCO
Gloucester County   **Site**

The word means "where the werowances live." A *werowance* was a war chief who did not have to bother about the day-to-day problems of his village and lived here to serve the great chief Powhatan. The representatives of the thirty-two tribes formed a council to give advice on serious matters, but neither the council nor the individual members had any independent powers. Here at Werowocomoco, on the north bank of the York River, Powhatan had the largest lodge, of course, and lived in primitive regal splendor. He was protected by his selected band of tall warriors (his Praetorian Guard) plus a host of women who had been given to him by the tribes as part of their annual tribute. This was the capital village of the loosely-knit confederacy which Powhatan ruled through fear and intimidation. Since it was inhabited by the collected werowances and other people from the various tribes, it was not identified by any tribal name.

Captain John Smith was brought here in December 1607 after his capture by the Chickahominies, and it was at Werowocomoco that Pocahontas saved his life. As a peace gesture, the colonists built Powhatan a house similar to the ones they had constructed for themselves at Jamestown. The great chief was then the only Indian to have a house with a fireplace and chimney, a singular honor. The house fell down after a few decades but the marl chimney stood as a monument to the chief for nearly 300 years. When Powhatan's chimney fell down in the middle of the twentieth century, all traces of Werowocomoco disappeared. *See: Orapax; Purton*

WEST CREEK ORDINARY
Amelia County   **Site**

Here in July 1781 Peter Franciscus, Virginia's "Hercules of the Revolution," encountered a troop of Tarleton's dragoons. Flighting alone with a broadsword against ten seasoned soldiers, he killed one and chased the others away. They retreated in such haste that they left their dead companion and all of the horses behind.

Franciscus (sometimes spelled Francisco) was an orphan whose origin is obscure. Some suggest he was born in Spain, kidnapped while young, and abandoned in Virginia. Found near City Point in 1766, he was adopted by Judge Anthony Winston. When the Revolution brought a need for soldiers, the foundling, then a strapping lad of about sixteen, joined the Continental Army. A muscular giant, well over six feet tall when he signed up, he continued to grow while in the army. Once he hauled an 1,100 pound cannon up a hill by himself during a battle and saved the day. On another occassion, he picked up a man and threw him onto the roof of a house.

There is also the story of a stranger who came up from Kentucky after the war. He announced that he had come to see who was the better man. Peter Franciscus not only tossed the braggart over a fence but threw the man's horse after him. He remained in the vicinity of West Creek Ordinary for the rest of his life, a kind, silent, strong giant.

WESTMORELAND COUNTY

Formed in 1653 from Northumberland, this county was named for the English shire of the same name. Many famous estates lie within this county, particularly those of the Lee family. The county seat is Montross. *See: Leedstown; Montross*

WESTOVER
Charles City County

Lord Delaware sent a group of men to this remote, upper portion of the James River in 1610 to look for gold. When they found none, he commanded them to remain there for the winter. They built a small fort to surround their small houses and hunkered down to wait for spring. The commander of the group was the governor's nephew, Henry West, who was killed by an arrow shot at random over the wall by an Indian. To keep a closer eye on the land outside the palisade, the men built a tower which they called West's Tower in memory of their slain captain. In 1611 Sir Francis West, the governor's brother, claimed this land and had plans to found a town of his own. His huge tract was called West and Shirley Hundred, a name that was soon dropped for the shorter West Tower.

The Massacre of 1622 forced the abandonment of this claim for the next fifteen years. In 1637 Thomas Paulett repatented the land and named it Westover. By then the old tower was just a memory. When Paulett died in 1666, Westover was sold to Theodoric Bland for 300 pounds sterling and 10,000 pounds of tobacco. The sale included 1,200 acres and the standing buildings. William Byrd I bought Westover from Bland in 1688 as an invest-

WESTOVER, CHARLES CITY

ment but remained at his trading post at the falls of the James. The original house is thought to have been near the site of the first church of Westover. Old gravestones, still standing, date back to 1637.

When William Byrd II, known as the Black Swan, returned to Virginia after completing his education, he found life at his father's remote trading post much too tame. With his mother, he moved to Westover and built the center portion of the present mansion in 1730. During his life-time, he expanded the lands of Westover to 26,000 acres and became a very wealthy gentleman farmer.

He wrote his own epitaph which was carved on a tombstone over his grave near the mansion: "Here lieth the Honourable William Byrd, Esq, being born to one of the amplest Fortunes in this Country. He was sent to England for his Education, where, under the care and direction of Sir Robert Southnell, and even favored with his particular instructions, he made a happy Proficiency in polite and various learning. By the means of the same noble Friend, he was introduced to the acquaintance of many of the first Persons of the Age for Knowledge, Wit, Virtue, Birth or high Station; and particularly contracted a most intimate and bosom Friendship with the learned and illustrious Charles Boyle, Earl of Orrery. He was called to the bar in the Middle Temple, studied for some time in the Low Countries, Visited the Court of France, and was chosen a Fellow of the Royal Society. Thus eminently fitted for the Service and Ornament of his Country, he was made Receiver-General of his Majesty's Revenues here. Was thrice appointed publick agent to the Court and Ministry of England, and being Thirty-Seven years a Member, at last became President of the Council of this Colony. To all this were added a great Elegancy of Taste and Life. The well-bred Gentleman and polite Companion, the splendid Occonomist and prudent Father of a Family, was the constant Enemy of all exhorbitant Power and hearty Friend of the Liberties of his County; Nat. Mar 28:1674, Mort Aug 26:1744, An Aetat 70."

He did not bother to mention his two wives or name his five children. His son and heir, William Byrd III, was the lord of Westover during the Revolution. A compulsive gambler, William III had to sell great sections of Westover land to cover his debts. He, too, had two wives. The second, Mary Shippen Willing of Philadelphia, was the sister of General Benedict Arnold's second wife. For

that she was suspected of being a Tory, especially when her brother-in-law, the famous traitor, stayed in her house at Westover for a few days in the summer of 1781. Mary Willing Byrd excused this visit by saying, "What could I, a helpless widow, do?" She held on to Westover for as long as she could, but was forced to sell in 1814. *See: Belvedere; Dismal Swamp; Evelynton; Marlboro; Richmond; Shirley; Stone House*

WESTOVER CHURCH
Charles City County

Established in 1613, the first church of the parish was erected sometime between 1630 and 1637 near the main house of Westover, then owned by Thomas Paulett. The parish had been organized for the benefit of the families of Westover, Berkeley, Shirley and adjoining properties along this bank of the James River.

The present structure was built about 1737 at a new site on Herring Creek. Tradition says the move was instigated by Mrs. William Byrd II because she became weary of so many guests for Sunday dinner every week. Since there was a brewery and a jail near the original building, it is also likely the sounds and smells were offensive enough to warrant the selection of a new site. The Reverend Peter Fontaine, who served the parish from 1716 to 1757, wrote that he felt the new location enhanced the dignity by being away from the "common" places. A tombstone bearing the date 1637 is located at the site of the first church. Marking the grave of William Perry, this may be the earliest existing tombstone in Virginia.

Attendance in Anglican churches ended during the Revolution, since the rectors had been supported through a poll tax and the people of Virginia wanted to sever all connections with the power of England. When the Statute for Religious Freedom was written into the new Commonwealth's constitution by Thomas Jefferson, other denominations organized congregations which attracted many former Anglicans. Westover Church stood empty and idle for decades. It had been used as a barn for forty years when missionaries from England came to Virginia to reorganize the Episcopal church in 1830. Even so, this church building was not reconsecrated until after its restoration in 1867. It has been faithfully used ever since.

This tidy, quaint house of worship was attended by Presidents Washington, Jefferson, William Henry Harrison, and Tyler. The parish still preserves a communion service made in London in 1694. Another piece of silver is inscribed "The Gift of Col. Francis Lightfoot, Anno 1727."

WEST POINT
King William County   Town

The triangle of land formed where the Pamunkey and Mattaponi rivers join to form the York is thought to have been the site of Opechancanough's village. He was the heir to Powhatan's confederacy. Some say he was a brother of the famous chief, others a nephew. Opechancanough planned the massacres of 1622 and 1644. In both uprisings, the Indians killed many settlers but could not eliminate the English from Virginia.

In 1650 Captain John West sold his land at Chischiak and built a new home about a mile up the Pamunkey River from the point of land. His home was West's Plantation and, because of his early influence in this region, Pamunkey Neck was called West's Point for many years. In 1701 John West III gave a tract of land at the point for a port, a fort, and a town. The port was lightly used, the fort was of no importance, and the town, called Delaware Town for the old Indian village, was slow to develop.

When the town was incorporated in 1870, it had a population of seventy-five it was at this time that the name West Point was adopted. The main industry today is the Chesapeake Corporation, a manufacturer of heavy paper products. *See: Bellfield; Chischiak; Delaware Town; Port Richmond; Utimara*

WEST'S PLANTATION
King William County   Site

Captain John West, a brother of Lord Delaware, patented 3,000 acres on the Pamunkey River about a mile upstream from the confluence of the Pamunkey and Mattaponi rivers where they form the York. His holdings included the site of the old Indian town of Cinquotek which had been deserted since the death of Chief Opechancanough in 1644. West occupied the northern portion of this tract in 1650 and built a modest home. When he died in 1659, the estate was inherited by his son, John II, who was the first white child born at Chischiak.

John West II was given lifetime immunity from taxes in 1660 because of "the many important former services to the country of Virginia by the noble family of West." He was a Burgess from the region and remained loyal to Governor Wiliam Berkeley during Bacon's

Rebellion of 1676. His son, John III, also a Burgess, gave fifty acres to the county for the port at Pamunkey Neck in 1701. He had one son, Charles West, who died unmarried in 1734. The plantation was claimed by his cousin, Thomas West, whose son was a Tory during the Revolution. John West IV was considered a dangerous threat during the siege of Yorktown. French General Rochambeau sent artillery to Delaware Town as a precaution but there was no action here.

A military map of 1781 shows that a portion of West's Plantation was then owned by Carter Braxton, a local area resident, who was one of the signers of the Declaration of Independence for Virginia. Braxton was forced to sell his farm to Charles Carter in 1805 in a mortgage foreclosure. *See Chischiak; Delaware Town; Elsing Green*

WEST VIRGINIA

Until 1863, this was Northwestern Virginia, the beginning of the Northwest Territory that stretched endlessly toward the Great Lakes. The Commonwealth of Virginia relinquished its claim to the Northwest Territory as its concession to the formation of the new republic, keeping only the region that today is known as the state of West Virginia. For years this sparsely inhabited, mountainous land was organized into four huge counties, all extremely remote from Wiliamsburg and Richmond. When the Republicans needed two Senators and eight Congressmen from a free state during the Civil War, the people of this region were persuaded to secede from Virginia and form a new state. *See: East Virginia; Southside Virginia*

WEYANOKE
Charles City County

George Yeardley, the Captain of Militia under Governors Dale and Argall, patented a tract of land on the north bank of the James River above the mouth of the Chikahominy River. He called it *Tanks Weyanoke,* meaning "Little Weyanoke" for the sub-tribe of the Weyanoke Indians who were living there when the Jamestown settlers arrived in 1607. The Indians were moved to a new village by Powhatan when the chief gave Yeardley the 2,200-acre tract. Although Yeardley tried to plant settlers on his land while he was the Governor from 1618 to 1620, his plantation did not succeed and the people drifted away.

His widow, Temperance Flowerdew Yeardley, sold the land to Joseph Harwood in 1644. William Hardwood, a descendant, replaced the early house with a brick dwelling in 1740. Harwood's daughter married Fielding Lewis of Warner Hall, Gloucester County. *See: Mulberry Island; Queen's Hith; Warner Hall*

WEYANOKE
Fairfax County
This relatively new community, due west of Alexandria, probably was named for the Indian tribe that lived on the James River in several villages when the Jamestown settlers first arrived. When the Weyanokes were forced to leave their James River homes, they moved west, not to this region. *See: Weyanoke Indians*

WEYANOKE INDIANS
Nobody knows what this tribe's real name was. Captain Gabriel Archer made the first contact with them in 1607. He could not understand their language but made out one word, *winauk*, which he took to be the tribal name. Actually, the Indians were telling him the name of a shrub that grew in abundance on their land from which they made a potion by boiling the fragrant root. Thus, unwittingly, Captain Archer named the tribe Sassafras, for that was the shrub that the Indians called *winauk*.

These people had at least five separate villages on both sides of the James River and could collect a small army of at least 300 braves if needed. Powhatan forced them to give up one of their villages, near the mouth of the Chickahominy River, when he made a gift of land to George Yeardley. It is possible they took part in the Massacre of 1622, but when things did not go as planned, those who escaped the war of retaliation moved up the James River to build a new town at the present site of Howardsville. After the Massacre of 1644, in which these Indians most probably did not participate, they realized their survival depended upon moving even farther west. Eventually, they blended with the other tribes that had migrated from the Chesapeake Bay area and came together as the Delaware Nation.

During the Indian troubles of the 1790s, a small tribe that was a part of Chief Little Turtle's Miami confederacy was known as the Weas. They might have been the remnants of the Weyanokes of the James River. Midwestern historians say they were named the Weas by French trappers because they were ready to say *oui* to almost any trade. No one knows for sure.

WEYER'S CAVE
Augusta County
A cavern was accidentally discovered under the floor of the Shenandoah Valley in 1806 by Bernard Weyer. It became known as Weyer's Cave, a name that was adopted by a community that developed near its mouth. Here, in the local high school, the first chapter of the Future Farmers of America was organized in 1927. The idea spread so quickly that a national society, with the same name, was put together in Baltimore one year later.

WHALEYVILLE
Suffolk
This town was founded by and named for S. M. Whaley. Once a separate community in Suffolk County, it is now a part of Suffolk city. *See: Suffolk*

WHITE CLIFF
Accomack County   Site
Thomas Savage settled here in 1619. His son, John Savage, married Ann Elkington and built his house on a white marl cliff about 1645. The marl here is an outcropping of the same material upon which Yorktown rests. The homes of Thomas and John Savage are long gone, but their names continue as Savage Neck. *See: Cherry Grove of Northampton; Dale's Gift; Savage Neck*

WHITE HALL
Albemarle County
A man whose last name was White bought Maupin's Tavern on the Three Chopt Road during the latter part of the eighteenth century. Acquiring land behind the tavern, he built a house near the former Revolutionary War barracks for Hessian soldiers, painted it white, and named it White's Hall. It was not too far from Black's Tavern near Yancey's Mill.

WHITE HALL
Gloucester County
Francis Willis, a member of the First Assembly of 1619, and later a member of the Council, settled here. When he died in England, all of his Virginia property was inherited by a nephew who promptly came to the colony and claimed it. The old house, originally known as Edge Ware, for the nearby Ware River, stood here prior to 1750.

WHITE HOUSE
New Kent County   Site
This was the home of Daniel Parke Custis

MARTHA WASHINGTON
WHITE HOUSE, NEW KENT

and his wife, Martha Dandridge. He was the son of the irascible Colonel John Custis IV of Arlington on the Eastern Shore and Queen's Creek Plantation near Williamsburg. Custis had so obediently "deferred to his father's prejudices, parsimony and alternate displays of affection and wrath" (as Daniel wrote), that he was thirty-seven years old before he dared to take a wife. At the time of the marriage in 1749, his bridge was eighteen years old. They had two children, a son named John Parke, and a daughter named Lucy Parke, both named for Daniel's mother, the former Frances Parke.

When Daniel Custis died rather suddenly in 1757, Martha became one of the richest widows in Virginia. After a brief courtship, the Widow Custis married George Washington on January 6, 1759. For a brief time they lived at White House, a charming residence on the Pamunkey River, but Martha wanted to live in a bigger house on the Potomac. For her, George remodeled and enlarged the home at Mount Vernon. They retained title to White House and its land, renting it out for income.

Almost exactly 100 years later, White House was inherited by William Henry Fitzhugh ("Rooney") Lee, the second son of Robert E. Lee.

During the Peninsula Campaign, General George McClellan used White House as his

base of supply. The Federals moved their base of supply to Harrison's Landing on the James River. On June 28, 1862, White House was evacuated and burned.

The land is now owned by ITT Corporation. *See: Arlington; Mount Vernon; Poplar Grove; Queen's Creek Plantation; Saint Peter's Church*

WHITE MARSH
Gloucester County

This estate once was part of a land grant given to Lewis Burwell of Fairfield in 1648. The elegant mansion at White Marsh began as a rather simple Georgian dwelling that was built about 1750. It remained in the Burwell family until 1798 when it was sold to Thomas Rootes, a lawyer, who is thought to have added to the original building by erecting the wing on one side and the porch on the other. Its most impressive front entrance is graced by tall columns. This estate was inherited by a member of the Tabb family and was owned by them until 1905. It has passed through several owners since then and was restored to its original appearance in 1965. *See: Elmington; Fairfield of Gloucester; Haw Branch*

WHITE PLAINS
Brunswick County

Possibly named for the Revolutionary War military activities near White Plains, New York, the name of this village first was Richardson, then Harrison. Both names came from early postmasters. The name White Plains was selected in 1925.

WHITE POST
Clarke County

Legend has it that the roadway leading to the home of Thomas, sixth Lord Fairfax, was marked by a sturdy post the servants kept continually whitewashed for visibility. It would have been poor taste to have either the name Greenway Court or Fairfax painted on a sign since anyone who wanted to visit knew where he lived. *See: New Post*

WHITING'S MOUNT
Gloucester County

This was the original seat of the Whiting family which became connected, through marriages, with all of the prominent families of the Middle Peninsula and the Eastern Shore. This tract was called Pig Hill during the latter part of the eighteenth century when Colonel Scaife Whiting lived here. *See: Elmington; Exchange; Mount*

WICOMICO
Northumberland County

This is another spelling of Yeocomico, an Indian tribe that lived on Northern Neck when this region was first settled. The name is pronounced Why-KOM-eye-co. A church was built on the edge of this creek in 1771. When the church fell to ruin, it was replaced by the present structure next to the original site. The congregation proudly owns a silver communion chalice inscribed "Ex Dono Hancock Lee to ye Parish of Lee 1711." Near this church are two Lee estates, Cobbs Hall and Ditchley. *See: Yeocomico*

WILDERNESS
Orange County

This tangle of scrub pines, thickets, vines, and miscellaneous thin hardwood trees covers an unsettled region of ridges and ravines. The works of man made it a wilderness. To feed his Tubal Furnace at Germanna, where iron ore was smelted as early as 1716, Alexander Spotswood purchased great amounts of charcoal. The suppliers cut the hardwood trees, cleared large circles of land for their kilns, and left behind two acres of cleared land for every filling of Tubal Furnace. It is estimated that 180 bushels of charcoal and two-and-one-half tons of ore produced one ton of pig iron. After twenty-five years of continuous production, the charcoal burners had cleared the entire region. The topsoil eroded until it supported only scrub oak, conifers, and other weed trees.

The spring of 1864 renewed Civil War action between the opposing armies.

General Lee met the forces of Grant in the Wilderness May 5-7 in one of the most savage battles of the war.

Lee tried to use the natural thickness of the terrain to limit the maneuvering of the Federals.

The Wilderness Battle began a drive that ended with the fall of the Southern forces.

Today, the area is under the direction of the National Park Service.

WILDERNESS ROAD

Many were the pioneer settlers who traveled this famous road from Virginia to Kentucky and Tennessee. It began a few miles from Fort Chiswell, crossed the New River at Ingle's Ferry (now Radford), and continued on beyond Abingdon to Block House. For the travellers of the eighteenth century, the road was little more than a horse

trail that gradually was widened by the passage of countless wagons and ox carts. After General Anthony Wayne crushed the Miami and Delaware Indians in the Midwest in 1792, the way was clear for easterners to build new homes and villages on the western side of the Ohio River.

WILLIAM AND MARY, COLLEGE OF
Williamsburg

Through the efforts of the Reverend James Blair, the Virginia representative of the Bishop of London, a royal charter was granted in 1693 to establish a college in Williamsburg. The grantors were the co-sovereigns King William III and Queen Mary II. The cornerstone of the first building, possibly designed by Sir Christopher Wren, was laid in 1695. Classes were held for younger children in the Grammar School and for a few selected young men in the Divinity School. For the next seventy-five years, the college was supported by the Anglican Church of Virginia.

In 1779 the Reverend James Madison was elected the president of the college. In a reorganization, the Grammar and Divinity schools were dropped and other academic courses were added. The first law school in America was created with George Wythe as the law professor. The college organized a medical school and added courses in modern foreign languages. Still, without government support, the college struggled to stay alive. It was not until 1906 that the college was accepted as a state-supported institution. It did not become coeducational until 1918.

The Reverend James Madison was the first Episcopal Bishop of Virginia. He was secretly ordained in Scotland without the consent of the king. *See: Varina Grove; Williamsburg*

WILLIAMSBURG
James City County   City

Middle Plantation, in the center of the long palisade erected across the Peninsula after the Massacre of 1622, was the headquarters of the militia that patrolled the barricade. No Indians were allowed to cross this line into the Kecoughtan district without a special badge. The terrain was higher at Middle Plantation than at Jamestown, the land was fertile and well drained, and the militiamen on permanent duty built homes here for their families. When the fourth statehouse at Jamestown caught fire in 1699, the House of Burgesses authorized movement of the seat of government to Middle Plantation. The

WILLIAM AND MARY, COLLEGE OF

Governor, Francis Nicholson, who fancied himself a city planner, worked out a design for the new town that placed the Capitol at one end of a wide street with the College of William and Mary at the other. The major streets were to be in the shape of the letters "W" and "M," a plan that was never fully carried out. By the time the government moved in 1699, the queen was dead and the new town was named in honor of King William III who remained on the throne. Williamsburg was the hub of political life in Virginia.

When the government moved to Richmond in 1780, while Thomas Jefferson was the Governor of the new Commonwealth, Williamsburg began to wither on the vine. It declined into a sleepy little village, half forgotten, until John D. Rockefeller, Jr. brought it to life again with the restoration and reconstruction of many of the old colonial buildings. The reconstructed Raleigh Tavern opened to the public in 1932. The Capitol and the Governor's palace, both rebuilt on the original foundations, were completed in 1934. Today Williamsburg is a mecca for all who wish to learn more of the vital contribution that Virginia made to the founding of the United States. *See: Jamestown; Middle Plantation; Richmond; Virginia*

WILLIAMS' FERRY
King William County   **Site**

Philip Williams' ferry which crossed the Pamunkey River was in operation here as early as 1716. In addition to being the ferryman, Williams was the manager of the public warehouse. Those who came from Northern Virginia to conduct business in Williamsburg usually crossed the Pamunkey at this point. The road to the old ferry can be made out today from the mounds of earth that are flanked by old trees.

WILLIAMSVILLE
Hanover County

This little hamlet took its name from the massive brick house built here in the nineteenth century by "Billy Particular," William Pollard II. While he was the clerk of Hanover County, a position he held from 1781 until 1824, Pollard supervised and fussed over the construction of his home. Begun in 1794, "Billy Particular" did not declare it finished and ready for occupancy until 1803. The three-story house, resting on an English basement, remained in the Pollard family until 1936.

WILLIS' TAVERN
Goochland County

An ordinary stood here beside the Three Chopt Road, the first tavern encountered by a traveller going west from Richmond. Little else is known about it. Obviously, it was operated by a Mr. Willis.

269

WILLIS WHARF
Northampton County
Edward Willis purchased land here in 1854 and built a wharf. Since it was on the Atlantic Ocean side of the Eastern Shore, only shallow-draft boats could use it. The tiny hamlet today retains the name.

WILLOUGHBY SPIT
Norfolk
A severe hurricane struck the lower portion of the Chesapeake Bay in 1680. The heavy action of the water and winds added 217 acres of sand on the south side of the entrance to Hampton Roads, just across from Old Point Comfort. Had it not been for the strong tidal action twice a day, as Hampton Roads empties into the ocean, the huge anchorage might have been completely sealed by sand. As it is, the opening now is but two miles wide and the expanded Willoughby Spit causes a heavy running of the tides at a point known as Rip Rap where Fort Wool was built just a few decades prior to the Civil War. The extension of the spit also increased the length of Willoughby Bay, just off the Norfolk Naval Air Station, which for a number of years was a quiet, protected landing place for military sea planes.

The name Willoughby has two possible origins. Captain John Smith grew up on his father's farm in Lincolnshire, England on land owned by Lord Willoughby of d'Eresby. The lord was an adventurer who inspired young John to lead a similar life even though he was a commoner. Smith did not place the name on his map of Virginia in 1612.

The spit most probably was named for Captain Thomas Willoughby who settled in the Norfolk area in 1636. Later in the seventeenth century, a home of the Willoughby family was located in what is now the Ocean View section of the city of Norfolk. *See: Fort Wool; Spit*

WILSONIA
Northampton County   Site
When John Custis first came to Virginia about 1640, he settled on the ocean side of the Eastern Shore at Magothy Bay. His son, John II, expanded the family lands by purchasing a huge tract on the bay side on Old Plantation Creek. The northern portion of this newly-acquired land, located on a neck between Mattawoman and Hungars creeks, was called Chiconessex for a former Indian village that once was located here. While John Custis II built his home on the southern fringe, which

he named Arlington, John Custis III built his home at Chiconessex. He was a Burgess for over fifty years and was appointed to the Council to replace his father in 1699. John Custis IV inherited both tracts in 1713, plus his grandfather's estates in James City County and became one of the wealthiest men in the colony. Many years after his death, the Chiconessex lands were purchased from the Custis family and the farm was renamed Wilsonia, most probably for the new owner. The neck of land is now called Wilsonia Neck. *See: Arlington; Mount Custis; Queen's Creek Plantation*

WILSONS
Dinwiddie County
The family name Wilson is common throughout Virginia. One branch of the family migrated to this region in pre-Revolutionary times and built a home on a stream that feeds into Namozine Creek. The tributary was called Wilson's Creek. Of course, the farm was called Wilson's, too. This tiny hamlet was named for either the creek or the farm and the punctuation was dropped for the benefit of the postal authorities who seem to object to the use of "apostrophe s." *See: Mouth of Wilson*

WILTON
Henrico County   Site
William Randolph III, a descendant of the Randolphs of Turkey Island, built Wilton in 1753 on a farm he called World's End since it was six miles below Richmond. Across the James River was Ampthill, the home of Henry Cary II. Both Wilton and Ampthill show so many similarities in plan and interior decorations that it is thought the same person may have designed them, possibly Richard Taliaferro.

The first owner of Wilton was active in the affairs of his county. By the time he was twenty-six, he had been elected a vestryman, a colonel of the militia, and a Burgess. In 1735 he married Anne Carter Harrison of Berkeley and thus joined two important and influential families. His youngest son, Peyton Randolph, inherited the estate. This Peyton Randolph was not the Speaker of the House of Burgesses, although they were closely related. Wilton remained in the family for three more generations, but by the nineteenth century, most of the Randolphs lived in Richmond, feeling, probably, that Wilton was still at the world's end.

In 1934 the old house, sadly neglected and

in need of repair, was purchased by the Virginia Society of Colonial Dames. The building was moved to its present location in the west end of Richmond where it now enjoys restored glory as the organization's Virginia headquarters. *See: Ampthill; Berkeley; Chesterville; Tuckahoe, Turkey Island*

WILTON
Middlesex County

One of the collateral ancestors of Winston Churchill lived in Middlesex County in the eighteenth century. William Churchill built this T-shaped house in 1763 and today, it is one of the least-altered colonial houses in Tidewater. Typical of the family's aggressive nature, William Churchill was actively engaged in county politics.

WILTON
Westmoreland County

One of the oldest inhabited houses in the Northern Neck section of Virginia, this Wilton was built about 1680 by John Gerard on land he patented in 1651. It is not a large house but it has great dignity, nestled into a perfect setting at the head of Jackson's Creek. Wilton is an old English name was used in many locations in Old Dominion.

WINCHESTER
Frederick County   City

First settled in 1738 near a former Shawnee Indian village called Opequon, the collection of dwellings was recognized by the Assembly in 1744 as Frederick Town, in honor of Frederick, Prince of Wales, the father of King George III. When the town was chartered in 1752, the name was changed to Winchester by Colonel James Wood for his native city in England. Lord Thomas Fairfax, the proprietor of Northern Neck, used this town as his frontier headquarters and eventually built his home, Greenway Court, not too far away.

When Lord Fairfax met George Washington at Belvoir, where he was learning to be a surveyor under the direction of his Lordship's nephews, he hired the young man in 1748 to survey his western lands. During Washington's three years in the wilderness, he had his office in a small building in this town at the corner of Cork and Braddock streets. While he was a colonel in the militia from 1756 to 1758, he used his old survey office as his headquarters. Lord Fairfax, who died shortly after the surrender at Yorktown in 1781, lies buried in the yard of Christ Church in Winchester. *See: Fort Loudoun; Greenway Court*

WINDINGDALE
Accomack County

In 1665 Richard Kellem purchased a huge tract of land on the Eastern Shore to create a new town of his own. He planned to build a church, a public market, a new courthouse, and a jail. The project fell through. The house now standing contains a portion of the first house which was not built until about 1722 by Thomas Kellam. His nearest neighbors at the time lived in Occahannock. *See: Hermitage*

WINDMILL POINT
Lancaster County

There were several points by this name up and down the various rivers that empty into Chesapeake Bay, but this is the only one that retains the name. The first windmill in America was built at Flowerdew Hundred in 1621. A second was built a few years later almost directly across the James on Mulberry Island (now Fort Eustis). Both were highly visible from ships and were marked on charts as navigational checkpoints. After windmills were constructed, the colonists began to build tide mills and other water mills that harness the movement of streams. It was not until the middle of the seventeenth century that dams were attempted to create mill ponds with mill races. *See: Mill*

WINDSOR
Caroline County

Here in 1734 was born General William Woodford, the commander of the Virginia militia during the Battle of Great Bridge in December 1775. General Woodford continued an active military career during the remaining years of the Revolution and later retired to his farm. Because of his fame, Windsor was better known as Woodford. *See: Great Bridge; Norfolk*

WINDSOR
Isle of Wight County   Town

This was the location of the palatial home of Colonel Augustine Claiborne, a lawyer, Revolutionary soldier, and the first clerk of Sussex County. His father was Thomas Claiborne II, a Captain of Virginia troops. His great-uncle, William was active on behalf of the Governor during Bacon's Rebellion. Others of the family were members of the Council, one was the Secretary of the colony, and another the Treasurer of Virginia. All were descended from William Claiborne of New Kent Island.

Colonel Augustine Claiborne's home is

nothing but a ruin now, as is the mill that provided needed services for the people of this region. One thousand acres of Windsor were purchased by the College of William and Mary in 1777 and leased to the citizens of the county at such a high rent that Colonel Claiborne felt it his duty to lodge an official complaint. There is no record of the reason the name Windsor was selected, but more than likely it was named for Windsor Castle in England. *See: Romancoke; Sweet Hall*

WINDSOR
Mathews County   **Site**

Astride the line between Mathews and Gloucester counties lie the lands of John Clayton, a noted botanist during colonial times. He wrote *Flora Virginica* in collaboration with the Dutch botanist, Gronovius, and had his book published in Leyden. Thomas Jefferson, Benjamin Franklin, and William Byrd II studied this monumental work about the flora native to Virginia. The house at this Windsor has disappeared, but traces of the experimental gardens remain, tended by the Garden Club of Virginia. *See: Banister River*

WINGINA
Nelson County   **Village**

This tiny village on the north bank of the James River was named for the Indian chief Wingina. He and his tribe welcomed the first Englishmen who arrived in 1581 to begin a colony on the Outer Banks of present-day North Carolina. The easy mixing of the two races quickly turned sour when the newcomers developed "gold fever" and attempted to force the natives to reveal the location of the mine. Wingina was killed in the conflict and his severed head was stuck on a pole at the water's edge. This heartless, needless action by the first settlers sealed the fate of the "Lost Colony" of 1585. No one knows why the name was adopted for a site in Virginia. *See: Virginia*

WISE COUNTY

Formed from parts of Lee, Russell, and Scott in 1856, this county was named for a man whose roots were on the Eastern Shore. Henry A. Wise was the Governor of the Commonwealth at the time the county was organized. This is one of the coal producing areas of the state. The county seat was named Gladeville for many years, named for Glade Creek that ran nearby. Today it is called Wise. *See: Onley*

WOLF'S SNARE
Virginia Beach

Adam Keeling sold this plantation to John Pallet in 1714. It was known as Wolf's Snare for reasons unknown, although wolves were common in all parts of Virginia until the present century. Lately, there have been reports of big grey wolves in the mountains as Virginia's deer population increases. John Pallet II built the house here about 1719. He began the custom, still retained, of coating the bricks with a pink whitewash.

WOLFTOWN
Madison County

The major structure here for many years was the Rose Tavern, a stage stop of the road between Alexandria and Charlottesville. When a post office opened at the tavern in 1828, the name was Rapidan, for the river that runs close by. For some unrecorded reason, the name was changed to Wolftown twenty-nine years later.

WOODBERRY FOREST
Orange County

William Madison, President James Madison's brother, built his home here in 1793. He named it Woodbury for an old English manor that probably was connected to the family. The old house is now the residence of the headmaster of Woodberry Forest School, a college prep school for boys which was founded in 1889 by Robert Stringfellow Walker, a Captain in Mosby's Rangers in the Civil War. It is not known why the name was changed from Woodbury to Woodberry Forest, but the connection with the Madison home has been established.

WOODBRIDGE
Prince William County

A toll bridge, made of wood, was erected across the Occoquan River in 1795 by Thomas Mason, the son of George Mason of Gunston Hall. This bridge lasted for 103 years and was replaced by a steel truss crossing in 1878. By then the name Wood Bridge had been firmly implanted in the minds of those who lived near it and, steel or not, the new bridge went by the old, familiar name. When a community developed at the south end, on the highway between Richmond and Washington, it adopted the name Woodbridge (spelled as one word). The first steel bridge was swept away in 1972 when a huge wave of water came from behind an upstream dam during Hurricane Agnes. It was replaced by a higher structure that arches from bank to bank in a graceful sweep. *See: Chain Bridge; Occoquan*

WOODFORD
See: Windsor of Caroline County

WOODLAWN
Carroll County
Colonel James Wood received a grant of 2,800 acres during the days of King George II. Modestly, he named it Woodlawn.

WOODLAWN
Fairfax County
The land of this estate was taken from the many acres of Mount Vernon and was given to Nelly Custis and Lawrence Lewis as a wedding gift. They were married at Mount Vernon on February 22, 1799, on their famous relative's last birthday. The bride was Eleanor Parke Custis, Martha Washington's granddaughter. The groom was the grandson of George Washington's sister, Betty Lewis. Included in the parcel was Dogue Run Farm, a grist mill, and a distillery. Construction of the mansion took five years. The couple moved into one of the wings in 1803 and occupied the entire house by 1805. After the death of Lawrence in 1839, Nelly moved to Audley in Clarke County, taking her son with her and leaving the Woodlawn plantation vacant and unused.

In 1846 it was offered for public sale. It was purchased by a group of Quakers who revitalized the farm lands, built their own modest dwellings, and used the mansion for a meeting house. Although the surrounding communities voted for secession at the beginning of the Civil War, the Quakers of Woodlawn remained staunchly loyal to the Union and lived out the war in isolation.

After a series of owners, during which the original large tract was reduced to a mere 500 acres, it was purchased in 1925 by Senator Oscar Underwood of Alabama. He was Woodrow Wilson's chief rival for the Democratic nomination in 1912. After again unsuccessfully seeking his party's nomination in 1924, Underwood retired from the Senate and spent his remaining five years at Woodlawn. The estate remained in the Underwood family until it was purchased by the Woodlawn Public Foundation in 1948. *See: Audley; Kenmore*

WOOD'S GAP
Tazewell County
Abraham Wood was an early explorer of the mountains of western Virginia. In 1653 he traveled in the company of William Claiborne and Henry Fleet. All three were searching for good lands to claim. Later, Wood returned by himself, found a new river, which he named for himself, and followed it to the mountains where he located a pass now known as Wood's Gap. For a while Virginia had two Wood's Gaps, the other one being in the Blue Ridge between Nelson and Albemarle counties which was discovered by Michael Wood in 1734. This second Wood's Gap was later renamed Jarman's Gap. *See: Petersburg*

WOODSTOCK
Shenandoah County   Town
Jacob Mueller donated the land and founded this town prior to 1761. He gave no reason for selecting the name Woodstock except that he did not want his name used. In a log church in this town, the Reverend John P. Muhlenberg preached a stirring sermon in 1776 that called for the men of the region to take up arms in the Revolution. He was the son of the man who had organized the first Lutheran Synod in America. The Reverend Muhlenberg, however, was an ordained Anglican priest, having taken Holy Orders in London in 1772. He was a leader in opposition to the taxes imposed upon the colonies by Parliament. In June of 1774, he and his congregation drafted a resolution in which they declared they would "pay due submission to such acts of government as His Majesty has a right to exercise over his subjects, and to such only."

Muhlenberg's resentment of the Crown reached a climax on a Sunday in January 1776 when he preached a sermon based on the text, "There is a time for every purpose . . . A time to war, and a time for peace." As a dramatic finale, he cried out, "The time to fight has come!" Casting off his black cassock, he stood before his congregation in the buff and blue uniform of a colonel in the Continental Army. Immediately he enlisted all eligible men into the eighth Virginia Regiment.

Woodstock, the seat of Shenandoah County, has a courthouse that dates to 1791. *See: Shenandoah County*

WOODVILLE
Rappahannock County
At one time the rector of Saint Mark's

church here was the Reverend John Woodville. This hamlet was named for him. *See: Ivy
Tavern*

WORMELEY CREEK
York County

Christopher Wormeley settled on the east
bank of this creek in 1635. Upon his death, the
property was inherited by Ralph Wormeley, a
member of the Council, who welcomed Sir
Thomas Lunsford, Sir Henry Chicheley, Sir
Philip Honeywood, and several other noted
Cavaliers who left Cromwell's England about
1649. The next year, Ralph Wormeley moved
his home to Middlesex County where he built
Rosegill and renamed Nimcock Creek there
for himself. The second Wormeley Creek,
fortunately, is now called Urbanna Creek.
This York County creek, a tidal inlet of the
York River, provides a haven for small
pleasure craft at private piers. It is subject to
shoaling by shifting sandbars and is difficult
to enter. *See: Creek; Rosegill; Urbanna*

WRENN'S MILL
Isle of Wight County   **Site**

About two miles northwest of Smithfield,
George Hardy operated a mill as early as
1646. Forty years later, the mill was
purchased by a miller whose last name was
Wrenn. Several mills have been erected on
this spot over the past 300 years. *See: Smithfield*

WYLLIESBURG
Charlotte County

The Wylie family was dominant here many
years ago when a name was required for the
post office.

WYNDALE
Washington County

In 1772 William Wyyn erected a fort on a
branch of the Holston River. At that time,
both the Cherokee and the Shawnee Nations
were on the warpath, although they spent
more time fighting each other than attacking
settlers. The fort was mainly used to defend
against the Shawnee. William Wynn also
found a good crossing of the Dan River which
bore his name. *See: Danville*

WYTHE COUNTY

Formed in 1798 from Montgomery, this
county was named for George Wythe, one of
the signers of the Declaration of Independence for Virginia. He was the first professor
of law in America, teaching at the College of
William and Mary in Williamsburg. Thomas
Jefferson was one of his students. George
Wythe was born in Elizabeth City, lived much
of his adult life in Williamsburg, and died in
Richmond. He was buried in that city's Saint
John's churchyard. The name of this county is
pronounced "With." *See: Chesterville*

WYTHEVILLE
Wythe County   **Town**

An early settler, Jesse Evans, named this
town Abbeville for his birthplace in South
Carolina. When the town was officially
recognized in 1792, the name was Evansham.
However, when it was incorporated in 1839,
the name was changed to Wytheville. It is the
seat of Wythe County.

YANCEY MILLS
Albemarle County

Among the first settlers in Albemarle County was Jeremiah Yancey who came to this part of the Piedmont about 1765. He and his son, Robert, ran a tavern, a distillery, and a mill. Later, the public house was called May's Tavern and, later still, Cocke's Tavern for the successive owners. The old mill is gone, but the settlement retains the name. Once named Yancey's Mill, the current spelling misplaces the "s."

YEOCOMICO RIVER
Northumberland County

This deep water inlet of the Potomac River, on the lower end of Northern Neck, is hardly a river in the true sense. Actually a creek, it carried important commerce from the local plantations for scores of decades until the end of the era of steamers in the Chesapeake Bay. The name is Indian in origin. This was in the Chicacoan Indian district. *See: Creek; Kinsale; Pecatone; Wicomico*

YORK COUNTY

One of the original eight shires formed in 1634, this area was first called Chischiak. At the time of the founding, it was called Charles River Shire for the river which formed its boundary. The first major landholder of note was Governor John Harvey who called his plantation Yorke. The first courthouse was built on his land, now occupied by the Yorktown Coast Guard Reserve Training Base. In 1643, the name of the river and the county were both changed to York because of the confusion with Charles City County. By then a new courthouse had been erected in the little village of Yorktown. *See: Charles City County; Yorktown*

YORKE
York County   **Site**

In 1630, Governor John Harvey encouraged men to settle on the south bank of the Charles River in the Chischiak region. To lead the way, he patented a tract at the mouth of the Charles River where it joins Chesapeake Bay. At the time, by luck, a Frenchman arrived in the colony, Nicholas Martiau by name, who had been sent by King Charles I to erect fortifications as protection against possible Dutch incursions. Harvey sent the engineer

to his land first to give his servants the use of a well-constructed fort. Today the Harvey plantation is occupied by the Coast Guard Reserve Training Facility. *See: Chischiak; Utimara; York River*

YORK HALL
Yorktown

According to a descendant, York Hall at Yorktown was built between 1725 and 1740 by the first Thomas Nelson, known as Scotch Tom. He came to Virginia from Penrith in Cumberland near the border between England and Scotland. He was a great merchant who established a prominent family, leaving two sons and a daughter. His first house was rather modest in size and the foundations have been located and preserved.

The present York Hall, also known as the Nelson House, was built by his son, William, who was the President of the Council when Lord Dunmore came to Virginia in 1771. William Nelson, rather elderly at the time, died two years later. His brother Thomas became both the President of the Council and the Secretary of the colony. He was presiding when Lord Dunmore left Williamsburg and sought refuge on a ship in the York River in the summer of 1775. According to custom, Nelson should have been appointed the acting governor, but Dunmore refused to do this since he wanted to preserve the legal position that the colony was in revolt and that he had not given up the reigns of government.

William Nelson married Elizabeth Burwell, the granddaughter of Robert "King" Carter of Corotoman. Their son (the grandson of Scotch Tom and the nephew of Thomas Nelson, Sr.) was a general in the Continental Army. During the siege of Yorktown in 1781, Thomas Nelson, Jr. noticed that his home, York Hall, was being spared by the cannoneers although Cornwallis had occupied it as his headquarters. He ordered the guns trained upon it and offered five guineas to the first gunner to hit it. The house was damaged and a cannonball, carefully preserved, is still lodged in the outer brick wall.

After the war, Thomas Nelson, a signer of the Declaration of Independence, and an elected Governor of the Commonwealth, was reduced to near poverty. He sold his property to pay the debts he had acquired as his contribution to the war effort. When the

275

Virginia Assembly debated the cancellation of all war debts to English firms. General Nelson rose and stated, "Others may do as they please; but, as for me, I am an honest man and, so help me God, I will pay my debts." When he died, he was buried in the yard of Grace Church in Yorktown. For many years his grave lay unmarked. A descendant placed a stone above his remains inscribed, "He gave all for Liberty." *See: Chischiak; Corotoman; Moore House; Nelson County*

YORK RIVER

The York River has had several names. Captain John Smith first called it the River Powhatan because the Great Chief's main village was upon its north bank. When Powhatan died in 1618, the river's name was changed to Pamunkey for the Indian tribe that lived at its head where the Pamunkey and Mattaponi join. When Charles I became the head of England in 1625, the colonists renamed this major waterway in his honor, thinking it was only good politics to have the two major streams, on either side of the region of population, bear the names of English monarchs. The shire on the south bank, Chischiak, also was renamed for the king but over the years it was often confused with Charles City County.

Having honored the king with the old county and Cape Charles, both the land mass and the river were redesignated York in 1643. This was one not-too-subtle way the Virginians proclaimed their loyalty to the Crown during the heyday of Oliver Cromwell and his Commonwealth. It is not clear if the chosen name honored the troubled king Charles I, who had been the Duke of York, or his younger son, James, who had been given his father's former title to follow the custom of identifying the king's second son this way. When James followed his brother, Charles II, to the throne in 1685, he became highly disliked for his Catholic leanings and was forced to flee the country in the wave of Protestantism that brought William and Mary to power as co-sovereigns. Leaning on the fact that the beheaded Charles I once had been the Duke of York, and finished with changing the name of the river at last, the colonists let the present name stand. *See: James River*

YORKTOWN

York County   **Town**

Settlement began here under orders from the Council issued in October 1630 to occupy the former lands of the Chischiak Indians.

Captain Nicholas Martiau followed Captains West, Utie, and Felgate to receive his fifty acres where the present town now stands. Martiau, a French engineer, and naturalized English subject, came to Virginia at the request of the king to build a system of forts as protection against possible Dutch incursions. For his work he was granted 1,550 acres, which he added to his original 50. All of this land was inherited by his son-in-law Colonel George Reade in 1657. Colonel Reade became the deputy Secretary of the colony and was appointed to the Council. After his death in 1671, his house and land was inherited by his son, Benjamin Reade.

In 1680, the House of Burgesses passed the "Act for Ports" which was designed to control all of the export and import trade of the colony. At these ports public warehouses were built where all tobacco was inspected and graded before being shipped abroad. Yorktown, located on a bluff above the mouth of the York River, was a natural point for a customs station. In 1691 Benjamin Reade sold fifty acres to the colony to establish a town which was properly laid out. In 1698 Yorktown was designated the county seat and a new courthouse was built. Except for customs collections, the town had no spectacular trade of its own, although it was well-known for its bawdy taverns and bordellos at the river's edge near the wharf.

*GENERAL GEORGE WASHINGTON
YORKTOWN*

The people of the business and social set maintained their homes higher up on the bluff.

In late summer of 1781, Yorktown was rudely awakened from its peaceful ways when Lord Cornwallis arrived with his army and prepared to winter here. While General Lafayette kept the English busy with a series of brief attacks and a group of French and American marines captured the fort across the river at Gloucester Point, Washington hurried from New York with his army and a French army under the command of the Comte de Rochambeau. They caught Cornwallis unprepared to defend against a siege. His rescue by a British fleet was foiled after a naval engagement off the Virginia Capes was won by the Comte de Grasse. Lord Cornwallis was forced to surrender.

Yorktown fell into a sleepy way of life for the next 100 years. It was awakened in time for the celebration of the Centennial in 1871 at which time the Yorktown monument was dedicated. After another 100 years of peaceful sleep, Yorktown was again awakened, in the autumn of 1981, for the Bicentennial celebrations. *See: Chischiak; Ringfield; Utimara; Yorke*

Z

ZION CROSSROADS
Louisa County

Near here, on the Three Chopt Road, stood Zion Church—and that was just about all there was for many, many years. The nearest tavern was Boyd's, a few miles to the west, where the River Road and the Three Chopt Road intersected. During the early decades of the twentieth century, the old River Road was relocated (now US 15) and the Three Chopt Road (now US 250) was straightened. The new intersection was named Zion Cross-roads for the old church.

In the days before Interstate 64 made movement of autos and trucks smooth and rapid, the challenge was to drive the fifteen miles from Free Bridge, on the Rivanna River outside Charlottesville, to Zion Crossroads in fifteen minutes without being caught by the state police. Many young men died trying. *See: Mount Zion*

ZUNI
Isle of Wight County

Despite many colorful attempts to connect this name with the Zuni Indians of south-western America, the name Zuni was selected by the wife of the president of the N & W Railway when the line was built through the counties on the south side of the James River from Richmond and Petersburg. Mrs. Billy Mahone named this flag stop, and several others, for the novels of Sir Walter Scott. *See: Ivanhoe; Ivor; Waverly*

BIBLIOGRAPHY

Abernathy, Thomas P. *University of Virginia Historical Sketch* Richmond, VA.: Dietz Press, 1948

Alden, John R. *Robert Dinwiddie, Servant of the Crown* Williamsburg, Va.: Colonial Williamsburg Fdn., 1973

Andrews, Matthew P. *Virginia, The Old Dominion* New York: Doubleday, Doran & Co., 1937

Andrist, Ralph K., ed. *The Founding Fathers: George Washington* New York: Newsweek Books, 1974

Arthur, Major Robert *History of Fort Monroe* Fort Monroe: Coast Artillery School Printing Plant, 1930

Ayling, Stanley *George the Third* New York: Alfred A. Knopf, 1972

Bagby, Rev. Alfred *King and Queen County, Virginia* New York: Neale Publishing Co., 1908

Billings, Warren M. *The Old Dominion in the Seventeenth Century* Chapel Hill, N.C.: University of North Carolina Press, 1975

Bland County Centennial Corporation *History of Bland County* Radford, Va.: Commonwealth Press, 1961

Blanton, Wyndham B. *Medicine in Virginia in the Seventeenth Century* Richmond, Va.: William Byrd Press, 1930

Boddie, John B. *Colonial Surry* Richmond, Va.: Dietz Presse, 1948

Bodine, A. Aubrey *Chesapeake and Tidewater* New York: Hastings House, 1954

Bodine, A. Aubrey *The Face of Virginia* Bodine, 1963

Bradshaw, Herbert Clarence *History of Prince Edward County, Virginia* Richmond, Va.: Dietz Press, 1955

Brodie, Fawn M. *Thomas Jefferson, An Intimate History* New York: W. W. Norton & Co., 1974

Brown, Alexander C. *Newport News' 325 Years* Newport News, Va.: Golden Anniv. Corp., 1946

Brown, Robert E. *Virginia 1705-1786, Democracy or Aristocracy* Ann Arbor, Mich.: University of Michigan Press, 1964

Bruce, Phillip A. *History of Virginia* Chicago: Lewis Publishing Company, 1929

Bruce, Phillip A. *Social Life in Virginia in the Seventeenth Century* Lynchburg, Va.: J. P. Bell, Inc., 1927

Brydon, George M. *Virginia's Mother Church* Church Historical Society, 1952

Burgess, Robert H. *Chesapeake Circle* Cornell Maritime Press, 1865

Burgess, Robert H. *This Was Chesapeake Bay* Cornell Maritime Press, 1965

Caperton, Helena L. *Legends of Virginia* Richmond, Va.: Garrett, 1931

Caywood, Louis R. *Greenspring Archeological Report* Williamsburg, Va.: Colonial National Historical Park, 1955

Chamberlaine, Samuel *Springtime in Virginia* New York: Hastings, 1947

Chitwood, Oliver Perry *Richard Henry Lee, Statesman of the Revolution* Charleston, W.Va.: West Virginia University Fdn., McClain Printing Co., 1967

Clarke, Peyton Neale *Old King William Homes and Families* Loisville: Ky.: John P. Morton & Co., 1897

Clement, Maud Carter *History of Pittsylvania County* Lynchburg, Va.: J. P. Bell Company, 1929

Cohen, Stan *Historic Springs of Virginia* Charleston, W. Va.: Pictorial Histories Publishing Co., 1981

Colonial Williamsburg, Inc. *Colonial Williamsburg Official Gudiebook and Map* Williamsburg, Va.: 5th edition, 1965

Colonial Williamsburg, Inc. *Peyton Randolph House* Williamsburg, Va.: (Mary Stephenson, 1952; revised by Jane Carson, 1967)

Couture, Richard T. *Powhatan, A Bicentennial History* Richmond, Va.: Dietz Press, 1980

Cox. V. D. and Weathers, W. T. *Old Houses of King and Queen County, Virginia* King and Queen Historical Society, 1973

Culpeper Historical Society *Historic Culpeper* Culpeper, Va.: 1974

Davis, Burke *A Williamsburg Galaxy* Williamsburg, Va.: Colonial Williamsburg Fdn., 1968

Davis, Julia *The Shenandoah* New York: Farrar & Rinehart, 1945

Davis, Margaret G. *Madison County, Virginia, A Revised History* Ephrata, Va.: The Science Press, 1977

De Samper, Hugh *Petersburg* Petersburg, Va.: Town Crier Publishers, 1975

Dowdey, Clifford *The Virginia Dynasties* New York: Little, Brown and Company, 1969

Dowling, Albert W. *On Chesapeake Shores* Richmond, Va.: Dietz Press, 1959

Duke, Jane Taylor *Kenmore and the Lewises* New York: Doubleday & Co., 1949

279

Dutton, Joan Parry *Plants of Colonial Williamsburg* Williamsburg, Va.: Colonial Williamsburg Fdn., 1979

Earle Swepson *The Chesapeake Bay Country* Baltimore, Md.: Thomsen Ellis Co., 1929

Eaton, David W. *Historical Atlas of Westmoreland County, Virginia* Richmond, Va.: Dietz Press, 1942.

Evans, M. Louisa *An Old Timer in Warrenton and Fauquier Counties* Berryville, Va.: Virginia Publishing, Inc., 1955

Ewan, Joseph, and Ewan, Nestra *John Banister and His Natural History of Virginia* Chicago: University of Illinois Press, 1970

Fairfax County Board of Supervisors *Fairfax County, Virginia—A History* Fairfax, Va.: 1978

Farrar, Emmie Ferguson *Old Virginia Homes Along the James* New York: Bonanza Books, 1957

Farrar, Emmie Ferguson *Old Virginia Houses Along the Fall Line* New York: Hastings House, 1971

Farrar, Emmie Ferguson *Old Virginia Houses: The Mobjack Bay Area* New York: Hastings House, 1955

Farrar, Emmie Ferguson *Old Virginia Houses: The Northern Peninsula* New York: Hastings House, 1972

Finberg, G. P. R. *The Formation of England 550-1042* Suffolk, England: Hart-Davis, Mac-Gibbon, Ltd., 1974

Fishwick, Marshall W. *Gentlemen of Virginia* New York: Dodd, Meade, 1961

Fithian, Philip Vickers *A Plantation Tutor of the Old Dominion* Williamsburg, Va.: Col. Williamsburg, Inc., Hunter D. Farish, editor, 1957

Foster, A. J. *Early James River History in and Around Richmond, Virginia* Falls Church, Va.: 1965

Gloucester Historical Society *Six Periods in the History of Gloucester County* Gloucester, Va.: 1970

Gold, Thomas D. *History of Clarke County* Berryville, Va.: Chesapeake Book Co., 1962

Goolrick, John T. *Fredericksburg and the Cavalier County* Richmond, Va.: Garrett and Massie, 1935

Gray, Ryland Simmons *Historic Buildings in Middlesex County, Virginia 1650-1875* Charlotte, N.C.: Delmar Printing Co., 1978

Hagemann, Mutter W. "Queen Anne" Monograph, unpublished; Hampton, 1970

Hale, Nathaniel C. *Virginia Venturer* Richmond, Va.: Dietz Press, 1951

Hanson, Rans McDill *Virginia Place Names* Verona, Va.: McClure Press, 1962

Harris, Malcolm H. *History of Louisa County, Virginia* Richmond, Va.: Dietz Press, 1936

Harris, Malcolm H. *Old New Kent County* vol. 1 and 2 West Point, Va.: 1977 (private printing)

Harris, Marlene R. *Virginia Antiques* Exposition, 1953

Harrison, Fairfax *Landmarks of Old Prince William* Berryville, Va.: Chesapeake Book Co., 1964

Havighurst, Walter *Alexander Spotswood, Portrait of a Governor* New York: Holt, Rinehart & Winston, 1967

Haynie, Miriam *The Stronghold: A Story of the Historic Northern Neck of Virginia and its People* Richmond, Va.: Dietz Press, 1959

Homes and Gardens *Photographic Studies of Old Virginia* Richmond, Va.: Dietz Press, 1953

Hudson, J. Paul *A Pictorial History of Jamestown, Virginia* Richmond, Va., 1957

Hume, Ivor Noel *Here Lies Virginia* New York: Alfred A. Knopf, 1965

Huntley, Elizabeth Valentine *Peninsula Pilgrimage* Princeton, N.J.: Pyne Press, 1941

Jefferson, Thomas *Notes on the State of Virginia* Chapel Hill, N.C.: University of North Carolina Press, 1954

Jester, Annie Lash *Newport News, Virginia, 1607-1960* Richmond, Va.: Whittett & Shepperson, 1961

Johnston, Henry P. *The Yorktown Campaign and the Surrender of Cornwallis 1781* New York: Harper and Bros., 1881

Junior League of Hampton Roads *Virginia Hospitality* Richmond, Va.: Dietz Press, 1975

Kellam, S. C., and Kellam, V. H. *Old Houses in Princess Anne, Virginia* Portsmouth, Va.: Portsmouth Press, 1931

Kern, E. Ethel Kelley *Trail of the Three Notch Road* Richmond, Va.: William Byrd Press, 1929

Kibler, J. Luther *Colonial Virginia Shrines* Richmond, Va.: Garrett & Massie, 1936

Kibler, James Luther *Sketches of One Hundred and Thirty-Three Historic Virginia Landmarks from Cape Henry to Richmond* Richmond, Va.: Garrett & Massie, 1929

Lancaster, Robert Alexander *Historic Virginia Homes and Churches* (1915) Spartanburg, S.C.: The Reprint Company, 1973

Lancaster, Robert B. *Hanover County, Virginia: A Sketch of the Early History* Hanover Chapter, Association for the Preservation of Virginia Antiquities, 1957

Lankford, John, editor *Captain John Smith's America* New York: Harper and Row, 1967

Lee, Mrs. Marguerite DuPont *Virginia Ghosts* Berryville, Va.: Virginia Book Company, 1966

Lewis, Margaret Lynn *The Commonplace Book of Me* Richmond, Va.: Nat'l. Soc. Colonial Dames of Amer. in Commonwealth of Va., 1976

Little, John P. *The History of Richmond* Richmond, Va.: Dietz Press, 1932

Mackenzie, Compton *Sublime Tobacco* London: Chatto and Windus, 1957

Mansfield, James Rogers *A History of Early Spotsylvania* Orange, Va.: Green Publishers, 1977

Mason, George Carrington *Colonial Churches of Tidewater, Virginia* Richmond, Va.: Whittet & Shepperson, 1945

Maury, Mrs. Anne F. *Intimate Virginiana* Richmond, Va.: Dietz Press, 1941

Moncrief, M. C. Scott *Kings and Queens of England* England: Blandford Press, 1966

Moore, Gay M. *Seaport in Virginia: George Washington's Alexandria* Richmond, Va.: Garrett, 1949

Moore, John Hammond *Albemarle, Jefferson's Country 1727-1976* Charlottesville, Va.: The University of Virginia Press, 1976

Mordecai, Samuel *Richmond in By-Gone Days* Richmond, Va.: Dietz Press, 1945 ,

Morton, Louis *Robert Carter of Nomini Hall* Richmond, Va.: Dietz Press, 1945

Morton, Oren F. *A Centennial History of Alleghany County (1923)* Reprint. Dayton, Va.: Reubush Co., 1970

Morton, Richard L. *Colonial Virginia* Chapel Hill, N.C.: University of North Carolina Press, 1960

Norris, J. E. ed. *History of the Lower Shenandoah Valley (1890)* Berryville, Va.: Reprint. Virginia Book Company, 1972.

Nugent, Nell Marion *Cavaliers and Pioneers — Abstracts of Virginia Land Patents and Grants 1623-1666* Baltimore: Geneological Publishing Co., Inc., 1963

Nutting, Wallace *Virginia Beautiful* Framingham, Mass.: Old America Company, 1930

Ollard, Richard *The Image of the King, Charles I & Charles II* New York: Atheneum, 1979

O'Neal, William B. *Architecture in Virginia* New York: Walker & Co., 1968

Parker, Rowland *The Common Stream* Suffolk, England: The Chaucer Press, Ltd., 1975

Peterson, Merrill D., ed. *The Founding Fathers: James Madison* New York: Newsweek Books, 1974

Quinn, S. J. *The History of the City of Fredericksburg, Virginia* Richmond, Va.: Hermitage Press, 1908

Rankin, Hugh F. *George Rogers Clark and the Winning of the West* Virginia Independence Bicentennial Commission, 1976

Rawlings, James S. *Virginia's Colonial Churches* Richmond, Va.: Garrett & Massie, 1963

Rawlings, Mary *Albemarle of Other Days* Charlottesville, Va.: The Michie Company, 1925

Reps, John W. *Tidewater Towns* Williamsburg, Va.: Colonial Williamsburg Fdn., 1972

Robertson, John William *On Land and Sea—A Pictorial Review of the Eastern Shore of Virginia* Accomac, Va.: The Eastern Shore News, 1961

Rosenberger, Francis C., ed. *Virginia Reader— A Treasury of Writings from the First Voyage to the Present* New York: Dutton, 1948

Rothery, Agnes *Houses Virginians Have Loved* New York: Rinehart and Company, 1954

Rothery, Agnes *New Roads in Old Virginia* New York: Houghton Mifflin Co., 1937

Rothery, Agnes *Virginia, The New Dominion* New York: D. Appleton Century Co., 1940

Rouse, Parke, Jr. *The English Heritage in Virginia* New York: Hastings House, 1966

Rutland, Robert A. *George Mason, Reluctant Statesman* New York: Holt, Rinehart & Winston, 1961

Sale, Edith T. *Interiors of Virginia Houses of Colonial Times* Richmond, Va: William Byrd Press, 1927

Sale, Edith T. *Manors of Virginia in Colonial Times* Philadephia: J. B. Lippencott Co., 1909

Sams, Conway Whittle *The Conquest of Virginia: The Forest Primeval* New York: Putnam & Sons, 1916

Sanchez-Saavedra, E. M. *Description of the Country—Virginia's Cartographers and Their Maps 1607-1881* Richmond: Virginia State Library, 1975

Scott, W. W. *A History of Orange County, Virginia* Richmond, Va.: Everette Waddey Co., 1907

Shepperson, Archibald B. *John Paradise and Lucy Ludwell* Richmond, Va.: Dietz Press, 1952

Simkins, Hennicutt and Poole *Virginia— History, Government, Geography* New York: Scribner's Sons, 1957

Sinclair, Caroline B. *Stories of Old Gloucester* Verona, Va.: McClure Printing Co., 1974

Starkey, Marion L. *In and Around Hampton* Hampton, Va.: Carr, 1948

Starkey, Marion L. *The First Plantation—History of Elizabeth City County* Hampton, Va.: Houston Printing Co., 1936

Stephenson, Mary A. *Old Homes in Surry and Sussex* Richmond, Va.: Dietz Press, 1942

Stetson, Charles W. *Washington and his Neighbors* Richmond, Va.: Garrett & Massie, 1956

Stevens, William T. *Virginia House Tour* Charlottesville, Va.: 1962

Summers, Lewis Preston *A History of Southwest Virginia and Washington County* Baltimore: Genealogical Publishing Co., 1966

Templeman, Eleanor Lee *Arlington Heritage* New York: Avenel Books, 1959

Templeman, Eleanor Lee *Northern Virginia Heritage* New York: Avenel Books, 1966

Truett, Randle B. *Monticello* New York: Hastings House, 1957

Tucker, George Holbert *Norfolk Highlights 1584-1881* Norfolk Historical Society, 1972

Turner, W. R. *Old Homes and Families in Nottoway* Blackstone, Va.: Nottoway Publishing Co., 1932

Tyler, Leon G. *History of Hampton and Elizabeth City County, Virginia* Hampton, Va. Board of Supervisors of Elizabeth City County, 1922

U.S. Department of Interior *Signers of the Constitution* Robert G. Ferris, ed., Washington, D.C.: Government Printing Office, 1976

Virginia Academy of Science *The James River Basin: Past, Present and Future* Richmond, Va., 1950

Virginia Department of Conservation and Development *State Historical Markers* 6th revision; Richmond, Va.: Virginia Association of Realtors, 1975

Virginia Education Secretary; Director of State Planning *Virginia Cultural Facilities and Historic Landmarks Inventory* Richmond, Va., 1976

Virginia State Library *Handbook of Virginia* Richmond, Va.: Virginia State Library, 1965

Waterman, Thomas T. *Mansions of Virginia 1706-1776* New York: Bonanza Books, 1945

Wayland, John W. *A History of Rockingham County (1912)* Reprint. Dayton, Va.: Ruebush-Elkins Co., 1972

Wayland, John W. *A History of Shenandoah County* Strasburg, Va.: Shenandoah Publishing House, 1969

Wertenbaker, Thomas J. *Norfolk: Historic Southern Port* Durham, N.C.: Duke University Press, 1962

Wertenbaker, Thomas J. *Patrician and Plebeian in Virginia* New York: Russell, 1959

Wertenbaker, Thomas J. *The Planters of Colonial Virginia* New York: Russell, 1959

Wertenbaker, Thomas J. *Virginia Under the Stuarts* New York: Russell, 1959

Wheeler, Roy *Historic Virginia* Charlottesville, Va.: Roy Wheeler Company, undated (ca. 1939)

Whitelaw, Ralph T. *Virginia's Eastern Shore* 2 vols., (1951) Revised by Peter Smith, Gloucester, Mass, 1968

Williams, Harrison *Legends of Loudoun* Richmond, Va.: Garrett & Massie, 1938

Williams, Henry L., and Williams, Ottalie K. *A Treasury of Great American Homes* New York: G. P. Putnam's Sons, 1970

Williams, Lloyd H. *Pirates of Colonial Virginia* Richmond, Va.: Dietz Press, 1937

Willis, Carrie H. *Legends of the Skyline Drive and the Great Valley of Virginia* Richmond, Va.: Dietz Press, 1940

Willison, George F. *Behold Virginia: The Fifth Crown* New York: Harcourt, Brace & Co., 1951

Wilstach, Paul *Potomac Landings* Indianapolis: Bobbs, Merrill Co., 1932

Wilstach, Paul *Tidewater Virginia* Indianapolis: Bobbs, Merrill Co., 1929

Wingfield, Marshall *A History of Caroline County, Virginia* (1924) Reprint. Baltimore: Baltimore Regional Publishing Co., 1969

Wise, Jennings Cropper *Ye Kingdoms of Accawmacke, of the Eastern Shore of Virginia in the Seventeenth Century* Richmond, Va.: Bell Book and Stationery Co., 1911

Wood, Leonora W. *Guide to Virginia's Eastern Shore* Richmond, Va.: Dietz Press, 1952

Woods, Rev. Edgar *Albemarle County in Virginia* Charlottesville, Va.: The Michie Company, 1901

Wright, Louis B. *The First Gentlemen of Virginia* San Marino, Cal.: Huntington Library, 1940

Wright, Louis B. and Tinling, Marion *The Secret Diary of William Byrd* Richmond, Va.: Dietz Press, 1941

Writers Program, WPA *Dinwiddie County* Richmond, Va.: Whittett & Shepperson, 1942

Writers Program, WPA *Jefferson's Albemarle* Charlottesville & Albemarle Chamber of Commerce, Va., 1941

Writers Program, WPA *Prince William, The Story of its People and Places* Richmond, Va.: Whittett & Shepperson, 1941

Writers Program, WPA *Sussex County, A Tale of Three Centuries* Richmond, Va.: Whittett & Shepperson, 1942

Writers Program, WPA Virginia *A Guide to the Old Dominion* London: Oxford University Press, 1940

Wyatt, Edward A. IV *Plantation Houses Around Petersburg* Petersburg, Va.: Petersburg Progress, 1955

A

Adams, Pres. John: *Bushfield*
Adams, Robert: *Alta Vista*
Anne (Princess of England): *Princess Anne County*
Anne (Queen of England): *Anna River, Federal Hill, Fluvanna River, Fort Christanna, Germanna, James River, King George County, Rapidan River, Rivanna River, Sarah Creek, Urbanna*
Albemarle, Earl of: *Albemarle County, Dinwiddie County*
Alexander, John: *Abingdon of Arlington, Alexandria, Christ Church of Alexandria, Summer Hill*
Allen, Arthur: *Bacon's Castle, Claremont*
Allen, Benjamin B.: *Glen Allen*
Allen, Floyd: *Hillsville*
Allison, Charles: *Allisonia*
Allsworth, Robert Warner: *Warner*
Amherst, Lord Jeffrey: *Amherst County, Fauquier County*
Amiss, Joseph: *Amissville*
Ammon, Rev. Thomas: *Crooked Run Baptist Church*
Anderson, Charlie: *Anderson's Tavern*
Anderson, R. M.: *Andersonville*
Andrews, Frank: *Franktown*
Ansbury, Thomas: *Blenheim*
Appomattox Indians: *Appomattox County, Bermuda Hundred*
Archer, Capt. Gabriel: *Hope, Littletown, Weyanoke Indians*
Argall, Gov. Samuel: *Argall's Gift, Chippokes, Henricus, Martin's Hundred, Paspehegh Indians, Powell's Creek, Warwick County*
Ariss, John: *Blandfield, Fairfield of Clarke, Powhatan*
Armistead, William: *Hessee*
Arnold, Gen. Benedict: *Battersea, Blenheim, Bollingbrook, Colonial Heights, Cuckoo, Elk Hill, Petersburg, Portsmouth, Providence Forge, Westover*
Ashbury, Bishop: *Benn's Church*
Ashby, John: *Ashby's Gap*
Astor, Lady Nancy: *Mirador*
Austin, Stephen F.: *Austinville*
Aylett, Philip: *Fairfield of King William, Montville*

B

Bacon, Nathaniel, Jr.: *Bacon's Castle, Bacon's Quarter, Belmont of Stafford, Brunswick County, Curles, Dogue Indians, Governor's Land, Jamestown, Jordan's Point, Kerr Reservoir, Mecklenburg County, Occaneechee, Poplar Spring Church*

Bacon, Nathaniel, Sr.: *Curles, Utimara*
Baker, Isaac: *Bristol*
Baldwin, Mary Julia: *Mary Baldwin College*
Ball, Mary: *See: Washington, Mary*
Ball, Col. Joseph: *Epping Forest*
Ball, Maj. James: *Bewdley of Lancaster*
Ballard, Thomas: *Bacon's Quarter*
Ballendine, John: *Rockledge*
Baltimore, Lord Cecelius: *Little Hunting Creek, Maryland, New Kent County, Occohannock, Romancoke*
Banister, Richard: *Banister River, Battersea*
Barbour, Gov. James: *Barboursville, Catalpa*
Barbour, Justice Philip: *Barboursville*
Barham, Bennett: *Barhamsville*
Barlow, Maria: *Sully*
Barnes, R. P.: *Barnes Junction*
Barton, Clara: *Chatham of Stafford*
Bassett, Col. William: *Eltham*
Bates, John: *Skimino Meeting House*
Baylor, Col. John: *New Market of Carolina*
Bayly, Edward: *Hermitage*
Baynum, John: *Magpie Swamp*
Beauregard, Gen. P.T.G., CSA: *Turkey Island*
Bellwood, James: *Bellwood, Defense Gen. Supply Center*
Belches, Hugh: *Greenyard*
Bennett, Edward: *Bennett's Choice*
Bennett, Richard: *Bennett's Choice, Bennett's Welcome, Utimara*
Bennett, Robert: *Bennett's Welcome*
Berkeley, Lady Frances: *Bolthrope, Chippokes, Claiborne's Neck, Green Spring*
Berkeley, Norborne: *See: Botetourt, Baron*
Berkeley, Gov. Sir William: *Arlington of Northampton, Bacon's Castle, Bacon's Quarter, Bennett's Choice, Bolthrope, Brickhouse of New Kent, Carolina, Chippokes, Chopawamsic, Curles, Eastover, Governor's Land, Green Spring, Gwynn's Island, Occohannock, Portsmouth, Powhatan, Stratton Manor, Timberneck Hall, Totopotomoi Creek, Wareham*
Berry, Benjamin: *Berryville*
Berry, Sir John: *Swann's Point*
Beverley, Harry: *Delaware Town*
Beverley, Maj. Peter: *Elmington*
Beverley, Robert I: *Barm Elms, Beverley Park*
Beverley, Robert III: *Blandfield*
Beverley, William: *Beverley Park, Blandfield, Manor Mansion, Staunton*
Black, James: *Black's Tavern*
Black, Samuel: *Monterey*
Black, William: *Blacksburg, Draper's Meadow, Montross*

Blackbeard (pirate): *Parramore Island*
Blackburn, Col. Richard: *Rippon Lodge*
Blackmore, Capt. John: *Fort Blackmore*
Blair, Rev. James: *Varina Grove, William & Mary, College of*
Blair, John: *Blairs*
Bland, Giles: *Barkeley*
Bland, Richard II: *Cawsons, Jordan's Point*
Bland, Theodoric: *Belvedere, Cawsons, Westover*
Bolling, Jane: *Curles*
Bolling, John: *Cobb's Hall of Chesterfield*
Bolling, Robert: *Bollingbrook, Brick House of Chesterfield, Cedar Level, Fort James, Kippax*
Bondurant, Charles: *Saint Charles*
Boone, Daniel: *Boone's Mill, Cumberland Gap, Kentucky County*
Boone, Jacob: *Boone's Mill*
Booth, John: *Belleville*
Booth, Thomas: *Rosewell*
Boswell, John: *Belleville*
Botetourt, Baron de: *Botetourt County, Gloucester County*
Bottom, John: *Bottom's Bridge*
Bowler, Thomas: *Bowlers*
Bowman, Edward: *Bowman's Folly*
Bowman, George: *Harmony Hall*
Boyd, Judge Alexander: *Boydton*
Boyd, Lizzie: *Oaks*
Braddock, Gen. Edward: *Ashby's Gap, Dinwiddie County, Fourt Loudon, Newgate, Richfield*
Braxron, Carter: *Chericoke, Elsing Green, Newington, West Point*
Braxton, George: *Newington*
Breckinridge, James Cabell: *Cloverdale, New Market of Shenandoah*
Brent, George: *Wellington*
Brent, Giles: *Aquia Creek, Brentsville, Marlborough, Piscataway Indians, Potomac Creek, Wellington*
Brent, Margaret: *Little Hunting Creek*
Brewer, John: *Stanley Hundred*
Bridgeforth (family): *Kenbridge*
Brock, George: *Forestville*
Brooke, Gov. Robert: *Federal Hill*
Brooks (family): *Brookneal*
Brown, John: *Harper's Ferry*
Brown, Rev. Samuel: *Brownsburg, Providence Church of Augusta*
Brown, Sarah: *Essex*
Browne, Col. Henry: *Eastover, Four Mile Tree Plantation*
Buchanan, Pres. James: *Buchanan County, Cloverdale*
Buck, Nathan S.: *Craig Springs*
Buckland, William: *Gunston Hall, Rockledge*
Buckner, John: *Marlfield*
Burgoyne, Gen. John: *Barracks, Charlottesville, Saratoga*
Burke, Samuel: *Burkeville*

Burns, Robert: *Kilmarnoc*
Burns, Judge W. E.: *Coeburn*
Burras, Ann: *Oares Plantation*
Burrows, John: *Four Mile Tree Plantation*
Burwell, Carter: *Carter's Grove, Trebell's Landing*
Burwell, Elizabeth: *York Hall*
Burwell, Lewis: *Fairfield of Gloucester, Penniman, White Marsh*
Burwell, Martha: *Hesse*
Burwell, Nathaniel I: *Burlington, Carter's Grove, Corotoman, Cownes, Wakefield of King William*
Burwell, Nathaniel II: *Carter Hall, Carter's Grove, Fairfield of Gloucester, Harrison's Landing, Millwood of Clarke*
Burwell, Rebecca: *Fairfield of Gloucester*
Burwell, Robert Carter: *Long Branch*
Bush, Abraham: *Ceeleys*
Bushrod, Richard: *Bushfield*
Bute, Earl of: *Audley, Bedford County*
Butler, Gen. Benjamin: *Turkey Island*
Byars, Capt. James: *Glade Spring*
Byrd, Evelyn: *Evelynton*
Byrd, Mary Willing: *Marlboro, Westover*
Byrd, Ursula: *Beverley Park, Blandfield*
Byrd, William I: *Banister River, Belvedere, Columbia, Richmond, Stone House*
Byrd, William II: *Ampthill, Belvedere, Beverly Park, Blue Stone Castle, Buffalo Springs, Dismal Swamp, Evelynton, Fort Chiswell, Germanna, Huguenots, Manchester, Matrimony Creek, Petersburg, Richmond, Rocketts, Virginia, Westover, Westover Church, Windsor of Mathews*
Byrd, William III: *Blue Stone Castle, Cloverfield of Charles City, Manchester*

C

Cabell, William: *Union Hill*
Cabell, Dr. William: *Clifford*
Caldwell, John: *Cub Creek Church, Fort Wool, Spencer*
Callaway, Jacob H.: *Callao*
Callaway, James: *Alta Vista, Callaway, Evington*
Calvert, Cecelius: *See: Baltimore*
Camp, Paul D.: *Dismal Swamp*
Campbell, Gen. William: *Campbell County, Loudoun County*
Cannon, William: *New Canton*
Capp, William: *Little England of Hampton*
Carr, Dabney: *Bear Castle, Carrsbrook*
Carr, Elias: *Carrsville*
Carr, Martha Jefferson: *Bear Castle, Shadwell*
Carr, Peter: *Carrsbrook*
Carroll, Charles: *Carroll County*
Carter Charles: *Cleve, West Point*
Carterm Edward: *Blenheim*
Carter, George: *Oatlands*
Carter, John I: *Corotoman*
Carter John II ("Secretary"): *Blenheim, Secretary's Ford, Shirley*

Carter, Landon: *Cleve, Ringsneck, Ripon Hall, Sabine Hall*

Carter, Robert ("King"): *Bladensfield, Carter's Grove, Christ Church of Lancaster, Colchester, Corotoman, Fairfield of Gloucester, Frying Pan Run, Hesse, Newington, Ripon Hall, York Hall*

Carter, Robert II: *Coles Point, Liberia, Nomini Hall*

Carter, Robert III ("Councillor"): *Bladensfield, Nomini Hall*

Carter, St. Leger Landon: *Cleve*

Carver, Capt. William: *Portsmouth*

Carvin, William: *Hollins College*

Cary, Archibald: *Ampthill*

Cary, Henry: *Ampthill, Forest of Newport News*

Cary, Mary: *Belvoir of Fairfax, Carter's Grove, Ceeleys*

Cary, Miles I: *Claiborne's Neck, Forest of Newport News, Joyles Neck, Magpie Swamp, Richneck of Newport News, Stanley Hundred*

Cary, Miles II: *Carysbrook, Claiborne's Neck, Warwick Town*

Cary, Judge Richard: *Peartree Hall*

Cary, Thomas: *Magpie Swamp*

Cary, Thomas Miles: *Elmwood of Langley Field*

Cary, Wilson Miles: *Ceeleys, Forest of Newport News, Richneck of Newport News*

Catesby, Mark: *Catalpa*

Catlett, John: *Catlett, Timberneck Hall*

Cave, Benjamin: *Montebello*

Ceeley, Thomas: *Ceeleys*

Chamberlayne, Richard: *Poplar Grove of New Kent*

Chancellor, George: *Chancellorsville*

Chanco: *Pace's Paines*

Chapman, Francis: *Swann's Point*

Chapman, Nathaniel: *Summer Hill*

Chapman, Gen. Samuel: *Hampton University*

Charles I (King of England): *Capes Charles, Cape Henry, Carrsbrook, Charles City County, Fort Charles, Little England of Hampton, Maryland, New Kent County, Virginia, Yorke*

Charles II (King of England): *Audley, Bellfield, Boscobel, Carolina, Castle Hill, Curles, Grafton, Green Spring, Kinsale, Northern Neck, Rokeby, Virginia, Ware Church, York River*

Charlotte (Queen of England): *Charlotte County, Charlottesville, Mecklenburg County*

Chase, Justice Salmon P.: *Chase City*

Chastain, Peter: *Monacan*

Chastellux, Marquis de: *Boswell's Tavern*

Cheatham, Adm, Joseph J.: *Cheatham Annex*

Cherokee Indians: *Battle Knob, Peaks of Otter, Pearisburg*

Chichley, Gov. Henry: *Barn Elms, Christ Church of Middlesex, Culpeper County, Rosegill, Wormeley Creek*

Chickahominy Indians: *Chippokes, Fort James*

Chiles, Macajah: *Chilesburg*

Chiswell, Charles: *Rockett's Mill, Scotchtown*

Chiswell, John: *Fort Chiswell, Lead Mines, Scotchtown*

Christian, Israel: *Fincastle*

Christian, Col. William: *Christiansburg, Fort Christian*

Churchill, Sir John: *Blenheim, Marlborough*

Churchill, Sarah: *Little England of Gloucester, Sarah Creek*

Churchill, William: *Wilton of Middlesex*

Claiborne, Augustine: *Windsor of Isle of Wight*

Claiborne, Thomas: *Sweet Hall*

Claiborne, William: *Bennet's Choice, Hampton, Kecoughtan, Magpie Swamp, Maryland, New Kent County, Northumberland County, Romancoke, Wood's Gap*

Clark, Charles: *Keswick of Chesterfield*

Clark, George Rogers: *Black's Tavern, Caroline County, Clarke County, Kentucky County*

Clarke, Maj. James IV: *Keswick of Chesterfield*

Clay, Henry: *Ashland, Clay Spring*

Clayton, John: *Windsor of Mathews*

Clifton, James: *Clifton Forge*

Clifton, William: *Wellington*

Cobb, Ambrose: *Cobbs Hall of Chesterfield*

Cockburn, Adm. Sir George: *Pungoteague, St. John's of Hampton, Tangier Island*

Cocke, James Powell: *Malvern Hills*

Cocke, John Hartwell: *Bremo Recess*

Cocke, Richard: *Bremo, Mount Pleasant*

Cocke, Richard Hartwell: *Bremo Recess*

Cocke, Thomas: *Malvern Hills*

Cockrell, Lillian: *Lilian*

Coe, W. W.: *Coeburn*

Cole, William: *Bolthrope, Cloverfields of Charles City*

Coles, John: *Enniscorthy*

Collier, Sir George: *Gosport, Portsmouth*

Columbus, Christopher: *Columbia, District of Columbia*

Conoy Indians: *Piscataway Indians*

Constable, Joan: *Church Hill*

Cooke, John, *Saratoga*

Cooke, Phillip: *Saratoga*

Cooke, Mordecai: *Church Hill, Wareham*

Corbin, Gawen: *Peckatone*

Corbin, Richard: *Laneville*

Core, Dr. James: *Mount Wharton*

Cornwallis, Lord Charles: *Portsmouth, Tyndall's Point, Yorktown*

Cowne, William: *Cownes, Wakefield of King William*

Crafford, Carter: *Mulberry Island*

Crafty, Tony: *Copper Hill*

Craig, Col. James: *Christiansburg*

Craig, Rev. James: *Craig's Mill*

Craig, Rev. John: *Augusta Meeting House*

Craig, Robert: *Craig County*

Craik, Dr. James: *Bel Air*

Crawford, Col. William: *Gosport, Portsmouth*

Crews, James: *Turkey Island*
Crigler, Jacob: *Criglersville*
Cripps, Zachary: *Forest of Newport News*
Cromwell, Oliver: *Aquia Creek, Bennett's Choice, Castle Hill, Kinsale, Oatlands*
Cropper, Gen John: *Bowman's Folly*
Crow, John: *Crows*
Crozet, Col. Flaudius: *Crozet, Fluvanna River*
Culpeper, Lord Thomas: *Culpeper County, Green Spring, Leedstown, Marlfield, Northern Neck*
Cumberland, Duke of: *Castle Hill, Cumberland County, Cumberland Gap, Patrick County, Prince William County*
Curry, Samuel: *Mount Sidney, Mount Solon*
Curtis, Daniel P.: *Endview*
Curtis, Edmund: *Bennett's Choice*
Custis, Daniel Parke: *Arlington of Northampton, Mount Stirling, Saint Peter's Church, White House*
Custis, George Washington Parke: *Arlington of Arlington county, Chatham of Stafford, Queen's Creek Plantation, Romancoke, Wakefield of Westmoreland*
Custis, Lt. Col. Henry: *Mount Custis, Ravenswood*
Custis, John I: *Wilsonia*
Custis, John II: *Arlington of Northampton*
Custis, John IV: *Arlington of Northampton, Queen's Creek Plantation, White House, Wilsonia*
Custis, John Parke: *Abingdon of Arlington, Eltham, White House*
Custis, Lucy Parke: *White House*
Custis, Nelly: *Audley, Fairfield of Clarke, Woodlawn*

D

Dabney, Benjamin: *Elmington*
Dangerfield, Col. William: *Belvidera*
Dale, Gov. Sir Thomas: *Dale's Gift, Dutch Gap, Eastern shore, Farrar's Island, Governor's Land, Henricus, Jamestown*
Dalton, Lady Catherine: *Charlotte Court House*
Dames, John: *Fort George*
Dandridge, Anna Maria: *Eltham*
Dandridge, Col. John: *Chestnut Grove, Elsing Green*
Dandridge, Martha: *See: Washington, Martha*
Danner, Jacob: *Middletown*
Dare, Virginia: *Carolina*
Darsie, Thomas: *Findowrie*
Davis, Alexander Jackson: *Virginia Military Institute*
Davis, Jefferson: *Bellona Arsenal, Cloverdale, Danville, Fort Monroe, Liberia, Richmond*
Dawber, Edmund: *Elmington*
Debedeavon, Chief: *Cheriton, Mattawoman, Oak Grove of Northampton, Savage Neck*
Delaware, Lord Thomas West: *Appomattox County, Borough, Brandon, Delaware Indians, Delaware Town, Dutch Gap, Hampton, Hog Island, Jamestown, Martin's Hundred, Shirley, Westover*

Deynes, William: *Elmington*
Dickenson, Henry: *Dickensonville*
Dickenson, W. H.: *Dickenson County*
Dickson, Rev. Thomas: *Donation Church*
Digges, Cole: *Bolthrope, Brandon*
Digges, Dudley: *Hesse*
Digges, Edward: *Bellfield, Chischiak, Kiskiack*
Dinwiddie, Gov. Robert: *Ashby's Gap, Dinwiddie County, Loudoun County, Norfolk*
Divers, George: *Farmington*
Dixon, John: *Airville, Belmont of Stafford*
Dogue Indians: *Belmont of Stafford, Colchester, Gunston Hall, Occoquan*
Donelson, Col. John: *Callaway, Markham of Pittsylvania*
Donelson, Rachel: *Callaway, Markham of Pittsylvania*
Dooley, James: *Maymont, Swannanoa*
Douglas, George: *Poplar Grove of Accomack*
Douglas, Rev. William: *Dover Church School*
Drake, Sir Francis: *Buckland, Jamestown, Virginia*
Drake, Mary: *Hill's Farm*
Drummond, John: *Poplar Grove of Accomack*
Drummond, Richard: *Hill's Farm*
Drummond, Spencer: *Little Scotland*
Drummond, William: *Brickhouse, Carolina, Governor's Land, Lake Drummond*
Dudley, William: *Dogue Indians*
Dulaney, Benjamin: *Shuter's Hill*
Dunlap, Alexander: *Dunlap Pass*
Dumore, Lord John Murray: *Botetourt County, Camp Peary, Cricket Hill, Doncastle's Ordinary, Fincastle, Fort Nelson, Gosport, Great Bridge, Gwynn's Island, Hampton, Kentucky County, Laneville, Montgomery County, Norfolk, Porto Bello, Richfield, Shenandoah County*
DuPont, William: *Montpelier*
Dutch: *Dutch Gap, Fort Algernourne, Hampton, Orange County, Richneck*

E

Early, Jacob: *Leesville*
Early, Col. Jeremiah: *Evington*
Eaton, Thomas: *Bull Island*
Edward (Duke of York): *Prince Edward County*
Edwards, Ambrose: *Cherry Grove of King William*
Edwards, Dr. Richard: *Waverly of Gloucester*
Edwards, William: *Pleasant Point*
Effingham, Francis Howard, Baron: *Cumberland County, Howardsville*
Eggleston, Richard: *Powhatan*
Ekeeks, Chief: *Clifton of Accomack*
Elizabeth (Princess of England): *Elizabeth City County, Elizabeth River, Hanover County, King George County*
Elizabeth I (Queen of England): *Jamestown*
Elkington, Ann: *White Cliff*
Emory, Bishop John: *Emory & Henry College*

Eppes, Francis (17th century): *City Point, Eppington, Hopewell, Weston*
Eppes, Francis (18th century): *Appomattox Manor, Forest of Charles City*
Eppes, John Wayles: *Eppington, Poplar Forest*
Eppes, Richard: *Hopewell*
Eppes, Robert F.: *Weston*
Eskridge, Col. George: Epping Forest, Sandy Point, Wakefield of Westmoreland
Eustis, Gen. Abraham: *Fort Eustis*
Eustis, Cocoran: *Oatlands*
Evans, Jesse: *Wytheville*
Ewell, Maj. Charles: *Bel Air*
Eyre, Littleton: *Eyre Hall*

F

"Fair Belinda": *Fairfield of Gloucester*
Fairfax, Anne: *Belvoir of Fairfax*
Fairfax, George William: *Belvoir of Fairfax, Pohick Church*
Fairfax, Hannah: *Fairfield of Clarke*
Fairfax, Sally: *Belvoir of Fairfax, Ceeleys*
Fairfax, Thomas, Fifth Lord: *Culpeper County*
Faifax, Thomas, Sixth Lord: *Belvoir of Fairfax, Fairfax County, Greenway Court, Leedstown, Washington (town), White Post, Winchester*
Fairfax, Col. William: *Audley, Belvoir of Fairfax, Fairfax County, Fairfax Hall, Fairfield of Clarke, Fort Belvoir*
Farrar, William: *Dutch Gap, Farrar's Island, Henricus, Jordan's Point, Powhite Plantation*
Fountleroy, Col. Moore: *Naylor's Hole*
Fauquier, Gov. Francis: *Charlotte Court House, Fauquier County, Loudoun County*
Felgate, Capt. Robert: *Chichiak, Yorktown*
Fincastle, Lord: *Botetourt County, New Castle*
Finch, Barbara: *Cherry Grove of King William*
Fithian, Phillip: *Blandensfield, Buchfield*
Fitzhugh, Henry: *Chatham of Stafford*
Fitzhugh, Thomas: *Boscobel*
Fitzhugh, William II: *Chatham of Stafford*
Fitzhugh, William, Jr.: *Corotoman*
Fitzhugh, William, Sr.: *Bedford of King George, Marmion, Ravensworth*
Flannagan, John W.: *Pound River*
Fleet, Henry: *Wood's Gap*
Fleming, Tarleton: *Rock Castle*
Fletcher, Elijah: *Sweet Briar College*
Flint, Capt. Thomas: *Stanley Hundred*
Flood, Col. John: *Eastover*
Flowerdew, Temperance: *Flowerdew Hundred, Weyanoke of Charles City*
Floyd, Gov. James: *Floyd County*
Fosque, Simon: *Neville's Neck*
Franciscus, Peter: *West Creek Ordinary*
Frederick (Elector of Palatine): *Elizabeth City County*

Frederick (Prince of Wales): *Augusta County, Frederick County, Fredericksburg, Prince Edward County, Winchester*
Fry, Col. Joshua: *New River, Shadwell, Viewmont*
Fulcher, Lowe: *Lowesville*
Funk, Joseph: *Singers Glen*

G

Gardiner, Julia: *Sherwood Forest*
Garnett, James Mercer: *Elmwood of Essex*
Garnett, Muscoe: *Elmwood of Essex*
Garrett, Dr. John Bolling: *Black's Tavern*
Garth, Thomas: *Chestnut Ridge*
Gates, Sir Thomas: *Bermuda Hundred, Chippokes, Dutch Gap, Elmington, Hampton, Jamestown, Kecoughtan*
George I (King of England): *Brunswick County, Hanover County, King George County*
George II (King of England): *Amelia County, Bedford County, Caroline County, Castle Hill, Fort George, Frederick County, Halifax County, Leesburg, Lunenburg County, Orange County*
George III (King of England): *Buckingham County, Charlotte County, Charlottesville, Chatham of Pittsylvania, Kentucky County, Mecklenburg County, Rockingham County, Winchester*
Gerard, John: *Wilton of Westmoreland*
Gibson, Charles Dana: *Mirador*
Gilmer, George: *Pen Park*
Gist, Christopher: *Mountain Lake*
Gooch, Gov. William: *Catalpa, Fort George, Goochland County, Staunton*
Goode, Thomas F.: *Buffalo Springs*
Gookin, Daniel: *Marie's Mount, Marry Point, Newport News*
Gordon, John A. B.: *Post Oak*
Gordon, Andrew James: *Locust Dale*
Gordon, Nathaniel: *Gordonsville*
Gordon, Col. W. W.: *Hampstead*
Gore, Thomas: *Lucketts*
Gourgany, Edward: *Curles*
Graffenried, Baron von: *Germanna*
Graham, Thomas: *Bluefield, Pocahontas*
Grant, Gen. Ulysses S.: *Appomattox County, Blandford Church, Cold Harbor, Dutch Gap, Petersburg, Richmond, Wilderness*
Gray, Thomas: *Smith's Fort Plantation*
Green, James: *Green Valley*
Greene, Gen. Nathaniel: *Greene County, Greenville, Lee County, Peytonsburg*
Grenville, George: *Bedford County*
Grenville, Sir Richard: *Greensville County*
Griffin, Cyrus: *Farnham*
Grimes, Lucy: *Carter's Grove*
Grimes, Susanna: *Carter's Grove*
Gwathmey, Owen: *Burlington, Wakefield of King William*

H

Hack, Dr. George: *Evergreen*
Hagan, Capt. Patrick: *Dungannon*
Haggoman, John: *Oak Grove of Northampton*
Haight, Jacob: *Sully*
Haight, Phebe: *Sully*
Hall, Dr. Richard: *Peckatone*
Hamilton, Lt. Col. Henry: *Kentucky County*
Hampden, John: *Hampden-Sydney College*
Hancock, George: *Fotheringay*
Hardin, Isaac: *Greenwood*
Hardy, George: *Wrenn's Mill*
Harman, Henry: *Hollybrook*
Harmon, Adam: *Eggleston*
Harmon, John: *Keller*
Harper, Robert: *Harper's Ferry*
Harris, Frederick Overton: *Frederick's Hall*
Harris, John: *Millwood of Powhatan*
Harris, Maj. William: *Millwood of Powhatan*
Harris, Capt. Samuel: *Fort Mayo*
Harrison, Anne Carter: *Wilton*
Harrison, Benjamin I: *Wakefield of Surry*
Harrison, Benjamin II: *Pace's Paines*
Harrison, Benjamin III: *Berkeley, Eastover, Harrison's Landing, Hunting Quarter*
Harrison, Benjamin IV: *Berkeley, Harrison's Landing, The Oaks*
Harrison, Benjamin V., Pres: *Berkeley*
Harrison, Carter Henry: *Clifton of Fluvanna*
Harrison, Capt. Henry: *Hunting Quarter*
Harrison, Nathaniel: *Brandon, Wakefield of Surry*
Harrison, Thomas: *Harrisonburg, Keestown*
Harrison, William Henry, Pres.: *Berkeley, Charles City County, Greenway, Hampden-Sydney College, Shawnee Indians, Sherwood Forest*

Harrod, James: *Kentucky County*
Hartwell, Elizabeth: *Mount Pleasant*
Hartwell, John: *Mount Pleasant*
Harvey, Gov. John: *Buckland, Chischiak, Claiborne's Neck, Harrop, Littletown, Utimara, York County, Yorke*
Harvey, Tobert: *Cloverdale*
Harvie, John, Jr.: *Barracks*
Harvie, John, Sr.: *Belmont of Charlottesville, Belvedere, Pen Park*
Harwood, Joseph: *Weyanoke of Charles City*
Harwood, Thomas: *Harwood's Mill, Mulberry Island, Queen's Hith*
Haskins, Cr. Creed: *Brunswick County*
Hatcher, William: *Half Way House*
Hawes, Capt. Richard: *Epping Forest*
Hayter, Charles: *Haysi*
Heath, John: *Heathsville*
Heathen, William Ratcliffe: *Skimino Meeting House*
Henry, Elizabeth: *Fairfield of King William*
Henry, John: *Michie Tavern, Mount Brilliant, Slash Church, Studley*

Henry, Patrick, Jr.: *Bizarre, Doncastle's Ordinary, Emory & Henry College, Hampden-Sydney College, Hanover Town, Hat Creek Presbyterian Church, Henry, Henry County, Lanesville, Long Island, Marlborough, Montville, Mount Brilliant, Patrick County, Pine Slash Farm, Red Hill, Richmond, Roundabout, Rural Point, St. John's of Richmond, Salisbury, Scotchtown, Studley*
Henry, Rev. Patrick, Sr.: *Slash Church, Studley*
Henry (Prince of Wales): *Cape Henry, Fort Charles, Fort Story, Henricus*
Hess, Henry: *Forestville*
Hicks, Joseph: *Rawley Springs*
Hill, Gen. A. P., CSA: *Fort A. P. Hill*
Hill, Col. Edward: *Pamunkey Indians, Shirley, Totopotomoi Creek*
Hill, Elizabeth: *Corotoman*
Hill, Richard: *Hill's Farm, Poplar Grove of Accomack*
Hite, Isaac: *Lacey Spring*
Hite, Col. John: *Springdale*
Hix, Robert: *Emporia*
Hobbs, Jacob: *Tappahannock*
Hoggard, Thomas: *Poplar Hall*
Holland, Michael: *Farmington*
Hollingsworth, Abraham: *Abram's Delight*
Holstein, Stephen: *Holston River*
Holt, William: *Jerdone's Castle*
Honeywood, Sir Phipip: *Wormeley Creek*
Hooker, Gen. Joseph: *Chancellorsville*
Hoomes, John: *Milford*
Hoomes, Maj. Thomas: *Bowling Green*
Hornbarger, Parker: *Bastian*
Houghwout, Mrs. Braithwaite: *Providence Forge*
Houston, Sam: *Rockbridge County, Timberneck Ridge Church*
Howard, Allen: *Howardsville*
Howard, Gov. Francis: *See: Effingham*
Hunt, Gen. Henry: *Fort Hunt*
Hunter, Bushrod W.: *Abingdon of Arlington*

I

Ingles, Mary Draper: *Draper's Meadow*
Iroquois Indians: *Fort Chiswell, Iroquois Trail*
Isham, Henry: *Dogham*

J

Jackson, Andrew, Pres.: *Callway, Markham of Pittsylvania, Mount Jackson, Shawnee Indians*
Jackson, Gen. "Stonewall", CSA: *Chancellorsville, Guinea, Lexington, Manassas*
Jackson, Thomas: *Austinville, Shot Tower*
James I (King of England): *Dutch Gap, Elizabeth City County, James City County, James River, Jamestown, Little England of Hampton, York River*
James II (King of England): *Brentsville, Bristow, Fort James, King & Queen County, Occohannock, Potomac Creek*

Jamieson, Malcolm: *Berkeley*
Janny, Amos: *Waterford*
Jefferson, Jane Randolph: *Shadwell*
Jefferson, Maria: *Eppington, Forest of Charles City*
Jefferson, Martha: *Edgehill of Albemarle,*
Hope Ferry, Tuckahoe, Tufton, Varina Grove
Jefferson, Martha Wayles: *Elk Hill, Forest of*
Charles City, Monticello, Poplar Forest
Jefferson, Peter: *Albemarle County, Bear Castle,*
Belmont of Charlottesville, Dungeness, Keswick of
Albemarle, New River, Shadwell, Tuckahoe

Jefferson, Randolph: *Shadwell, Snowden*
Jefferson, Thomas, Pres.: *Albemarle County,*
Ashlawn, Barracks, Battersea, Bear Castle, Belmont
of Charlottesville, Brandon, Bremo Recess,
Carrsbrook, Colle, Cuckoo, Dover Church School,
Dungeness, Edgehill of Albemarle, Enniscorthy,
Eppington, Fairfield of Gloucester, Farmington,
Fauquier County, Forest of Charles City, Hope Ferry,
Lee County, Lexington, Locust Hill, Monticello,
Natural Bridge, Oak Hill of Loudoun, Oriskany,
Poplar Forest, Richmond, Rockbridge County,
Shadwell, Snowden, Tuckahoe, University of
Virginia, Varina Grove, Westover Church,
Windsor of Mathews

Jeffreys, Gov. Herbert: *Barn Elms*
Jenings, Gov. Edmund: *Camp Peary, Ripon Hall*
Jenkins, John: *Bladensfield*
Jerdone, Francis: *Farmington, Jerdone's Castle,*
Mount Stirling, Providence Forge
Johnson, Mary Montague: *Epping Forest*
Johnson, Richard: *Turners*
Johnson, Thomas: *Turners*
Johnston, Gen. Joseph E., CSA: *Cheatham*
Annex, Longwood, Prince Edward County
Johnston, Peter: *Longwood*
Jones, Frederick: *Jonesville*

Jones, John Gabriel: *Kentucky County*
Jones, Mathew: *Bourbon*
Jones, Peter: *Folly Castle*
Jones, Capt. Peter: *Fort Henry, Petersburg*
Joplin, Col. Joseph: *Argyle*
Jordan, Cecily Bayly: *Farrar's Island,*
Jordan's Point
Jordan, Col. George: *Eastover, Four Mile*
Tree Plantation
Jordan, Samuel: *Farrar's Island, Jordan's Point*
Jouett, Jack: *Cuckoo*
Joyner, Walter: *Walters*

K
Keeling, Adam: *Wolf's Snare*
Keeling, John: *Princess Anne County*
Keene, Hannah: *Buchfield*
Keisell, George: *Kessletown*
Keith, Rev. George: *Skiffe's Creek*
Kellem, Richard: *Windingdale*

Kemp, Richard: *Airville, Claiborne's Neck,*
Kempsville, Richneck of Newport News
Kendall, Col. William: *Oak Hall*
Kennedy (family): *Kenbridge*
Kennon, Mary: *Cobb's Hall of Chesterfield*
Kennon, Richard: *Brick House*
Kerr, John: *New Hope*
Kerr, Cong. John H.: *Bugg's Island Lake,*
Kerr Reservoir, Staunton River
Key, Francis Scott: *Key's Gap*
Keys, John: *Keysville*
Kilmer, Willis S.: *Renlik*
Koonrad, Frederick: *Spring Hill*
Koontz, John: *Lacey Spring*

L
Lafayette, Marquis de: *Blandford Church,*
Bollingbrook, Boswell's Tavern, Colonial Heights,
Doswell, Paris, Petersburg
Lamb, Wilnot: *Lambsburg*
Lambden, Joseph: *Rosslyn*
Langhorne, Chiswell: *Mirador*
Langley, Samuel Pierpont: *Langley Field*
Latrobe, Benjamin: *Green Spring*

Lawne, Capt. Christopher: *Lawne's Plantation*
Lawrence, William: *Brickhouse*
Laydon, John: *Chesterville, Oares Plantation*
Lear, Col. Tobias: *Wellington*
Ledered, John: *Dunlap Pass, Massinacak*
Lee, Arthur: *Marlborough*
Lee, Charles: *Leeton Forest*
Lee, Gen. Charles: *Portsmouth*
Lee, Edward: *Blenheim*
Lee, Gen. Fitzhugh, CSA: *Trevillians*
Lee, Francis Lightfoot: *Leesburg, Menokin,*
Stratford Hall
Lee, George: *Burnt House Field, Machodoc*
Lee, Hancock: *Ditchley, Wicomico*
Lee, Hannah: *Peckatone*
Lee, Henry (17th century): *Chischiak, Kiskiack*
Lee, Henry ("Black Horse Harry"): *Stratford*
Lee, Henry ("Light Horse Harry"): *Lengley,*
Lee County, Leesylvania, Matildaville, Shirley,
Stratford Hall
Lee, John: *Leesville*
Lee, Kendall: *Ditchley*
Lee, Ludwell: *Belmont of Loudoun, Shuter's Hill*
Lee, Philip Ludwell: *Leesburg, Stratford Hall*
Lee, Richard (17th century): *Burnt House Field,*
Cobb's Hall of Lancaster, Ditchley, Green Spring,
Kiskiack
Lee, Richard Bland: *Chantilly of Fairfax,*
Langley, Sully
Lee, Richard Decator: *Lee Hall of Newport News*
Lee, Richard Henry: *Chantilly of Westmoreland,*
Leedstown, Leeton Forest, Stratford Hall
Lee, Richard ("Squire"): *Lee Hall of Lancaster*

Lee, Gen. Robert E., CSA: *Appomattox County,*
Arlington of Arlington, Brompton, Cold Harbor,
Five Forks, Fort Belvoir, Fort Lee, Fort Monroe,
Harper's Ferry, Jetersville, Leesylvania, Lexington,
Petersburg, Richmond, Seven Pines, Shirley,
Stratford Hall, Washington & Lee University,
White House
Lee, Thomas (17th century): *Burnt House Field,*
Clifts, Leeton Forest, Lee Hall of Lancaster,
Machodoc, Stratford Hall
Lee, Thomas (18th century): *Belmont of Loudoun,*
Frying Pan Run
Lee, Thomas Ludlow: *Berry Hill*
Lee, William Harrison: *Kiskiack*
Lee, William Harrison: *Kiskiack*
Lehew, Peter: *Front Royal*
Lester, G. W.: *Figsboro*
Lewis, Gen. Andrew: *Cricket Hill, Dunlap Pass,*
Fort Lewis, Richfield, Staunton
Lewis, Anne Jefferson: *Snowden*
Lewis, Betty: *Brompton, Kenmore, Woodlawn*
Lewis, Charles: *Farmington*
Lewis, Lt. Charles: *Fort Lewis*
Lewis, Col. Fielding: *Brompton, Kenmore,*
Millbrook
Lewis, George: *Marmion*
Lewis, John: *Argyle, Poropotank, Scottsville,*
Staunton
Lewis, Lawrence: *Audley, Fairfield of Clarke,*
Woodlawn
Lewis, Meriwether: *Locust Hill*
Lewis, Thomas: *Lynwood*
Lightfoot, Col. Francis: *Westover Church*
Lightfoot, John: *Lightfoot*
Lightfoot, Col. Philip: *Dancing Point*
Lincoln, Abraham, Pres.: *Lacey Spring,*
Liberia, Rocketts
Lomax, John: *Bristol Iron Works*
Loudoun, Earl of: *Cherokee Indians, Fort Loudoun*
Louisa (Queen of Denmark): *Louisa County*
Lovett, David: *Lovettsville*
Loving, James: *Lovingston*
Low, Augustus: *Low Moor*
Ludlow, George: *Moore House*
Ludwell, Col. Phillip: *Chippokes, Claiborne's Neck,*
Green Spring, Richneck of Newport News
Lumpkin, Griffin: *Salem*
Lumpkin, Col. Jacob: *Newington*
Lunsford, Rev. Lewis: *Marattico*
Lunsford, Sir Thomas: *Claiborne's Neck, Richneck*
of Newport News, Wormeley Creek
Lybrooks, Pem: *Pembroke*
Lynch, Col. Charles: *Alta Vista, Chestnut Hill,*
Lynchburg, Pen Park
Lynch, John: *Lynchburg*

M
Mack, William: *Max Meadows*

Macon, Nathaniel: *Randolph Macon College*
Macon, Sarah: *Jerdone's Castle*
Madison, Dolley: *Montpelier, Pungoteague,*
Scotchtown
Madison, Francis: *Madison Mills*
Madison, Bishop James: *William & Mary*
Madison, James, Pres.: *Bloomsbury, Hampden-*
Sydney College, Madison County, Madison
University, Montpelier, Port Conway, Providence
Church of Louisa, Rokeby, Somerset, University
of Virginia
Madison, William: *Woodberry Forest*
Mahone, Mrs. William: *Ivanhoe, Ivor, Wakefield*
of Sussex, Waverly of Sussex, Zuni
Makemie, Rev. Francis: *Assawoman, New*
Church, Providence Church of Augusta,
Temperenceville
Mann, John: *Timberneck Hall*
Marks, Capt. John: *Locust Hill*
Marlborough, Duke of: *See, John Churchill*
Marriott, Obadiah: *Bewdley of King & Queen*
Marshall, Gen. George C.: *Virginia Military*
Institute
Marshall, James Markham: *Markham of Fauquier*
Marshall, Justice John: *Bealton, Germantown,*
Marshall, Midland, Oak Hill of Fauquier
Marshall, Thomas: *Germantown, Oak Hill*
of Fauquier
Martiau, Capt. Nicholas: *Chischiak, Yorktown*
Martin, John: *Borough, Brandon, Jamestown,*
Martin's Brandon, Surry County
Martin, Gen. Joseph: *Martinsville*
Martin, Sir Richard: *Martin's Hundred,*
Merchant's Hope Plantation
Mary (Queen of Scots): *Fotheringay, Hermitage,*
Richneck of Surry
Mary II (Queen of England): *King & Queen*
County, Queen's Creek, William & Mary
Marye, Col. Lawrence: *Brompton*
Marye, William Staige: *Luray*
Mason, George III: *Marlborough*
Mason, George IV: *Dumfries, George Mason*
University, Gunston Hall, Marlborough,
Pohick Church
Mason, Gen. John: *Roosevelt Island*
Massie, Thomas: *Massies Mill, Woodbridge*
Massie, Judge Thornton: *Hillsville*
Mathews, Samuel, Jr.: *Chopawamsic, Denbigh,*
Harrop, Maryland, Warwick Town
Mathews, Samuel, Sr.: *Denbigh, Magpie Swamp*
Matthews, Gen. Edward: *Fort Nelson,*
Portsmouth, Suffolk
Maury, Rev. James: *Bear Castle, Maury's School*
Maury, Matthew Fontaine: *Maury River*
Maycock, Samuel: *Maycock's Plantation*
Mayo, Maj. William: *Richmond*
Mazzei, Filippo: *Colle*
McArthur, Sgt. Moses: *Bellona Arsenal*

McClellan, Gen. George: *Berkeley, Fort Monroe, Henrico County, Manassas, Peninsula, The, Richmond, Seven Pines, White House*
McCormick, Cyrus: *Rockbridge, Vesuvius, Walnut Grove*
McGahey, Tobias: *McGaheysville*
McGavock, John: *Fort Chiswell*
McGuire, Dr. Hunter Holmes: *McGuire Medical Center*
McKeel, John: *Mount Custis*
McKinney, William R.: *McKenney*
McNider, Stanley: *Stanley*
Meade, David: *Matcock's Plantation*
Meade, Fol. Richard Kidder: *Merchant's Hope Plantation*
Mease, Rev. William: *Saint John's of Hampton*
Menefie, George: *Buckland, Harrop, Littletown, Timberneck Hall, Utimara*
Mercer, Charles F.: *Aldie*
Mercer, James: *Marlborough*
Mercer, John: *Marlborough*
Mercer, George: *Marlborough*
Mercer, Dr. Hugh: *Ferry Farm*
Merrimac (CSS Virginia): *Gosport, Hampton Roads, Oriskany*
Meriwether, Nicholas I: *Cismont, Locust Hill, Roundabout*
Meriwether, Nicholas II: *Cloverfields of Albemarle*
Michie, John: *Michie Tavern*
Miller, Samuel: *Miller School*
Milne, George C.: *Lyndhurst*
Minor, Gen. John: *Cleve*
Mitchell, Gen. Billy: *Langley Field*
Mode, Dr. Giles: *French Ordinary*
Monacan Indians: *Chickahominy Indians, Columbia, Manakin, Monacan, Rassawek, Scottsville*
Monitor (Ironclad): *Gosport, Hampton Roads*
Monroe, Andrew: *Marlborough, Monrovia*
Monroe, James, Pres.: *Ashlawn, Colonial Beach, Fort Monroe, Monrovia, Oak Hill of Loudoun, Pope's Creek, Providence Church of Louisa, University of Virginia*
Montague, George, Earl of Halifax: *Halifax County*
Moore, Col. Augustine: *Chelsea*
Moore, Samuel: *Providence Church of Augusta*
Moore, Thomas: *Waterford*
Moorman, Charles: *Moorman's River*
Morgan, Gen. Daniel: *Millwood of Clarke, Saratoga*
Morris, Gouverneur: *Bizarre*
Morton, Joseph: *Roanoke Bridge*
Moryson, Gov. Francis: *Swann's Point*
Moseby, John S., CSA: *Loudoun County*
Mossom, Rev. David: *Mount Stirling, Saint Peter's Church*
Mottrom, John: *Chicacoan, Coan Hall*

Muce, Marquis de la: *Manakin*
Mueller, Jacob: *Woodstock*
Muhlenburg, Rev. John P.: *Woodstock*
Muir, Adam: *Evergreen, Mullins, James, Pound*
Murray, Rev. Alexander: *Ware Church*
Murray, John: *See: Lord Dunmore*
Myer, Gen. Albert J.: *Fort Myer*
Myles, Alyce: *Eastover*

N

Namontack: *Savage Neck*
Neal (family): *Brookneal*
Nelson, Adm. Horatio: *Collingwood*
Nelson, Jordan: *Pocahontas*
Nelson, Gov. Thomas: *Grace Church of Yorktown, Nelson County, York Hall*
Nelson, Thomas ("Secretary"): *Hesse*
Nelson, Gov. William: *York Hall*
Newce, Sir William: *Marie's Mount*
Newport, Capt. Christopher: *Cherry Grove of Northampton, Christopher Newport College, Jamestown, Massinacak, Richmond, Turkey Island*
Newton, John: *Bedford of King George*
Newton, Willoughby: *Lee Hall of Lancaster*
Nicholas, George: *Blenheim*
Nicholas, Robert Carter: *Retreat*
Nicholson, Gov. Francis: *Eastville, Grace Church of Yorktown, Hesse, Lightfoot, Middle Plantation, Williamsburg*
Nottoway Indians: *Assamoosick Swamp, Courtland, Fort Christanna*
Nutte, Col. William O.: *Nittsville*

O

Okiawampe, Chief: *Occohannock*
Opechancanough, Chief: *Argall's Gift, Chischiak, Cinquoteck, Pamunkey Indians, West Point*
Oulds, J. W.: *Craig Springs*

P

Pace, Richard: *Pace's Paines*
Page, Gov. John: *Page County, Rosewell*
Page, Mann I: *Rosewell*
Page, Mann II: *Mannsfield, Rosewell*
Page, Mann III: *Mannsfield, Shelly*
Page, Matthew: *Rosewell*
Pallett, John: *Wolf's Snare*
Palma, Amasa: *Palmer Springs*
Parke, Daniel: *Queen's Creek Plantation*
Parke, Frances: *Arlington of Northampton, Queen's Creek Plantation*
Parke, Lucy: *Evelynton*
Parkins, Isaac: *Spring Hill*
Paspehegh Indians: *Argall's Gift*
Pasteur, Dr. William: *Ringfield*
Patterson, John: *Poplar Grove of Mathews*

Patton, Col. James: *Blacksburg, Chilowie, Draper's Meadow, Smithfield Plantation*
Paulett, Thomas: *Westover*
Payne, John: *Scotchtown*
Pearis, Capt. Richard: *Pearisburg*
Peary, Adm. Robert E.: *Camp Peary*
Peirce, William: *Harrop, Utimara*
Pendleton, Edmund: *Edmundsbury, Moon's Mount, Piscataway, Port Royal, Turners*
Penn, John: *Penola*
Perciful, Joseph: *Church View*
Percy, Sir George: *Fort Charles, Hampton, Paspehegh Indians*
Perrin, Capts. John, Thomas: *Little England of Gloucester*
Perrin, Keokee: *Keokee*
Perry, Capt. William: *Pace's Paines, Swann's Point*
Peteet, Dr. John: *French Ordinary*
Peterborough, Earl of: *Evelynton*
Peyton, Sir John: *Isleham*
Phillips, Gen. William: *Barracks, Blandford Church, Blenheim, Bollingbrook, Petersburg, Saratoga*
Pickett, Gen. George, CSA: *Turkey Island*
Pierce, Joane: *Mulberry Island*
Piersey, Abraham: *Bolthrope, Denbigh, Weyanoke of Charles City*
Pitt, William (Elder): *Chatham of Pittsylvania, Pittsylvania County*
Pitt, William (Younger): *Chatham of Stafford*
Pleasanton, Gen. Alfred: *Brandy Station*
Plovier, Dr. Peter: *French Ordinary*
Pocahontas: *Argall's Gift, Gwynn's Island, Henricus, Matoaca, Pocahontas, Pocahontas State Park*
Pochin, Chief: *Kecoughtan*
Poindexter, George: *Criss Cross*
Pollard, William: *Williamsville*
Pollock, George Freeman: *Shenandoah State Park*
Pompadour, Madam de: *Belle Vue*
Pooley, Rev. Greville: *Jordan's Point*
Pope, Nathaniel: *Clifts, Pope's Creek*
Porteus, Edward: *Poropotank*
Portobago Indians: *Coleman*
Pory, John: *Borough*
Pott, Dr. John: *Harrop*
Powell, Capt. Nathaniel: *Powell's Creek*
Powell, Capt. William: *Chippokes*
Powhatan, Chief: *Argall's Gift, Cappahosic, Chickahominy Indians, James River, Orapax, Powhatan's Chimney, Powhatan County, Purton, Werowocomoco*
Poythress, Jane: *Fort James*
Poythress, Sally: *Lee Hall of Lancaster*
Pratt, William C.: *Camden*
Preston, Gen. Francis: *Saltville*
Preston, Gov. James Patton: *Smithfield Plantation*

Preston, Col. William: *Alta Vista, Smithfield Plantation, Stuart's Draft*
Purcell, Valentine: *Purcellville*

Q
Queensbury, John: *Green Bay*
Quiney, Richard: *Martin's Brandon*

R
Radcliffe, John: *Fort Algernourne, Nansemond Indians*
Raleigh, Sir Walter: *Virginia*
Randolph, Anne: *Chatham of Stafford*
Randolph, Gov. Edmund: *Carter Hall*
Randolph, Isham: *Dungeness, Shadwell*
Randolph, John: *Bizarre, Cawsons, Randolph Macon College, Roanoke Plantation*
Randolph, Nancy Mann: *Bizarre*
Randolph, Col. Peter: *Chatsworth*
Randolph, Peyton: *Wilton of Henrico*
Randolph, Richard: *Bizarre, Curles*
Randolph, Thomas Jefferson: *Tufton*
Randolph, Thomas Mann, Jr.: *Colle, Edgehill of Albemarle, Tuckahoe, Varina Grove*
Randolph, Thomas Mann, Sr.: *Dover Church School, Tuckahoe*
Randolph, William I: *Curles, Dungeness, Shadwell, Tuckahoe, Turkey Island*
Randolph, William II: *Tuckahoe, Wilton of Henrico*
Ratcliffe, Richard: *Fairfax*
Ravell, Edward: *Metomkin, Ravenswood*
Reade, Benjamin; George: *Yorktown*
Rebecca, Lady: *See: Pocahontas*
Rector, John: *Rectortown*
Reed, Elijah: *Reedville*
Reed, George: *Lilian*
Reed, Isaac: *Greenfield*
Revere, Paul: *Cuckoo, Warrenton*
Rice, Col. James: *Lawrenceville*
Rich, Robert: *Harrop, Richneck, Warwick County*
Richardson, William T.: *Church View*
Riedesel, Baron de: *Colle*
Ring, Joseph: *Ringfield*
Robertson, Rev. Frank: *Lignum*
Robins, John: *Level Green*
Robinson, Benjamin: *Hewick, Moon's Mount*
Robinson, Christopher: *Hewick*
Robinson, Edwin: *Ashland*
Robinson, Dr. George: *Locust Grove*
Robinson, Henry: *Mount Pisgah*
Robinson, John ("Speaker"): *Bewdley of King & Queen, Doncastle's Ordinary, Hewick, Piscataway, Robinson River*
Rochambeau, Comte de: *West Point, York County*
Rockefeller, John D., Jr.: *Smith's Fort Plantation, Williamsburg*

Rogers, Henry H.: *Huddleston*
Rogers, William B.: *Mount Rogers*
Rolfe, Jane: *Kippax*
Rolfe, Jane Pierce: *Stanley Hundred*
Rolfe, John: *Argall's Gift, Hog Island, Mulberry Island, Smith's Fort Plantation, Stanley Hundred, Varina Grove*
Rolfe, Thomas: *Cedar Level, Fort James, Hog Island, Kippax, Smith's Fort Plantation, Varina Grove*
Rookings, William: *Bacon's Castle, Flying Point*
Rose, Rev. Robert: *Roseland*
Ross, William H.: *Rosslyn*
Rostow, William: *Ceeleys*
Rowlett, Mackness: *Green Bay*
Roy, Benton: *Bentonville*
Roy, John: *Moon's Mount*
Roy, Thomas: *Port Royal*
Royall, Joseph: *Dogham*
Royster, Clark: *Clarksville*
Royston, Thomas: *Fredericksburg*
Ruffin, Edmund; Robert: *Richneck of Surry*
Ruffner, William H.: *Longwood College*
Rupert (Prince of Holland): *Kinsale*
Russell, Rev. James S.: *Saint Paul College*
Russell, Walter: *Stingray Point*
Russell, Dr. Walter: *Swannanoa*
Russell, Gen. William: *Russell County, Saltville*
Rust, Jeremiah: *Rustburg*

S

Saarinen, Eero: *Dulles Airport*
Sadler, John: *Martin's Brandon*
Sandys, Sir Eedwyn: *Smythe's Hundred, Toddsbury*
Saunders, Jonathan: *Pembroke Manor*
Savage, Nathaniel Littleton: *Cherry Grove of Northampton*
Savage, Thomas: *Cherry Grove of Northampton, Eastern Shore, Savage Neck, White Cliff*
Sayers, Alexander: *Fort Chiswell*
Scarburgh, Charles: *Fairfield of Accomack, Occohannock*
Scarburgh, Col. Edmund: *Accomack County, Corbin Hall, Craddockville, Deep Creek Plantation, Guilford, Metomkin, Occohannock, Ravenswood*
Scarburgh, William: *Hedra Cottage*
Schooler, Samuel: *Edgehill of King George*
Scott, Rev. Alexander: *Gordonsdale*
Scott, Gen. Charles: *Powhatan County*
Scott, Dred: *McLean*
Scott, Edward: *Glendower*
Scott, John: *Mount Walla*
Scott, John Baytop: *Scottsburg*
Scott, Red. John: *Gordonsdale*
Scott, Gen. Winfield: *Buena Vista, Scott County*
Selden, Dr. Wilson Cary: *Exeter*
Seneca Indians: *Alexandria, Pamunkey Indians, Piscataway Indians, Susquehannock Indians*

Senseny, Dr. Peter: *Middletown*
Serene, James: *Schuyler*
Sewell, Henry: *Sewell's Point*
Shawnee Indians: *Battle Knob, Castlewood, Cherokee Indians, Delaware Indians, Draper's Meadow, Fort Blackmore, Fort Lewis, Hungry Mother State Park, Kentucky County, Shawnee Indians*
Sheffield, Sir Charles: *Buckingham County*
Shelby, Evan: *Bristol*
Shelton, John: *Hanover Town, Pine Slash Farm, Rural Point*
Sheridan, Gen. Phillip: *Belle Grove, Charlottesville, Five Forks, Trevellians*
Sherley, Sir Thomas: *Shirley*
Sherwood, Grace: *Princess Anne County*
Sidney, Sir Philip: *Mount Sidney*
Sigel, Gen. Franz: *New Market of Shenandoah*
Sikes, Robert: *Saxis*
Simon, Robert E.: *Reston*
Sims, Edward: *Arvonia*
Skeen, Alexander: *Nora*
Skelton, Bathurst: *Forest of Charles City*
Skinner, William: *Haymarket*
Skipwith, Sir Peyton, Bart.: *Blue Stone Castle, Prestwould, Skippers*
Slaight, E. E.: *Seaford*
Smith, Armistead; Thomas: *Centerville*
Smith, Col. Arthur: *Smithfield*
Smith, Charles: *Jerdone's Castle*
Smith, Maj. Charles: *Battletown*
Smith, Rev. Charles: *Providence Forge*
Smith, Daniel: *Fort Christian*
Smith, Efie: *Evington*
Smith, Gideon: *Smith Mountain Lake*
Smith, Giles: *Craig Springs*
Smith, Henry: *Oak Hall*
Smith, Capt., John (1607): *Cappahosic, Chickahominy Indians, Cinquoteck, Colchester, Copper Hill, Jamestown, Occoquan, Old Point Comfort, Smith Point, Smith's Fort Plantation, Smith's Island, Stingray Point, Strawberry Bank, Tangier Island, Werowocomoco, Willoughby Spit, York River*
Smith, Capt., John (1628): Four Mile Tree Plantation
Smith, Lawrence: *Moore House*
Smith, Capt. Lawrence: *Fredericksburg*
Smith, Capt. Roger: *Lawne's Plantation, Warescoyak*
Smith, Sylvatus: *Sylvatus*
Smith, William: *Rescue*
Smyth, Gen. Alexander: *Smyth County*
Smythe, Sir Thomas: *Smythe's Hundred*
Snead, Joseph: *Chester*
Snickers, Edward: *Bluemont, Snicker's Gap*
Soane, Henry: *Mount Stirling*
Southampton, Earl of: *See: Wriothesly, Henry*

Spain: *Appalachia, Cape Henry, Carolina, Dutch Gap, Fort Algernourne, Gold Mines, Hampton, Jamestown, Kentucky County, Virginia*

Spencer, Nicholas: *Coan Hall*

Spotswood, Gov. Alexander: *Bloomsbury, Chelsea, Criglersville, Ellerslie of Brunswick, Federal Hill, Fort Christanna, Germanna, Germantown, La Grange, Hebron Church, Massaponnox, Mine Run, New Post, Saponi Indians, Shenandoah Valley, Spotsylvania County, Swift Run Gap, Tubal Furnace, Wilderness*

Spotswood, Anne: *Anna River, Germanna, La Grange, Lake Anna*

Sprowle, Andrew: *Gosport*

Stanards, Robert: *Stanardsville*

Stanhope, Philip: *Chesterfield County*

Stanley, Thomas B.: *Stanleytown*

Stanton, Edward: *Arlington*

Stebbins, Charles: *Chester*

Stegge, Thomas: *Richmond, Stone House*

Stegge, Thomas II: *Bennett's Choice, Belle Aire of Charles City*

Stephen, Peter: *Stephens City*

Stephenson, Augustus: *Littletown*

Stevens, Gen. Edward: *Stevensburg*

Stevens, Richard; Samuel: *Bolthrope*

Stewart, Mrs. Victor: *Chippokes*

Stockley, Dr. William S.: *Cheriton*

Storey, Thomas: *Skimino Meeting House*

Story, Maj. John Patton: *Fort Story*

Stover, Peter: *Strasburg*

Stratton, Thomas: *Stratton Manor*

Strother, William: *Ferry Farm*

Stuart, Gen. J.E.B., CSA: *Brandy Station, Patrick County, Stuart*

Stubbs, Capt. John: *Cappahosic*

Susquehannock Indians: *Curles, Ocaneechee, Piscataway Indians*

Swann, Col. Thomas: *Mount Pleasant, Swann's Point*

Swann, William: *Swann's Point*

Sweeney, George: *Chesterville*

Sydney, Algernon: *Hampden-Sydney College*

Syme, Col. John: *Rock Hill, Studley*

Syms, Benjamin: *Bull Island*

T

Tabb, John; Thomas: *Haw Branch*

Tabb, Phillip: *Toddsbury, Waverly of Gloucester*

Taliaferro, Lawrence: *Belvidera*

Taliaferro, Richard: *Chesterville, Powhatan, Wilton of Henrico*

Taliaferro, Warner T.: *Belleville*

Tarleton, Lt. Col. Banastre: *Craig's Mill, Cuckoo, Elk Hill, Providence Forge, Rock Castle*

Tayloe, John: *Bristol, Bristol Iron Works, Dumfries, Hazlewood, Mount Airy, Tayloe's Furnace*

Tayloe, Mary: *Mannsfield*

Tayloe, William: *Ultimara*

Taylor, James: *Bloomsbury*

Taylor, Capt. James: *Magpie Swamp*

Taylor, Rebecca: *Menokin*

Taylor, Williams: *Charlottesville*

Taylor, Zachary, Pres: *Bloomsbury, Buena Vista, Mineral, Montebello, Monterey*

Teakle, Rev. Thomas: *Craddockville*

Tebbs, Maj. Fouchee: *Dumfries*

Temple, Rev. Peter: *Moore House*

Thomas, George: *Mount Wharton*

Thompson, Rev. John: *La Grange*

Thompson, William: *Darvills*

Thornton, Francis: *Fall Hill*

Thornton, William: *Cappahosic*

Thorpe, Rev. George: *Berkeley*

Throckmorton, Gabriel: *Church Hill*

Thruston, Rev. Charles: *Mount Zion*

Todd, Martha Vickers: *Belmont of Stafford*

Todd, Thomas: *Toddsbury*

Todd, William: *Todd's Tavern, Todd's Wharf*

Tomkins, Capt. Sally, CSA: *Goshen*

Trebell, William: *Trebell's Landing*

Tucker, Sarah: *Bedford of King George*

Tuley, Joseph: *Tuleries*

Turner, Nat: *Southampton County*

Turney, Richard: *Gunston Hall*

Tyler, John, Pres.: *Charles City County, Elliston, Greenway, Sherwood Forest*

Tyng, Hannah: *Savage Neck*

U

Underwood, Oscar: *Woodlawn*

Upshur, Judge Abel P.: *Vaucluse*

Upshur, Arthur: *Brownsville, Essex, Warwick*

Utie, Capt. John: *Chischiak, Harrop, Penniman, Utimara, Yorktown*

V

Vause, Capt. Ephraim: *Shawsville*

Venable, Nathaniel: *Slate Hill*

Vernon, Adm. Edward: *Mount Vernon, Porto Bello*

Vestal, John: *Key's Gap*

Vickers, Thomas: *Belmont of Stafford*

Victoria (Queen of England): *Alberta, Benn's Church, Brunswick County, Spring Valley, Victoria*

W

Wachawampe, Chief: *Chincoteague*

Walker, John: *Belvoir of Albemarle*

Walker, Joseph: *Ringfield*

Walker, Robert Stringfellow: *Woodberry Forest*

Walker, Schuyler: *Schuyler*

Walker, Dr. Thomas: *Abingdon of Washington, Belvoir of Albemarle, Blenheim, Castle Hill, Cuckoo, Cumberland Gap, Grace Church of Albemarle, Mount Walker, Walkerton*

Wallace, Dr. Michael: *Ellerslie of Stafford*
Ward, Alexander W.: *Wardtown*
Ward, John: *Gretna*
Warner, Augustine: *Abingdon Church, Epping Forest, Warner Hall*
Warren, Thomas: *Bacon's Castle, Smith's Fort Plantation*
Warwick, Earl of: *See: Robert Rich*
Washington, Augustine: *Ferry Farm, Little Hunting Creek, Pope's Creek, Sandy Point, Wakefield of Westmoreland*
Washington, Booker T.: *Rocky Mount*
Washington, Bushrod: *Bushfield, Mount Vernon, Rippon Lodge*
Washington, Charles: *Oak Grove of Westmoreland, Wellington*
Washington, George, Pres.: *Bel Air, Belvoir of Fairfax, Bushfield, Carter's Grove, Dinwiddie County, Dismal Swamp, District of Columbia, Edmundsbury, Elmington, Eltham, Epping Forest, Ferry farm, Fort Loudoun, Fort Mayo, Greenway Court, Kenmore, Liberty Hall Academy, Little Hunting Creek, Lynwood, Matildaville, Merchant's Hope Plantation, Mount Stirling, Mount Vernon, Naylor's Hole, Northern Neck, Oak Grove of Westmoreland, Patowmack Canal, Pohick Church, Pope's Creek, Poplar Grove of New Kent, Porto Bello, River Farm, Romancoke, Saint Peter's Church, Scottsburg, Viewmont, Wakefield of Westmoreland, Warner Hall, Washington, Washington & Lee University, Washington County, Waterford, Wellington, White House, Winchester, Woodlawn, Yorktown*
Washington, John: *Mount Vernon, Pope's Creek*
Washington, John Augustine: *Bushfield, Rippon Lodge*
Washington, Lawrence: *Belvoir of Fairfax, Mount Vernon*
Washington, Martha Custis: *Arlington of Northampton, Audley, Bushfield, Chestnut Grove, Eltham, Mount Stirling, Poplar Grove of New Kent, Queen's Creek Plantation, Saint Peter's Church, White House, Woodlawn*
Washington, Mary Ball: *Bewdley of Lancaster, Epping Forest, Ferry Farm, Mary Washington College, Saint Mary's White Chapel, Sandy Point, Wakefield of Westmoreland, Warner Hall*
Washington, Mildred: *Fall Hill*
Washington, Warner: *Audley, Fairfield of Clarke*
Watts, James Monroe: *Monroe*
Wayles, John: *Elk Hill, Eppington, Forest of Charles City, Poplar Forest*
Wayne, Gen. Anthony: *Delaware Indians, Waynesboro*
Webb, George: *Hampstead*
Webb, Stephen: *Chippokes*
Webb, Rev. Robert: *Bourbon*
Weems, Parson Mason Locke: *Bel Air*

Weir, William J.: *Liberia*
Welbourne, Samuel: *Corbin Hall*
Wellford, Dr. Armistead N: *Sabine Hall*
Wesley, Rev. Charles: *Virginia Wesleyan College*
West, Sir Francis: *Shirley, Westover*
West, Henry: *Westover*
West, John I: *Bellfield, Chischiak, Harrop, West's Plantation*
West, John II: *Deep Creek Plantation, Kiskiak, Pamunkey Indians, Ripon Hall, West Point, Yorktown*
West, John III: *Delaware Indians, Delaware Town, West Point*
West, Thomas: *See: Lord Delaware*
West, Thomas: *West Point*
Westhorpe, John: *Merchant's Hope Church*
Whaley, S. M.: *Whaleyville*

Wharton, John: *Mount Wharton*
Whipple, Gen. Amiel W.: *Fort Myer*
White, Ambrose: *Tangier Island*
Whiting, Beverley: *Elmington*
Whiting, Henry: *Elmington, Exchange*
Whitman, Walt: *Chatham of Stafford*
Whittington, Capt. William: *Chincoteague, Neville's Neck*

William III (King of England): *Fluvanna River, Hesse, King & Queen County, King William County, William & Mary, Williamsburg*
Williams, Evan; John: *Arvonia*
Williams, Indiana Fletcher: *Sweet Briar College*
Williams, Philip: *William's Ferry*
Willis, Edward: *Willis Wharf*
Willis, Elizabeth: *Corotoman*
Willis, Francis: *White Hall of Gloucester*
Willoughby, Capt. Thomas: *Norfolk, Willoughby Spit*
Wilson, Maj. William: *Ceeleys*
Wilson, Woodrow, Pres.: *Staunton, Woodlawn*
Wingfield, Edward Maria: *Jamestown, Littletown*
Winston, Judge Anthony: *West Creek Ordinary*
Wise, Gov. Henry A.: *Clifton of Accomack, Onley, Wise County*
Wise, Col. John: *Clifton of Accomack*
Wise, Tully Robinson: *Deep Creek Plantation*
Wittaker, Rev. Alexander: *Argall's Gift, Henricus*

Witten, Thomas: *Fort Witten*
Wood, Capt. Abraham: *Fort Henry, New River, Petersburg, Totopotomoi Creek, Wood's Gap*
Wood, Henry Clinton: *Clintwood*
Wood, Col. James: *Woodlawn of Carroll*
Woodford, Gen. William: *Windsor of Caroline*
Woodlief, Capt., John: *Berkeley*
Wool, Gen. John E.: *Fort Wool, Norfolk*
Woreley, John: *Ringfield*
Wormeley, Christopher: *Wormeley Creek*
Wormeley, Ralph: *Claiborne's Neck, Hesse, Rosegill*

Wren, Sir Christopher: *Christ Church of Alexandria, William & Mary*
Wright, Peter: *Covington, Peter's Mountain*
Wriothesly, Henry: *Hampton, Hampton Roads, Smythe's Hundred, Southampton County*
Wyatt, Gov. Francis: *Farrar's Island, Timberneck Hall*
Wynn, William: *Danville, Wyndale*
Wythe, George: *Chesterville, Clay Springs, Oares Plantation, St. John's of Richmond, Wythe County*
Wythe, Thomas: *Chesterville, Oares Plantation*

Y

Yeardley, Argoll: *Peachburg*
Yeardley, Gov. George: *Appomattox County, Argall's Gift, Bermuda Hundred, Chuckatuck, Corporations, Flowerdew Hundred, Henricus, Jamestown, Mattawoman, Mulberry Island, Oak Grove of Northampton, Powell's Creek, Savage Neck, Stanley Hundred, Tyndall's Point, Warescoyak, Weyanoke of Charles City*
York, Duke of: *Cape Charles, Prince Edward County, York River*
Young, Richard: *Elmington*

Z

Zane, Izaac: *Marlborough*